Perspectives in Pentecostal Eschatologies

Perspectives in Pentecostal Eschatologies

World without End

Edited by

PETER ALTHOUSE *and* ROBBY WADDELL

PICKWICK *Publications* · Eugene, Oregon

Pickwick Publications
An Imprint of Wipf and Stock Publishers
199 W. 8th Ave., Suite 3
Eugene, OR 97401

www.wipfandstock.com

ISBN 13: 978-1-60899-372-7

Cataloguing-in-Publication data:

Perspectives in Pentecostal eschatologies : world without end / Peter Althouse and Robby Waddell.

xvi + 428 pp. ; 23 cm. Includes bibliographical references and index.

ISBN 13: 978-1-60899-372-7

1. Pentecostalism. 2. Pentecostal churches—Doctrine. 3. Eschatology. I. Althouse, Peter. II Waddell, Robby. III. Title.

BX8762.Z5 A48 2010

Manufactured in the U.S.A.

To those visionaries
who had the foresight
to bring together
the body of Pentecostal thinkers:
The Society for Pentecostal Studies.

Glory to the Father, and the Son, and the Holy Spirit;
As it was in the beginning, is now, and ever shall be,
world without end.
Amen.

Contents

Contributors

J. Ayodeji Adewuya, PhD (University of Manchester) is Professor of New Testament, Pentecostal Theological Seminary, Cleveland, Tennessee. He is author of *Holiness and Community in 2 Corinthian 6:14—7:1: Paul's View of Communal Holiness in the Corinthian Correspondence* and other commentaries.

Sammy Alfaro, PhD (Fuller Theological Seminary) is Assistant Professor of Christian Studies, Grand Canyon University, Phoenix, Arizona. He is the author of *Divino Compañero: Toward a Hispanic Pentecostal Christology*.

Peter Althouse, PhD (University of St Michael's College at the University of Toronto) is Associate Professor of Theology, Southeastern University, Lakeland, Florida. He is author of *Spirit of the Last Days: Pentecostal Eschatology in Conversation with Jürgen Moltmann*.

John A. Bertone, PhD (University of St Michael's College at the University of Toronto) is the English Pastor at Kitchener-Waterloo Chinese Alliance Church, Ontario, and an independent New Testament scholar. He has authored *"The Law of the Spirit": Experience of the Spirit and Displacement of the Law in Romans 8:1–16* and various articles and book reviews.

Daniel Castelo, PhD (Duke University) is Associate Professor of Theology, Seattle Pacific University, Washington. He is author of *The Apathetic God: Exploring the Contemporary Relevance of Divine Impassibility*.

Blaine Charette, PhD (University of Sheffield) is Professor of New Testament, Northwest University, Kirkland, Washington. He is author of two monographs on the Gospel of Matthew.

Murray W. Dempster, PhD (University of Southern California) is Distinguished Professor of Social Ethics, Southeastern University, Lakeland,

Florida. He is coeditor of *The Globalization of Pentecostalism* and *Called and Empowered: Global Mission in Pentecostal Perspective.*

JEFFREY GROS, FSC, PhD (Fordham University) is Distinguished Professor of Ecumenism and Historical Theology, Memphis Theological Seminary, Tennessee. He is coeditor of *Growth in Agreement II & III* and *Introduction to Ecumenism.*

FRANK D. MACCHIA, DTh (University of Basel) is Professor of Theology, Vanguard University, California. He is author of *Baptized in the Spirit: A Global Pentecostal Theology.*

MICHAEL J. McCLYMOND, PhD (University of Chicago) is Associate Pro-fessor in Theological Studies, Saint Louis University, Missouri. He is author of *Encounters With God: An Approach to the Theology of Jonathan Edwards, Familiar Stranger: An Introduction to Jesus of Nazareth,* editor of *Encyclopedia of Religious Revivals in America,* and co-author of *The Theology of Jonathan Edwards.*

LARRY McQUEEN, PhD candidate (Bangor University) is an independent scholar and author of *Joel and the Spirit: the Cry of a Prophetic Hermeneutic.*

NESTOR MEDINA, PhD (University of St. Michael's College at the University of Toronto) is Adjunct Professor at Master's College and Seminary, Seminario Evangélico de Teología, Matanzas Cuba, and Emmanuel College, University of Toronto; and author of *Mestizaje: (Re)mapping Race, Culture and Faith in Latina/o Catholicism.*

DAVID MOORE, PhD (Regent University) is Historian for The International Church of the Foursquare Gospel and has published *The Shepherding Movement: Controversy and Charismatic Ecclesiology.*

JOHN CHRISTOPHER THOMAS, PhD (University of Sheffield) is Clarence J. Abbott Professor of Biblical Studies, Pentecostal Theological Seminary, Cleveland, Tennessee; and Associate Director of the Centre for Pentecostal and Charismatic Studies at Bangor University, North Wales. He is co-author of the forthcoming commentary on the Apocalypse for Eerdmans' Two Horizons Commentary Series.

MATTHEW K. THOMPSON, PhD (Luther Seminary) is Assistant Professor of Religious Studies, Southwestern College, California. He is author of *Kingdom Come: Revisioning Pentecostal Eschatology*, 2010.

WILLIAM RACCAH, PhD (Université Laval) is an educational philanthropist and Executive Director of Project Consulting and author of *Widows at the Gate*.

ROBBY WADDELL, PhD (University of Sheffield) is Associate Professor of New Testament, Southeastern University, Lakeland, Florida. He is author of *The Spirit of the Book of Revelation*.

Acknowledgments

THE IDEA FOR THIS book came about after a classroom discussion in the area of eschatology. With Robby Waddell's skills as a biblical scholar and Peter Althouse's skills as a theologian, we thought that a constructive collaboration in Pentecostal and Charismatic eschatology was sorely needed given the undue emphasis on fundamentalist dispensationalism within the movement, which quite frankly undercuts the sustainability of its pneumatological foundations. The chapters that follow are an attempt to broaden the horizons of research on Pentecostal and Charismatic eschatology in an effort to discover the diversity that exists. We would especially like to thank Southeastern University for providing a generous grant to hold a symposium—Fresh Perspectives in Pentecostal Eschatologies—in which the authors of these chapters came together to discuss their research with faculty and students. Thanks especially to Esteban Felix who helped with preparing the manuscript. And an overwhelming thank you to our families who sacrificed their time as we worked to bring this book to completion.

Abbreviations

ABD	*Anchor Bible Dictionary.* 6 vols. Edited by David Noel Freedman. New York: Doubleday, 1992.
AJPS	*Asian Journal for Pentecostal Studies*
BNTC	Black's New Testament Commentaries
BSac	*Bibliotheca Sacra*
CBQ	*Catholic Biblical Quarterly*
CD	Karl Barth, *Church Dogmatics.* 4 vols.
DPCM	*Dictionary of Pentecostal and Charismatic Movements.* Edited by Stanley M. Burgess, Gary B. McGee, and Patrick H. Alexander. Grand Rapids: Zondervan, 1988.
EA	*Encyclopedia of Apocalypticism.* 3 vols. Edited by Bernard McGinn, John J. Collins, and Stephen J. Stein. London: Continuum, 2000.
EgT	*Église et Théologie*
GTJ	*Grace Theological Journal*
HCL	*The 'Higher Christian Life': Sources for the Study of the Holiness, Pentecostal, and Keswick Movements.* 48 vols. Edited by Donald W. Dayton. New York: Garland, 1985.
IBMR	*International Bulletin of Missionary Research*
IRM	*International Review of Mission*
JACT	*Journal of African Christian Thought*
JECS	*Journal of Early Christian Studies*
JES	*Journal of Ecumenical Studies*
JETS	*Journal of the Evangelical Theological Society*
JPT	*Journal of Pentecostal Theology*
JPTsup	Journal of Pentecostal Theology Supplement Series
JRA	*Journal of Religion in Africa*

JRS	*Journal of Religious Studies*
JTS	*Journal of Theological Studies*
NCB	New Bible Commentary
NICNT	New International Commentary on the New Testament
NIDNTT	*New International Dictionary of the New Testament.* 4 vols. Edited by Colin Brown. Grand Rapids: Zondervan, 1975–1979.
NIDPCM	*New International Dictionary of Pentecostal and Charismatic Movements.* Rev. ed. Edited by Stanley M. Burgess and Eduard M. Van Der Mass. Grand Rapids: Zondervan, 2002.
NTS	*New Testament Studies*
TDNT	*Theological Dictionary of the New Testament.* 10 vols. Edited by Gerhard Kittel and Gerard Friedrich. Translated by Geoffrey W. Bromiley. Grand Rapids: Eerdmans, 1964–1976.
Transformation	*Transformation: An International Dialogue on Mission and Ethics*
WBC	*Word Biblical Commentary*
WTJ	*Wesleyan Theological Review*

The Landscape of Pentecostal and Charismatic Eschatology

An Introduction

PETER ALTHOUSE

THE CONTOURS OF THE ESCHATOLOGICAL LANDSCAPE

MAKING SENSE OF THE eschatological landscape is a daunting task to say the least. Eschatology is that area of Christian dogmatics that investigates the culmination of divine activity in what is traditionally called the doctrine of the last things. It deals with the issues of death, judgment, heaven, and hell as well as the end of world history, the coming of the kingdom of God, and the future cosmos. However, eschatology cannot simply be reduced to the end, but recapitulates in itself all of human history. Eschatology cannot be reduced merely to individual redemption of the soul, but includes social and cosmic dimensions in that the culmination of socio-historical life and the non human elements of the earth, and indeed the entire universe will be transformed by God. Theological concepts related to eschatology include apocalypticism—the belief in divine revelation of the end through the ongoing historical struggles between good and evil; millennialism—a thousand year reign at the end of history; and messianism—the belief in a divine savior who will bring about a better age.[1] The meaning of apocalyptic can vary, however, depending on whether one is denoting an ancient Near Eastern literary genre, theological notions of divine disclosure or unveiling in revelation, or the event of the end itself.

---

1. Collins, McGinn, and Stein, "General Introduction," ix–x.

On the one hand, evangelical eschatology tends to be inundated with millennial views of the end. Taking the one thousand year reign of Christ at the end of the age as significant, millennialists argue that God will come to judge the world and establish the divine reign on this earth. Yet millennial views vary substantially. Historically, premillennialism can be traced back into the second century in Tertullian and Montanism. Two female prophets Priscilla and Maximila, predicted that the world would end in their lifetime, but their prophecies were disconfirmed with Maximila's death in CE 179. However, Tertullian's response was that since the church was in the age of the Comforter, believers were given prophetic insight that all biblical prophecies must be fulfilled before the coming of Christ and the end of the world. Tertullian criticized the Roman elite of his day, placing Christian hope in the eschatological age to come, thereby establishing the pattern of millennialism.[2] Twelfth-century theologian Joachim of Fiore likewise proposed a millennial eschatology. He argued that salvation history was divided into three ages: the age of the Father (creation to birth of Christ), which he believed to have been seven thousand years earlier, the age of the Son (from the incarnation until the return of Christ), and the age of the Spirit (which would begin with the eschaton). Interpreting the book of Revelation historically, Joachim believed the church was living through tribulation, specifically seven tribulations. Six had already been fulfilled in history, starting with Nero and Herod and including Saladin's defeat of the Christian Crusaders. The last tribulation would be that of the Antichrist, whose reign was foretold, Joachim insisted, in the book of Daniel. Although Joachim resisted predicting a specific time for Christ's return, expectations were high in CE 1200 and some of his followers identified CE 1260 as the end of the world, forty-two generations from the birth of Christ. Significant for the pre-Reformation era, Joachim claimed that as the second age drew to a close the papacy would experience moral decline.[3] For the next three hundred years, there was an expectation that the Antichrist would arise through the papacy, providing a powerful internal critique for moral and papal reform within Roman Catholicism but also providing the basis for Martin Luther's Protestant criticism of the papacy and its identification with the apocalyptic end of the world.[4]

2. Stackhouse, *End of the World?* 35–40.

3. Ibid., 41–45.

4. See McGinn, "The Last Judgment in Christian Tradition," 361–401; Rusconi,

Prophets of millennial expectation and predictions of the imminent end arose occasionally throughout the next four hundred years. Predication became the fodder of millennialism as charismatic prophets interpreted biblical prophecy according to current historical events and offered predictions as to the exact time for Christ's return. During the Reformation, a radical fringe of Anabaptist prophets asserted a chiliastic eschatology, and ultimately alienated itself from the Lutheran Reformation. Anabaptist Melchior Hoffman expected the start of the millennium in Strasbourg in 1533 and Jan Matthys believed that Münster would be the site of the New Jerusalem. His vision was thwarted by his own death, the Roman Catholic siege of the Anabaptist radicals, and the disillusionment of the city's inhabitants, who eventually opened the city gates to the Roman bishop.[5] Later German Pietist Johann Albrecht Bengel also adopted chiliastic beliefs and expected the imminence of the coming kingdom in the parousia. Using elaborate prophetic calculations, Bengel predicted the coming of Christ and the end of the world to occur in 1836.[6] During the nineteenth century, millennial expectations brought with it numerous predictions of the coming of Christ and the end of the world. Millennial preaching of the coming of God grew intense, especially in the American postbellum period, as religious sentiments became increasingly antagonist against the American establishment. Disciples of Christ leader, Alexander Campbell proclaimed the imminent return of Christ in millennialist and cataclysmic categories. However, it was William Miller, a self-taught Baptist and founder of the Millerites (later to form the Seventh-day Adventists Church), who using a historicist approach to prophetic interpretation and developing complex calculations, predicted that Christ would return in about 1843, later to be refined to October 22, 1844. Miller's disconfirmation resulted in the movement's denunciation, though its anti-government rhetoric and cynicism regarding human efforts for social betterment in the present (the basis of both modernist theologies and nineteenth-century evangelicalism) was carried into subsequent millennial thinking, and provided

---

"Antichrist and Antichrists," 287–325; Anderson, "A Catholic and Ecumenical Response to the *Left Behind* Series," 209–30; Obermann, *Luther: Man between God and the Devil*, 42–44.

5. González, *The Story of Christianity*, vol 2. *The Reformation to the Present Day*, 57–59.

6. Macchia, *Spirituality and Social Liberation*, 9–11.

impetus for theological changes in evangelicalism. Evangelical theology shifted from postmillennial hope with its emphasis on social transformation and successes such as the abolition of slavery, human rights and emancipation, and women's suffrage, to premillennial dispensational pessimism with its withdrawal from efforts for social transformation.[7] Charles Taze Russell, founder of the Watchtower Bible and Tract Society, which eventually incorporated into the Jehovah's Witnesses, likewise adopted a historicist interpretation to argue that the millennium had already dawned in 1874, but that Christ's return would occur forty years later in 1914.[8] Russell's heterodox teachings of the separation of Christ from Jehovah and elimination of the Spirit as deity, belief in the 144,000 saints of God, and annihilation of the unregenerate would place him on the radical fringe (though one can see his influence on early Pentecostal Charles F. Parham), but his apocalyptic and millennial teachings created disillusionment with modernity's optimism in progress and social reconstruction typical in mainstream Christianity.[9]

Disconfirmation, that is, the disillusionment that comes to expectant Christians when the return of Christ does not occur as predicted, has placed millennialism in a minority position in the broad contours of Christian eschatology. The disappointment that Christ did not return as expected and that the world was still continuing as always created disbelief among believing Christians and secular onlookers alike. The problem of disconfirmation would change, however, with the rise of nineteenth-century dispensationalism. Beginning with a small group of theological thinkers at Oxford University and Trinity College Dublin, and popularized through the efforts of John Nelson Darby and the publication of the *Scofield Reference Bible*,[10] the problem of millennial disconfirmation was resolved with the inclusion of a secret and unexpected rapture for the faithful church saints, at which point prophetic calculations, having been suspended for a time beginning at Pentecost with the age of the church, would resume. Speculations of the end would then come to fruition. In other words, prophecy calculations of the old covenant did not apply to the age of the church, because God was acting in grace to redeem the

7. Boyer, "The Growth of Fundamentalist Apocalyptic in the United States," 145–46; also Moorehead, "Apocalypticism in Mainstream Protestantism: 1800 to the Present," 82.

8. Forty is a common number in prophecy calculations and symbolically significant in Scripture.

9. Boyer, "Growth of Fundamentalist Apocalyptic," 157–60.

10. Gribbens, *Writing the Rapture*, 5–7.

church. At the rapture, however, a seven-year tribulation would commence in which the Antichrist would arise and the post-rapture saints
(however defined) would be persecuted, culminating in the defeat of the
Antichrist and the forces opposed to God in a battle at Armageddon.
The genius of dispensational premillennialism was that the imminent
expectation and prophetic predictions could be maintained, but without
the embarrassing problem of disconfirmation. Fundamentalist thinkers
could argue over the details of the Tribulation without reprisal—and
argue they did, over when the rapture would occur, what type of tribulations the world would experience, the specific calculations of certain
prophecies, who would be raptured and who would be left behind. The
rapture was an unpredictable wildcard in the dispensational schemata,
but everything else could be calculated. Dispensational millennialism
has taken root in the fertile ground of evangelicalism, though with varying degrees of success. For the most part, premillennial dispensationalism has been affirmed mostly in the modern West, as well as perhaps in
areas of Western missionary expansion, and tends to be proclaimed in
the USA more in the southern states than in the northern ones.[11]

Although premillennial dispensationalism has had a major influence on the Pentecostal movement, particularly in the mid-twentieth
century, on the horizon of eschatological options, millennialism has
played a fairly minor role. A thousand year period is mentioned only
once in the entire New Testament (Rev 20) and is perhaps implied in the
redemption of the 144,000 (Rev 14), but the literary style of the book of
Revelation is highly symbolic. Other eschatologies have emerged historically within the traditions of Christianity and are part of the theological
make-up of Christianity today. Reginald Stackhouse argues, for instance,
that throughout the history of Christianity three types of eschatology
have emerged: (1) millennialism (above), which uses a literal interpretation of Scripture to understand the end as a historical event in time and
space; (2) the pastoral, which understands eschatology as the present
activity of God in human beings and the church militant, i.e., the church
presently here on earth. This approach is more psychological in helping
people of faith prepare for their spiritual development and their own
mortality; and (3) the social, which understands the eschatological as the
promise of the new age in the present, the end of the present social order

---

11. Gribbens, *Writing the Rapture*, 53, 64, 160; Boyer, "Growth of Fundamentalist
Apocalyptic," 159.

and the beginning of a new age. Social change is the outcome of eschatological imagination.[12] In the pastoral and social types of eschatology the Apocalypse of John is taken to be symbolic; consequently, imposing a "literal" thousand year reign would distort New Testament eschatology. Although within the millennial traditions alternatives to *pre*millennialism can be found—namely, *post*millennial (the manifestation of God on the earth after a period of societal construction according to the ideals of the kingdom of God), and *a*millennial (an understanding of eschatology in non-millennialist, or realized-millennialist, terms)—those outside the millennialist traditions would unlikely even use the terminology. Yet even in the premillennial camp, the expected and imminent reign of God on the earth often functions symbolically.[13]

Jürgen Moltmann argues that four types of eschatology have emerged in theological discourse: personal, social-historical, cosmic, and divine. Personal eschatology probes the question of the ultimate destiny of the individual, not in terms of the platonic ascension of the soul devoid of material life, but as body and soul together in the resurrection of the dead. Social-historical eschatology probes the question of the ultimate destiny of the socio-political developments of history, the end of world history and the beginning of the kingdom of God. Cosmic eschatology probes the question of the ultimate destiny of the earth and the entire universe, in which God's creation finds its divine fulfillment. Divine eschatology probes the question of divine being, in which the dynamic Trinitarian self-giving will be glorified and God will be all in all.[14] Moltmann also makes a distinction between historical millenarianism and eschatological millenarianism. The former is the premature location of the reign of God in a particular historical-political reality (i.e., papal reign in the Holy Roman Empire, or the policy of manifest destiny of the USA in which the kingdom of God is

---

12. Stackhouse, *End of the World?* 26–27.

13. While Gribbens argues that premillennial dispensationalism functions as a critique of modernity by appropriating and supporting modernist ideology (Gribbens, *Writing the Rapture*, 4–5), Damien Thompson's socio-scientific analysis of a Pentecostal congregation in Great Britain argues that one needs to distinguish between predictive millenarianism, which is a prophetic proclamation of the impending apocalyptic doom, and explanatory millenarianism, which functions as a rhetorical narrative addressing current social issues as a means to reduce anomie and stabilize social institutions. Thompson, *Waiting for the Antichrist*, 22–31.

14. Moltmann, *Coming of God, passim.*

equated with its civil religion). However, in the end historical millennialism succumbs to socio-political and economic powers and creates other forms of oppression. The latter is legitimate hope in the reign of God on this earth as a sovereign and free act of God. In millennial terms, historical millenarianism is a form of postmillennialism, while eschatological millenarianism is a form of premillennialism. Yet, whereas the current American dispensational premillennialism encourages passive withdrawal in the hope of escape from the present, apostolic premillennialism inspires resistance to the oppressive powers in hope for the coming reign of God.[15] Moltmann's eschatology of hope would fit into Stackhouse's social type owing to its emphasis on critical, political theology as a reflection of eschatological hope.

Bernard McGinn's investigation into apocalyptic themes of the Middle Ages demonstrates that the apocalyptic themes of the monastic traditions brought reform, in which the religio-political beliefs and practices were used either to reform and to support the social order, or to subvert it.[16] Even in the Antenicene era, apocalyptic literature was subversive of the political order of the Roman Empire initially, and to dominating powers thereafter. Once Christianity became the official religion of the Roman Empire, the harsh critique of the status quo found within apocalyptic literature fell out of favor with many of the early Christians, adding to delayed acceptance of the book of Revelation in some parts of the Christian world. Nevertheless, the apocalyptic literature proved to be resilient and found popularity, especially among the marginalized sects.

Apocalyptic images both inform and transform the socio-political contexts inside and outside Christianity. In the modern context, apocalyptic images informed the subversion and reforms of the dominating powers of monarchies and the church hierarchies, in order to establish new systems of power around rationality. Robin Barns' insightful thesis argues that the changes brought about by apocalyptic themes contributed to the rise of modernity. "The broad outlines of this picture suggest that the changes commonly associated with emerging 'modernity,' including the religious reformations, the rise of experimental science, and even the development of political liberalism, were themselves intimately related to the continuing evolution of Western prophetic and apocalyp-

---

15. Moltmann, *Coming of God*, 146–78.

16. McGinn, "Apocalypticism and Church Reform: 1100–1500," 74–109.

tic visions."[17] Dealing with the tensions between pessimistic despair and optimistic hope, early modern apocalypticism contributed to the rise of modernity in transforming millennial hope at the end of the age to a "forward-looking" hope in historical progress. Progress therefore acts as a variation of providence, in which the Spirit is present in the historical process. Conversely, apocalyptic despair contributed to the practical use of skeptical reason and methodological atheism.[18]

Likewise, Altizer argues that it was Hegel who brought the apocalyptic thrust of modernism to the fore in his declaration of the end of history and the self-negation of the divine. His dialectic method of negation proposed that consciousness itself was evolving from sense certainty to absolute knowing, in which the events of history are fundamentally the evolution of absolute Spirit, represented in the New Testament category of the kingdom of God. *Phenomenology of Spirit* is an apocalyptic work in that it locates absolute knowing as the death of God.[19] For Hegel, the kenosis in the cross, which touches the divine as well as the human in Christ Jesus, is the realization of divine self-negation. The cross is, for Hegel, the death of God and as such the beginning of secularization, in that self-consciousness is now certain of itself as absolute freedom. In the dialectic of negation, the essential is itself negated and the subject becomes totally free. However, in the freedom of the self through the negation of divine essence death itself is emptied of significance so that in absolute freedom the self realizes the terror of its own negation in death.[20] ". . . [D]eath is objectively meaningless and insignificant. But it is subjectively more real than ever before, and thus death becomes the one and only portal to a full and final subjective and interior resolution and fulfillment. Hegel's term for this form of consciousness that realizes itself by losing all the essence and substance of itself is the Unhappy Consciousness, a consciousness which realizes itself by interiorly realizing that *God Himself is dead* (author's emphasis)."[21] For Hegel, the French Revolution embodied the end of history and the terror of death in the vacuous abstraction of God, the death of God, but in that event there is a new beginning, the beginning of modernity. Yet the death of

17. Barns, "Images of Hope and Despair" 143–84.

18. Ibid., 166–71.

19. Hegel, *Phenomenology of Spirit*.

20. Altizer, *Apocalypticism and Modern Thinking*, 329–31.

21. Ibid., 332.

God is realized in Spirit's self-alienation and self-negation from itself and the fulfillment of kenosis. "Thus it is dialectically and apocalyptically necessary that Spirit become wholly estranged and alienated from itself before it can realize and effect its own death or self-negation. Yet this is the ultimate apocalyptic event, one finally releasing an absolutely new world, but only insofar as it is the actual death of God."[22] The logic of Hegel's dialectical method is progressive, forward moving, open to a new future, and therefore eschatologically progressive, but at the cost of the apocalyptic dislocation of God and the end of history.[23]

Hegel's philosophy was influential on subsequent philosophical and theological thinkers. On the one hand, the forward movement of Hegel's dialectical method informed biological and social evolutionary theories. It also informed the social critique of Feuerbach, who inverted Hegel's dialectic to reflect a more humanist perspective, and Marx, who argued for a materialist understanding of history that borrowed from Hegel's dialectic in which the means of production is progressing through feudal, industrial, and communist modes. Marx also embodied Hegel's apocalyptic view in both a collapse of transcendence as the "opiate of the people" and the revolutionary end of history in the communist revolt, which establishes a utopian society as the *telos* of history. On the other hand, Hegel's philosophy influenced the nihilistic developments in existentialism. The one is teleologically open to the future as human or social self-realization, the other apocalyptic in vacuous transcendence, the collapse of essence into pure existence.

We can therefore speak of secular eschatologies rooted in the Christian tradition and inherent within modernity. The scientific age embodied an eschatological outlook that resisted apocalyptic despair and death, and sought to change the future age by applying the principles of rationality to the betterment of the plight of humanity. In order to accomplish this task, the dominance of the political and religious powers were challenged, their "myths" deconstructed, in order to assert the authority of scientific reason. Hans Schwarz notes a number of scientific perspectives with eschatological impulses. The positivism of Auguste Comte attempted to explain natural phenomena as subject to natural laws, and these rules of scientific materialism could be applied to

---

22. Ibid., 333.
23. Ibid., 335–37.

social and human betterment.[24] Both J. Robert Mayer's postulate of the law of conservation and Julien Offray de la Mettrie's naturalistic views of humanity explained nature as the totality of matter (including the so-called spirituality of the soul), in which the future is merely modification of the past.[25] Ludwig Feuerbach modifies Hegelian thought and reinterprets the resurrection, arguing that no disembodied existence is possible in material life. Notions of an immortal soul or heavenly existence deny bodily, material existence in which the human ceases to be human. Christianity has cheated humanity, argues Feuerbach, because it denies the human ability to apply rationality to its own problems and seek its own solutions.[26] Suffice it to say, the point is that scientific materialism contributed to a type of secular eschatology, which sought its own fulfillment in the application of reason to the orders of nature in which the future betterment of humanity would be accomplished through human progress.

According to Schwarz, the evolutionary theory proposed by Charles Darwin can also be viewed as an eschatological perspective. Although Darwin's developmental theories attempt to understand the causal connections between organisms by examining their biological histories without assertions regarding their future states, he hints at an eschatological goal. In the conclusion of *Origin of the Species* he writes: "And as natural selection works solely by and for the good of each being, *all corporeal and mental endowments will tend to progress toward perfection.*"[27] Had Darwin limited his examination to an understanding of the development of biological life based in the fossil records of the past, he would have remained within the realm of the natural sciences. However, in suggesting biological life was progressing toward a *telos*—perfection, Darwin insinuates forward-looking possibilities.[28] The evolutionary view was a paradigm shift that influenced many areas of research. While some attempted to remain strictly scientific based on biological present and past conditions, others applied his progressive theories to both biological and social spheres in an effort to change the future. The application of eugenics, for instance, was an attempt to produce a more perfect hu-

24. Schwarz, *Eschatology*, 174.

25. Ibid., 175–76.

26. Ibid., 176–78.

27. As quoted in ibid., 186 (my italics); cf. Darwin, *Origin of the Species*, 528.

28. Schwarz, *Eschatology*, 185–88.

man race. The dark side of this approach was the rise of Nazi Germany and its program to exterminate undesirables, though eugenics was also used in North America to justify selective sterilization of physically and mentally disabled individuals.[29] Eugenics is also the theory supporting current efforts to map the genome and develop genetic therapies for overcoming inherited diseases.

From a theological perspective, Pierre Teilhard de Chardin can be taken as representative of an evolutionary eschatology, though he was heavily criticized. Teilhard de Chardin believed that the universe is evolving toward an ultra-human state of increased consciousness. The evolutionary process was not simply naturalistic in the biological advancement of life, but a Christological process in which the teleological goal is the "Christification" of the universe. Through the cosmic Christ, redemption and fall are not limited to humans but extend to the whole cosmos. The evolution of humanity to its fullest potential is the precondition for the parousia, but both an anthropogenesis ascent and the permeation of the Christogenesis descent form a unity in salvation history.[30] The details of Teilhard de Chardin's theology are not important here, except to note that he offers an eschatological proposal that includes the evolutionary process.

While Teilhard de Chardin represents an evolutionary cosmic eschatology as a counterbalance to secular evolutionary perspectives, Hegel's methodological progressivism and apocalyptic nihilism influenced the development of a number of existential eschatologies of both secular and theological stripes. On the one hand, various secular existential philosophies formally hold to an atheistic methodology that eschews any form of metaphysical impositions. Nietzsche picks up on the death of God in Hegel to argue that nihilism is the consequence of Western history, beginning with the death of God at Golgotha. For Nietzsche, the death of God is a historical event and an ultimate event, in which the collapse of transcendence brings the inauguration of absolute immanence. Thus the will to power is the energy of life in its "becoming."[31] Consequently, death becomes a leitmotif in existentialist philosophy in that nothing beyond death has any bearing on our existence, and therefore we must

29. See for instance, Black, *War Against the Weak*; and Bruinius, *Better for All the World*.

30. Schwarz, *Eschatology*, 189–94; Moltmann, *Way of Jesus Christ*, 292–96.

31. Altizer, "Apocalypticism and Modern Thinking," 342–43.

live authentically in this present life. Existential meaning is not generated from outside of us, but from "Being-in-the-world" (Heidegger), from radical "freedom" from metaphysical reference points (Sartre), or nihilistic absurdity (Camus); living for something beyond our own existence would be inauthentic. For Camus, evil does not emerge from unjust social institutions, but from the human heart. Camus does claim that human help can come only from human solidarity serving human purposes, and not from metaphysical sources, prompting Hans Schwarz to suggest that implied in Camus' claim is the idea that a metaphysical purpose can serve to fulfill a human need.[32] Nevertheless, death can be seen as a negative apocalypse on human life, the cessation of human existence and therefore an apocalyptic annihilation on all life.

On the other hand, Christian existentialism proposes the eschatology of the eternal in-breaking into the present. Rudolph Bultmann was perhaps the most influential Christian existentialist in the last century. Drawing on the philosophy of Heidegger, Bultman understood eschatology as the personal decision of faith in the crisis of the present. The existential encounter with Christ is a decision of faith in the moment that is devoid of biblical mythologies or historical realities. What is important is "my history," in which eternity breaks into my present existence, enabling me to live authentically. However, Moltmann notes that for Bultmann the future collapses into the present, making judgment and resurrection a present reality.[33] Where death becomes an apocalyptic pronouncement of annihilation for secular existentialism, in Christian existentialism the anxieties over the annihilation of death point to the crisis of faith as a radical moment of faith in order to live an authentic life. However, nothing survives the apocalypse of death. Curiously, Karl Barth's crisis theology can also fit into this existentialist model, though Barth would have resisted such a comparison; he sees death as the gateway to life hereafter. For Barth, the breaking of eternity into present life calls people to a radical decision of faith. The eternal moment overcomes chronological time because there is no past or future in God, but once again the future is collapsed into the now.[34]

The problem of eschatology therefore is the problem of navigating the tension between the present and the future, or more accurately, the

32. Schwarz, *Eschatology*, 210–16.

33. Moltmann, *Coming of God*, 19–21.

34. Barth, *Epistle to the Romans*, 92; cf. Moltmann, *Coming of God*, 13–15.

tension between the already and not yet of the coming kingdom of God. The eschatological tension between the present age and the future age to come can be collapsed into the present, relegated to the distant future, or held in tension. Correlate to the already and not yet tension is the comparable concepts of hope and despair. The eschatological vision of the coming of God can bring great despair in the dread of divine judgment on this world and the creatures that inhabit it, or the eschatological vision can bring great hope in the culmination of divine purposes in the spiritual and material redemption of humanity, the world, and the cosmic orders of the universe.

The landscape of eschatology ranges, therefore, between the present and the future, on the one hand, and hope and despair on the other. If one were to organize the eschatological options on a grid, the x axis consisting of present on the left and future on the right, and the y axis consisting of hope in the upper position and despair in the lower, one can start to make sense of the theological options of eschatology. The upper left quadrant of present hope could include various secular eschatologies with the modernist hope of progress and emancipation. Marxist materialism and utopian visions, and social Darwinianism are all secular versions of Christian hope. This quadrant could also include the Christian eschatologies of Karl Barth's eternal in-breaking, realized eschatologies, Christian evolution, and Christian existential eschatologies. The upper right quadrant of future hope might include such eschatology as secular futurism, postmillenarianism, latter rain eschatology, and Moltmann's theology of hope, though some of these can span the upper left quadrant. In fact, a number of eschatologies hold the present-future in tension, such as inaugurated or covenantal and proleptic eschatologies. Shifting from hope to despair, the lower end of the graft entails anxieties regarding apocalyptic judgment. The lower left quadrant could include explanatory premillennialism, existential nihilism, ecological and political holocausts of both secular and Christian varieties, whereas the lower right quadrant could entail futuristic millenarianism with its tribulationist theories, predictive millennialism or apocalyptic nihilism in the divine, human, or even cosmic destruction of the world. However, these eschatologies can span across quadrants, so that premillennial dispensationalism, which is predominantly a function of future despair (lower right) can spur hope in escape through a secret rapture (upper right). Another example could be an ecological apocalyptic seen in present concerns over pollution or nuclear waste (lower left), which can operate as signs pointing to future apocalyptic of world destruction through nuclear holocaust (lower right), or conversely could span into the upper left quadrant in the offer of hope through liberation in socio-political activity of hope. The point is that while some eschatologies offer hope and others lead to despair, some are futuristic and others are present, none truly fit one type exactly but span across quadrants. Needless to say, the grid we are suggesting is a heuristic tool, a kind of ideal type. When one starts to look into the nitty-gritty details, the differing eschatologies can span across multiple quadrants of the grid, and it therefore starts to break down. However, this grid is helpful for understanding the contours of eschatological options.

PRESENT HOPE	FUTURE HOPE
Secular Eschatologies	**Secular Eschatologies**
Marxist materialism	Futurism
Darwinism–natural and social	
varieties	
Christian Eschatologies	**Christian Eschatologies**
19th century evangelical	Theology of Hope
postmillennialism	Historic millennialism
Amillennialism	Latter Rain eschatology
Social Gospel	
Existentialism	

Bridging Eschatologies
Covenantal, Proleptic, and Inaugural Eschatologies

PRESENT DESPAIR	FUTURE DESPAIR
Secular Eschatologies	**Secular Eschatologies**
Existential nihilism	Secular apocalypticism
Cosmological and ecological	
nihilism	
Christian Eschatologies	**Christian Eschatologies**
Explanatory premillennialism	Premillennial dispensationalism
Doomsday cults	Predictive millennialism

PENTECOSTAL AND CHARISMATIC ESCHATOLOGIES

What then is the landscape of Pentecostal eschatology? In this volume Pentecostalism is broadly defined to include its classical, charismatic, and independent or non-denominational expressions. Classical Pentecostalism—which has its American roots in the Azusa Street Mission but finds its global expressions in Wales, India, Korea, Toronto, Germany, etc.[35]—consists of some of the oldest Pentecostal denominations such as Church of God (Cleveland), Church of God in Christ, Assemblies of God, International Church of the Foursquare Gospel, Pentecostal Assemblies of Canada, and a variety of Apostolic denominations. To varying degrees, these denominations have been influenced by the development of dispensational premillennialism, though its earliest expressions were closer to the tripartite millennialism of Joachim of Fiore mediated through Wesleyan sources, and covenantal eschatologies, articulated as the theology of the latter rain. Instead of passive withdrawal from society in anticipation of a secret rapture and the expression of divine judgment on the wicked, early classical Pentecostals anticipated an intensification of the charismatic outpouring of the Spirit in expectation of a final, glorious harvest of souls prior to the coming of the Lord. Fundamentalist forces would soon be felt among Pentecostals and they would abandon their latter rain eschatology for dispensational premillennialism, yet at the cost of the foundation of their dearest doctrine—speaking in tongues as the expression of the baptism of the Spirit. Dispensationalism is undergirded by a cessation doctrine, which argues that all the spectacular charismatic gifts ceased in the apostolic age.[36] The problem of wedding dispensationalism to Pentecostal pneumatology is immediately obvious, and, as Gerald Sheppard skillfully argues, undercuts Pentecostal ecclesiology and the doctrine of Spirit baptism. The meaning of the Blessed Hope thus changed from the advent of the Second Coming to this new view of the rapture.[37] Passive withdrawal from society thus replaced the original vision of hope in Pentecostal eschatology.

Charismatic expressions of Pentecostalism officially began in 1960 with Episcopal priest Dennis Bennett at St Marks in Van Nuys,

35. Anderson, *Introduction to Pentecostalism*, 24, 35–37, passim.

36. Althouse, *Spirit of the Last Days*, chapter 1; Althouse, "Left Behind—Fact or Fiction," 187–207.

37. Sheppard, "Pentecostalism and the Hermeneutics of Dispensationalism," 5–34.

California. Although Pentecostal forms of spirituality and glossolalia were finding expression in the historic traditions prior, Bennett's public announcement became a symbolic focus for the origins of the Protestant Charismatic Renewal. By the early 1960s, experiences of glossolalia and other charismatic demonstrations were finding their way into every major Protestant denomination. The official beginning of the Roman Catholic Charismatic Renewal was in 1967 in Duquesne University and the University of Notre Dame. Unlike its Protestant counterpart, the Catholic Charismatic movement was among educated Catholic laypersons and later priests in the renewal context of Vatican II, and was therefore theologically nuanced.[38] While the Charismatic Renewal adopted Pentecostal-like spirituality and practices such as glossolalia and healing, participants remained within their own traditions and interpreted their new practices within the context of their traditional theologies. Thus glossolalia, healing, and spontaneous worship were read through the lens of an already given eschatology. In the late 1970s and 1980s, non-denominational or independent expressions of Pentecostalism emerged with an emphasis on networks of trans-congregational leaders and fellowships. The non-denominational charismatic movement includes diverse groups and networks such as the National Leadership Conference, People of Destiny, the House Church Movement, Covenant Ministries, International Convention of Faith Ministries, the Vineyard Fellowship, and its offshoot known as the Toronto Blessing, or New Frontiers International and Salt and Light in the United Kingdom. It also includes charismatic personalities such as Ken Sumrall, Charles Simpson, Kenneth Hagin and Kenneth Copeland, Pat Robertson, Earl Paulk, Steven Strang, Oral Roberts, John Wimber and Peter Wagner, Randy Clark, and John Arnott, to name only a few.[39] The emphasis in these networks vary greatly, but often include the five-fold apostolic and prophetic ministry, exuberant worship, healing and charismatic gifting. Pentecostalism in this work is taken in the broadest sense to include classical, Charismatic and non-denominational varieties, and as its expressions vary, so too does its eschatology.

---

38. Hocken, "Charismatic Movement," 481.

39. Ibid., 487–89.

PURPOSE AND OUTLINE OF THE BOOK

The collection of essays in this volume addresses the question of Pentecostal eschatology from biblical, theological, and contextual perspectives. The first section is a biblical evaluation of eschatology, under the premise that while the whole of the biblical canon must be taken into account in the construction of theology, each of the biblical authors has particular theological points of view, and therefore one can observe variances in eschatological perspectives. The approach taken here is not intended to be comprehensive, but biblical snapshots that provide contours for understanding biblical eschatology. William Raccah's inaugural chapter "Early Jewish Eschatology" nicely summarizes and places eschatology within the context of the ancient Jewish worldview. Creation itself is made meaningful in its eschatological culmination. God as Creator transcends creation, but also chooses to covenant with the people of Israel in history. The messianic hope was a hope for Israel, the world, and creation, to which other eschatological symbols point. Blaine Charette explores the Lukan question of Israel's destiny in "Restoring the Kingdom to Israel: Kingdom and Spirit in Luke's Thought." In response to the disciples query regarding the restoration of national Israel, Jesus offers the eschatological Spirit depicted in the event of Pentecost. The kingdom is restored to Israel in so far as the Spirit of God is restored to the people of God in entirety, and the gift of the Spirit is eschatologically significant in that the signs of the kingdom are present among God's people. In "Seven Dispensations or Two-Age View of History: A Pauline Perspective," John Bertone explores the Pauline corpus to argue that dispensationalism is incongruent with Paul's emphasis on the multiplicity of the spiritual gifts. Where dispensationalism teaches that the charismatic gifts ceased with the age of the church, Paul clearly advocates the edifying purpose of these gifts as the work of the one Spirit. Significantly, for Pentecostals, dispensationalism lacks biblical support and severely undercuts the logic for the operation of the gifts of the Spirit. Robby Waddell offers biblical support for an ecologically responsible eschatology in "Apocalyptic Sustainability: The Future of Pentecostal Ecology." He eschews the notion of a cataclysmic destruction of the earth, not only because of his ethical concerns that apocalyptic destruction is incongruent with social ministry and justice, but because the biblical tradition points to the renewal of the earth thereby supporting ecological responsibility. John Christopher Thomas', "The Mystery of the Great Whore: Pneumatic Discernment of

Revelation 17," concludes the biblical section with a biblical appraisal of the Whore of Babylon. The Great Whore alludes to a socio-political critique of the worldly powers (Rome) by reference to earlier cities of destruction (Egypt and Sodom). Yet God will bring about the demise of the Whore and by implication the demise of ungodly rulers.

The next section engages Pentecostal eschatology in historical and theological dimensions. In "Early Pentecostal Eschatology in Light of *The Apostolic Faith*, 1906–1908," Larry McQueen seeks to uncover the eschatology that emerges from *The Apostolic Faith*, the periodical connected to the Azusa Street Mission and its relation to Pentecostal spirituality, in order to assess whether or not early Pentecostal eschatology aligned with classical dispensationalism. The theology of Azusa Street was holistic and contingent on the outpouring of the Spirit. It was apocalyptic in the sense that heaven was believed to be a future state, but also an experience that could be partially realized in the present activity of the Spirit's gifting. He argues that Azusa Street's eschatology cannot be understood as another type of dispensational premillennialism. Murray Dempster explores the relationship between eschatology and social ethics in "Eschatology, Spirit Baptism, and Inclusiveness: An Exploration into the Hallmarks of a Pentecostal Social Ethic." Integrating biblical theology with ethical insight, Dempster seeks to explore the relationship between the Pentecostal doctrine of Spirit baptism and eschatology in order to construct a Pentecostal social ethic, which moves beyond individual piety and proclamation to social transformation in identity with the work of Christ.

In "Eschatology as Soteriology: The Cosmic Full Gospel," Matthew Thompson draws on Wesleyan theology to argue for an eschatologically infused soteriology. This eschatology is neither realized nor individualistic, but progressive and cosmic in scope. It corresponds with the patristic concern for *theosis* and the divine movement of descent and ascent. Thompson then sketches how *theosis* can be applied to an understanding of the full gospel. Peter Althouse's chapter "Pentecostal Eschatology in Context: The Eschatological Orientation of the Full Gospel" dovetails nicely with Thompson's, but where Thompson proposes an eschatologically infused soteriology that is Wesleyan in orientation, Althouse proposes an eschatological reading of Pentecostal theology informed by a Reformed perspective. Althouse understands eschatology as proleptic, in which the kingdom is inaugurated in the life, death, and resurrection of

Christ Jesus, who offers the eschatological Spirit on the day of Pentecost, and will find its culmination in the eschaton. He suggests an eschatological reading of the fourfold gospel[40] informed by Moltmann, Barth, and N. T. Wright rather than the continental tradition. Daniel Castelo's chapter "Patience as a Theological Virtue: A Challenge to Pentecostal Eschatology" argues that Pentecostals would do well to reassess their frenetic emphasis on eschatological immediacy with an appropriation of the theological tradition of patience. By looking to the virtue of patience, Pentecostals can maintain the expectancy of the eschatological coming of Christ, while at the same time surrendering to the mystery of the coming kingdom as a divine act, with all the ambiguities, tensions, frustration, and hope the coming kingdom entails.

The next section explores various Charismatic developments in eschatology. Written from a Roman Catholic Charismatic perspective, Jeffrey Gros' chapter "Hope for Eternal Life: Perspectives for Pentecostals and Charismatics" bridges the Pentecostal and Catholic perspectives on eschatology in order to encourage ecumenical dialogue. Noting those eschatological elements both Pentecostals and Roman Catholics have in common, though with varying degrees of emphases, Gros unpacks the role of popular piety and imagination in forming eschatological beliefs, and how these create misunderstandings between the two traditions. In order to move forward in the process of reconciliation, an investigation of each other's popular beliefs, and their role, if any, in forming core beliefs, needs to be determined. Gros then unpacks the historical developments of dispensational and millenarian views from as far back as the patristic era, in order to discuss the rise of Roman Catholic popular piety. The chapter is an invitation for a Pentecostal response to further the dialogue. In "'Discerning the Times': The Victorious Eschatology of the Shepherding Movement," David Moore explores the historical developments and eschatological perspectives of five independent charismatic leaders who willingly submitted themselves to each other's authority, in an effort to produce moral reform. The eschatological leaning of the Shepherding movement was restorationist: in the

---

40. The major difference between Wesleyan Holiness and Reformed Pentecostal perspectives is their view of sanctification. The former assumes Wesley's theology of entire sanctification, whereas the latter follows William H. Durham and believes sanctification is objectively "finished on the cross" though with an accent on its progressive development throughout the Christian life and fully realized in glorification.

last days God was restoring the five-fold ministry of apostle, prophet, evangelist, pastor, and teacher. While controversial for other Pentecostal and Charismatic groups, the Shepherding movement's apostolic brand of leadership and authority, which encouraged people to submit to a leader's authority, was inherently coherent with its restorationist eschatology. Michael McClymond's chapter "Prosperity Already and Not Yet: An Eschatological Interpretation of the Health and Wealth Emphasis in the North American Pentecostal-Charismatic Movement" probes the eschatological understanding of that brand of charismatic Christianity labeled the "Prosperity Gospel." McClymond argues that the Prosperity Gospel must be interpreted in the context of the Latter Rain Revival of the 1940s, in which the restoration of prophets and apostles and an optimistic eschatology shapes the idea of the church as the dominion of God's reign and demonstrates a partial realization of the eschaton. Both Moore and McClymond's chapters can be seen as companion pieces revealing the eschatological thrust of two representatives of the independent charismatic movement.

Section four looks at how Pentecostal eschatology has been ethnically and geographically contextualized. Nestor Medina leads the section with "The New Jerusalem versus Social Responsibility: The Challenges of Pentecostalism in Guatemala." Medina offers a socio-political critique of Pentecostalism in Guatemala, in which the paradoxical tension between an otherworldly eschatology retards constructive socio-political engagement, but the emphasis on the missionary expansion of Christianity brings Pentecostals squarely into a socio-political arena. Guatemalan Pentecostals are generally conservative, though at times they have periodically supported repressive regimes and democratic reforms. Sammy Alfaro investigates the funeral rites of Hispanic Pentecostals in "'*Se Fue con el Señor*': The Hispanic Pentecostal Funeral as Anticipatory Celebration," as an anticipatory celebration of hope in the coming kingdom, which at the same time brings liberation to the present. Funeral rites bring comfort in the hope that God will triumph over sin and death in the age to come, but that the faithful can also receive a present foretaste of the heavenly kingdom in signs of healing, salvation, and even liberation. In "Constructing an African Pentecostal Eschatology: Which Way?" J. Ayodeji Adewuya reflects on the contributions of African Pentecostal eschatology. Cautioning that African worldviews cannot be taken as monolithic and therefore neither can African

Pentecostalism, Adewuya draws from his Nigerian roots to argue that African Pentecostal eschatology must start with reflection on an African worldview. This worldview points to hope beyond this world, salvation as relief in time of distress in which healing, deliverance, empowerment, and successful life are important elements, death is the only portal into continued human existence, and especially a core belief in the Holy Spirit in a context of a cosmology of spirits and demon possession. Added to this mix is the influence of dispensationalism through the proclamations of Western evangelical missionaries. This influence brings typical eschatological elements such as the return of Jesus Christ, the certainty of a future resurrection, and the defeat of Satan. However, Adewuya insists that Africa cannot oscillate between Western eschatological views and its own worldview, but must construct its own eschatological voice. Finally, Frank Macchia's chapter "Jesus is Victor: The Eschatology of the Blumhardts with Implications for Pentecostal Eschatologies" offers a European Pentecostal eschatology. Though prior to the outbreak of charismatic worship at Azusa Street in the USA, Johann and Christoph Blumhardt emphasized a Pentecostal-type spirituality in the stress of divine healing and social transformation. Their recovery of eschatology under the concept of the kingdom of God influenced major German theologians such as Karl Barth, Paul Tillich, and Jürgen Moltmann. Moltmann even claims that the "Pentecostalism of Blumhardt" can be a corrective to the futuristic eschatology of dispensationalism.[41] Macchia's contribution is to investigate how Johann's emphasis on divine healing was transformed into an emphasis on the liberating activity of social action and justice with the theology of Christoph, in which the eschatology of the kingdom of God played a significant role. The implication for Pentecostal eschatology is that the liberative reign of the kingdom of God must shift away from narrow piety and futuristic events, in order to focus on the renewal of life in all its diversity and global dimensions.

The chapters that follow are a modest and preliminary contribution to the developing Pentecostal scholarship, in an effort to trace the vast and diverse landscape of Pentecostal eschatology, and to contribute to its further development. We hope that you will be encouraged, inspired, and even challenged by these chapters, as you reflect on the meaning of Christian hope.

---

41. Moltmann, Foreword, in Althouse, *Spirit of the Last Days*, viii.

PART ONE

Eschatology in Biblical Perspectives

1

Early Jewish Eschatology

WILLIAM RACCAH

INTRODUCTION

ESCHATOLOGY IS THAT BRANCH of theology concerned with last things, such as, death, resurrection, judgment, the messiah, and immortality. Derived from the Greek *eschatos*, the term "eschatology" means "furthest" or "last" and the Oxford English Dictionary defines it as "the science of the four last things: death, judgment, heaven and hell." Paradoxically, although it is concerned with "last things," as with the termination of this world and this life, the religious meaning of the term emphasizes at the same time the ideas of a new life and a new world. The old world—this present world—will give way to the ushering in of the new world of eternity.[1]

Eschatology is essentially a religious symbol.[2] Dealing as it does with the symbols of the religious experience, it is not conducive to philosoph-

1. Harshbarger and Mourant, *Judaism and Christianity*, 332–33.

2. "By *symbol* we mean that which represents or expresses some form of reality, whether that be a particular thing, person, or action in the past, present, or future. The religious use of symbols excludes the conceptual for the existential. In the words of Mircea Eliade, 'Symbols still keep their contact with the profound sources of life; they express one might say, the "spiritual as lived"' (*le spirituel vécu*). That is why symbols have, as it were, a numinous aura; they reveal that the modalities of the spirit are at the same time manifestations of life, and consequently, they directly engage human existence. The religious symbol not only unveils a structure of reality or a dimension of existence; by the same stroke, it brings a *meaning* into human existence. This is why

ical conceptual analysis. Nor can it be reduced to scientific knowledge, for scientific knowledge is conceptual and factual. Transcending both philosophy and science, eschatology relates to a cosmic reality based upon revelations apprehended and accepted by the individual, which we call symbols. Occasionally, of course, eschatology may touch upon certain problems frequently treated within philosophical investigation, such as the demonstration of the immortality of the soul or the attempt to discover the laws of history, but the symbols are the symbols of religious experience with the premise that truths are accepted as revealed. Thus, the main method of eschatology is essentially the explication and interpretation of such truths and symbols, and many of the conclusions concerning the basic symbols of either Judaism or Christianity, being quite speculative, frequently admit of more diversity of opinion than agreement.[3]

As a religious symbol, eschatology is concerned with the interpretation of history as meaningful, purposeful, and ethical. This interpretation of history contrasts sharply with the views of many historians and philosophers. So, while the historian is not concerned with the end of history nor strives to transcend history and relate it to some higher cosmic reality, and the philosophers are agreed that the study of history does not yield demonstrative knowledge and that to determine its purposes is a hazardous undertaking, these considerations have not prevented many philosophers from speculating about the nature and course of human history.[4] Indeed, like the writer of Ecclesiastes, the philosopher of history may be satisfied to affirm, "there is nothing new under the sun" (Eccl 1:10, NIV).

History, most religions claim, moves in cycles of time throughout eternity rather than in a linear time that culminates in some specific goal. This cyclical view, or the myth of the eternal recurrence, holds that history is endlessly repetitive, directionless, and devoid of end or purpose. However, that history is meaningful, that it has a purpose and a goal, and that it holds out hope is nowhere better exemplified than in the whole Jewish-Christian tradition. Both Judaism and Christianity are unique in their conception of history. Following certain interpretations

---

even symbols aiming at the ultimate reality conjointly constitute existential revelations for the man who deciphers their message." Eliade, *History of Religions*, 100.

3. Harshbarger and Mourant, *Judaism and Christianity*, 332.

4. Ibid.

found in the Jewish writings of the intertestamental period and the first few centuries of the CE, early Christian writers and those who followed throughout the centuries have affirmed that hope lies in God and in the conviction that God's purposes are realized in history. This is why the people of Israel, and Christians later, place their hopes in the expectation of a great good, the coming of the messianic kingdom.[5] In a kingdom where ultimate happiness and salvation will be achieved.

Thus when looking at the religious concept of eschatology, we find that the meaning of history is revealed in Scripture rather than in the attempted speculations of the philosophers. The meaning of history may be said to be contained in a theology of history, and such a theology of history has certitude and meaningfulness based upon the faith of the individual, which is not found in a philosophy of history.[6] Consequently, for Judaism, as for Christianity, the meaning of creation is revealed in its end, and only in its valuation as good is creation made meaningful.

Interestingly, we can observe that what is said at the beginning and the end of the universe is highly symbolic or speculative. There are many symbols in the Jewish-Christian tradition for the meaning of the end of history, symbols that must be held together in a kind of pattern for their total understanding. In addition, these symbols must be placed within an ordered structure, which is history itself.[7] Since for the Jews the meaning of history centers upon the covenants God made with Noah and Abraham, which were ratified in the covenant with Moses at Sinai, the Law given to Moses gives meaning to history, for observance of the Law perfects humanity and society. Thus, only at the consummation of history and the realization of the kingdom of God will the Law disappear.

The historical reality, for both Jews and Christians, refers not so much to the relations of nations and of persons as it does to their relationship to God. History, therefore, is not reduced to mere human happenings, a much later Renaissance and Enlightenment development, for this would undermine human personality and significance in the ebb and flow of events. The importance of being a person is to take one's place, one's role in the drama of humanity in the presence of God. In that drama, no individual is a mere thing or event. Each individual is a subject of unlimited destiny and great significance, and each individual

5. Ibid., 334–35.

6. Ibid., 335.

7. Ibid., 336.

is challenged to make a decision that will make history as far as that individual is concerned. Another way to express this is to say that the *kairos* gives meaning to the *chronos*, for the *kairos* is the intersection of our time with eternity, making every moment of time (*chronos*) significant. With the manifestation of God in and through history, every moment of time is charged with significance and value.[8]

THE MESSIAH AND THE MESSIANIC KINGDOM

When we turn our attention to early Jewish eschatology, it is very important to remind ourselves of a basic premise, often taken for granted, and more often ignored: Jesus, his disciples, the Apostles, the various writers of the New Testament (with the possible exception of Luke), Paul, and the majority of those who composed the very early church were Jews. Not only were they Jews, but they were also full participating members and typical representatives of the Jews who lived in first-century Palestine and the Diaspora. As such, whatever they affirmed, argued about, wrote or pronounced was within a context that defined their identity, of which one part was theological, while another portion concerned itself with eschatological questions. Therefore, while others in this book will address the writings, pronouncements, and interpretations of what we find within the pages of the New Testament, we will focus our attention for the next few pages on eschatological elements found in the period preceding and contemporaneous with the rise and development of the early church.

One of the first things we can observe when looking at the relevant material is that the rabbis of the early period, it seems, show a carelessness and sluggishness in the application of theological principles,[9] which is rather astonishing considering the care with which they addressed various subjects, especially those dealing with the Jewish people, their relationship toward God, and vice versa. As already mentioned, Judaism is essentially an historical religion. In history, God is revealed to the Jewish people and intervenes for the Jewish people and for all the nations. To these rabbis, Israel's election was predestined before the creation of the world and sanctified unto the name of God even before the universe

---

8. Ibid., 336.

9. Schechter, *Aspects of Rabbinic Theology*, 13.

was called into existence.[10] Accordingly, for the rabbis, "Israel was there before the world was created and is still existing now and will continue to exist in the future."[11] For this reason God has covenanted with God's chosen people and has led them out of Egypt to the promise land. This recital could be continued at length, but it should be obvious that Israel has a future, that God has given the history of Israel a meaning and has endowed it with divine promises and hopes, and that these promises and hopes center upon the central symbol of Jewish eschatology: the messiah and the messianic kingdom.[12]

For Judaism there is a messiah and a messianic kingdom. Both are intimately connected and bound up within history. The messiah *will* appear in history and the messianic kingdom *will* appear within history. This contrasts sharply with Christianity, which teaches that the messiah, as Jesus, appeared and that he has established his kingdom both now and in the future. The future messianic kingdom foretold in the Hebrew scriptures envisions the destruction of the present evils and the realization of a completely new set of values. It is important to stress that for Jewish and Christian eschatology this point is thoroughly ethical. The vision of the messianic kingdom as one in which the highest ethical values will be achieved is the logical consequence of the belief in a personal God who has established a moral relationship with a chosen group of people. Furthermore, to say that the messiah and the messianic kingdom will appear in history means for the Jewish tradition that the messiah and the messianic kingdom are essentially of *this* world, although their realization lies in the future.[13]

The coming of the messiah and the messianic kingdom is closely bound up in the early development of Judaism and the Jewish monarchy. The term "messiah" is adjectival in the Old Testament where it occurs thirty-eight times, whereas the noun usage came much later.[14] It means "anointed" and, in the early monarchy, it referred to a person anointed

10. See *Gen Rabba* 1:4, "It is forbidden to inquire what existed before creation, as Moses distinctly tells us (Deut 4:32) 'Ask now of the days that are past which were before thee, since the day God created man upon earth.' Thus the scope of inquiry is limited to the time since the Creation."

11. Schechter, *Aspects of Rabbinic Theology*, 59.

12. Harshbarger and Mourant, *Judaism and Christianity*, 337.

13. Ibid., 337.

14. Stewart, *Rabbinic Theology*, 46.

with holy oil (2 Kgs 5:3). In the early history of Israel, the monarchy, especially under king David, attained considerable prestige and Jewish expectations concerning the messiah centered around the conception of the Davidic, royal messiah.[15] Thus, the monarchy established by David became not merely an ideal for the future, but was given a religious sanction and ratification. It had the duty of maintaining the covenant and preparing for the future salvation of humanity in the messianic kingdom that is to come. The close relationship between the Davidic monarchy and God is evident in much of 2 Samuel, which covers the reign of David. In particular, the divine character and direction of the monarchy is marked in the words of God as reported by the prophet Nathan (2 Sam 7:12–16). In verse 12, where we read "I will raise up your son after you, who shall come forth from your body . . ." the immediate reference is to the reign of king Solomon. Jewish theologians, however, add that this verse also refers to the sanctification of the coming rule of the messiah as king. In fact, the entire chapter appears to ratify the Davidic monarchy and establishes its messianic character for all time to come.[16]

Furthermore, the very prosperity and greatness of the Davidic monarchy is a type of what is to come in the future realization of the messianic kingdom. The religious character of the monarchy, evident in its important role in the maintenance of the Covenant, was coupled with its political prestige and its economic prosperity. All these factors contributed not only to the strong sense of nationalism in Israel, but served as the basis for some nationalistic hopes that came to be centered on the vision of the messianic kingdom. In particular, such hopes included the strong conviction that the new kingdom would be of this world and that it would be especially marked by material blessings and prosperity.[17]

However, despite the ratification of the Davidic monarchy and its more immediate and phenomenal success, its increasing failures in the years following led to prophetic criticism and denunciation. One of the strongest and most significant critics of the monarchy in its later period

15. De Jonge, *Jewish Eschatology, Early Christian Christology and the Testaments of the Twelve Patriarchs*, 65.

16. Harshbarger and Mourant, *Judaism and Christianity*, 338.

17. This notion of material prosperity as a concomitant of spiritual values is not an uncommon one. While very much present today, it already was so in the beliefs of certain Puritan theologians of the seventeenth century who identified material wealth as a sign that the individual who possessed it was one of the elect, whereas poverty was a sign of future damnation.

was the prophet Isaiah whose prophecy for the future of the monarchy is the vision of an ideal monarchy, of a kingdom of God ruled over by the messiah who shall be a descendant of David. For Isaiah, the messiah as an ideal king will come to rule over an ideal kingdom, one who will restore the golden age of humankind, an age in which there is no evil, no sickness, and no death.[18] All this is clearly brought out in Isa 11:1–10. Yet, the term "messiah" is neither the central title nor is it only connected with a prince of Davidic descent.[19]

Considerable confusion also arises from unclear terminology. The terms "messiah" and "messianic" are often used in a wider sense than attributed them by later theologians. They denote any eschatological mediator, regardless of whether the person is called "anointed" or not.[20] It is, therefore, not very helpful to call every future "redeemer/savior" or agent of divine deliverance a "messiah." In fact, the word "anointed" is used surprisingly seldom of future mediating figures in the literary sources around the beginning of the Christian era and, apart from the uncertain instance in 1Qsa 2:11–16, the absolute use of the term "messiah" is found only in some places in the Syriac *Apocalypse of Baruch*[21] and *4 Ezra*.[22] The appearance of a mediating figure, whether human, angelic or divine, whatever name or title may be used, is not a regular or indispensable element. However, to speak about messianism without a messiah does not contribute greater clarity of thought. In the Old Testament, "anointed" and "anointing" are used in connection with kings, high priests and other priests, and with prophets. The term is used for Saul, David and Davidic kings, and even once for Cyrus.[23] In four places, we find the term

18. Ibid., 338.

19. See De Jonge, "Use of the Word 'Anointed' in the Time of Jesus," 132–48; De Jonge, "Role of Intermediaries in God's Final Intervention in the Future according to the Qumran Scrolls," 44–63; De Jonge and Van Der Woude, "11Q Melchizedek and the New Testament," 301–26.

20. De Jonge, "Use of the Word 'Anointed' in the Time of Jesus," 110.

21. Also known as 2 Baruch, a Jewish pseudepigraphical text thought to have been written in the late first century CE or early second century CE, after the destruction of the Temple in 70 CE.

22. The book known as 4 Ezra is a compilation of three textual traditions that make up sixteen chapters, and was composed at the end of the first century CE in Palestine. The central chapters of the book (3–14) are a Jewish apocalypse, with a later Christian addition added to the front (chapters 1–2) and a later Christian addition added to the end as an appendix/conclusion (chapters 15–16).

23. Isa 45:1, "Thus says the LORD to Cyrus His anointed, Whom I have taken by

"the anointed high priest" (Lev 4:3, 5, 16; 6:15). As far as prophets are concerned, 1 Kgs 19:16 announces the anointing of Elisha by Elijah to be prophet in his place. The varied usage of the term in the Old Testament is reflected in later Jewish sources, in particular in the picture of David, who acts as the idealized description of Davidic kings in a number of royal psalms (e.g., Ps 2, 89, 110, and 132) and prophetic texts about the coming of a true son of David (see in particular Isa 11:1–10.) where the term "anointed" ("messiah") does not occur. De Jonge admonishes, "we should not speak of a royal, priestly, or prophetic messiah but of a future king, high priest, and prophet who is in a few places called 'anointed.'"[24]

Interestingly, the Maccabean documents, which disdain the revival of the Davidic dynasty, ignore the term and there is no mention of the "messiah" in the Book of Jubilees, nor is there in *1 Enoch* 1–36 and 91–104, in the *Assumption of Moses*,[25] in *2 Enoch*, or in the *Sibylline Oracles*;[26] yet, "all of these contain prophetic passages in which some messiah

---

the right hand, To subdue nations before him. And to loose the loins of kings; To open doors before him so that gates will not be shut." See, Stewart, *Rabbinic Theology*, 46.

24. De Jonge, "Use of the Word 'Anointed' in the Time of Jesus," 111.

25. Also known as the *Testament of Moses*. Based on the literal translation of idioms within the text, it is generally accepted that the extant Latin version is a translation from Greek, itself probably a translation from Hebrew. It purports to be secret prophecies revealed by Moses to Joshua when close to the end of his life. In it, a brief outline of Jewish history up until the first century CE is sketched out. Most scholars date the work to the early first century CE, contemporary with the latest historical figures described in it. A significant number of others, however, date it to the previous century and suggest that the first century CE references are later insertions into the text. A far smaller number of scholars place it in the second century CE.

26. A chaotic medley, the *Sibylline Oracles*, as we now have them, consist of twelve books (originally fourteen) of various authorship, date, and religious conception, oftentimes of unrelated fragments. The unknown editor of the final arrangement is thought to be Alexander (sixth century CE) and seems to have been guided by caprice as often as by any discernible principle of editing. Anonymous in origin, these oracles were apt to modification and enlargement at will by Hellenistic Jews and by Christians for missionary purposes. The oldest of the surviving *Sibylline Oracles* seem to be books 3–5, which were composed partly by Jews in Alexandria around 140 BCE. The third oracle seems to have been composed in the reign of Ptolemy VI Philometor. Books 1–2 may have been written by Christians, although there may have been a Jewish original that was adapted to Christian purposes. The *Sibylline Oracles* appear as a pastiche of Greek and Roman pagan mythology, employing motifs of Homer and Hesiod; Judeo-Christian legends such as the Garden of Eden, Noah and the Tower of Babel, Gnostic and early Christian homilies and eschatological writings, as well as thinly veiled references to historical figures such as Alexander the Great and Cleopatra.

might reasonably have been expected to make an appearance."[27] For Ecclesiasticus, or Ben Sira,[28] who has no interest in a future redeemer, the "anointed one" or "messiah" is the Israelite king. The Qumran Scrolls, for their part, mention at least two messiahs, one Davidic and one priestly, each of which is not necessarily an eschatological figure.[29] To confuse the situation further, the Scrolls also apply the term to the prophets.[30] In the *Psalms of Solomon* 17,[31] which is neither apocalyptic nor eschatological, the messiah is an idealized, future Davidic king who also exhibits traits of sage and teacher. *The Similitudes of Enoch*,[32] for their part, allude not to a king, but to a transcendent heavenly figure, preferring such titles as "Chosen One" and "the Son of Man" (*1 Enoch* 37–71).[33] The conflicting pictures of the messiah found in *4 Ezra* add another dimension to the concept of the messiah within the varied ancient Jewish literature. In 7:28ff., the messiah dies an unredeeming death before the *eschaton* (end times), but later chapters portray him as announcing and executing the final judgment. In *2 Baruch*, the term "messiah" applies primarily to a warrior, the slayer of Israel's enemies. Finally, in the Mishnah's legal contexts, the appellation "messiah" refers to an anointed priest, and the concept of the messiah as redeemer is negligible.

In view of the data above, "one may legitimately wonder about the reasons for conceiving of 'the messiah' as a fundamental and generative component of both Israelite religion and early Judaism."[34] One may wonder about the justification for the assertion that "from the first century BCE, the messiah was the central figure in the Jewish myth of

---

27. Smith, "What is Implied by the Variety of Messianic Figures?" 68.

28. Ecclesiasticus is the only apocryphal work whose author is known: Ben Sira. Written in Hebrew in Palestine around 180–175 BCE, Ben Sira was probably a scribe well-versed in Jewish law and custom.

29. Collins, *Apocalyptic Imagination*, 123.

30. Green, "Messiah in Judaism: Rethinking the Question," 3.

31. Group of eighteen religious songs or poems dating from the first century BCE; originally written in Hebrew or Aramaic and then translated into Greek, the *Psalms of Solomon* form part of the Pseudepigrapha.

32. *The Similitudes of Enoch* is the second part of a larger composite work known as *1 Enoch*. They are very difficult to date, but the general consensus of scholarship seems to be the first century CE, but pre-70.

33. See Collins, "Son of Man in First-Century Judaism," 448.

34. Mowinckel, *He That Cometh*, 3.

the future,"[35] or for the claim that 'the belief in the messiah' is one of the four "good gifts which the people of Israel have left as an inheritance to the entire world,"[36] or for the widespread assumption that "In the time of Jesus the Jews were awaiting a messiah."[37] One may wonder how so much has come to be written about an allegedly Jewish conception in which so many ancient Jewish texts manifest such little interest.[38]

For Jewish theologians, and indeed the majority of Jewish people throughout the centuries, the coming of the messiah is still part of the dream of Israel. Also, for the Jews, the expected messiah is a person—a human being and not a god. The human nature of the messiah is often signaled in terms of "the suffering servant of the Lord" (Isa 52–53). The messiah will also be poor, humble and despised. Jonathan ben Uzziel's Targums on this passage, dating from the first century CE, begin Isa 52:13 by immediately identifying the suffering servant as the messiah saying, "Behold my servant messiah shall prosper."[39] Any idea of his death as an atonement or as a "ransom" was unknown to the rabbis, but there are occasional allusions to his sufferings. However, these allusions are much later than the period under consideration.[40]

Early on, the conception arose that the messiah already existed in heaven from the creation,[41] and that he had been born as a human long

35. Patai, *Messiah Texts*, xxvii.

36. Klausner, *The Messianic Idea in Israel*, 13.

37. Mowinckel, *He That Cometh*, 3.

38. Lindars, *New Testament Apologetics*, 251, "The primacy of 'the messiah' as a subject of academic study derives not from ancient Jewish preoccupation, but from early Christian word-choice, theology, and apologetics. Early Christians, and particularly the earliest Christian writers, had to establish a discourse that made Jesus' career reasonable, His unexpected death believable, and their audacious commitment and new life plausible."

39. Quoted in Neubauer, *Fifty-Third Chapter of Isaiah According to the Jewish Interpreters*, 5.

40. Montefiore, *Rabbinic Literature and Gospel Teachings*, 305.

41. The preexistence of the messiah first appears in the apocryphal book of *1 Enoch* (46:1–3; 48:4–6; 62:7–9), which was originally written in either Hebrew or Aramaic around 150 BCE. From that period on, the concept of the messiah who was created in the six days of Creation (*B. Pesachim* 54a; *B. Nedarim* 39a; *Gen Rabba* 1:4; 2:4), or even prior to them, or who was born at variously stated subsequent dates and was then hidden to await his time, became a standard feature of Jewish messianic eschatology. In one version, it is the name of the messiah that was created in the beginning (*1 Enoch* 48:2–3; *B. Sanhedrin* 98b; *Y. Berachot* 5a; *B. Sanhedrin* 98b; *B. Baba Bathra* 75b: *Pereq Shalom* p. 101; *Sifre on Deuteronomy* 65a; *Lam Rabba* 1:51), while in another, his spirit or his

ago but had been kept hidden away, probably on account of Israel's sins. His public manifestation as messiah was still to come. In this hidden life, he had to endure many sufferings for Israel's sake. Thus, "Sufferings are divided into three portions, of which one part has been allocated to all the generations of the world, and one part to the age of the Persecutions [under Hadrian], and one part to the messiah, as it is written, 'He was wounded for our transgressions.'"[42] The suffering in this same verse from Isaiah is referred to in *Ruth Rabba* on 2:14 where we read, "Dip thy morsel in the vinegar: these are the sufferings of the messiah, as it says, He was pierced for our iniquities.'"[43]

The *Midrash Sifre*, dating from the middle of the third century CE, but with the majority of its core material dating back to the schools of Rabbi Akiva and Rabbi Ishmael, applies Isa 53:5–6 to the messiah. The argument is: if the transgression of Adam (the first human who was given one prohibition) resulted in such consequences upon all of his descendants ("all generations"), and since the attribute of goodness is greater and more powerful than vengeance, how much more will the sufferings of the messiah justify all generations.[44] Interestingly, this argument is strikingly similar to that made by Rav Shaul (the apostle Paul) in Rom 5:15–19.

The *Babylonian Talmud* states, "The Rabanan[45] say that messiah's name is The Suffering Scholar of Rabbi's House (or The Leper Scholar) for it is written, 'Surely He hath born our grief and carried our sorrows,

---

souls, and in yet a third, he himself was actually born and even his celestial throne was fashioned. See Patai, *The Messiah Texts*, 16.

42. *Midrash Samuel* xix. 29b.

43. *Midrash Ruth* v. § 6 on ii. 14.

44. "R. Yosé the Galilaean said, "Come forth and learn the righteousness of the King messiah and the reward of the just from the first man who received but one commandment, a prohibition, and transgressed it: consider how many deaths were inflicted upon himself, upon his own generations, and upon those that followed them, till the end of all generations. Which attribute is greater, the attribute of goodness, or the attribute of vengeance? He answered, The attribute of goodness is the greater, and the attribute of vengeance is less; how much more, then will the King messiah, who endures affliction and pains for the transgressors (as it is written, "He was wounded," etc.) justify all generations! And this is what is meant when it is said, "And the Lord made the iniquity of us all meet upon him." Quoted in Neubauer, *Fifty-Third Chapter of Isaiah according to the Jewish Interpreters*, 10–11.

45. The Rabanan (explainers) was a group of sages who, during the middle fifth century CE in Babylonia, were entrusted to provide final explanations on the almost completed Talmud.

yet we did esteem him stricken, smitten of God and afflicted.'"[46] From this it seems evident that the Babylonian Talmud applies Isaiah 53:4 to the messiah. It further adds, "The messiah—what is his name? . . . Our teachers have said, His name shall be the Leprous One of the house of Rabbi [perhaps in reference to Rabbi's sufferings for thirteen years], even as it says, 'Surely he bore our sickness and carried our pains: yet we esteemed him as one stricken with leprosy, and smitten of God.'"[47]

Thus, within Jewish theology, the messiah will be a concrete reality and his appearance will come in God's own time, and that will be the end of time and the establishment of God's kingdom.[48] Since the knowledge of the end of history lies with God, God alone will consummate the end of history with the coming of the true messiah.[49]

In the historical development of this notion of the messiah, it should be observed that a transition is made from the conception of the messiah as a political ruler and liberator, one who will merely free the Jews from the oppressive rule of others, to the conception of an ideal monarch, one who will effect the spiritual regeneration of all people. Although originally only a national savior, the messiah now becomes the perfect type of ruler who will sanctify and establish the rule of God's law for all. The uniqueness and nationalism involved in the original conception of the messiah merges into the conception of a messiah for all humanity, one who will redeem not merely Israel but the whole world. With this conception of a more universalistic reign, we find that the emphasis upon the messiah is replaced more and more with an emphasis upon the messianic kingdom, the benefits of which will extend not merely to the Jewish people but to all peoples for all times.[50] We find this new conception of the messiah and the messianic kingdom present in the revelation of the prophet Daniel (7:13–14). It is important to note that the context

46. *Sanhedrin* 98a.

47. *Sanhedrin* 98b in Neubauer, *Fifty-Third Chapter of Isaiah According to the Jewish Interpreters*, 7. "Rabbi" in this passage is the title of Rabbi Judah the Saint, the redactor of the Mishnah. The fullest and most interesting passages of those dealing with messiah's sufferings come from the late Midrashic compilation homilies on special Pentateuchal and Prophetic lessons known as the *Pesikta Rabbati*, which dates from the early eighth century CE. See in particular *Pesikta Rabbati* 146b, 159b, 161a, 161b, 162a, 163a.

48. See the familiar passage found in Sanhedrin 98a, which bases its conclusion on Ps 95:7b.

49. Harshbarger and Mourant, *Judaism and Christianity*, 339.

50. Ibid., 339.

within which Daniel is writing was not Ancient Palestine, but Medo-Persia, which was then controlling various peoples and nations. All were under some form of bondage or control and all aspired to freedom and a reaffirmation of who they had been. The message of Daniel thus became universal and inclusive in its proclamation, and saw itself appropriated a few centuries later by some of the people living in that region.[51]

The religion of Israel is to be world encompassing, revealed by the fact that Israel is to be not only a witness to God—a partner of God in a historical relationship—but Israel is also concerned to bring its truth to other nations. For if there is but one God why should there not be one humanity, one law, one justice, and one set of moral values for all rather than for a chosen few?[52]

Leo Baeck states, "Judaism's messianic conception may also be contrasted with that of Christianity. Judaism stressed the kingdom of God not as something already accomplished but as something yet to be achieved, not as a religious possession of the elect but as the moral task of all. In Judaism, man sanctifies the world by sanctifying God and by overcoming evil and realizing good. The kingdom of God lies before each man so that he may begin his work; and it lies before him because it lies before all. For Judaism, the whole of mankind is chosen; God's covenant was made with all men."[53] Simply expressed, for Christianity, the kingdom of God is not to be attained through the individual's own efforts. The individual requires the grace of God; Judaism, for its part, leaves the attainment of such an end up to the individual. Accordingly, for Judaism, the messiah will be either a wholly human person or a sym-

---

51. In the first half of the first century CE, according to Josephus, in a small Parthian dependency called Adiabene on the eastern side of the middle Tigris, king Izates and his wife Helena converted to Judaism. The ruling house had close dealings with Jerusalem, where queen Helena and her two sons lived for a while and contributed funds to the Temple. It is quite probable that at that time these rulers had at least the Torah translated into their Eastern Aramaic dialect for their own use and for the use of their subjects. At the same time, the Targumim were being produced in the West Aramaic dialect. It has been posited that the translation of the Old Testament produced for the Syrian Church in East Aramaic Syriac manifests evident relationships with a preliminary stage of the Palestinian Targum of the Pentateuch. This suggests that there was at least a partial Jewish translation of the Old Testament in East Aramaic Syria. See Noth, *Old Testament World*, 323.

52. Harshbarger and Mourant, *Judaism and Christianity*, 340.

53. Baeck, *Essence of Judaism*, 252.

bol of the product of the collective endeavors of all humanity to bring the messianic age into being.[54]

Despite differences of opinions among Jews, even during the inter-testamental and early Common Era, it must be emphasized that the messianic expectation was and continues to be a vital and living thing for the believing Jews. Not only is it stated frequently in Scripture, it is diffused throughout the Jewish holy days, the Sabbath, and indeed throughout the whole calendar of Judaism. Maimonides[55] expressed this expectation thus, "He may come on any day."[56] A more recent Jewish rabbi and editor

54. Harshbarger and Mourant, *Judaism and Christianity*, 340.

55. Maimonides' full name was Moses ben Maimon (1135–1204); in Hebrew, he is known by the acronym of Rabbi Moses ben Maimon, or Rambam. He was born in Spain, but to avoid persecution by the Muslims, Maimonides fled with his family, first to Morocco, later to Israel and finally to Egypt, where he served as physician to the sultan of Egypt, wrote numerous books on medicine, and, in his "spare time," served as leader of Cairo's Jewish community. His two best-known works are the *Mishneh Torah* and *Guide to the Perplexed*. See Telushkin, *Jewish Literacy*.

56. The traditional Jewish understanding of the messiah is non-supernatural, and is best elucidated by Maimonides, in his commentary to tractate Sanhedrin, of the *Babylonian Talmud*. He writes:

The messianic age is when the Jews will regain their independence and all return to the land of Israel. The messiah will be a very great king, he will achieve great fame, and his reputation among the gentile nations will be even greater than that of King Solomon. His great righteousness and the wonders that he will bring about will cause all peoples to make peace with him and all lands to serve him ... Nothing will change in the messianic age, however, except that Jews will regain their independence. Rich and poor, strong and weak, will still exist. However it will be very easy for people to make a living, and with very little effort they will be able to accomplish very much ... it will be a time when the number of wise men will increase ... war shall not exist, and nation shall no longer lift up sword against nation ... The messianic age will be highlighted by a community of the righteous and dominated by goodness and wisdom. It will be ruled by the messiah, a righteous and honest king, outstanding in wisdom, and close to God. Do not think that the ways of the world or the laws of nature will change; this is not true. The world will continue as it is. The prophet Isaiah predicted, "The wolf shall live with the sheep, the leopard shall lie down with the kid." This, however, is merely allegory, meaning that the Jews will live safely, even with the formerly wicked nations. All nations will return to the true religion [monotheism, although not necessarily Judaism] and will no longer steal or oppress. Note that all prophecies regarding the messiah are allegorical—only in the messianic age will we know the meaning of each allegory and what it comes to teach us. Our sages and prophets did not long for the messianic age in order that they might rule the world and dominate the gentiles ... the only thing they wanted was to be free for Jews to involve themselves with the Torah and its wisdom.

expresses this messianic expectation as follows, "The chief feature of the belief in the messiah can then be summarized: (1) his rule of truth and goodness will extend over all humankind; (2) Israel will be restored in its pristine glory and security; (3) his sovereignty will be ushered in by God's enactment, not by human achievement; (4) the messiah will be a single human person through whom God will perform the ultimate miracle."[57]

Hell, heaven, resurrection, and immortality are symbols of less significance in Jewish eschatology when compared to the all-important symbol of the messiah and the messianic kingdom and are therefore considered "lesser symbols." Yet, they were, and continue to be, debated issues. Whereas there is virtual unanimity of faith in the messiah and the messianic kingdom, however these might be conceived, Jewish theologians and believers are in much disagreement about these lesser symbols. Also, and very importantly, the evidence, both scriptural and traditional, for the lesser symbols is less substantial and is often a matter of differences in interpretation. Since it is extremely difficult to give them an essential historical coherence with one another, it does not matter with which of these lesser symbols we begin. We will confine our attention to the symbols of hell, heaven, and the resurrection because each of them (and the beliefs associated with them) acquire significance from the moral retribution for the individual. Actually, and very interestingly, the way in which this moral retribution may be worked out is of much less importance than the idea of moral retribution itself. "This explains why," according to Harshbarger and Mourant, "once the symbols are affirmed, little more is said of them. In this connection it should be pointed out that for some scholars the more significant doctrine in Judaism is that of the redemption of man to be effected by the messiah in days to come."[58]

HELL: SHE'OL AND GEHINNON

Similar to Christian belief, Jewish belief in heaven and hell is bound up with the moral conviction that God will mete out retribution in accordance with the actions of the individual in this life. In Judaism, this notion of retribution in association with the afterlife developed gradually.

---

57. Millgram, *Great Jewish Ideas*, 189.

58. Harshbarger and Mourant, *Judaism and Christianity*, 341.

In the Bible, beginning with the prophetic writings of the eighth century BCE, the belief in a "Day of the Lord" is attested as an old popular principle. The people expected and hoped that a day would come in which God would execute judgment over the nations of the world. Amos cautioned that the Day of the Lord would be "darkness and no light" (Amos 5:18–20), meaning that Israel itself would also have to undergo the stern scrutiny by God and receive punishment for its injustice. Thereafter the Day of the Lord was expected to be a day of national calamity. When, less than two centuries after Amos, the Babylonians destroyed Jerusalem, this was interpreted as the fulfillment of those expectations (see Lamentations). Following the Babylonian exile, the hope arose that the Day of the Lord would be a day of rejuvenation, restoration, and redemption, on which the enemies of Israel would, in turn, receive retribution.[59]

Toward the end of the biblical period, the Day of the Lord assumed a growing "supranatural" coloring and an eschatological character. This appears fully developed in *1 Enoch*, written in the first century BCE. The recurring message throughout is that God will deliver the kings and the mighty of the nations to the angels for punishment. In the *Sibylline Oracles*, dating only a few decades later, the Day of the Lord is connected to the appearance of a "king" who has definite messianic features.[60] By the time of the *Psalms of Solomon*, written around 63 BCE, the "Son of David" or messiah had definitely become the agent carrying out God's vengeance on the "godless nations."[61]

The Talmudic teachers elaborated this idea and present lively arguments taking place between God and the wicked nations who try to plead a fraudulent defense of their evil deeds, of course to no avail. In these texts, repeated numerous times, we find the punishment of the idolatrous nations and of the wicked of Israel, as well as their sentencing to Gehinnon. Typically, though, while the Last Judgment is projected into the messianic era, the messiah plays no role in the proceedings. God, sitting on the exalted Throne of Judgment hears the cases, examines the culprits, and sentences them.[62]

---

59. Patai, *The Messiah Texts*, 211.

60. *Sybylline Oracles* 3:652–72.

61. *Psalms of Solomon*, 17:21–36.

62. See, for example, B. *Avodah Zarah* 2a-b; *Ecclesiastes Rabba* 3:9; *Sefer Eliyahu* 3:67; *Nistarot di Rabbi Shim'on ben Yohai* 3:80–81; *Midrash va Yosha'* 1:56–57; *Midrash Hallel* 5:107; B. *Sanhedrin* 91a–b. See Bauckman. "Early Jewish Visions of Hell," 355.

Now, while Judaism concentrates on the importance of the present world, the fact is that all of classical Judaism does posit an afterlife.
Jewish tradition affirms that the human soul is immortal, and thus, in
some way, survives the physical death of the body. The existence of the
soul after death is sometimes described with terms such as *Olam Haba*
(the world to come),[63] Gan Eden and Gehenna or Gehinnon.

There is much rabbinic material on what happens to the soul of the
deceased after death, what it experiences, and where it goes. At various
points in the afterlife journey the soul may encounter: *Hibbut ha-kever*
(the pains of the grave), *Dumah* (the angel of silence), the angel of death,
the *Kaf ha-Kela* (the catapult of the soul); Gehenna and Gan Eden (heav-
en or paradise). All classic rabbinic scholars agree that these concepts are
beyond typical human understanding. Throughout rabbinic literature
these ideas are expressed through many parables and analogies.

The early Jewish belief in the death of the individual centered on
the term *nefesh* (Gen 2:7; Lev 7:20–21), in which death was conceived as
a virtual ebbing away of the life force of the individual person to a mere
shadow of the former self (*nefesh*). Such a shadow or "shade" reflects
the notion of the dead leading a somewhat drab, ghostly existence. The
abode of the dead in this sense was called *she'ol*, apparently derived, according to some, from "hole" or "pit." Thus in Ps 30:3 we read, "O LORD,
You have brought up my soul from *she'ol*; You have kept me alive, that I
would not go down to the pit" (NASB).

She'ol is clearly subterranean and is similar to the Hades described
by Homer.[64] In the early development of Jewish doctrines little emphasis was placed upon rewards and punishments in the afterlife for the
individual. Rather, such rewards and punishments were assumed to be

---

63. The end of the world is called the *acharit hayamim* (end of days). It is worth
noting that the Talmud, in tractate *Avodah Zarah* 9a, states that this world as we know
it will only exist for six thousand years, "The Tanna Debey Eliyahu taught: The world
is to exist six thousand years; the first two thousand are to be 'void' [of Torah], the
next two thousand are the period of the Torah [from Abraham until the completion of
the Mishnah—the first part of the Talmud], and the following [last] two thousand are
the period of the messiah [i.e., the messianic age could commence during this time];
through our [the Jews'] sins a number of these [times for the messiah's coming] have
already passed [and the messiah has not come yet]."

64. Hades (aidēs) refers both to the ancient Greek underworld, the abode of Hades,
and to the god of the underworld. In Homer's *Odyssey*, Hades, whose brothers were
Zeus and Poseidon, referred just to the god associated with the underworld. Hades was
also called Pluto (*Ploutōn*), meaning "rich one."

meted out in this life in the justice imposed by the community. After the Exile, the social justice imposed by the community broke down. This led the Jewish theologians of the period to develop an affirmation and an emphasis upon a retribution for each individual in the afterlife. It was felt that only in this way could divine justice be maintained. Apparently, in the pre-exilic period there seems to have been little relation between Yahweh and the inhabitants of *she'ol*, but, after the Exile, the rule of Yahweh over *she'ol* was asserted; each individual was to be judged by Yahweh and made subject to divine justice. Eventually, *she'ol* disappeared as an important concept and, interestingly, there appears to be no description of the final judgment in the Old Testament. Eventually, in the apocryphal book *1 Enoch* 45–69, we find that the final judgment will be turned over to the messiah.

After the Exile, the term "*Gehinnon*" (or Gehenna) became prevalent. The thinking, then, was that the wicked must suffer individually for their misdeeds since they were no longer considered mere shades living a dull existence with their equals in *she'ol*. The term of choice to describe the place where the dead were gathered was "*Gehinnon*," taken from Ge-Hinnon, the valley of Hinnon. This valley was located just outside Jerusalem, where the pre-Israelites were believed to have sacrificed children to the god Moloch. Later, the early Jews were said to have used it to dispose of the bodies of criminals and animals, which were left to decay and to be burned. The description of such a place—the fire and smoke, the sufferings and the cries—easily came to be identified with the horrors of hell. As early as the eighth century BCE, the prophet Isaiah affirmed an endless punishment for the wicked (Isa 66:24) and, later, the rabbinic writings and the New Testament identified Gehinnon as a place of punishment.[65]

The School of Hillel, in later Talmudic times, taught a much more moderate and humane conception of *Gehinnon*. Premising their argument upon the compassion of God, the rabbis belonging to this school of thought held that after the retributive justice of God was satisfied and all sinners purified, then *Gehinnon* would cease and all souls would share in the world to come.[66] This thinking is reinforced by the develop-

---

65. *Erubin* 19a, *Sukkah* 32b; Matt 5:22, 29.

66. It has been taught (that) the school of Shammai says, "(There will be) three groups on Judgment Day [yom ha din]: (a) one that is completely righteous, (b) one that is completely wicked, (c) and one that is in between." The completely righteous will

ment of the concept of purgatory. An instance of the conception of the
dead in their purgatorial period is found in a Baraita,[67] which implies
that the dead are beneficially affected by the prayers, or the sufferings,
of the living. Thus, a son is to honor his father among other things by
saying, "*Behold I will be the atonement for his death-bed.*" He is to say this
for twelve months after his father's death, because the idea was that the
purgatorial period in *Gehinnon* would only last twelve months at most.
By his readiness to accept sufferings in lieu of his father, the son could
shorten the period his father spent in purgatory.[68]

A more profound interpretation of this doctrine was that *Gehinnon*,
like *Gan Eden*, is made by humans and exists in humanity. Thus, according to some rabbis, the saying of the School of Hillel that "*Gehinnon will
cease*" means that man will abolish it by righteous living.[69]

HEAVEN: GAN EDEN

The Gan Eden (Garden of Delight) in early Jewish writings was regarded
as an abode of bliss. It may have been derived by linguistic analogy from
the account of the Garden of Eden in the Book of Genesis. Many early
Jewish interpreters regarded the Garden of Eden as a prototype of a heavenly paradise, although they tended to treat the descriptions of heaven
in a figurative sense and considered them primarily as exemplifying the
divine justice. As Friedlander puts it:

> As the life of Adam and Eve in the Garden of Eden was free
> from care and trouble, and such a life was the ideal of human

---

be recorded and sealed at once for eternal life. The completely wicked will be recorded
and doomed at once to Gehinnom, as it says, "And many who sleep in the dust of the
earth shall rise up, some to eternal life and some to shame and eternal rejection" (Dan
12:2). Those in between will go down to Gehinnom and cry out and rise up, as it says,
"And I will bring the third part through the fire and refine them as silver is refined and
test them as gold is tested. They will call on my name and I will answer them" (Zech
13:9). (But) the school of Hillel says, "He who is Master of grace tends towards grace."
Babylonian Rosh HaShanah 16b–17a.

67. The term "baraita" designates a tradition in the Jewish oral law not incorporated
in the Mishnah.

68. See *Kiddushin* 31b. The overwhelming majority of rabbinic thought maintains
that people are not tortured in Gehenna (Gehinnon) forever; the longest that one can
be there is said to be twelve months, with extremely rare exception. Some consider it a
spiritual forge where the soul is purified for its eventual ascent to Gan Eden (heaven),
where all imperfections are purged.

69. Harshbarger and Mourant, *Judaism and Christianity*, 343.

hopes and wishes, the Garden of Eden [literally, the "garden of pleasure"] became the symbol of man's happiness in its perfection, such as will fall to the good and the righteous. On the other hand, the valley of Hinnom, near Jerusalem, was a place of horror and disgust; a place where at one time children were sacrificed to Moloch, and where later the refuse of the city was cast. Dwelling in the valley of Hinnom became the symbol of the punishment to be inflicted on the wicked. Gan-Eden or Paradise, and Gehinnon or hell, are thus mere figures to express our idea of the existence of a future retribution, and must not be taken literally as names of certain places. The detailed descriptions of Paradise and Hell as given in books both profane and religious are nothing but the offspring of man's imagination.[70]

RESURRECTION

The idea of the resurrection appears occasionally in the Hebrew Scriptures (e.g., Job 19:26; Isa 26:19; Dan 12:2), and it is certainly a part of the Jewish tradition. The Old Testament speaks of several noteworthy people being "gathered to their people,"[71] while others take for granted that death is not the end of one's existence.[72] This gathering is described as a separate event from the physical death of the body or the burial.[73] On the other hand, certain sins are punished by the sinner being "cut off from his people."[74] This punishment is referred to as *kareit* (literally, "cutting off," but usually translated as "spiritual excision") and is traditionally understood to mean that the soul will have no part in the afterlife, or "world to come."[75]

In Lev 19–20 and Deut 18, Israelites are prohibited from contacting the spirits of the dead, thus indicating that something of a person lives on after physical death. As well, Saul, in 1 Sam 28:19, employs a sorceress to raise the spirit of the prophet Samuel who had died some

---

70. Michael Friedlander, *Jewish Religion*, 223.

71. See, for example, Gen 25:8 (Abraham), 25:17 (Ishmael), 35:29 (Isaac), 49:33 (Jacob), Deut 32:50 (Moses and Aaron), 2 Kgs 22:20 (King Josiah).

72. See, for example, Job 19:26, Isa 26:19, Eccl 12:7, Dan 12:2.

73. Johnson, "Resurrection of the Body in Early Judaism and Early Christianity," 235.

74. See, for example, Gen 17:14 and Exod 31:14.

75. See Chilton, "Resurrection of the Body in Early Judaism and Early Christianity," 157–60.

time prior. One of the more frequently cited passages from Scripture is the vision of the dry bones in Ezek 37:1–14 which is contemporary with the destruction of the First Temple of Jerusalem in 586 BCE. This has been interpreted as symbolical of the future restoration of Israel or, as Raphael Patai wrote, "[the] Resurrection becomes a messianic miracle, the diachronic counterpart of the synchronic ingathering of the exiles."[76] More positive affirmations of a belief in the resurrection are to be found in Isa 26:19 and Dan 12:1–3. Jewish prayers and services also emphasize the resurrection of the dead.[77]

The earliest mention of a future resurrection is found in the Apocrypha. In 2 Macc 7:14, 23,[78] the hope for the resurrection forms an integral part of the story of the woman and her seven sons who suffered martyrdom for the sanctification of the Name of God. In *2 Baruch*,[79] written in the early first century CE, the resurrection is tied to the appearance of the messiah, and in rabbinic literature[80] the belief in the resurrection to the messianic days.[81]

To perceive more clearly the nature of the resurrection, a number of specific questions concerning it need to be raised, such as: Does the resurrection apply to all people? What form does the resurrection take—does it apply only to the spirit or to the body as well? What specific relation does it have to the symbol of immortality, and how is the latter interpreted?[82] To the first question no clear-cut answer can be given. There are texts in the extracanonical books that unequivocally exclude the wicked from the resurrection. This seems to be the meaning of chapters 3 and 4 of the *Book of Wisdom*, at one time attributed to Solomon.[83] And in the extra-

76. Patai, *The Messiah Texts*, 197.

77. Typical of these prayers is this, "There is none but Thee, oh our Redeemer, even in the days of the messiah, and there is none comparable to Thee, oh our Savior, [who is capable of bringing] about the resurrection of the dead."

78. 2 Macc is an abridgment of a lost book originally written in Greek by Jason of Cyrene about 150 BCE.

79. 2 [Syriac] Baruch 30:1–5.

80. *B. Taanit* 2a; *B. Ketubot* 111a; 111b; *Targum of the Songs of Solomon* 8:5; *Gen Rabba* 28:3.

81. On that basis, it was included among the "Thirteen Articles of Faith" by Maimonides.

82. Harshbarger and Mourant, *Judaism and Christianity*, 343–44.

83. This apocryphal book represents the most classical Greek language found in the Septuagint, having been written during the Jewish Hellenistic period (the first or second

canonical book of the *Psalms of Solomon* we are told, "The destruction of the sinner is forever. And he shall not be remembered when [the Lord] visits the just. This is the portion of sinners forever; but they that fear the Lord shall arise to eternal life."[84] However, there seem to be no clear and explicit statements on this question in the Hebrew Scripture. Hence, it is difficult to decide these matters based on these few texts. Once the messianic kingdom is established, then the resurrection would apply to the righteous of all people.[85] A sequence of virtues, properly carried out, will lead to the resurrection of the dead. There is no break between this life and the next if one is to carry out this-worldly traits, for example, cleanliness, abstinence, holiness, modesty, and the like; these would, in turn, carry out to other-worldly events, such as the encounter with the Holy Spirit, the resurrection of the dead, and onward.[86]

The second question opens the way to similar difficulties. Some early writers interpreted the symbol of the resurrection as meaning literally a physical resurrection. The reasoning was that God could easily repeat the miracle of creation, and could re-create the physical body and unite it with the soul. This is well brought out in the prophecy of Ezek 37:10–14. The physical resurrection of the body[87] also involves a return to this earth in the messianic kingdom of the future. While most contemporary Jewish writers reject any literal interpretation of the resurrection of the body,[88] inquiry concerning the resurrection was very much a hot issue during the first century CE, as is well documented in Matt 22:23–33. Dubious evidence from the rabbinic literature indicates that in the life of the resurrection people would marry and would beget and bear children. It seems more probable that the evidence refers to the life of the messianic era. In a familiar passage from *Berachoth* 17a, Rav, who died about CE 250, said, "In the world to come there is no eating and drinking, or procreation and child-bearing, or trade and business, or enmity and strife, but the righteous sit with crowns on their head

---

century BCE). The author of the text appears well versed in the popular philosophical, religious, and ethical writings adopted by Hellenistic Alexandria.

84. Quoted in Sutcliffe, *Old Testament and the Future Life*, 170.

85. Harshbarger and Mourant, *Judaism and Christianity*, 344.

86. *Sotah* 9:15; *Y. Shabbat* 1:3 v3; *Y. Sanhedrin* 6:9.III. See Neusner, *Theology of Normative Judaism*, 129–47; Neusner and Chilton, *Jewish-Christian Debates*, 172–73.

87. There seems to be no specific teaching of a spiritual body within Judaism.

88. Harshbarger and Mourant, *Judaism and Christianity*, 344.

and enjoy the radiance of the Shechinah." This passage may refer to the intermediate state between death and the resurrection and not to the life after the resurrection. In this intermediate state, the soul lives without the body. This notion seems to be supported by a passage from a small tractate, *Kallah Rabbati*.[89] However, according to Montefiore, it is more probable that both during the first century CE and the time of the first Amoraim, Abba Arika, respectfully referred to as Rav, there was a popular view according to which the life of the resurrection would be thoroughly material, and assimilated, except for its duration and joy, to our own. The rabbis often quoted Psalm 50:12–13 for the purpose of showing that, "there is no eating or drinking in heaven." Thus, much later, we read in *Pesikta* 57b, "If Moses, while he was on the sacred mountain for forty days, neither ate nor drank, how much less is there eating and drinking before God? That is what the words of Psalm 50:12 imply."[90]

IMMORTALITY

Second in importance only to the belief in the messiah and the messianic kingdom is the belief in immortality. Without this belief, there would be little meaning to such doctrines as the resurrection, retribution in the hereafter, and other eschatological notions. The belief in immortality probably arose during the second temple period. At any rate it was not held at the time the Book of Job was written, for Job does not have the consolation such a belief might offer. The group primarily responsible for the development of this belief is that of the Pharisees. In opposition to the Sadducees, who emphasized a national God for Israel alone, the Pharisees affirmed the existence of a universal God of all. Stressing the relations and the responsibility of the individual to God, the Pharisees argued for the necessity of the survival of the soul and its reward or punishment in the hereafter.[91]

89. The Minor Tractates are normally printed at the end of *Seder Nezikin* in the Talmud; the tractate *Kallah Rabbati*, an elaboration of the tractate *Kallah*, deals with engagement, marriage and sex. It takes its name from the teachers' convention that was held twice a year in Babylonian Academies, by the Jews then in captivity in Babylon, after the beginning of the Amoraic period (230 to 500 CE), in the two months Adar (February–March) and Elul (August–September).

90. This Midrash is held to be a work from Erets Israel, edited in the sixth or seventh century CE.

91. Harshbarger and Mourant, *Judaism and Christianity*, 344. Among the medieval Jewish philosophers, the notion of immortality is quite prevalent. Generally, they tend

The conception of immortality involves more than mere survival beyond the grave, but calls upon humans to cooperate with God and to continue the divine relationship. A person must merit immortality—"and the dust returns to the earth as it was, and the spirit returns to God who gave it" (Eccl 12:7).

CONCLUSION

The subject of immortality has given rise to many discourses, debates, speculations and esoteric thinking. When everything is said and done, though, it all boils down to the topics of the resurrection of the dead, the state of the dead, and the person and mission of the messiah.

What has been attempted in this chapter was an exploration of these subjects, with the understanding that delving into any one of them is a task not easily achieved in just a few pages. The symbols focused upon are only the most prevalent ones. Our goal has been to be descriptive, rather than propositional or prescriptive, setting up a good foundation of the varied perspectives prevalent within early Judaism that will be a help in better understanding the context(s) in which Jesus, Paul, and the early Christian writers set about to present their message.

---

to regard immortality as wholly spiritual and as applicable to the soul rather than to the body. In this way, Maimonides might be said to give a figurative interpretation to what others regard as a physical resurrection. Maimonides teaches that the functions of the body are no longer needed (but he does not teach that the body is evil) and that immortality applies only to the soul. In his *Essay on the Resurrection of the Dead*, he describes this immortal existence.

2

Restoring the Kingdom to Israel

Kingdom and Spirit in Luke's Thought

BLAINE CHARETTE

COMMONPLACE IN PENTECOSTAL ESCHATOLOGY, at least at the popular level, is to link the final events of the present age to the fortunes of the nation state of Israel. This is due, of course, to the significant impact that dispensationalist approaches to eschatology have had on Pentecostal reflection and preaching, especially since the establishment of the state of Israel in 1948. Accordingly, the outworking of God's purpose is frequently interpreted with reference to the ever changing and frequently volatile situation that characterizes Middle East politics. A weakness inherent in much of Pentecostal eschatology is the reluctance to critique the legitimacy of the dispensational paradigm and to adequately assess its impact on Pentecostal thought. Many Pentecostals have been content to embrace a theological approach that does not cohere with the essential structure and aims of a Pentecostal theology and which in fact may be inimical to them.

The purpose of this chapter is to examine one facet of New Testament eschatology that touches on these broader concerns. It relates to Luke's treatment of the last question the apostles put to Jesus before his ascension: "Lord, is this the time when you will restore the kingdom to Israel?" Jesus responds to the question in part by directing their attention to the eschatological Spirit who is about to be poured out. The matter to be explored in what follows is the extent to which the national goals of Israel are most fully realized when at Pentecost the redemptive activity of the Spirit of God begins to move beyond the sphere of Israel to the ends of the earth. The kingdom is restored to Israel when the nation becomes the centerpiece and starting point of the eschatological redemption that touches all people.

The opening scene of the Book of Acts consists of a dialogue between Jesus and his disciples, which addresses two topics of key importance to the succeeding narrative.[1] First, Jesus speaks of the gift of the Holy Spirit ("the promise of the Father") that his disciples are about to receive, which will empower their witness to the ends of the earth (1:4–5, 8). Second, the disciples wish to know if this is the time when Jesus will restore the kingdom to Israel (1:6). The significance of the Holy Spirit to the narrative of Acts does not require argument; it is sufficient to observe the defining reference to the Holy Spirit in Acts 1:8, the thematic verse of the narrative. The idea of the kingdom may not appear to be as significant for Acts as it is for the Gospel of Luke (8 uses of *basileia* in Acts compared with 46 uses in Luke); yet the importance of kingdom for Acts is not a matter of its frequency but of its placement. It is significant that the narrative opens with the observation that during the forty days following his resurrection Jesus spoke to his apostles about the kingdom of God (1:3) and concludes with Paul in Rome proclaiming the kingdom of God to all who came to him (28:31).[2] By choosing to open and close his narrative with reference to the kingdom Luke is drawing attention to the importance of the concept.

It might appear as though Jesus and his disciples are talking past each other. He wishes to prepare them for the coming of the Spirit, whereas they seek an answer to a question concerning the national fortunes of the people of Israel. Their question is not altogether out of place, however, since according to the preamble to Acts (1:1–3) Jesus spoke to his disciples about the kingdom of God when he appeared to them

1. One might more accurately speak of "the opening scenes" since Jesus' directive to the apostles in vv. 4–5, to wait in Jerusalem for the promised Spirit, occurs prior to the question and answer of vv. 6–8. Yet the two parts constitute a single dialogue in which the apostles' question about the kingdom in v. 6 is bracketed between Jesus' two statements about the imminent gift of the Spirit.

2. When noting the *inclusio* formed by these references to the kingdom in Acts, Dunn observes that "[t]his is presumably Luke's way of indicating that although the post-Easter proclamation focused on Jesus' death and resurrection, the content and central concerns of Jesus' pre-Easter preaching and teaching continued to be a fundamental feature of the post-Easter preaching and teaching." Dunn, *Beginning from Jerusalem*, 143.

during the forty day period after his resurrection. Yet, more to the point, it appears to be Luke's intention to draw together these two topics at the very outset of the narrative in such a way that readers might begin their own dialogue on the connection between kingdom and Spirit in the outworking of the divine purpose.[3] The intention of the present discussion is to enter into this dialogue through consideration of this nuanced exchange between Jesus and his disciples and of the pivotal questions raised by this juxtaposing of kingdom and Spirit.

To understand the question of the disciples ("Lord, is this the time when you will restore the kingdom to Israel?"), it is helpful not only to recognize that it is prompted by the earlier teaching of Jesus on the kingdom of God and by his more recent declaration that they will soon be baptized in the Holy Spirit but also to see it within the larger framework of expectation for Israel that is outlined in Luke-Acts.[4] In the Lukan infancy narrative John the Baptist and especially Jesus are associated with the soon to be fulfilled hopes of Israel. John is described in relation to the repentance of the people. He is the one who will turn many in Israel to the Lord their God (1:16) so they might obtain the promised restoration. Jesus, however, relates to this expectation in a much fuller way. His birth marks the Lord's assistance (*antilambanō*) of Israel (1:54), the redemption (*lutrōsis*) of the people (1:68; cf. 2:38), the consolation (*paraklēsis*) of Israel (2:25), and the appearance of light for the glory of Israel (*doxa*; 2:32). Moreover, Jesus will effect this salvation of Israel in his role as the messianic son of David. To him the Lord will give the throne of his father David (1:32). He is to be "the horn of salvation" (*keras sōtērias*) raised up in the house of David (1:69), the savior (*sōter*) who is Christ the Lord (2:11). At the same time, this introduction to the gospel sounds an ambivalent note: this child is destined for the falling and rising of

3. With respect to the fact that the question of the kingdom is framed by the promise of the Spirit, Dunn comments that "the promised Spirit is in fact the presence and activity of God's royal power." Dunn, *Beginning from Jerusalem*, 144. This is preferable to the conclusion of Pervo that the "narrative invites the readers, like the apostles, to look for the coming of the Spirit rather than the advent of God's rule." Pervo, *Acts*, 43. It is best to see the concepts of kingdom and Spirit as related and complementary.

4. Even though Luke and Acts are distinct narratives that can be read independently of each other, they nonetheless form a theological whole to the extent that each narrative assists in the interpretation of the other and are thus best read together. Worth observing is the dual concepts of kingdom and Spirit are combined very early in Luke in the words of the angel Gabriel to Mary (Luke 1:33, 35) and in Paul's final preaching in Rome (Acts 28:25, 31).

many in Israel and for a sign to be opposed (2:34).[5] The purpose of this resonant language is to identify that the time of the eschatological restoration of Israel has come.

The work of John, through proclaiming a baptism of repentance (3:3), is to prepare the people for the work of the coming mightier one who will baptize in the Holy Spirit and fire (3:16). Through the anointed ministry of Jesus the redemption of Israel begins to take place. Yet, the central irony of Luke's Gospel is that Israel fails to recognize in the activity of Jesus the time of their visitation from God (19:44). Many are blind to the realities of redemption (19:42: "now they are hidden from your eyes,")[6] because they do not understand how the fulfillment is to take place. Jesus does not match expectations and as a result he indeed becomes the cause of the falling of many in Israel.

Even those closest to Jesus do not recognize the full meaning of the redemption centered in him. This is emphasized in the final scenes of the gospel. In the penultimate scene two disciples find themselves in conversation with the risen Jesus on their way to Emmaus. They speak of their frustrated hopes respecting Jesus (24:21: "we had hoped [*elpízō*] that he was the one to redeem Israel.") In response Jesus rebukes their foolishness and slowness of heart because their hopes were not fully informed by the words of Moses and of the prophets (24:25–27).[7] In the final scene Jesus appears to a larger group of disciples, including these two who had returned to Jerusalem, to confirm the reality of his resurrection. Their response is joy mixed with disbelief and wonder (24:41).

---

5. It is best not to follow the opinion of Bovon that the "falling" applies to Luke's Gospel and the "rising" to the Book of Acts. Bovon, *Luke 1*, 104. Both narratives include references to Israelites who reject and who accept the message centered in Jesus.

6. The activity of God is implied in the passive *ekrubē*. The people lack perception but this itself is part of the judgment of God; cf. Marshall, *Gospel of Luke*, 718, I have argued elsewhere ("Tongues as of Fire," 174–76) that, as the one who will baptize in the Holy Spirit and fire, Jesus effects a separation within Israel. Those who are open to the work of the Spirit in Jesus' ministry come to know the redemption of God whereas others who refuse the work of the Spirit present in Jesus face judgment.

7. The fact that these disciples are prevented from recognizing Jesus throughout their conversation and up to the point where he breaks bread with them indicates their ignorance regarding the necessity that the messiah must suffer before entering his glory, which for Luke is declared in Moses and the prophets and demonstrated also in Jesus' earlier breaking of bread at the last supper. Thus, to a significant degree, even the disciples of Jesus share in Israel's ignorance of the manner in which the nation's redemption will occur.

Jesus once again meets their misapprehensions with reference to what is written in Moses, the prophets, and the psalms, "opening their minds to understand the scriptures" so they might appreciate that the messiah must suffer and rise from the dead (24:45–46). Jesus had indeed come to redeem Israel, yet the nature of that redemption is susceptible to misunderstanding.

In view of the fact that the disciples at the end of Luke are just beginning to come to terms with how the hopes of Israel find fulfillment in Jesus, it is most probable that their question in Acts 1:6 reflects a further misunderstanding. Jesus answers the question by turning their attention to the power they are to receive when the Spirit comes upon them and to the worldwide witness they will then carry out.[8] If it is true that at this stage in the narrative the followers of Jesus are still unsure how the kingdom proclaimed by Jesus relates to the eschatological hopes of Israel, perhaps it is helpful to look at the ideas articulated by followers later in the narrative when presumably their understanding is more complete. The perspective of Paul on this subject is very instructive, especially as it is presented in his words to the leaders of the Jews in Rome. These words have the particular advantage of coming near the end of the narrative. On that occasion he informs the Jewish leaders that he wishes to speak with them since it is "for the sake of the hope (*elpizō*) of Israel" that he has arrived in Rome in chains (28:20). What is this hope of Israel to which Paul refers?

Based on Paul's use of the term hope (*elpizō*) earlier in Acts, it is clear that for him this hope is centered in the reality of the resurrection.[9] Before the Sanhedrin Paul declares that he is facing judgment on account of the hope of the resurrection of the dead (23:6); before Felix he attests that even his Jewish accusers have the expectant hope that there

---

8. That their question follows forty days of Jesus' instruction on the kingdom of God might suggest that it issues from an informed perspective. Yet Jesus' immediate response, that it is not for them to know the times or seasons set by the authority of the Father, indicates otherwise. Pervo observes that literary tradition permitted pupils "to ask dull and inappropriate questions so that teachers could promulgate the correct view." Pervo, *Acts*, 41. Jesus' two part response to the disciples' question is best understood as an initial rebuke of their ignorance followed by a positive declaration that does not ignore their question but transposes it by placing it within a new framework of meaning.

9. Fitzmyer reviews the various interpretive options for "the hope of Israel" and correctly decides on hope in the resurrection of the dead. Fitzmyer, *Acts of the Apostles*, 793.

will be a general resurrection (24:15); finally, before Agrippa Paul again reiterates that he is accused by Jews and now stands on trial because of this hope in the promise God had made to Israel, a promise that Israel hopes to attain (26:6–7). Paul wishes to speak to the Roman Jews since it is because of his hope in the resurrection that he has arrived in Rome in chains. What is of particular interest is that when he then speaks to them he testifies to the kingdom of God by seeking to convince them about Jesus by appealing to Moses and the prophets (28:23).[10] Noted above, such reference to Moses and the prophets draws attention to the necessity that the messiah of Israel must die and be raised. It would seem that for Paul in Acts the message of the kingdom has become merged with that of Jesus' resurrection.[11] In the resurrection of Jesus the hopes of Israel, especially those hopes that find expression in the concept of the kingdom of God, are becoming realized.

This correlation of resurrection and kingdom is articulated even earlier in Paul's preaching to the synagogue in Pisidian Antioch (13:16–41). Following an overview of Israel's history that directs attention to God's choice of David as king, Paul turns to the Jesus narrative emphasizing God's raising of Jesus. In 13:32–33 Paul summarizes the good news he brings by noting that the promise (*epangelia*) God made to the fathers is fulfilled for the children in the raising of Jesus. Moreover, the "holy promises" (*hosia*) made to David find their fulfillment in the raising of Jesus (13:34–37). The promises to David alluded to here (by way of Isa 55:3) are those made when the Davidic covenant is confirmed in 2 Sam 7:12–16. God will "raise up" a son for David and establish the throne of his kingdom forever.[12] Through this son David's house, throne,

10. The close connection in Acts 28:23, 31 between Paul's announcement of the message of the kingdom and his teaching about Jesus indicates that they are substantially identical.

11. Luke's use of the verb *prosdechomai* (7 times in Luke-Acts) might provide a key to how the Jewish hope is to be understood. In the gospel Simeon is described as "looking forward to" the consolation of Israel (Luke 2:25), Anna speaks about Jesus to all who were "looking for" the redemption of Israel (Luke 2:38), and Joseph of Arimathea is described as "looking for" the kingdom of God (Luke 23:51). In Acts the verb is used of Paul's Jewish accusers who "look for" the hope of resurrection (24:15). It is very probable that Luke intends for his readers to recognize that "consolation," "redemption," and "kingdom" all come to Israel by means of the "resurrection" of Jesus, especially in view of the eschatological centrality Luke attaches to Jesus' resurrection.

12. Noteworthy, the verb *anistēmi*, used consistently by Luke with reference to the resurrection of Jesus, is also used at 2 Sam 7:12 (LXX) with reference to the offspring of David whom God will raise up.

and kingdom will be established forever. These same promises are referred to at the beginning of Luke's Gospel. The angel Gabriel announces to Mary that God will give to her son the throne of his father David and of his kingdom there will be no end (Luke 1:32–33). The resurrection of Jesus fulfils these promises made to David inasmuch as the direct consequence of Jesus' resurrection is his exaltation to the right hand of God. It is on this exalted throne, positioned at the right hand of God, that Jesus' rule begins to be established.

This belief is already articulated in the first sermon of Acts where Peter interprets the meaning of the Pentecost event. According to Peter, David knew that God would place one of his descendents on his throne. Moreover, being a prophet, David foretold the manner in which this would occur, that is through the resurrection and exaltation of the messiah (2:25–32). In the sermon Peter notes a further result of Jesus' resurrection: being exalted at the right hand of God and having received the promise of the Holy Spirit, Jesus has now poured out that Spirit (2:33). Later Peter informs his audience that this promised Spirit is for them, their children, and for all who are far away (2:39). The phrase "to all those far away" (*pasin tois eis makran*), although evocative of OT passages referring to the scattered exiles of Israel, in the context of Acts refers to the Gentiles whom God calls[13] (note the telling use of *makran* at 22:21: the risen Jesus informs Paul that he will send him "far away" to the Gentiles). This grouping of ideas in Peter's programmatic Pentecost sermon points to the fact that Jesus ascends to the eternal rule promised to David through his resurrection and exaltation. From this position of authority he pours out the Holy Spirit on all who call upon his name.[14] All this suggests that for Luke the kingdom (or rule) of God is experienced primarily through the blessings that flow from the outworking of the eschatological Spirit now poured out.[15] The rule of Jesus is established over the earth by means of the transformative work of the promised Spirit.

13. Johnson observes that the phrase *tois makran* in Isa 57:19 (LXX) could be read as applying to Gentiles. Johnson, *Acts of the Apostles*, 58.

14. "Promise" (*epangelia*) in Luke-Acts is connected with both resurrection (Acts 26:6; cf. 13:12) and the gift of the Holy Spirit (Luke 24:49; Acts 1:4; 2:33, 39). The fulfillment of the former in Jesus' resurrection is both antecedent to and the basis of the fulfillment of the latter.

15. The thesis of Cho that for Luke the primary connection between the Spirit and the kingdom is that the Spirit empowers the proclamation of the kingdom is far too limiting. In Luke-Acts the Spirit is more than the divine agent behind such proclama-

In view of this understanding of the kingdom the meaning of the Davidic text at Acts 15.16 is clear. According to James' interpretation, Amos 9:11–12 finds fulfillment in God's favorable acceptance of Gentiles as his own people. In its original setting the Amos passage concerns the restoration of the Davidic dynasty in terms signifying the renewal of national strength and the attendant subjugation of other peoples. By way of the language of the Septuagint, James reads the promise in a different way. God's restoration of the Davidic house (*anoikodomēsō tēn skēnēn Dauid*), through the resurrection and exaltation of Jesus,[16] creates a new ordering of affairs so that all people, including the Gentiles, may seek the Lord and enjoy the benefits of salvation. The fact that James' remarks follow Peter's reminder of the Cornelius event and the testimony of Barnabas and Paul about the signs and wonders God had done through them among the Gentiles indicates that it is through the redemptive activity present in the Spirit's operation that the restored Davidic rule now finds its realization. Nationalistic aspirations have been replaced by new realities created by the eschatological Spirit, which benefit all peoples. The question of the disciples "Lord, is this the time when you will restore the kingdom to Israel?" finds its answer. The kingdom is being restored to Israel, although it appears in a way they did not expect.

Luke prepares his readers for such an understanding of the kingdom in his description of Jesus' activity relative to the kingdom. As Jesus goes about proclaiming the good news of the kingdom its presence is evident primarily through healings and exorcisms. Following his baptism he begins to function in the authority and power of the Spirit. When his ministry begins in Capernaum he not only teaches with authority but also with authority and power (note the use of language resonant with kingly associations) he affects a series of exorcisms (4:36) and performs

---

tion; the Spirit generates the many benefits that distinguish God's rule. Cho, *Spirit and Kingdom*, 194–95. Closer to the mark is the assertion of Smalley that "God's eschatological reign in history is both mediated and characterized by the Spirit." Smalley, "Spirit, Kingdom and Prayer," 68. With respect to the impact on Israel, Turner observes that "the gift of the Spirit is not merely empowering to witness, but that the varied activities of the Spirit of prophecy . . . will together also constitute the purging and restoring power of God in the community which effects Israel's transformation/salvation." Turner, "Spirit of Prophecy," 345.

16. Although not followed by many interpreters the exegesis of Haenchen is persuasive that the rebuilding of the fallen tent of David adumbrates "the story of Jesus, culminating in the Resurrection, in which the promise made to David has been fulfilled." Haenchen, *Acts of the Apostles*, 448.

several healings for the people of the city (4:38–41).[17] The next morning he informs the crowds of the city that he must "bring the good news" (*euangelizō*) of the kingdom of God to other cities as well (4:43). The context indicates that for Luke the verb *euaggelio* means much more than mere verbal proclamation of the beneficent kingdom but the actual demonstration of the transforming goodness of God's rule.

This emphasis continues in 9:1–2 when Jesus calls together the twelve and gives them power and authority over all demons and to heal diseases. He then sends them out to proclaim (*kērussō*) the kingdom and to heal. Similarly, in his instructions to the seventy at 10:1–12, Jesus commands them to heal the sick and say to them, "The kingdom of God has come near (*engizō*) to you" (v. 9). The clearest evidence that God's rule is at hand is found in the exorcisms and healings accomplished by Jesus and his disciples through the power and authority conferred on Jesus when the Holy Spirit comes upon him at his baptism. The rule of God is being established in Israel through such Spirit empowered activity.

This description of how the kingdom manifests itself is of particular importance to the understanding of Luke 17:20–21. The Pharisees ask Jesus when (*pote*) the kingdom of God is coming. Jesus responds by stating that the kingdom of God is not coming "with observation" (*meta paratērēseōs*); rather, the kingdom of God is "among you" (*entos humōn*).[18] This question can be seen as previewing the question asked by the disciples at the beginning of the Book of Acts to the extent that it concerns the timing of the coming of the kingdom and most probably reflects an understanding of kingdom largely informed by national political aspirations. Jesus' response is consistent with the idea of kingdom that has been emerging up to this point in Luke. The coming of God's kingdom is not seen in the same things that indicate the rise of a typical kingdom (note, for example, the very different exercise of power and

17. Noteworthy, the demons that are cast out respond with the declaration, "You are the son of God" (v. 41), addressing Jesus with a title that evokes the Davidic ruler (cf. Ps 2:7; 2 Sam 7:14).

18. The term *paratērēsis* ("observation") is used only here in the Greek Bible. Luke's use of the related verb *paratēreō* (four of six NT appearances are in Luke-Acts) might suggest that the observations of the Pharisees will be unsuccessful in detecting the appearance of the kingdom since their prior observations of Jesus' activity were directed at discrediting him. They reveal themselves to be people who are deliberately blind to the redeeming work of God. Green notes that, although Luke presents them as keen observers of Jesus' activity, "the Pharisees consistently measure his ministry against their own, fallacious canons." Green, *Gospel of Luke*, 629.

authority; cf. Luke 22:25: "the kings of the Gentiles lord it over them.") Nevertheless, God's kingdom is at work in their midst. The kingdom is among them and is evident in the healings and exorcisms that stand at the very center of Jesus' messianic work.

The argument advanced in this chapter, that the kingdom is restored to Israel in the restoring of the full people of God through the power of the Holy Spirit, receives additional support through interesting catchword connections present in the larger Lukan narrative. For example, Luke 6:6–11 describes the healing of a man with a withered hand. The healing occurs on the Sabbath, an act that Jesus defends before the accusations of the scribes and Pharisees by noting that it is lawful to do good and to save life on the Sabbath.[19] Jesus heals the man by commanding him to stretch out his hand and when he does so Luke notes that his hand is restored (*apokathistēmi*). The only other time Luke uses this term is in the question of the disciples at Acts 1:9: "Lord, is this the time when you will restore the kingdom to Israel?"[20] The act of restoration in the healing provides an important clue as to how that question is to be answered.

Similarly, Luke 13:10–17 relates the healing of a crippled woman with a spirit who had been bent over for eighteen years. Jesus is once again criticized for performing the healing on the Sabbath and responds by arguing that it is appropriate that this daughter of Abraham whom Satan had bound for so long should be set free on the Sabbath. In describing the healing Luke notes that when Jesus laid his hands on her she "stood up straight" (*anorthoō*). The only other time Luke uses this term is in James' quoting of the divine promise respecting the fallen house of David at Acts 15:16: "I will set it up (*anorthoō*)."[21] The act of liberating this daughter of Abraham from bondage points to the realities effected

19. In this context the scribes and Pharisees are described as observing (*paratēreō*) Jesus' activity so that they might level charges against him. Their focus on a potential violation of Torah causes them to miss the demonstration of God's kingly rule that plays out before them.

20. In the LXX *apokathistēmi* is used with reference to the eschatological restoration of Israel from the lands to which that had been exiled. Green observes that in this one scene "we are to see an expression of Jesus' mediation of God's eschatological redemption." Green, *Luke*, 256.

21. Note that in the LXX *anorthoō* can be read as a technical term for the establishment of the Davidic dynasty (2 Sam 7:13, 16; 1 Chr 17:12, 14, 24; 22:10).

by the Davidic rule. In such acts of healing and deliverance the eternal rule promised to David is manifest.

It is important to recognize that Luke connects the healing of the woman to the kingdom parable of the mustard seed in 13:18–19. The parable is introduced by the phrase "He therefore (*oun*) said," which indicates that the parable is a corollary of and thus related to the meaning of the earlier healing.[22] The purpose of the parable is to describe what the kingdom of God is like. It is like a seed that grows to become a sizeable tree. The point is that the rule of God is discernible even in this healing of the woman. Though a seemingly insignificant event in the larger scheme of things, it nonetheless defines the essence of the kingdom of God that will grow in magnitude in a way consistent with this embryonic representation.

Luke's concern in the gospel is to show that the coming of God's rule particularly benefits those in Israel who are infirmed or afflicted. The very people who do not receive benefit from those exercising earthly power become the beneficiaries of the power of God's rule.[23] In Acts this concern continues and finds its complement in God's acceptance of the Gentiles who for so long stood outside of the covenant and thus beyond the blessings of God's rule.[24] Through the Spirit's power God is now bringing to all people the benefits of the kingdom. The kingdom is restored to Israel in the bringing of good news to the poor (cf. Luke 4:18) and in the fulfillment of Israel's covenant obligation to the nations (cf. Acts 13:47). The answer Luke offers to the question the disciples ask at the beginning of Acts is of continuing relevance to the people of God. Only when they truly understand the nature of God's kingdom and how the Spirit seeks to establish that kingdom are they able to be effective witnesses of Christ. If they misinterpret the character and means of God's rule their witness becomes uncertain or muted and the power of

22. According to Marshall, the presence of *oun* suggests that Jesus is now commenting on what has just happened. Marshall, *Luke*, 560.

23. Tannehill correctly observes that "the kingdom over which Jesus wants to rule must stretch to include people excluded by the holy people as previously defined." Tannehill, "Kingdom," 20.

24. In Acts it is only Philip and Paul who proclaim the kingdom, Philip in Samaria (8:12) and Paul in Pisidian Antioch (14:22), Ephesus (19:8; cf. 20:25), and Rome (28:23, 31). It is not so much the persons as the locations that are important. The kingdom is now announced outside the land of Israel. Luke thus underscores that the good news first brought to Israel is now for all people.

the Spirit given for witness becomes misdirected or misused. Yet when God's people know their king and seek his kingdom they are able to bear effective witness to his salvation to the ends of the earth.

It is probable that dispensationalist eschatology has prevented Pentecostals from recognizing the full eschatological significance of the gift of the Spirit. Due to the influence of such theology the eschatological focus often shifts to "signs of the end" and to dramatic scenarios detailing the final outworking of God's plan. As a result it is possible for Pentecostal believers to become blind to the evidence of God's eschatological activity in their midst. An important lesson can be learned from Jesus' contemporaries. Many of them assumed they understood well how God would establish his rule in the world and the role Israel would play in that purpose. Yet these assumptions kept them from recognizing the actual work of God and in some cases caused them to oppose that work. Luke can be read as a cautionary tale on the dangers that attend an overconfident attachment to a faulty eschatological perspective. Pentecostals should always seek to be people of discernment, not attached to a particular theological agenda but open to what the risen and exalted Christ continues to do and to say through his Spirit. As people of the Spirit they should be sensitive to what the Spirit is doing and wishes to do in the sphere of their own involvement. When Pentecostal believers choose to operate in faithful submission to Christ's agenda, the Pentecostal movement will become an even more effective instrument in the establishment of God's rule.

3

Seven Dispensations or Two-Age View of History

A Pauline Perspective

JOHN A. BERTONE

STATUS QUAESTIONIS: PAUL THE DISPENSATIONALIST?

THE FERVOUR OF PENTECOSTALISM in the early twentieth century
was based on the conviction that God was restoring the manifestations of the Spirit in the last days, such as healing, miracles, prophecy,
and tongues. Pentecostals believed the outpouring of the Spirit was an
indication of the "latter rain" or restoration of "last days" in the apostolic church, which would soon culminate with the return of Christ.[1]
Ironically, Pentecostals found common ground with dispensationalists
on the idea of the imminent return of Christ and embraced a dispensational ideology.[2] William Menzies describes the early Pentecostal movement with the following words: "Imbued with a sense of the nearness
of the end of the age, and that the Pentecostal revival was the harbinger
of the cataclysm, the cry was heralded abroad, 'Jesus is coming soon.' It

---

1. Sheppard, "Pentecostals and the Hermeneutics of Dispensationalism," 5–31, esp. 7.

2. Dispensationalism is constantly evolving ideology. For example, C.A. Blaising
and D. L. Block advocate a system known as "progressive" dispensationalism, modifying
some of the teachings of J. N. Darby, one of the pioneers credited for advancing dispensationalist ideas. Blaising and Block, *Progressive Dispensationalism.*

61

was an easy exercise to adapt the teaching and literature of Scofieldian dispensationalism to the Pentecostal emphasis."[3]

However, while Pentecostals could agree with dispensationalists with respect to the imminent return of Christ, the Pentecostal position was a point of contention for dispensationalists. Scofieldian dispensationalism advocated the view that the sign gifts were confined to the apostolic age, "Chapter 14 [1 Cor] regulates the ministry of gifts in the primitive, apostolic assembly of believers in Christ . . . Tongues and the sign gifts are to cease."[4] Pentecostals could not reconcile themselves to the cessation of the sign gifts. Sociologist Margaret Poloma states, "The belief that God once granted 'dispensations' (allowing manifestations of the gifts of the Spirit, including 'miracles' and 'tongues,' as reported in the Bible) that have since been withdrawn is opposed by the Pentecostal doctrine that gifts of the Holy Spirit are for all time and for all believers."[5] As a result, many of the Pentecostal denominations such as the Assemblies of God, Church of God (Cleveland, Tennessee), and the Pentecostal Holiness Church did not completely commit themselves to dispensationalist ideology. Apart from its disagreement over the sign gifts, the Pentecostal movement conveniently aligned itself with dispensational thinking, adopting the language of "dispensations,"[6] and especially emphasizing the events associated with the Second Coming: the rapture of the church, the seven-year tribulation, the millennium, and cataclysmic judgment.[7] Both Pentecostalism and dispensationalism advocated the

---

3. Menzies, *Anointed to Serve*, 329. Note that Scofield was able to maintain the unexpectedness of the Lord's coming. Crutchfield, *The Origins of Dispensationalism*, 178.

4. Scofield, *Oxford NIV Scofield Study Bible*, 1210.

5. Poloma, *Charismatic Movement*, 126. See below under "A Reductionism of the Spirit?"

6. Myer Pearlman mentions the "dispensational mission" of both Christ and the Spirit and the respective roles they have in the inclusion of the Gentiles. Subsequent to this period, he describes the Spirit's role in the world as having "another and different relationship." Pearlman, *Knowing the Doctrines of the Bible*, 341. This corresponds to distinctions made between the "dispensations" of "grace" and "kingdom" by dispensationalists, where the former emphasized God's grace as a blessing to all humankind (Gentiles especially), but the latter focuses on fulfilling the covenantal promises made to Abraham and David. Ryrie, *Dispensationalism Today*, 63.

7. Note the promotion of the rapture of the church, the seven-year tribulation, the millennium, and the judgment of the nations under the heading of the Second Coming by influential Pentecostal theologians. Pearlman, *Knowing the Doctrines of the Bible*, 390–94; Duffield and Van Cleave, *Foundations of Pentecostal Theology*, 519–53.

literal or grammatical-historical method of interpretation.[8] As a result, the predictive prophecies were also understood literally.[9]

Dispensationalism teaches that God deals with the human race in seven successive phases of history: Innocence (Gen 1:1—3:7), Conscience (Gen 3:8—8:22), Government (Gen 9:1—11:32), Patriarchal Rule (Gen 12:1—Exod 19:25), Mosaic law (Exod 20:1—Acts 1:26), Grace (Acts 2:1—Rev 19:21), Kingdom (Rev 20:1–6).[10] Each of these periods is marked off in Scripture by a change in the manner in which God responds to sin and human responsibility.[11] These were the super-impositions of John N. Darby on scripture, which found their way into the Scofield Study Bible in 1909 and subsequent editions and impacted many early Pentecostals.[12]

---

8. "Consistently literal or plain interpretation is indicative of a dispensational approach to the interpretation of the Scriptures," Ryrie, *Dispensationalism Today*, 45–46; see also Pentecost, *Things to Come*, 9–15. These texts were used widely in Pentecostal Bible colleges throughout North America.

9. Dispensationalists interpreted the bizarre images and numbers literally, ignoring the multivalent symbols and poetic nature of apocalyptic literature. Consequently, repeated numbers in the Book of Revelation such as four (7:1; 8:1), seven (1:4; 5:1; 6:1; 13:1; 15:1; 17:1), ten (17:12), and twelve (7:5–8) and their inherent symbolism usually gave way to a literalistic interpretation. Furthermore, the Jewish practice of gematria, the practice of assigning numerical values to letters of the alphabet, was not even considered. For example, it is generally accepted among biblical scholars that the number 666 in Rev 13:18 was a reference to the Neronian antichrist figure Domitian in the year 88–89 CE (Witherington, *Revelation*, 177–79). The major problem with a literal reading of Revelation is a hermeneutical one; apocalyptic literature and its poetic language are read as prose instead of poetry. Suffice to note for our purpose here, that if one interprets the Book of Revelation literally and uses it as a template to fit Paul's understanding of the events associated with the Second Coming, a distorted view of Paul's understanding of the second advent of Christ emerges, since all of Paul's writings fall under another literary genre, that of "letter." (See Achtemeier et al., *Introducing the New Testament*, 4–6; Witherington, *Jesus, Paul, and the End of the World* and *Jesus the Seer*).

10. Crutchfield, *Origins of Dispensationalism*, 34–44; for a fuller explanation see Ryrie, *Dispensationalism Today*, 50–64.

11. Rossing, *Rapture Exposed*, 23.

12. The Scofield Study Bible had extensive notes throughout, coupled with maps, charts, and dispensational headings. The majority of the prophetic texts were explained and coordinated with the dispensations according to Darby's teachings. The notes were woven into the text itself, appearing as self-evident teaching. Millions of Scofield Study Bibles were sold, in part due to its promotion by Moody Bible Institute and William E. Blackstone, a wealthy Chicago businessman, see Canfield, *Incredible Scofield and His Book*, 1988; see also the positive references to the *Scofield Study Bible* in Duffield and Van Cleave, *Foundations of Pentecostal Theology*, 470, 531.

When we turn to the writings of the Apostle Paul there is no mention of "dispensations" or anything that complies with seven successive phases of redemption history. Even if we adopt a completely literal reading of Paul, we are struck with the fact that he never mentions a millennial reign of Christ, preceded by the secret rapture of the church that is distinct from the second advent of Christ, and a seven-year tribulation period, events that are said to be features of dispensational eschatology.[13] Yet surprisingly, writings that promote a dispensationalist viewpoint extensively quote the writings of Paul in support of their theological positions.[14] The purpose of this chapter is to examine the letters of Paul to determine if they can be used to support a dispensationalist view of biblical history, and to determine whether they can be used to support a dispensational eschatology. We will also examine the proposition that Paul promoted the cessation of the sign gifts (healing, miracles, prophecy, tongues) at the end of the apostolic age.

THE FUTURE AGE IMPOSED UPON THE PRESENT

A Definition of "Dispensation"

C. I. Scofield writes, "A dispensation is a period of time during which man is tested in respect of obedience to some specific revelation of the will of God."[15] Important concepts are implied in this definition: there is a deposit of divine revelation concerning God's will, the requirement of humans to conduct themselves appropriately, time periods, and divine revelation is dominant in the testing of a person's obedience to God.[16] Etymologically, the English word *dispensation* is the anglicized form of the Latin *dispensatio*, the Vulgate rendering of the Greek word *oikonomia*.[17] The Greek feminine noun *oikonomia* occurs nine times in the New Testament (Luke 16:2, 3, 4; 1 Cor 9:17; Eph 1:10; 3:2, 9; Col 1:25; 1 Tim 1:4.), which can mean, the "responsibility of management [i.e., of a household], state of being arranged, program of instruction [i.e.,

---

13. Ryrie, *Dispensationalism Today*, 159–61.

14. In Ryrie's, *Dispensationalism Today*, there are approximately 72 references made to Paul's letters (Rom, 1—2 Cor, Gal, Phil, Col, and 1—2 Thess) and approximately 38 references made to Eph, 1—2 Tim, or Titus (see 220–21).

15. *Scofield Study Bible*, 3.

16. Ibid.

17. Skeat, *Etymological Dictionary of the English Language*, 174.

in the way of salvation]."[18] According to dispensationalists the Greek word *oikonomia* implies the concept of *time* (i.e., *period* of time) and indicates a *divinely given stewardship based on the unfolding divine truth.* For example, John F. Walvoord describes a dispensation in the following manner, "A dispensation is considered a divinely-given stewardship based upon a particular rule of life revealed in the progressive unfolding of divine truth in Scripture. Each new major deposit of truth had its own demand for faith and obedience . . . a dispensation . . . is often marked off from the preceding period by some spiritual crisis in the history of God's people."[19] A dispensation is inevitably related to time because a specific "period" is implied. However, the *sine qua non* of a dispensation is the distinctively revealed truth in the redemptive plan of God during this specific period of time and the appropriate response by humans to that truth.[20]

In order to buttress this definition, a scriptural appeal is often made by dispensationalists to the writings associated with Paul. For example, it is said that Paul[21] mentions at least three dispensations: in Eph 1:10, he writes of "the dispensation [*oikonomia*] of the fullness of times," referring to the future period of the kingdom, in Eph 3:2 he designates the "dispensation [*oikonomia*] of the grace of God," referring to the present period of grace, and in Col 1:25–26 it is implied that another dispensation preceded the present one.[22] Ryrie writes, "It is very important to notice that in the first two of these instances [Eph 1:10 and 3:2] *there*

---

18. Danker, *A Greek-English Lexicon of the New Testament and Other Early Christian Literature*, 697–98.

19. Walvoord, "Dispensational Premillenialism," 11; see also the explanation given by Ryrie, *Dispensationalism Today*, 25–33.

20. Chafer, *Major Bible Themes*, 126.

21. There is some question regarding whether or not Paul was the author of the Epistle to the Ephesians. In Ephesians, the style of Greek is noticeably different than Paul's major letters. The literary similarities indicate that the author of Ephesians depended on Colossians for many of the ideas and language employed. There are also a significant number of words found in Ephesians that do not occur in the other Pauline letters. Furthermore, many key phrases that Paul uses in his main letters do not occur in Ephesians (Achtemeier et al., *Introducing the New Testament*, 379–80). Some even question Paul's authorship of Colossians based on both linguistic and doctrinal grounds (Achtemeier et al., *Introducing the New Testament*, 418–20).

22. Ryrie, *Dispensationalism Today*, 27

can be no question that the Bible uses the word dispensation in exactly the same way the dispensationalist does [his emphasis]."[23]

However, Eph 1:10 is to be understood within the context of vv. 7–10 as a whole. These verses address God's redemption procured through Christ's sacrificial death, similar to Rom 3:25. The words, "redemption through his blood" in Eph 1:7 are parallel to "sacrifice of atonement through his blood" in Rom 3:25. In Eph 1:7 the present tense verb is employed, indicating that it is a redemption taking place and enjoyed in the present and also that it is a continuous: "In him *we receive (and continue to receive [echomen])* our redemption . . ." There are subsequent and future aspects of this redemption yet to be realized, which are all associated with the decisive and sacrificial death of Christ.[24] This is a potential problem for dispensationalist thinking, which understands the time described in Eph 1:10 specifically as the future dispensation of kingdom, distinct from the present dispensation of grace. On the contrary, there is no such distinction made in these verses. The "*oikonomia* of the fullness of times" in Eph 1:10 is simply considered to be part of a unified whole, the direct result of the redemption already obtained through Christ's sacrificial death in the past, which will flourish and culminate in various ways in the future as already planned by God. Further examination of the subsequent verses will confirm this.

In Eph 1:9 we read, "He [God] has made known to us the mystery of his will." "Mystery" is a recurring term in Eph 3:3, 4, 9; 5:32; 6:19, referring to "a truth once hidden but now made known" (see Rom 11:25; Col 1:26 cf. Matt 13:11, 35). In both Jewish apocalyptic literature and in the Dead Sea Scrolls the word denotes the secret plan of God, which is disclosed at the end of the age.[25] Here in Eph 1:9, however, the unlocking of the mystery of the secret plan of God has already been made known to God's children because it has already been set in motion in the present. There is no need to wait for the future to know what God's strategy or revelation is regarding redemption and the kingdom. The verification is the sacrificial work of Christ in the past: "He [God] has made known to us the mystery of his will, according to his good pleasure *that he set forth*

---

23. Ryrie, *Dispensationalism Today*, 27.

24. In Eph 1:11 the aorist verb *eklērōthēmen* is used, which is translated "we have been chosen," indicating that followers of Christ *in the present* have already been destined to obtain their inheritance as children.

25. Bornkamm, "μυστήριον μυέω," 802–28, esp. 813–17.

in Christ" (Eph 1:9). This understanding counters the dispensationalist idea that the future dispensation of the kingdom has its own revealed truth regarding the redemptive plan of God. Quite the opposite, it has already been disclosed and enacted in the present.

In Eph 1:10, the word *oikonomia* is used to describe a further "administration" or subsequent phase in God's redemptive plan that has already been implemented: "for *the administration* in the fullness of times, to gather up all things in him, things in heaven and things on earth." The phrase "fullness of time" refers to God's putting into effect the far-reaching redemptive plan inaugurated at the death of Christ as described in Eph 1:7. Gal 4:4 reads, "But when *the fullness of time* had come, God sent his Son, born of a woman . . . in order to redeem." Here in Eph 1:10 it refers to the second advent of Christ, when salvation history reaches its climax.[26] This is confirmed by the words, "to gather up all things in Christ, things in heaven and things on earth" (Eph 1:10). "All things" refers to the whole creation (Col 1:17; Heb 1:3). Elsewhere we read how at the second advent of Christ everything will be subsumed under Christ (1 Cor 15:27; Phil 2:10). The idea conveyed here is that the redemptive plan of God first implemented with the sacrificial death of Christ has future, far-reaching effects, which will eventually take on a cosmic dimension as well, extending beyond the human race. Again, we can note that any notion of a separate and successive dispensation is foreign to Paul's thought.

In Eph 3:2 the word *oikonomia* refers to the grace associated with Paul's apostleship: "the stewardship [*oikonomia*] of God's grace given to me" (Eph 3:7–8).[27] This grace involves the proclamation of the gospel message to the Gentiles. Paul has been given special responsibility with regard to the evangelization of the Gentile world ["that the Gentiles should be fellow-heirs, members of the same body, joint-partakers of the promise fulfilled in Christ Jesus through the gospel" (Eph 3:6; 1 Cor 9:17)]. Similar to Eph 1:9, he describes this as a "mystery" that was made known to him (Eph 3:3). In this context the referent for *oikonomia* in Eph 3:2 is not the present dispensation of "grace." It is more likely a reference to the administration of Paul's apostolic office ("the stewardship [*oikonomia*] of God's grace given *to me*").[28] This becomes even more

26. Wood, "Ephesians," 26.

27. Bruce, *Epistles to the Colossians to Philemon and to the Ephesians*, 311.

28. "Paul is not now referring to saving grace as in Eph 2:5, 8 but to the equipment

apparent in Col 1:25, the other verse that Ryrie claims functions as the biblical basis for a distinct "dispensation." Col 1:25 reads: "I became its [church's] servant according to God's *stewardship* [*oikonomian*] that was *given to me* for you, to make the word of God fully known." It suggests that Paul understood the work to which God appointed him to be a sacred appointment and trust. This cannot be, as Ryrie claims, "another dispensation preceding the present one in which the mystery of Christ in the believer is revealed."[29]

In our examination of Eph 1:9 we noted that the word *oikonomia* is a reference to the redemptive plan of God as a unified whole that was first implemented with the sacrificial death of Christ and which is currently unfolding. In Eph 3:2 and Col 1:25 the word *oikonomia* refers to the special appointment and trust of Paul's apostleship to the Gentiles. In none of these contexts do we encounter the idea of seven distinct and successive periods of time characterized by special revealed truths with respect to the salvific plan of God. Instead, there is consistent attestation that God has imposed the future age of his kingdom upon the present with the sacrificial death of Christ, and because of this decisive act, there will be subsequent realizations associated with it, in particular, it will culminate with the second advent of Christ. The kingdom of God is considered both present and still future, but, nevertheless, a unified whole.

THE FUTURE AGE ONTO THE PRESENT

The Greek word *aion* is another word that warrants consideration. Dispensationalists are hesitant to equate this with their conception of dispensation because they claim it does not include the idea of stewardship arrangement in the progressive redemptive program of God.[30] However, Paul consistently uses this word in a salvation-historical context, particularly to contrast the present era of sin with the future era of salvation.[31] His thinking was shaped by Jewish apocalyptic eschatology, which advocated a simple twofold division of history.[32] In Hebraic

---

that enabled him to fulfill his calling as a missionary to the Gentiles (cf. vv. 7, 8; 4:7–13)." Wood, "Ephesians," 45.

29. See explanation above and Ryrie, *Dispensationalism Today*, 27.

30. Ehlert, *Bibliographic History of Dispensationalism*, 33; Ryrie, *Dispensationalism Today*, 29; Crutchfield, *Origins of Dispensationalism*, 24.

31. See Sasse, "αἰων αἰώνιος" 197–209, esp. 205–6.

32. "And he has revealed the wisdom of the Lord of the Spirits to the righteous and holy ones, for he has preserved the portion of the righteous because they have hated and

thought time was typically conceived as a succession of two ages and history was understood as forward movement beginning with creation and ending with final judgment. The major sign that the future age had arrived was the coming of the royal messiah who would usher in the messianic age.[33] Paul shared this eschatological schema, referring to the present age as "this age" (Rom 12:2; 1 Cor 1:20; 2:6–8; 3:18; 2 Cor 4:4), associating it with sin (Gal 1:4), and describing the future age as "the end of the ages" (1 Cor 10:11) and the "new creation" (2 Cor 5:17; Gal 6:15).

With the coming of Jesus, whom Paul believed was the Christ (i.e., the royal messiah), and his death and resurrection (Rom 1:3–4; 1 Cor 15:20, 23; 2 Cor 5:14–15, 17), the previous Jewish eschatological schema was disrupted and needed to be modified. The future age had already imposed itself upon the present and the eschatological climax had already occurred. Paul associates the incarnation with the "fullness of time" in Gal 4:4, instigated by God. In Rom 1:4 Paul describes Jesus' resurrection generally as "the resurrection *of* the dead" rather than the more restrictive, "*his* resurrection *from* the dead" (Rom 4:24; 6:4; 6:9; 7:4; 8:11, 34; 10:7, 9; Gal 1:1; Col 1:18; 2:12; 1 Thess 1:10, cf. 1 Cor 15:13, 21, 42; 1 Cor 15:12), indicating that he understood Jesus' resurrection to be the beginning of the general resurrection of the dead reserved for the future age.[34] This is the reason Paul can represent Jesus as the "first fruits of those who have died" in 1 Cor 15:20, that is, Jesus was the first who had been raised in the general resurrection, the first sheaf of the ongoing harvest (1 Cor 15:22–23).

At the same time the eschatological climax was incomplete because the dead have not yet been raised and judgment has not yet taken place. The completion of God's redemptive plan required a further climactic end, the second advent of Christ. Only then would the rest of the final

---

despised this *world* [*aion*] of oppression (together with) all its ways of life and its habits in the name of the Lord of the Spirits" (*Ethiopic Enoch* 48:7) cf. "He shall proclaim peace to you in the name of the *world* [*aion*] that is to become" (*Ethiopic Enoch* 71:15) (Translations from Isaac, *1[Ethiopic Apocalypse of] Enoch*, 35) ; see also *4 Esdras* 4:2; 9:19 cf. 7:13.

33. See particularly 2 Sam 7:14, which says that a descendant of David would sit on his throne and establish his kingdom forever. The phrase "descended from the seed of David" (Rom 1:3) used by Paul is part of a creedal formula and signifies the common hope for a royal messiah in Israel; see also Petersen and Nickelsburg, "Eschatology," 575–94.

34. Dunn, *Theology of Paul the Apostle*, 240.

events, including the resurrection of the believing dead, unfold (1 Thess 4:13—5:11; 1 Cor 15; Rom 8:31–39; 11:26–27; Phil 3:20-21; Col 4:4–5). As a result, Paul believed the present age and the future age co-existed.[35] "We are those," he reminds the Corinthians, "upon whom the ends of the ages have come" (1 Cor 10:11). However, at the same time, his recipients are still said to be living in "the present evil age" (Gal 1:4) of sin, even though it is "passing away" (1 Cor 7:31). This tension between the future age being "here" and "not yet" is also evident in the manner he understands redemption and salvation. For example, on the one hand, he can describe redemption as a benefit already possessed by his readers (Rom 3:24; Col 1:14) but on the other hand, they still await the "the redemption of the body" (Rom 8:23). Likewise, salvation is something that is already possessed (Rom 8:24, cf. 8:15), but at the same time is not completely finalized (1 Cor 1:18). Still outstanding is the full arrival of the kingdom of God at Jesus' Second Coming (1 Cor 15:23-28; 1 Thess 4:13—5:10; 2 Thess 2:2). Consequently, for Paul, those who have believed in Christ live out their lives as Christ's "between the times," that is, between this time of the overlap of the present and future ages, and the still outstanding Second Coming, when the present age will be no longer and the future age will be completely brought to fruition.

Paul's understanding of history poses important corollaries. First, Paul did not conceive of seven distinct and successive phases of "dispensations" or anything that complied with seven separate stages in God's redemption history. His thinking was shaped by Jewish apocalyptic eschatology, which advocated a simple twofold division of history: the present age and the future age. Paul associated the future age with "life" (Rom 5:17, 18, 21), "Christ" (Rom 5:15, 17, 21), and the "Spirit" (Rom 7:6; 8:2, 4–16). He associated the present age with "evil" (Gal 1:4), "Adam" (Rom 5:12-21; 1 Cor 15:21–22), "death and corruption" (Rom 5:12), "flesh" (Rom 7:14, 25), and the Law (Rom 7:1–6). Paul's definition of the "present age" would correspond with what dispensationalists call the dispensations of Conscience, Government, Patriarchal Rule, and Mosaic Law. Even though Paul makes a distinction between the period before the Law and the giving of the Law with Moses, his underlying theological premise was the universality of sin brought about by the disobedience of Adam and the reign of the power of sin and death in Adam's

---

35. This is identical to the "here, but not yet" or "begun, but not complete" tension described by Cullman, *Christ and Time*, 145, 154-55.

race, extended up until the time of Christ (Rom 5:12–21). His ideas were driven by the common Jewish thought of universal sinfulness associated with the "the fall."[36] Paul did not conceive of the period between Adam and Christ as separate and disconnected units in redemptive history as dispensationalists do.

Second, and more importantly, the demarcation between the so-called dispensations of grace and kingdom is an artificial one. As we have demonstrated above, Paul understood the future age, that is, what dispensationalists would call the dispensation of the "kingdom," to have begun with the most decisive event in Jewish history—the death and resurrection of Christ. The future age was already a present reality. "Kingdom" (i.e., the future age) expectations have already taken place in the present with the coming of Christ and followers of Christ experience the resultant benefits such as sanctification, justification, redemption, and salvation now in the present. The coming of Christ secured these benefits in the present, even though there are further complements to them in the future at the Second Coming. Paul understood these consequences of the death and resurrection of Christ to be benefits, both those experienced in the present and those that are still outstanding, but nevertheless they are all directly related to Paul's definition of the future age that has exerted itself onto the course of history.

For example, Paul's use of the "first fruits" (1 Cor 15:20) metaphor conveys the idea that we cannot posit a distinction of "dispensations" (i.e., a separate and unrelated phase in the redemptive plan of God based upon new and revealed "truth"[37]) between the resurrection of Christ and the general resurrection of the believing dead: "Now if it is proclaimed that Christ was raised from the dead, how can some of you say there is no resurrection of the dead? If there is no resurrection of the dead, then Christ has not been raised" (1 Cor 15:12–13). The resurrection of Christ and the resurrection of his followers are considered to be an inextricable whole, even though they take place at different times. For Paul, the resurrection of Christ means that the general resurrection previously reserved for the future age had already begun in the present. The resur-

---

36. Gen 6:5; 8:21; 1 Kgs 8:46; 2 Chr 6:36; Job 4:17; 14:4; 25:4; Pss 51:5; 130:3; 143:2; Prov 20:9; Eccl 7:20; Jer 17:9 (Fitzmyer, *Paul and His Theology*, 71–72); cf. "From a woman sin had its beginning, and because of her we all die" (Sir 25:24); Wis 2:23–24 cf. 2 Cor 11:3; Wis 2:23–24 cf. Rom 1:19–21.

37. See the important characteristics of the concept of "dispensation" above.

rection of Christ has set in motion the general resurrection of the dead and the future age.

"RAPTURE" THEOLOGY EXPOSED

The tendency among dispensationalists to posit distinct and separate periods in the course of redemption history is evident in their understanding of Paul's eschatology as well. One of the salient features of dispensational eschatology includes a precise chronology of end-time events. At the end of the church age there will be a secret rapture where the church will go up, followed by the seven-year tribulation.[38] At the conclusion of the tribulation, Christ will return and come down with those previously raptured and fight the battle of Armageddon, during which Satan will be bound. After Satan's forces have been neutralized, there will be the millennium, a thousand years of peace and righteousness on earth during which time the promises to Israel find their fulfillment. At the conclusion of the millennium, Satan is released; he attempts to revolt but is defeated and cast into the lake of fire for eternity.[39]

An important feature for dispensational eschatology is the distinction between the church and Israel. The church will be taken out to meet Christ in the air at the rapture but it is during the millennial reign of Christ that the prophetic promises made to ethnic Israel will come to fruition.[40] Ryrie states, "If the prophecies of the Old Testament concerning the promises of the future are made to Abraham and David are to be literally fulfilled, then there must be a future period, the millennium, in which they can be fulfilled, for the church is not now

---

38. "The church will be taken from the earth before the beginning of the tribulation . . . Pretribulationalism has become a part of dispensational eschatology." Ryrie, *Dispensationalism Today*, 159. However, those that hold to the belief in a literal seven-year tribulation are divided on whether the rapture occurs before (pretribulation), during (mid-tribulation) or after (post-tribulation) the tribulation. Pentecost, *Things to Come*, 164–218; Crutchfield, *Origins of Dispensationalism*, 41; Ryrie, *Basis of the Premillennial Faith*, 139.

39. See Crutchfield's description of the "Eschatology of Dispensationalism" under the chapter title of "Normative Dispensational Theology," *Origins of Dispensationalism*, 40–42; compare with Ryrie's description of "The Features of Dispensational Eschatology" under the chapter title of "Dispensational Eschatology," *Dispensationalism Today*, 157–61.

40. Ryrie, *Basis of the Premillennial Faith*, 145–46.

fulfilling them in any literal sense."[41] This is the motivation for holding to a separate rapture of the church and a subsequent Second Coming and millennial reign of Christ. The one thousand years is the interval when God will honour his commitments to ethnic Israel, namely the Abrahamic (Gen 17:1–22), Davidic (2 Sam 7:12–17), and new covenants (Jer 31:31–34). Ryrie adds, "The dispensational premillennialist says that the Church is in no way fulfilling these prophecies [Israel's prophecies] but that their fulfillment is reserved for the millennium and is one of the features of it."[42]

However, Paul does not always discriminate, as dispensationalists would have us believe, between the covenantal benefits to be enjoyed exclusively by Israel in a future "millennial reign of the messiah" and those blessings experienced by the church in the present "dispensation of grace." On the contrary, he understands that some of the benefits of Israel promised in the various covenants are applicable to the church during his day. For example, in Gal 3:6–9, 16–18, 29 Paul states, "those who believe are descendants of Abraham" (v. 7) and later claims, "if you belong to Christ then you are Abraham's offspring, heirs according to the promise" (v. 29).[43] In this case Paul does not make a definite and clear distinction between those promises made for believing ethnic Jews and those who believe in Christ, whether Jew or Gentile. Elsewhere, however, Paul does make a distinction between those who believe in Christ, who are part of ethnic Israel, and those who are Gentiles. In Rom 11 Paul addresses believing Jews as the recipients of God's covenantal blessings.[44] This is especially clear in v. 25, "I want you to understand this mystery: a hardening has come upon part of Israel, until the full number of the Gentiles has come in." In v. 26 he states, "all Israel will be saved" indicating that Israel as a corporate identity is meant.[45] Paul is most likely refer-

41. Ryrie, *Dispensationalism Today*, 158.

42. Ibid., 159.

43. Note further, Paul's allegory of Hagar and Sarah and the statement to the believing Galatians, "Now you, my friends, are children of the promise, like Isaac" (Gal 4:28); see also Jeremiah's new covenant language in 2 Cor 3:3–18 applied to the ministry of Paul and those who receive the Spirit. There is no delineation between Jews and Gentiles in these examples.

44. Dunn, *Romans 9–16*, 634–83.

45. "Paul writes, 'all Israel,' not 'every Israelite'—and the difference is an important one. 'All Israel' . . . has a corporate significance, referring to the nation as a whole and not to every single individual who is a part of that nation." Moo, *Epistle to the Romans*,

ring to a mass conversion of Jews taking place at the climactic parousia of Christ.[46] In the very next verse (v. 26), he explains this more fully with a scriptural basis. Paul follows Isa 59:20 from the LXX with slight modification and writes, "the *redeemer* will come out of Zion . . . And this is my covenant with them." Elsewhere in his writings, Paul identifies Jesus as this *redeemer* at his Second Coming "to wait for his Son from heaven, whom he raised from the dead—Jesus, *the one who redeems* us from the coming wrath" (1 Thess 1:10). Paul most likely has the new covenant promise of Jer 31:31–34 in mind when he wrote Rom 11:27.[47] When Christ comes out of heaven he will fulfill the covenant with Israel. However, in Paul's discussion there is no mention of a one thousand year reign of Christ.

Dispensationalists insist that there is a significant time span between 1 Thess 4:13–18 and 5:1–11. Highlighting the phrase, "the Day of the Lord" in 1 Thess 5:2, they claim this is a term encompassing multiple events: the seven-year tribulation period, the Second Coming, and the entire millennial age.[48] Prior to "the Day of the Lord" there was a separate event, the rapture of the church, as described in 1 Thess 4:13–18. The idea of a separation between the parousia and the Day of the Lord is an artificial one and requires special pleading. Paul does not describe an interim seven year period between the parousia of the church in 1 Thess 4:13–18 and the Day of the Lord in 1 Thess 5:1–11. In addition, the element of surprise evident in the description of the Day of the Lord coming "like a thief in the night" (1 Thess 5:2), cannot be reconciled with the precision associated with a seven-year tribulation period and one thousand-year period. As we shall argue, the notion of a separate "rapture" of the church followed by an interval of seven years before the Second Coming and millennial reign[49] of Christ was foreign to Paul.

722.

46. Rom 11:15 gives us an indication as to the specific point in the future when Israel will turn to Christ. There is an association made between Israel's acceptance and the eschatological resurrection of the dead at the parousia of Christ: "For if their [Israel's] rejection is the reconciliation of the world, what will their acceptance be, if not life from the dead."

47. Dunn, *Romans 9–16*, 692.

48. Pentecost, *Things to Come*, 174.

49. Some use 1 Cor 15:24–27 ("*Then* comes the end, when he hands over the kingdom to him who is God and Father for *he [Christ] must reign* until he has put all enemies under his feet. The last enemy to be destroyed is death. For God *has put* all things

The differentiation between a secret "rapture" of the church and the Second Coming did not appear to have arisen before the nineteenth century. In 1830 in Glasgow, Scotland, Margaret MacDonald attended a healing service and claimed to have received a vision of the two-stage return of Christ.[50] This idea would have fallen into obscurity except that John Nelson Darby, founder of the Plymouth Brethren, heard about the story and spread it far and wide. He used Paul's discussion of the "parousia" in 1 Thess 4–5 to substantiate this theological position.[51]

The term *rapture* does not occur anywhere in the New Testament. It comes from the Latin word *raptus/raptio*, a translation of the Greek word *harpazō*, which means, "to grab or seize suddenly so as to remove or gain control, *snatch/ take away*"[52] used in 1 Thess 4:17. In 1 Thess 4:13–18 Paul focuses on the current state of the dead and their fate in

---

in subjection under his feet.") as a complement to Rev 20:1–6, which explicitly mentions a one thousand-year reign of Christ. Ladd, *The Gospel of the Kingdom*, 35–36, 43–46. However, it seems unthinkable that if Paul understood a one thousand year reign of Christ here that he would pass it over without a word. It is most likely that the word *then* ("*Then* comes the end . . .") simply means *thereupon*—the parousia of Christ, accompanied by the resurrection of Christians, ushers in the end, *at which time* the main event is handing over the kingdom by Christ to God, Barrett, *The First Epistle to the Corinthians*, 356. Also significant is the verb *has put in subjection* (hupataxen) ("For God *has put* all things *in subjection* under his feet" (1 Cor 15:27). It is written in the past tense, indicating that God has already set in motion the process of subjecting things under the feet of Christ, that is, Christ is already reigning. This explanation best coincides with what Paul states elsewhere. Paul understood Christ's reign to have begun already at his exaltation and the completion of this reign entails the annihilation of death and the resurrection of the dead (cf. 1 Cor 15:54–55). For example, in Phil 2:9–11 we read, "Therefore, God also highly *exalted* (*huperupsōsen*, aorist tense) him [Christ] and gave him the name that is above every name so that at the name of Jesus every knee should bend, in heaven and on earth and under the earth and every tongue should confess that Jesus is Lord, to the glory of God the Father." The past tense verb *exalted* indicates that Christ is already reigning, and with the resurrection of the dead (cf 1 Cor 15:24–25), the reign of Christ will have been fully realized and the kingdom is then handed over to God. See Plevnik, *Paul and the Parousia*, 76.

50. Rossing, *Rapture Exposed*, 22.

51. Under the heading of "The Rapture," Darby claims "It [the church] will physically go up to meet Christ in the air (1 Thess 4:15–17)," Darby, *Collected Writings*, #6, 361–62. However, Darby is quick to point out that the rapture does not establish the kingdom. At the conclusion of the tribulation period, Christ will return with the saints to destroy Satan's power on earth and to deliver the world from his evil influence. Darby, *Collected Writings*, #6, 362.

52. Danker, *Greek-English Lexicon of the New Testament and Other Early Christian Literature*, 134.

the future coming of Christ, "For we do not want you to be uninformed, brothers, concerning those who have fallen asleep . . . For if we believe that Jesus died and rose, so also God will bring with him those who have fallen asleep in Jesus" (1 Thess 4:13–14). Paul is not discussing the end of history for its own sake but for the purpose of bringing encouragement to the converts in Thessalonica. The issue there was whether or not the Christian dead would participate with Jesus in the air when he returned and whether they would be with him forever.[53]

In 1 Thess 4:15 Paul speaks of "the *parousia* of the Lord," which can be translated as "presence" or "coming" and often denoted the ceremonial arrival of a royal visit to a city where the king was greeted with honors.[54] This connotation is confirmed in 1 Thess 4:17, when Paul states that at the parousia those who are alive will "*meet* (*apantēsis*) the Lord in the air." The word *apantēsis* was often used with parousia to describe the visits of dignitaries who would be ceremonially escorted back into the city.[55] In v. 16 Paul connects the resurrection of believers who had died, to the parousia and meeting of Christ in the air. Clearly this will be a public event and not a secret or invisible return. Paul speaks of a "loud command" like the one given on a battlefield to signal troops.[56] The underlying motif of the command signals God's decisive action on the Day of the Lord.[57] Along with the voice of the archangel (Jude 9, 1 Enoch 20:1–7, 4 Ezra 4:36) and the trumpet call of God, these images communicate the idea of Jesus summoning his army. Angels are regularly associated with the Second Coming (Mark 8:38; 13:27; Matt 24:31). The trumpet was often sounded during a theophany like the Second Coming

---

53. "It appears that the Thessalonian Christians fear that the deceased faithful will not be united with Christ, as the living would be, at his coming. For some unexplained reason they think that death has robbed the deceased of this." Plevnik, *Paul and the Parousia*, 69.

54. Diessmann, *Light from the Ancient Near East*, 368–73; Danker, *Greek-English Lexicon of the New Testament and Other Early Christian Literature*, 780–81.

55. See Josephus, *Ant* 11:327f.

56. Schmid, "κέλευσμα," 656–59.

57. The word *keleusma* ("loud command") that Paul uses in 1 Thess 4:16 occurs only here in the New Testament but see Plevnik who identifies the underlying motif of the "loud command" to occur in the context of the Day of the Lord, for example, in *4 Ezra* 12:31–32; 13:1–13; *2 Bar* 21:19–23; *Ps Sol* 17:23–24. Plevnik, *Paul and the Parousia*, 45–50.

as well (Zeph 1:14–16; Isa 27:13; Matt 24:31) and in 1 Cor 15:52 Paul links it with the resurrection of the dead and the End.

In vv. 16–17, Paul makes it clear that Christ is to come *down* out of heaven and meet his followers in the clouds, not in heaven. There is no discussion of a "rapture" into heaven here: "For the Lord himself . . . *will descend from heaven*, and the dead in Christ will rise first. Then we who are alive, who are left, will be caught up *in the clouds* together with them *to meet the Lord in the air.*" Clouds regularly accompanied a theophany when God comes down to the human level, not when humans are taken up into the presence of God in heaven (Exod 19:16; 40:34; 1 Kgs 8:10–11; Ps 97:2). Paul then reassures the Thessalonians that "the dead in Christ will rise first" (v. 16). Evidently Paul is concerned only with the Christian dead here, not with what happens to the non-believers. Nothing is said of the resurrection body or of the transformation that is to take place in those who are alive at the parousia (1 Cor 15 and Phil 3:21). Then the living Christians will be "snatched away" (*harpagēsometha*) and meet the Lord in the air. Paul does not tell us what will happen next after the reunion in the air except that believers "will be with the Lord forever." His primary concern is to convey the idea that the Christian dead will in no way be disadvantaged, in fact, they will take precedence and be raised first. With these words the Thessalonians are to be encouraged (v. 18).

In 1 Thess 5:1 Paul is now taking up a new angle on the previously discussed topic of the parousia in 1 Thess 4:13–18. Rather than bringing encouragement to the converts in Thessalonica with new information of the active participation of the Christian dead in the parousia, he is now exhorting the Thessalonians based on the knowledge they already have. In 5:2 he writes, "For you yourselves know very well that the Day of the Lord will come like a thief in the night." Subsequent to this he exhorts them to be diligent as they wait for the Day of the Lord to arrive: "let us keep awake and be sober" (v. 6), "let us be sober" (v. 7), "put on the breastplate of faith and love and for a helmet the hope of salvation" (v. 8). The exhortations for believers in Christ to be diligent would be pointless if in fact they were not envisioned as still on earth until the Day of the Lord. What motivation would Paul have for writing 1 Thess 5:4: "But you, beloved, are not in darkness, for that Day [the Day of the Lord] to surprise you like a thief"? The exhortations that follow in vv. 5–7 to be sensitive to the inevitable redemption would be pointless if he believed they would be taken away prior to the Day of the Lord. Paul concludes his exhortations in 1 Thess 5:1–11 in the same manner as 1 Thess 4:13–18. Both reveal how believers will be "with the Lord" (1 Thess 4:18; 5:10) and both end with the admonition to "encourage one another" (1 Thess 4:18; 5:11). The reason for these similarities is because in both passages Paul is describing only one Second Coming of Christ but from two different perspectives. 1 Thess 4:13–18 describes the Second Coming from the perspective of the rescue of believers whereas 1 Thess 5:1–11 examines the same event from the perspective of judgment on unbelievers.[58]

In 1 Thess 5:2 Paul tells us how Jesus will come—like a "thief in the night," in an unexpected manner. The idea of a sudden and unexpected coming appears in passages such as Mal 3:1; Mark 13:34ff; Luke 12:35–40 and partially in Job 24:14; Joel 2:9; Obad 5 but nowhere is it linked to the Day of the Lord. There are variant forms in 2 Pet 3:10; Rev 3:3; 16:15 and in the last two passages in the book of Revelation it is the exalted One and not the Day of the Lord who comes. The metaphor "thief in the night" is found in Q (Luke 12:39 = Matt 24:43), which contains the earliest sayings of Jesus. In the Q sayings it is Jesus himself who is said to come like the thief in the night. Paul applies the metaphor to the Day of the Lord in 1 Thess 5:2. He uses several phrases to refer to this future event—*the Day* (1 Thess 5:4; 1 Cor 3:13; Rom 2:5 cf. 13:12), *that Day* (2 Thess 1:10), *the Day of the Lord* (1 Thess 5:2; 2 Thess 2:2; 1 Cor 5:5), *the Day of our Lord Jesus Christ* (1 Cor 1:8), *the Day of the Lord Jesus* (2 Cor 1:14), *the Day of Jesus Christ* (Phil 1:6), or *the Day of Christ* (Phil 1:10; 2:16). The various phrases go back to Jewish history and refer to a decisive or final intervention of God. Essentially it is a time of judgment but it also came to mean a day of deliverance for God's people (Amos 5:18–20; Joel 1:15 cf 1:32; Isa 13:6, 9; Obad 15–17; Zech 14). The Day of Yahweh became the Day of the Lord, Christ for the early Christian move- ment.[59] The phrase *Day of the Lord* for Paul is used in contexts when he speaks of the coming judgement (Rom 2:5). Clearly Paul's special use of the phrases *the Day* in 1 Thess 5:4 and *the Day of the Lord* in 1 Thess 5:2 is motivated by their specific associations with the themes of judge- ment for unbelievers and deliverance for the faithful, ideas he received from his Jewish tradition.[60] He is not describing a different event than

---

58. Best, *First and Second Epistles to the Thessalonians*, 219; Howard, "Literary Unity of 1 Thessalonians 4:13—5:11," 163–90.

59. Witherington, *Jesus, Paul, and the End of the World*, 163–65.

60. In 1 Thess 5:3–9 Paul writes, "When they say, 'there is peace and security,' then

the one he already mentions in 1 Thess 4:13–18. For believers, the Day of the Lord will result in salvation, which includes a life lived together with Jesus Christ as Paul has already described in 1 Thess 4:13–18 and reiterated here in 1 Thess 5:8–10. We can confidently deduce that 1 Thess 5:1–11 is not a reference to a separate coming of Christ that occurs seven years after the "rapture" of the church. Rather, it is but one of the events that will transpire with various others at the one and only second advent of Christ.

When we examine the details of 1 Thess 4:13–18 and 5:1–7, there is a striking resemblance to the synoptic tradition in Matt 24:30–49. These parallels make it likely that Paul is drawing upon the tradition associated with the Second Coming, which was already prominent during the time of Jesus. The discourse in Matt 24 is about "the sign of your [Jesus'] coming" (v. 3) (i.e., the Second Coming). Dispensationalists rely on Matt 24 to substantiate their position for a seven-year tribulation (vv. 21–22) followed by the glorious return of Christ (vv. 29–30), while turning to the writing of Paul (1 Thess 4:13–18) to bolster their idea of a separate rapture of the church that will precede both of these events.[61] However, when we examine 1 Thess 4:13–18 and 5:1–11, we notice that *these passages together* correspond with the details Matt 24.[62]

sudden destruction will come upon them . . . and there will be no escape! . . . God has destined us not for wrath but for obtaining salvation through our Lord Jesus Christ."

61. Scofield's understanding of the relationship between Matt 24 and 1 Thess 4:13–18 is as follows: Christ will first return from heaven to raise the dead saints who together with those still living, will be caught up to meet the Lord in the air and remain forever with Him (rapture of the church—1 Thess 4:16–17). This will be followed by the seven-year tribulation (Matt 24:21, 22; Dan 12:1; Jer 30:5–7; Zeph 1:15–18). Then the Lord will return in power and glory to judge the earth and prepare the way for the last dispensation, the dispensation of the kingdom (Matt 24:29, 30; 25:31–46). Scofield, *Rightly Dividing the Word of Truth*, 15; see also the description by Crutchfield, *Origins of Dispensationalism*, 126.

62. Witherington, *Problem with Evangelical Theology*, 117.

	1 Thessalonians	Matthew
Christ returns from heaven	4:16	24:30
Accompanied by angels	4:16	24:31
With a trumpet of God	4:16	24:31
Believers gathered to Christ in clouds	4:17	24:30–31, 40–41
Time unknown	5:1–2	24:36
Coming like a thief	5:2, 4	24:43
Unbelievers unaware of coming judgment	5:3	24:37–39
Judgment like a mother's birth pangs	5:3	24:8
Believers not deceived	5:4–5	24:43
Believers to be watchful	5:6	24:37–39
Warning about drunkenness	5:7	24:49

These parallels confirm our analysis of 1 Thess 4:13–18 and 5:1–11. Paul was describing the one in the same Second Coming of Christ, following the tradition of Matt 24, not a two-stage return of Christ with an intervening seven-year tribulation. For Paul, "the coming of the Lord" (4:15) was relating the same event as "the Day of the Lord" (5:21) and "the sign of your [Jesus'] coming" (Matt 24:3).

Dispensationalists make the same artificial distinction between the rapture of the church and the Day of the Lord in 2 Thess 2. Commenting on 2 Thess 2, Darby writes, "[The] course of reasoning of the whole chapter [2 Thess 2] [*Darby's inclusion of the scriptural passage*], which shews (*sic*) the distinction of the rapture of the saints before Christ appears, and the coming of the day when He is admired in them. . . ."[63] Darby proposes a difference between 2 Thess 2:1 and 2:2. He claims 2 Thess 2:1 is a reference to the rapture of the church when Paul speaks of "our gathering with him." For Darby, 2 Thess 2:2 refers to "the Day of the Lord," which is a description of a time of judgment occurring on a separate occasion at the Second Coming. However, the noun *episunagōgēs*[64] ("gathering" in

63. Darby, *Collected Writings*, vol. 11: *Prophetic No. 46.*, 115.

64. The noun *episunagōgēs* ("gathering") used in 2 Thess 2:1 is rare in the New Testament (found elsewhere only in Heb 10:25). Both the noun and the cognate verb were used for the re-gathering of the dispersed Jews into Palestine (Isa 52:12; 2 Macc 1:27; 2:7, 8). Understandably, used in these previous contexts it quickly took on an eschatological significance in Matt 24:31 and Mark 13:27. See Best, *First and Second Epistles to the Thessalonians*, 274.

the phrase "our *gathering* with him") in 2 Thess 2:1 has verbal cognates in Mark 13:27 and Matt 24:31, which refer to the gathering of believers at the coming of the Son of Man (i.e,. the Second Coming). In 2 Thess 2:1 Paul is using the same cognate alluding to his previous discussion on the parousia in 1 Thess 4:17, the same subject he was addressing there—the Second Coming. In the very next verse, in 2 Thess 2:2, it is evident that Paul's subject all along had been "the Day of the Lord": "As to the coming of our Lord Jesus Christ and *our gathering with him*, we beg you, brothers, not to be quickly shaken in mind or alarmed, either by spirit or by word or by letter, as though from us, to the effect that *the Day of the Lord is already here*" (2 Thess 2:1–2).

Does Paul promote a "rapture" theology? Perhaps he does promote the "rapture" of the church if this is defined as the church being taken up into the air to meet Christ there, followed by various other occurrences at this time such as the judgment of unbelievers, which will both transpire at the one time event of the Second Coming. However, Paul did not envision a secret "rapture" of the church in order to spare it from any form of tribulation that was to follow. Dispensationalists rely on 2 Thess 2:3–11 to promote an intense period of persecution, but where the church has already been "raptured."[65] As we have already shown in 2 Thess 2, Paul did not conceive of a seven year time interval between the time when believers are gathered with Christ (v. 1) and "the Day of the Lord" (v. 2), since both refer to the one in the same second advent of Christ. In addition, the theme of suffering runs throughout both 1 and 2 Thessalonians, indicating that throughout the church age believers in Christ endured and will continue to experience suffering and persecution even up until the time of the end.[66] In 2 Thess 1:4 Paul writes, "Therefore we ourselves boast of you among the churches of God for your steadfastness and faith during all your persecutions and the afflictions that you are enduring. This is evidence of the righteous judgment of God, and is intended to make you worthy of the kingdom of God, for which you are also suffering." For Paul, suffering, persecution, and martyrdom are common

65. According to Scofield, "The Manifestation of the Man of Sin, and of Anti-Christ" will take place (2 Thess 2:3–10; Matt 24:15; Rev 13:1–8, 11–18; 1 Jn 2:18) shortly after the rapture, beginning the first three and a half years of the tribulation (*Scofield StudyLeaflets*, Series C, Lesson 20).

66. "For what is our hope or joy of crown of boasting before our Lord Jesus at his coming? Is it not you? . . . no one would be shaken by these persecutions. Indeed, you yourselves know that this is what we are destined for" (1 Thess 2:19—3:3).

for the church in the past and in the future, extending up to the time of the Second Coming (cf. Mark 13:19, 24, 26–27; Matt 24:9–14; Luke 21:12–19). Ben Witherington argues, "The church of the last generation will go through the fire, just as every other generation of Christians has had to do . . . There will be no 'beam me up Scotty' effect for the last generation of Christians."[67]

A REDUCTIONISM OF THE SPIRIT?

One of the most significant disagreements between dispensational-ism and Pentecostalism occurs over the subject of the Holy Spirit. Dispensationalists adopted a cessationist position. Scofield asserted that "the sensational gifts" or "sign gifts," that is, the gifts of healing, faith, working of miracles, and tongues, ceased after the apostolic age and should be forbidden because God no longer bestows such gifts. A varia-tion of this same conclusion is the idea that the sign gifts were relevant only for the era prior to the completion of the canon of Scripture.[68] They are no longer necessary since the written record of God's revelation in the canonized scriptures replaces them.[69] Dispensationalists believe the Spirit operates in a limited manner, complementing the current stage

67. Witherington, *Problem with Evangelical Theology*, 130.

68. It should be noted that not all cessationists hold to a dispensational view of sal-vation history. For example, Richard Gaffin is a proponent of the view that the gifts of prophecy, tongues, and knowledge endure only through the course of "inscripturation," that is, the process of writing Scripture (*Perspectives on Pentecost*, 111). The underlying premise is that the content conveyed through these gifts becomes redundant in light of the complete and the authoritative supremacy of scripture. Ironically, Pentecostal, Charismatic and cessationists together hold to the same view of the verbal, plenary in-spiration of scripture (see Duffield and Van Cleave, *Foundations of Pentecostal Theology*, 24–25; Pearlman, *Knowing the Doctrines of the Bible*, 15–29). However, Pentecostals and Charismatics believe the information conveyed in the gifts of prophecy, knowl-edge, and the interpretation of tongues complement the truths revealed in scripture and are relevant for changing contemporary situations. If genuine, these gifts would never contradict scripture. Pentecostals have always been advocates for the authorita-tive supremacy of scripture as the ruling standard. As Pearlman states, "The inspiration manifest in the gift of prophecy is not on a level with that of Scripture" (*Knowing the Doctrines of the Bible*, 325). Likewise Duffield and Van Cleave state, "All Spirit-filled believers have known, to some degree, the miracle of Divine inspiration by the Holy Spirit, *but never to the extent experienced by the writers of Scripture* [italics and emphasis added]" (*Foundations of Pentecostal Theology*, 27).

69. Walvoord, "Contemporary Issues in the Doctrine of the Holy Spirit: IV, Spiritual Gifts Today," 315–28; Fraikin, "'Charismes et ministères' àl lumière de 1 Cor 12–14," 462.

in salvation history. This is a fundamental point of contention within Pentecostal and Charismatic circles. Pentecostals commonly thought of the twentieth-century outpouring of the Spirit, in particular, the gift of speaking in tongues and the working of miracles, as evidence of the "latter rain," a sign of the "last days" restoration of apostolic church prior to the return of Christ.[70] With the outpouring of the Spirit a continuum is created with the original proclamation of the gospel message in the apostolic age and the operations of the Spirit that accompanied it. In addition, one of the distinctive theological convictions in classical Pentecostalism is the teaching of a subsequent experience to conversion, the baptism in the Holy Spirit, which is evidenced by the manifestation of speaking in tongues.[71]

Our purpose in this section is to examine the writings of the Apostle Paul to determine if he proposed a distinction between the apostolic and post-apostolic periods with respect to the Spirit's operation. If, in fact, there was no such distinction envisioned by Paul, dispensational ideology would have created an artificial dichotomy between an apostolic era Spirit and a post-apostolic era Spirit. This, in turn, runs the risk of promoting a reductionism of the Spirit in the post-apostolic era and for today, minimizing the potential benefit the complementary gifting of the Spirit can have for the church of Christ (1 Cor 12:7).

Cessationist positions commonly rely on 1 Cor 13:8 as their scriptural basis, "Love never ends. But as for prophecies, they will come to an end; as for tongues, they will cease; as for knowledge, it will come to an end."[72] In 1 Corinthians 12—14 Paul interrupts his discussion of spiritual gifts with chapter 13, in which he intends to put the entire discussion of gifts in proper perspective. He demonstrates the superiority of love. Love lasts forever, whereas the gifts are all temporary. 1 Cor 13:9–12 further explains why the gifts are temporary. Through a series of comparisons and analogies, Paul will show how these manifestations of the Spirit are

70. Arrington, "Dispensationalism," 247–48.

71. Pearlman, *Knowing the Doctrines of the Bible*, 313–15.

72. "Ch. 14 regulates the ministry of gifts in the primitive, apostolic assembly of believers in Christ. . . . Tongues and the sign gifts are to cease." Scofield [ed.], *Oxford NIV Scofield Study Bible*, 1210; see also Reymond whose argument hinges on Paul's contrast between "the imperfect" and "perfect" in 1 Cor 13:10. The "perfect," he claims, refers to a completed means of revelation, the time when the canon of scripture will be complete (*What about Continuing Revelations and Miracles in the Presbyterian Church Today?* 32–34).

especially relevant for the church up until the time of the final consummation.[73] In vv. 9–10 Paul describes knowing and prophesying to be "in part" compared to a future time when "the complete" comes and what is "in part" will disappear. When this time of "completion" comes, the gifts of prophecy, knowledge, and tongues, and other charismatic gifts, will disappear.[74]

Did Paul have the post-apostolic age in mind, the completion of the canon itself or the maturity of the church as the time when the charismatic gifts would cease? On a cursory reading it is difficult to believe that Paul could have expected the Corinthians to think that by "completion" he was referring to the post-apostolic age or a fixed canon or the maturity of the church. In v. 11 he picks up the themes of "in part" and "the complete" and proceeds to the point of vv. 9–10 by way of the analogy of "the child" and "the adult." The adult does not continue to "talk" or "think" or "reason" like a child. The use of the verb "to talk," which is the same verb used to describe the phenomenon of "tongues" (1 Cor 12:30 cf. 1 Cor 13:11), and the contrast in 14:20 between thinking like children and adults, has been thought by some to indicate that the purpose of the analogy in 13:11 was intended to convey the idea that speaking in tongues was evidence of a state of immaturity that the Corinthian church had to outgrow.[75] But this line of reasoning is faulty in many ways. First, in 13:11 Paul writes using the past tense and first person singular,[76] including himself in the analogy: "When *I was* a child,

73. Fee, *First Epistle to the Corinthians*, 643; Carson, *Showing the Spirit*, 69–72.

74. Paul intentionally named the gifts of prophecy, tongues, and knowledge in 1 Cor 13:8 because they reflect the current situation in the Corinthian church. For example, in 1 Cor 14:1ff, the discussion emphasizes the greater value of prophecy over unintelligible tongues when the church gathers for worship because when the gift of prophecy is exercised it is spoken in the vernacular language and benefits the entire church. The terminology, the "tongues of angels" (1 Cor 13:1), indicates the possibility of an over-realized eschatology. When the Corinthians exercised the gift of tongues they believed they had already reached a heavenly status like that of angels. In addition, Paul's argument consistently appears to take up the hypothesis of speaking in tongues, "if I come to you speaking in tongues" (1 Cor 14:6), which is a sure indication that the Corinthians were fascinated with this specific gift (see also the emphasis on "wisdom" and "knowledge" in 1 Cor 2). The logic implies that what Paul says of the gifts of prophecy, tongues, and knowledge is also relevant for the other charismatic gifts as well.

75. Thomas, "Tongues . . . Will Cease," 81–89.

76. "It would be impossible to draw the analogy: *lalein* [to speak] = speak with tongues, etc.; this is already counter to the figure and its form (first person, past tenses)" (Conzelmann, *1 Corinthians*, 226 n. 85).

I spoke like a child . . ." It would be illogical for Paul to write later on in 14:18, "I thank God that *I speak* in tongues more than all of you," if he thought that he had personally "outgrown" the experience of speaking in tongues. The use of the present tense verb *lalō* ("I speak") in 14:18 describes Paul's current experience of the gift of tongues when he wrote this letter to the Corinthians. Second, the extended discussions in 1 Cor 12:4–11 and 14:1–40 would be pointless if in fact Paul believed that the gift of tongues was something to be "outgrown." He goes to great lengths to emphasize the variety of gifts (including the manifestation of tongues, 12:10) bestowed by the Spirit in 12:4–11, and in 14:1–40 he engages in an extended discussion of the greater benefit of intelligible prophecies over tongues that are not interpreted when people gather for worship.

In the analogy Paul is attempting to illustrate the difference between the present and the future times, not immaturity associated with being a child and maturity that goes with being an adult. He is seeking to demonstrate types of behaviour characteristic of various periods of time in one's life. For example, a child will demonstrate the speech appropriate to his current age, but when the child becomes an adult, this type of speech is no longer suitable for the life of an adult. The analogy demonstrates a time when the gifts will not be appropriate just like the adult who no longer speaks as a child. There will come a time when the gifts will be "put to an end" (1 Cor 13:11). When will this time be? The next analogy in v. 12 explains this more clearly. The use of the conjunction "for" in v. 12 is a confirmation that our understanding of the previous analogy in v. 11 refers to the contrast of two periods of time rather than the contrast between immaturity and maturity (1 Cor 13:11b–12a).

In v. 12 Paul sets up this time distinction between the present and future more definitively: "For *now* we see but a poor reflection in a mirror, *but then* we will see face to face. *Now* I know only in part; *then* I will know fully, even as I am fully known." The word translated "a poor reflection"[77] is used to describe the indirect vision of reality in a mirror. On the other hand, the words "face to face," is a biblical idiom for direct personal communication and is intended to bring a contrast with the in-

---

77. The word *ainigmati* ("a poor reflection") is used only here in the New Testament and most likely alludes to Num 12:6–8 (LXX), where God spoke with Moses directly ("mouth to mouth") in contrast to the prophets, whom he spoke through visions or dreams "in a riddle, or in a figurative way" (v. 6), which implied that they received less clear truths than the ones received by Moses (Fee, *First Epistle to the Corinthians*, 647 n. 42).

direct vision of reality from a mirror. This phrase conveys the direct and complete vision of God like someone experiences in a theophany.[78] This is most certainly a reference to the future new state brought about by the parousia. The analogy conveys the idea that in our present existence we have only an indirect vision of God through the communication we receive when the gifts of the Spirit are in operation.[79] As great as this present state is, however, in the future there is no need for the gifts of the Spirit since we will have direct and personal access to God.[80]

In addition, the words in v. 12, "Now I know in part; then I will know fully, even as I am fully known [by God]" are informative for us. Again Paul contrasts the present ("now") with the future time ("then"). As with the previous comparisons, future time refers to the time of the end enacted by the second advent of Christ. Paul uses two different verbs for "knowing" in this verse. He states, "Now *I know* in part." This verb *ginōskein* is the same verb he uses previously in 13:9 to describe the "knowing" that is partial in the present. However, when he describes the future type of "knowing," ("*then I will know fully*, even as *I am fully known* [by God]" Paul employs the verb *epiginōskein*, which means "to know exactly, completely, through and through."[81] This verb was intended to bring out the completeness of future knowledge, that is, "present knowledge will be done away not in the interests of ignorance but of full understanding."[82] Paul intends to delineate the difference between "the knowing" that is available through the gift of the Spirit in the present and is partial,[83] and the future "knowing" that is complete (1 Cor 13:10) and made possible by the state of affairs brought on by the Second Coming of Christ.[84]

---

78. The words "face to face" are not found in the New Testament but are found in the Septuagint (LXX): Gen 32:30; Deut 5:4; 34:10; Judg 6:22; Ezek 20:35; Exod 33:11.

79. This corresponds to the description of the present knowledge and prophesies being "partial" in contrast to "completion" at a future time (1 Cor 13:9–10).

80. Fee proposes that a comparable metaphor would be the difference between seeing a photography and seeing someone in person, *First Epistle to the Corinthians*, 648.

81. Danker, *Greek-English Lexicon of the New Testament and Other Early Christian Literature*, 369.

82. Barrett, *First Epistle to the Corinthians*, 306–7.

83. "For we know (*ginōskein*) in part" (1 Cor 13:9).

84. "Paul . . . is thinking . . . in eschatological terms. This also indicates the sense in the present context: even the charismatic does not attain the full vision of God in this world. It is future." Conzelmann, *1 Corinthians*, 228.

In v. 12, the nature of the final knowing is expressed by the words, "even as I am fully known." Paul equates this type of "knowing" in the future to God's type of "knowing" Paul ("*as* I am fully known [by God]"). He envisions a time when his knowledge will be in some way comparable with God's present knowledge of him. It does not mean that he expects God to grant him omniscience rather it refers to a time when Paul expects to be free from the inabilities to understand God and his will, which are part of this present life, even when he exercises the gift of knowledge through the Spirit. It is most likely comparable to God knowing us completely, as the previous analogy of the mirror indicates. In the future Paul's knowledge will be part of God's present knowledge of him without limitations as to what can be perceived in this age and under the present conditions in which Paul currently finds himself.[85]

In v. 13, Paul states, "And now[86] these three remain: faith, hope and love. But the greatest of these is love." The first observation is that now, in addition to love, he mentions the permanency of faith and hope: "And now these three *remain* (or *abide*)." In contrast with v. 8, which speaks of the temporary use of prophecies, tongues, and knowledge, which are limited to the present age, faith, hope and love endure also in the age to come, that is, in the period that Paul has previously described as when "the complete comes" (v. 10), the direct form of seeing—"face to face" (v. 12) "knowing fully" (v. 12). Paul most likely adds faith and hope to love in order to form a triad that was common in early Christianity (Rom 5:1–5; Gal 5:5–6; Eph 4:2–5; Col 1:4–5; 1 Thess 1:3; 5:8; Heb 6:10–12; 10:22–24; 1 Pet 1:3–8, 21–22). Faith, hope, and love summarize Christian existence. Here faith no longer refers to the miracle-working faith of 1 Cor 13:2 but the trustful acceptance of God (Rom 1:16, 17; 3:21–22 particularly). Hope is not simply directed towards what is not seen in a blessing yet to come, but also refers to a foundational hope in God and in Christ (1 Cor 15:19). Paul says love is "the greatest" in 13:13 because it exempli-

---

85. Grudem, *Gift of Prophecy*, 231–32.

86. The words "and now" can be understood temporally: "*now, during this age*, only these three virtues remain: faith, hope, and love." Moss, "1 Corinthians xiii.13," 93. They can also be taken to imply a logical force: "*now in fact*, only these three virtues remain: faith, hope, and love," Barrett, *First Epistle to the Corinthians*, 308. But given the time comparison between "the present" and "the future" and the present tense of the verb "remain" (i.e., "continue to remain") it is not unlikely that Paul could have intended both meanings—"*now in fact during this age*, only these three virtues remain: faith, hope, and love." Fee, *First Epistle to the Corinthians*, 649–50.

fies the very character of God and it is foundational, even to faith and hope ("faith working through love," Gal 5:6). Understood in this manner, love is in a different category than the gifts of the Spirit because love is both for the present and the future. In the present, love is said to accompany the gifts of the Spirit, not replace them, "If I speak in the tongues of mortals and angels, but do not have love . . . if I have the gift of prophecy . . . but have not love . . . If I give all I possess to the poor and surrender my body to the flames, but have not love . . ." (13:1–3). In contrast to the spiritual gifts, love endures even into eternity.

When we analyze 1 Cor 13:8 in its context there is no sufficient exegetical warrant for banning tongues, prophecy, the so-called "sign" gifts, and by implication, any of the spiritual gifts on the grounds that Paul anticipates their demise at the close of the apostolic age, or completion of the canon, or the maturity of the church. Furthermore, for Paul, the spiritual gifts are indispensable for the proper functioning and sustaining of the church up until the time of the second advent of Christ. In Rom 8:17–27, we note how the Spirit takes on a primary role between the time when God first implemented his redemptive plan at the death and resurrection of Christ until the time of the Second Coming of Christ.[87] In v. 23 Paul refers to the "*first fruits* of the Spirit." The term *aparchē* ("first fruits") is used in the LXX in Num 15:19–21, referring to the bread made from the first harvest to be used in a "sheaf-offering," implying that the harvest has begun. Paul picks up the first harvest metaphor and uses it in the context of eschatological harvest. Here, Paul understands the Spirit as the first harvest and as a basis of guarantee and hope for the final eschatological harvest in the future, which includes the full benefits of *adoption* and *the redemption of the body*: "We ourselves, who have the first fruits of the Spirit groan while we wait for adoption, the redemption of our bodies" (v. 23).

In vv. 26–27, Paul conveys a specific example of how the Spirit assists individuals in this phase of redemption history. He writes, "The Spirit takes share in our weakness; for we do not know what we should pray for, but the Spirit himself supplicates on our behalf with inarticulate groanings. And he who searches our hearts knows the mind of the Spirit." There are good reasons to believe that Paul has the experience of speaking in tongues in mind when he describes the Spirit's supplication as "inarticulate groanings." Rom 8:26 makes a direct correlation with

87. Bertone, "Function of the Spirit," 85–97.

1 Cor 14. In 1 Cor 14 Paul states three positive characteristics of exercising the gift of tongues: (1) it is speaking to God (v. 2), which is a circumlocution for praying,[88] (2) those who speak in a tongue edify themselves (v. 4), (3) Paul wished for all to speak in tongues (v. 5). Regarding (2), one might ask how "unintelligible" glossolalic utterance might be edifying to the speaker. Paul answers this in 1 Cor 14:14: "For if I pray in a tongue, my spirit prays, but my mind is unfruitful." The possessive "my spirit" is juxtaposed with "my mind" and indicates that Paul is here referring to his own human "spirit" at prayer, particularly as the center of human emotions. It is as if Paul was saying, "When I pray in a tongue, the very depths of my emotions are stirred but my cognition is unaffected."[89] The result of this phenomenon of speaking in tongues is not the benefit received through intelligible speech, which requires human rationality and reasoning, rather, the Holy Spirit connects with the human spirit, where the individual senses emotional alignment with the Spirit in communication with God. When Paul describes the Spirit's intercession in Rom 8:26 as "inarticulate groaning," he is referring to the "groanings" that accompany the whole experience of the gift of tongues. The experience of the Spirit's "groaning" sustains the believer in this transitional period between the "here, but not yet." In this manner, "The Spirit takes share in our weakness" (Rom 8:26).

As we have demonstrated above, Paul unequivocally taught that the Spirit dispenses a variety of gifts, whose primary purpose is to strengthen and sustain the church until God's redemptive plan has been fully realized at the Second Coming of Christ. Dispensationalism would not deny that the Spirit played a central role in the church after the Day of Pentecost. But at the same time the "sign gifts" (healing, faith, working of miracles, and tongues) are no longer operative in the post-apostolic era.[90] This forces a dichotomy between an apostolic-era Spirit and a post-apostolic era Spirit and implies an artificial shift in the course of salvation-history. It is as if dispensationalists are saying that when the good news of the kingdom of God is proclaimed, the Spirit operates in a more restrictive manner today than when the original gospel message

---

88. "For if I *pray* in a tongue, my spirit *prays* but my mind is unfruitful" (1 Cor 14:14).

89. Bertone, "Experience of Glossolalia and the Spirit's Empathy," 59–60.

90. Ironically, Darby calls the period between the Day of Pentecost and the rapture, "the dispensation of the Spirit," Darby, *Collected Writings of J N Darby*, 1:127.

was proclaimed. This is especially odd in light of the fact that healing, faith, miracles, and tongues are all tangible expressions of the kingdom of God exerting itself on earth.[91] Paul describes his missionary success in the following manner: "By the power of signs and wonders, by the power of God's Spirit . . . from Jerusalem and as far as Illyricum I have fully proclaimed the good news of Christ."[92] The various operations of the Spirit brought humans face to face with the reality of the Living God.[93] To say these gifts have ceased today is to whittle the gospel message to a "signless" kingdom of God and to make God obscure.

The whole dispensational notion of a distinction between an apostolic and a post-apostolic era is ironic given that they both fall under the same umbrella of "the dispensation of grace" according to the dispensational scheme of history.[94] Again, the dispensational tendency to break up time into separate phases in salvation history poses a problem for Paul and his understanding of the role of the Spirit. Certainly Paul would be both surprised and displeased to see his words penned in 1 Cor 13:8 used to legitimize a future, more "mature" church that has "outgrown" the gifts of healing, faith, working of miracles, or tongues.

IMPLICATIONS FOR PENTECOSTALISM

To their credit both dispensationalists and Pentecostals recognize Paul's emphasis on the imminent return of Christ. However, Paul did not want to scare the living daylights out of Christians living at the dawn of the twenty-first century by advocating a severe and unique seven-year tribulation period and a great time of apostasy,[95] apart from tribulations that

91. "My speech and my proclamation were not with plausible words of wisdom, but with a demonstration of the Spirit and of power, so that your faith might rest not on human wisdom but on the power of God" (1 Cor 2:5).

92. Rom 15:19–20; in Acts 19:6 describes Paul's missionary activities more vividly, being accompanied by the manifestations of inspired speech (tongues and prophecy).

93. "But if all prophesy, an unbeliever or outsider who enters is reproved by all and called to account by all . . . that person will bow down before God and worship him, declaring, 'God is really among you.'" (1 Cor 14:24–25). See also Gee, *Concerning Spiritual Gifts*, 30–31.

94. Dispensationalists generally believe "the dispensation of grace" covers the period between Acts 2:1—Rev 19:21.

95. The "lawless one" referred to in 2 Thess 2:3 will be instrumental in deceiving many, resulting in a time of apostasy. However, we learn later in v. 7 that Paul was describing someone or something already evident during his day: "For the mystery of lawlessness is *already at work*." This cannot refer to a distant future seven-year tribulation period.

Christianity throughout the ages have already experienced and will continue to experience until the end. Many popular and so-called prophecy experts have been known for their overly creative interpretations of Scripture, using Paul and the book of Revelation to predict the precise time of a global nuclear war, the identity of a world dictator and the like, and have written books that are immensely popular within contemporary Pentecostal circles. Consequently, many Pentecostals have worked themselves into a state of frenzy, praying that their pretribulation rapture theory is the correct one, trying to avoid products with bar codes numbering 666, or trying desperately to identify any political or religious figure who speaks of anything that comes close to "a new world order." On the contrary, both Paul and the book of Revelation call believers not to live in fear but to live their daily lives on the basis of faith. Their words were meant as comfort for those enduring persecution.[96] This faith includes trust that history is in the hands of God and of Jesus.

A fear for the future can also result in a form of escapism and idleness, one that leads believers to abandon interest in the world and its problems. One of the distinctive teachings of dispensationalism is the idea that at the end of the "dispensation of grace," the church itself will become "the center and the power of evil and corruption in the world"[97] and nothing at all can be done to restore this dispensation.[98] Darby himself said, "I believe from Scripture that ruin is without remedy" and Christians should expect "a progress of evil."[99] This dispensation, it is said, will culminate in great apostasy with the presence of many antichrists and the one main Antichrist.[100] The end result will be judgment.[101] The belief in such soon-approaching conditions can lead to pessimism, fatalism, and forsaking of political responsibility.[102]

Idleness was one of the major concerns Paul had for the Thessalonians, who were overcome with fear and grief concerning the Lord's

96. After describing the coming of the Lord in 1 Thess 4:13–17, Paul writes, "Therefore encourage one another with these words;" see also Rev 1:17–18; 6:10; 7:15–17; 21:3–7.

97. Darby, *The Collected Writings of J. N. Darby-Doctrinal No. 1*, 278.

98. Darby, *The Collected Writings of J. N. Darby-Prophetic No. 2*, 349.

99. Carter, *Anglican Evangelicals*, 220, 226.

100. Carter, *Anglican Evangelicals*, 302–3.

101. Scofield claims that at the end of the dispensation of grace the church "is irremediable and awaits judgment," *Oxford NIV Scofield Study Bible*, 1012–13.

102. Hill, *In God's Time*, 208.

return. In his first letter to them he writes, "Admonish idlers, and encourage the faint hearted" (1 Thess 5:14). By the time of his second letter this problem had escalated to the point where many no longer worked to provide for either themselves or their families. Paul writes, "Anyone unwilling to work should not eat" (2 Thess 3:10) and warns them to "Keep away from believers who are living in idleness" (1 Thess 3:6). We should learn from Paul in that he was ever active in proclaiming the gospel message, constantly looking for new venues (Rom 15:20), no matter how dire the circumstances in which he found himself. Furthermore, he demonstrated a concern for the environment (Rom 8:21) and political matters as well (Rom 13:7). The Pentecostal movement should never buy into a "sit, wait, and do nothing" mentality, motivated by fear. On the contrary, it must live up to one of its defining theological and pro-active distinctives—empowerment *for service* (Acts 1:8).

In the previous section, we discussed some of the theological corollaries of the dispensationalist notion that the "sign" gifts have ceased with the close of the apostolic age and concluded that this position, in reality, conveys a reductionism of the Spirit. We have also demonstrated how one of the original convictions of the Pentecostal movement was the idea that the church was living in the "latter rain," where God had restored various manifestations of the gifts of the Spirit, which would soon culminate with the return of Christ. Some classical Pentecostals understand Paul's list of spiritual gifts in 1 Cor 12:8–10 as a definitive and, in some sense, a complete list of the varieties of the Spirit's operations.[103] For example, L. Thomas Holdcroft states, "Only Paul's list in Corinthians sets forth a systematic enumeration of the divine charismata. . . ."[104] Others have gone so far as to claim, "every supernatural happening in the Bible or out of it, except of course counterfeit miracles of satanic origin, *must be included in the sweep of the Nine Supernatural Gifts* [emphasis added]."[105] Statements such as these express the thoughts of many sincere Pentecostal believers today. There has been a growing tendency

103. Other classical Pentecostals, however, correctly understand Paul's list in 1 Cor 12:8–10 as a sampling, not a complete or comprehensive list. For example, commenting on this passage in 1 Corinthians, Stanley M. Horton states, "The emphasis is on the fact that all come from the one Holy Spirit, not that all the gifts are being named," *What the Bible Says about the Holy Spirit*, 209. See also Duffield and Van Cleave, *Foundations of Pentecostal Theology*, 329, 355.

104. Holdcroft, *Holy Spirit*, 145.

105. H. Horton, *Gifts of the Spirit*, 80.

to categorize[106] and over-emphasize these particular nine spiritual gifts to the point of missing the original purpose for which Paul listed them in the first place. This puts unnecessary restrictions on the Spirit's role and inadvertently runs the risk of putting God in a box.

Paul's main point in 1 Cor 12:4–11 simply stated, is that there are a variety of gifts, but it is the same Spirit who operates within each individual for the benefit of the community as a whole.[107] Consequently, there should be "no room for rivalry, discontent, or a feeling of superiority" among the Corinthian Christians.[108] In 12:4–6 Paul emphasizes that diversity has its roots in God: "There are *diversities* of gifts, but *the same Spirit*. There are *diversities* of service, but *the same Lord*. There are *diversities* of workings, but *the same God* who works all of them in all people." In v. 7 he states, "*To each* is given the *manifestation of the Spirit* for *the common good*." Paul places "to each" in the emphatic first position in the Greek sentence structure in order to further emphasize his point on diversity. In "each" person there is a unique disclosure of the Spirit's activity ("*manifestation* of the Spirit") and this diversity serves to benefit the community as a whole.[109] He then proceeds to demonstrate this more fully in vv. 8–10: "to one is given *the message of wisdom*, through *the Spirit*; to another *a message of knowledge*, by *the same Spirit*; to another *faith*, by *the same Spirit*, to another *gifts of healings*, by *the one Spirit*." Paul is attempting to illustrate that diversity originates in God (vv. 4–6) and in turn diverse gifting is evident in believers through the operation of the Spirit (vv. 7–11).

Paul's purpose is not to give a comprehensive and exhaustive list of gifts, but simply to illustrate the point that the Spirit dispenses diverse gifts. Upon closer examination, we notice that the spiritual gifts, "word of wisdom," (12:8), "word of knowledge" (12:8), "kinds of tongues" (12:10) reflect the Corinthian situation itself. The subjects of "wisdom"

---

106. Holdcroft categorizes the spiritual gifts enumerated in 1 Cor 12:8–10 in the following manner: (1) Gifts of Revelation (word of wisdom, word of knowledge, discerning of spirits), (2) Gifts of Power (faith, working of miracles, gifts of healing), (3) Gifts of Utterance (prophecy, different kinds of tongues, interpretation of tongues), *Holy Spirit*, 145.

107. Fee, *First Epistle to the Corinthians*, 584.

108. Barrett, *First Epistle to the Corinthians*, 283–84.

109. The pronoun "to each" is a distributive, emphasizing the individualized instances in a collective sense expressed in the words "in all people" from the previous verse (1 Cor 12:6).

and "knowledge" are addressed within a different context previous to chapter 12 (see 1 Cor 1:17; 2:1–16; 8:1–13) and the benefits of the gift of "tongues" are compared to those of "prophecy" in 1 Cor 14 (1 Cor 14:1–25, 27–28; 1 Cor 12:10). In all likelihood some of the gifts in 1 Cor 12:8–10 are listed, in part, to suit the situation. The other gifts may simply be a sampling. Paul has six other lists of spiritual gifts in the very same context of 1 Cor 12 (1 Cor 12:28, 29–30; 13:1–3, 8; 14:6, 26), no two exactly alike either in language, number, or character, suggesting that the list of gifts in 12:8–10 is neither exhaustive, nor organized with respect to their particular nature or quality.[110]

Since its inception the Pentecostal movement has understood the important role of the Spirit, taking Paul's teaching in 1 Cor 12–14 seriously. The manifestations of the Spirit authenticate and confirm that the kingdom of God is a present reality and the time is soon approaching for the return of Christ. However, if we follow Paul's logic closely, his point was to highlight a multiplicity of gifts bestowed by the Spirit. This was to counter the Corinthian fascination with the gift of tongues. The Pentecostalism movement today cannot afford a restrictive view of the Spirit, one that in the end puts limitations on the work of God in our world today. This would, in effect, create a dysfunctional church as Paul has already spelled out in his metaphor of the body in 1 Cor 12:17–26, "For just as the body is one and has many members . . . so it is with Christ. For in the one Spirit we were all baptized into one body. . . . If all were a single member, where would the body be"? Biblical history teaches us that God does not work within the confines of humans schemes, even within the confines of ecclesiastical organizations. History teaches us that Spirit-ual revivals happen in the most unexpected places and ways. Believers are responsible to keep their eyes open to God's diverse manifestations of the Spirit.

The greatest gift that God can bestow is the gift of the Holy Spirit, creating new life, residing within every believer, and conferring familial status, "You received the Spirit of adoption, by whom we cry, 'Abba, Father.' The Spirit testifies with our spirit that we are children of God" (Rom 8:15–16). All other diverse gifts are the result of the Spirit's creation of new life.[111] *Emitte Spiritum tuum et creabuntur.*

---

110. Conzelmann states, "The enumeration in vv. 8–10 is *unsystematic* [emphasis added]." *1 Corinthians*, 209.

111. Bertone, "Law of the Spirit," 192–204.

4

Apocalyptic Sustainability

The Future of Pentecostal Ecology

Robby Waddell

Resolving the ecological crisis of our planet . . . is no longer a problem we can leave to the scientists. Just as we are all part of the problem, so we are all also part of the solution. We all need to come to terms with the forces that have created this crisis and the resources within our traditions that can motivate us to resolve the crisis. One of those traditions is our biblical heritage.[1]

INTRODUCTION

IN THE EPIGRAPH, DESMOND Tutu claims "our biblical heritage" is a resource that can motivate us to resolve the ecological crisis. On the one hand, there are biblical texts that support ecojustice, for example Rom 8:21, "the creation itself will be set free from its bondage to decay and will obtain the freedom of the glory of the children of God" (NRSV). On the other hand, there are a number of texts that have fueled ambivalence and at times even hostility toward creation care, a prime example being 2 Pet 3:10, "But the day of the Lord will come like a thief, and then the heavens will pass away with a loud noise, and the elements will be dissolved with fire, and the earth and the works that are upon it will be burned up" (RSV). 2 Pet 3:10 has unfortunately been far more influential

---

1. Tutu, Forward, *Earth Story in the New Testament*, vii.

among Pentecostals than Rom 8 in relation to the ecological responsibility of the church, or the lack thereof.

Notwithstanding the sentiments of Archbishop Tutu, the Christian tradition has not been at the forefront of ecological thought or praxis, leading many to question whether Christianity is compatible with environmental concerns. In fact, Christianity has received a significant amount of the blame for the ecological crisis, an indictment supported by a number of separate, though related, arguments. One argument is that the cultural mandate in Gen 1:28 encourages an anthropocentric view of the world, which inevitably leads to the degradation of nature.[2] Offering a more comprehensive reading of the creation narratives, Miroslav Volf challenges the assumption that Genesis sanctions human abuse of nonhuman creation, though he qualifies that "human work is *the* cause of ecological problems."[3] He concludes, "Both ecological alarmists and optimists must agree that the quality of life for the human race, and indeed its future, depend on the capacity of human beings to learn how to work in a way that is cooperative with, and not destructive of, their nonhuman environment."[4]

Equally prevalent is the complaint that some forms of Christian eschatology are hopelessly otherworldly in orientation and thus render Christians incapable of ecological concern. For instance, Ludwig Feuerbach claimed that, "Nature, the world, has no value, no interest for Christians. The Christian thinks only of himself and the salvation of his soul."[5] In this chapter, I shall respond to both the protological and eschatological criticisms that Christianity contributes to ecological degradation, briefly reexamining the role humanity has in the created order, followed by an analysis of a key biblical text that is often used to support ecological abuse, namely 2 Pet 3:10–13.

CARING FOR CREATION IN THE BEGINNING

Although Lynn White is not the first to hold Christianity responsible for the ecological crisis, his oft-cited article, "The Historical Roots of

---

2. For example, White, "Historical Roots of Our Ecological Crisis," 1203–7.

3. Volf, *Work in the Spirit*, 42. Emphasis original.

4. Ibid., 42.

5. Feuerbach, *Essence of Christianity*, 287.

Our Ecological Crisis,"[6] has become the hallmark of the anti-Christian critique. White, who describes western Christianity as "the most anthropocentric religion the world has ever seen," argues that the monotheism of the Judeo-Christian worldview is unique in establishing a hierarchical theology of creation that logically leads to the use and abuse of nature. According to White, the cultural mandate which instructs humans to subdue and have dominion over the rest of creation not only permits but encourages people to dominate nature and utilize it to meet their needs. In White's interpretation of Genesis, "no item in the physical creation had any purpose save to serve man's purposes."[7]

Alternatively Wendell Berry rightly argues, "Such a reading of Genesis 1:28 is contradicted by virtually all the rest of the Bible, as many people have now pointed out . . . (God) thinks the world is good, and He loves it. . . . If God loves the world, then how might any person of faith be excused for not loving it or justified in destroying it?"[8] Although humanity is called upon to subdue and have dominion over the rest of the natural order, it does not necessarily follow that humans should *dominate* nature in a self-serving manner. Humanity has been created in the image and likeness of God; therefore, human rule on the earth ought to resemble God's loving rule over creation. Often in the biblical narratives, terms such as "ruling" or "having dominion" are tied to the idea of sustaining and nurturing rather than dominating and abusing (cf. Ps 104). In Ps 72, the king is entreated to use his dominion as a means to bring justice to the poor and for the good of children. Likewise, in the New Testament Jesus defines his own leadership as that of being a servant (Mark 10:45). Defining dominion as stewardship fits best with the creation narrative in Gen 2:15 where Adam is instructed to work and care for the garden. "The purpose of human dominion over nature is the preservation of the integrity of the nonhuman creation, not simply the satisfaction of human needs and wants."[9] In the end, White's anthropocentric interpretation of the creation narrative is simply too selective.

White also argues that Christianity is further culpable for the ecological crisis, because it was the impetus for rise of modern science and technology, which in turn has been the means of so much of the world's

6. White, "Historical Roots of Our Ecological Crisis," 1203–7.

7. Ibid., 1205.

8. Berry, *What Are People For?* 98.

9. Volf, *Work in the Spirit,* 147.

ecological degradation. This criticism is also problematic. Though many of the scientists throughout western history have been Christian, it is far too unrealistic to think that Christianity alone provided the motivation for their discoveries. In response, Wolfhart Pannenberg comments that the domination of nature by human power corresponds more to the time in the eighteenth century "when modern humanity in its self-understanding was cutting its ties with the creator God of the Bible."[10] In actuality, the philosophical ground for the dichotomy between humans and the material world can easily be traced further back to the radical dualism between the soul and the body popularized by the philosophy of René Descartes. In *Discourse on Method*, Descartes suggests that his philosophical project, if successful, will render humanity as the "masters and possessors of nature," enabling a person "to enjoy trouble-free the fruits of the earth and all the goods found there."[11]

Significantly influenced by Cartesian (and Platonic) philosophy, "Christian theologians have for centuries," according to Volf, "stripped the human spirit of everything corporeal and emptied corporeality of everything spiritual."[12] Despite the popularity of this belief, a careful reading of the creation narratives supports a more integrated anthropology. A human is not simply a soul that inhabits a body, but rather the integration of both body and soul. The goodness of nature ought not to be reduced to a utilitarian function providing the necessary though transitory conditions for humans to exist. God affirms the innate goodness of creation by pronouncing it as such even prior to the formation of humans (cf. Gen 1:4–25). An emphasis on the unique position of humanity as the sole bearers of the image of God often overshadows the fact that humanity was not created on a separate day but rather shares the sixth day of creation with the rest of the animal kingdom, implying a basic human naturalness.[13]

---

10. Pannenberg, *Anthropology in Theological Perspective*, 78. While at the end of the day White's assessment of the cause of the ecological crisis is too narrow, he does, nevertheless, suggest an interesting solution to the problem. Seeing the industrial and technological culture as being morally bankrupt, White proposes a revival of Franciscan Christianity, following the lead of its founder, Francis of Assisi. Francis, who White describes as "the patron saint of ecologists," is legendary for his care and concern for animals and nature.

11. Descartes, *Discourse on Method*, 35.

12. Volf, *Work in the Spirit*, 143.

13. See Moltmann, *God in Creation*, 244ff.

On the one hand, my comments thus far should not be read as an apologetic for the neglect of environmental sensitivity for which Christians share responsibility. As Christians we need to confess our sin of failing to care for the rest of creation. To reiterate Tutu, "we are all part of the problem." On the other hand, I wish to highlight the ways in which our biblical heritage contains an alternative voice, which both repudiates the destructive history of ecological exploitation and degradation and promotes a holistic theology of creation care. In other words, Judeo-Christian protology, rightly understood, encourages ecological concern.

CARING FOR CREATION IN THE LIGHT OF THE END

The ecological argument against Christian eschatology focuses primarily on a widespread form of eschatology most popular among North American evangelicals and Pentecostals, which foresees the future of creation as an inevitable downward spiral ending in cosmic destruction. By implication, if the church is going to be raptured and the world destroyed, what is the need for ecological care? Al Truesdale comments, "Until evangelicals purge from their vision of the Christian faith the wine of pessimistic dispensationalist premillennialism, the Judeo-Christian doctrine of creation and the biblical image of stewardship will be orphans in their midst."[14] The incompatibility between dispensational millennialism and ecological concern means that apocalyptic eschatology "makes it religiously unnecessary and logically impossible to engage in the long-range commitments to the environment."[15] When I have personally advocated energy conservation or protested various forms of ecological degradation, I have had students innocently, if naively, question my motivation. If everything is going to burn up in the final judgment, then why concern ourselves with the temporary material world?[16]

The response to this question will depend on one's understanding of the eschatological nature of the kingdom of God. Both popular and scholarly opinions are divided in regards to how the kingdom of God should be understood. The various views can be divided into three areas: (1) an apocalyptic eschatology, which expects an abrupt end to the status

14. Truesdale, "Last Things First," 116.

15. Ibid.

16. The logic behind this question is faulty. Even if the premise is granted that the world is temporary, it does not necessarily follow that this grants humanity license to abuse or neglect it. Cf. Bouma-Prediger, *For the Beauty of the Earth*, 78.

quo brought about by a radical divine intervention; (2) an inaugurated eschatology, which understands the kingdom to be both already present and not yet fully consummated; and (3) a realized eschatology, which sees the kingdom being fully present whether in the words and deeds of Jesus or in the contemporary words and deeds of the followers of Jesus.

Pentecostalism in its various forms seems to oscillate historically between the two extremes of an apocalyptic eschatology, which has been influenced by fundamentalist dispensationalism and currently popularized by *The Left Behind* series, and a realized eschatology represented in both the postmillennialism of the Kingdom Now movement and the hyper-faith doctrine proposed by Kenneth Hagin, Kenneth Copeland, and others. These extremes seem to be determined at least partially by the socio-economic status of the perspective groups. The poor and socially marginalized gravitate toward the apocalyptic eschatology with its annihilationist tendencies while the middle class and upwardly mobile gravitate toward the realized eschatology, functionally if not theoretically. The irony of the mega-church tendency in Pentecostal circles is that it maintains a verbal commitment to an apocalyptic eschatology and therefore preaches that the salvation of souls is the only ministry goal of ultimate value; yet the mega-church simultaneously constructs multi-million dollar buildings, commits itself wholeheartedly to political campaigns (usually Republican), and offers seminars that promise to maximize the personal and financial success of its membership in the here-and-now.[17] This theological bipolarization has plagued the Pentecostal movement for decades.[18]

Further problems arise between theology and ethics. Despite the otherworldly orientation of apocalyptic eschatology and its expectation of a sudden and destructive end to the world, Pentecostals have endorsed and engaged in various forms of social ministry.[19] The failure of

17. Althouse, "In Appreciation of Jürgen Moltmann," 31. It is interesting to note that the popularity of fundamentalist dispensationalism seems to be waning among Pentecostal ministers. According to Margaret Poloma's research, only 58 percent of Pentecostals surveyed agreed or strongly agreed with the statement, "I believe in a dispensationalist interpretation of Scripture." Poloma "The Future of American Pentecostal Identity," 162.

18. Many early Pentecostals who held an apocalyptic view of the kingdom avoided political involvement thereby displaying as certain consistency in their theological ethics. See Wacker, *Heaven Below*, 19–20.

19. Theologically Pentecostalism has been for the most part an otherworldly religion, but practically its adherents have been committed to and involved in a variety

the church to address this tension has resulted in a theological ambivalence in which "beliefs are permitted to head in one direction, while the practice of ministry heads in another."[20] Theologically, this conundrum has been addressed by the construction of a distinctively Pentecostal eschatology. Over the last few decades, Pentecostal scholars have opted for neither the apocalyptic nor the realized eschatology and instead have advocated an "already/not yet" eschatology.[21]

In the gospels, the kingdom of God (and Matthew's verbal equivalent, "kingdom of heaven")[22] is present on earth, introduced by the words of Jesus, "The time is fulfilled." Gordon Fee makes an important distinction that the kingdom of God "refers to a *time* that was *promised* and was to be *fulfilled*, not to a place where people were to go . . . Those around Jesus, therefore, never ask about *what* or *where*, but "*when* does (the kingdom) come?"[23] Supporting this idea and contrary to popular opinion, the final vision of Revelation does not contain an image of Christians being resurrected and going off to the wild blue yonder, but

---

of social ministries. Although inconsistent with their eschatology, the endorsement of social ministry proved to be a natural fit with Pentecostal pneumatology. The Spirit has empowered them in the last days to minister in the world. In 1968, Michael Harper rationalized a renewed call to social ministry stating that "the Holy Spirit in the Acts of the Apostles was constantly destroying social barriers, and reconciling deeply entrenched prejudices." Harper, *Walk in the Spirit*, 60. Also in 1968, the General Presbytery of the Assemblies of God drafted a statement on social concern which included a final pledge "to exert (their) influence as Christian citizens to justifiable social action in areas of domestic relations, education, law enforcement, employment, equal opportunity and other beneficial matters." For the complete statement see Menzies, *Anointed to Serve: The Story of the Assemblies of God*, 394–95. Ironically, the 1968 General Presbytery also removed the fellowship's official statement on pacifism. For an assessment of these and other Pentecostal efforts for social justice in the 1960s see Dempster "Soundings in the Moral Implications of Glossolalia," 1–2. Cf. Sepúlveda, "Reflections on the Pentecostal Contribution to the Mission of the Church in Latin America,"108; Alexander, *Peace to War*.

20. Dempster, "Christian Social Concern in Pentecostal Perspective," 53.

21. See Kuzmič, "History and Eschatology," 135–64; Volf, "Loving with Hope," 28–31; Dempster, "Evangelism, Social Concern and the Kingdom of God," 22–43; Land, *Pentecostal Spirituality*; Macchia, *Spirituality and Social Liberation*; and Petersen, *Not By Might Nor Power*.

22. Although he shows a strong penchant for the phrase "kingdom of heaven," on four occasions Matthew uses the more common phrase "kingdom of God." For a nuanced look into Matthew's verbiage see Thomas, "Kingdom of God in the Gospel according to Matthew," 136–46.

23. Fee, "Kingdom of God and the Church's Global Mission," 8.

rather of the kingdom of God coming down to earth (i.e., the descent of the New Jerusalem). In the new creation, heaven comes to earth and the two become one. The throne of God, which was once hidden in the heavenly realm (Rev 4–5) is now on earth (21:3, 5), thus providing a final consummation of the Lord's Prayer, "Thy kingdom come and thy will be done *on earth* as it is in heaven."[24]

By praying "thy kingdom come" the Christian is acknowledging the future elements of the kingdom, a prayer of "kingdom-expectation." By praying "thy will be done" the Christian is making supplication for a present transformation, a prayer of "kingdom-participation."[25] Drawing attention to the latter aspect of the kingdom, Fee explains, "[Our] gospel is not simply that of 'saving souls'; it is rather, as with Jesus, the bringing of wholeness to broken people in every kind of distress."[26] To focus solely on either the spiritual dimensions or the physical realities is to misconstrue the global mission of the church. The Christian mission, indeed the mission of God (*missio Dei*), is indivisible. In other words, eschatology and social ethics inevitably go hand-in-hand.

Although a number of Pentecostals have written on the correlation between eschatology and social ethics, Miroslav Volf has been the most unequivocal in connecting eschatology, social responsibility, *and ecological concerns.*[27] In his article "On Loving with Hope: Eschatology

---

24. In a number of ways this chapter, focusing on the ecological implications of a transformational eschatology, builds on my previous work on the cosmic implications of transformation. See Waddell, "Revelation and the (New) Creation," 30–50.

25. Kuzmič, "History and Eschatology," 150–54.

26. Fee, "Kingdom of God," 17.

27. Other Pentecostal constructions of an eschatological social ethic are by no means devoid of ecological concern. Volf's work, however, is the most explicit about the ecological implications. See especially Macchia, *Spirituality and Social Liberation*. Macchia's work is most helpful in identifying an early, theologically motivated, concern for ecology in the ministry of Johann Blumhardt who advocated for the "liberation" of the whole creation, and even more conspicuously this idea can be found in Johann's predecessor Friedrich Oetinger who fully expected the eschatological transformation of nature, 1–12. Perhaps no one has been more influential in the construction of a Pentecostal social ethic than Murray Dempster (see Dempster's chapter in this volume). For the relationship between Pentecostal social concern and the Old Testament mandate for justice see Dempster, "Pentecostal Social Concern and the Biblical Mandate of Social Justice," 129–53; for the role of glossolalia in social justice see idem, "Soundings in the Moral Implications of Glossolalia;" for the social dimension of the kingdom of God see idem, "Evangelism, Social Concern and the Kingdom of God;" for the eschatological role of social ethics see idem, "Christian Social Concern in Pentecostal Perspective."

and Social Responsibility," Volf responds to a claim that questions the value or even adequacy of using apocalyptic eschatology for justification of a Christian social ethic.[28] He concedes that it is *logically* possible to advocate for creation care even if one expects the annihilation of the world. In fact, appropriately utilizing natural resources as long as they last is a fundamental way of caring for other humans, i.e., loving one's neighbor. Be that as it may, if a belief in annihilation is united with an expectation of an imminent return of Jesus, then ecological concerns lose all rational support.[29] Such a combination of theological viewpoints led Assemblies of God member James Watt, Ronald Reagan's first Secretary of the Interior, to support the reckless consumption of the USA's natural resources. When questioned about his policy, Watt replied, "I do not know how many future generations we can count on before the Lord's return."[30]

Although logically someone expecting annihilation (and not an imminent parousia) may be involved in social and ecological preservation, *theologically* the doctrine of cosmic annihilation is inconsistent with the protological doctrine of the goodness of creation. Apocalyptic destruction implies that "what God will annihilate must be either so bad that it is not possible to redeem it, or so insignificant that it is not worth being redeemed."[31] Volf contends that the Christian doctrine of bodily resurrection and the cardinal Pentecostal doctrine of divine healing make little sense if in the end all matter is annihilated. Rather than being annihilated, our bodies, indeed the whole creation, will be transformed (cf. Phil 3:20–21 and Rom 8:19–23 respectively).

An implication of this bodily and cosmic transformation is that it presupposes continuity between the present and the future. According to Volf, this continuity includes an integration of human work in cultural, social, and ecological development. "Through their work," he writes, "hu-

---

Further developing and applying Dempster's work to the setting of Latin American Pentecostalism is Petersen, *Not by Might nor by Power.*

28. Volf, "Loving with Hope," *op. cit.* Volf is responding to Williams, "The Partition of Love and Hope: Eschatology and Social Responsibility," 24–27. Arguing in favor of an ethic based solely on the command to love one's neighbor, Williams questions the legitimacy of the role of eschatology in the formation of social responsibility.

29. Volf, "Loving with Hope," 29.

30. Cited in Fowler, *Greening of Protestant Thought,* 47. Cf. Wolf, "God, James Watt, and the Public Lands," 58–65.

31. Volf, "Loving with Hope," 30.

man beings contribute in their modest and broken way to God's new creation."[32] In the words of Paul, "Therefore, my beloved, be steadfast, immoveable, always excelling in the work of the Lord, because you know that in the Lord *your labor is not in vain*" (1 Cor 15:58, NRSV).[33] The labor to which Paul refers can certainly not be limited to spiritual matters. After all, the context of his statement is a discussion on the resurrection of the body, which requires a material, albeit glorified environment.[34] According to Jürgen Moltmann, "Christian eschatology cannot be reduced to human eschatology, and human eschatology cannot be brought down to the salvation of the soul in heaven beyond. There are no human souls without human bodies, and no human existence without the life system of the earth, and no earth without the universe."[35] Commenting on Paul's statement in Rom 8:21 that "the creation itself will be set free from its bondage to decay," F. F. Bruce explains, "if words mean anything, these words of Paul denote not the annihilation of the present material universe on the day of revelation, to be replaced by a universe completely new, but the transformation of the present universe so that it will fulfill the purpose for which God created it."[36]

Given the argument thus far, it is possible to conclude that the new creation is not *ex nihilo* (out of nothing) but rather *ex vetera* (out of the old). This raises questions however as to how to interpret the biblical texts that purport the destruction of the earth without simply dismissing them as hyperboles. In the next section, I examine what is perhaps the most difficult of this type of passage, 2 Pet 3:10–13, the most common "proof text" for those who maintain an annihilationist view.

---

32. Volf, "Loving with Hope," 31.

33. Cf. Wright, *Surprised by Hope*, 208–9.

34. Volf, "Loving with Hope," 29.

35. Moltmann, *Science and Wisdom*, 71. Cf. Richard Bauckham echoes a similar sentiment, "We recognize that, in continuity with the Old Testament (the New Testament) assumes that humans live in mutuality with the rest of God's creation, that salvation history and eschatology do not lift humans out of nature but heal precisely their distinctive relationship with the rest of nature." Bauckham, "Jesus and the Wild Animals (Mark 1:13)," 4.

36. Bruce, *Epistle of Paul to the Romans*, 170. Bruce continues, "There is no discontinuity between here and hereafter, as far as God's working in and for His people is concerned. If inanimate creation longs blindly for the day of its liberation, the community of the redeemed . . . strain forward intelligently for that same consummation" (170–71).

2 PET 3:10–13 AND THE (RE)NEW(ED) EARTH

2 Pet 3 contains a response to accusations by false teachers who are saying that the return of the Lord is doubtful, evidenced by the fact that his coming has been impeded beyond all reasonable expectation. The author suggests that the apparent delay ought not to be measured by a person's shortsightedness, because God's reckoning of time is far different than ordinary human calculations (2 Pet 3:1–9; cf. Ps 90:4/ LXX 89:4). In fact, the purpose of the so-called delay is a direct result of God's forbearance, not wishing that any would continue to adhere to the questionable ethics of the false teachers, but would rather repent. Notwithstanding God's longsuffering, judgment is nevertheless unavoidable and will arrive unexpectedly. The author describes the suddenness of the Day of the Lord coming like a thief, a simile used in the parables of Jesus to illustrate the coming of the Son of Man (Matt 24:36–44; Luke 12:35–40).[37]

At the Day of the Lord, "the heavens will pass away with a roar, and the heavenly bodies will be dissolved while burning, and the earth and the works in it will be found" (v. 10). The final phrase, which is certainly the most difficult to interpret, is described by Richard Bauckham as a "*crux interpretum*" (an interpreter's cross).[38] Although the manuscript evidence is divided, the final verb *ehurethēsetai* (will be found) is unquestionably the best reading as the *lectio difficilior*.[39] According to Bruce Metzger,[40] various ancient attempts were made to correct the opaque passage, including the addition of either a negation (*oux ehurethēsetai*),[41] thus translated, "the earth and the works in it will *not*

---

37. The time of Noah serves as an apparent backdrop for both the Gospel of Matthew and 2 Peter, albeit in different ways. Matthew compares the unexpectedness of the people in Noah's time to the unexpectedness of the people in Jesus' time (24:36–39). 2 Peter alludes to Noah's flood as the first destruction of the world, which will be followed by a second judgment and destruction with fire (3:5–7).

38. Bauckham, *Jude, 2 Peter*, 316.

39. Despite the fact that this variant is the oldest and the one which best explains the other extant variants, Bruce Metzger, nevertheless, doubts that it is original. The textual support for this reading includes: ê B K P et al. The UBS 3rd edition gives the reading its lowest possible grade, "D." Metzger, *Textual Commentary on the Greek New Testament*, 705–6.

40. Metzger, *Textual Commentary on the Greek New Testament*, 705–6.

41. The textual evidence for this reading is sparse, including only the Sahidic version and a single manuscript of the Harclean Syriac version. With no attestation in the Greek manuscripts, this variant is certainly not original, though a number of commentators prefer it. For more discussion see Bauckham, *Jude, 2 Peter*, 317.

be found," or by providing an additional verb at the end of the verse (*luomena*), which would be translated, "the earth and the things in it will be found *dissolved*."[42] Other attempts at harmonization include omitting the last phrase altogether (Jerome, Pelagius, and others) or the substitution of an alternative word that made better sense of the passage, for example "will be burned up" (*katakaēvsetai*).[43] Reinforcing the idea that the new creation is completely discontinuous with the present, many modern translations have opted for this final variant or something very similar.[44] Despite the difficulty of the translation "to be found," it remains the best textual option and therefore requires a closer look to see if a sensible interpretation can be presented.

Some of the older commentators understood the verse to be a reference to an unveiling of the evil works of humanity in preparation for a divine verdict.[45] In other words, the earth and the works upon it become visible and therefore susceptible to final judgment once the heavens have been burnt away. This revelation of the wicked in 2 Peter can be contrasted with those who attempt to hide themselves from God's wrath (e.g., Rev 6:15–16). "The Judgment is here represented not so much as a destructive act of God, as a revelation of him from which none can escape."[46] Even in the face of a cosmic inferno, humans will still have to face the consequences of their actions.[47] It is important to note that the theme of judgment has been the author's consistent concern rather

42. This emendation also lacks sufficient manuscript support, appearing only in P[72]. As Bauckham notes, this reading has not "commended itself to any scholar. In spite of our author's tendency to repeat words, the clumsy repetition of *luesthai* three times in vv 10–11 is unlikely." Bauckham, *Jude, 2 Peter*, 317.

43. The textual support for this reading is codex Alexandrinus and a host of later minuscules. For a number of modern attempts at emendation see Metzger, *Textual Commentary*, 706.

44. The versions which translate the final phrase as "will be burned up" are the RSV, NASB, KJV, JB, ASV. The TEV translates, "the earth with everything in it will vanish." As noted by Steven Bouma-Prediger, "the French and Spanish equivalents of the TEV render the last verb 'will cease to exist' (*cessera d'exister*) and 'will be burned up' (*sera quemada*). The 1985 update of Luther's German Bible comes closer to the true meaning when it translates the last clause 'the earth and the works upon it will find their judgment' (*werden ihr Urteil finden*)." Bouma-Prediger, *Greening of Theology*, 3.

45. Wilson, "Εὑρεθησεται in 2 Peter iii.10," 44–45. This interpretation is endorsed by Bauckham, *Jude, 2 Peter*, 319–21, and Skaggs, *1 Peter, 2 Peter, Jude*, 137–38.

46. Wilson, "Εὑρεθησεται in 2 Peter iii.10," 44–45.

47. Cf. Roberts, "A Note on the Meaning of II Peter 3.10d," 32–33; Lenhard, "Ein Beitrag zur Übersetzung von II Ptr 3.10d," 128–29.

than an ultimate cosmic destruction (cf. 2 Pet 3:7, "the present heavens and earth are reserved for fire, being kept for the day of judgment and destruction of ungodly men"). The judgment motif is carried forward in the following verses as well (2 Pet 3:11–14). The readers of 2 Peter are encouraged to pursue lives of holiness and godliness in order "to be found (*ehurethēai*) by him without spot or blemish and at peace" (v. 14). As opposed to the evil works of humanity which will be found by God for condemnation, the faithful are encouraged *to be found blameless.*[48]

Understanding the verse primarily as a prophetic announcement of judgment rather than an annihilation of the cosmos helps to clarify other anomalies in the text. For example, the familiar paring of the heavens and the earth is abbreviated in this verse, simply saying "the heavens will pass away (*pareleusontai*) with a loud roar and the heavenly bodies will be dissolved."[49] While the passing away of the heavens and the earth may seem like a necessary prerequisite for the new heavens and the new earth promised in v. 13, it is not altogether clear that an annihilation of the original is required. Early Christians understood the Day of the Lord as a renewal rather than a destruction of creation. Eusebius of Emesa writes, "Like a cloak, (a person's) body grows old with time. But although it grows old, it will be renewed again by your divine will, O Lord. The heavens will not be destroyed, but rather they will be changed into something better. In the same way our bodies are not destroyed in order to disappear altogether but in order to be renewed in an indestructible state."[50] In their visions of the future, both Isaiah[51] and John

48. In v. 10, the passive voice of the verb (*ehurethēsetai*) implicitly implies a divine action, though in v. 14 the grammar is more explicit as the righteous are to be found *by him* (*auto ehurethēai*).

49. For the use of *parérxomai* with the fuller phrase "heavens and earth" see Matt 5:18; 24:35; Luke 16:17; 21:33. Cf. *Didache* 10:6 where the verb is used to refer to the passing away of the world (*kósmos*). Most commentators agree that the word translated "heavenly bodies" (*stoixeia*) refers to the sun, moon, and stars (cf. Isa 34:4 LXX; 2 Clement 16:3). Alternatively, Bede understood the word to refer to the basic elements of nature. He wrote, "There are four elements, earth, air, fire and water. All of which will be swept away by a great fire. Yet that fire will not devour them all but only two of them (fire and water), for there will be a new heaven and a new earth after this destruction has passed." Bede, "On 2 Peter," 239.

50. Eusebius of Emesa, "Catena," 100.

51. In Isa 65:17–35 the Hebrew verb for "create" (*bârâ*) is used three times in the first two verses, emphasizing the creative activity of God; however, the description of this new creation is so continuous with the former life of Israel that to believe in it requires hardly any eschatological imagination. Although the infant mortality rate will be zero

the revelator[52] seem to imply a transformation of the first creation. In 2 Peter, the addition of the adverbial modifier "with a roar" (*rhoizēdón*) reinforces the connotation of judgment given the frequent use of this metaphor in Jewish literature as an accompaniment of divine judgment.[53] 2 Clement 16, which almost certainly shares a common Jewish apocalyptic source with 2 Peter, provides a corroborative parallel, in which the theme of cosmic conflagration is used as a means to reveal the deeds of humanity. Clement writes, "But you know that 'the day' of judgment is already 'approaching as a burning oven, and some[54] of the heavens shall melt,' and the whole earth shall be as lead melting in the fire, and then shall be made manifest the secret and open deeds of (humans)" (16:3).[55]

The argument of 2 Peter 3 can be summarized as follows: (1) the false teachers are incorrect when they interpret the delay of the Lord's coming as evidence that it is not going to happen; (2) the apparent delay

---

(v. 20) and the standard life expectancy will be considerably lengthened ["those dying at a hundred years will be considered youth" (v. 20)], the life of the people seems strikingly similar to their former way of living. Extraordinary long life, while remarkable, would not have been totally foreign for the Israelites given the life span of their patriarchs as recorded in Gen. In Isaiah's vision of the new creation, people are living in Jerusalem, building houses, planting vineyards, enjoying the fruits of their labor, and providing a secure future for their children and grandchildren. The discontinuity lies not in the kind of life which they live, full of peace and hope, but the prevalence with which they live it, no longer in a partial or threatened way but to the fullest extent. The first hint that life in the new creation represents a radically different ecosystem comes in the final verse with references to the domesticated lifestyle of wolves, who will feed not on the sheep but with the sheep, and lions, who will eat straw like the oxen (v. 25).

52. In the final chapters of Revelation, John recounts his vision of a new heaven and a new earth, the first heaven and the first earth have passed away (21:1) and all things are being made new (21:5). Notice that it does not say that God is making *all new things* but making *all things new*. This distinction is of the utmost importance. Although John borrows imagery from Isaiah, he explicitly contradicts his prophetic exemplar by describing life in the new creation as everlasting, "death will be no more" (21:4). The former things that pass away are death, sorrow, and pain. The death of death, to a large extent, is what makes the new creation new, i.e., different.

53. An alternative understanding of the onomatopoeic metaphor (*rhoizēdón*) is that it denotes the crackling of the heavenly elements as they burn in the conflagration rather than a thunderous announcement of divine judgment. Cf. Oecumenius, "Commentary on 2 Peter," 616.

54. In this passage, Clement alludes to Isa 34:4, which in a variant reading of the LXX says "the powers (*dunámeis*) of heaven shall melt away." J. B. Lightfoot recommends substituting *dunámeis* for *tines* (some) in the translation of 2 Clement 16:3. Lightfoot, *Apostolic Fathers*, 250.

55. The translation of 2 Clement comes from *Apostolic Fathers*, 1:155.

is a result of God's longsuffering not wanting any to perish but rather that all should reach repentance; (3) the delay, however, should not be presumed as an acquittal, for judgment is unavoidable; (4) God will make a place for righteousness to dwell; and therefore (5) *caveat lector,* let the reader beware to live at peace with God. According to the interpretation offered above, this argument does not necessitate annihilation. The seventh-century monk Andreas wrote, "It is not just we, says Peter, but the whole creation around us also, which will be changed for the better. For the creation will share in our glory just as it has been subjected to destruction and corruption because of us."[56]

IS "APOCALYPTIC SUSTAINABILITY" AN OXYMORON?

Following the lead of other Pentecostal scholars, I have advocated for an inaugurated eschatology, which is both biblically sound and theologically practical. By adopting a transformational understanding of eschatology, Pentecostals are able to maintain the tension between the already and the not yet. On the one hand, creation is already good and all of life has value; therefore, the social ministries of the church are theologically viable. So we should continue to pray and care for the sick, feed the hungry, house the homeless, embrace the marginalized, speak out against injustice, and care for the environment. On the other hand, our hope is in the coming of God, who alone has the power to transform this world. In order to prevent social activism from becoming a thinly veiled atheism, we must continue to pray, sing, worship, and discern what the Spirit is saying to the churches.

Contrary to popular belief, the word *apocalypse* does not mean *end times* or *cosmic dissolution,* but rather *unveiling* or *revelation.* Jewish and ancient Christian apocalyptic texts have more to do with discerning the spiritual significance of the present than predicting the future. The power of the apocalyptic language is its drastic metaphors, which have become quite common among those who speak about the ecological crisis (e.g., the documentary, *An Inconvenient Truth*). The dualistic nature of apocalyptic literature (and early Christianity for that matter) is often overstated. It is true that apocalyptic literature purports a dualism between good and evil, Creator and creation, the present age and the age to come. However, religious historians and critics are mistaken

56. Andreas, "Catena," 101.

when they assume that this apocalyptic dualism necessarily includes a denunciation of all physicality in favor of an ethereal spiritual reality.[57] The early Christians and the Jews before them expected an end to the *"present world order"* but not a cosmic end to the space-time universe.[58] When *apocalypse* is rightly defined, the phrase apocalyptic sustainability is not an oxymoron.

In closing, I want to make a few final remarks about why I think ecological sustainability is an important issue for Pentecostals. Among the various challenges facing the world today, the ecological crisis intersects and overlaps with a number of other issues of justice. Pentecostalism has been and continues to be the religion of choice among the global poor and because of this Pentecostal theology has often found a corresponding connection with theologies that champion the cause of the marginalized. This may be seen in the appreciation for various forms of liberation theology, whether Latin American, Black, or Feminist. Ecological theology, as one of the many branches of political theology, is a natural next step for Pentecostals. By addressing the ecological crisis, Pentecostals will find their efforts intersecting with other social ministries, because environmental degradation and poverty go hand-in-hand. Again in the words of Archbishop Tutu, "We all need to come to terms with the forces that have created this crisis and the resources within our traditions that can motivate us to resolve the crisis."

57. Cf. Wright, *New Testament and the People of God*, 297–98.
58. Ibid., 299.

5

The Mystery of the Great Whore

Pneumatic Discernment in Revelation 17

John Christopher Thomas

O NE OF THE MORE intriguing eschatological images found in the Apocalypse is that of the Great Whore, located in Revelation 17. She is a favorite amongst artists who seek to bring the images of the Apocalypse to visual expression and is oft-depicted in their work. Her relationship to a variety of eschatological figures such as the beast, the seven horns of the beast that are seven kings, the ten kings who reign for one hour, those whom she dominates by her power, and the saints from whose blood she is drunk makes her a significant character who often is part of contemporary end-time speculations. In this chapter I seek to engage in an exercise of pneumatic discernment, called for within the text of the Apocalypse itself. Rather than allow a variety of issues external to the text I here seek to allow the text of the Apocalypse to inform us as to the significance of the Great Whore, as well as any number of other characters within the text with whom she comes into contact or is related. Methodologically, this chapter employs a combination of narrative and intertextual analyses, which seeks to determine, as nearly as possible, the effect of the text upon the hearers. I seek to honor both the visionary nature of the book and the clear priority given in the book to hearing the words of this prophecy.

THE CONTEXT OF THE PASSAGE
WITHIN THE APOCALYPSE

As the second and largest section of the Apocalypse comes to a close, the next major section begins with the occurrence of the third "in the Spirit" phrase (17:3). This extended passage takes the hearers from the destruction of Babylon the Great City to the New Jerusalem descending from heaven. Thus, in this section the hearers encounter an accounting of the final things. Beginning with a description of Babylon the Great City (17:1–18) the section moves to an extensive description of her destruction (18:1–24). Following this is an account of great shouting in heaven accompanying the marriage supper of the Lamb (19:1–10), the victory of the King of Kings and Lord of Lords over his enemies (19:11–21), the one thousand year reign of Jesus and those who overcome (21:1–6), Satan's final rebellion and defeat (20:7–10), the final judgment (20:11–15), and the description of the New Jerusalem descending from heaven (21:1–8).

THE WOMAN ON THE BEAST: BABYLON THE WHORE
(17:1–18)

Once again the hearers may be forgiven if they are unprepared for the fact that the Apocalypse has not quite come to an end. For despite the fact that the last seven plagues of God's wrath have now been poured out, culminating in the destruction of the Great City and the fall of the cities of the nations, the narrative continues, "And one of the seven angels having the seven bowls came and spoke with me saying, 'Come, I will show to you the judgment of the great whore who sits upon many waters, with whom the kings of the earth have committed sexual immorality and the inhabitants of the earth have become drunk with the wine of her sexual immorality.'" Though these words do not designate which of the seven angels is here in view, the hearers would likely understand this angelic figure to be the seventh angel who poured out the seventh bowl,[1] which leads to the destruction of the Great City, now described as the judgment of the Great Whore. The fact that this angel is one of those who poured out the seven last bowls of the plagues of God's wrath would also suggest to the hearers that the description of judgment to follow is closely

---

1. Smalley, *Revelation to John*, 426.

connected to the pouring out of the bowls that precedes it.[2] Perhaps the hearers would also appreciate the fact that although many angels have been described to this point in the book, this is the first time an angel addresses John directly. Such a dramatic encounter is made all the more significant by the specific words the angel speaks to John. While the very first word to come to John from the angel, (*deuro*, "come"), could be taken as a simple command on the angel's part, Johannine hearers would likely recall that its only other occurrence in the whole of the Johannine tradition is in Jesus' command to Lazarus to "come forth" from his tomb (John 11:43). Such an association would no doubt underscore the idea that in this angelic command John encounters a divine invitation. The significance of this invitation is further revealed by the next word from the angel, (*deixo*, "I will show"), as its meaning for Johannine hearers would include two specific aspects given its earlier occurrences within the Apocalypse and its usage in the broader Johannine tradition.

First, the hearers have previously encountered this term in Rev 1:1 and 4:1, where the term is closely associated with those things that must take place soon, suggesting that the judgment of the Great Whore must take place soon. Second, the term also has a rich history in the Fourth Gospel where it is often used to describe divine revelation, which comes from Jesus and/or God (John 5:20; 10:32; 14:9; 20:20).[3] Thus, in Rev 17:1 the term would strike the hearers as pregnant with divine revelatory meaning. Specifically, the angel promises to show John "the judgment of the Great Whore who sits on many waters." It is difficult to believe that the hearers would not see in the judgment of the Great Whore an answer to the prayer of the souls under the altar for God to judge those who shed their blood (6:10). Such an act of judgment would fit nicely with the fact that in the Apocalypse the time for judging the dead has already come (11:18; 14:7) and that the judgments of God are indeed deemed to be righteous (16:5, 7). Such connections would also suggest to the hearers that a description of the final judgment immediately awaits them. The occurrence of the word *pornes*, "whore," would both remind the hearers of its earlier occurrences, as well as introduce a word group in this context, which will have unrivaled prominence as the section unfolds. Earlier the hearers encountered the verbal form of this term in close association with eating food sacrificed to idols (2:14), specifically

---

2. Prigent, *L'Apocalypse de saint Jean*, 375 and Murphy, *Fallen Is Babylon*, 348.

3. Schneider, "δείκνημι, δεικνύω" 280–81.

with reference to the activities of the woman who calls herself a prophet, but whom the resurrected Jesus calls Jezebel, who teaches the servants of God to commit sexual immorality and eat food sacrificed to idols (2:20). With regard to this woman the resurrected Jesus warns that judgment awaits her and her children if she does not repent of her sexual immorality (2:21–23). Perhaps it would not be going too far to suggest that the hearers would see in the judgment of the Great Whore in 17:2 an ultimate fulfillment of the warning the resurrected Jesus gives in his prophetic message to the church in Thyatira. At the same time, the hearers would not be unaware of the ways in which this term is often applied in the OT to Israel (Hos 5:3) and a variety of cities including Jerusalem (Isa 1:21; Ezek 16:15; 23:1), Tyre (Isa 23:16), and Nineveh (Nah 3:4). But perhaps more than anything else the hearers would think of the words Jer 51 speaks with regard to the destruction of Babylon.[4] The description of the Great Whore in Rev 17:1 as "sitting upon many waters" would not only remind the hearers of the description of Babylon in Jer 51:13, as well as the physical qualities of historic Babylon through which the Euphrates ran and which was criss-crossed with canals,[5] but would also reveal something about the Great Whore's idolatrous ambitions as the hearers would likely remember that it is Yahweh who is enthroned upon the flood (Ps 29:10).[6] The words that follow this description make clear that the Great Whore is deserving of her title, for the Great *pornes*, "whore," is identified as the one with whom the Kings of the earth *eporneusan*, "have committed sexual immorality," and from whose wine of *porneias*, "sexual immorality," the inhabitants of the earth have become drunk. Such a concentration of variations of the same Greek word in this sentence would serve to underscore her role in the seduction of others in her idolatrous activity. The fact that both "the kings of the earth" and "the inhabitants of the earth," a phrase that normally has negative associations in the book (3:10; 6:10; 8:13; 11:10; 13:8, 12, 14), are described as her active partners in sexually immoral activity indicate that her seduction to idolatrous activity has been universally successful, including both the world's leaders and its constituency. Mention of the wine of her sexual immorality would communicate at least two others things to the hearers. First, it would serve to heighten the context of judgment in which these words

4. Prigent, *L'Apocalypse de saint Jean*, 375.

5. Aune, *Revelation 17–22*, 929.

6. Smalley, *Revelation to John*, 427.

occur, given the hearers' earlier encounter with this phrase in 14:8, which occurs in the angelic words, "Fallen, fallen is Babylon the Great." Second, this association would encourage the hearers to make the connection between the Great Whore and Babylon the Great, a connection made explicit in 17:5.

While the hearers at this point may well be impressed by the many points of continuity between these first words of chapter 17 and those that have preceded, they quickly discover that they are standing at the beginning of the next major section of the Apocalypse as they hear the words, "And he took me away into the wilderness in the Spirit." For the third time, the hearers encounter the "in the Spirit" phrase. From their earlier encounters with the phrase in 1:10 and 4:2 they would have come to expect that several things are significant about its appearance here in 17:3. First, since there is no hint in the text that John was no longer "in the Spirit" as chapter 17 begins, the phrase's appearance here would convey a sense of continuity between John's experience in chapters 1–3, his experience in chapters 4–16, and his experience in chapter 17 and following. Second, owing to what the hearers learn from their last encounters with this phrase, they likely expect additional prophetic words from or about Jesus in what follows. Third, as the Apocalypse has unfolded they may now suspect that this phrase is central to the book's structure and further discern that the means by which the revelation is given is "in the Spirit." Fourth, there appears to be a connection between certain geographical locations and being "in the Spirit." In chapter one there was a connection between John being on the island of Patmos when "in the Spirit" (1:9–10), while in Rev 4:2, there appears to be a connection between John being "in the Spirit" and being in heaven. This trend continues in Rev 17:3 where John is transported to the wilderness while "in the Spirit," no doubt reminding the hearers of Ezekiel's experience (3:12, 14; 8:3; 11:1, 24; 37:1; 43:5). While the location to which John is transported "in the Spirit" might surprise contemporary hearers it is not likely to have surprised Johannine ones. In the Johannine tradition the wilderness is a place where God is active in prophetic and redemptive ways. Not only is the wilderness the location of the prophetic work of John (the Baptist), who is likened to "a voice crying in the wilderness" (John 1:23), but the redemptive sign of the serpent being lifted up also takes place in the wilderness (3:14).[7] In the bread of life discourse Jesus

7. On the salvific dimension of this text cf. Thomas, *Spirit of the New Testament*, 175–89.

twice makes reference to the gracious provision of manna for Israel in the wilderness (6:31, 49). In addition to these associations the wilderness also functions as a place where Jesus and his disciples take refuge after the raising of Lazarus from the dead (11:54). From Rev 12:6, 14 the hearers would know that the wilderness is a place prepared by God for the protection and sustenance of God's people. Thus, when John is transported to the wilderness "in the Spirit" the hearers would, no doubt, discern that what awaits John will be no less filled with prophetic and salvific significance than other "wilderness" events in the Johannine tradition.[8] As soon as John has been so transported he immediately begins to see a number of things, "And I saw a woman seated upon a scarlet beast, full of blasphemous names, having seven heads and ten horns." In the Spirit John sees the Great Whore who sits upon many waters morph into a woman who sits upon a scarlet beast. Her presumptuous, idolatrous enthronement upon the waters, in the place of Yahweh, is revealed actually to be an enthronement upon an idolatrous beast. The hearers may not be surprised that the woman is enthroned on this beast, for this beast's color is reminiscent of the Great Red Dragon,[9] while its physical appearance bears striking resemblance to the Beast that emerges from the sea in 13.1, who also has ten horns, seven heads, and blasphemous names.[10]

If this woman is indeed enthroned on the scarlet beast, the hearers would have little doubt as to her character or intentions. Her power comes from the Great Red Dragon who opposes the woman clothed with the sun, her child, and her other seed; the Dragon who is cast down out of heaven. Eventually the Great Red Dragon gives his authority to the Beast from the sea, who is a parody of the Lamb, who worships the Dragon, who is himself worshipped by the whole earth as invincible in battle, who blasphemes God and his dwelling, and who makes war upon the saints. The fact that this beast is described in 17:3 as being full of blasphemous names would not be difficult for the hearers to imagine as such blasphemous names reveal his presumptuous and idolatrous actions and nature. If the woman is enthroned upon such a one, there

---

8. Contra Aune, *Revelation 17–22*, 933 who suggests that wilderness here carries a negative connotation.

9. Ladd, *Revelation*, 223.

10. Murphy, *Fallen Is Babylon*, 335.

can be absolutely no doubt as to her own presumptuous and idolatrous actions and nature.

Before the hearers can ponder the relationship between the woman and the scarlet beast, their attention is directed to her attire, "And the woman was clothed in purple and scarlet and covered with gold in gold and precious stones and pearls, having a gold cup in her hand full of abominations and the uncleanness of her sexual immorality." The occurrence of the term *peribeblemene*, "clothed," would likely draw the hearers' attention to the contrast between how this woman is described and the last time this verb is used, where it describes the woman clothed with the sun (12:1). In fact to this point in the Apocalypse every occurrence of the verb *periballo*, "clothe," carries with it a positive connotation (3:5, 18; 4:4; 7:9, 13; 10:1; 11:3), suggesting the contrast the hearers are to discern is not simply between these two women, as striking a contrast as that is, but also the contrast between this woman and all those clothed in white. Specifically, this woman is clothed in purple, a color conveying the pretensions to royalty,[11] which to Johannine hearers would be associated with the mockery of Jesus by the soldiers during his passion, as they clothe and display him in a purple garment (John 19:2, 5) in order to mock him as "the King of the Jews" (19:3). Thus, not only does her relationship with the beast reveal the presumptuous and idolatrous nature of this woman, but so does the first article of clothing that she is described as wearing! The fact that she is also clothed in scarlet would make clear to the hearers that this woman is dependent upon the beast as the basis of her authority and that she actually shares in his nature.[12]

The next detail of her appearance suggests that she is literally covered in gold, as the phrase *kechrusomene chrusio*, "covered with gold in gold," underscores the extraordinary amount of gold she wears, the same root word appearing in both verbal and noun forms to convey the point. As with the previous details, so this one reveals a contrast between all those individuals and things associated with gold to this point in the Apocalypse (1:12, 13, 20; 2:1; 3:18; 4:4; 5:8; 8:3; 9:13, 20; 14:14; 15:6, 7) and this opulent portrayal.[13] Even the mention of the *litho timio*, "precious stones," is significant, likely reinforcing the presumptuous and idolatrous character of this woman. To this point only God and one of the angels

11. Aune, *Revelation 17–22*, 935.

12. Gause, *Revelation*, 221.

13. The only possible exception to this positive usage is found in 9:7.

have been described as wearing stones (4:3; 15:6) and only to God and the Lamb has the term *timen*, "honor" or "value," been ascribed (4:9, 11; 5:12, 13; 17:12). Thus, the wearing of precious stones reveals something of the woman's nature. Given all these associations the hearers might well expect mention of the pearls that the woman wears also to convey a similar message. However, at this point they are left to wonder, as they will have to wait until 21:21 to have their suspicions confirmed. Suffice it to say, in ways not always apparent to modern interpreters, the attire of this woman reveals a great deal about her presumptuous and idolatrous nature and character.

If the attire of the Great Whore reflects her character, even more is revealed by the golden cup in her hand. For in contrast to the golden bowl filled with the prayers of the saints (8:3), this golden cup is filled with abominations and the uncleanness of her sexual immorality.[14] The contents of the cup would be especially meaningful to the hearers for the phrase conveys several things to them. First, it may strike them as significant that both *bdelugmaton*, "abominations," and *ta akatharta*, "uncleanness," appear in the plural, underscoring the extent of her abominable and unclean activities. Second, while *bdelugmaton*, "abominations," might carry with it the general idea of that which is loathsome before God,[15] the hearers would likely discern a more concrete understanding of this term as in the Prophets (in the LXX) it often appears with reference to idols (Jer 13:27; 39:35; 51:22; Ezek 5:9, 11; 6:9).[16] Third, the hearers would likely see in the words *ta akatharta tes porneias autes*, "uncleanness of her sexual immorality," a reference to the unclean spirits of idolatry, which come from the mouths of the dragon, the beast, and the false prophet in 16:13, who through demonic seduction gather the kings of the whole inhabited world together to make war with God (16:14).[17] The appetites of the woman match her appearance. She constantly drinks in idolatrous abominations and the uncleanness of her sexual immorality, which characterizes her own idolatrous identity.

If there is any confusion on the hearers' part as to this woman's identity, they are given additional divine assistance to help in their pneumatic discernment with the words, "And upon her forehead a name had

14. Wall, *Revelation*, 206.

15. Zmijewski, "βδέλυγμα," 209–10.

16. Prigent, *L'Apocalypse de saint Jean*, 377.

17. Smalley, *Revelation to John*, 431.

been written, mystery, 'Babylon the Great, the Mother of whores and of all the abominations of the earth.'" The very first words of this phrase would catch the attention of the hearers for they have come to know the significance that the forehead of an individual plays in the Apocalypse, for to this point it is the place where the seal of God (7:3; 9:4) and/or his name (14:1) has been placed upon those who identify with him, and conversely the place where the mark of the Beast has been placed upon those who identify with him (13:16; 14:9). Thus, mention of the woman's forehead would raise the level of the hearers' expectancy in which they will soon have a clear indication of the woman's identity. Their expectations are not disappointed as they learn that a name has been written upon her forehead, a name written in the past that continues to be valid, as the perfect tense *gegrpammenon*, "had been written," indicates. But there is more, as for a third time in the book the hearers encounter the word mystery. While it is possible the hearers might take the word mystery as part of the woman's name, it is likely that the earlier occurrences of this term (1:20; 10:7), along with the other divine aids given to facilitate the hearers' pneumatic discernment, would put the hearers on notice that the name of the woman must be discerned, as many of the other names occurring in the book to this point (Balaam, Jezebel, Sodom, Egypt, the city where their Lord was crucified, the number of the Beast, etc.).[18] Consequently, when the hearers learn that the name of the Great Whore is Babylon the Great, they understand they must discern its meaning, as they have discerned numerous other names, titles, and events throughout the Apocalypse.

What exactly would the hearers discern in this regard? Perhaps the most obvious thing would be that this Babylon the Great is the same as the Babylon the Great of 14:8, whose fall was declared by the second other angel and out of whose wine of the wrath of her sexual immorality all the nations have drunk. Such reflection would go some way toward closing the gap between this figure and the description of the Great Whore with which this section begins, specifically the angelic words to John with regard to the judgment of the Great Whore in 17:1 and the fact that the inhabitants of the earth have become drunk from the wine of her sexual immorality. The hearers would also likely remember that the Babylon the Great named in 17:5 is the same Babylon the Great who, in the context of judgment (16:17–21), was remembered before God to

18. Aune, *Revelation 17–22*, 936.

give her the cup of the wine of the wrath of his anger (16:19). Would the hearers also think of Babylon the Great who destroyed Jerusalem, exiled her inhabitants, was seated on the waters, and whose king eventually acknowledged the God of heaven (Dan 4:4–37)? If so, perhaps they would discern that just as the Beast continues to exist despite the death of Nero, so Babylon the Great continues to exist despite the destruction of Babylon of old![19] But the title "Babylon the Great" does not stand alone for her name also includes the words "the Mother of Whores and the Abominations of the Earth."[20] Such words make clear that the Great Whore and Babylon the Great are indeed the same as this Great Whore and is the source or origin, the Mother, of all whores, those who practice and advocate idolatrous activity. This Mother of all Whores stands in direct contrast to the Woman Clothed with the Sun who gives birth to the Male Child who is taken up into heaven (12:1–6) and the rest of her seed who are characterized by "keeping the commands of God and having the witness of Jesus" (12:17).[21] In contrast, the Mother of all Whores brings forth those like the false prophetess Jezebel, who commits and advocates sexual immorality (2:20–21), just like her mother. The additional description of Babylon the Great as the mother of "the abominations of the earth" makes clear her relationship to the abominations of idolatry, for not only does she hold in her hand a gold cup filled with such abominations (17:4), she also produces children who both practice and actively propagate idolatrous activity.

Despite these earlier descriptions of the Great Whore, her description becomes even more graphic with the next words the hearers encounter, "And I saw the woman drunk out of the blood of the saints and out of the blood of the witnesses of Jesus." The second occurrence of *ehidon*, "I saw," in this passage confirms for the hearers that the woman

---

19. Cf. Cheung, "The Mystery of Revelation 17:5 & 7," 1–19, esp., 18.

20. This graphic depiction of the Great Whore has led Bruns ("The Contrasted Women of Apoc 12 and 17," 459–63) to conclude that Valeria Messalina, the wife of the emperor Claudius (41–54 CE), sat for this portrait. Her exploits, as depicted by Juvenal (Satire 6:116–32), Tacitus (Annals 11:1, 2, 12, 26–38) and Pliny (Natural History 11:171), suggest that "Messalina was remembered . . . as (1) a Roman Empress who (2) literally played the Harlot and (3) crowned her adulteries amid the luxurious surroundings of a drunken orgy." According to Juvenal's description she literally bore an assumed name (on her forehead?)—"Lycisca," "The Wolf Girl." Bruns suggests that her ignominious death parallels that of the Great Whore in Rev 17:16.

21. Smalley, *Revelation to John*, 432.

John saw sitting upon a scarlet beast (17:3) is the same woman he now sees drunk on the blood of the saints. Within this repulsive imagery a number of ideas converge. First, for the hearers there could hardly be any question that the blood of the saints and the blood of the witnesses of Jesus here emphasized is tightly connected to the blood of the souls under the altar (6:10) and the blood of the saints and the prophets (16:6). Such continuity reinforces the reality of persecution and death for those who would be faithful witnesses of Jesus. Second, mention of the blood of the saints and the blood of the witnesses *of Jesus* would serve once again to draw attention to Jesus' own faithful witness involved the shedding of his blood from which salvific consequences result and for which he is often praised. Thus, the hearers have yet another reminder that those who would follow the Lamb wherever he goes (14:4) must be prepared to follow him into death. Third, the hearers would also likely wonder whether there is not a connection between the blood from which this woman has become drunk and the gold cup in her hand, which is full of abominations and sexual immorality.

Though the contents of the cup do not morph into the blood of the saints and the blood of the witnesses of Jesus before the eyes (or ears) of the hearers, like the transformations that have taken place with a variety of other images in the Apocalypse to this point, the hearers are likely to discern a deep connection between the two. As the Apocalypse has unfolded, an increase in idolatrous activity upon the earth brings the death of the saints in its wake. This is learned in part from the way in which the Great Red Dragon makes war against the saints (12:17) and the way in which the Beast from the earth will allow no dissent from the first beast's universal worship (13:15). Those who remain faithful in their witness to Jesus and refuse to worship the Beast, his image, his name, or his number inevitably face death. Thus, the contents of the gold cup and the blood from which the Great Whore becomes drunk share a deep connection.[22] The increase of the one entails the increase of the other. Fourth, the hearers might also discern a connection between the wine of her sexual immorality *ek*, "out of," which the inhabitants of the earth have become drunk, the gold cup full of abominations and the uncleanness of her sexual immorality, and the blood of the saints and the blood of the witnesses of Jesus *ek*, "out of," which the Great Whore has become drunk. Such a connection makes clear the Great Whore is

22. Smalley, *Revelation to John*, 432.

not alone in her culpability; it is shared by the kings of the earth who have committed sexual immorality with her (17:2) and the inhabitants of the earth who have become drunk from her wine, having worshipped the Beast (13:8, 12, 14). Finally, the hearers might also wonder as to the relationship between the blood of the saints and the witnesses of Jesus from which she has become drunk and the blood God has given his enemies to drink owing to the fact that they have poured out the blood of his saints and prophets (16:6). Whether or not the hearers would in retrospect see the blood with which God inundates the earth and its inhabitants with the pouring out of the last bowls of his wrath and the blood with which the Great Whore has become drunk, they would likely appreciate the connection between the faithful witness of the saints, their shed blood, the prayers they offer, and God's ultimate judgment of the earth. If so, her drunken state resulting from the orgy of idolatrous activity leading to the death of the saints and witnesses of Jesus reveals that the Great Whore has become intoxicated and unable to function in a clear-headed fashion, having consumed the witness who could have led to her salvation!

Even the disturbing nature of the description of the Great Whore to this point might not prepare the hearers for the shock that comes from the next words they encounter, for John says, "And I marveled seeing her a great marvel." Several aspects of this sentence would be of significance for the hearers. Perhaps the first thing to strike them would be the grammatical structure, for the words "seeing her" stand in the middle of the Greek sentence, surrounded by a cognate accusative where both the verb and the direct object employ the same Greek root word, in this case *ethaumasa*, "I marveled," . . . *thauma mega*, "a great marvel." Thus, grammatically the sight of this woman is surrounded by John's marveling, underscoring her appearance has generated such an effect. What would heighten the hearers' sense of concern is their memory that this very verb has appeared once before in the Apocalypse to describe the response of the whole world to the healing of the Beast's wounded head (13:3), a response that results in the universal worship of the Dragon and the Beast (13:4)![23] Is it possible John could here be susceptible to the same idolatrous seduction, which has resulted in the worship of the Dragon and the Beast by the whole world?[24] Such a possibility would be

---

23. Caird, *Revelation of Saint John*, 213.

24. Schüssler Fiorenza, *Book of Revelation*, 96.

an additional emphasis on the recurring theme of true and false worship. If John, who is "in the Spirit" at the time, could be so tempted, could anyone be immune from such seduction? Such a possibility would serve as a stark warning to the hearers about the vigilance required to withstand temptation. At the same time, Johannine hearers would likely recall that this term is used to describe a response that often accompanies aspects of Jesus' teaching or actions, difficult to understand for various individuals in the Fourth Gospel (John 3:7; 4:27; 5:20, 28; 7:15, 21). In addition to heightening the significance of vigilance with regard to temptations to idolatrous worship, the hearers would perhaps also see in these words an indication of John's puzzlement in interpreting this detail of the vision.[25]

If the hearers are still concerned about John's response to the seductive power of the Great Whore, so it seems is the angel, as John recounts, "And the angel said to me, 'On account of what are you marveling? I will show you the mystery of the woman and the beast who bears her who has seven heads and ten horns.'" With these words the hearers learn that the angel addresses both aspects of their own reflection about John's response to the vision of the Great Whore. The angel begins with a question that can hardly be taken as anything other than a rebuke to John.[26] For the hearers the question would provide some space, however brief, for reflection upon John's response to the Great Whore. Perhaps it would also provoke the hearers to answer the same question themselves. Is there some seduction in this vision that could result in idolatrous activity on their part? Or to put it the other way round, what is it about this vision that proves seductive to them? The hearers learn various things from the rest of the words spoken to John. First, they are informed that they, like John, are to receive additional divine assistance in their pneumatic discernment when told the angel will explain the mystery of the woman and the beast who bears her. Specifically, the hearers may well suspect the meaning of the beast's seven heads and ten horns will be revealed by the angel, just as the resurrected Jesus revealed the mystery of the seven stars and the seven golden lampstands in 1:19–20. Second, the hearers learn of the close relationship between the woman and the beast, as their mystery is to be explained together.[27] Third, in discovering that the woman is being borne by the beast (*bastazontos*, "who bears,")

25. Aune, *Revelation 17–22*, 938.
26. Gause, *Revelation*, 223.
27. Ladd, *Revelation*, 226.

the hearers would no doubt contrast this beast and what it bears and the church in Ephesus who was "not able to bear (*bastasai*, 'bear,') evil ones or things" (2:2), but who "have patient endurance and bear (*ebastasas*, "bear") on account of my name" (2:3).

Perhaps contrary to the hearers' expectations the angel begins his explanation of the mystery of the woman and the beast with attention focused on the beast, "The beast which you saw was and is not and is about to come up out of the Abyss and go into destruction, and the inhabitants of the earth will have been made to marvel, those whose names have not been written upon the book of life from the foundation of the world, seeing the beast that was and is not and will be present." The first thing to catch the attention of the hearers may well be the words "the beast," which stand first in the Greek sentence as a point of emphasis, and is followed by the words *ho eides*, "which you saw," a literary marker that directs the hearers' attention to various details of the vision for which the angel now offers the interpretation.[28] While focusing attention on the beast the hearers learn that it is described with an appellation, "was and is not and is about to raise from the Abyss," which is simultaneously a parody of both the One Who Sits on the throne and the Lamb.

This three-fold appellation could not help but to bring to mind the three-fold description of God as "the One Who is and the One Who was and the One Who is coming" (1:4, 8; 4:8). By this appellation, the beast's idolatrous presumption would be seen for what it is and in keeping with the Great Whore. The hearers might also discern that this appellation, as idolatrous as it may be, carries with it the testimony of the beast's destruction for they would hardly encounter it without remembering the three-fold appellation for God has given way to a two-fold appellation, "the One Who was and the One Who is" (11:17), indicating that God is no longer described as the coming one—for he has come! At the same time, the description of the beast as "and was not" would no doubt be taken as having reference to the slaughter suffered by one of the beast's heads (13:3), which is a parody of the Lamb, who himself was slaughtered (5:5). The description of the beast as "about to come up from the Abyss and goes into destruction" reveals something of his character,[29] owing to

---

28. The phrase *ho eides*, "that which you saw," will occur five times in 17:8–18 (vv. 8, 12, 15, 16, 18).

29. Caird describes these as permanent qualities of the beast, not a description of one-off events; the beast is always arising from the Abyss and always heading for destruction. Caird, *Revelation of Saint John*, 216.

his origin and end, and confirms for the hearers that this beast is identical to the one who makes war against and overcomes the two witnesses (11:7), as he too comes from the Abyss. Thus, their earlier suspicion that the beast who comes from the Abyss (11:7) and the beast who comes from the sea (13:1) are one and the same is confirmed.

With such thoughts still in mind, attention is directed to the "the inhabitants of the earth are made to marvel," words that remind the hearers that the world's earlier astonishment at the healing of the beast's slaughtered head led to the universal worship of the dragon and the beast (13:3–4) and that John himself (and they with him?) has been made to be astonished at the sight of the Great Whore (17:6). For a second time in the book, the identity of the inhabitants of the earth, who are made to marvel by the beast, is made clearer by the description, "whose names have not been written upon the book of life from the foundation of the world." Earlier the book of life has been closely associated with the resurrected Jesus (3:5) and the Lamb slaughtered from before the foundation of the world (13:8). Here, despite the lack of exactitude in language, Johannine hearers would be reminded of the fact that those who are so taken with the beast have made a decision to identify with him disregarding the salvific provisions made by the slaughtered Lamb, salvific provisions which in fact predate the foundation of this world and are grounded in the pre-temporal relationship of the Father and the Son. Ultimately, they are reminded that such ones as these do not have their names written upon the book of life because they have chosen the one whose ways lead to destruction over the One Who is Life, in whose book their names do not appear. The amazement of the inhabitants of the earth comes from "seeing the beast that was and is not and is coming." With these words perhaps it would dawn upon the hearers that the description of the inhabitants of the earth, who are astonished at the beast and whose names have not been written in the book of life, are bounded on either side by descriptions of the beast's three-fold appellation, which underscores his presumptuous and idolatrous character. The intensity of the latter appellation is made even greater by the fact that it ends with the word *parestai*, "comes," which not only is used exclusively for the activity of Jesus in the Fourth Gospel (John 7:6; 11:28), but is also the verb from which the noun parousia, "coming," is derived,[30] a term used on at least one occasion in the Johannine tradition for the return of

---

30. Schneider, "πάρειμι," 36.

Jesus (1 John 2:28). Thus the parody of the One Who sits on the throne and the Lamb by the beast continues in the last word of Rev 17:8.

As the hearers reflect on such astonishing details they encounter words that once again encourage their pneumatic discernment, "Here is the understanding, the one who has wisdom. The seven heads are seven mountains, where the woman sits upon them. And they are seven kings." For the hearers it hardly matters whether this call is one to reflect back on the words of 17:8[31] or one that calls them forward into the explanation offered by the angel, for the words of 17:8 and those following are intricately connected to one another. The call to pneumatic discernment is reminiscent of a similar call in 13:18, where, following the words "Here is Wisdom" a call is given for "the one who has understanding" to calculate the number of the beast.[32] Significantly, the call in 17:9 combines the words "understanding" with "wisdom" and the verse is also concerned with spiritually discerning the aspects of the beast's identity, suggesting that the discernment called for in 13:18 and 17:9 are not unrelated activities. The first words to follow this call for pneumatic discernment assist the hearers in this task, for they reveal something about the identity of the beast's seven heads, just as Jesus had revealed the mystery of the stars and the seven lamp stands earlier in the book (1:20). In 17:9 the angel reveals that the seven heads are seven mountains, an identification that might well prompt the hearers to think of the seven hills of Rome owing to such a description in numerous ancient authors (Vergil, *Geor.* 11:535; Aen vi.783; Horace, *Carm* 7; Ovid, *Trist* 1:5.69; Mart iv:64; Cicero, *ad Att* vi:5).[33] Such identification would also confirm the connection between the pneumatic discernment to which they had been called in 13:18 and the pneumatic discernment in 17:9—just as there had been a resemblance between Nero and the beast in the former, so there is a resemblance between Rome and the beast in the latter. But just as the beast was not confined to the identification with Nero in the hearers' earlier pneumatic discernment, so the imagery of the seven mountains would not be exhausted by the identification of Rome with the beast.[34] The significance of the number seven throughout the Apocalypse would likely convey the imagery of Rome, the imagery of the seven hills would

31. See Aune, *Revelation 17–22*, 941 and Smalley, *Revelation to John*, 435.

32. Murphy, *Fallen Is Babylon*, 359.

33. Caird, *Revelation of Saint John*, 216.

34. Smalley, *Revelation to John*, 435.

likely convey the idea of universal power, not unlike the way in which mountains and hills were closely associated with political power in the OT (Jer 51:25).[35] Such identification would surely not come as a shock to the hearers owing to the universal power with which the beast rules in chapter 13. Neither does it come as a surprise that the Great Whore, Babylon the Great, sits upon them, for they are the seven heads of the beast!

But before the hearers can fully take in such an interpretation, the image of the seven heads, which has morphed into the seven hills, now morphs into the image of seven kings. Though sometimes challenging to modern interpreters,[36] such a transformation confirms the hearers' initial discernment that the hills do indeed have reference to political powers, even universal political powers. Though not as overt as in the case of the seven hills, the imagery of the seven kings would possibly remind the hearers of Rome, for in Roman and Etruscan histories (Tacitus, *Histories*, 3:72; Pliny, *Natural History*, 34:139) there were seven kings (Romulus, Numa Pompilius, Tullus Hostilius, Ancus Marcus, Tarquinus Priscus, Servius Tullius, and Tarquinius Superbus), with later historians going so far as identifying minor figures with major ones to preserve the number seven![37] At the same time, the imagery of seven kings would reinforce for the hearers the idea of universal or complete rule, which the seven hills first generate and the beast earlier exhibits in chapter 13.

With the image of the seven kings now in mind, the hearers encounter additional words, "And five have fallen, one is, another has not yet come, and when he comes it is necessary for him to remain a little while." Several aspects of these enigmatic words would be significant for the hearers. First, these words clearly extend the description of and focus upon the imagery of the seven kings, as their corporate description now takes on a threefold shape. Second, this threefold shape is reminiscent of the threefold way in which the Beast is spoken, "was and is not and is coming" (17:8), suggesting that the identity of the seven kings is to be understood as intimately connected to the identity of the Beast. Third, the fact that "five have fallen, one is, and one has not yet come" indicates

35. Wall, *Revelation*, 207.

36. For example, Ladd sees no connection between the seven hills and the seven kings, preferring to take the seven kings as representing seven kingdoms. Ladd, *Revelation*, 227.

37. Aune, *Revelation 17–22*, 948.

that the hearers who have already encountered the Beast in the form of the "five who have fallen," are currently facing the Beast in the form of the one that is, and are sure to face him in the form of the one "who has not yet come" but will reign for a little while. Fourth, the fact that "five have fallen" and "one (now) is" suggest to the hearers that they indeed stand near the end of all things for they await the emergence of the one who brings the "seven" to their completion.[38] Fifth, the words spoken of the seventh, that "it is necessary for him to remain *oligon*, 'a little,'" might well remind the hearers of similar words spoken of the Devil, who knows that he has but *oligon*, "a little" time (12:12), underscoring the connection between the Devil, the Beast, and the seven kings all the more. Sixth, reference to "remaining a little (while)" might even call to the hearer's mind the relatively short length of the Beast's forty-two month reign (13:5), again pointing to the connection between the identity of the seven kings and the Beast.

Attempts to calculate the identity of these seven kings would be virtually impossible owing to the high number of variables involved, such as the starting point for the calculations (does one begin with Julius Caesar, Augustus or even Tiberius?), the parameters determining which kings are included and which are excluded (does one include all those who ruled, even the relatively minor figures Galba, Otho, Vitellius?), and the identity of the one who is (Galba, Otho, Vitllius, Vespasian, Titus, Domitian?).[39] While little consensus would likely emerge even amongst the hearers as to the identity of the seven kings,[40] the likelihood of the close connection between the Devil, the Beast, and the seven kings would be clear.[41]

The relationship between the Beast and the seven kings is made even clearer in the next words the hearers encounter, "And the Beast which was and is not and he is eighth and is of the seven, and he goes into destruction." Perhaps one of the first things to strike the hearers when encountering these words is the way in which they, together with those in the last part of 17:8, serve as an *inclusio* around the mystery to which the hearers are called to discern in vv. 9–10. Thus, the Beast

38. Beasley-Murray, *Revelation*, 257.

39. For the various possibilities cf. the helpful overview by Aune, *Revelation 17–22*, 945–50.

40. For a similar point cf. Kiddle, *Revelation*, 350.

41. For a similar conclusion cf. Murphy, *Fallen Is Babylon*, 358.

and his identity are integrally intertwined with the seven hills, which are the seven kings. The threefold formula by which the Beast has come to be known in a parody of both God and the Lamb is expanded in this verse drawing attention to elements of the Beast's identity, which to this point have not been made clear. Two aspects of this expansion are particularly noteworthy. First, in this verse the Beast is identified as "the eighth," a startling detail owing to the fact that reference has been made to this point only to seven kings. Though the hearers might conceivably be tempted to take these words to mean that the seven kings have morphed into an eighth king, such an interpretive option is unlikely, owing to the prominence of the number seven throughout the book generally and its prominence with regard to the Beast in particular. Rather, this enigmatic detail would likely generate more reflection on the identity of the Beast. Perhaps reference to the Beast as "eighth" would remind the hearers of the discerning reflection to which they were earlier called in calculating the name of the Beast and his number, 666.

Among the many things discerned about the number of the Beast was the fact that the number 666 is a triangular number, the sum of every number from 1 to 36, and that triangular numbers are exceedingly rare. In point of fact, the number 666 is only the *eighth* such triangular number to occur (1, 6, 21, 55, 120, 231, 406, and 666).[42] At one level, then, the identification of the Beast as "eighth" in 17:11 would likely call the hearers' attention back to the calculations of the Beast's number in 13:18, further revealing the connection between the seven kings and the Beast. On this understanding the Beast is not the eighth king after the seven, but is "eighth" whose number is 666. Second, such an understanding would make clear for the hearers why the Beast is *ek*, "out of," "the seven" not one of the seven,[43] for his identity is coterminous with the seven as a whole, not as one of the seven individually. Thus this eighth (666) is of the seven. Before leaving a discussion of v. 11 it should perhaps be noted that the words with which this verse concludes, "and he goes into destruction," is a reminder that despite the Beast's relationship to the seven kings, he is ultimately doomed for destruction. It is characteristic of his identity, a detail he cannot escape!

The description of the Beast continues with the next words, "And the ten horns which you saw are ten kings, who have not yet received

---

42. Bauckham, *Climax of Prophecy*, 395–96.

43. Mounce, *Book of Revelation*, 316.

their kingship, but they will receive authority as king for one hour with the Beast." For the second time in the description of the Beast the hearers encounter the words *ho eides*, "that which you saw," indicating a new detail is being revealed about the mystery of the Beast upon whom the Great Whore sits. Specifically, attention is now focused upon the Beast's ten horns, divinely revealed to be ten kings. As the hearers discover this detail a number of previous ideas would likely converge for them. For from this vantage point the connection between the ten days of suffering tribulation brought on by the Devil (2:10), the ten horns of the Great Red Dragon (12:3), the ten horns and ten diadems of the Beast (13:1), the number of the Beast (666) which in Greek includes the word/number *deka*, "ten," in it, the ten horns of the Beast upon whom the Great Whore sits (17:3, 7), and the ten kings which are the ten horns (17:12) are all intimately connected to the Great Dragon, the ancient serpent, the one called the Devil and Satan, the one who deceives the entire inhabited world (12:9). In this regard, their work is one and the same. Thus, once again the work of the Beast is concretized in human terms. While the identity of these ten kings is something of a mystery at this point, perhaps the hearers would see some continuity between them and the ten eschatological horns/kings of Dan 7:24, on the one hand, and the kings from the east (Rev 16:12) who appear to morph into all the kings of the whole inhabited world (16:14), on the other hand. The connection between the ten kings and all the kings of the inhabited world would fit nicely with the way in which "ten" is itself a number of completion in the Apocalypse. What would perhaps be clearer to the hearers at this point than the identity of the ten kings is the way in which the following description of these kings parallels part of the description of the seven kings mentioned earlier. The description of the ten kings as "not having received their kingship" and "receiving authority as king for one hour" (17:12) stands in remarkable parallel to the previous description of the final of the seven kings described as "the other has not yet come, and when he comes it is necessary for him to remain a little (time)" (17:10). Such similarities would at the least underscore the tight connection between these ten horns of the Beast and one or more of the Beast's seven heads. The short duration of the reign of these ten kings, one hour, stands in stark contrast to the forty-two month reign of the Beast (13:5), indicating their reign is for only the shortest portion of his activity. The derived nature of their authority is made clear by the fact that they have

authority as kings "with the Beast." The relationship of the ten kings to
the Beast is made even clearer in the next words the hearers encounter,
"These have one purpose and their power and authority they will give to
the Beast." The grammatical construction suggests that their "one" purpose is the giving of their power and authority to the Beast, underscoring the intimate connection between the ten kings and the Beast. When
the hearers encounter one (the ten kings) they encounter the other (the
Beast)!

The intensions of the ten kings are made clear in the next words,
"These will make war with the Lamb and the Lamb will overcome them,
because he is Lord of Lords and King of Kings and those with him are
called and chosen/elect and faithful." In ways reminiscent of the demonic seduction of all the kings of the whole inhabited world who gather
together at Harmagedon to make war (16:16), these ten kings will make
war on the Lamb. At various points in the Apocalypse attention has been
drawn to the ability of the Beast (11:7) and the Great Red Dragon (12:7,
17) to make war upon God's people. In fact, songs were even sung by the
inhabitants upon the earth to the Beast extolling his alleged invincibility
in war (13:4). Despite such activities, 17:14 is the first text in which it is
explicitly stated that war was made upon the Lamb! It probably does not
surprise the hearers to learn that the efforts at war upon the Lamb by the
ten kings (the ten horns of the beast) end in utter defeat, for this Lamb is
uniquely connected with overcoming in the Apocalypse, as he has previously identified himself as one who has overcome (3:21), is described as
having overcome as the Lion of the tribe of Judah (5:5), and his followers
are said to overcome by the blood of the Lamb and the word of their testimony (12:11). This same Lamb, who earlier had promised to make war
with the sword of his mouth on those who refuse to repent at Pergamum
(2:16), proves victorious against the ten kings (of the Beast).

The hearers are told explicitly why the Lamb overcomes, "for he
is Lord of Lords and King of Kings," an extraordinary attribution! To
this point in the Apocalypse the term *kurios*, "lord," has been frequently
applied to "the One Who Sits on the throne," "the Lord, God, the all powerful One" (1:8; 4:8, 11; 11:4, 15, 17; 15:3, 4; 16:7), with the word used in
reference to Jesus on only one occasion (11:8). The use of this title for the
Lamb in 17:14 would highlight the close relationship between God and
the Lamb, and the superiority of Jesus over all the kings of the earth (the
ten kings in particular). He is without any rivals.

The second part of the title would be especially significant to
Johannine hearers for several reasons. First, Jesus' identification as king
is a rich one in the Johannine tradition (John 1:49; 6:15; 12:13, 15; 18:33,
37, 39; 19:3, 12, 14, 15, 19, 21). Second, one of the first things the hearers
learn about Jesus in the Apocalypse is that he is the ruler of the kings
of the earth (Rev 1:5). Third, the kings of the earth sometimes function in the Apocalypse either as those being at enmity with God and
the Lamb (6:15; 16:12, 14) and/or as those to whom prophetic witness
is to be given (10:11). Fourth, on occasion God himself is spoken of as
king (15:3). Thus, for the Lamb to here be called the King of Kings underscores Jesus' inherent identity as king and ruler of all the kings of
the earth, especially the ten kings who will seek to make war on him! In
this he is also king over the Beast, whose ten horns are these ten kings.
Further, the hearers now learn the Lamb does not stand alone, but, just as
in 14:1–5 where he stands with the 144,000 who follow him wherever he
goes, has certain ones with him. These are not described as participating
in the war directly but simply referred to as those who are "called and
chosen and faithful."

This threefold designation underscores the character of those who
stand with the Lamb, drawing upon the hearers' knowledge in a very
subtle fashion. While the term *kletoi*, "called," does not appear elsewhere
in the Johannine literature, the verb form from which it is derived would
likely inform its usage here. Johannine hearers would be aware of the
way in which it is closely associated with discipleship, as it is used to
describe the renaming of Simon as Cephas by Jesus (John 1:42), as well
as functioning as a term of invitation for the disciples to the wedding
at Cana (2:2), where they are described as believing in Jesus (2:11). At
the same time, from the Apocalypse they would discern that this term
is one that reveals the identity and even spiritual significance of places
and/or individuals (Rev 1:9; 11:8; 12:9; 16:16). In the light of these connections the hearers would likely understand the occurrence of *kletoi*,
"called," as indicating those who stand with the Lamb are his disciples,
who have been named or called by Jesus himself. The second term to
appear in this threefold designation, *elektoi*, "chosen" or "elect," would
also be of significance to Johannine hearers for this term of honor is
used for either an individual or community in right standing with the
Elder (2 John 1, 13). At the same time, when the verb form from which
it is derived occurs in the Fourth Gospel it is always found on the lips of

Jesus in contexts underscoring his own divine selection or choosing of his disciples (John 6:70; 13:18; and esp. 15:16). Thus, for those who stand with the Lamb to be called "chosen" or "elect" underscores the fact that their relationship with the Lamb rests upon divine initiative. The third term to appear in this threefold designation, *pistoi*, "faithful," would be immediately recognizable to the hearers for it has become the term *par excellence* for the faithful obedience unto death that exemplifies Jesus (Rev 1:5; 3:14), those called upon to withstand the suffering inflicted by the Devil even unto death (2:10), and Antipas who was killed owing to his faithful witness (2:13). Thus, for those who stand with the Lamb to be called "faithful" underscores the fact that such ones as these, like the 144,000 who follow the Lamb wherever he goes, are overcomers owing to their faithfulness even unto death![44]

With these words of praise for those who stand with the Lamb the hearers' attention is directed to still another dimension of this mystery, "And he says to me, 'The waters which you saw, upon which the Whore sits, are peoples and crowds and nations and tongues.'" The third occurrence of the words *ho eides*, "that which you saw," in this angelic explanation guides the hearers to another aspect of John's vision. It is a return to the Whore with whom this vision began, with specific reference made to the waters upon which she sat. Here the waters are identified as people by means of a by now familiar fourfold listing: peoples, crowds, nations, and tongues. For a seventh time in the Apocalypse this fourfold formula appears (with slight variations), a formula conveying a sense of universality.[45] By this point the hearers have come to understand the formula to designate all those who worship God and the Lamb (5:9; 7:9), those who are opposed to God and are under the authority of the Beast (11:9; 13:7), those to whom John must prophesy a second time (10:11), and those to whom the everlasting gospel must be preached (14:6). Not only would the hearers be struck yet again by the blasphemy of the Whore, who presumes to sit in the place of God (17:1), but would also understand even more fully than before that those to whom their pneumatic witness is to be directed find themselves under the oppressive authority of the

---

44. It may be that these terms would be understood as building upon one another, as Prigent observes, "Cette fidélite c'est la réponse de l'homme qui reconnaeît et accepte la vocations et l'élection." Prigent, *L'Apocalypse*, 383.

45. Smalley, *Revelation to John*, 440.

Whore, just as they earlier were said to be under the authority of the Beast (13:7).

With such ideas about the peoples dominated by the Whore in their minds, the hearers' attention is directed to still another aspect of the vision with the words, "And the ten horns which you saw and the Beast will hate the Whore and will make her ruined/desolate and naked and will eat her flesh and will burn her in fire." As had the three previous occurrences of the words *ho eides*, "that which you saw," so their fourth occurrence in this angelic explanation of the words alerts the hearers to yet another dimension of the vision to be explained. Mention of the ten horns and the Beast would serve to underscore for the hearers the solidarity of the actions of the ten kings and those of the Beast. Amazingly enough, the Beast (and his ten horns), who has to this point supported the Whore and her domination of the peoples of the world, turn upon her with a viciousness normally associated with the actions of wild animals![46] Their treatment of the Whore would likely generate a visceral response amongst the hearers as they encounter the language of hatred, desolation, nakedness, eating flesh, and burning with fire. Specifically, such graphic language would likely remind the hearers of the words of Ezekiel (23:1–49) in describing the divine judgments brought on by the actions of two whoring sisters, Oola (Samaria) and Ooliba (Jerusalem). Owing to their opulence, unrestrained adulteries and sexual immoralities, they are turned over to those who hate them, they are stripped naked, their flesh is mutilated, and their remnant burnt with fire![47] In addition to the message of divine judgment conveyed by the similarities to the Ezekiel passage the hearers would also likely pick up on a variety of other nuances in the text. The fact that the Beast and the ten horns will hate the Whore might convey the idea that their actions are tied to God's judgment in some way, in as much as the resurrected Jesus himself has earlier claimed to "hate" the works of the Nicolaitans (Rev 2:6), perhaps suggesting a connection between their works and the Great Whore's. Words of warning that the Whore will be ruined or made desolate are given in anticipation of the event which is to follow (18:19).

The fact that the Whore will be made naked would make clear the real nature of her spiritual state, as it had with the church in Laodicea (3:17), exposing her shame (16:15). Neither would the stark juxtapo-

---

46. Ladd, *Revelation*, 233.

47. Murphy, *Fallen Is Babylon*, 364.

sition of her naked state with her earlier opulent attire be lost on the hearers. Perhaps they would wonder if there is not a deeper connection between the fact of eating of the Whore's flesh and her idolatrous sexual immoralities would no doubt have included the seduction to eat food sacrificed to idols, a temptation with which more than one of the seven churches struggled (2:14, 20). These gruesome words might also remind the hearers of Jezebel's ultimate fate (2 Kgs 9:30–37).[48] Though the hearers would not realize it at this point, this description of the Beast and his ten horns eating the flesh of the Whore serves as a harbinger of things to come (19:18). Owing to the close association between burning (8:7) and the display of fire as a near universal activity of God in the Apocalypse (the lone exception being 13:13), mention of her fiery fate could hardly be taken as anything other than divine judgment.

If the previous verse leads the hearers to suspect the hand of God in the demise of the Whore the next words they encounter confirms that suspicion, "For God gave into their hearts to do his purpose and to do one purpose and to give their kingship to the Beast until the words of God might be fulfilled." Now the hearers discover that even the one purpose of the ten kings, to give their authority to the Beast as they go out to make war against the Lamb (vv. 13–14), is not beyond the activity of God. Just as the hearers had earlier learned that the pouring out of the sixth bowl had caused the Euphrates to dry up so a way might be made for the kings of the east to invade (16:12), they now learn that God has a hand in the cooperative venture of the ten kings and the Beast! Their *mian gnomen*, "one purpose," is in reality his *mian gnomen*, "one purpose." Such activities are part of the divine plan and will play a role in bringing to completion "the words of God."[49] The occurrence of the term *teles-thesontai*, "will have been completed," would be of special significance to Johannine hearers for it is the same verb Jesus utters at the end of his life on the cross ("It is completed"—John 19:30), but it also functions in the Apocalypse to describe the completion of extraordinarily important things: the mystery of God (Rev 10:7), the witness of the two prophetic witnesses (11:7), and the wrath of God (15:1, 8). Here the hearers would likely take these "words of God" as coterminous with "the words of this prophecy" (1:3; 22:7, 9, 10, 18, 19). The actions of these ten kings in ac-

---

48. Aune, *Revelation 17–22*, 957.

49. Gause, *Revelation*, 227.

cord with the divine will, and these actions are being revealed in the book John has written!

At long last the angelic explanation returns to where it began with the words, "And the woman which you saw is the great city which has the kingship over the kings of the earth." The mystery of the woman, which the angel earlier promised to reveal (17:7), is now taken up directly again as she is identified with the great city. With these words a number of things converge for the hearers about the Woman's identity. The first mention of the great city in the Apocalypse described the city in which the body of the two prophetic witnesses would lay, a city called pneumatically Sodom, Egypt, the place where their Lord was crucified. They would likely recall this universal city was a location, the identity of which could only be discerned by means of the Spirit (11:8). In conjunction with this city the first mention of the Beast in the Apocalypse occurs (11:7), underscoring the close relationship between the two. Now in 17:18 they learn this woman is identified with this "great city," which is none other than Babylon the Great! With such words the hearers would be reminded that, despite her unrivaled power, this woman's fate is as certain as Babylon the Great, which had earlier fallen!

PART TWO

Theological Engagements on Pentecostal Eschatology

6

Early Pentecostal Eschatology in the Light of *The Apostolic Faith*, 1906–1908

LARRY McQUEEN

INTRODUCTION

HISTORIANS WRITING ABOUT EARLY Pentecostalism agree that eschatology played a major role in the formation and development of early Pentecostal thought.[1] Furthermore, most believe that many early Pentecostals adopted (with modifications) the eschatology of classical premillennial dispensationalism to varying degrees.[2] Those scholars who examine the eschatology of early Pentecostalism often point out how Pentecostals modified the dispensational script in order to maintain their understanding of the work of the Holy Spirit.[3] A number of scholars point out the theological tension that developed between the spirituality of Pentecostalism and the dispensational eschatology it has embraced.[4] The question remains, however, as to how influential dispensationalism was during the *earliest* period of the movement. This chapter seeks to address this question by examining early Pentecostal eschatology from the perspective of *The Apostolic Faith*, the periodical produced by The Apostolic Faith Mission at Azusa Street in Los Angeles

---

1. Cf. Dayton, *Theological Roots of Pentecostalism*; Faupel, *Everlasting Gospel.*

2. Prosser, *Dispensationalist Eschatology.*

3. Cf. Wacker, *Heaven Below*, 251–65.

4. Cf. Sheppard, "Pentecostalism and the Hermeneutics of Dispensationalism," 5–33.

from 1906 through 1908.[5] Representing the earliest published articulation of Pentecostal thinking, *The Apostolic Faith* quickly became a primary means of spreading the "full gospel" message, both nationally and internationally. Thus, it contains a broad representation of thought at the grassroots level as well as from those who would later become leaders of the movement.

THE DYNAMICS OF DISCERNMENT

With the advent of the Pentecostal outpouring in 1906, a multitude of theological issues was forced into a period of re-examination. Spiritual discernment became a necessity. The primary issue to be rethought was, of course, the meaning of baptism in the Spirit, especially in relation to sanctification. Many other issues, however, were brought into this process, including eschatology. At Azusa Street, the discerning process centered on submitting experience to the Word of God understood as a dialectical relationship of Scripture and the Spirit, resulting in a distinct Pentecostal hermeneutic. William Seymour wrote, "If we remain in the scriptures and follow the blessed Holy Spirit all the way, we will be able to measure up to the Word of God in all its fullness."[6] Experience was measured against Scripture, resulting in either the denial or affirmation of its validity. For example, the practice of writing in "tongues" was judged to be unscriptural and was not encouraged in the meetings,[7] whereas, various biblical texts and the perceived anointing of the Spirit were sufficient to validate women in ministry.[8] At times the discerning process resulted in a shift of understanding, as in the issue of what constituted the "Bible evidence" of baptism in the Spirit. Speaking in tongues was eventually viewed to be deficient in itself, requiring the larger context of love to be

5. The methodology employed here is inductive analysis. Thus, the question of historical antecedents or sources is outside the scope of this study.

6. *AF* 1.5 (Jan 1907), 2. The Holy Spirit was deemed crucial in the interpretive process. A brief exhortation in *AF* 1.1 (Sep 1906), 2, encourages, "Dear ones, do not puzzle yourselves by theorizing, but tarry in Jerusalem, and the Spirit will throw light upon God's word and you will see it just as it is. He will reveal the whole word from Genesis to Revelations [*sic*]."

7. *AF* 1.10 (Sep, 1907), 2.

8. *AF* 1.9 (Jun–Sep 1907), 3, references Joel 2:28; 1.10 (Sep 1907), 2, references Gal 3:28; 1.12 (Jan 1908), 2, references Acts 2:17–18; 21:9 and notes, "Before Pentecost, the woman could only go into the 'court of women' and not into the inner court. But now, 'It is the same Holy Spirit in the woman as in the man.'"

a convincing confirmation of Spirit baptism.[9] The discerning process in relation to eschatology followed the same pattern as with many other issues. What was valid for eschatology was formed by bringing relevant biblical passages into conversation with present spiritual experiences, all understood as obedience to the Spirit.[10] How compatible a particular understanding of eschatology was with the overall spiritual experiences of the believer became a primary factor, those experiences also subject to the discerning process. The results of this process will be elaborated in the following paragraphs.

HOLISTIC SPIRITUALITY

The eschatology of Azusa Street was embedded in a holistic spirituality. The sense that eschatology was not so much a formulated doctrine as it was a lived reality is immediately evident in the pages of *The Apostolic Faith*. This is demonstrated by the fact that, on the one hand, eschatology was never made part of the statement of faith published in almost every issue,[11] and yet, on the other hand, it permeates the personal testimonies, poems, letters, reports of tongues-speech, and articles as a constant reminder that "Jesus is coming soon." The sense of Jesus' imminent return was woven tightly into the spiritual experience of the participants.

9. *AF* 1.1 (Sep, 1906), 2; 1.9 (Jun–Sep 1907), 2; 1.11 (Oct 1907), 3.

10. A brief exhortation in *AF* 1.12 (Jan 1908), 3, enjoins, "If there is too much reading the word without prayer, you get too argumentative, and if you pray too much without reading you get fanatical." The entirety of Scripture was brought into this process. In an article dealing with whether married persons could be part of the bride of Christ, Seymour wrote, "We must rightly divide the Scriptures and compare Scripture with Scripture so that there be no confusion and no deceptive spirit or wrong teaching may creep in."

11. The repeated statement includes "repentance, godly sorrow for sin, confession of sin, forsaking sinful ways, restitution, justification, sanctification, baptism with the Holy Ghost, and healing." Robeck, *Azusa Street Mission and Revival*, 119–23, notes that Seymour made the statement of faith at the mission available as a one-sided flyer (date unknown; cf. reprint, 120). The flyer contained an additional section than that printed in *The Apostolic Faith* which included a list of "Steps into Heaven," the final ones being: "Redemption—Dead Raised; Living Changed in a moment; the one, true Glorious Church set in order; Adoption; Perfect Bodies; Glorification." In 1915, Seymour published *The Doctrines and Discipline of the Azusa Street Apostolic Faith Mission*, in which brief statements of belief concerning eschatology are included, but within *The Apostolic Faith* papers, this was not done. Even in *Doctrines and Discipline*, the statements are not comprehensive, as they are focused on the immortality of the soul and the final state.

Within the holistic worldview presented in *The Apostolic Faith,* the new understanding of, and experience in, the Holy Spirit was linked closely with eschatology.[12] The present work of the Spirit was understood to be the fulfillment of the "latter rain," characterized as "the last days when He is pouring out His Spirit upon all flesh."[13] Historically, then, participants at Azusa Street located themselves "in the evening of the dispensation of the Holy Ghost" (the day of Pentecost being "the morning"). As John the Baptist warned people to prepare the way of the Lord, so "the voice of warning is going out to the world today to prepare for the Second Coming of the Lord Jesus Christ."[14] Thomas Hezmalhalch wrote, "How we rejoice at the hope, each day bringing to us a deeper experience and a brighter assurance that we, ourselves, will never see the grave! His approach is so nigh at hand, one almost thinks they can hear the songs of the angels who are to accompany Him in His coming. Without a shadow of a doubt, we are living in the latter days and that "Latter Rain" is being poured upon us . . ."[15]

The primary message or "burden," which the Holy Spirit was understood to be bringing to the church, was "that Jesus is coming soon and we must prepare to meet Him."[16] Indeed, it was frequently reported that messages in tongues from around the world were being interpreted as "Jesus is coming soon."[17] The very fact that people all across the world were seeking God for the baptism of the Holy Spirit indicated that "the Lord is preparing His people for His soon coming."[18] The testimony of A. H. Post concludes:

> Surely the glorious coming of our blessed Lord is very near, and
> all this supernatural work of God is needed for the work to be

12. Eschatology was only one area of belief subjected to rethinking in the light of the outpouring of the Spirit. Alexander, *Pentecostal Healing,* 78–79, notes that a similar process was occurring in relation to healing.

13. *AF* 1.3 (Nov 1906), 2.

14. *AF* 1.2 (Oct 1906), 3.

15. *AF* 1.9 (Jun–Sep 1907), 4.

16. *AF* 2.13 (May 1908), 4. Cf. the testimony of E. C. Ladd, *AF* 1.6 (Feb–Mar 1907), 3: "The burden of the Spirit seems to be the blindness of the people, the soon coming of the Lord, the awful judgments that are coming, and to prepare messengers and a bride for His coming."

17. *AF* 1.1 (Sep 1906), 1; 1.7 (Apr 1907), 1; 1.8 (May 1907), 3; 1.11 (Oct 1907), 3; 2.13 (May 1908), 4.

18. *AF* 1.4 (Dec 1906), 1.

completed. This is only the beginning of the gracious latter rain, which our risen Lord will pour out upon all flesh, and as the Holy Spirit shall temper each vessel meet for service, He will fully restore all the gifts, or rather manifest each as needed. For all is inherent in Himself, and all thus baptized will indeed be one. The Holy Spirit is now leading us into much prayerful study of His Word. He makes Christ increasingly all in all, the flesh nothing, God's children one, and the coming of the Lord increasingly real. Beloved, don't criticize, but join us in prayer.[19]

The holistic spirituality at the Azusa Street mission had a Christological foundation and focus. According to Seymour, the benefits of the atonement included "justification, sanctification, healing, and baptism with the Holy Ghost."[20] Eschatological concerns were also brought under the umbrella of Christology. Significantly, the only inclusion of eschatological concerns within a list of beliefs in *The Apostolic Faith* appears under the heading: "The principles of the doctrine of Christ." The list includes:

1. Repentance

2. Faith in our Lord and Savior Jesus Christ

3. Water baptism

4. Sanctification

5. The baptism with the Holy Spirit

6. Second coming of our Lord Jesus Christ

7. Final white throne judgment[21]

The preaching of Christ's birth, death, resurrection and Second Coming was naturally extended to include, "His reigning in His millennial kingdom, and His white throne judgment, and then the new heavens and earth and the New Jerusalem coming down from God out of heaven, when He shall have put all enemies under His feet and He shall reign eternally, and we shall abide with Him forever and ever."[22]

19. *AF* 1.5 (Jan 1907), 2.

20. *AF* 1.1 (Sep 1906), 2.

21. *AF* 1.11 (Oct 1907), 4.

22. *AF* 1.6 (Oct 1907), 7.

The following testimony of a reader from England reveals a similar integration of eschatology within Christology—expressed in a holistic spirituality, "On the evening of our next united gathering for prayer and waiting, revelation after revelation was given of the Lamb; the glory of the Lamb, the power of the Lamb, the victory of the Lamb, the marriage supper of the Lamb, and the reign of the Lamb with His glorified bride. I knew from that moment that Christ Jesus was on the throne of my heart as the Lamb slain from the foundation of the world, and that His purpose was to demonstrate the Lamb's life through me."[23]

THE BRIDE OF CHRIST AND THE MARRIAGE SUPPER

The most frequent and consistently applied biblical metaphor used in reference to the Second Coming of Jesus in *The Apostolic Faith* was that of the bride of Christ viewed in the contexts of the parable of the ten virgins (Matt 25:1–13) and the marriage supper of the Lamb (Rev 19:9). This complex of images provided a comprehensive framework within which to connect the new understanding of the baptism in the Holy Spirit, the spiritual experiences of the believer, and anticipated future fulfillment. In the eschatology of Azusa Street, the baptism in the Holy Spirit was "the real type" of the "double portion" of oil obtained by the wise virgins in the parable of the ten virgins. Thus, only those who were baptized in the Spirit were thought to be prepared to meet the coming Bridegroom and attend the marriage supper.[24] A. G. Johnson wrote, "Please tell the saints of the Lord that Christ is coming soon and that the time is very short. Jesus is looking for His bride, a few out from the body, the church, the chosen ones, the first fruits to God and unto the Lamb, the wise virgins who have oil in their vessels with their lamps."[25] Mrs. T. M. Rist reported a vision in which she was handed a dazzling garment and understood it to be "the wedding garment." She noted, "It was revealed to me that this 'latter rain' was getting people ready for the

---

23. *AF* 1.11 (Oct 1907), 2. Cf. *AF* 1.6 (Feb–Mar 1907), 7.

24. Seymour makes this clear in *AF* 1.5 (Jan 1907), 2: "Dearly beloved, the only people that will meet our Lord and Savior Jesus Christ and go with Him into the marriage supper of the Lamb, are the wise virgins—not only saved and sanctified, with pure and clean hearts, but having the baptism with the Holy Ghost. The others we find will not be prepared. They have some oil in their lamps but they have not the double portion of His Holy Spirit." Cf. *AF* 1.3 (Nov 1906), 4; 1.6 (Feb–Mar 1907), 6.

25. *AF* 1.5 (Jan, 1907), 3.

'Marriage Supper of the Lamb,' and this is the time when the wise virgins are getting the oil in their vessels with their lamps."[26] Membership in the bride of Christ and participation in the marriage supper were not merely theological labels, but were integral to the lived reality of those who professed Spirit baptism. Lillian Garr noted, "He longs for a bride who shares both His sufferings and joy. I want to enter into His own heart and feel as He felt, letting His joy be my joy, His sorrow my sorrow."[27] Similarly, G. B. Cashwell closed a letter to the readers of *The Apostolic Faith* with the words, "I long to see you all in life, but if not I will meet you at the marriage supper of the Lamb."[28]

In an article entitled, "Behold the Bridegroom Cometh!" based upon Matt 25:1–13, the bride of Christ metaphor (wise virgins-oil-marriage supper) is central in William Seymour's explanation of the sequence of future events. I quote at length:

> Christ is speaking in this parable about the church and its condition at His coming. Many precious souls today are not looking for the return of their Lord, and they will be found in the same condition as the five foolish virgins. . . . They think they have enough [oil]. They have some of God's love in their souls, but they have not the double portion of it. The thing they need is oil in their vessels with their lamps. It is just as plain as can be. Dearly beloved, the Scripture says, "Blessed are they which are called to the marriage supper of the Lamb." Rev 19:9. So they are blessed that have the call. Those that will be permitted to enter in are those who are justified, sanctified, and filled with the Holy Ghost—sealed unto the day of redemption. O may God stir up His waiting bride everywhere to get oil in their vessels with their lamps that they may enter into the marriage supper . . . Those that are not ready at the rapture will be left to go through the awful tribulation that is coming upon the earth. The wise virgins will be at the marriage supper and spend the time of the great tribulation with the Lord Jesus . . . It seems that people will be able to buy oil during the rapture. It seems that the Spirit will still be here on earth and that they could get it, but it will be too late for the marriage supper . . . Those that get left in the rapture and still prove faithful to God and do not receive the mark of the beast, though they will have to suffer martyrdom, will be raised to reign with Christ . . . But we

26. *AF* 1.10 (Sep, 1907), 4.

27. *AF* 1.9 (Jun–Sep, 1907), 4.

28. *AF* 1.8 (May, 1907), 1.

that are caught up to the marriage supper of the Lamb will escape
the plagues that are coming on the earth. [29]

An unsigned article that shares many characteristics with Seymour's
signed contributions continues these thoughts,[30] adding that "nothing
but holy people will meet the Lord Jesus in the skies, when He comes in
the rapture."[31]

If the baptism of the Holy Spirit was discerned to be the identifying
mark of the bride of Christ, this means that sanctification, Spirit-baptism,
and the anticipation of attending the bridal supper were integrated within a continuum of spiritual experience. This integration was supported
by means of language used consistently within the periodical, denoting
spiritual experience in terms of direction: sanctification required *"going
down"* into spiritual humility, forsaking all claims of self-identity; Spirit-
baptism resulted from *"coming through"* into a new spiritual identity, thus
becoming a member of the bride of Christ; and future hope anticipated
"rising up" into spiritual fulfillment to meet the Lord in the air to go to
the marriage supper.

BAPTISM IN THE SPIRIT AS THE SEAL OF GOD IN THE FOREHEAD

Another prominent image used in *The Apostolic Faith* to refer to the
baptism in the Holy Spirit is that of the seal of God in the forehead.[32]
In a clear reference to Rev 7:1–3, Seymour wrote, "I am so glad that the
Lord is holding back the winds until the angel has sealed all of the saints
of the living God in their foreheads, the baptism of the Holy Ghost."[33]

---

29. *AF* 1.5 (Jan 1907), 2.

30. Robeck, *Azusa Street Mission and Revival*, 116–19, notes that several unsigned
contributions to *The Apostolic Faith* may indeed have originated from the hand of
Seymour.

31. *AF* 1.10 (Sep 1907), 4. In a clear example of the discerning process, the author
notes, "Those that have no light on the baptism with the Holy Ghost but were sanctified
will have part in the first resurrection." This implies that once a person knows about
Spirit baptism, he or she is responsible to receive it in order to attend the marriage
supper.

32. *AF* 1.4 (Dec 1906), 2; 1.5 (Jan 1907), 2; 1.6 (Feb–Mar 1907), 1, 6; 1.9 (Jun–Sep
1907), 1, 4; 2.13 (Jan 1908), 2.

33. *AF* 1.9 (Jun–Sep 1907), 4; Cf. also *AF* 1.5 (Jan 1907), 2: "The Holy Ghost is sifting
out a people that are getting on the robes of righteousness and the seal in their foreheads. The angel is holding the winds now till all the children of God are sealed in their
foreheads with the Father's name. Then the wrath of God is going to be poured out."

Likening Spirit baptism to the writing of God upon the stone tablets
stored in the holy of holies, one unidentified writer commented, "When
we are baptized with the Holy Spirit we are sealed in the forehead until His coming."[34] Consistent with other aspects of spirituality at Azusa
Street, this sealing was not understood positionally (as a kind of eternal
security), but experientially (as a mark of character): "This oil keeps us
pure and sweet and preserved. He also seals you with the Holy Spirit
of God unto the day of redemption. Eph 4:30. He seals you to keep
anything from getting in that would sour or embitter."[35] Another writer
added, "God wants you to wear this seal, and not the badges of men and
devils."[36] Having been sealed, the waiting bride will be snatched away to
the marriage supper. Then, "the awful black night of tribulation as the
black night of Egypt will come upon all the world."[37]

The writer of an unsigned article entitled, "Full Overcomers—Rev.
14,"[38] expanded this complex of images to include the "man child" of
Rev 12 and the 144,000 of Rev 14. In an apparent symbolic treatment
of the number, the 144,000 that appear with the Lamb on Mount Zion
(Rev 14:1) are identified as "full overcomers" who were ready to go in
the rapture with Christ to the marriage supper. As the bride of Christ,
they are "represented" as the "man child" who came from the church and
are "caught up" to the throne of God (Rev 12:5).[39] Continuing in Rev 14,
the writer concludes that this group is sanctified, for "they are virgins;"
they are filled with the Holy Spirit, for "they follow the Lamb" (v. 4); and
they are kept from evil, for they "are without fault before the throne of
God" (v. 5). Only the "full overcomers," that is "those that are washed in
the Blood, made holy and sealed with the Holy Spirit of promise" will be
"ready for the rapture." The time of tribulation following the "catching
away of the bride," will be characterized by the preaching of the gospel

34. *AF* 1.4 (Dec 1906), 2.

35. *AF* 1.6 (Feb–Mar 1907), 7.

36. *AF* 1.9 (Jun–Sep 1907), 1. The writer identifies "badges of men and devils" with
human–made creeds and worldly associations.

37. *AF* 1.9 (Jun–Sep 1907), 4.

38. *AF* 1.12 (Jan 1908), 2. Although it is unsigned, this article shares many stylistic
characteristics with other articles attributed to William Seymour.

39. Another reference to the church bringing forth the "man child" also appears
in *AF* 1.11 (Oct 1907), 4. It may be noted that this view was maintained by Charles F.
Parham and is also found in various other early Pentecostal periodicals as well.

to all nations (v. 6).[40] Although not present at the marriage supper of the Lamb, those who are faithful to Jesus and do not bow down to the Antichrist during the tribulation will receive spiritual protection. The writer draws from Rev 12:6 to conclude that during the tribulation, "the Lord will feed the church and protect her from the face of the serpent." The church is warned in Rev 14:9–11 that those who worship the beast will be "tormented day and night;" but it is encouraged in verses 12–13 that those who keep the faith unto death will be blessed.

SUFFERING AND REIGNING

Azusa Street believers used another broad stroke of thought to connect present reality with the anticipated future beyond the marriage supper and tribulation: suffering in the present is prerequisite to reigning with Christ in the future. To suffer with Christ means to "bear all things and keep the faith of Jesus in our hearts."[41] According to a written prophecy by Mary Galmond, Christians are to prepare for wars, pestilences, floods, and earthquakes, and to be ready for the coming of the Lord. She wrote, "The time is coming when the poor will be oppressed and the Christians can neither buy nor sell unless they have 'the mark of the beast,' which mark she associated with labor unions."[42] Seymour believed that only the faithful who overcome "the world, the flesh, and the devil" would be worthy to reign "on this earth with our Lord."[43] One exhortation enjoins, "Our reigning time will come when Jesus comes in great power from the throne. Until then we are to be beaten, to be spit upon, and mocked. We are to be like His son."[44]

40. In an apparent effort to discern the meaning of Rev 14:6, the writer commented, "It *seems* that after the rapture, or catching away of the bride, that the Gospel will still be preached on the earth to the people that will be left and were not ready to go in to the marriage supper" (emphasis mine).

41. *AF* 1.11 (Oct 1907), 3.

42. *AF* 1.2 (Oct 1906), 2. Galmond predicted that the lack of food for the poor will cause rioting and bloodshed. The imagery in her prophecy echoes that of Rev 14:17–20. Seymour, *AF* 1.12 (Jan 1908), 2, mentions the mark of the beast in reference to the time of tribulation after the rapture, at which time many Christians that are not taken to the marriage supper will be martyred for resisting the Antichrist. In an article concerning the spiritual condition of married persons and parents, Seymour treats the tribulation of Matt 24:19–21 as a reference to the destruction of Jerusalem in 70 CE, and Christ's concern for mothers during that event. Cf. *AF* 1.12 (Jan 1908), 3.

43. *AF* 1.11 (Oct 1907), 3.

44. *AF* 1.9 (Jun–Sep 1907), 2.

The metaphor of reigning with Christ dominates the descriptions of the millennium and beyond. Those who are ready at the rapture will come back with Christ on white horses to help him execute judgment on the earth and make way for the millennial kingdom. The millennium will be a time of reigning with Christ "over unglorified humanity" for "a thousand years in a jubilee of peace."[45] In the millennium, the bride will "sit with the glorified Christ in His throne as His queen, the Lamb's wife," helping him rule "this old world . . . when righteousness shall cover the earth as waters cover the sea. Then afterwards at the white throne judgment, we shall sit with Him and judge the world. Then after the new heavens and new earth, when He shall have delivered up the kingdom into the Father's hands, we shall reign with Him throughout eternity. O beloved, are you ready?"[46]

OLD TESTAMENT TYPOLOGY

Several passages from the Old Testament were treated in *The Apostolic Faith* as "types" or prefigures of the full salvation of the bride of Christ and of Christ's coming. In an article by William Seymour entitled, "Rebecca, Type of the Bride of Christ–Gen 24," the search of Eliezer to find a bride for Isaac among Abraham's kindred typifies the search of the Holy Spirit for a bride for Christ "among His brethren, the sanctified."[47] Seymour concludes, "Now we are living in the eventide of this dispensation, when the Holy Spirit is leading us, Christ's bride, to meet Him in the clouds."

An unsigned article, "Old Testament Feasts Fulfilled in Our Souls Today," explains that the four feasts of the Old Testament "typify complete salvation."[48] Passover, First Fruits, and Pentecost are types of justification, sanctification, and the Spirit baptism, respectively. The Feast of Trumpets, as the "feast of the full harvest" "typifies the coming and reigning of our Lord and Savior, Jesus Christ, when He shall spread the tabernacle and feed us."[49]

Noah's ark is also viewed as "a type of the coming of Jesus." One writer explained, "Just as when the flood arose, the people of God were

45. *AF* 1.5 (Jan 1907), 2.

46. *AF* 1.10 (Sep 1907), 4. Note that the focus here is on the future experiences of the bride of Christ.

47. *AF* 1.6 (Feb–Mar 1907), 2.

48. *AF* 1.9 (Jun–Sep 1907), 2.

49. *AF* 1.9 (Jun–Sep 1907), 2.

lifted by the ark toward the sky, so when Jesus Christ, who is our Ark, shall appear, we shall also appear with Him in glory. Then as the ark came back and rested on Mt. Arrarat, so when the Lord Jesus comes back, we shall stand with Him on Mt. Olivet. Christ comes and gets His saints before the great tribulation, which corresponds with the flood. The same conditions are prevailing now as in the days of Noah. (Matt 24:37)."[50]

APOCALYPTIC SPIRITUALITY AND THE FORETASTE OF THE FUTURE

The holistic worldview of the Azusa Street participants may be called apocalyptic in that the realms of heaven and earth were often perceived to be intermingled. While they certainly believed in heaven as a future state, they also experienced an immediate sense of "heaven below."[51] Nellie Burnwell wrote, "It is heaven to go to heaven in."[52] G. B. Cashwell testified, "Heaven seems to be nearer every day. I hear the music. I see the city."[53] Another participant testified, "These great blessings have come upon the lowly and humble. Many have seen visions of Jesus and of heavenly fire and the interpretations speak of the soon coming of Jesus."[54] Maggie Geddis reported a vision of "the New Jerusalem coming down out of heaven, and the rainbow-encircled throne, just a portion of that given in Revelation."[55] A vision of hell convinced Thomas Junk that hell is a literal place, and that he should preach it that way.[56] Two believers in Minneapolis reported receiving identical visions of "the New Jerusalem, the table spread, and many of the saints there."[57] Such visions were usually accompanied by exhortations to be prepared for Jesus' coming.

---

50. *AF* 1.9 (Jun–Sep 1907), 4. Noah's ark is also treated as a type of the rapture in the article, "Full Overcomers," noted above, that appeared in *AF* 1.12 (Jan 1908), 2.

51. *AF* 1.4 (Dec 1906), 2. Another writer commented that "heaven and earth came together" in a recent baptismal service. *AF* 1.2 (Oct 1906), 4.

52. *AF* 1.6 (Feb–Mar 1907), 8.

53. *AF* 1.7 (Apr 1907), 4.

54. *AF* 2.13 (May 1908), 1.

55. *AF* 1.6 (Feb–Mar 1907), 4.

56. *AF* 1.3 (Nov 1906), 4. Junk spoke of hell as a warning to "those who scorn this holiness and baptism," including religious people. Annihilation was repudiated because in the story of Lazarus and the rich man, the rich man was not burned up in hell, but was "tormented by this flame." Cf. *AF* 1.4 (Dec 1906), 1; 1.6 (Feb–Mar 1907), 2.

57. *AF* 1.11 (Oct 1907), 4.

Visions and dreams were also subject to the discerning process of being "tried" or "proven" by Scripture.[58]

Within such an apocalyptic spirituality, images in the book of Revelation, such as the river of life and leaves for healing in Rev 22:1–2, were sometimes used to describe present spiritual experiences.[59] The terminology found in Alberta Hall's testimony is commonplace in *The Apostolic Faith*: "The third night I lay under the power of God for about three hours. I was drunk on *the wine of the kingdom*" (emphasis mine).[60] Such present kingdom language is most often associated with the baptism of the Holy Spirit as "the earnest of our inheritance" or as "a foretaste of heaven." Concerning Spirit baptism, one writer commented, "People do not have to travail and agonize for the baptism, for when our work ceases then God comes. We cease from our own works, which is the very type of the millennium."[61] Joseph Grainger looked back to the time he spent at Azusa Street as "a foretaste of the glad millennial day."[62]

POWER FOR THE PRESENT MISSION

This apocalyptic vision impelled the recipients on a world-wide mission to spread the "full gospel" message because "the time is short."[63] The global aspect of the mission was captured in the following announcement, "One token of the Lord's coming is that He is melting all races and nations together, and they are filled with the power and glory of God. He is baptizing by one spirit into one body and making up a people that will be ready to meet Him when He comes."[64] *The Apostolic Faith* quickly became an international paper as reports of revival from across the nation and from other countries such as England, Sweden, India, Norway, and Africa were published.[65] In an interesting reference to Rev 10:1–7, the

58. *AF* 1.6 (Feb–Mar 1907), 1.

59. *AF* 1.4 (Dec 1906), 1. To partake of the fruit of the tree of life, the believer is encouraged to "launch out by faith into the river."

60. *AF* 1.6 (Feb–Mar 1907), 8.

61. *AF* 1.11 (Oct 1907), 1.

62. *AF* 1.12 (Jan 1908), 4.

63. *AF* 1.1 (Sep 1906), 1.

64. *AF* 1.6 (Feb–Mar, 1907), 7.

65. The staff of *The Apostolic Faith* viewed the paper as an evangelistic tool. See *AF* 1.3, 3: "This Gospel must go, for the time is short. . . . As workers cannot get to the fields fast enough, the Lord is using the paper." Alexander, *Pentecostal Healing*, 70–72,

commission of those who were Spirit-baptized to evangelize the world would not cease "till the angel stands with one foot on the land and one on the sea and declares that time shall no longer be."[66] In a paraphrase of Matt 24:14, the editor of *The Apostolic Faith* summarized it best: "This Gospel, the full Gospel of Jesus must be preached in all the earth for a witness then shall the end come."[67]

CONCLUSION

This brief overview of *The Apostolic Faith* has highlighted the holistic nature of Pentecostal spirituality as the starting point of the study of eschatology within early Pentecostalism. Eschatology, along with many other issues, was caught up into an intense discerning process in the light of the outpouring of the Spirit. Eschatology became essential to their philosophy of history as adherents viewed the early twentieth-century outpouring as "the latter rain," creating time boundaries for a "Holy Ghost dispensation." More than anything, the outpouring at Azusa Street signaled the soon return of Jesus. Within this large framework, baptism in the Holy Spirit was discerned to be the defining mark of membership in the bride of Christ. Using the parable of the ten virgins (Matt 25:1–13) and the marriage supper of the Lamb (Rev 19:9) as controlling metaphors, the earliest Pentecostal witnesses weaved eschatology into their daily experience of the Spirit by envisioning a continuum of spiritual advancement: justification, sanctification, Spirit-baptism, marriage supper of the Lamb, reigning with Christ in the millennium and afterward for eternity. The secondary metaphor of Spirit baptism as the seal of God in the forehead (Rev 7:1–3) and the consequent identification of the bride of Christ with the sealing of the 144,000 (Rev 14:1–5) supported the primary vision by providing a complementary image consistent with the first: the experience of baptism in the Spirit had personal eschatological significance. Moreover, the apocalyptic nature of Spirit baptism had multiple ramifications. Being viewed as a foretaste of Christ's coming

---

describes the importance of publishing in early Pentecostalism, especially as a means of spiritual formation.

66. *AF* 1.9 (Jun–Sep 1907), 2. The writer does not comment further, leaving the question open as to whether this was a general reference to "the end of time," or whether the angel's appearance will signal the rapture of the bride.

67. *AF* 1.10 (Sep 1907), 1.

kingdom, it also meant that the kingdom was near. Thus, the time was short to do the work of global evangelism.

This assessment of eschatology in the earliest of the Pentecostal written sources calls into question previous historical analyses, which posit that early Pentecostal eschatology was merely a modification of classical dispensationalism.[68] In the light of *The Apostolic Faith*, this clearly is not the case. The alleged connections between classical dispensationalism and the eschatology articulated here are transformed in the light of the holistic and apocalyptic nature of early Pentecostal spirituality.[69] First, the Old Testament was not compartmentalized but was viewed as a rich source of texts that "typified" early Pentecostal soteriology and eschatology. Second, the images in the book of Revelation were not relegated to the future, but had contemporary importance for the spirituality of the believer. Third, the teaching of the rapture was not primary but was molded by the bride of Christ complex of metaphors mentioned above, becoming supplementary to the event of the marriage supper. Fourth, the church was not defined in terms of its distinction from Israel but was seen as the group from which the bride of Christ would emerge. Though

68. Bass, *Backgrounds to Dispensationalism*, 18, lists the following distinguishing features of classical dispensationalism: "its view of the nature and purpose of a dispensation; a rigidly held applied literalism in the interpretation of Scripture; a dichotomy between Israel and the church; a restricted [parenthetical or intercalational] view of the church; a Jewish concept of the kingdom [fulfillment of promises to Abraham]; a postponement of the kingdom [not fulfilled in the church]; a distinction between law and grace that creates a multiple basis for God's dealing with man; a compartmentalization of Scripture; a pre-tribulation rapture; its view of the purpose of the great tribulation [to gather the remnant of Israel]; its view of the nature of the millennial reign of Christ [to fulfill the Jewish kingdom]; its view of the eternal state, and its view of the apostate nature of Christendom [separatism]."

69. My conclusions here support those of Dayton, *Theological Roots of Pentecostalism*, 146–47. The eschatology of early Pentecostalism is not a non-critical assimilation of classical dispensational categories, for the following reasons: (1) the emphasis on the "latter rain" and "restoration of spiritual gifts" does not fit within the dispensational categories that easily; (2) Pentecostalism generally adopted different periodizations of history (tripartite) than the classic dispensational model; and (3) the biblical hermeneutic of Pentecostals allowed the application of OT promises and several NT texts directly to the church (sermon on the mount, etc.), which dispensationalists relegate to the millennium. Rather, Dayton proposes that Pentecostal eschatology is a parallel development (or occasionally an antecedent) to the rise of dispensationalism, with common dynamics and much intermingling. Furthermore, he indicates that the eschatology of the holiness and ethnically defined branches of Pentecostalism show less dependence upon dispensational categories.

excluded from the marriage supper, the church would continue in the care of Jesus during the tribulation. Fifth, the millennium was not viewed as a fulfillment of promises to the Jews but was characterized as a time when faithful Christians who suffered now would reign with Christ and help judge the world. Immersed in a different worldview, Pentecostals of Azusa Street did not merely modify the script of dispensationalism, but departed from it significantly.

7

Eschatology, Spirit Baptism, and Inclusiveness

An Exploration into the Hallmarks
of a Pentecostal Social Ethic

MURRAY W. DEMPSTER

THE OVERALL PURPOSE OF my chapter is to develop a Christian social ethic that provides a theological and ethical rationale for the Pentecostal church to carry on its mission of blending together the tasks of evangelism, strengthening the church's own congregational life in worship and *koinonia*, and creating social ministries for people both inside and outside the church, which promote human welfare, social justice, and personal dignity. This wholistic vision of church mission and ministry is designed to affirm the growing sense of Christian social concern among Pentecostals in the various sectors of the movement, which has generated an increasing number of social programs designed to minister the full gospel to the whole person. These various social programs often exist, however, as awkward appendages to—and in some quarters as an unwelcome distortion of—the church's "priority" task of world evangelization.

Biblical eschatology organized around a dispensational framework, as it has existed in Pentecostal understanding, is a major, perhaps the major, theological factor that has sparked and perpetuated the controversy over the social involvement of the church. In contrast, I aim to demonstrate that belief in the triumphant return of Jesus Christ, when it is grounded in Jesus' own mission, ministry, and message about the kingdom of God, actually entails an eschatological warrant and a moral mandate for the church's engagement with society. Further, I will argue that the moral character of God's coming reign, proclaimed by Jesus as the basis of his own mission and ministry, identifies the ethical principles to construct a social ethic to guide the church's engagement in social service and social transformation.

After a brief discussion of the connection between eschatology and world evangelism in Pentecostalism, and its neglect in developing a social ethic, I will identify the mission and ministry of the church portrayed in Luke-Acts by exploring the Pentecost/kingdom connection, but with an eye to the synoptic gospels. For Luke, Jesus' eschatology of the kingdom was central to his mission, ministry, and message. Based on the eschatological portrayal of the kingdom by Jesus, the corresponding social ethics of the kingdom will be developed as a theological and ethical basis for the church's social engagement within a wholistic approach to church mission.

ESCHATOLOGICAL MOTIVATION FOR WORLD EVANGELISM IN EARLY PENTECOSTAL MISSIOLOGY

Pentecostals typically make a connection between the empowerment of Spirit baptism and eschatological urgency for the church's global mission to spread the gospel. Pentecostal leaders highlighted Peter's reference to Joel's prophecy in his sermon from Acts 2, which explained the outpouring of the Spirit on the Day of Pentecost (especially vv. 17–18). They also deftly connected Peter's quote from Joel's prophecy in Acts with various other Old Testament prophetic verses, which distinguished between the time of "the latter rain" and "the former rain" in the cycle of the annual agrarian harvest. By such a hermeneutical arrangement of biblical texts, Pentecostals portrayed the coming of the Spirit in the upper room in Jerusalem as "the former rain" and the coming of the Spirit at the Azusa Street Mission in Los Angeles as "the latter rain." As a consequence of this logic, Pentecostals believed that "the latter rain" outpouring of the Spirit at Azusa Street and beyond was a telltale "sign" of the impending return of Jesus Christ.[1] Robert Mapes Anderson noted that given the repeatable experiential nature of Spirit baptism—with its fillings and

---

1. For example, see Myland, "Latter day Lectures," *The Latter Rain Evangel* 1 (May 1909) through 2 (October 1909), later published in *The Latter Rain Covenant and Pentecostal Power*.

refillings—the eschatological fervor of the Pentecostal movement at its beginnings seemed to rival the New Testament church.[2]

Pentecostal missiologist L. Grant McClung, Jr., has noted that the premillennial dispensational belief in the imminent return of Jesus Christ coupled with the experience of Spirit baptism for empowerment of believers to "Go into all the world and preach the gospel to all creation" (Mark 16:15) combined to forge a potent motivational force for world evangelism. Based on his missiological analysis of the early formative years of the twentieth-century Pentecostal movement, McClung draws this conclusion, "Eschatological urgency is at the heart of understanding the missionary fervor of early Pentecostalism."[3] Pentecostal historian Dwight J. Wilson concurred with McClung in his analysis of the role of eschatology in motivating global evangelism. He made the additional insightful observation that the premillennial dispensational eschatology of early Pentecostalism also unwittingly promoted a withdrawal of the church from social involvement, because such social concern might sidetrack the church from its priority of evangelistic mission. Wilson characterized the impact of premillennial dispensational eschatology in forming the predominant Pentecostal mindset on social ministry: "Since the end is near, they are indifferent to social change and have rejected the reformist methods of the optimistic postmillennialists and have concentrated on 'snatching brands from the fire' and letting social reforms result from humankind being born again."[4] Eschatological intensity, therefore, had the *manifest* function of inspiring the Pentecostal church to Spirit-empowered evangelism; but as Wilson noted, belief in the imminent return of Jesus Christ had the *latent* function of producing within the Pentecostal movement a spirit of social quietism.

Ironies emerge when the practical ministries of the Pentecostal churches from the early years to the present, especially in the ministries of the movement's missionary force, are compared with the theological rationale for an eschatological-driven focus on evangelism. The first irony is that the eschatologically driven focus on evangelism did not

2. Anderson marshals considerable historical evidence to support his thesis that belief in an imminent, apocalyptic return of Christ was the unifying concept in a Pentecostal world view. *Vision of the Disinherited*, 79–97. See also Wilson, "Eschatology, Pentecostal Perspectives on," 267.

3. McClung, "Missiology," 607.

4. Wilson, "Eschatology, Pentecostal Perspectives on," 267. Cf. Sheppard, "Pentecostalism and the Hermeneutics of Dispensationalism," 5–33.

keep ministers at home and abroad from developing social programs. Despite the eschatological beliefs at the theological level, church leaders at the practical level who ministered at home in decaying urban centers or abroad in various geographical regions marked by hunger, disease, and poverty developed social programs to meet human need. From the early days of the movement, church leaders established orphanages, hospices, rescue homes, and lepersariums as expressions of Christian compassion for the homeless, the poor, the hungry, and the outcasts of society. In more recent times, social programs have expanded beyond social welfare programs to include involvement designed to change the unjust social conditions that perpetuate human ills such as poverty and hunger.[5]

A second irony is related to the success the Pentecostal movement has enjoyed in world evangelism, which has been spawned by eschatological fervor and Spirit-empowerment. By some estimates the movement has now grown to an estimated five hundred million adherents worldwide in only about a century of time.[6] The irony is that the astonishing growth of the movement with its global mobility has brought church leaders into contact with the world's political, economic, and social ills, as well as its structural injustices. Witnessing to God's love through a proclamation of salvation without addressing human need had the hollow ring of a truncated gospel. Responding to human need within a global context with its various cultural matrixes became a practical component in gaining a hearing for the "good news" of God's salvation and has generated a staggering proliferation of social programs in all sectors of the Pentecostal movement. These programs aimed at social service and social change have been part of the untold story that has fostered Pentecostal growth around the world.[7]

---

5. See my Presidential Address, "Christian Social Concern in Pentecostal Perspective," that highlighted the various ministries of social concern in three of the largest Pentecostal denominations. The expansion of social ministry documented in the presentation represented the proliferation of social programs among Pentecostals.

6. The estimation of growth of the Pentecostal movement on a global scale is reported by Barrett in every January issue of the *International Bulletin of Missionary Research (IBMR)*.

7. To provide an analysis of this growth of social concern within the Pentecostal movement, I had the privilege of guest editing a special theme issue, "Church Mission and Social Concern" in *Transformation*, 1–33.

A third irony is the fact that after multiple decades of proliferating social programs within the Pentecostal movement, missionaries and other church leaders were still receiving mixed signals about the biblical and theological validity of ministries of social service and social transformation as part of the integral mission of the church. The Pentecostal church remained a house divided.[8] Division regarding social ministry is clearly illustrated in back-to-back editorials in *Mountain Movers*, the missions magazine of the Assemblies of God. On one side of the divide is the view that concentrating efforts on social programs gets the evangelistic mandate of the church off track. In light of the premillennial dispensational character of Pentecostal eschatology the church's task should be focused on evangelism of the lost before the Second Coming of Jesus.[9] On the other side of the divide is the view that the church's involvement in social service and social transformation is justified because Jesus himself engaged in social ministry to the needy.[10] Neither position seeks to integrate evangelism and social concern into a wholistic approach to church mission. Yet all ministry expressions of the church—whether designed to evangelize, to nurture congregational life, or reach out in service and programmatic action to the hurting and oppressed—need to be rooted in, and give expression to, the church's mission.[11]

Mission is the benchmark for the determination of ministry. Only when the church's multiple and diverse ministry programs are authenti-

8. This lack of an integrated sense of evangelism and social concern in Pentecostal church mission within the Assemblies of God led to a Consultation of the Division of Foreign Missions of the Assemblies of God in Brussels, Belgium on May 27–31, 1998. The purpose was to address the "gap" between compassionate outreach and evangelism by developing an understanding of the biblical foundations to guide these efforts. The mandate was to develop a coherent theological stance integrating biblical concepts with the church's evangelistic efforts and its ministries of social concern. The consensus document, "Brussels Statement on Evangelization and Social Concern" was produced by the Brussels Consultation of the Division of Foreign Missions of the AG. Sadly, the Brussels Statement was never used by the Division of Foreign Missions. The "Brussels Statement" as well as two of the papers and responses presented at the consultation were published in a special issue, "A Pentecostal Approach to Evangelization and Social Concern," in *Transformation*, 41–66.

9. "Sidetracked!" 3.

10. Hogan, "Because Jesus Did," 10–11.

11. Orlando Costas persuasively argues that "The true test of mission is not whether we proclaim, make disciples or engage in social, economic and political liberation, but whether we are capable of integrating all three in a comprehensive, dynamic and consistent witness." Costas, *Integrity of Mission*, 75.

cally related to church mission will there be integrity and wholeness in the church's witness to the world on behalf of Jesus Christ.[12] Theological reflection on ministry and mission needs to be thoroughly grounded in Scripture. For Pentecostals, the Pentecost narrative of Acts is the natural place to begin formulating the rudimentary principles of a biblically based theology of church mission aimed at the integration of social concern with evangelism and discipleship.

TOWARD A PENTECOSTAL WHOLISTIC CHURCH MISSION: THE CONNECTION OF THE EMPOWERMENT OF THE SPIRIT AND THE ESCHATOLOGICAL KINGDOM OF GOD

As noted earlier, today's Pentecostal church took its identity, mission, and ministry from its understanding of the early church's mission and ministry recorded in Luke's Acts. As a consequence, the Pentecostal church of today shared with the apostolic church of Acts the conceptual connection between church mission, the empowerment of the Holy Spirit, and the eschatological hope in Jesus Christ's return. In developing a wholistic approach to church mission, this conceptual pattern honors the past tradition while providing a theological vantage point from which to develop a biblically-based integrated understanding of evangelism, discipleship, and social concern for today's church, and laying the foundation for constructing a Pentecostal social ethic. Recent biblical scholarship on Acts and the synoptic gospels can help us to interpret Luke's theology of church mission accurately within a Pentecostal framework.

12. A watershed event affirming a wholistic approach to church mission and ministry and inviting the development of a Pentecostal social ethic within the AG occurred at the fifty-third General Council, in Florida, 2009. The General Council adopted resolutions to amend the General Council Constitutional Declaration, concerning the reason-for-being of the AG Fellowship by adding an additional priority: *to be a people who demonstrate God's love and compassion for all the world.* The amendment to the Constitution on the Assemblies of God's *raison d'être* was subsequently used in the resolution to amend two of the sixteen articles in the AG Statement of Fundamental Truths. This change is cause for celebration, recognition of the social concern in the ministry of missionaries and church leaders from the beginning of the movement and the denominational leadership in promoting a wholistic approach to church mission and ministry, integrating evangelism, worship, discipleship, and social concern. The challenge now is to design curriculum for theological education that supports the developing Pentecostal social ethic in providing social service for human welfare and social change to bring about social justice. See 2009 Resolutions Committee, *Resolutions Processed for Presentation to the 53rd General Council*, 7–11.

Of particular help in identifying Luke's theology of church mission in Acts is the groundbreaking work of Professor Roger S. Stronstad. Based on his insight that Luke's theology of church mission in Acts is connected to Luke's portrayal of Jesus' mission in his gospel, Stronstad claims that Luke's Gospel and Acts constitute two volumes of a single theological treatise.[13] The mission of the church portrayed in Acts is connected to the mission of Jesus portrayed in Luke's Gospel. Stronstad characterizes Luke's theology as "charismatic" in order to highlight the point that Luke used the theme of the Holy Spirit to bind his Gospel and the Acts together as one story in two volumes. The Gospel focused on the activity of the Holy Spirit in the story of Jesus; the Acts focused on the activity of the Holy Spirit in the early church. At the beginning of Jesus' ministry, the Holy Spirit came upon him and anointed him for his mission; at the beginning of the early church's ministry, the Holy Spirit came upon the disciples and empowered them for their mission. Jesus proclaimed his message, performed his ministry, and accomplished his mission as the "charismatic" Christ; the disciples accomplished their mission and performed their ministry as members of the "charismatic" church.

Given this literary continuity and pneumatological homogeneity between Luke's Gospel and Acts, Stronstad argued that the outpouring of the Holy Spirit at Pentecost had an essential relationship with the prior descent of the Holy Spirit on Jesus at his baptism.[14] Stronstad identifies the following didactic purpose for Luke in his portrayal of the coming of the Holy Spirit on the day of Pentecost, "The Pentecost narrative is the story of the transfer of the charismatic Spirit from Jesus to the disciples. In other words, having become the exclusive bearer of the Holy Spirit at His baptism, Jesus becomes the giver of the Spirit at Pentecost . . . By this transfer of the Spirit, the disciples become the heirs and successors to the earthly charismatic ministry of Jesus; that is, because Jesus has poured out the charismatic Spirit upon them the disciples will continue to do and teach those things which Jesus began to do and teach (Acts 1:1)."[15]

---

13. Stronstad, *Charismatic Theology of St. Luke*, 2–5. The "Pentecost/Kingdom" terminology is shorthand to convey the historical continuity of the coming of the Holy Spirit in Luke's Acts with the kingdom of God as the essential concept that Jesus used to identify his mission in Luke's Gospel and the other synoptic gospels.

14. Ibid., 33–62.

15. Ibid., 49.

Stronstad's concept of "the transfer of the Spirit" needs to be unpacked because of its potential to clarify the eschatological character of Luke's theology of church mission. Transference of the Spirit meant that the early church was anointed to continue Jesus' mission, ministry, and message. At the Pentecost festival, the same Holy Spirit who had earlier anointed and empowered Jesus of Nazareth was outpoured to call out and empower the disciples to form the church in order to perpetuate Jesus' mission, ministry and message. Consequently, Luke made clear in his prologue in Acts that the church continued to do and teach those things which Jesus began to do and teach (Acts 1:1). The eschatological concept of the kingdom of God was the focal point of all those things that Jesus began to do and teach. As Gordon Fee emphasizes, "the universal witness of the synoptic tradition is that the absolutely central theme of Jesus' mission and message was 'the good news of the kingdom of God.'"[16] When the Holy Spirit came upon Jesus, he was anointed to proclaim the gospel of the kingdom and to inaugurate God's right to reign through his ministry. When the Holy Spirit came upon the early church, the disciples were empowered to continue Jesus' mission and ministry of proclaiming the good news of the kingdom in the form of announcing God's reign "in Christ."[17]

The book of Acts when connected with Luke's Gospel makes clear that the mission and ministry of the Church are to replicate the mission and ministry of Jesus through the power of the Holy Spirit. The Pentecost/kingdom connection is essential to understand Luke's own theology of church mission and ministry. To comprehend the mission and ministry of the Spirit-empowered church in Acts requires an understanding of what Jesus meant when he adopted the kingdom of God as the core theological concept to portray his mission, ministry, and message.

Jesus opened his ministry in Galilee with this succinct manifesto, "The time is fulfilled, the kingdom of God is at hand, repent and believe

16. Fee, "The Kingdom of God and the Church's Global Mission," 8.

17. Peter Kuzmič observes that the apostolic proclamation translated the messianic language of the kingdom of God into a "dynamic equivalent" more suited to the broader audience of the early church's preaching, which included both Jews and Gentiles. "Kingdom of God," 525–26. Pomerville notes the change in language is a pivotal transition in salvation history, initiated by the coming of the Holy Spirit in power at Pentecost. See *Third Force in Missions*, 148–57.

the good news." (Mark 1:14–15 = Matt 4:13–17 = Luke 4:14–21).[18] Here are three aspects of Jesus' kingdom teachings and ministry, which are crucial to understand his eschatology and the connection of the eschatological kingdom of God to his ethical teachings and moral responses in the section to follow. First, when Jesus announced that he would inaugurate God's reign again in human history through his ministry, he connected God's kingdom within a framework of history, which divided "this age" and "the age to come" with the Day of the Lord ushering in the reversal in the order of life, a concept popularized by the Jewish apocalyptic. The Day of the Lord will bring an end to human history as we know it and the end of "this age" will be brought about by God's direct intervention through a deliverer, the Son of Man. The Son of Man would descend from heaven with supernatural divine intervention and human history would end in the apocalyptic destruction of the demonically oppressive social order. For the apocalyptics, the Day of the Lord was "the age to come" *beyond* history when God would establish his eternal kingdom. The kingdom of God in the age to come would be established on the ashes of this age and would bring about a reversal in the order of life. However, Jesus broke with the apocalypticists by proclaiming that the reversal in the order of life would happen *within* history just as the Old Testament prophets had said.

Second, when Jesus announced that he would inaugurate God's reign again in human history through his ministry, he declared that the kingdom of God was an eschatological reality. Eschatology is related to the end time. *Eschaton* is the Greek word for the time of the end. When Jesus proclaimed that the kingdom of God was an eschatological reality, he was declaring that the kingdom of God belonged to the category of time rather than a geographical reality that belonged to the category of space.[19] The kingdom of God was the time of God's blessing. The kingdom of God was the time of the reversal in the order of life. Jesus clearly

---

18. The content of this section is indebted to Fee, "Kingdom of God and the Church's Global Mission," 7–21, and reflects many of the exegetical insights and conclusions made by Ladd, *Jesus and the Kingdom.* For a Pentecostal exposition on the kingdom of God in Jesus' mission and ministry as both already present and a future event within a pneumatalogical perspective, see Kuzmič, "Kingdom of God," 521–26.

19. Ladd, *Jesus and the Kingdom,* 118–44, illustrates the difference between the kingdom as a spatial realm identified by geographical boundaries and the time when a King has authority to reign. Luke 19:11–15 makes a similar distinction in order to identify the kingdom of God explicitly with the time of God's reign.

identified the kingdom of God, which he was inaugurating through his ministry with the time of God's reign. Through his ministry God was establishing his authority to reign in human history.

Third, when Jesus announced that he would inaugurate God's reign again in human history through his ministry, he declared the eschatological kingdom was related to both present time and future time. There is sufficient textual support to suggest that Jesus held both of these assertions.[20] It seems clear that the kingdom of God was present for Jesus,[21] and it seems equally clear that the kingdom of God was future for Jesus.[22] The kingdom of God, according to Jesus, was both a present reality and a future reality. The kingdom of God was "already" present in the messianic signs associated with his ministry but "not yet" consummated in the transformation of a new heaven and a new earth. For Jesus the kingdom of God was "now" and "not yet."

In responding to the good news of the gospel, Jesus declared that repentance and belief become a person's greatest joy. The radical change that attends repentance and belief in response to God's reign was elaborated on by Jesus in Matt 11:12 and its Lucan parallel in 16:16. Matt 11:12, 13 reads, "From the days of John the Baptist until now the kingdom of heaven has suffered violence, and the violent take it by force. For all the prophets and the law prophesied until John came." Luke 16:16

20. When Jesus proclaims "the Kingdom of God is at hand," one can infer that the kingdom of God is at hand and therefore the time of God's reign is about to begin with his ministry. One can also infer that that the kingdom is at hand and therefore the time of God's reign still belongs to the future.

21. Four groups of texts suggest that the kingdom was present for Jesus. One group chronicles Jesus' view that the reversal in the order of life was already present, i.e., Luke 4:18–19 and Luke 7:28–35. A second group suggests the kingdom of God was already present because Jesus declared that the old age of the Law was already giving way to the new age of kingdom, i.e., the Sermon on the Mount. A third group shows that the eschatological banquet was already celebrated by Jesus, i.e., Mark 2:18ff., arguing the bridegroom is present to celebrate the eschatological banquet. The final group in which Jesus casts out demons reveals God's already inaugurated right to reign in history, i.e., Luke 11:20.

22. Three groups of texts suggest that the kingdom of God was in the future for Jesus. One group makes it clear that for Jesus the reversal in the order of life was still in the future, i.e., Matt 8:11–12, which implies that the eschatological banquet was still in the future and the blasphemy sayings of Matt 12:32. The two other groups of future texts include the "Son of Man sayings," which identify the kingdom of God as coming in the future and the "watchfulness sayings" in which Jesus admonishes his disciples to watch and wait for the coming kingdom.

reads, "The law and the prophets were in effect until John came; since then the good news of the kingdom is preached, and everyone enters it by force." Or, everyone presses one's way into it. Or, everyone enters it with radical changes.

The meaning of this text is connected to the apocalyptic view of history used by Jesus to frame his kingdom teaching: this age—the *eschaton*—the age to come. The tendency is to think along this time line with God's people moving forward chronologically from this age into the age to come. But the text does not imply such a chronological sequence of time. It says that the law and the prophets were until John, since then the kingdom of God has been advancing or proclaimed as coming. Jesus declared that it was not that the present historical moment was moving into the future of God's reign. Rather, it was the reign of God, which belonged to the future, and was moving into the present. The imagery Jesus used was that the future eschatological kingdom was pressing against the time line of this age. It was the *kairos* moment—a new era was dawning—God's Day of Salvation was pressing in. The time of the old age was fulfilled; the kingdom of God was breaking into the present moment.

Jesus said, as the kingdom was pressing into this age, people could press *against* it and already experience the transforming power of God's messianic salvation. It was like new wine placed in old wineskins; it begins to bleed through the leather and just a bead of the new wine of the age to come is powerful enough to unstop a deaf ear, or to loose a dumb tongue, to restore sight, to cure a leper, or to gladden the heart of the poor. It is God's Day of Salvation. In George Ladd's fine phrase, Jesus declared the kingdom of God as "the presence of the future."[23] When people press into God's kingdom, God's gracious reign is powerful enough to overthrow the old self-centered kingdom. To experience God's reign is to come under divine management. God's gracious rule overmasters and violates the self's right to rule. In that transforming moment of radical change God's future reign becomes the center of human loyalty.

Two insights can be drawn from this Pentecost/kingdom paradigm that are particularly germane for today's Pentecostal church in need of a biblically-based eschatological validation of wholistic mission and ministry. First, the Pentecost/kingdom framework calls for the doctrine of the return of Jesus Christ to be interpreted in the broader eschato-

---

23. Ladd, *Presence of the Future*.

logical context of Jesus' kingdom teaching. Such a hermeneutical move has profound implications for providing an eschatological impulse in the already/not yet kingdom of God toward a Pentecostal social ethic, which can empower and integrate social ministry with evangelism and discipleship. No longer is all the work of human hands in caring for the needy and building a more just society going to be swept aside, as if it counts for nothing in the eschatological drive of God's mission.[24]

The historical continuity and theological homogeneity, which Jesus posited between the anticipatory reign of God "already" present in his ministry and the consummated reign of God "not yet" come, is crucial to keep in mind when interpreting the nature of the kingdom of God as "an apocalyptic act" at the end of the age when Jesus Christ returns. Historical continuity and theological homogeneity between the kingdom already come in Jesus' ministry and the kingdom not/yet consummated until Jesus' return implies that the apocalyptic act at the end of this age will not be one of *total annihilation* of the world but one of *total transformation* of the world purged of evil. This transformation, which makes all things new in Jesus Christ and the consummation of the kingdom of God, most surely requires God's judgment in rewarding the good works and moral deeds of God's people, in the annihilation of evil from the cosmos, in the balancing of the scales of justice for those innocents who suffered as victims of wrongdoing, and in the purging of evildoers who persisted in resistance to God's right to reign. The justice we are not able to achieve in this age will be rendered in the age to come. This transformed world of God's future reign, however, has historical continuity and theological homogeneity with the reign of God, which was present in the person and ministry of Jesus and continues to press into our human history to this very day through the person and empowerment of the Holy Spirit.[25]

To come under God's reign is to become part of an eschatological people—a people of God who live in the present age by the future kingdom "not yet" consummated. The theological context of the already/not yet coming kingdom is essential to understand the ethical teachings

---

24. Smith, "Eschatological Drive of God's Mission."

25. For the transformation of human work into God's future reign, see Volf, "On Loving with Hope: Eschatology and Social Responsibility," 28–31; Williams, "Partition of Love and Hope," 24–27; cf. Dempster, "Christian Social Concern in Pentecostal Perspective," 51–64.

of Jesus as well as the moral responses of Jesus to the social issues of his own day. The ethical teachings and moral responses of Jesus identify the behavioral expressions, which demonstrate what life looks like when people respond to God's reign in concrete situations. The ethical teachings of Jesus are designed to create a people who provide a visible witness in the present age of what the future will look like. The eschatological kingdom, with its ethics centered on the mission, ministry, and message of Jesus, provides the firm foundation to develop a Pentecostal social ethic to guide the church in its work of social service and social transformation.

TOWARD A PENTECOSTAL SOCIAL ETHIC: THE CONNECTION OF THE ESCHATOLOGICAL AND THE ETHICAL KINGDOM OF GOD

Whether the ethical teachings of Jesus are found in the Sermon on the Mount, the parables, or individual *logia*, the teachings describe what life looks like where God reigns. Accordingly, the moral imperatives of Jesus' ethic need to be interpreted in the context of the theological indicatives that define the nature of God's rule. This theological indicative/moral imperative structure of Jesus' ethical teachings has roots deep in Jewish life and the moral traditions of the Old Testament, particularly the eighth-century prophets.[26] Thoroughly woven into the fabric of Israel's moral consciousness in Old Testament times was this central organizing principle, "What God is in his character, and what God wills in his revelation defines what is right."[27] To determine what is morally good and morally right required the prior theological determination of who God is in moral character and how God acts in moral conduct. Every theological statement indicating who God is in his moral character and conduct is by definition a moral imperative prescribing who God's people ought to be in character and how they ought to act in conduct.

---

26. See Dempster, "Pentecostal Social Concern and the Biblical Mandate of Social Justice," 129–53. Stemming from the Brussel's Consultation, I organized this chapter around three moral principles in Jesus' kingdom ethics. Much of the content, however, is abstracted verbatim from that presentation. For a copy of the Brussels Statement on Evangelization and Social Concern, as well as my paper on "Social Concern in the Context of Jesus' Kingdom Mission and Ministry," 41–53. My Brussels presentation was subsequently also published in an anthology as, "Theology of the Kingdom," 44–75.

27. Kaiser, *Toward Old Testament Ethics*, 3.

This ethical axiom of the *imitatio Dei*, which is embedded in the theological indicative/moral imperative structure of Old Testament ethical thinking, rests at the heart of Jesus' ethics. Standing firmly in the prophetic tradition, Jesus taught that God is a God of ethical character. God's kingly rule discloses God's moral character and will, which simultaneously defines the moral principles by which human life under God's rule ought to be governed. On the one hand, the moral norms that Jesus enunciated in his ethical teachings describe the moral features that characterize God's own redemptive action in human history. On the other hand, the moral norms define the kinds of human action that conform to God's kingly rule. For example, Jesus' admonition to love one's enemies is transformed from a perfectionist ideal into a kingdom life principle. When God reigns he loves his enemies, so God's people who live under his reign ought to love their enemies. Put within this organizational structure, the moral imperative is binding if indeed the theological indicative is true that God does love his enemies.

Much more, however, is provided in the theological indicative/ moral imperative relationship than a means to structure ethical thinking. The moral demands embodied in the ethics of Jesus presuppose that his hearers had been, in fact, overmastered by God's gracious reign. The ethics of Jesus can and will only be practiced successfully if the actions are the behavioral expressions of God's overmastering rule in the believer and the community of faith. The ethics of the kingdom presuppose that Jesus' hearers had "entered" the kingdom by experiencing the joy of repentance and the believing faith that connects God's people to the good news of the gospel. Rather than being expressions of "law," the ethics of Jesus are expressions of the "gospel." Jeremias makes this point cogently, "To each of the sayings belongs the message: the old aeon is passing away. Through the proclamation of the gospel and through discipleship you are transferred into the new aeon of God. And now you should know that this is what life is like when you belong to the new aeon of God . . . This is what a lived faith is like. This is what the life of those who stand in the salvation-time of God is like, of those who are freed from the power of Satan and in whom the wonder of discipleship is consummated."[28]

Contextualized within this theological framework, the ethical teachings of Jesus are designed to portray what life looks like when humans

---

28. Jeremias, *Sermon on the Mount*, 23, 30–31.

respond to the Good News. The ethics of Jesus in the gospels, as Jeremias emphasized, are not so much *"prescriptions of law"* as they are *"descriptions of grace."*[29] Therefore, Jesus' ethic is neither a call to repentance in light of an imminent kingdom nor a blueprint for bringing about the perfect society on earth. Instead, as Ron Farmer correctly emphasizes, "Jesus' ethics is a response ethic," describing "the proper response of people who have experienced the saving activity of God."[30] Within Jesus' response ethic, ethical reflection is guided by this fundamental theological-ethical principle, "God is acting in all actions upon you, so respond to all actions upon you as to respond to his action."[31]

Before identifying some of the content of Jesus' kingdom ethics one last comment on ethical structure is needed. Jesus did not provide his followers with a complete system of ethics. Most of his moral assertions were made either in an impromptu debate with his critics or in responding to the questions of his disciples. No attempt was made by Jesus to articulate regulations for every aspect of life. Further, even when specific ethical instruction was given—for example, on the state, marriage and the family, and human work—the scope of the teaching was not comprehensive but tailored to the specific concerns of his hearers. To speak of a "social ethic" grounded in Jesus' kingdom teachings, therefore, is somewhat of a misnomer since Jesus himself never constructed such an ethic. Even so, Jesus did give specific ethical teachings. And given the theological indicative/moral imperative structure in which ethical teachings come to life, the corpus of moral sayings and parables provide rudimentary principles of a social ethic.

Commenting on the "incompleteness" of the Sermon of the Mount from a moral point of view, Jeremias makes the point that even though incomplete the sayings collected in the Sermon provide a sufficient basis for determining moral responsibility even in areas not specifically addressed in the moral catechism. When other sources of Jesus' ethical teaching are added to the Sermon, what Jeremias says is made even more poignant:

> [W]hat is here taught is symptoms, signs, examples, of what it means when the kingdom of God breaks into the world which is still under sin, death, and the devil. Jesus says, in effect: I in-

29. Jeremias, *Sermon on the Mount*, 30–31.

30. Farmer, "Kingdom of God in the Gospel of Matthew," 127.

31. This axiom is taken from H. R. Niebuhr, *Responsible Self*, 126.

tend to show you, by means of some examples, what the new life is like, and what I show you through these examples must apply to every aspect of life. You yourselves should be signs of the coming kingdom of God, signs that something has already happened. Through every aspect of your lives, including those aspects beyond which I speak, you should testify to the world that the kingdom of God is already dawning. In your lives rooted and grounded in the *basileia*, the kingdom of God, the victory of the kingdom of God should be visible.[32]

In his ethical teachings, as Jeremias suggests, Jesus revealed the moral principles by which the moral actions of God's people could give God's redemptive action a visible form in the concrete world of everyday life. Three of the basic moral norms in Jesus' ethics—love, justice, and respect of persons—are particularly germane in formulating a social ethic designed to portray what life looks like where God reigns.

Where God reigns, love creates a moral bond with brothers and sisters, with neighbors and strangers, and even with enemies.

One of the moral trademarks of Jesus' disciples, who had responded to his proclamation of the good news of the gospel, is a commitment to the law of love. The expanding moral bonds that God's love creates among people can be charted by looking at each of these moral commands in turn love of the brothers and sisters (John 13:34–35), love of the neighbor (Matt 22:34–40 = Mark 12:28–34 = Luke 10:25–27) and love of enemies (Matt 5:43–48 = Luke 6:2–28).

According to Jesus, love of the brothers and sisters within the community of disciples was "a new commandment" (John 13:34). In-group love was certainly nothing new. However, as Professor Stephen Mott points out, Jesus established a new order of life in which Jesus loved his disciples in order to make their love possible for one another. What Jesus taught here has profound social implications. Some people cannot give love because they have never received love. Daily life is chalked full of cases in which the chains of domestic violence link the generations: the abused become the new abusers—"thus the tragic spiral of parents, deprived as children, recreating their own misery in their children."[33] In the face of such inexorable forces of social conditioning a command-

---

32. Jeremias, *Sermon on the Mount*, 33.

33. Mott, *Biblical Ethics and Social Change*, 40–41.

ment to love falls limp to the ground. But there is "a new commandment." What is new is a commandment to love one another that presupposes a community of disciples who function together as a surrogate family. Belonging to a community in which love is modeled and experienced as a real social bond can simultaneously activate the capacity to love and break the chains of incorrigible destructive behavior and relationships.

Once activated, though, love creates moral bonds not only among the members of the believing community, but also with those outside the walls of the church, transforming strangers into neighbors. Jesus elevated the moral question of love of neighbor to the theological question of love of God. He did so in response to a lawyer's question that asked for the "first" or the "greatest" one of the commandments. Jesus answered with the so-called double commandment of love, clearly communicating his conviction that love of God and love of neighbor are inextricably bound together (Mark 12:28–31 = Matt 22:34–40 = Luke 10:25–28). There can be no authentic love of God without love of neighbor. Conversely, love of neighbor is the tangible moral expression of love of God. Jesus took the love of God from Deut 6:4, 5 and the love of neighbor from Lev 19:18 and put them together as a unified commandment.

The lawyer asked, "Who is my neighbor"? to clarify who was included within the circle of his moral responsibility. He wanted to know where the limits of love could be drawn. The lawyer's question brought Jesus into a rabbinical debate regarding the neighbor referred to in Lev 19:18. The position that came into ascendancy in later Judaism was that neighbor, in Lev 19:18, referred to members of the covenant community. The law of love of neighbor was limited, applying only to Israelites and full proselytes. Even so, there were others who championed the removal of limits. Noting that the case commentary that followed Lev 19:18 alluded to responsibility for strangers dwelling in the land, the rabbis on the other side of the controversy argued that the stranger, or resident alien, was included in the scope of the commandment.[34] Within the context of this rabbinical dispute, Jesus tells the story of the Good Samaritan.

In telling his parabolic story, Jesus ironically reversed the social roles and expectations of the main characters: the priest, the Levite, and the Samaritan. The Samaritans included Israelites who had been assimilated into Assyrian Gentile culture after they were conquered by the Assyrians. The "Samaritan" Jews were not recognized as true Jews by

---

34. Schrage, *Ethics of the New Testament*, 73–74.

those Jews who returned from the Babylonian exile. Samaritans were considered "unclean" bastardized Jews and were treated with disdain. In contrast, the priests and the Levites were highly respected members of the Jewish community. With the rabbinical debate in full swing over whether or not aliens should be regarded as neighbors, Jesus intentionally cast the villain into the role of a hero and turned the heroes into the villains in order to add a bite to his story. The "alien" Samaritan identified with the victim who needed help; the Jewish priest and Levite, who likewise saw that the man was robbed, beaten, and left half dead, passed by, forsaking the victim to suffer his own fate. The Samaritan, feeling compassion for the brutalized man, involved himself in the life of the needy person. He provided the form of assistance that matched the victim's need and alleviated his suffering. The Samaritan acted on behalf of the highest good of the needy person, demonstrating that love begins with compassion but ends in "active and concrete involvement on behalf of those who suffer."[35]

After Jesus tells the story he turns the question back on the lawyer. And he turns the question itself on its head. "Who is my neighbor"? was the starting question of the lawyer to Jesus. "Which of these three proved to be a neighbor to the man who fell among thieves"? was the concluding question of Jesus to the lawyer. The lawyer sought to define the neighbor starting with himself as the point of reference. Jesus made the victim in need the reference point for the definition of who was a neighbor to him. By shifting the subject of the question, Jesus told the story from the viewpoint of the person who was robbed. The lawyer, in final analysis, did not get to define which neighbors are to be loved and which are not. The victimized person on the roadside actually defined who acted like a neighbor by identifying the one who loved him. Indeed, the "alien" was a "neighbor" to the victim in distress. Jesus made the lawyer himself say it, the "alien" Samaritan showed mercy—the alien proved himself to be a neighbor. So, Jesus brings the lawyer to the conclusion that aliens are included in the neighborhood of God's love and in the circle of moral responsibility of God's people.[36]

35. Schrage, *Ethics of the New Testament*, 78.

36. The Samaritan's love showed mercy beginning with "compassion," which was stimulated by a capacity to interchange places with the victim. The feeling of compassion also motivated Jesus to acts of love for the "harassed and helpless" (Matt 9:36; 14:14 = Mark 6:34), "sick" (Matt 14:14), "hungry and malnourished" (Matt 15:32 = Mark 8:2, 3), "the blind" (Matt 20:34), "the leper" (Mark 1:40–42), and a rebellious son (Luke 15:11–32).

Any doubt that Jesus intended to universalize love of neighbor is dispelled when Jesus embraced enemies within the love commandment. The moral imperative, "Love your enemies," (Matt 5:44 = Luke 6:27) made it clear that *all* neighbors are included in the geography of love. As Larry Rasmussen correctly observed, "If the enemy is *in*cluded, no one is *ex*cluded since the enemy is the one most likely to be an exception."[37] Further, all enemies—personal antagonists, legal adversaries, economic competitors, national foes—are brought under the umbrella of love's obligation. No category of enemy is excluded. Given love's unconditional character and global scope, "the commandment to love our enemies censures love that is mere social solidarity."[38] Family ties, class standing, national interests, cultural values, and religious identity can no longer confine the boundaries where the law of love is normative. Love of enemies shatters such limitations, and according to Stephen Mott, "generates a way of life," not merely an attitude, anchored in the "recognition of the common humanity of all persons."[39]

Because love of enemies requires the positive content of boundless neighbor-love associated with the love of God, and because love of enemies breaks with the powerful conventional patterns of reciprocity that govern the old age, Allen Verhey states, and correctly so I believe, that "to welcome this saying is to welcome the coming kingdom."[40] Verhey's assertion gets to the theological heart of the moral issue. To enter the kingdom and come under God's rule is to be incorporated into the new order of life in which love is normative. Such unconditional love reflective of God's own moral character, however, runs against the grain of human nature, and as a consequence, the law of love is experienced as an "ought." Experiencing the "ought" of the moral imperative to love, therefore is both the gift of the kingdom demonstrating its presence and the call to realized discipleship to live out the values of the future eschatological kingdom. But love is not the only moral principle in the new order of God's reign. So is the principle of justice, a principle that Jesus taught and practiced to validate his mission, ministry and message that he was inaugurating God's reign.

---

37. Rasmussen, "Creation, Church, and Christian Responsibility," 188.
38. Schrage, *Ethics of the New Testament*, 78.
39. Mott, *Biblical Ethics and Social Change*, 44
40. Verhey, *Great Reversal*, 25.

Where God reigns, justice is established for the poor, the sick,
the powerless, and the disinherited

In his theological teachings and social behavior Jesus consistently portrayed God's reign as a rule of justice. Three aspects of Jesus' ministry
bear directly on formulating an integrated understanding wholistic
mission and ministry, which promotes social service and social action
in the service of God's will for justice. Jesus—in both word and deed—
proclaimed that the reversal in the order of life to redressed past injustices, created a sense of solidarity with the socially marginalized, and
promoted a spirit of generosity in calculating what was due to those in
need. These three aspects of social justice related to Jesus' own view of
life where God reigns.

Jesus' identification with the social ethics of the Year of Jubilee
sounded the keynote of his mission: God's coming kingdom will put in
motion a reversal in the order of life. Luke places this kingdom manifesto in his gospel to indicate the way Jesus announced the beginning
of his mission and ministry of inaugurating God's reign. According to
Luke 4:18–19, after Jesus entered the synagogue he received the scroll
for the lectionary reading from the attendant. Breaking with the order of
the passage scheduled to be read, Jesus found the portion of the Servant
Songs of Isaiah that spoke of the messianic promise of the Jubilee. With
every eye upon him, he read, "The Spirit of the Lord is upon me because
he has anointed me, to preach the good news to the poor, to proclaim
release to the captive, to recover the sight of the blind, to set at liberty
the oppressed, to proclaim the year of the Lord's favor." He rolled up
the scroll, gave it to the attendant, and sat down but the custom was to
preach the sermon. What they heard did not correspond to custom. He
said, "Today this Scripture has been fulfilled in your hearing."

Initiation of "the year of the Lord's favor" or "the acceptable year of
the Lord" with which Jesus identified his mission was nothing less than
the fulfillment of the Jubilee instituted by Moses. One of the major functions of the Jubilee Year was to correct the accumulated inequities that
arose in Israel's social structure over a period of fifty years, especially the
widening gap between the rich and the poor. The purpose of the Jubilee
ordinances was to maintain the egalitarian nature of God's covenant
community. Emphasizing the social ethics of Jubilee, Stephen Mott notes,
"The provisions of the Year of Jubilee exemplify biblical justice. Among
its stipulations is the provision that after fifty years all land, whether sold

or foreclosed, is to be returned to the family whose heritage it is (Lev 25:25–28). The effect of this arrangement was to institutionalize the relative equality of all persons in the landed means of production. It was a strong equalitarian measure and a far-reaching means of redress."[41]

This particular stipulation of Jubilee land equalization continued to be recognized in the prophetic tradition as a key measure of correcting past injustices.[42] In addition to prescribing the return to one's patrimony, the Jubilee required letting the land lay fallow, the liberation of slaves, and the forgiveness of debts. All these measures were designed to prevent the accumulation of wealth by a minority of people in perpetuity, to give an opportunity to start life over again every fiftieth year with a relatively level playing field, and to supply every member of society with necessary landed means to obtain food, clothing, and shelter.[43] When combined with the social regulations of the sabbatical year (seven year cycle), the law of tithing (three year cycle), and the law of gleaning (annual cycle), the Jubilee was part of a social and legal system that created institutional social structures and mechanisms to provide care for the poor, the alien, the widow, and the orphan until the social conditions, which fostered the inequitable distribution of the nation's wealth, could be equalized through measures implemented in the Year of Jubilee.[44]

Within this context of the Jubilee Year, Jesus' kingdom manifesto in the synagogue at Nazareth announced that God's time to reverse the fortunes of life by redressing injustices and social inequities had now started. In his excellent analysis of Jesus and the Jubilee, André Trocmé, notes that those who heard Jesus' announcement would be drawn to this inescapable conclusion, "By proclaiming the Jubilee, Jesus wanted to transform the present from the perspective of the future according to the code of justice God had promulgated in the past."[45] Accordingly, the reversal in the order of life associated with the Jubilee meant good

41. Mott, *Biblical Ethics and Social Change*, 68.

42. The prophet Ezekiel proposed a land redistribution scheme along the lines of the Year of Jubilee (Ezek 45:8–9; 46:18). See Mott, *Biblical Ethics and Social Change*, 68–69.

43. Trocmé, *Jesus and the Nonviolent Revolution*, 19–76.

44. An examination of these four ordinances demonstrated they were institutional structures in Israel's life, which were designed to care for the poor. See Sider, *Rich Christians in an Age of Hunger*, 79–99. Cf. Dempster, "Pentecostal Social Concern and the Biblical Mandate of Social Justice," 143–46.

45. Trocmé, *Jesus and the Nonviolent Revolution*, 30. The Jubilee analysis is on pages 19–76.

news for the poor, release for the captives, sightedness for the blind, and liberation for the oppressed.

These characteristic features of his own ministry were represented by Jesus as the "signs" that authenticated his messianic credentials as the One who was anointed to announce the kingdom of God. Where God establishes his right to reign, Jesus declared in the spirit of Jubilee and the prophetic tradition, the first subjects with whom God is concerned are the poor, the enslaved, the infirm, and the oppressed. God's justice is the kind that corrects unfairness, redresses evil, and reverses misfortunes as the first plank in building a just social order.

Once again in John's imprisonment narrative, proclaiming good news to the poor and healing the sick were "signs" that validated the presence of God's reign. When John was awaiting execution, having never witnessed any of the miracles and healings associated with Jesus' ministry, he sent his disciples to inquire of Jesus whether or not he was the messiah. As John's messengers approached, Luke reported that Jesus gave sight to the blind and healed many from their "infirmities and plagues and evil spirits" (7:21). Jesus then instructed John's emissaries, "Go and tell John what you have seen and heard: the blind receive their sight, the lame walk, lepers are cleansed, and the deaf hear, the dead are raised up, the poor have good news preached to them. And blessed is he who takes no offense at me" (7:22–23). Echoed in Jesus' response to John, one can hear the messianic "signs" from Isaiah, which Jesus quoted earlier in Nazareth. Jesus authenticated his messianic credentials again by "signs" proclaiming glad tidings to the poor, sight to the blind, and healing of the lame, the deaf, and the leper.

Besides their suffering from a physical infirmity, the one thing that the blind, the lame, the deaf, and the leper all shared in common was the fact that their affliction typically caused them to be socially marginalized and economically disenfranchised from mainstream society. Often they were reduced to begging for a living; lepers bore the additional stigma of being designated as social outcasts. In this context, Jesus healing ministry tangibly authenticated in deed the good news he preached to the poor in word. His miracles, healings, and exorcisms were not a supernatural fireworks display to prove he was the messiah. Rather, they were indigenous "signs" that God's day of salvation had dawned and that the reversal in the order of life had already begun. The poor, the blind, the lame, the deaf, the leper, as well as Gentiles, and women of that time, tasted already the social justice of God's future order through the healing power of Jesus ministry.[46] "Jesus' healing activity demonstrated that the saving grace of God extends not only to personal guilt and broken relationships but to human bodies, to societal structures, to mysterious forces that hold creation in check."[47] Moreover, Jesus' healing ministry demonstrated that redressing the conditions of the poor required more than the gifts of daily bread: poverty created deep scars in the human psyche and the healing of the whole person was required if injustice was to be genuinely reversed.

When emphasizing Jesus' proclamation to, and healing of, the poor, it is important to keep the inclusive spirit of Jesus' ministry in mind. To be sure, the gospels record occasions in which Jesus did heal a rich or a powerful person, clearly demonstrating his own conviction of God's love for all people independent of their economic or social standing. Neither such healings nor Jesus' accepting hospitality from the wealthy or the religious establishment should be construed to mean, however, that Jesus acquiesced in the status quo.[48] His predominant focus outlined in the kingdom manifesto and repeated throughout his ministry was made incontestably clear in the gospels. Jesus, healer of the sick and weak, was friend of sinners, liberator of the oppressed, and champion of the underdog and disinherited. Verhey claims that God's benediction of blessedness was upon the poor and the disinherited. They were the recipients of the eschatological blessing inherent in "the great reversal" of the kingdom inaugurated by Jesus.[49]

The social implications for church mission and for constructing a social ethic within this perspective are twofold. On the one hand, it becomes clear that before justice can be a positive achievement enhancing human equality and fairness, injustice must be rectified. The wrongs must be righted before the good can be achieved. On the other hand, it becomes clear that the achievement of perfect justice is not required in order to redress the injustices that do exist. Jesus himself lived in the realization that the transformation of the social and ecological order was a future event. Yet, he put the full supernatural and human resources of his ministry in redressing the injustices he encountered by reversing the

---

46. Cassidy, *Jesus, Politics and Society*, 20–24.

47. Senior and Stuhlmueller, *Biblical Foundations for Mission*, 151.

48. Cassidy, *Jesus, Politics and Society*, 24.

49. Verhey, *Great Reversal*, 16–21.

order of life when it was in his power to do so. In so doing, Jesus ministry pictured in microcosm what the future was going to be like.

Jesus not only represented God's reign as a reversal in the order of life that rectified human injustices, but he also personally welcomed the weak, the despised, and the impoverished into the fellowship of his messianic community. He invited the materially poor and repentant sinners, along with others, into his entourage of followers and exalted these lowly ones by portraying them as the vanguard of the kingdom of God. Such a powerless crew might appear to be as insignificant as "a mustard seed," but in Jesus' view they were the "great shrub" of God's kingdom already making its embryonic appearance (Mark 4:3–20 = Matt 13:3–23 = Luke 8:4–15). With the lowly and the outcast Jesus enjoyed public table fellowship, which he enacted as the eschatological banquet of the kingdom (Mark 2:15–28 = Luke 5:27–6:11). It was the poor, the maimed, the lame, and the blind who responded to his invitation to the banquet feast in the eschatological hour, while the righteous made excuse (Luke 14:16–24). Jesus dignified the poor, the despised, and the sinners by refusing to weed them out of his band of followers (Matt 13:24–30).[50] Jesus' justice meant personal involvement in the cause of the poor, infirm, and helpless.

Perhaps nowhere did Jesus state his profound identification with the powerless and the needy more dramatically than in the "identity sayings" (Matt 25:31–46) and the "*paidion* (child) pericope" (Mark 9:33–37 = Matt 18:1–5 = Luke 9:46–48). The identity sayings were part of the parable of the Last Judgment. At first glance it appears that the separation of the sheep from the goats was based on the criteria of the six corporal works: providing food for the hungry, water for the thirsty, hospitality for the stranger, clothing for the naked, care for the sick, and companionship for the prisoner. Not so. The text has Jesus inviting the righteous into the kingdom, saying "*I* was hungry and you gave *me* something to eat, *I* was thirsty and you gave *me* something to drink, *I* was a stranger and you invited *me* in, *I* needed clothes and you clothed *me*, *I* was sick and you looked after *me*, *I* was in prison and you came to visit *me*" (Matt 25:35–36). The same language was used in banishing the cursed from the kingdom. Both the righteous and the cursed inquired as to when they saw Jesus hungry, thirsty, homeless, without clothing, sick, or in prison. To the righteous, Jesus responded, "I tell you the truth,

50. Jeremias, *Rediscovering the Parables*, 179–89. Also see Jeremias, *New Testament Theology*, 113–16.

whatever you did for one of the least of these brothers of mine, you did for me" (v. 40). To the condemned, Jesus answered, "I tell you the truth, whatever you did not do for one of the least of these, you did not do for me" (v. 45). Separation of the sheep from the goats was not based on the six corporal works, but on the encounter with Jesus Christ. Jesus himself made the astonishing claim that he was encountered *incognito* in the destitute, the desperate, the disabled, and the disenfranchised. So great was Jesus' sense of solidarity with "the least of these" that he actually shared identity with them—to minister to these poor ones, Jesus said, was to minister to him.[51]

Jesus' identification with the least as a defining characteristic of justice in God's reign was also portrayed in the various child narratives. In Mark 10:13–15—the "blessing of the children" narrative—the disciples scolded the parents who were bringing their children to Jesus for a blessing. Mark records that Jesus became "indignant," or literally translated, *he was boiling inside*. What Jesus said to his disciples, therefore, should not be heard as a polite reprimand, but expressive of his deep feelings of anger, "Let the children come to me, and do not hinder them, for the kingdom of God belongs to such as these" (v. 14). Becoming like a child in this context, according to Allan Boesak, has little to do with the romantic notions of the child's simplicity, purity, or innocence. "Rather, the child stood more or less on a par with those who counted for nothing, those peripheral to the real world, the good life; they were the 'little people' who claim no status at all." The point Jesus made was that where God reigns the unimportant and powerless who possess no status are also recipients of the eschatological blessing of the kingdom.[52]

Jesus' fury with his disciples and their failure to grasp this kingdom principle is explained by the fact that Jesus had earlier emphasized this teaching to them in the context of their discussion about who was the greatest in the kingdom. Jesus, in response to this dialogue, picked up a child in his arms, and said, "Whoever receives one such child in my name receives me" (Mark 9:37). By such a visible object lesson Jesus made it abundantly clear that the greatest in the kingdom was the one who re-

---

51. Gray, *Least of My Brothers Matthew 25:31–46*, provides an comprehensive treatment of the history of interpretation of Matt 25:31–46. The phrase "the least of my brothers" has been understood at different times to refer to the Jewish people (as a whole or particular group), humanity in general, or in a universal sense, 347.

52. Boesak, "Eye of the Needle," 8.

ceived and gave service to the least. Bruce Chilton and J. McDonald suggest that the main point that Jesus emphasized in this incident was his own identification with the least, "One must 'receive' such a *paidion* as if he were Jesus himself. . . . Jesus identifies with those of lowest status: to serve them is to serve him."[53]

An inescapable implication for church mission and social ethics arises from the kingdom teaching and justice-embodying acts of Jesus concerning the poor and "the least." Active concern for the poor is not part of the elective curriculum of the church. Rather, service to the poor and the least penetrates to the heart of church mission in the tradition of Jesus. To neglect the poor, the deprived, and those with no or little status is much more than a moral failure; it also symbolizes a theological blindness to the real identity of Jesus and to God's own ethical character. To neglect to service the poor and so-called "nobodies" is to neglect to serve Jesus, who opts to represent them because they are God's concern. To minister to the needs of the poor and the least is to minister to Jesus, who has vested his own identity with them.

Added to the kingdom accent on redressing injustice and cultivating solidarity with the poor Jesus enunciated a third feature of the kind of justice which reflected God's reign. In the parable of the good employer (Matt 20:1–15), Jesus identified both the theological basis and the regulatory rule by which to calculate what is due people as a matter of justice. The plot centered on the identical wages a landowner paid to workers who were hired at different times of the day. When the first laborers were hired at daybreak, they agreed on a wage of a denarius for the day. Apparently, in order to get the job done, the owner hired workers at the third, sixth, ninth, and the last hour before nightfall. Each time he said, "Whatever is right, I will give you." When the day was done, the foreman paid the laborers who worked the last hour the same denarius he paid those who had worked since daybreak. The workers who had toiled long through the heat of the day felt wronged because all the laborers were paid equally without regard to who merited more or less. Hearing their complaints, the employer asks, "Friend, I am doing you no wrong; did you not agree with me for a denarius? Take what belongs to you, and go; I chose to give to this last as I give to you. Am I not allowed to do what I choose with what belongs to me? (vv. 13–15)."

---

53. Chilton and McDonald, *Jesus and the Ethics of the Kingdom*, 82.

Joachim Jeremias points out that in this parable Jesus provided the following defense against his critics, "'Do you begrudge my generosity?' God acts like that householder who sympathized with the unemployed and their families. That is the way he acts now. He gives tax-collectors and sinners a share, all undeserved, in his salvation. So, too, he will deal with them on the last day. That, says Jesus, is what he is like; and because he is like that, so am I, as I am acting under his orders and in his stead. Are you going to grumble at God's goodness? That is the core of Jesus' vindication of the gospel: See what God is like—all goodness."[54] Two worlds were thrown into sharp contrast. In the old order, human justice is achieved by merit, making sure people got their due. From this perspective, the all-day laborers had a legitimate gripe. In the new eschatological order, however, justice based on the discrimination of merit is brought under the expansive generosity of God. From this perspective, everyone received "what was right" from God's generous bounty, whether it was merited or not. Real human need, rather than difference in human merit, was the reference point of God's justice. Deprivation was no more right for the last-hour workers than for the first-hour workers. God is so good, said Jesus, that God compensates generously so that none is deprived and, as a consequence, real justice reigns.

Informed by this expansive kingdom perspective on justice, the mission of the church in ministering to the needs of people takes on a distinctive character. Only a spirit of generosity in ministering to the needy can adequately witness to the kind of justice that is inherent in God's reign. God's generosity in establishing his reign by grace, or unmerited favor, forever overrides human merit as the discriminating rule of social justice in church mission. In contrast, the basic rule of justice, which aligns the church and its mission with God's own reign of equity and fairness, is this: to give generously to each and every person what is needed in order to function fully as a human being in relation to others and the creation. Because this rule presupposes that people—regardless of all other considerations—ought to be treated equally and fairly by virtue of their common humanity, it naturally leads to the third principle in a social ethic reflective of God's eschatological kingdom, the value of human beings as God's image bearers.

---

54. Jeremias, *Rediscovering the Parables*, 111.

Where God reigns, respect of persons is promoted for men and women created in God's image within the institutions of society

Two instances stand out most prominently in the story of Jesus in which he based the value of persons on the theological grounds that human beings are God's image bearers. One instance is captured in the poll-tax narrative (Mark 12:13–17), which concluded with the pronouncement saying, "Render to Caesar, the things that are Caesar's and to God the things are God's" (v. 17). The other instance is found in Jesus' divorce and remarriage teachings (Matt 19:3–9 = Mark 10:2–12) in which Jesus referred back to the creation narrative (Matt v. 4 = Mark v. 6).

In the first incident of the poll-tax narrative, Jesus was asked by the Pharisees and Herodians to take sides on a burning issue in the political ethics of Judaism. The question was whether the imperial tax, and the paying of it, was morally right or morally wrong. This was a loaded question because of the generalized sense of the exploitive nature of taxes. Then, violent measures often used to collect taxes also caused disenchantment to spread. In particular, the head tax elicited feelings of oppression because it tangibly symbolized the domination of Rome. Within this context, Jesus stated forthrightly that he knew the question from the religious establishment was designed to trap him, and then he requested a coin. When he received the denarius he asked his detractors to look at it and tell him whose "image and inscription" was on it? "Caesar's", they responded. "Render to Caesar the things that are Caesar's, and to God the things that are God's," Jesus retorted. Wolfgang Schrage correctly contends that proper interpretation of this saying depends largely on knowing what "image and inscription" was on the coin. Noting that a denarius was a Roman silver coin which visibly represented Roman power and supremacy, Schrage provides the following description of the sacral character of the "image and inscription": "Its obverse depicted the emperor with a laurel wreath symbolizing his divinity; the reverse depicted his mother seated on a divine throne as the earthly incarnation of heavenly peace. The reference to the emperor's apotheosis in the inscription made it no less offensive than the portrait: the obverse read 'Emperor Tiberius, venerated son of the venerated God,' and the reverse 'High Priest.'"[55] Knowledge of the "image and inscription" engraved on the coin make clear the error of this dualistic view, in that it contends

---

55. Schrage, *Ethics of the New Testament*, 113. Cf. Stauffer, *Christ and the Caesars*, 133–34, 135–36.

that Jesus taught that God and the emperor had autonomy and absolute authority in their respective realms. Jesus critiqued the view that
Caesar ruled the secular and God ruled the spiritual in a world of two
kingdoms.

Against the backdrop of the depiction of the sacral emperor,
Schrage rightly emphasizes that "Jesus' saying effectively secularizes civil
authority and removes it from the realm of ideology."[56] Jesus' saying not
only desacralized the Roman state but set specific boundaries around its
legitimate sphere of authority. Taxes belonged in the sphere of Rome's
legitimate authority. Why? Because Caesar made the coin, it bore his image, and therefore "belonged" to him. However, Caesar's ownership was
not without proper delimitation, according to Jesus, because some things
"belonged" to God. The incontestable parallelism of v. 17 makes the un-
stated premise of what indeed did belong to God the most provocative
truth claim in the pronouncement saying. If the tax rightfully belonged
to Caesar because the coin was made in his image, then what belonged to
God was that which was made in God's image. Only one thing was made
in God's own image and that was humankind. Taxes belonged to Caesar,
said Jesus, human beings belonged to God. The implications are pictured in the coin and structured in the argument. By desacralizing and
delimiting Caesar's power, Jesus refused to give Caesar an autonomous
sphere even in terms of taxation. If taxation dehumanized, exploited,
and oppressed people, then Caesar was usurping his authority by rob-
bing what rightfully belonged to God. God created men and women in
God's own image (Gen 1:27). Humanity does not possess intrinsic value
based solely on being human; rather, men and women have value because of their relationship to the Creator. They belong to God and God
did not create men and women to be exploited by an unjust tax system.
Therefore, people deserved a tax system that treated them with respect
because people are God's image-bearers and God wills that they should
be treated with dignity.

Jesus enunciated this same moral principle of the value of persons
created in God's image in his ethical response to the divorce and remarriage laws found in Matt 19:3–19 and its parallel in Mark 10:2–12. While
the issue shifted from the political and economic system to the judicial
system, it was also a hot button one filled with personal emotion, social
divisiveness, and religious acrimony, pitting one rabbinical school over

56. Schrage, *Ethics of the New Testament*, 113.

against another. The rabbinical debate concerned the lawful reasons permitted by the Mosaic bill of divorcement (Deut 24:1–4) in which a man could divorce his wife. The rabbinical school of Shammai held that only the sin of sexual unchastity provided a sufficient ground for divorce, while the rabbinical school of Hillel held that any displeasing or indecent behavior on the wife's part justified the husband divorcing his wife.[57] When the question was posed to Jesus, he responded, according to Mark's Gospel, "What did Moses command you"? (v. 3). The Pharisees cited the Mosaic legal code requiring a certificate of divorce. This ordinance, according to Jesus, was not an expression of God's will, but was permitted as a historical concession to human sinfulness (v. 5). Instead, Jesus emphasized the creation story as the basis for his claim that God intended marriage to be a permanent and monogamous bond between a husband and a wife (vv. 6–9).

By shifting away from the argument of how stringent or lax the divorce law should be and focusing instead on the divine intent for marriage portrayed in the creation story, Jesus put his own unique twist on the rabbinical dispute. Divorce, in Jesus' view, called into question the permanent bond of marriage. The "transgression" involved in the practice of divorce, therefore, was not determined solely by reference to legal grounds as the rabbinical dispute suggested but by reference to the fidelity that one owed to one's spouse. The issue was moral not legal. Based on the belief that faithfulness between husband and wife was a constituent element in marriage, Jesus carried his logic to its conclusion: divorce was tantamount to adultery (Mark 10:10–11).

That divorce was equivalent to adultery would have struck a discordant note with Jesus' Jewish audience, and as Schrage has noted, when Jesus added that the adultery was "against her," his male contemporaries in particular would have been dumbfounded. Schrage explains:

> This would be a provocative statement to a Jewish audience, because the Jewish notion of marriage, defined solely from the perspective of the husband, treats the wife as property and includes marriage under property law. A man's wife is his property, acquired through the payment of the bride price. . . . Jesus' prohibition of divorce grants protection to the wife, who had virtually no legal standing; this protection goes far beyond the legal

---

57. For a discussion of the rabbinical dispute between Hillel and Shammai over the grounds for divorce, see Lillie, *Studies in New Testament Ethics*, 118–25.

institution of divorce, which at least gives the woman the right
to remarry. If the original prohibition of divorce was addressed
only to the husband, Jesus was taking the side of the wife, who
had no legal protection. Jesus' "strict interpretation of marriage"
is therefore the appropriate contemporary expression of the protection and respect proper to a woman, who had no standing in
Jewish marital law.[58]

Jesus made his viewpoint uncompromisingly clear. Because men
and women were created in God's own image, Jesus had to break with
both rabbinical traditions and take the side of justice and respect of persons against the exploitation of women. Women should not be dehumanized by an oppressive divorce law, even when quotations from Moses are
evoked to legitimate the institution and the social practices associated
with it. A social institution—even though existing under the cover of
law—that permitted woman to be demeaned and trivialized as subservi-
ent objects of male domination was debunked by Jesus. As God's image-
bearers, Jesus unhesitatingly stated that women should be treated with
respect and human dignity and not be made into an object of male ownership. Moreover, divorce wreaked havoc on a woman's life because she
would lose the source of her legal entitlement, which was the basis of her
well-being within the socio-economic system. Jesus, therefore, refused
to make either rabbinical tradition morally normative. Both rabbinical
traditions viewed the divorce law as a concession to human sinfulness
and moral failure. Ethics for Jesus was never valued in relationship to
human fallenness but was connected to portray what life looked like
under God's reign. Given those institutional practices codified into law,
Jesus stood in solidarity with women who often were demeaned as chattel, and he sought to disempower men in their use of divorce practices,
which treated women like chattel, while at the same time supporting the
view of maintaining lifelong marital vows of commitment.

Unmasking systemic injustice in the laws governing institutional
life—such as the institution of marriage and the divorce law—and desacralizing the political policies and practices of governments—such
as the tax laws—identify the prophetic side of the church's mission in
the service of enhancing human value, human dignity, and the respect
of persons. The other side is for the church to be the advocate for the

---

58. Schrage, *Ethics of the New Testament*, 95, 97. The quotation that Schrage cited
from was from Braun, *Jesus*, 103. English translation: *Jesus of Nazareth*.

weak and the powerless against oppressive political power and social institutions. God's eschatological rule—to which the church owes its allegiance—aims at transforming the political order and its social institutions into agencies that create an environment in which the sacredness of human life is promoted as a basic moral value. In bearing witness to God's kingdom, the church needs to resist compliance with the notion that human governments and social institutions are granted legitimacy just because they exist. Where God reigns—and Jesus himself stated the principle in the poll-tax and divorce narratives—political systems and social structures demonstrate their moral legitimacy by the concrete practice of respecting human beings as God's image bearers. Discriminatory practices based on class, race, or gender, which systematically oppress or marginalize the weak and the powerless, belong categorically to the old social order that is already passing away.

In sum, love, justice, and respect of person are the normative moral principles in a Pentecostal social ethic reflective of God's kingly rule. Practices and actions that embody love, justice, and respect of persons give a tangible witness to what life looks like when God's people respond to God reigns. This social ethic not only guides the church in its social service and social action in the world, but it also directs the church to structure it own life in becoming a community of character and conduct, which models what life looks like when the people of God respond to God's eschatological reign. The Pentecost/kingdom paradigm of Luke focuses the theological reflection on the church and its mission birthed on the day of Pentecost back to the mission, ministry, and message of Jesus inaugurating the kingdom of God. Against that kingdom backdrop and the transfer of the Spirit from Jesus to the disciples, Luke also shows in Acts that the church was anointed by the Spirit to continue the mission and ministry of Jesus as an eschatological community. The coming of the Spirit at Pentecost, creating the church as an eschatological community, had continuity with the coming of the Spirit on Jesus at his baptism, empowering him to announce his anointing to inaugurate the already/not yet reign of God.

CONCLUSION ON SPIRIT BAPTISM AND INCLUSIVENESS

In conclusion, by observing the way Luke used glossolalia to organize his narratives about the Spirit, we can identify the main thrust of his apologetic in the Acts.[59] For Luke, the Holy Spirit was the One who empowered the early church to provide both a spiritual and a moral witness to the world. Spiritually, the Spirit empowered the church's witness of proclamation, which heralded the truth that Jesus Christ provided a saving way of life. The church's spiritual mission was to proclaim a Spirit-empowered gospel, which initiated new believers through repentance and faith into Jesus Christ's redemptive order of life. Morally, the Spirit created the church's *koinonia* as a tangible social witness to a divided world. The church's moral mission was to demonstrate visibly that this future redemptive social order was already beginning to structure its own inclusive communal life. Spirit baptism empowered the believing community to walk its talk, to put creed into conduct, to confirm proclamation with practice. Spirit baptism, for Luke, did not simply empower individual disciples to witness in verbal proclamation. Spirit baptism empowered the church in its corporate life to witness to the moral dynamic of the gospel to transform people, change deep-seated prejudices, and restructure relationships so the participants incorporated into the inclusive believing community possessed an equally valued status in Christ.

For today's Pentecostal church, Luke's theology of Spirit baptism provides a formidable challenge. At the heart of this challenge is Luke's portrayal of the church as the eschatological community, which already gives visible witness in its *koinonia* to the future redemptive order of life. The challenge can be met by the coming and renewing of the Spirit. Only the Spirit can empower the Pentecostal church to experience true *koinonia* and create the possibility of living by the values of the future order of life in the context of the present socially fragmented and morally divided world. Only the Spirit can empower Pentecostal believers of different gender identities and economic statuses, and from different ethnic and religious backgrounds to regard one another with equal value and to experience how diversity enriches an inclusive community of faith.

From the Pentecost/kingdom paradigm constructed from Luke's two volumes we have developed a Pentecostal social ethic, which provides a theological rationale for the church's engagement in social service and social action to work toward the social welfare of individuals and the transformation of the institutions of society. At the same time this

---

59. Dempster, "Church's Moral Witness," 1–7.

Pentecostal social ethic provides a theological rationale for the church to transform its own life in providing a moral witness, which embodies love, justice, and respect of persons. These two areas of the church's social ministry need to be integrated with the calling of the church to proclaim the gospel with the evangelistic intent of inviting people who have yet to experience the joys of repentance and the new life in Christ to bring their lives under the new management of God's reign.

8

Eschatology as Soteriology

The Cosmic Full Gospel

Matthew K. Thompson

INTRODUCTION

PENTECOSTALISM IS A MOVEMENT fired by the eschatological imagi-nation, an apocalyptic revival looking to the soon return of the Lord. Early Pentecostals preached the "full gospel" of Jesus Christ as savior, sanctifier, Spirit baptizer, healer and soon coming King, accenting a dis-tinctive Christological emphasis anchored in a robust pneumatology. The Pentecostal revival preached the "latter rain" restoration of charismatic gifts, which would herald the end of the age and the return of Christ. However, second generation Pentecostals shifted from the imminence of the Lord's return to a new fundamentalist dispensationalist doctrine of the pretribulational rapture of the church to define its eschatology. Pentecostals repudiated most of the rest of the dispensational system, but eventually came to embrace the system itself as they forged alliances with popular evangelicalism in the mid-twentieth century.[1]

The dispensational system, with its rigidly compartmentalized and predetermined blueprint of history (which assumes a cessationist hermeneutic), and its jigsaw approach to biblical prophecy, is inimi-cal to the vibrant spirituality and participatory scriptural approach of Pentecostalism. The call is coming from many quarters for Pentecostals

---

1. See Sheppard, "Pentecostals and the Hermeneutics of Dispensationalism," 5–33.

to rethink their "uneasy relationship" with Scofieldian dispensationalism. The vagaries resulting from the adoption of an alien eschatology are becoming more apparent. Since Pentecostal theological scholarship is coming into its own, the time has come to formulate a Pentecostal eschatology, which does justice to the sensibilities of early Pentecostals before the movement allied with fundamentalism and conservative evangelical theology.

Pentecostals would benefit from an articulation of a fresh eschatology, one consistent with their spirituality and identity as a renewal movement. Helpful in constructing such an eschatology are two key convictions, which have a long and venerable history in strands of the Christian tradition amenable to Pentecostalism:[2] the anthropological doctrine that the human person as steward of creation (Gen 1:26–30) is a microcosm of the universe, and the soteriological conviction that salvation is a process that begins in this life and reaches its consummation in the next. With these two convictions in place, we will then be in a position to construct a cosmic eschatology as the full gospel writ large for all creation.[3] This affords Pentecostalism a distinctive and self-consistent eschatology, which reflects its key orienting theological concerns. I will proceed by discussing the eschatological elements of salvation available in this life, drawing primarily from the Wesleyan tradition but with an eye to the Eastern patristic tradition, before exploring what these facets of salvation entail on a cosmic scale.

SOTERIOLOGY IS ESCHATOLOGY

Though contemporary Pentecostalism is and always has been something of a melting pot of earlier theological ideas, even those who champion Reformed influences in the movement will typically not deny its Wesleyan heritage. John Wesley, deeply influenced by his high church Anglican tradition and his reading of Eastern patristic theology, construed salvation as a process punctuated by moments of crisis (i.e., justification, the new

2. I have here in mind Orthodoxy, the Anglo-Catholic and Wesleyan streams. See Bundy, "Visions of Sanctification," 104–36, and Rybarczyk, "Spiritualities Old and New," 7–25 and idem, *Beyond Salvation*.

3. This chapter is to some extent a selective summary of the constructive portion of my 2010 monograph, *Kingdom Come*. The larger work contains a much fuller articulation of each of the five "Full gospel" themes featured in the soteriological eschatology I am here presenting, as well as a discussion of many related biblical and theological themes and questions that come to the fore in any discussion of the last things.

birth, sanctification, etc.). This soteriological process demonstrates far more continuity with Orthodoxy, Roman Catholicism and Anglicanism than with the continental Reformation traditions, which have often either implicitly or explicitly promulgated justification in such a way that it becomes the sum total of soteriology. For Wesley, "initial" justification is just the beginning of the process of salvation, which has as its centerpiece a growing communion with the triune God through the Holy Spirit, culminating in entire sanctification. The Orthodox theology of *theosis*, or deification, correlates with the Wesleyan doctrine of entire sanctification in which an ontological change (not merely a relational one) has occurred in the believer. The believer is made a new creation through participation in the Trinitarian life and love of God. Perseverance of the sanctified believer will result in "final" justification in the eschaton. [4]

Wesley's eschatology is inextricably tied to his soteriology: for him they are "two parts of one system of understanding."[5] Many have thus supposed that Wesley held only a "realized" eschatology in which the kingdom is now entirely present in the process of each individual Christian's sanctification. Perhaps the notion would have some merit if not for two significant factors. First, Wesley understands salvation as a process that begins now and finds completion in the eschaton, whether or not entire sanctification is granted in this life. Wesley features a Cappadocian[6] understanding of perfection as dynamic rather than static, which allows for continual progression in perfection throughout eternity, and ties our present experience of salvation to our future life. Christ's incarnation, life, death, resurrection, and ascension has inaugurated the last days, seeking fulfillment in the eschaton.[7] This view maintains the Pauline "already/not yet" eschatological tension.

Second, Wesley's eschatological soteriology is not as rankly individualistic as contemporary notions of personal eschatology. Consistent with the Eastern patristic orientation typical of his thought, Wesley sees the salvation of the individual as microcosmic of the whole of creation. "For [Wesley], as for Jesus and Paul, the salvation of the individual directly involves and reflects God's larger plan of redemption for history

---

4. See Maddox, *Responsible Grace*, 157–91.

5. Greathouse, "John Wesley's View of the Last Things," 142.

6. Cf. Gregory of Nyssa, *Life of Moses*, 30 and passim; and Maddox, *Responsible Grace*, 253.

7. Greathouse, "John Wesley's View of the Last Things," 149.

and the created order. The devastating ravages of sin must give way to the redemptive power of Christ. Salvation must mean 'the restitution of all things.'"[8] Several of Wesley's sermons, particularly "The New Creation" and "The General Deliverance," express his holistic vision of cosmic soteriology.

John Wesley's protégé, John Fletcher, follows Wesley in tightly associating soteriology and eschatology. With Fletcher, however, the connection becomes more structured in his notion of a triune dispensational pattern discernible in both the individual believer's spiritual developmental progress and in the movement of the broader sweep of salvation history.

Fletcher exhibits remarkable similarity to the approach of the Eastern Father Gregory Nazianzen, who construes history as comprised of three dispensations, corresponding to the Trinitarian Persons in which God is revealed progressively in dispensing salvific knowledge through gracious interactions with creation.[9] The first age, the dispensation of the Father, stretches from creation to John the Baptist and reveals God as creator and sustainer; the Son's dispensation, which spans from John the Baptist (the forerunner of Christ) to Pentecost, reveals God as the redeemer; and the dispensation of the Holy Spirit, stretching from Pentecost to the eschaton, reveals God the Spirit as sanctifier, the one who perfects the work begun in creation and redemption.[10] These ages or dispensations will culminate in the fullness of time to usher in the eschatological kingdom. They are sequential, but perichoretic (mutually interpenetrating or indwelling), so that each successive stage deepens and qualifies the others, each containing the foretaste of, and thus the promise of, the next.[11] The age of the Father anticipates and promises the Son, the age of the Son promises the full revelation and real presence of the Spirit (see John 14:26), and the age

---

8. Greathouse, "John Wesley's View of the Last Things," 154. Cf. Maddox, *Responsible Grace*, 253.

9. Strieff, *Reluctant Saint?* 201–2. See also Wood, *The Meaning of Pentecost in Early Methodism*, 113–44. Though he is nearly unanimously depicted as following Joachim's schema, Fletcher's dispensational designations correspond much more closely to the specific historical transitions delineated by Gregory the Theologian.

10. Strieff, *Reluctant Saint?* 202; cf. Dayton, *Theological Roots of Pentecostalism*, 51.

11. Dayton, *Theological Roots of Pentecostalism*, 51.

of the Spirit both promises the new creation and gives us access to its powers in the here and now (Heb 6:5).[12]

Summarizing both Gregory of Nazianzen and John Fletcher, salvation comes through divine self-revelation in which the history of salvation finds its *telos* in the inner life of the triune God. All of salvation history is eschatological, as God progressively penetrates back into history, in order to redeem it from the corruption of human sinful self-centeredness. Salvation, understood as participation in the Trinitarian life of God, becomes possible in the glorification of Christ and the sending of the Spirit. "Fletcher referred to this development of grace in salvation history as a progressive shining forth of God's being like different rays of light until the fullness of his Triune grace was made known. When the fullness of the divine rays was revealed, then the fullness of salvation took effect. And that did not happen until Jesus was glorified and the Spirit was given to the Church."[13] The understanding of the age of the Spirit as the completion of God's salvific self-revelation in history illustrates the importance of pneumatology for both personal and cosmic soteriology.

Fletcher's pneumatological emphasis is clearly discernable in his understanding of the dispensational pattern of salvation history, which correlates to the stages of spiritual developmental in the believer's life. Fletcher descries correspondence between progressive works of grace in the individual believer's salvation and the dispensations of the Son and the Spirit. Justification is found in the appropriation of the work accomplished by Christ in the Son's dispensation, whereas entire sanctification is actualized in a full reception of the Holy Spirit,[14] a personal Pentecost event that completes the experienced reality of the new birth (symbolized by Easter), and the entrance into the "promised land" of life in Christ, who delivers from bondage to sin and death.[15] Christian perfection then is the province of the age of the Spirit. "The dispensation of the

---

12. Dayton, *Theological Roots of Pentecostalism*, 150.

13. Wood, *Meaning of Pentecost in Early Methodism*, 126.

14. Dayton, *Theological Roots of Pentecostalism*, 150.

15. See Wood, *Meaning of Pentecost in Early Methodism*, 117: "Easter was incomplete without Pentecost, even as the exodus from Egypt was incomplete without the entrance into Canaan. This is why the church could not be formed until the day of Pentecost. Fletcher interpreted 'baptism with water' (Easter) and 'baptism with the Spirit' (Pentecost) as the two liturgical moments of Christian initiation."

Spirit brings the inbreaking of Christian perfection already in this life."[16] The developmental stages of growth in grace for the individual also hold true for the ecclesial (communal) and cosmic levels. As with Orthodox anthropology and the theology of Fletcher, the human is a microcosm of the universe. For Fletcher, the experiences of justification and entire sanctification (which for Fletcher is synonymous with Spirit baptism) are reflective of the broader scope of the salvation of all creation.

As a consequence, the suggestion that Fletcher's eschatology is a "realized" personal eschatology is overstated. Fletcher holds that no one is saved alone. Individual salvation is consummated in the salvation of all creation, thereby holding intact the Pauline "already/not yet" eschatological tension. What happened to the community of the church at Pentecost in which the Spirit is available to each individual believer on a personal experiential plane, is a foretaste of divine glory awaiting the final, cosmic fulfillment in the eschaton. "Fletcher often spoke of the coming kingdom of God, its initial fulfillment on the day of Pentecost, its personal appropriation by faith in the lives of individual believers, and the final arrival of the kingdom when a global Pentecost would engulf the whole world. The essence of the millennium when the whole world would be baptized in the Holy Spirit, was loving God with all the heart, mind, and soul."[17]

The understanding of the individual *via salutis* writ large to encompass the whole of creation is in keeping with anthropological convictions of the human as steward of creation, and should find resonance among Pentecostals since many early Pentecostals were influenced by Fletcher.[18] This reading of eschatology offers a valid alternative to the fundamentalist dispensationalism promoted by Darby and popularized by the Scofield Bible. Fletcher's triadic dispensational pattern did not feature sharp distinctions between dispensations. The dispensational ages of the kingdom interpenetrate each other because they are reflective of the perichoretic relationships of the triune God. The Father created all through the Son (John 1) by the power of the Spirit. The Son was incarnate in Christ by the power and anointing of the Spirit to make the Father known, for "he is the reflection of God's glory and the exact im-

---

16. Strieff, *Reluctant Saint?* 208.

17. Wood, *Meaning of Pentecost in Early Methodism*, 147.

18. Land, *Pentecostal Spirituality*, 193. Cf. Wood, *Meaning of Pentecost in Early Methodism*, xvi.

print of God's very being" (Heb 1:3 NRSV). The Spirit proceeds from the Father and is sent by the Father in the Son's name (John 14:26) to make the eschatological presence of the resurrected Christ known through the church in the world as a foretaste of the coming kingdom of glory.

The dispensational distinction is appropriate due to the progressive nature of God's self-revelation and the resultant corresponding degree of receptivity achieved by creation in response to the ongoing activity of the divine hypostases in their respective, particular missions.[19] The threefold pattern also ties pneumatology more explicitly to soteriology and eschatology by conceiving of the first Pentecost as a penultimate eschatological event in God's economy,[20] which testifies to the content of the kingdom to come by currently granting access to its powers (Heb 6:5). Furthermore, early Pentecostals, who were deeply influenced by Fletcher, assumed a progressive view of God's self-revelation.[21]

Salvation history is not just for humans, and certainly not only, or even primarily, for individuals. The Spirit, as *Creator Spiritus*, perfects *all* the Spirit has created.[22] Human salvation is the necessary and facilitating avenue for the salvation of the cosmos. Material creation is saved precisely and requisitely through the salvation of humanity. This is the case because humans uniquely inhabit both the spiritual and material realms,[23] which is what made them initially fit prior to their fall to be God's vice-regents in creation, the stewards of the earth by God's directive (Gen 1:28).

However, our primordial parents opted to cut themselves off from the source of their spiritual life. The result was the impairment of the *imago Dei*, the enslavement of our spiritual nature to the perversions of our physical nature, and the encroachment of death upon God's originally good creation. The entire story of salvation history is the triune God calling us back to true life and drawing all creation back to partici-

---

19. Cantalamessa, *Come, Creator Spirit*, 44–45.

20. Althouse, *Spirit of the Last Days*, 25.

21. See, for example, the discussion of J. H. King's thought on this matter in Jacobsen, *Thinking in the Spirit*, 170–71. Fletcher's dispensational schema became particularly popular in the late nineteenth century in Wesleyan and Holiness circles, which are the same circles many of the original Pentecostals moved. See Dayton, *Theological Roots of Pentecostalism*, 152.

22. Bergmann, *Creation Set Free*, 53.

23. Ibid., 97.

pation in God.[24] The entire triune history of God's interactions with our fallen cosmos consists of a two part movement of descent and ascent: God's descent to the world and creation's responsive ascent, which itself is elicited and enabled by God.[25] The world's response is through the steward of humanity. "The redemptive mystery of our salvation should be centered on the theme . . . of the identification of God and of the human being, between which there is a double movement of conferring and receiving love. St Athanasius, inspired by St Irenaeus of Lyons said, 'God became man so that man might become God.' This short, incisive formula sums up the mystery of salvation."[26] This double movement begins with Noah, as God seeks to save a remnant from the chaos of the flood. The remnant survives and repopulates the world, but sin and death remained, evident in Noah's drunkenness and Ham's impudence (Gen 9:20–27).

The Father's dispensation commences with the ancestral history and Abra(ha)m's calling (Gen 12). Abraham receives the revelation of God as the one true God, in contrast to the polytheistic and idolatrous religious cultures of the day. These are God's initial overtures toward reconciliation. Though YHWH can, from a Christian perspective, be seen as connoting the Trinity, it would have been too much too soon to reveal God's true identity as Trinity at such a time and in such a religious climate, when the truth of only one true God was not fully established.[27] The revelation of the one God becomes clearer when God discloses God's name to Moses (Exod 3:14–15), and calls YHWH's chosen people Israel out of Egyptian slavery, as they are spared God's judgment of death on the land by the application of the blood of the lamb upon the post and lintel of their homes, a typological cruciform gesture that constitutes a "less definite" proclamation of the Son.[28] Throughout the years of the tribal confederacy, the monarchy (first united, then divided) and the exile and return to the "promised land," the divine Name abides with God's chosen people, keeping them accountable to the divinely issued

24. Bergmann, *Creation Set Free*, 96: "For Gregory the dynamic process of redemption consists in the Creator drawing the entire world up to himself. Everything now below is ultimately to move upward."

25. Bergmann, *Creation Set Free*, 95.

26. Bobrinskoy, *Compassion of the Father*, 55.

27. Gregory of Nazianzus, *Or.* 31.26, *On God and Christ*, 137.

28. Ibid.

mosaic law, the obedience of which constitutes a Godward movement to creation through Israel in the age of the Father, while YHWH teaches the infantile and sin-sick creation to take its first steps of redemption (Hos 11:3), and promises a suffering servant, a messiah, whose work will not stop at the mere restoration of Jacob, but will extend to all the nations (Isa 49:6).

The Son's dispensation begins with the annunciation of his birth to the Virgin Mary and then the onset of his adult ministry by John the Baptist. In the incarnation, God is truly Emmanuel, God with us, one of us, even as the Son remains God. The Eastern Church has always insisted that the incarnation itself is salvific because it is the union in one person of the divine and the human, the reunion of humanity with divinity in close intimate fellowship. Continental Protestantism unwisely truncates Christology and soteriology in its tendency to depict the crucifixion/ atonement as the primary salvific event in the life and ministry of Jesus. The incarnation, miracles, and preaching of Jesus declare God's will and plan to redeem God's good creation whatever the cost, even the cost of the death of God's Son. God made Jesus, who was without sin, *to be sin* (2 Cor 5:21), to absorb the fallenness and sickness of creation within God's self and to condemn corruption to death within the triune fellowship of love. The Father's resurrection of Jesus through the Spirit is both the declaration of Christ's divinity as God the Son incarnate and the inauguration of the new creation, for Jesus was raised bodily, the first among many sisters and brothers (Rom 8:29). Christ's resurrection culminates in his ascension to the Father, which also carries the created order, via his humanity, back to the Father.[29] Jesus Christ, as the representative of humanity in particular and the material creation in general, has, in his own person, in principle accomplished the salvation of the cosmos. Now it remains for the Spirit, sent by the Father in Jesus' name, to prepare the world for the full presence of God in the eschaton.

After the Son ascends, the Spirit descends at Pentecost, which marks the beginning of the age of the Spirit, "a new period in God's history with his world. . . . The Father and Son have already been revealed; now it is time for God's Spirit to become visible as well."[30] The Spirit's dispensation extends the redemptive powers of the incarnation throughout the world[31]

29. Bergmann, *Creation Set Free*, 95.

30. Ibid., 169.

31. Ibid.

in preparation for the end, preparing creation for the full union between God and the world. The Spirit leads us into all truth, beginning with the truth of the Spirit's own identity as the third person of the trinity, which completes the salvific self-revelation of God to the world.[32] This trinitarian, revelatory process, culminating in the first Pentecost completes the initial downward movement of God toward the world in the provision and offer of salvation.

The Spirit applies the salvation provided by Christ to the world, which effects the new creation.[33] This reverses the flow of the economy of salvation, the "eschatological trinitarian [sic] process,"[34] which constitutes God's saving relations with God's world. "Thus salvation history is a progression from the Father through the Son in the Spirit, then in the Spirit through the Son to the Father."[35] Even now, the Spirit is enervating creation with the eschatological powers of the kingdom and recalling to life that which was always meant to live forever. This penultimate age will culminate with the parousia in the presence of the glorified triune God filling in the new creation. But before examining the facets of the coming kingdom illustrated by the "full gospel" formula, we must examine the corollaries of this cosmic salvation at the microcosmic level, the salvation of the human person.

As we have seen, John Fletcher saw the dispensations in not only the cosmic scale of the redemption of the entire creation, but as also mirrored in the process of salvation within the individual believer.[36] The revelation of the Father advances us from the condition of "Gentilism," a state wherein the person possesses a bare acknowledgment of a deity, or pantheon of gods, or supernatural realities, to "Judaism," the specific confessional acknowledgment of the one true God revealed as the creative Father. The revelation of the Son moves us from Judaism to gospel, which is the good news of the fulfillment (as opposed to abolishment) of the law in Jesus Christ. The revelation of the Spirit applies to us the powers of the resurrection and teaches us the mystery of salvation in this post-Pentecost era.[37] For the believer, this reflects the process of salva-

32. Gregory of Nazianzus, *Or.* 31.27, *On God and Christ*, 138.

33. Bergmann, *Creation Set Free*, 139.

34. Land, *Pentecostal Spirituality*, 198.

35. Ibid., 200.

36. Dayton, *Theological Roots of Pentecostalism*, 150.

37. Wood, *Meaning of Pentecost*, 6.

tion, wherein one moves from awareness of deity to the acknowledgment of God as God, with all the attendant demands such revelation holds for fallen creatures. We find relief from these demands when we accept the merits of Christ's work on our behalf and when we appropriate the justification accomplished and provided by the Son, with the *imputation* of his righteousness covering our sinfulness, enabling a preliminary restored relationship with God. We then experience the sanctifying and empowering work of the Holy Spirit, which *imparts* the truly transforming grace of God to us in sanctification and Spirit baptism,[38] which for Pentecostals are not synonymous but are, I contend, nevertheless intricately related.[39] This is all provisional as the "already" aspect of salvation awaiting its final fulfillment in the "not yet" of the eschaton. The "already" of the kingdom includes the initial works of grace, which will then be consummated in the second movement in which creation is drawn up in God by God in concert with the creation's growing receptivity to divine grace, not yet here.[40] The logic of a Pentecostal perspective of Fletcher's[41] theme can be construed in the following chiastic pattern of concentric parallelism, moving inward from A. Initial Justification, B. Initial Sanctification, C. Initial Spirit Baptism and finally D. Entire Sanctification to Parousia; then moving outward from D. Parousia to Entire Sanctification, C. Final Spirit Baptism, B. Theosis, and A. Final Justification.[42] Everything that happens in this current age is a result of the downward movement of God toward creation, which enables and

38. These terms are synonymous in Fletcher and the later Holiness movement.

39. See Thompson, *Kingdom Come*, ch. 8.

40. See Bulgakov, *Bride of the Lamb*, 418. Bulgakov here speaks of the necessity of the world being conformed to its original purpose, a fit dwelling place for God and humanity in communion. The Spirit is the divine agent, in synergy with creation, who accomplishes this act. Bulgakov, *The Comforter*, 350.

41. Fletcher's contribution here is a Spirit-facilitated *via salutis*, a pneumatologically inspired process of salvation. He would not make a distinction between entire sanctification and Spirit baptism, and referred to the entire process as the new birth. See Streiff, *Reluctant Saint?* 53–54.

42. Pentecostal theologian Amos Yong, explicitly following Wesley, argues for a teleological process of full salvation populated by a variety of interpenetrating crisis moments. Yong chooses the appellation of Spirit baptism as the primary category for this process, without denying the reality of the particular crisis experience classical Pentecostals call by that name. Yong's use of terms may be debated (my own preference is *theosis*), but the fluid eschatological-soteriological complex accords well with what I am here proposing. See Yong, *Spirit Poured Out on All Flesh*, 81–120, esp. 119.

evokes the movement of creation upward to God, finding its completion[43] in the relational reunion of *theosis*. All the crisis moments that punctuate the process of the Pentecostal *via salutis* anticipate and principally pre-accomplish microcosmically what will occur on the macrocosmic scale in the eschaton.[44] "Transformation of the believer is the first step in the transformation of the world . . ."[45] The interconnectivity of humanity with the material cosmos and the salvation is wrought by the Holy Spirit.[46] The Spirit facilitates the final salvation of the entirety of creation in all its myriad interrelationships and dimensions.[47]

ESCHATOLOGY IS SOTERIOLOGY: THE FULL GOSPEL OF THE ESCHATON

As noted above, the five-fold Wesleyan-Pentecostal full gospel was Christologically articulated as Jesus as savior (justification), sanctifier, Spirit baptizer, healer, and coming king, but the emphasis was on the Spirit's work in the believer and the world. The Christocentric flavor must be maintained, but with the recognition of its patrocentric and pneumatocentric accents, and thus fully Trinitarian. Specifically, the Word (Son) and the Spirit, the *Logos* and the *Pneuma*, are the two hands of the Father (Irenaeus), eternally begotten and eternally breathed, respectively. Thus, the Spirit inheres perichoretically in the work of Christ, and Christ inheres perichoretically in the work of the Spirit. The short shrift the Spirit has received in most eschatology in the West, popular or otherwise, can be redressed through a pneumatological Pentecostal eschatology of cosmic soteriology. The five-fold pattern will serve as the organizing principle in what follows.

The Second Coming

In keeping with the ancient Trinitarian doctrine of Irenaeus, the "two hands" of the Father in the Word and Spirit, and the ancient principle

---

43. Entire sanctification is not denied availability in this life, but entire sanctification this side of the eschaton does not free us from "sin improperly so called," the fallenness of our finitude. It frees us from willful sin that results from disordered affections (Wesley).

44. Land, *Pentecostal Spirituality*, 78–79.

45. Althouse, *Spirit of the Last Days*, 183.

46. Yong, *Spirit Poured Out on All Flesh*, 95.

47. Ibid., 97.

of *perichoresis*, the parousia of Christ also precipitates the parousia of the Holy Spirit.[48] The Spirit is the active Trinitarian agent in the kenotic act of the incarnation via the conception of Christ in the Virgin Mary, and the Spirit anoints Jesus for ministry at his baptism. By the Spirit Jesus performs healings and exorcisms in illustration of the arrival of the kingdom. The Spirit raises Christ from the dead at the Father's behest. After ascending to the Father, Christ sends the Spirit as Comforter at Pentecost. The Spirit is present now kenotically, empowering us rather than overpowering us, and the Spirit now reveals to us the nature of the coming kingdom by the Spirit's own sanctifying and empowering presence. Through Jesus, the Spirit is concretely present in the world. The Spirit in turn now makes Jesus spiritually present in the world, particularly and most fully in the church. "In His earthly life Jesus was the place of the Spirit of God, His favorite place, total and unique. Today, in the time of the church, the Spirit is the place of the presence of Jesus."[49] When the Father sends the Son in full glory to inherit his rightful kingdom, the Spirit will also be manifest in full glory and splendor, for the world will have been prepared to the degree necessary for the Spirit's unrestricted presence.

Pentecostalism is restorationist in orientation. Whatever merit this claim has, Pentecostalism certainly constitutes a significant moment in the process of the restoration of holistic Christian spirituality. "But this process of restoration is part of the larger restoration of all things which will finally issue in that which is greater than the initial creation. It is a 'restoration plus', for God will be 'all in all.'"[50]

Healing

Healing has served as a soteriological and eschatological sign within Pentecostalism. The healings performed by Jesus in his earthly ministry underscore his claim that the kingdom had come among the people.[51] "Healing was in anticipation of the final healing of all things. The material was meant for the spiritual and vice-versa. Healing anticipated a

---

48. See Bulgakov, *Bride of the Lamb*, 404–5. Bulgakov describes the Spirit's first advent at Pentecost as a kenosis of the Spirit in the same manner of the Son's kenosis in the incarnation.

49. Bobrinskoy, *Compassion of the Father*, 63.

50. Land, *Pentecostal Spirituality*, 200–201.

51. Ervin, *Healing*, 2.

millennial restoration of all things: heaven come to earth and no more sickness or sorrow."[52] When Jesus raised the dead it was illustrative of the fact that "death is not the natural consequence of life."[53] The bodily healing of the saints signifies the healing of all created matter.

The sinful destructiveness of technology and war on God's good creation will be healed, as will the finite processes of nature that wreak violence in the course of their functioning (earthquakes, volcanic eruptions, seasonal storms, etc.), for the new earth will have no sea ("chaos," Rev 21:1). The emphasis on healing both now and in the eschaton points to the intended sacramental nature of creation, realized in the new heavens and the new earth. Indeed, the Christian dogma of the resurrection of the body logically and theologically requires a remade physical cosmos. "Theologically it makes little sense to postulate a nonearthly eschatological existence while believing in the resurrection of the body . . . The resurrection body demands a corresponding glorified but nevertheless material environment. The future *material* existence therefore belongs inalienably to the Christian eschatological expectation."[54] *This* world will be renovated and made fit for the dwelling of the triune God and God's perfected creatures. All will be healed and made whole, brought into conformity with the Word of God, as the saints are nurtured to full health by the Marriage Supper of the Lamb.[55]

Spirit Baptism

The Second Coming of the king and of the Spirit constitutes a cosmic Pentecost, as all the cosmos is baptized in the Spirit by the full presence of Jesus, the Spirit-baptizer, and thereby energized by the empowering presence of God through the Son and the Spirit. The saints are empowered to reign perfectly with Christ in the new creation. "Tongues of fire" were manifest in the kenotic, first coming of the Spirit (Acts 2), and are now surging through creation as the dross of ungodly elements afflicting the created order is burned away. The old heavens and the old earth,

---

52. Land, *Pentecostal Spirituality*, 54.

53. Ervin, *Healing*, 43.

54. Volf, *Work in the Spirit*, 95, italics in original.

55. This also implies the need for a significant overhaul in popular Pentecostal attitudes toward creation-care. If this world is to be healed rather than destroyed, our efforts, or lack thereof, in the present to fulfill our original mandate as stewards of creation will have eternal significance.

which are the patterns of this present fallen age, will be destroyed by the holy and powerful fires of the Spirit of God (2 Pet 3:7, 10).[56]

Tongues shall cease (1 Cor 13:8), for there will now be no need for them. We, and the Spirit with us and for us, will no longer groan for the revealing of the children of God (Rom 8:19–27), for we will be revealed, transfigured with the whole cosmos *by* the Spirit and transformed into the beings we were always meant to be. The power and intimacy with the triune God, which is a hallmark of the Pentecostal experience in this world, is merely a foretaste of the intimacy we will have with this God in the next, when we will no longer lack the expressive means, evidenced now by tongues, to express accurately intimacy with the Father, Son and Spirit. We shall see God as God is, a perfect triune community of love, and the limits of finite linguistic mediation will fall away. We will perfectly praise God throughout eternity.

Entire Sanctification

The fullness of the Spirit's presence in the cosmic Spirit baptism sanctifies creation entirely. The surging fires of the cosmic Pentecost are purging, purifying powers, melting away the dross, making the creation fit for the unmediated presence of its Creator. Just as Spirit baptism in the individual believer is a sanctifying experiential reality, the cosmic Spirit baptism results in cosmic sanctification, for nothing that is not in conformity with the Spirit can remain in the Spirit's presence. Thus, the cosmos will then realize its true nature, as the sanctuary of the living God. The growing presence of God in creation, which began as a small compartment in the tabernacle of the Hebrews, later became installed in the temple of Israel, and still later expanded into the world as the church is now thrown open to the whole cosmos, so that the new creation becomes the cosmic Holy of Holies. The unapproachable light (1 Tim 6:16) will now enfold and illuminate the entirety of reality. Humanity and the rest of creation will be perfected together by the full presence of the Trinity in God's holy city, the New Jerusalem, which will be the state of our final, entirely perfected, existence.

---

56. Bulgakov, *Bride of the Lamb*, 400.

Justification

When our primordial parents fell into sin, all of creation, over which they had been given stewardship, fell with them (Rom 8:20). Just as creation lapsed out of right standing with God due to humanity's fall, so humanity's rise in salvation entails the rise of creation to the same. When the full presence of God is manifest at the parousia, we, through our faith and the works performed on its basis (Jas 2:24), will be finally justified. As creation's stewards, our final justification provides for the justification of all the created order. This justified condition, the result of the deification of the cosmos through the sanctifying presence of the triune God, is a complement to healing, Spirit baptism and sanctification: to be finally, fully and rightly related to God means to be finally, fully and rightly related to one another. All oppositional relationships, including unjust social structures and adversarial dynamics between humanity and nature will be done away.

CONCLUSION

As Pentecostals develop their contributions to the broader church's theology, they must find a way to situate their distinctiveness within the broader patterns of historic Christian traditions amenable to their own, and strive for theological coherence. The foregoing has been an earnest attempt at integrating Pentecostal eschatology with soteriology, as it accounts for the rightly cherished vibrant spirituality and theological formulation of classical Pentecostalism, while finding continuity with prior Christian thinking on these matters. From the perspective of systematic theology, this construction has the benefit of couching anthropological soteriology within the broader creation-consummation nexus in a far more consistent way than Scofieldian dispensationalism, with its covenantal dualism and patchwork view of biblical revelation. Whether or not this particular proposal finds acceptance, Pentecostals need to leave the largely discredited hermeneutic of dispensationalism behind.

9

Pentecostal Eschatology in Context

The Eschatological Orientation of the Full Gospel

PETER ALTHOUSE

INTRODUCTION

JÜRGEN MOLTMANN IS PERHAPS the foremost Protestant theologian of
the latter half of the twentieth century to push for the recovery of
eschatological hope. He insists that all theology is eschatological in orientation.[1] If Moltmann's claim is true, and I believe that it is, then what
does this mean for the ongoing construction of Pentecostal theology?
In other words, what would the theology of Pentecostals look like if it
consistently founds its truth claims in an eschatological orientation?

One is immediately faced with a problem however: What is Pentecostal theology? Pentecostalism as a movement is a fluid and diverse
constellation of claims, experiences, ethos and norms. Pentecostals have
no confessions of faith, no consistently articulated doctrines, though
some have produced statements of faith, albeit in an inconsistent and
hodge-podge manner. Pentecostals and non-Pentecostals alike have
tended to define the movement in terms of its practice of glossolalia, or
what Pentecostals call "speaking in tongues." Donald Dayton, however,
has argued that the focus on glossolalia has resulted in its theological impoverishment, subjecting theological analysis to ahistorical assumptions

---

1. Moltmann, *Theology of Hope*, 16.

and sociological and psychological categories.[2] Instead, Dayton argues that the analysis of Pentecostalism must look at the broader theological *gestalt* of the "full gospel," defined in terms of four Christological themes of salvation, healing, baptism in the Spirit and the Second Coming.[3]

Dayton's proposal is an important starting point for any discussion of Pentecostal theology in that it extrapolates and draws together the major components of Pentecostalism despite its theological and experiential diversity. However, within the matrix of the full gospel only the "Second Coming of Christ" is defined in terms of eschatology. If Moltmann's statement that the entirety of theology is eschatological is true, then the fourfold gospel remains underdeveloped. My proposal is that Pentecostal theology must be rearticulated within the context of eschatological hope, in a way that the future hope of the entire cosmos is accessible in the present. In other words, the world and creation together is the context for eschatology and therefore any holistic eschatological construction must be founded in a creational eschatology. I shall argue that a holistic eschatological hope must undergird Pentecostal theology and propose to construct a holistic Pentecostal eschatology by addressing the strands of the fourfold gospel.

THE ESCHATOLOGICAL DIMENSIONS
OF THE COMING KING

The doctrine of the "coming King," "Second Coming," or "imminent return" of Christ had a prominent place in the theological orientation of early Pentecostals. There is even evidence that the eschatological vision was already integrated to a certain degree into the other strands of the full gospel. For instance, the development of the doctrine of the baptism in the Spirit, in which speaking in tongues was the "Bible evidence" that one had indeed been baptized, was oriented to a great end-time revival

2. Dayton, *Theological Roots of Pentecostalism*, 15–16.

3. Ibid., 19–23, 173–74. Dayton acknowledges the tension between the fourfold and five-fold patterns, the latter focusing on the doctrine of sanctification as defined by Wesleyan Holiness concerns, but claims "the fourfold pattern expresses more clearly and cleanly the logic of Pentecostal theology." The four- or even five-fold gospel has its limitations however. The Christological dimension is presupposed but needs to be made more explicit. Also, mission is an important theological focus that must be assessed and ecclesiology, which Pentecostals tend to approach pragmatically, needs explicit theological grounding. Otherwise it will be susceptible to the whims of contemporary culture.

preceding the coming of the Lord. For Parham, speaking in tongues was a supernatural endowment to speak the languages of the world, in order for the gospel to be preached to all nations as the last sign ushering in the return of Christ. In other words, both the urgency in preaching the gospel to the whole world and the supernatural endowment of speaking in tongues were eschatological. As one early Pentecostal writer proclaimed, *"The second coming of the Lord Jesus Christ is not a feature of the program, but it is THE program.* The preaching of regeneration, the restoration of man back to God, the outpouring and the Baptism of the Holy Spirit upon believers, the working of signs and wonders and miracles in the earth, are features of this program, leading up to its grand and glorious fulfillment."[4]

The turn to an eschatological understanding of the emergence of Pentecostalism began with the publication of Robert Mapes Anderson's *Vision of the Disinherited.* Adopting a social deprivation model, Anderson argued that the rise of Pentecostalism must be understood as yet another fundamentalist movement, which emphasized the ecstatic experience of speaking in tongues as an indication of the imminent return of Christ.[5] The eschatological thrust of the movement was defined in terms of dispensational millennialism, which embodied revolutionary potential for social change, but was ultimately frustrated by conservative political forces.[6]

As mentioned, Dayton identified the "coming King" as an important Christological category in the full gospel. Disagreeing with Anderson, Dayton insisted that in the connection between pneumatology and eschatology the "personal infusion of the Spirit seem to long most ardently for a return of Christ and a corresponding cosmic transformation of this world order."[7] Pentecostalism emerged in a period of history when American evangelicalism was shifting from a postmillennial to a premillennial eschatology. While Pentecostalism may have had some affinity to premillennial dispensationalism, its cessationist assumptions severely undercut Pentecostal pneumatology and ecclesiology. Dayton argues:

4. McDowell, "Purpose of the Coming of the Lord," 2. Italics mine.

5. Anderson, *Vision of the Disinherited*, 4.

6. Ibid., 195–96, 221–24.

7. Dayton, *Theological Roots of Pentecostalism*, 144.

> . . . it is not clear that Pentecostal eschatology, with its emphasis
> on the inauguration of the "new order of the latter rain" and the
> "restoration of spiritual gifts" as a prelude to the return of Christ,
> fits as easily into dispensational categories as it is sometimes as-
> sumed. It was generally premillennial in expecting a millennial
> kingdom to be inaugurated by an imminent return of Christ, but
> contradicted dispensational distinctives by adopting different
> (generally tripartite) periodizations of human history by applying
> many Old Testament promises to the church, by appropriating
> more directly texts (the Lord's Prayer, the Sermon on the Mount,
> and so forth) that dispensationalists relegate to the millennial
> kingdom, and so forth.[8]

In other words, dispensationalism created a serious threat to the Pentecostal insistence that the apostolic gifts were for today's church.

D. William Faupel also argues that eschatology was the primary
impulse of early Pentecostalism and emerged as a species-specific
paradigm shift in the millenianism of nineteenth-century perfection-
ism.[9] Moreover, Faupel constructs five models through which early
Pentecostals self-identified. The "full gospel," which argues that the theological motifs of justification, sanctification, healing, baptism in the Holy
Spirit and Second Coming of Christ were the myriad of core beliefs;
the "latter rain," which uses the weather patterns of Palestine to explain
charismatic outpouring of the Spirit like that of the early church precipitates the eschaton; the "apostolic faith," which argues for the restoration of charismatic gifts; the "Pentecostal movement, which looks to the
event of Pentecost as narrated in Acts as the inaugurated new era and
experience of God's working in the church; and the "everlasting gospel,"
which looks to the imminent, premillennial return of Christ as the basis
for missionary and evangelistic work.[10] Faupel prefers the "everlasting
gospel" as the model that best expressed the eschatological impulse in
early Pentecostalism. However, I would suggest that the eschatological
impulse is integrated with all five models. The models of the everlasting
gospel, latter rain, and full gospel already have an implicit eschatological
focus. The Pentecostal model with its orientation to Acts 2 potentially
imbibes the eschatological nuances of the narrative, and the apostolic
model, while looking back to the early church would also imbibe the es-

---

8. Dayton, *Theological Roots of Pentecostalism*, 145.

9. Faupel, *Everlasting Gospel*, 17.

10. Faupel, "Function of 'Models,'" 53–63.

chatological anticipation of the in-breaking Day of the Lord, as opposed, for instance, to a secular eschatology in which progress and evolutionary development are the eschatological categories.[11]

While the historical evidence of the role of eschatology in the emergence of Pentecostalism is ongoing, theological reassessments have also been underway. Steven Land launched a renewed theological interest in Pentecostal eschatology with the publication of *Pentecostal Spirituality*. Land reconstructs Pentecostal eschatology in a way that makes sense to the contemporary mind. For Land, Pentecostal eschatology is better suited to inaugural or proleptic eschatology: "This 'promise-fulfillment, already-not yet' is a tense dynamic which characterizes Christianity's eschatological passion. From time to time when the tension is resolved prematurely—either in the direction of an otherworldly, 'not yet' escapism or a this worldly, 'already' accommodation—there arise movements of restoration, revival, awakening and renewal to remind the church that it is the 'eschatological mother' whose sons and daughters are meant to prophesy."[12] The proleptic tension situates Pentecostalism within the socio-historical framework, which inspires believers to acts of social benevolence and justice. Issues in the world such as racism, poverty, chauvinism, or spiritual lostness were addressed within the context of its eschatological impulse, so that a reconciled church would realize racial equality, social justice, women in ministry and mission. We are "involved in cosmic struggle with powers and principalities—in all these respects Pentecostalism lived and lives in an apocalyptic existence made existentially palpable by the presence, manifestations and power of the Holy Spirit."[13] Within the already-not yet tension, Land proposes a holistic understanding of eschatology, which not only included the personal but social and cosmic as well. "Hope is not given by and in and for the present order that is passing away. This does not mean they demeaned this world. It was a hope which had continuity—a new body, a new earth, a new heaven. But this hope was at the same time discontinuous because it is new—a new creation."[14] Although Land's work is perhaps idealist in its reading of the movement—overlooking some inherent tensions and squabbles, its value lies in the construction of an eschatology more in

11. See Schwartz's *Eschatology*, chapter 4.

12. Land, *Pentecostal Spirituality*, 15.

13. Ibid., 66.

14. Ibid., 65

keeping with the heart and vision of Pentecostal spirituality, one which embodies hope and the spiritual motivation to tackle dehumanizing concerns in the world.

Frank Macchia also addressed Pentecostal eschatology in *Spirituality and Social Liberation*, through a Pentecostal reading of Wuerttemburg Pietism. Macchia looks to the pietistic theology of Johann and Christoph Blumhardt, in which the "kingdom of God" was the primary metaphor for eschatological anticipation. Briefly, Pietism experienced shifting tensions between belief in the apocalyptic, future in-breaking of the kingdom, with the realization of its presence in history, belief that the kingdom will bring the cosmic transformation of creation with its concrete presence in the liberation of the poor and oppressed, and belief in the apocalyptic outpouring of the Spirit in the future with its universal outpouring in the present age. These tensions were captured in Johann and Christoph Blumhardts' belief that the kingdom was a matter of prayerful "waiting" for the kingdom to arrive and Christian "hurrying" to work for the kingdom.[15] My purpose here is not a detailed discussion of their eschatology (see Macchia's chapter in this volume), but to note the implications of Macchia's work on the Blumhardts for Pentecostal eschatology. The kingdom of God cannot be wholly futuristic (apocalyptic) in which Christians passively allow the powers and principalities of this world to overrun the good in hope for spiritual escape through mystical experience or a rapture, nor can it be wholly present (realized) in which current social and political realities are sanctioned by the church as the "new Christendom," but must be seen in tension between God's sovereign in-breaking and human participation in the work of the kingdom. Eschatology needs to be prophetic in its witness to the kingdom as it speaks to our concrete social and cosmic contexts.[16] History and creation are included in the eschatological fold, not as something that must ultimately be opposed and overcome, but as something that is incorporated into eschatological glory.

My own work in *Spirit of the Last Days* is an attempt to demonstrate the diversity of Pentecostal eschatology by showing three different eschatological positions in the history of the movement: the first was a latter rain eschatology, which anticipated a wondrous outpouring of the Spirit unseen since apostolic days. The belief was that as the new age dawned

---

15. Macchia, *Spirituality and Social Liberation*, 42.

16. Ibid., 159.

that the Spirit would pour out spiritual gifts to empower Christians to prepare for the kingdom; the second was the rise of dispensational millennialism (what I call fundamentalist dispensationalism) in the mid-twentieth century, in part a reaction to the 1940s Latter Rain movement, a divisive movement that used latter rain theology to castigate established Pentecostal denominations, and in part due to the evangelicalization of Pentecostalism, in which dispensational millennialism played a major role in reshaping Pentecostal theology.[17] The third phase is ongoing, in which Pentecostals are dissatisfied with dispensationalism and are articulating a proleptic eschatology, which focuses on the already-not yet, or the inauguration and fulfillment of the eschaton.[18]

My point is that Pentecostal eschatology is diverse, both in the early movement and in its current manifestations. Latter rain, threefold dispensationalism, historic millennialism, covenantal and inaugural eschatologies are just some of the options Pentecostals employed to understand their role in God's plan for the world and the kingdom-to-come.

THE ESCHATOLOGICAL ORIENTATION OF HEALING

Bodily healing was and is an integral part of Pentecostalism's full gospel, believed to bring physical, emotional, psychological, or spiritual wholeness. Inheriting its theological position from the nineteenth-century healing movement,[19] and contextualized in diverse forms throughout the twentieth century,[20] early Pentecostals believe that healing is made universally available in the atonement as a soteriological benefit of the work of Christ[21] or that healing is available but may not be actualized until after death.[22] Kim Alexander hints at a position that healing is a

17. Althouse, *Spirit of the Last Days*, especially chapter 1.

18. Ibid., especially chapter 2.

19. See Chappell, "Divine Healing Movement in America." Van De Walle, *Heart of the Gospel*, chapter 4; Dayton, *Theological Roots of Pentecostalism*, chapter 5; Alexander, *Pentecostal Healing*, chapter 1.

20. Warrington, *Pentecostal Theology*, 267–68. Early Pentecostals followed in the footsteps of the healing movement and established healing homes where people could rest and pray, follow a nutritional diet, and receive healing. The mid- to late- twentieth century witnessed the rise of healing evangelists who would hold revival type campaigns for the primary purpose of bodily healing.

21. Kydd, *Healing through the Centuries*, especially pertinent is part 6, which highlights the soteriological model of Pentecostals.

22. Warrington, *Pentecostal Theology*, 271.

partial realization of the in-breaking kingdom of God as a foretaste of the resurrection.[23] This latter view is the position I shall explore but with an eye to a soteriological integration.

Frank Macchia's work on the healing theology of the Blumhardts highlights its eschatological framework. Without going into detail, the healing of Gottlieben Dittus[24] spurred Johann Blumhardt to develop a holistic theology of healing, which envisioned the liberative healing of the suffering of all creation in the in-breaking of God's kingdom.[25] The Christological work of the cross brought victory in overcoming the forces of darkness[26] in which Jesus comes in time for the healing of both body and soul.[27] Christoph Blumhardt developed his father's theology is a social direction in which the Spirit was poured out to remove greed and eliminate class struggle.[28] Healing was seen as the alleviation of social ills, poverty and oppression.[29] He also saw the outpouring of the Spirit of Pentecost environmentally as the transformation of creation, contextualized in the struggle to oppose the "poisoning of trees."[30] Both father and son came to understand healing as an eschatological category of the in-breaking kingdom into this world longing for the transformation of creation.[31]

Miroslav Volf notes the materiality of the doctrine and its correlation with theologies of liberation. "Both liberation and Pentecostal theology emphasize what I will call," claims Volf, ". . . the *materiality of salvation*. Salvation is not merely a spiritual reality touching only an individual person's inner being but also has to do with *bodily* human existence."[32] Unlike conciliar Protestantism which interpreted salvation as an inner spiritual change, Pentecostalism (and liberation theology) claims that there are concrete material implications to divine healing. Volf also casts the Pentecostal doctrine of healing in an eschatological

23. Alexander, *Pentecostal Healing*, 241.

24. Macchia, *Spirituality and Social Liberation*, 64–65.

25. Ibid., 67.

26. Ibid., 70–71.

27. Ibid., 74.

28. Ibid., 126–27.

29. Ibid., 128.

30. Ibid., 116.

31. See Macchia's chapter in this volume.

32. Volf, "Materiality of Salvation," 448.

light as a partial realization of the kingdom in the world. "Healing is rather '*one aspect of the Gospel*,' but one without which the gospel is not complete because healing of the body is conceived of as a partial fulfillment of the promise of the resurrection of Christian bodies. Healing is the future redemption of the body's happening in the present by the Spirit's power on the basis of Christ's atoning work."[33] The already/not-yet of the eschatological new creation means that healing is a partial realization of the resurrection.[34] Because the resurrection of Christ and the outpouring of the Spirit have already been "inaugurated," God's reign is already here and calls Christians to both expectation and participation in the kingdom, though with caveat that the arrival of the kingdom is definitively not a human achievement.[35] The consequence, of course, is that healing cast in the light of the eschaton as its partial realization, also has social-political implications as Christians work in service to God's righteousness to change the material conditions of the world to "ensure bodily well being."[36]

I would like to draw on Macchia and Volf to propose a strengthened eschatological view of healing, which correlates to the resurrection as the eschatological fullness of healing but also to the cosmic redemption of the new creation, in which creation itself groans for its redemption. Such a position does not deny the soteriological position that healing is a provision of the atonement, but expands it within the totality of the salvific work of Christ. If one looks at healing from an eschatological perspective, then the Pentecostal conundrum of the universal application of healing as a provision of the atonement, and the reason why some are not healed, is overcome. Why are some healed and others not? Simply, we have not experienced the eschatological resurrection yet. Healing is a partial realization of the new creation, anticipatory signs of the cosmic reign of Christ. The bodily implications of the resurrection and healing as a sign of resurrection hope is immediately obvious, in that redemption is not construed solely as a spiritual redemption in which the soul ascends into heaven and the body is left behind as corruptible, but a bodily resurrection. As the apostle Paul claims, if there is not resurrection then our

33. Ibid., 458.

34. Ibid., 459.

35. Volf relies heavily on his brother-in-law Peter Kuzmič to make this argument, ibid., 462.

36. Ibid., 463–64.

faith is in vain (1 Cor 15:12–19), and therefore the resurrection of Christ and healing as signs of the eschatological resurrection are soteriological in that they are objectively accomplished in Christ's atoning work of the cross. In agreement with Moltmann, a bodily resurrection presupposes creation's transformation in that the human person, body and soul, is an integrated whole and must both be transformed by the resurrection in order to complete salvation.[37]

As a corollary, healing as a sign of creation's eschatological transformation in the context of the proleptic eschatology I am proposing has implications for social action and justice, and especially for ecological responsibility. Creation is the context from which God's eschatological transformation will emerge, thereby calling us to participate "already" in the care of God's good creation, as we await its apocalyptic transformation. By apocalyptic I do not mean cataclysmic, but rather the elimination of sin and death, which are antithetical to the kingdom of God. In other words, if the doctrine of healing is cast in the eschatological vision of the new creation, present healing (bodily or otherwise) is ultimately a characteristic of the resurrection and penultimate signs of the hope for which we await, then it also has implications for our participation in the transformation of creation, not that we can somehow bring about the new creation, but we are called to participate with God in God's sovereign enactment to transform all creation.

THE ESCHATOLOGICAL ORIENTATION OF THE BAPTISM IN THE SPIRIT

The Pentecostal doctrine of the baptism in the Holy Spirit and its concomitant phenomenon of glossolalia, or what Pentecostals prefer to call "speaking in tongues," emerged within the specific historical context of Wesleyan Holiness, Revivalist, and Keswick evangelicalism. Biblically, the distinctive hinges on a pneumatological reading of Luke-Acts, in which a subjectivizing hermeneutic is employed allowing Pentecostals to place themselves in the narrative and then reading their own narrative through the Lukan narrative.[38] Acts 2:1–39, 8:14–17, 10:44–46 and 19:1–17 are viewed as describing Spirit baptism and speaking in tongues as a normal practice in the apostolic church from which Pentecostals derive

---

37. Moltmann, *God in Creation*, 256–59

38. Dayton, *Theological Roots of Pentecostalism*, 23–24.

their doctrine. Historically, baptism in the Spirit is distinguished from the reception of the Spirit in the baptism of water, which is ordained as the confession of the initiation of faith. Spirit baptism is understood as a "subsequent" stage in the life of faith, indicated by the physical phenomenon of glossolalia, a link referred to as "initial evidence" or "initial physical sign."[39] Curiously, the first decade of the Assemblies of God, one of the denominations that emerged from the Pentecostal revival, articulated its doctrine as "the full consummation of the Baptism in the Spirit."[40] Immediately obvious is the eschatological connotation of the term "consummation," which is suggestive of an inaugural eschatology in which Spirit baptism and its phenomenological indicator of glossolalia is the completion or fulfillment of the Spirit's activity already begun in the reception of the Spirit in the baptism of faith. However, these distinctions are not without controversy and have created tensions within the Pentecostal movement. Pentecostals also typically distinguish the practice of glossolalia in the baptism of the Spirit as depicted in Acts as the entry point into the higher Christian life from the charismatic gifts of tongues and interpretation in 1 Cor 12–14 for the edification of the community of faith. The former is potentially available to all believers, the latter according to one's spiritual gifting.

Keith Warrington is quick to note the tensions in Pentecostalism, in that while some Pentecostals affirm Spirit baptism as a doctrinal proposition and ferociously defend the doctrine through their particular reading of the Bible, others wish to explore the validity of the experience of glossolalia but realize that its biblical foundation is difficult to assert.[41] The problem from a biblical point of view is the different terminology indicating the reception of the Spirit ("filling," "indwelling," "outpouring" are likewise used),[42] which heightens the tensions among Pentecostals and with their Charismatic siblings. Thus neither a shallow biblical reading nor a historical analysis is adequate for a full explanation of the meaning of Spirit baptism. One must turn to a theological assessment of

39. There is an irony currently playing out in the Assemblies of God by one particular group wanting to recast "initial physical sign" as "initial evidence." The outcome of this tension has not yet been seen.

40. "Minutes of the General Council of the Assemblies of God in the United States, Canada and Foreign Lands, 1916," 11, Flower Pentecostal Heritage Center.

41. Warrington, *Pentecostal Theology*, 96.

42. Williams, "Baptism in the Holy Spirit," 355–56.

the doctrine, and my position is that Spirit baptism must be integrated within the horizon of a proleptic eschatology.

A number of Pentecostal theologians have started to think about the theology of tongues and Spirit baptism. Richard Baer argues that glossolalia "functions" in ways similar to the silence of Quaker prayer and the aesthetic of liturgical worship, all of which allow the analytical mind to "rest" so that the human heart and spirit can focus on God. Although glossolalia can heighten the emotions it is not emotional per se, but employs non-cognitive elements of the human mind and body. As a form of prayer, glossolalia expresses praise, sorrow or lament, intercession, and petition.[43] Baer's analysis highlights the contemplative and sacramental elements in glossolalia, but the eschatological context is missing.

Asian Pentecostal Simon Chan has picked up on the contemplative side of the argument and attempts to flesh out the doctrine of "initial evidence" by integrating the connection between glossolalia and Spirit baptism within the context of the Christian mystical tradition. He rejects the notion that Spirit baptism is for the purpose of the enduement of power as being too truncated, instead hoping to understand the doctrine as a form of contemplative prayer. Drawing upon the mystical theology of Theresa of Avila, Chan argues, "This aspect of the Pentecostal experience is in fact very similar to the 'passive' phases of contemplative prayer in the Christian mystical tradition."[44] As prayer progresses through its various stages, from acquired to infused contemplation, the pray-er draws closer to God. Glossolalia occurs at the lower levels of passive prayer and the transition from active prayer, as one transitions from striving to reception. "The main difference between the Pentecostal and the mystic is that the former's receptivity is signaled by glossolalia while the latter is signaled by silence," thereby drawing on Baer's functional insight.[45] The implication though is that glossolalia is a lower form of prayer than the higher levels of contemplation, though perhaps this is apropos since Spirit baptism initiates the recipient into the higher Christian life.

---

43. Baer, "Quaker Silence, Catholic Liturgy, and Pentecostal Glossolalia—Some Functional Similarities," 150–64.

44. Chan, "Evidential Tongues," 198–99; idem, "Language Game of Glossolalia, or Making Sense of the 'Initial Evidence,'" 87–88.

45. Chan, "Evidential Tongues, 200.

Chan develops his eschatology primarily in the context of the church. By contrasting the apocalyptic, interpreted as the abandonment of history to false millennial utopias, and biblical eschatology defined in the prolepsis of the already/not-yet, Chan argues that "glossolalic prayer" must be understood in the "unutterable groaning" of the Spirit, groaning for a broken world awaiting its liberation in God in solidarity with creation (human and non human). Otherwise glossolalic prayer is reduced to mere privatized longings and pious abdication.[46] However, Chan is critical of the attempt by Moltmann and liberation theologians to extend the Spirit's involvement beyond the church. Moltmann's use of the cosmic Spirit as a symbol for the eschatological transformation of creation, argues Chan, ends up validating Western liberal egalitarianism over other ideologies and severs the new creation from the gospel.[47] I disagree with Chan on this last point. By collapsing the cosmic reality of the Spirit to the church makes the church the locale for the totality of the Spirit's presence and work, rather than as a sign of God's presence anticipating the kingdom of God's new creation. A hint of triumphalism could easily creep into the church when it is deemed to possess the fullness of the Spirit.

Amos Yong investigates the theology of tongues from a philosophical perspective using the philosophy of Robert C. Neville, and in a way similar to the mystical stages suggested by Chan. According to Neville's theory, truth is defined semiotically in that symbols that make reference to that which it signifies in either literal (non-metaphorical) or metaphorical (non-literal) ways. With reference to the religious, imagination plays an important role as the basis for human experience and is the basis for world-making in its perception of the boundaries of human finitude and its ontological and existential contingency. Engagement of the theological imagination, which involves a dialectic between the imagination of the finite/infinite divide and also the ongoing work of symbols to shape the imagination, is an interpretive, theoretical, and practical process bringing about transformation. This transformation is the result of the ongoing process of individual and communal spiritual maturation.[48]

46. Chan, *Pentecostal Theology and the Christian Spiritual Tradition*, 109–10.

47. Ibid., 112–13.

48. Yong, "Tongues of Fire," 44–46. Macchia critiques Neville and therefore Yong on this point, in that the infinite/finite paradigm is a lingering preoccupation of liberal

Yong insists that glossolalia is a sign of the Spirit's presence, bringing about transformation and progresses through successive stages of innocence, growth and adept. The stage of innocence includes both the anticipation of the would-be tongues speaker focusing on the human aspects of glossolalia with the caveat that the phenomenon is divinely inspired. She is confronted by the majesty and glory of the infinite, ecstatically swept up into the Spirit's presence as a holistic response to God's self-disclosure by the Spirit. Glossolalia is "an unclassified free speech to an unclassified, free God," a sign denoting the liberating presence of the Spirit.[49] Growth shifts to the notion of "anointing" or "empowerment" in which the experience of tongues brings deeper reflection. At this stage, the glossolalic is empowered for social action—testimony, prophecy, witness, evangelism, mission, etc. Glossolalia is, in this stage, symbolic of divine proclamation and power, and serves to release the Spirit to proclaim the coming kingdom of God.[50] The adept is the mature tongues speaker who no longer sees glossolalia as a sign of the Spirit's presence or as a means to proclamation, but now participates in the divine life by worship through divine language. Glossolalia is transformed into "divine praise," "unutterable groans," "the language of angels" and "prayer without ceasing." The glossolalic is caught up into the divine life in personal "mystical" union and communal "playful" union without any purpose other than participation in the presence of God.[51]

Yong addresses the eschatology of glossolalia first by suggesting that premillennial dispensationalism was historically influential on the missiological emphasis of tongues, in which the purpose of Spirit baptism was for missiological engagement prominent in the growth stage. However, more interesting is Yong's appropriation of the patristic theology of *theosis* to argue that in the adept stage there is an upward eschatological movement by which Pentecostals conform to the will of the divine and the soul is brought into union with the divine life. "Glossolalia is interpreted regarding the infinite as symbolic of the unity of the divine life, but regarding the finite, it is interpreted both horizontally and verti-

---

Protestantism and needs to be replaced by an eschatological framework that contrasts this age of sin with the kingdom that is to come. Macchia, "Discerning the Truth of Tongues Speech," 70–71.

49. Hollenweger as cited by Yong, "Tongues of Fire," 52.

50. Yong, "Tongues of Fire," 53–56.

51. Yong, "Tongues of Fire," 57–62.

cally. This dual eschatological movement is what is observed in the doxa and praxis of the cultic community."[52] The vertical is the mystical ascent into the divine life and playful participation of the community of faith with the play of Word and Spirit (Suurmond). The horizontal is the ecumenical quest to realize the unity and diversity of the church catholic, and takes as its paradigmatic symbol the Pentecost event of Acts 2, in which the diversity of the body of Christ is united under the unity of the Spirit, in the dissonance that diversity brings, but is spiritually one. "This eschatological movement can be seen to instantiate on the historical level what is taking place spiritually in the visible church. As the church continues to be drawn into the divine life by the power of the Spirit, she is also extended as a universal *oecumene*."[53] In *The Spirit Poured Out on All Flesh*, Yong shifts the discussion from glossolalia to baptism in the Spirit, though theologically these two ideas are connected vis-á-vis the concept of "initial evidence." He gives the Pentecostal distinctive theological and eschatological weight. Yong proposes a nuanced view, in which the baptism of the Spirit is offered by Christ to all, in order to draw all into Christ. Spirit baptism is then seen as the culmination of Christian initiation and therefore connected to repentance, forgiveness of sins and adoption into the body of Christ. Yong also sees baptism in the Spirit in a metaphorical sense, in that the resurrection of Jesus for our justification is the activity of the Spirit, implying that justification is not limited to a forensic sense, but is intricately connected to sanctification, in that Christ "makes" sinners righteous through the purifying fire of the Spirit, and restoring them to God's image. Moreover, the baptism of the Spirit unites believers to Christ's resurrection, empowering them to minister to the church body and through the church to the world. Finally, the baptism of the Holy Spirit is an eschatological down payment, understood in the context of *theosis*, as making believers participants in the divine nature.[54] Significantly, by tying the initiation and the higher life meaning of baptism in the Spirit, Yong can then argue that baptism points to the resurrected life guaranteed by the resurrection of

---

52. Yong, "Tongues of Fire," 58.

53. Ibid., 61.

54. Yong, *The Spirit Poured Out on All Flesh*, 102. Yong looks to the Orthodox view of *theosis*, but this view can be seen in Wesley's discussion of partaking in the divine nature.

Christ and the participatory nature of Spirit baptism as the eschatological purpose of the *imago Dei*.[55]

Macchia is the foremost theologian on the Pentecostal doctrine of baptism in the Spirit and its connection to speaking in tongues, having explored the topic for almost twenty years now. Macchia interprets tongues within the context of eschatology as theophanic, sacramental and ecumenical. The Pentecost narrative of Acts 2 is an eschatological event, in which the coming of the resurrection Spirit renews the covenantal community in anticipation of the parousia, and tongues is a theophanic sign of divine self-disclosure like that of the burning bush in the calling of Moses and the giving of the Law.[56] As an eschatological foretaste, speaking in tongues is a cry for liberation, a "cry of abandonment," which symbolizes the liberating force of the Spirit in breaking down racial, gender and class barriers. Glossolalia embodies an equalizing impulse in leveling all languages and human strivings, pointing to the inauguration of divine justice and mercy in its "groaning" for the suffering of creation yearning for liberation.[57]

Macchia argues that speaking in tongues is sacramental, not in terms of an older Roman Catholic scholastic view of the sacrament operating as a means of grace in and of itself, but in a newer understanding that views sacrament as a sign value pointing to an eschatological reality. Drawing on the theology of Karl Rahner and Paul Tillich, Macchia claims that for Rahner the "sign value" of sacrament insists that the reality to which it points is in some way already present in the sign itself. When one encounters the free and spontaneous God in the sacrament, the eschatological presence of God is realized through signification.[58] For Tillich, God's free self-disclosure is found in the physical/audible reality of the sacrament and the physical/audible human response is taken up into God to become the *kairos* event through which God is encountered.[59] Macchia then argues that glossolalia is a physical/audible response to the presence of the Spirit, which "signifies the divine presence in the sense of actually participating in making it present. Tongues are signs given in

---

55. Yong, *Spirit Poured Out on All Flesh*, 102.

56. Macchia, "Tongues too Deep," 57.

57. Ibid., 59–66. Note the connections with the eschatological reading of healing discussed in the previous section.

58. Ibid., 63.

59. Ibid., 63.

divine freedom but also a visible context in which the experience of God is received and manifested. It is both free and sacramental."[60] Macchia summarizes his position well:

> The eschatological Spirit is free and unrestrained, representing the "powers of the age to come" (Heb 6.5). Yet the eschatological Spirit is not distant or hidden. The Spirit manifests itself through tangible signs of things to come. Tongues is a sign of the renewed language and renewed human relationships called forth by the dawning kingdom of God in our midst. The fact that language is transcendent points to the unfulfilled mystery of God's kingdom. The fact that we participate together in glossolalic utterances signifies that the Spirit invites, even requires, our participation in the breaking in of the kingdom in our world.[61]

Macchia also argues that the significance of tongues is ecumenical in scope. The Pentecost event of Acts 2 signifies the Spirit's presence in the early church and symbolizes a unity in diversity that is realized in the unfolding of the apostolic church. Tongues are a creaturely, broken language that point to the hope of the fullness of God's ultimate self-disclosure in the parousia, which embodies the unity in diversity of God's people. "Tongues are a sign of our fragmentation and promise of reconciliation. Tongues reflect the struggle and the hope, the tears and the joy. Implied is a catholicity that is ultimately eschatological, representing an ongoing challenge to realize the unity and life of God that is never possessed this side of eternity."[62] The contentious distinction made between the Spirit's work in initiation and gifted service can be ameliorated by an eschatological orientation. Empowerment of the Spirit is not the actualization of already possessed human capacities (via a doctrine of creation), but are infused by "radically new possibilities called forth by the eschatological Spirit of God."[63]

The baptism in the Spirit in the relationship between initiation and subsequent empowerment is an issue Macchia has recently taken up in his monograph *Baptized in the Spirit*, a work that is trinitarian, ecclesiological, ecumenical, and eschatological in scope. Although Macchia shifts away from the view that Pentecostalism is an eschatological movement

60. Ibid., 70.

61. Macchia, "Question of Tongues as Initial Evidence," 125.

62. Macchia, "Tongues of Pentecost," 7.

63. Ibid., 11–12.

par excellance in order to iterate Spirit baptism as its primary distinctive, he is careful to define it within an eschatological context. He reintegrates sanctification and eschatology, to define it as the eschatological indwelling of divine love in creation, and reintegrates sanctification and Spirit baptism, to define Spirit baptism along the eschatological plane from initiation through gifting and the indwelling of the Spirit at the end of the age. In this move, Macchia has potentially overcome the second and third works of grace tensions between Holiness and Reformed Pentecostals, and the sectarian tensions in Pentecostalism against the historical-liturgical traditions to argue that Spirit baptism encompasses the full range of Christian life as we "participate in the life-transforming presence of God."[64] Spirit baptism allows the church to participate in the sanctification of creation and the experience of new life, sacraments, and "prophetic consecration (with charismatic signs following) allows one to participate already in a Spirit baptism that is yet to come. It is always present and coming, emerging and encountering."[65] In other words, Spirit baptism which points to the presence of God is already here but not yet in its fullest. Its fullness will only come in the parousia of God.

Macchia's prophetic and apocalyptic distinctions make sense in the context of a Pentecostalism influenced by popular dispensationalism, but are in my opinion overstated. "The prophetic impulse of historical fulfillment and responsibility was set in tension with the apocalyptic hope for a deliverance that would bring final justice and restoration."[66] The significance is that Spirit baptism brings with it a prophetic critique of social, political and environmental practices, not to condemn them as unredeemable, but in order to judge and therefore liberate that which is counter to God to redeem the good. Tongues are a sign of the prophetic. However, apocalyptic—which has numerous ancient literary, social, political and theological meanings—need not call for our passive resignation to the powers-that-be and giving over creation to cataclysmic disaster in the hope for a sovereign act of God at the end of history, but rather needs to be seen as divine condemnation of sin, death and forms of oppression as the sovereign act of a graceful God to transform the cosmos. Macchia affirms, "The fact that the new does not annihilate creation but rather transforms it implies continuity of identity in God

64. Macchia, *Baptized in the Spirit*, 42.
65. Ibid., 86–87.
66. Ibid., 92.

throughout one's spiritual journey. God both indwells and continues to come in newness."[67] Apocalyptic need not be seen as disaster which brings the total destruction of the world. This is not divine apocalyptic, claims Jürgen Moltmann, but secular apocalyptic without a coming kingdom.[68] Divine apocalyptic can be integrated with Spirit baptism if one sees it as God's sovereignty and freedom to be present, both now and in the world-to-come.[69] For Macchia, Spirit baptism "inaugurates the kingdom, bestowed already by the Spirit as it moves us to the unfolding of the end of the age, but also a foretaste of the "final transformation of all things."[70] The baptism in the Spirit is the "first-fruits of the renewal of creation in the midst of cosmic upheaval,"[71] and "calls for such a life in the here-and-now in anticipation of the final victory of life over death, righteousness over unrighteousness."[72] Just as the kingdom seeks liberation and transformation in all spheres of life—personal, relational, political, creational—so too Spirit baptism in an eschatological anticipation of the final transformation that urges us to acts of liberation in the here and now.[73] In this sense, baptism in the Spirit empowers the people of God to confront the powers of destruction with the good news of Jesus Christ in both word and deed, for they have been given the Spirit of the charismatic Christ. Apocalyptic, as I see it, is the in-breaking of the presence of God in sovereign grace, and (with Moltmann) the ultimate judgment of sin and death. Apocalyptic and prophetic therefore stand together rather than being construed as polar opposites.

---

67. Ibid., 96.

68. Moltmann, *Coming of God*, 227.

69. Cf Macchia, *Baptized in the Spirit*, 95. Macchia wishes to shift Moltmann's coming "advent" for "presence," which fits well with what I have just argued, but risks a realized eschatology of the charismatic presence already and always here in the present without the not yet. Moltmann defines this as the epiphanic or eternal present, in which the eschatological is a vertical relationship between the infinite/finite, and not a hopeful promise of the eschatological *novum*. In my opinion, Macchia does not make this mistake, but a careless reading might assume such a position.

70. Macchia, *Baptized in the* Spirit, 98.

71. Ibid., 101.

72. Ibid., 106.

73. Ibid.

THE ESCHATOLOGICAL ORIENTATION OF SALVATION

Finally, the salvific dimension of the Christian life cannot be defined solely in theo-ontological categories, or in terms of individual versus corporate salvation, but must also be understood as eschatological. Within the doctrine of salvation broadly speaking, there are sub categories—repentance, conversion, justification, regeneration, sanctification, union, etc. Space does not permit a thorough examination of each of these doctrines from an eschatological perspective. I will therefore limit myself to a brief discussion of justification as eschatological in orientation. My two dialogue partners on this point will be Karl Barth and N. T. Wright.

A shift has occurred in the theology of justification known simply as the "new perspective." The new perspective started in the Reformed theology of Karl Barth and was taken up by Pauline scholars such as Krister Stendall, E. P. Sanders, James D. G. Dunn, Terrance Donaldson and N. T. Wright as well as theologians such as the New Yale school of Hans Frei and George Lindbeck, on the one hand, and Radical Protestants John Yoder and Stanley Hauwerwas, on the other. The new perspective argues that since the Reformation, justification has been read from an anthropological foundation, focusing on faith as a human existential or experiential work, a reading that has been intensified by the modern emphasis on anthropocentric subjectivity. Stemming from the "postliberal nonfoundationalism" of Karl Barth, the new perspective insists that faith must be Christological in orientation. The reading of *pistis Christou Iēsou* (from Gal 2:18 and elsewhere) has been read as "faith *in*" Jesus Christ but must instead be read as "the faith *of* Jesus Christ."[74] The shift changes the focus from human faith that is subjectively appropriated by the recipient and therefore just another form of anthropological experience, to the faithfulness of God in Christ Jesus, and his loyalty and obedience to the will of the Father. "*Pistis Christou* encapsulates a *story about God's faithfulness in relation to Jesus' faithfulness. . . .* It is in the first place, a story about Jesus' faithfulness or loyalty to God in doing what God sent him to do for humanity."[75] Brevity forces me only a brief glance at the current debates in Pauline scholarship, and to assess these debates from a theo-

---

74. Harink, *Paul among the Postliberals*, 15–18.

75. Ibid., 41.

logical perspective. However, my interest in the debates is to extrapolate how the faithfulness of Christ can be assessed eschatologically.

My starting point is Karl Barth's paradigmatic shift in the study of theology from German liberalism as influenced by modernist rationality and experientialism, to a postliberal position focusing on the revelation of the Word in Christ Jesus as the start and end of prayerful theological reflection. For Barth, neither rationalism nor experientialism could be used as independent criteria to adjudication the truth-claims of the gospel. God's self revelation was the only acceptable criterion. Reading apocalypse as the in-breaking of divine revelation, Barth emphasized that "God's revelation in Jesus Christ is *God's apocalyptic triumph* over all the enslaving powers and gods of the world, a triumph that in turn delivers idolaters (for Barth, this means all of humankind) from their imprisonment to these other, finally immanent and impotent, powers and gods."[76] The faithfulness of God is to be found in Christ Jesus and not in some independent individual experience of faith. *Dia pistēs Iēsou Christou* is rendered by Barth as "through his [God's] faithfulness in Jesus Christ" (Rom 3:22).[77] Barth claims, "The faithfulness of God and Jesus Christ confirm one another. The faithfulness of God is established when we meet the Christ in Jesus . . . Our discovery of Christ in Jesus of Nazareth is authorized by the fact that every manifestation of the faithfulness of God points and bears witness to what we have actually encountered in Jesus."[78] In the section "Justification by Faith Alone in CD 4/1," Barth retains this understanding of Christ's faithfulness and claims regarding justification: "he [the Christian] must not on any account regard it [faith] as his own . . . What is the meaning of it as the human action which makes a faithful and authentic and adequate response to the faithfulness of God, which does justice to the reality and existence of the justified man created by God's pardon, which meets with the divine approval in its suitability to this object, which is recognized and judged and accepted by Him as right, which therefore the knowledge of justification is a genuinely and concretely human event?"[79] Later Barth adds that one must reject the idea that "in virtue of an inner quality of what the believing man does, faith is the real means which man can use to

---

76. Harink, *Paul among the Postliberals*, 47–48.

77. Barth, *Epistle to the Romans*, 96.

78. Ibid.

79. Barth, CD 4/1: 617–18.

justify himself and himself to declare the divine pardon."[80] Hence faith is not an inward quality or experience of justification, but solely an act of God's faithfulness in Christ and his faithfulness to God, and we are engrafted into the family of God by Christ's faithful obedience.

I need not belabor the point here, but wish to highlight the eschatological character of justification. For Barth, the eschatological character of the gospel is found in the eternal in-breaking in time both in the past, present, and future. In *The Epistle to the Romans* he writes:

> Were we to know more of God then the groans of creation and our own groaning; were we to know Jesus Christ otherwise then crucified; were we to know the Holy Spirit otherwise then as the Spirit of Him that raised Jesus from the dead; were the incognito in which *salvation has come to us, does come to us, and will come to us,* broken through—then *there would be no salvation . . . If Christianity be not altogether thoroughgoing eschatological there remains in it no relationship whatsoever with Christ. Spirit which does not at every moment point from death to the new life is not the Holy Spirit* (emphasis mine).[81]

In reference to Rom 3:21, Barth declares: "*But now* directs our attention to time which is beyond time, a space which has no locality, to impossible possibility, to the gospel of transformation, to the imminent coming of the kingdom, to affirmation in negation, to salvation in the world, to acquittal in condemnation, to eternity in time, to life in death—*I saw a new heaven and a new earth: for the first heaven and first earth are passed away.*"[82] Yet for Barth, the eschatological is a crisis, in which the eternal breaks into history at any given moment, collapsing the past-future continuum into no time. The eschatological is primarily a vertical relationship of divine descending in apocalyptic crisis (Moltmann), though Barth's discussion of the "kingdom of God" as a present and future reality in the latter half of CD suggests Moltmann's critique is overstated.[83]

Pauline scholar N. T. Wright closely resembles Barth's position in many ways. Wright too is in the "new perspective camp," arguing that in Christ we see "the *faithfulness of the Messiah to the purposes of God*

---

80. Barth, CD. 4/1: 618.

81. Barth, *Epistles to the Romans,* 314.

82. Ibid., 92.

83. Busch, *Great Passion,* 279–88.

rather than the faith by which Jew and Gentile alike believe."[84] Wright also insists that apocalyptic cannot be defined in opposition to prophetic or as a divine in-breaking that corrects a corrupt historical process in which the new creation is a new *creatio ex nihilo*, or that it must be defined dualistically as division between heaven and earth. Reminiscent of Barth, Wright argues that "Paul believes that the ultimate dramatic apocalypse, the great unveiling of all God's mysteries, the full disclosure of God's secret plan, *has already come about* in and through the events concerning the Messiah, Jesus, particularly through his death and resurrection."[85] In this way apocalyptic and covenant converge as the unveiling of the covenant plan of God. Also like Barth, Wright argues that apocalypse (*parousia*) is not to be as "coming," but as "presence," his "appearance."[86] In the context of God's faithfulness to the covenant, Wright rightly argues for an inaugural eschatology. "The age has already arrived with Jesus; but it will be consummated in the future."[87]

> Paul's reworking of eschatology: that the complex event for which Israel had hoped had already happened in the events of Jesus of Nazareth. Jesus' resurrection indicated not just *that* something extraordinary had come to pass, but *what that extraordinary thing was*: the anticipation, the breaking in to the scene of ongoing history, of the ultimate End. Moreover, with this inaugural framework in which Paul reworks Jewish expectations, "the creative tension between the two, between what has already happened in the Messiah and what is still to happen at the ultimate end, is where we must locate some of his most characteristic themes (justification, the body, and so on).[88]

This reworking of justification, so that it is understood within the context of the eschatological, covenantal, and apocalyptic, is what I wish to probe here. "The whole point about 'justification by faith' is that it is something which happens *in the present time* (Rom 3:26) as a proper anticipation of the eventual judgment which will be announced, on the basis of the whole life led, in the future (Rom 2:1–6)."[89] As such, there

---

84. Wright, *Paul: In Fresh Perspective*, 47.

85. Ibid., 50–52.

86. Ibid., 54–55.

87. Ibid., 57.

88. Ibid., 136.

89. Ibid., 57.

is a close link between justification and resurrection, in that the resurrection is the corporate hope of Israel, her covenantal vindication and rescue from death and exile. "[J]ustification properly belongs not to an individualistic soteriology but in the context of God's affirmation that this or that person is a member of the covenant family. Resurrection is therefore, as in much contemporary Jewish thought, the ultimate 'justification.'"[90] However, the inauguration of covenantal renewal was not just about the expectations of a future for the people of God, but also about God's future, which has burst into the present in the messiah, and a future event when the messiah will receive "homage from the whole creation" and hand over the kingdom to the Father "so that—the ultimate in 'God's Future'—God will be all in all."[91] Wright is close to Moltmann's understanding of divine eschatology in which God's trinitarian dynamic is in movement to God's ultimate glorification in the messianic handing over of the new creation to the Father, when God will be all in all.[92]

In his recent publication *Justification*, Wright tackles the criticisms of conservative Reformed theologian John Piper to argue that justification is not about a disembodied soul ascending to heaven (or hell) after death, but about bodily resurrection; nor about the imputation of Christ's perfect righteousness in exchange for human sinfulness, but about the legal status in which the divine Judge finds in favor of his covenant people and declares them "in the right;" nor is it about the old covenant of the law that is now overcome by the new covenant of grace, but about a gracious God, who works faithfully in Christ as Israel's Messiah and Jesus' faithfulness to God and the covenant, begun in Abraham and continuing as the single plan of God to establish the new creation through Israel and into the world in order to eliminate sin and death. Justification has an eschatological sense of a "*final* justification where God puts the whole world right and raises his people from the dead, and the *present* justification in which that moment is anticipated."[93] To reiterate present justification is anticipation of eschatological justification. For Wright, eschatology includes the salvific purposes of God to redeem his people and rescue all creation, messianic in that the goal of God is already launched in the messiah, and inaugural in that the new

90. Wright, *Climax of the Covenant*, 204.

91. Wright, *Paul: In Fresh Perspective*, 135–36.

92. Moltmann, *In the End—The Beginning*, 150, 155, 158.

93. Wright, *Justification*, 10–12.

age has already been introduced, but not yet here. One caveat, however, is that Wright cautions that this inauguration cannot be thought of as progressive, but is apocalyptic in the sense that salvation has burst into this age, and anticipatory of the ultimate moment when God will be all in all (1 Cor 15:28).[94]

The messianic resurrection is the key to the dawning of the new creation and the locale for understanding the meaning of justification. Resurrection functions as both metaphor and metonym for the exilic return which is taken up by Paul as the eschatological renewal of Israel and human beings within the context of Roman occupation.[95] Jesus' messianic mission is vindicated in the resurrection, and in this sense he is justified after having been condemned in court by the ungodly powers of this age. The resurrection inaugurated God's promised new age, now awaiting its ultimate fulfillment, when corruption, decay, and death are overcome, and creation is renewed.[96] Yet this eschatology is collaborative in taking up the people of God in the messianic work. Those who are in Christ "were empowered by his Spirit were charged with transforming the present, as far as they were able, in light of the future."[97]

One final comment is that Wright's eschatological framework for justification does not make sense without a theology of the Spirit. The outpouring of the Spirit is the means by which covenant renewal occurs. Paul's references Joel, Ezek 36, and Jer 31 to insist that renewal is effected by the Spirit as the inauguration of the eschatological, in which Gentiles are brought into the covenant and Jews are renewed through baptism into the messianic body. However, I disagree with Wright's point that the outpouring of the Spirit was a confusion, in which speaking in tongues was not to be seen as a sign of God at work. If one moves from Pauline literature to Luke-Acts, the activity of glossolalia is a prophetic sign of the Spirit's presence at work in the renewal of Israel as the people of God, in which the Gentiles now have a part.[98] Nevertheless, the Spirit is understood by Paul as the down payment of what is to come, the messianic

94. Ibid., 101.

95. Wright, *Surprised by Hope*, 46–47.

96. Wright, *Justification*, 106.

97. Wright, *Surprised by Hope*, 46.

98. The ongoing debate has been taken up by James D. G. Dunn, Max Turner on the one hand and Roger Stronstad, Robert Menzies, Mathias Wenk and Martin Mittelstadt on the other.

heralding of the new age, as a gift from God's future and guarantee of the future in Christ. The Spirit heralds the eschatological age inaugurated in the death and resurrection of Christ and works to bring this age to completion. To walk in the Spirit is to walk in God's new age as a renewed people, to be part of the family of God's eschatological inauguration in Christ and delivered from the evil of the present age. Together, the resurrection and ascension of Christ, and the gift of his Spirit in Pentecost, are the agent of the transformation of creation, and in the eschatological journey makes us transformative agents as coworkers with God.[99]

Both Barth and Wright reworked theology to articulate an eschatological focus of salvation, from a fresh reading of faith that is thoroughly Christological in orientation. This new perspective challenges theo-ontological categories that view faith as founded in anthropological experience, especially reading the Reformation doctrines through modernist lenses, or as moral exchange between the atoning work of Christ and sinful humanity, a Protestant liberal reading with a conservative Christendom spin. However, salvation in all its dimensions is eschatological and seeks not merely the salvation of humanity (though this is an important part of the story) but the total renewal of creation transforming into its goal in the new creation.

CONCLUSION

My point is that theology proper needs to be re-forged within the eschatological context in order to be faithful to its Jewish-Christian origins. The new perspective of Barth and Wright articulates the theology of justification by faith along an eschatological axiom in which Christ as God's faithful messiah ushers in the new age which is anticipating its final reality. As Christians, we are grafted into the covenant by the Spirit, in which Christ's resurrection provides the first-fruits of the new age, and through the Spirit we are made bearers of Christ and his mission.

I have argued that this eschatological reworking of Pentecostal theology would provide Pentecostals with a more mature theology than simply taking on theology as a doctrine of the last things as passive withdrawal in a questionable doctrine of the rapture, and bring Pentecostalism closer to its original impulse. Christ as savior, healer, baptizer in the Spirit, and coming king makes more sense as a prolepsis of the already and not

---

99. Wright, *Surprised by Hope*, 202.

yet of the new creation, in which Christ is the messianic harbinger inaugurating the new reign but also the One who will bring that reign to its fulfillment in God's future. It makes more sense in envisioning healing and Spirit baptism as looking back to the work of Christ's life, death, and resurrection and forward to the end of days where healing and Spirit baptism find their ultimate fulfillment. Salvation, healing, Spirit baptism, and the Lord's coming are all interpreted along the continuum of the already and not yet of the eschatological parousia of God.

10

Patience as a Theological Virtue

A Challenge to Pentecostal Eschatology

Daniel Castelo

P ATIENCE IS NOT AN attribute one usually associates with Pentecostals. Pentecostals are sometimes characterized as reflecting uncritically modernist culture, technologically innovative, pragmatic, passionate, and even loud.[1] Pejorative characterizations include accusations of being, "fanatical," "possessed," "mentally unstable," "delusional," and "deprived."[2] Pentecostals are better known for their fervor, positively described as "sanctified urgency," or negatively as "reckless impulsiveness." Of all these characterizations, patience is not one that readily comes to mind.[3]

1. Pentecostals show a certain flair for and dependence on cultural modernism and pragmatism, despite their restorationist heritage, making R. G. Robins' depiction of A. J. Tomlinson as a "plainfolk modernist" a helpful representation of the movement as a whole. See Robins, *A. J. Tomlinson*. Grant Wacker notes, for instance, that Pentecostal primitivism must be placed alongside its modernist pragmatic methods. Wacker, *Heaven Below*, 12–14. Pentecostal pragmatism can be seen in the utilization of mass communication and travel technologies. Moreover, when one situates the movement historically and theologically, it is difficult not to escape the analysis of Fry that the mutual emphasis on human experience makes theological liberalism and Pentecostalism fraternal twins. Fry, "Pentecostalism in Historical Perspective," 182, 192, as quoted in Faupel, "Whither Pentecostalism?" 21–22.

2. The most famous diatribe, of course, can be attributed to G. Campbell Morgan's assessment of Pentecostalism as "the last vomit of Satan." See also Anderson, *Vision of the Disinherited*, in which he argues that the emergence of Pentecostalism was another conservative fundamentalist movement consisting of the disinherited.

3. I have remarked in another piece that a Pentecostal metaphor for understanding theological ethics could be the notion of "tarrying." See Castelo, "Tarrying on the

Early Pentecostals exhibited a missionary urgency that belied a sense of patience as a *habitus*. Commenting on the missionary impulse of the Azusa Street Mission, Cecil M. Robeck remarks:

> Essentially, when someone spoke in a tongue, the mission followed a simple four-step program. First, they attempted to identify the language. Second, if they felt they had identified it, they sought to establish whether the speaker believed he or she had received a missionary "call." Third, if the tongues-speaker claimed to have such a call, the mission staff tried to discern whether the call was genuine and whether the person was ready and willing to go. Finally, if the person testified to a readiness to go, and the mission discerned the necessary gifts and call, then they gave the candidate the money to reach the foreign field.[4]

This process was deliberate and prayerful, but due process gave way to expediency in that the candidate quickly "left town within days, if not hours" to carry out the call.[5] Missionary financial support provided a "one-way ticket" to the country of destination[6] in the sense that these missionaries received enough money to get to their destinations, but not enough for them to return. The theological reasoning was that the immediate return of the Lord negated the need for funds to return home. If the eschaton should be delayed then God would provide for the missionary's needs.

This practice reveals a theological rationale for a kind of "sanctified impatience" in Pentecostalism's eschatological self-understanding. D. William Faupel argues that eschatology was the heartbeat, a hermeneutical key for understanding early Pentecostalism,[7] and one can detect in

---

Lord," 31–56. However, note that "tarrying" is usually undertaken by Pentecostals with an expectation that God will answer in time; in other words, if one tarries long enough, God will act on behalf of the seeker. On the surface, therefore, tarrying appears to demonstrate patience but practically it can be located within the rubric of Pentecostal impatience. The present chapter attempts to expand the notion of "tarrying" in order to account for when God does *not* appear to answer the pleas made at the altar, a situation that calls into question the over-realized eschatology Pentecostals find so tempting.

4. Robeck, *Azusa Street Mission and Revival*, 239.

5. Particularly in reference to the Garrs; Robeck, *Azusa Street Mission and Revival*, 239.

6. Robeck, *Azusa Street Mission and Revival*, 240.

7. Faupel, *Everlasting Gospel*, 20. Faupel follows the lead of Anderson in *Vision of the Disinherited*, although Faupel develops this thesis considerably and helpfully in the direction of historical and theological reconstruction, but without Anderson's deprivation analysis.

Pentecostal testimonies and literature that Pentecostals operated from an "over-realized" or "hyper-realized" eschatology, in which the "already" was emphasized to the neglect of the "not yet," because Jesus' return was considered to be imminent. For first generation Pentecostals, the signs and miracles were indications that they were living and participating in the "latter rain," in a "time before the time," in which Jesus would return.[8] The Spirit was readying the world for the Second Coming of Christ, and those who knew and experienced this spiritual reality were called to share their faith in preparation of the "marriage supper of the Lamb."[9] Belief in Christ's immediate return was a catalyst for sacrificial endeavors, which included the uprooting of families and the experience of suffering hardship for the gospel. The theological and praxis-oriented impulse for the proclamation of the "full gospel" was expectation of God's in-breaking kingdom.

However, contemporary Pentecostals now live in a time when eschatological fervor has diminished. Reference is rarely made to Jesus' Second Coming in today's Pentecostal contexts. A shift in theology has taken place so that Pentecostal self-understanding now revolves around the role of glossolalia in the baptism of the Spirit, or the Spirit's activity in charismatic expression, rather than the end-time expectation of the kingdom in which the manifestation of tongues plays a role.[10] In other words, Pentecostal eschatological expectancy is in tatters, especially in those contexts in which Pentecostalism has settled for an extended period of time. Consequently, an editorial by Assemblies of God theologian Frank Macchia ponders the role of eschatology: "Were the Pentecostals mistaken at the turn of the century when they shared

8. Peter Althouse considers at length the metaphor of the "latter rain" within Pentecostalism in Althouse, *Spirit of the Last Days*, esp. chapter 1.

9. Althouse remarks that such metaphors as the "bride of Christ" served to explain to Pentecostals that what they were witnessing was a climax of history; such historical accoutrements helped explain the rationale for such signs in the present as well as the reason why they were believed to be largely absent in the post-apostolic period. Althouse, *Spirit of the Last Days*, 19.

10. This argument is first made by Anderson, *Vision of the Disinherited*, 96–97 and is largely assumed by Dayton, *Theological Roots of Pentecostalism*, and Faupel, *Everlasting Gospel*. I am aware that one group of scholars has maintained the distinctive of Pentecostal identity as Spirit baptism with the initial evidence of speaking in tongues, but I remain convinced by the historical work of Anderson, Dayton, and Faupel that historical and contextual issues are paramount for understanding the movement theologically, both in its past iterations and for its future possibilities.

the apostle's conviction [of Rom 13:11–12] in their time as well?"[11] The question raises broader issues related to Pentecostal identity and self-understanding: How do Pentecostals understand their history and their future in light of Christ's own eschatological tarrying? Christ has not yet returned despite expectations, so how can current Pentecostals deal with their heritage of "impatience" in light of the Lord's own patience in delaying the parousia?

The task for Pentecostals now is to recast their theological expectation. My contention is that eschatological expectation is not something Pentecostals have contrived, because it points to the reality of God's kingdom breaking into the world; but the kingdom is God's and its presence and manifestation are divinely initiated, thereby occasioning moments of ambiguity, tension, confusion, and frustration when believers fail to see God's manifest activity. The task at hand is to determine what features of eschatological expectation are reflective of God's own work through the Spirit, and what has been misconstrued by overzealous Pentecostals. Pentecostal zeal has the potential of diminishing, altering, and perhaps even corrupting the expectancy of early Pentecostal eschatology, with the concomitant shift from expectation to enthusiasm. These circumstances raise the question: How should Pentecostals live in the "already-not yet" tension now that the sense of the eschatological immediacy has dissipated with time?

I want to suggest that Pentecostals ought to look to the virtue of "patience" as a way to re-conceive their eschatological ethos. Despite the diverse tendencies current Pentecostals have inherited from their forebears, I believe a salutary understanding of the "not yet" aspect of the eschatological dyad would strengthen Pentecostalism so that eschatology is not cast in a way that requires immediate fulfillment. Despite its claims, Pentecostalism has institutionalized. Theological space is needed to support the developing tradition of the movement. To start the conversation, I will look at the virtue of patience in the Christian tradition with the aim of retrieving resources which can help address the current challenges facing Pentecostal eschatology. Through this interchange, I hope to offer possibilities for recasting Pentecostal eschatology so that Pentecostals can shift away from their "over-realized" eschatological heritage to a patient hope.

---

11. "The Time is Near!" 161.

THE TRADITION OF PATIENCE

Patience is a theological theme in Christian antiquity. As a virtue, it has served an important function in Christian reflection as a vital check to eschatological expectation within a myriad of challenging and difficult contexts.

Interestingly, early Christian reflection on patience culminated with the work of Tertullian, a figure whom Pentecostals extol for his charismatic exuberance. Ironically, Tertullian had no patience for philosophizing in Christian theology and showed a flair for hyperbole in opposing those whom he deemed in error. Yet he extolled the value of Christian patience. The irony was not lost on Tertullian himself who remarked, "So I, most miserable, ever sick with the heats of *im*patience, must of necessity sigh after, and invoke, and persistently plead for, that health of patience which I possess not."[12] Tertullian was well aware he was impatient and that his life did not correspond fully to the embodiment of the virtue of patience, and yet he recognized that reflection on divine patience served as solace for him. In *Of Patience* Tertullian proceeds in a manner similar to his other theological discussions: He begins with reflection on God and then moves to the human situation so that God is highlighted as the ultimate exemplar of patience for creatures to imitate. God endures the rejection of many, the disobedience of others, and in the process disparages God's self. In fact, God continues in godly patience despite occasions of disbelief among those who cannot fathom why God is not more active or "impatient" with the problems and suffering in the world. Most indicative of God's patience is the life and work of Christ. Whereas many of his contemporaries want to emphasize the deeds of Christ on earth, Tertullian notes the events and circumstances of Christ's life, which show that Christ indeed endured with great patience those who met, followed, tortured, and even killed him.

As for the role godly patience plays in the life of the believer, Tertullian makes a strong case that every sin is ascribable to impatience and that the deficiency of patience in the Christian life is detrimental to discipleship.[13] Patience breeds and vivifies humility, obedience, faith, charity, and mercy, while impatience promotes the opposite vices and behaviors. For instance, Abraham was patient, which led God to ac-

---

12. Tertullian, *Of Patience*, I. The translations of patristic sources are taken from the ANF and NPF (First Series) editions published by Hendrickson.

13. Ibid., V.

count him as righteous even in the midst of the great trial of Gen 22. Impatience fosters possessiveness and blurs mourning or loss with covetousness. Succinctly stated, impatience derails the Christian life to its core, whereas attributes necessary for a faithful and God-honoring life spring from divine patience. Tertullian states, "For where God is, there too is His foster-child, namely Patience. Whence God's Spirit descends, then Patience accompanies Him indivisibly."[14]

Cyprian was a Western father who further developed Tertullian's theology of patience. Reminiscent of his fellow Carthagite, Cyprian asks in contrast to the philosophical espousal of patience, "For whence can he be either wise or patient, who has neither known the wisdom nor the patience of God?"[15] In other words, patience is a function of knowing God, who is the true and only source of patience. As Cyprian remarks, "From Him patience begins; from Him its glory and its dignity take their rise. The origin and greatness of patience proceed from God as its author."[16] Living patiently reflects the Sermon on the Mount and implies obedience to the love commandments of being perfected in imitation of Christ. "Even he is made alive by Christ's blood," Cyprian writes, "who has shed Christ's blood. Such and so great is the patience of Christ."[17]

Cyprian argues that patience is not simply a matter of obedience but of survival for the Christian: "Nor can there be supplied any consolations to those that sweat and toil other than patience; which consolations, while in this world they are fit and necessary for all men, are especially so for us who are more shaken by the siege of the devil, who, daily standing in the battle-field, are wearied with the wrestlings of an inveterate and skilful enemy."[18] Cyprian recognizes that the Christian life is one of afflictions and sorrows, and fostering patience is a means by which to resist and endure the antagonisms that go with living in the "time between the times."

Augustine also contributes to the subject in his treatise *On Patience*, affirming that patience is a great gift from God bestowed on believers. Augustine asserts that God is impassible, i.e., God does not suffer, and yet Augustine whole-heartedly recognizes that the "long-suffering" God is

14. Ibid., XV.

15. Cyprian, *On the Advantage of Patience*, II.

16. Ibid., III.

17. Ibid., VIII.

18. Cyprian, *On the Advantage of Patience*, XII.

ineffably and mysteriously patient, just as he is ineffably and wondrously "jealous without any darkening of spirit, wroth without any perturbation, pitiful without any pain," and repentant without having to be set right.[19] Augustine highlights patience as a resource for the persecuted and suffering church as it attempts to endure the trials and tribulations that accompany Christ-followers.

Thomas Aquinas extends Augustine's arguments in an article on patience in the *Summa Theologiae*. Moving from Augustine's passing reference to patience as a "virtue of the mind," Thomas notes that patience is necessary for reason to not be impeded by the sorrow in the world.[20] But Thomas goes on to locate patience as a function of charity, the chief of the theological virtues.[21] In this way, patience is a function of grace while at the same time retaining some of its qualities as a virtue. Thomas concludes his discussion of patience by comparing it to longanimity or longsuffering. Thomas notes that patience endures certain evils for the sake of good, but over time the endurance becomes more difficult; the postponement of hope causes sorrow, but patience helps one in the endurance of sorrows.[22] Aquinas' commentary on Tully states, "For this reason Tully in defining patience, says that *patience is the voluntary and prolonged endurance of arduous and difficult things for the sake of virtue or profit*. By saying '*arduous*' he refers to constancy in the good; when he says '*difficult*' he refers to the grievousness of evil, which is the proper object of patience; and by adding *continued* or *long lasting*, he refers to longanimity, in so far as it has something in common with patience."[23]

For our purposes, the last figure worth considering is John Wesley. As a clergyman and educator in the Church of England, Wesley was steeped in the traditions of the church fathers and appropriates their theological views in the development of his own theology of Christian perfection. Taking Jas 1:4 as a guiding text, Wesley considers patience in light of the onslaught of trials and temptations in this life. He defines patience not as a heathen virtue but as "a gracious temper wrought in the heart of a believer by the power of the Holy Ghost" and "a disposition to

---

19. Augustine, *On Patience*, I.

20. IIa IIae, q. 136, art. 1.

21. Thomas considers the theological virtues generally in Ia IIae, q. 62 and charity specifically in IIa IIae, q. 23.

22. IIa IIae, q. 136, art. 5.

23. IIa IIae, q. 136, art. 5.

suffer whatever pleases God, in the manner and for the time that pleases him."[24] Through the use of the language of "tempers," Wesley is reiterating the perennial theme that patience is a work of God that takes place in the heart but nevertheless requires enactment. Patience leads to the fruits of peace and joy in the midst of sufferings, and these difficulties work in shaping our Christian character, in helping us grow in holiness.

The voices of these Christian thinkers are suggestive for the task of considering the value of eschatological expectation: First, patience is a gift from God, which can only come from God since God is the ultimate exemplar of patience. True patience is neither humanly achieved nor deceptively fabricated. Only God is the source and end of true patience, that which is needed to sustain the community of faith in the trials of this life. Second, this gift of God requires enactment; God's patience becomes the Christian's patience when it is embodied, attended to, and exercised as an affection or temper that bears fruit. In this light, the consideration of patience as a virtue, specifically within the logic of the theological virtues, is helpful in that such language suggests "habituation" and "performance" in the Christian life. Finally, patience is an indispensable gift when a community is facing both persecution and sorrow and can serve as a resource for sustained confrontation and resistance of evil in the world. Patience is crucial when the "not yet" aspect of kingdom living is outright and burdensome for communal life.

PENTECOSTALISM AND THE VIRTUE OF PATIENCE

Pentecostals would do well to learn from past articulations of Christian patience, for the complications resulting from their "sanctified impatience" have started to take their toll on the movement's theological coherence and current-day identity and practices. As Augustine notes in *De Patientia*, "The patience of a man . . . is understood to be that by which we tolerate evil things with an even mind, that we may not with a mind uneven desert good things, through which we may arrive at better."[25] Augustine suggests that patience is inherent to the practice of resisting evil and appreciating the good, making it a virtue that serves well in the long-term stability of any person or group over time. Pentecostalism is at a place in its history where it needs to draw from the deep wells of the

---

24. Wesley, Sermon 83 "On Patience," *The Works of John Wesley*, III, 171.

25. Augustine, *On Patience*, II

Christian faith in which theologians of godly patience can shed light on the particularities of Pentecostalism's eschatological self-understanding, in order to ameliorate the negative effects of impatient urgency in Pentecostal identity and practice.

For instance, Pentecostal impatience has inspired eschatological impatience in conceiving divine and human activity in the world in a way that truncates a theological understanding of the economy of salvation. For example, Faupel notes that many early Pentecostals believed not only that Jesus' return was imminent, but that their evangelistic practices could in fact *hasten* Christ's return. Though perhaps naïve, Pentecostals believed that Christ's return would be preceded by the preaching of the gospel unto the ends of the earth.[26] For all the "escapist" tendencies within Pentecostalism, on this point they tended to be quite optimistic about how human efforts could influence salvation history to reach its denouement. D. J. Wilson suggests as much when he notes that some early Pentecostals believed they could "*facilitate* [Jesus'] return by spreading the Good News."[27]

The perceived possibility of hastening the Second Coming is brimming with theological difficulties, not only for what it suggests about divine-human interaction in the economy of salvation history, but also in relation to the kind of expectancy that is envisioned, which can lead to frustration over the course of time. Pentecostals have tended to the Arminian side of the grace-free will debate vis-à-vis Wesley, and much of the revivalist camp-meeting ethos emphasized the value of human freedom, choice, enactment, and embodiment, even at the risk of blurring divine-human distinctions. Through practices such as miracle-working, healing, and prophecy, Pentecostals have operated with a strong conviction that through God's empowering work on their lives and in their communities, they have an important role on the stage of cosmic history. Yet this sense of empowerment brings with it the lurking temptation to assume that what occurs in this world directly influences features of the

---

26. *Everlasting Gospel*, 21–22. The logic worked well for thinking of tongues as *xenolalia*, as Charles Parham apparently did. As Althouse notes, "Parham believed that since the coming of Christ was going to occur in his lifetime, there was an urgent need to evangelize the world. The intensity of missions thinking, an intensity forged in the belief that preaching the gospel to the whole world was the last requirement to be fulfilled before Christ would return, provided a utilitarian function for tongue speaking as an empowerment for Christian service." Althouse, *Spirit of the Last Days*, 26–27.

27. Wilson, "Pentecostal Perspectives on Eschatology," 604–5 (emphasis added).

heavenly realm. This tendency has the potential to displace divine sovereignty and freedom with an anthropocentric self-willing and thereby diminishes the complexity of the relationship between humanity and God. In other words, the elevation of the human role at the cost of the divine freedom and majesty tragically overlooks human finitude and sinfulness. The risk for Pentecostals is a sense of religious triumphalism.

Perhaps illustrative of this theological danger is the assumption that one can expect a miraculous intervention of healing or blessing if one fulfills the assumed requirements. Yet disappointment ensues when the expected miracle does not occur. Overlooked in this scenario is God's sovereignty. The theological risk of ritualizing God's activity according to human "faith requirements" is that it represents an attempt to control God and to elevate the role of human activity.[28] Perhaps most anguishing are cases when human suffering is blamed on the sufferers because, it is assumed, they do not have enough faith or are hiding unconfessed sin. Certainly, one does not want to downplay the miraculous, which can be an occasion for revealing God's gracious character and for the prompting of both joy and assurance. But how do Pentecostals explain theologically the absence of divine miracles or blessings? On too many occasions, fault is ascribed to the seeker, and alternative explanations are overlooked, especially the possibility that God's ways are mysterious and often different from humanity's.[29]

The unfulfilled expectation of the miracle is a microcosmic analogy of the greater problem of Pentecostal eschatological expectancy today. Past expectation of the immediacy of Jesus' Second Coming and the

28. Of course, not all Pentecostal theologies of healing are prone to make healing a somewhat "automatic" event, but enough of them do that they can be situated between the extremes of "divine faithfulness" and "divine freedom." See Knight, "God's Faithfulness and God's Freedom," 65–89. On the former side of the continuum, people believe God has promised blessings or pronounced laws, which come into effect only when believers appropriately and sufficiently believe. Within such an understanding, healing occurs on the basis of one's faith more so than God's timing or sovereign will, thereby defining faith as "trusting in God's promises in Scripture rather than trusting in God," Knight, 69. This scenario reduces relationality, a key component of spirituality, to technique.

29. In surveying the beliefs of the charismatic Agnes Sanford, Knight remarks, "For Sanford, when a person we pray for is not healed it is usually due to our being an inadequate channel of God's healing energy . . . This does not mean we cannot be healed by our own prayers. But if we are not, again the problem is with us." Knight, "God's Faithfulness and God's Freedom," 71. Such a logic pervades Pentecostal settings as well.

fervor this created are logically precarious when they assume human creatures can force God's hand. Many early Pentecostals mistakenly believed that their work could hasten Jesus' return if all the signs of the last days, especially the preaching of the gospel to all nations, are fulfilled. However, Pentecostal eschatology needs to be cast in light of the virtue of patience. In their impatience, Pentecostals have negatively allowed their hope to shift from fervency to cynicism, contributing to the diminution of eschatology in Pentecostal circles today.

But the matter is more complex than to say simply that early Pentecostals were mistaken in what they believed. Admittedly, certain details about the unfolding of cosmic history were wrong, as time has shown, but their expectation of the eschatological coming of God was theologically feasible. Early Pentecostals were mistaken to think that in their historical lifetimes they would see Christ's return, but their conviction that they could hope to see their soon-coming king still applies. Yes, many of their illustrations and metaphors for interpreting history are less persuasive now with the passing of time, but the Christian reading of history continues to have one end, goal, and consummation in God. Admittedly, early Pentecostals may have aggrandized their role and place in the divine economy, believing their activity represented the culmination of history, but their claims stemmed from the deep conviction that God was actively working in their lives and communities in powerful and wondrous ways.

Expressed pithily, early Pentecostals were wrong about some of the details, but were right to expect and live in light of the eschatological kingdom. The task for contemporary Pentecostals, and especially Pentecostal scholars, is to preserve those positive features of early Pentecostal expectancy without succumbing to end-time scenarios based in hypothetical assumptions. If contemporary Pentecostals are to live in light of this vision, then like Tertullian their call is nothing less than to wait patiently for a patient God, despite their creaturely impatience. As Cyprian suggests, the patience Pentecostals are to cultivate can only come from God, and such cultivation ought to be undertaken with passion, commitment, and yes, a certain restlessness and equanimity. It means that God's tarrying, i.e., patience, is not eschatological misfortune or tragedy, at least from the human vantage point, but divine perseverance stemming from the sovereign God in whom we trust. These points can be held alongside the conviction that "what our eyes have seen" and "our hands have touched" really constitute the in-breaking kingdom of God. To summarize the dialectic, Pentecostals, as all Christians, need God in order to wait on God in hopeful and patient expectation.

To this end, Pentecostals can move forward in reconfiguring their particular species of expectancy through a multi-tiered process, one in which patience is practiced and cultivated through specific activities. First, the function of lament is worth pursuing within Pentecostal communal life.[30] In acknowledging that their expectancy has not been fulfilled, that Christ has not returned as expected, or that one is not healed or apparently shown blessing, Pentecostals can recognize in concrete circumstances the promise of hope. Admittedly, Christ's tarrying has allowed suffering to continue, but I believe Pentecostals have avoided talk of lament in their public pronouncements for fear that doing so would be perceived as a sign of inadequate faith.[31] Pentecostals ought to realize that being a community of hope implies being a patient people who participate in the *koinonia* of one another's sufferings, hoping for their soon-returning Lord in the midst (rather than in spite) of their plight.[32] The practice of lament can help Pentecostals be a more truthful community, one that lives in transparency to and vulnerability before God and one another.[33]

30. Pentecostals have begun to work with the topic of lament, including Ellington, *Risking Truth*. However, connections between lament and the Pentecostal ethos are not made in this work and are pressing in contemporary Pentecostal theology.

31. Kimberly Alexander notes how controversial it was for early Pentecostal publications to include obituaries. Certain strands of Pentecostalism, like the Finished Work camp, avoided obituaries altogether, and groups that included them, such as Wesleyan Pentecostals, did so by emphasizing that in death believers were victorious and "going home" occasions that should inspire joy and worship. See Alexander, *Pentecostal Healing*, 208–9. Given the absence of lament themes among Pentecostals, one wonders if lament practices, as biblically sound as they are, have been avoided because they are understood to betray vital features associated with the movement.

32. As Keith Warrington notes, "The recognition of the place of suffering in Pentecostal theology needs to be redeemed as an integral aspect of an authentic spirituality that acknowledges the value of suffering in the life of the believer and does not simply attempt to exclude it or assume that its presence is intrinsically illegitimate." Warrington, *Pentecostal Theology*, 303.

33. Walter Brueggemann has done much to retrieve the theme of lament for the contemporary life of the church based on his reading of the Psalms. In his view, avoiding lament implies the "loss of *genuine covenant interaction*" as well as "*the stifling of the question of theodicy.*" Brueggemann, *Psalms and the Life of Faith*, 102, 104, author's emphases. When lament is seen as impossible or unfaithful, the harshness of reality is minimized or explained away. As the Psalms prove, lament is an important part of a

If Pentecostals need God in order to wait on God, then activities that promote the "practice of the presence of God" ought to be cultivated. One way of considering these practices is the Wesleyan means of grace. For Wesley, "Means of grace are means through which persons experience and respond to the loving presence of God."[34] To quote Wesley, they are "outward signs, words, or actions ordained of God, and appointed for this end—to be the *ordinary* channels whereby he might convey to men preventing, justifying, or sanctifying grace."[35] Naturally, the use of the term "means" can be misleading: these activities were not meant to be ends in themselves, nor were they to be ways that automatically ensured God's presence. In both cases, the focus is on the activity rather than the object and purpose of the activity. The advocacy of the "means of grace" therefore required careful framing by Wesley, and his nuancing of this theme is helpful. Wesley considered the means of grace as "active forms of *waiting*" on God's presence. Wesley did not want to ascribe ultimate value to human activity, but he was also fighting against a form of Quietism lingering among his Moravian acquaintances. Wesley's way forward was to suggest that faith has an active and pathic component in that it is directed to God but lived by believers. As Wesley observes, "All who desire the grace of God are to wait for it in the means which he hath ordained; in using, not in laying them aside."[36]

In casting the means of grace as "active forms of waiting" on the presence of God, Wesley is advocating the cultivation of patience in the spiritual life. Wesley tries to avoid the "forcing of God's hand," which has become characteristic of certain forms of Pentecostal spirituality, while simultaneously attempting to render human activity as vital. The practice of patience in the Pentecostal context would mean "tarrying" and attending to that which they are able, while recognizing that at times God discloses God's self powerfully and at other times, perhaps in most cases, remains hidden. Either way, steadfastness in waiting must be a vital feature of a Pentecostal spirituality so that circumstances do not become harmfully determinative of the quality of Pentecostal piety.[37]

---

vital, engaged, fruitful, and honest faith.

34. Knight, *Presence of God in the Christian Life*, 2.

35. Wesley, "The Means of Grace," I, 381.

36. Wesley, "The Means of Grace," I, 384.

37. For a contribution within the vein of Wesleyan-Pentecostal spirituality, see Knight, "From Aldersgate to Azusa," 82–98. Steven Land's *Pentecostal Spirituality* also

Extrapolating Wesley, Pentecostals must attend to the means of grace patiently and consistently, regardless of whether they see God moving.

Finally, Pentecostals would do well to operate with a reverent sense of the mysteries of God in such a way that patience takes the form of practicing silence. Specifically, the tendency (and oftentimes felt need) to explain ought to be muted when clear and definitive answers are not available in attempting to understand how God works in the world.[38] The double-edged sword of Pentecostal belief in the imminence of God's presence carries with it the pressure to explain God's apparent absence. Such framing suggests that expectancy has a similar shape to faith, one that operates precisely in patience for its eventual resolution. Some mysteries remain, and God only will make them known in the eschatological landscape. In the meantime, the role of believers is to endure the "cognitive dissonance" and tests of faith that stem from both God's visibility and hiddeness, God's immediate work and God's tarrying. Rather than diminishing or dispelling suffering, Pentecostals need to recognize that part of the Spirit's work includes helping us overcome and endure both suffering and evil, as we patiently wait on the mystery of God's eschatological reign.

CONCLUSION

To conclude, Pentecostals are at an important juncture in their history, one in which because of God's patience they must wait in unexpected ways. Their waiting is centered on God's waiting, just as their expectancy is a result of God's free and gracious activity in their midst. In both cases, God's role is key. But in the former case, Pentecostals have little recourse in narrating theologically God's hiddenness in the midst of God's revealedness, God's apparent absence in addition to God's manifest presence. Theologically, this growing awareness of the need to be a patient people may be strange and unexpected for Pentecostals, but it certainly is not improper, and it may be even timely given where the movement

makes this case with the emphasis on the affections as the integrating center for this spirituality.

38. Another way of stating the matter is to suggest that Pentecostals ought to evolve into a post-theodical people who approach evil and suffering not via a cold, syllogistic, hard rationalism, but through practices of resistance and endurance and dispositions of compassion and empathy. John Swinton makes the case for a "practical theodicy." Swinton, *Raging with Compassion*.

currently finds itself. As with expectancy, so with waiting: As a people of God, Pentecostals and all Christians receive their hope and vitality from the God of Abraham, Isaac, and Jacob; the God revealed in the life of Jesus Christ; and the God who continues to wait patiently as a sign of grace to us all.

PART THREE

Theological Engagements
and Charismatic Issues

11

Hope for Eternal Life

Perspectives for Pentecostals and Catholics

Jeffrey Gros, FSC

God our maker, who knows the clay we are made of;
    God our father, who never can forget his child;
God our Redeemer, who died to save us, has a special providence
        for death.
He knows our utter need,
    He is most helpful when our need is sorest.
Therefore he has provided these three things,
    The last sacraments,
        The grace of contrition, and
            Holy hope.

        —Gerard Manley Hopkins, SJ, (1885)[1]

F OR ALL CHRISTIANS THE horizon of this earthly life is the gift of risen life promised in the resurrection of Jesus Christ. As Pope Benedict XVI reminded us in his April 18, 2008 address in New York City:

> Only by "holding fast" to sound teaching (2 Thess 2:15; cf. Rev 2:12–29) will we be able to respond to the challenges that confront us in an evolving world . . . Like the early Christians, we have a responsibility to give transparent witness to the "reasons for our hope," so that the eyes of all men and women of goodwill may be opened to see that God has shown us his face (cf.

---

1. Devlin, ed., *Sermons and Devotional Writings of Gerard Manley Hopkins*, 248.

2 Cor 3:12–18) and granted us access to his divine life through Jesus Christ. He alone is our hope! God has revealed his love for all peoples through the mystery of his Son's passion and death, and has called us to proclaim that he is indeed risen, has taken his place at the right hand of the Father, and "will come again in glory to judge the living and the dead (*Nicene Creed*)."[2]

Catholics and Pentecostals share this common calling.

The Catholic charismatic movement has been a major source of renewal for the church.[3] Catholics and Pentecostals share the affirmation of Christ's revelation of his Second Coming and judgment, though today with different emphases; everlasting life in heaven or hell; and death as the passage from this life to eternity with its promise of resurrection. "Eschatology, more than any other branch of theology, may be said to have undergone paradigmatic shifts in both content and methodology. In a nutshell, it moved from the margins to the center of theology."[4]

The contemporary world is fascinated with both the challenge of death and views of history, philosophy, and politics as well as religion.[5] Literature, poetry, and drama overflow with the challenge of human destiny and its meaning. Among the eschatological themes that Christians ponder are God's role and that of Christ and his disciples in the unfolding of the history of the world. Modern liberation and political theologies are also expressions of the eschatological Christian faith.

Among the many themes that can be addressed by Pentecostal and Catholic thinkers, I will focus on two: (1) the recent report of the

---

2. Http://www.vatican.va/holy_father/benedict_xvi/speeches/2008/april/documents/hf_ben-xvi_spe_20080418_incontro-ecumenico_en.html. Note: In reading the works of Joseph Ratzinger there are three roles in his career, all of which will be utilized in this essay: (1) Texts like this one, in his role as Bishop of Rome, Benedict XVI, as center and head of the college of Catholic bishops, with different levels of authority according to the documents. (2) Cardinal Joseph Ratzinger, twenty-five year president of the Congregation of the Doctrine of the Faith, with responsibility for the orthodoxy and discipline of Catholic teaching. In this capacity, the texts he has signed are repots of a Congregation, which he may or may not have had a hand in drafting. Likewise, these have a variety of levels of authority for Catholics. And finally, (3) there are his private writings as an individual scholar, which may have the level of influence in theological dialogues as any other theologian. He has continued to write as a private scholar during the periods of the other two responsibilities, with more or less success at keeping the distinctions clear.

3. *On Becoming a Christian.*

4. Phan, *Responses to 101 Questions on Death and Eternal Life,* 4.

5. See, for example, Fiddes, *Promised End*; Schonborn, *From Death to Life.*

international Catholic Pentecostal dialogue: *On Becoming a Christian: Insights from Scripture and the Patristic Writings with Some Contemporary Reflections*; and (2) elements of Pentecostal and Catholic popular piety that lead to misunderstandings.

It is the position of this author that the core of the faith in Christian hope in the last things is held in common by Catholics and Pentecostals, with different emphases. However, as any attentive student of religion will recognize, personal piety even when not at the center of the revealed faith in the death and resurrection of Jesus Christ, often has more power in the popular imagination of the majority of Christian people than the clear formulations of theologians, or the objective teaching of the Word of God. Therefore, understanding one another's popular beliefs and imaginative world views informed by faith, is a necessary step in the process of reconciliation and embarking, together, on a common eschatological pilgrimage as the people of God toward the future promised by Jesus Christ in the power of the Holy Spirit.

Only in this way "will we be able to respond to the challenges that confront us in an evolving world," and "give transparent witness to the reasons for our hope . . . [to] all peoples through the mystery of his Son's passion and death."[6]

PENTECOSTAL AND CATHOLIC CHRISTIANS IN DIALOGUE

In the more than thirty-five years of formal dialogue among Pentecostal and Catholic Christians, Christ's end time, and our entering with him into glory have yet to be approached directly. This probably can be attributed to the fact that there are more urgent issues dividing our communities, where there are deeper misunderstandings that diminish our ability to engage in common witness to the gospel. Likewise, the academic debates about biblical understandings of Jesus' own view, raised by the scholarship of Johannes Weiss and Albert Schweitzer; enlightenment rationalist reductionisms; and the European-originated eschatological utopianisms of Neoliberal capitalism or atheistic Marxism, not to mention the nihilist millennialism of Nazism; have not been the concerns of Pentecostals or many Catholics.[7]

6. Benedict XVI, Ecumenical Prayer Service, St. Joseph's Parish, New York, Friday, 18 April 2008, note 2 above.

7. For the state of the question from a European Catholic point of view see Ratzinger, *Eschatology*, 1–18. For more accessible Catholic overviews see Phan, *Responses* or Kelly, *Eschatology and Hope*.

However, in the most recent dialogue, finalized in 2006, the text *On Becoming a Christian*[8] provides an extended section on Christian experience. It notes Pentecostal and Catholic emphases including comparison of eschatological faith. While not the focal subject of the text, the authors lay the groundwork for further dialogue and reflective work.

For Pentecostal history of the last century there is a specificity to the role of the end of time in the development and the missionary impulse of the movement, and the theology of history and ecclesiology implicit in its view of the gospel and the world:

> Number 169. Given their Restorationist view of history, eschatology has played a significant role within Pentecostalism. Their belief that they are participating in the "Latter Rain" prophesied in Joel 2:23 and that they are living in "the last days" (Acts 2:17), has led them to place mission and evangelism at the center of their existence. Their view of the Kingdom of God as both present and yet coming has led them to view the Holy Spirit not only as the Comforter sent from above (John 14:16–17, 25–26; 15:26; 16:7–14), the One who sanctifies them (Rom 15:16), or even the One who empowers them through the distribution of various charisms (1 Cor 12:11), but also as a "down payment" or "guarantee" (2 Cor 1:22) of its future blessings, while providing power necessary for them to fulfil their calling between the times (Acts 1:8). They look forward, with hope, to the consummation, when "every knee shall bow" and "every tongue should confess that Jesus Christ is Lord to the glory of God the Father." (Phil 2:10–11)

While Catholics share this hope, and—at least implicitly in the faith of their church—this missionary impulse; the urgency of the last days and engagement of each believer in the missionary zeal by the power of the Spirit are often less central in their piety and religious practice. Indeed, in this they have much to learn from Pentecostal fellow Christians, and in many parts of Latin America have been stimulated to do so.[9] As we will note below, even the restorationist theology of history is not unknown

---

8. *On Becoming a Christian.* There have also been significant dialogues between Catholics and Evangelicals, which have implications for Pentecostals as well.

9. See Gill, *Rendering unto Caesar.* Also Catholics have been challenged to partner with Pentecostals in evangelization. Smith, *Religious Politics in Latin America.* Berryman, *Religion in the Megacity.*

in the renewal movements before the Reformation, and it is the impulse behind a variety of renewal movements in contemporary Catholicism.[10]

Catholic perspectives on the end of time do not exclude belief in the final judgement, Christ's role in history and the missionary impulse of the pilgrim people of God, but the experience is much more focused on the sacramental mediation of the end time in the living community, as noted poetically above:

> Number 183. Eschatology or the "Last Things" also shapes Catholic experience in a fundamental way. All the sacraments and our earthly liturgies are celebrated until the coming of the Lord. Christians exist between the times with the gift of the Holy Spirit as a "down payment" of what is to come (2 Cor 1:22, Eph 1:13–14). We hope for what we do not see and wait for it with patience (Rom 8:24–25). This extends to our personal mortality, which for Catholics becomes the subject of spiritual desire as traditionally expressed in the prayer of the "Hail Mary"—"pray for us now and at the hour of our death." Also, one's suffering in sickness is united with the passion and death of Christ through prayer and the sacrament of the anointing of the sick (CCC 1521–1522)[11] including one's final sufferings in death when reception of the body and blood of Christ in the final holy communion known as the "viaticum" has "particular significance and importance" as one "passes over" to the Father (CCC 1524). All of these are important dimensions of the spiritual life. It also makes us realize that we still await a "new heaven and new earth where God's righteousness will dwell" (2 Pet 3:13), where sin and death will be overcome, and "every tear will be wiped away" (Rev 21:4). Living in the time between Pentecost and the Parousia we experience the graced realities of Christian life imperfectly even as Catholics acknowledge that "[A]ll Christians in any state or walk of life are called to the fullness of Christian life and to the

10. Catholic self understanding of the ecumenical movement as eschatological renewal is neatly capsulated by Cardinal Walter Kasper, "The Second Vatican Council described the church as a pilgrim people, as a church which is on the way towards its eschatological fulfillment. That is, as a church that has to grow and to mature to the fullness of what it was from its very beginning and what it will be forever. To be in dialogue, to listen to each other, and to learn from each other does not mean to become a new church but to become a spiritually renewed church." "Preface," in Murray, ed., *Receptive Ecumenism and the Call to Catholic Learning Exploring a Way for Contemporary Ecumenism*, viii.

11. *Catechism of the Catholic Church* (hereafter CCC).

perfection of charity" (*Lumen gentium* 40, CCC 2013) until the consummation of salvation is brought to completion.

Of all the reforms of the second Vatican Council (1962–1965) among the most successful have been the renewal of rites dealing with eschatology: the funeral liturgy, from "day of wrath, day of woe" to "Resurrection, Alleluia" themes; and the anointing of the sick from the "last rites" to "celebration of healing."[12]

The redirection to the world is articulated in the *Pastoral Constitution on the Church and the Modern World*, "far from diminishing our concern to develop this earth, the expectancy of a new earth should spur us on, for it is here that the body of a new human family grows, foreshadowing in some way the age which is to come."[13] This reintegration of Catholic eschatology has generated a whole range of liberation, political, and inculturated theological developments. As Pope Benedict says in his second encyclical: "While this community-oriented vision of the 'blessed life' is certainly directed beyond the present world, as such it also has to do with the building up of this world—in very different ways, according to the historical context and the possibilities offered or excluded thereby."[14]

Even if Pentecostals are not so focused on the present reality of Christ's eschatological presence in liturgy or the ordinances, their vibrant worship can also be seen as a sign and foretaste of the kingdom for which we hope and begin to live into by the power of the Spirit. The call to perfection and charity is present in Pentecostal spirituality in service of God's eschatological calling in this life. Indeed, the Pentecostal emphasis on healing is not unlike the firm conviction Catholics have about the anointing of the sick being a sign of Christ's eschatological healing presence in the community embodying a foretaste of our final union with him, even in the midst of suffering.

The ecumenical encounter embodied in *On Becoming a Christian*, focused as it is on the initiation of the Christian life in Pentecostal and Catholic communities, is a harbinger of future work on the end and goal of the Christian life and its hope for eternal union with the Father in Christ by the power of the Spirit. This will undoubtedly entail important

12. For the Catholic shifts from devotional to liturgical piety see Dolan, *American Catholic Experience*, 384–90.

13. Number 39. For some of the history of this shift see Phan, *Responses*, 9ff.

14. *Spe Salvi*, number 15.

dialogues on the church and the understanding of history, both with their eschatological dimensions.

PENTECOSTAL AND CATHOLIC POPULAR PIETY

Even with this common faith at the center of our affirmation of Christ and his work of the Spirit, there are a variety of practices of piety and secondary popular beliefs that are not only different, between Pentecostal and Catholic Christians, but often seem unwarranted by the other. Having outlined these agreements, we will explore popular religious emphases in the light of core common affirmations. Daily prayer, views of the world, society and history, and popular evaluations, even stereotypes, of one another may have more impact on the imaginations and behavior of our people in relationship to one another than our careful theological formulations or relations with one another on a formal, institutional level.[15]

In this section I will outline several areas of popular evangelical piety, shared by many in the Pentecostal community, which are misunderstood by Catholics, or which lead Pentecostals to harbor prejudices about Catholics and their church. Both Catholics and Pentecostals can see the continuity with the medieval church in contemporary apocalyptic piety. Then I will note expressions of popular Catholic eschatological piety, which seem strange or biblically unwarranted to Pentecostals.

Popular piety is often messy and does not always conform to the core formulations of the tradition. Theology's role is to articulate the biblical content, to help discern the positive core of the faith within the development of these practices, and to purify devotion in service to authentic witness to the gospel. Often religious enthusiasm overflows the bounds of reason or biblical warrants. In order to appreciate the Christocentric piety of fellow Christians of different traditions, one must understand it, even if one does not like popular piety or even feels it is biblically warranted.

---

15. Gros, "Towards a Hermeneutics of Piety for the Ecumenical Movement," 1–12. See Faith and Order Commission, *Treasure in Earthen Vessels*, Paper No. 182. Bouteneff & Heller, *Interpreting Together*.

EVANGELICAL ESCHATOLOGICAL PIETY AND ITS
CATHOLIC ANTECEDENTS

The history and theology of spirituality is usually not a high priority for the common believer. In fact, piety has a much stronger hold on the religious imagination and on the style of discipleship of the ordinary follower of Christ, than the most accurate theology or the clearest biblical exegesis. In this section we will look at pre-Reformation catholic apocalyptic piety and its perspectives on (1) the millennium, (2) dispensations in Christian history, and (3) the Antichrist figure.

Throughout history one can notice the recurrence of apocalyptic readings of the biblical record, especially Daniel, Revelation, Thessalonians and segments of the Synoptic gospels. Apocalyptic approaches to history are also present in the Hebrew scriptures and extracanonical, intertestamental literature. Contemporary evangelical apocalyptic views of the future and interpretations of history demonstrate more continuity with the piety of the church through the ages than is acknowledged by critics and practitioners alike.

Many Catholics do not know that all of the prophetic interest, apocalyptic dispensationalism, detailed interpretation of historical events as presaging the immediate end of time, and characterization of particular figures, including the pope, as the Antichrist all have Catholic precedents. Many evangelicals[16] do not realize their readings of biblical apocalyptic and its application to specific epochs, events and persons have precedents in pre-Reformation Catholic religious speculation and devotion.

The outset of the sixteenth [and one might add twentieth] century does not mark an important change in the form or content of the apocalyptic tradition itself—most of the themes used by the Reformers and their Catholic opponents, including the identification of the papacy and the Roman Church with the Antichrist, had their origins in the late Middle Ages.[17]

---

16. Weber, *Living in the Shadow of the Second Coming*.

17. McGinn, *Visions of the End*, xiv. McGinn, in later work on the theme, does take account of some American Protestant contributions to Christian eschatology. See McGinn, *AntiChrist*. However, one may wonder if the scholar of the classical Middle Ages has the resources at hand to do the explorations necessary in this field. See, for example, Faupel, *Everlasting Gospel*; Althouse, *Spirit of the Last Days*.

Pentecostal scholars themselves are challenged to study patristic and medieval apocalyptic literature and trace the parallels and sources.[18] This challenge includes helping their own Pentecostal people to see their continuity with Christian visionary piety through the ages. "Christianity was born apocalyptic and has remained so, not in the sense that apocalyptic hopes exhausted the meaning of Christian belief, but because they have never been absent from it."[19]

In history there are two tendencies in interpreting the biblical prophecies, especially after the Christianization of the Roman Empire, given the direction of Revelation at the pagan, persecuting Rome. One continues to give specificity to the final struggle, immediacy to the final coming of Christ, and identifies concrete persons, events and eras with the biblical symbols. The other tendency attempts to come to terms with the delay of the end time and provide an interpretation spiritualizing the millennium and the biblical symbols. The latter emphasis was supported by Augustine and dominated until the High Middle Ages, though the former was never absent from Christian thinking.[20]

Since Augustine set the tone for the philosophy and theology of history in Western Christianity, much of apocalyptic speculation and piety were, and continues to be, marginalized. For example, theologian Joseph Ratzinger provides an accurate assessment of most Catholic attitudes today: "Christ's coming is quite incommensurable with historical time and its immanent laws of development, so it cannot in any way be calculated from the evidence of history. In so calculating, one works with history's inner logic, and thereby misses Christ, who is not the product of evolution or a dialectical stage in the possessive self-expression of reason, but the Other, who throws open the portals of time and death from

---

18. What the dialogue says about patristics may very well be true of medieval sources as well, "we have seen that there are patristic texts, which can cast light on each of the issues we considered (conversion, faith, Christian experience in community, discipleship and formation, and baptism in the Holy Spirit). These texts arise from the Fathers' reflections on the Scriptures and frequently provide insight and wisdom to contemporary questions and situations. Moreover, they remain relevant to contemporary experience. The writings of the Fathers are not *library* treasures from centuries ago. Their words are vibrant witnesses to Christians of today, and of every time." *On Becoming a Christian,* number 269.

19. McGinn, *Visions,* 11.

20. Ibid., 17, 26.

the outside."[21] This does not mean, of course, that in popular Catholicism it is impossible to find millennial movements, dispensational theories, and persons or institutions designated as the Antichrist even in today's church. With the Fifth Lateran Council (1512–1515) on the eve of the Reformation the Catholic eschatological debates diminished, though some of the end time urgency continued in the Latin American mission context.[22] Much of the apocalyptic thinking about history, the proximate end and the Antichrist was carried forward in Reformation rhetoric.

MILLENNIAL CONTEXTS

The crisis atmosphere that generates apocalyptic piety in every generation continued after the end of the Roman persecutions, which was the context for the book of Revelation. The Barbarian invasions and fall of old Rome in the West, the rise of Islam and Crusading wars, the feuds between Emperors and Popes within Christendom, the Avignon papacy and subsequent Great Schism with its two rival popes, corruption in church and empire, and the plagues and cataclysms characteristic of western European history all gave ample scope for apocalyptic analyses of history, signs of the immediate end and coming of Christ, and personages identified with the Antichrist.

The ultimate, positive religious meaning and the faith content of the extravagant prophecies, predictions, expectations, and conflict rhetoric in medieval apocalyptic[23] or contemporary Pentecostal piety is recognized if we look to its Christocentric core. "The most fundamental appeal of apocalypticism is the conviction it holds forth that time is related to eternity, that the history of man has a discernable structure and

---

21. Ratzinger, *Eschatology*, 194. He goes on to note, "Secondly, even a cursory glance at the actual reality of every century suggests that such 'signs' indicate a permanent condition of the world. The world has always been torn apart by wars and catastrophes, and nothing allows one to hope that, for example, 'peace research' will manage to erase this watermark of all humanity." 198.

22. See "Joaquinismos, Utopías, Milenarismos y Mesianismos en la América Colonial" in *Closa*, 613–88. When a Catholic Pentecostal dialogue begins, in earnest, in Latin America the theology of history and eschatology will be among the central topics.

23. Ratzinger characterizes the medieval developments as hysteria, while McGinn is more moderate in his assessment. *Visions*, 8.

meaning in relation to its end, and that this End is the product not of chance, but of divine plan."[24]

MEDIEVAL DISPENSATIONALISM

Throughout the Middle Ages the apocalyptic literature was a continual source of evangelical reform and internal critique of both the political and ecclesiastical realities of Christendom. The most influential dispensationalist was the Cistercian Abbot Joachim of Fiore (1135–1202). His visions of history, its stages and its dynamics, and later works attributed to him, influenced piety and theology for centuries.[25] His vision energized many reform movements, and a variety of critics of emperors and popes.[26] Much attention is given to the social and historical implications of Joachim's thought. However one can also see his contribution as an expression of the Christ centered, contemplative stream of western mysticism,[27] just as one needs to see behind the more demonstrative expressions of Pentecostal piety to the Trinitarian faith informing it.

Might not what was said about the thirteenth century eschatological speculation also be true of the twentieth century, from the point of view of some Pentecostals? "Joachim's stress on the domination of the spiritual and charismatic over the institutional and rational in the future church was diametrically opposed to the forces that triumphed in the thirteenth century . . . In this sense the concept of the third age in the writings of Joachim of Fiore was a radical critique of the thirteenth-century church."[28]

Later, St. Francis was interpreted as an eschatological harbinger of the end of time, and a splinter group of Spiritual Franciscans used Joachim's prophecies and a restorationist view of their movement as bringing back evangelical poverty into the church, to further their vision of reform and restoration.[29] In fact, to reconcile the charismatic,

---

24. McGinn, *Visions*, 36. This author questions whether these faith apprehensions of the mystery of time and eternity are any less worthy of consideration than the bland reductionistic scientific illusions.

25. McGinn, *Calabrian Abbott*.

26. See McGinn, *Apocalyptic Spirituality*.

27. Tavard, *Contemplative Church*.

28. McGinn, *Visions*, 129.

29. Ibid., 203–21. The Pentecostal Catholic dialogue has proposed looking together at the restorationist impulse in Christian history, *On Becoming a Christian*, number

restorationist Franciscan zeal and millenarian enthusiasm dividing the order, Bonaventure (1221–1274), had to be taken out of academics at the University of Paris into Franciscan leadership, where he integrated Joachimist apocalyptic into an orthodox theology of history, compatible with the church's ecclesiology.[30]

The most chilling secularized millenarian pretensions surfaced in the twentieth century with the Third Reich of Hitler's Nazi nihilism. A political component often accompanied the predicted final reign of the Last Emperor, the Antichrist, the Angelic Pope or Christ himself.[31] However, unlike many of the caricatures retrojected from the tragic twentieth century, millennial thinking prior to the fifteenth-century Hussite revolts remained pacific, even contemplative.[32] Contemporary evangelical millennialism has its own political dimension in the contemporary world.[33]

RECURRENT ANTICHRIST

The immanent end, coming final judgment, and the Antichrist figure were deeply engrained, not only in medieval popular piety, but also in philosophies of history and political rhetoric. During the eleventh-century reforms, the papal party would use the Antichrist rhetoric to characterize the Hohenstaufen emperors in their struggle within the Christendom of the day.

Emperors and popular reform movements would characterize popes with whose policies they disagreed as the Antichrist or his predecessor. The first such characterization is recorded in 1260, "Hence it is necessary that Antichrist appear in the place of the Supreme Pontiff [Innocent IV, 1243–1254], in which state his avarice and other vices will be most directly opposed to Christ and in which the Church will be most scandalized and corrupted."[34] This use of the Antichrist rhetoric to designate elements of catholic Christendom at the time was by no means

---

238, see also number 246 on the relationship of eschatology and restorationism in the Pentecostal view.

30. Ratzinger, *Theology of History in St. Bonaventure*, xvi.

31. Cohn, *Pursuit of the Millennium*.

32. McGinn, *Visions*, 226, 246–52, 263–69.

33. Weber, *On the Road to Armageddon*.

34. Friar Arnold, in McGinn, *Visions*, 175. The Friar quotes 2 Thess 2:4 and Rev 13:18 to underline his claims.

a rejection of the papacy, much less of the universal church, which was the Roman Catholic Church of the day. Rather it was a reforming rhetoric, which looked forward to a prophesied angelic pope, or later a series of such popes who would rectify problems of church and empire.[35]

As in Luther's vision, the Roman Catholic Church had to be the true church, for the Antichrist to be the "abomination of domination in the holy place" (Dan 12). The American evangelical use of the biblical symbol for the Roman Catholic Church is an ironic creativity in the Christian tradition because it is a continuation of Roman Catholicism's self critique.

Catholic views of the Antichrist motif today tend to also be spiritualized rather than personalized in history:

> The fact that the future antichrist is thus described [in Dan 11: 36, Ez 28:2] . . . naturally deprives him of any very well defined uniqueness . . . [C]hristological heretics contemporary with the writer are called "antichrist," leading to the conclusion that the "final hour" is now. In truth, however, this "hour" loses thereby its chronological content, becoming the expression for a central spiritual condition, a certain inner closeness to the End . . . The Easter Jesus is our certainty that history can be lived in a positive way, and that our finite and feeble rational activity has a meaning. In this perspective, the "antichrist" is the unconditional enclosure of history within its own logic—the supreme antithesis to the Man with the opened side . . .[36]

CATHOLIC ESCHATOLOGICAL PIETY IN PENTECOSTAL PERSPECTIVE

The core of the Catholic faith in the future is grounded in Christ's death, resurrection and promised return in judgment, and in Christians' unity with him in the communion of saints. In this section we will talk briefly about the practices of (1) praying for the dead, (2) praying to the saints, (3) purgatory, and (4) indulgences.

Faith in these eschatological practices is rooted in an understanding of the communion of saints, living and dead, to whom and for whom we pray in Christ. Associated with these ancient practices, for which Catholics feel there are biblical and historical warrants, there are also

---

35. See Friar Arnold, in McGinn, *Visions*, 186–95.

36. Ratzinger, *Eschatology*, 196–97, 214.

beliefs in the possibility of purgation for those who have been justified in Christ, as one moves into union with him after death. These practices of prayers to the saints, for the dead and indulgences, and the belief in purgatory while not central to Catholic faith in God's saving work in Jesus Christ are, however, alive in Catholic piety. They are among the most misunderstood elements. Likewise, they stand at the headwaters of the tragic divisions of the sixteenth century.

Prayer for the Dead

For Catholic and Orthodox Christians, prayers for the dead are rooted in the most ancient practice of the church. Christians recognize that there is a difference between our relationships in this life and the next, but our communion with the departed in Christ has not been interrupted, only changed. It is as normal to pray for the dead as is to pray for family members who are living or friends who are at a physical distance.

> The possibility of helping and giving does not cease to exist on the death of the Christian. Rather does it stretch out to encompass the entire communion of saints, on both sides of death's portals. The capacity, and the duty, to love beyond the grave might even be called the true primordial datum of this whole area of tradition.[37]

> The belief that love can reach into the afterlife, that reciprocal giving and receiving is possible, in which our affection for one another continues beyond the limits of death—this has been a fundamental conviction of Christianity throughout the ages and it remains a source of comfort today.[38]

Protestant-Catholic dialogues have clarified that there is not as much difference, especially for some of the Reformers, in our understanding as was once believed, and as many of our people still believe.[39]

---

37. Ratzinger, *Eschatology*, 233.

38. *Spe Salvi*, number 48.

39. Bilateral Working Group of the German National Bishops' Conference and the Church Leadership of the United Evangelical Lutheran Church of Germany, *Communio Sanctorum*.

Purgation

In the ancient church reflection on this venerable practice of prayer for the dead led theologians to use images from Paul about fires of purgation to illustrate how such prayers, for those already justified in Christ, might be effective (1 Cor 3:10–15). Of course, in the intermediate states between death and the final judgment; time, space and processes like fire, are only metaphorical, and cannot encompass a place or a period in the way we might understand it with human time. However, the pious imagination has created a rich iconography around the images of purgation proposed by Augustine and other fathers of the church, in giving concrete expression to this hallowed practice.[40]

Contemporary theology, in trying to be clear about the limitations of images of time, space and fire, have provided newer explanations more faithful to present understandings of biblical eschatology, modern anthropology, and the dynamics of human development in Christ by the power of the Holy Spirit:

> The essential Christian understanding of Purgatory has now become clear. Purgatory is not, as Tertullian thought, some kind of supra-worldly concentration camp where man is forced to undergo punishment in a more or less arbitrary fashion. [Often a favorite theme for medieval muralists, one might add, with all of one's enemies, popes and emperors brought into equality with the rank and file Christian peasant, in the flames of purgation!] Rather is it the inwardly necessary process of transformation in which a person becomes capable of Christ, capable of God and thus capable of unity with the whole communion of saints . . . It does not replace grace by works, but allows the former to achieve its full victory precisely as grace . . . Encounter with the Lord *is* this transformation. It is the fire that burns away our dross and re-forms us to be vessels of eternal joy.[41]

---

40. Goff, *Birth of Purgatory*. See Ratzinger, *Eschatology*, 228–29. For the official current formulation of the doctrine see CCC numbers 1030–31.

41. Ratzinger, *Eschatology*, 230–31. He goes on to elaborate the historical roots of the doctrine, "The identification of Purgatory with the Church's penance in Cyprian and Clement is important for drawing our attention to the fact that the root of the Christian doctrine of Purgatory is the Christological grace of penance. Purgatory follows by an inner necessity from the idea of penance, the idea of the constant readiness for reform which marks the forgiven sinner," 231.

"Some recent theologians are of the opinion that the fire which both burns and saves is Christ himself, the Judge and Savior. The encounter with him is the decisive act of judgment. Before his gaze all falsehood melts away. This encounter with him, as it burns us, transforms and frees us, allowing us to become truly ourselves."[42] Ratzinger's explanation tries to purify Catholic imagery of its confusions, which opened it to the abuses that both the Reformers and the Council of Trent (1545–1563) sought to correct.[43] He tries to make clear, in an ecumenical context, what is the core of the faith of the church.[44]

Prayer to the Saints

The practice of praying to members of the communion of saints who have gone on before, and who are presumed to be alive in Christ, goes back to the catacombs and prayers to those who have been martyrs for their faith.[45] Invoking fellow Christians, already deceased, and asking their intercession is integral to Catholic popular piety. For Catholics prayers to the Mother of God and the saints is a confession of the unique mediatorial role of Christ and his association with those whom he has justified and holds in eternal life with him.[46]

Furthermore, understandings of the Mother of Christ's role in the plan of salvation is intimately related to Christ's saving role by the power of the Spirit, as understood from the Scripture,[47] and the Council of Ephesus (431). For Catholics, the affirmation of Mary's union with Christ, in the doctrine of the Assumption, confesses eschatological hope for final union with Christ in the communion of saints.[48]

However, from the early days of the Reformation in the sixteenth-century Protestants have had reservations about this traditional practice of invoking the intercession of the saints in heaven. Lutherans and

---

42. *Spe Salvi* numbers 45–47.

43. The sixteenth century itself demonstrated a rich diversity of Catholic eschatological pieties. See, for example, Swanson, *Promissory Notes on the Treasury of Merits.* Eire, *From Madrid to Purgatory.* Duffy, *Stripping of the Altars.*

44. Duffy, *Stripping of the Altars,* 273.

45. Brown, *Cult of the Saints.*

46. H. G. Anderson et al., eds., *The One Mediator, Mary and the Saints.*

47. Brown, et al., *Mary in the New Testament.*

48. See Anglican Roman Catholic International Commission, "Mary: Grace and Hope in Christ."

Catholics, in their dialogue with one another in the last half-century have begun to resolve these historical discrepancies in the Christian heritage. These convergences lend themselves to Pentecostals for their own evaluation, and possible deepening, in light of common agreements with Catholics: "The discrepancy between Catholic and Lutheran teaching on the intercession of saints is not the decisive one. Lutherans do not deny the Catholic doctrine, but question its biblical basis and its certainty. They assert that Christ prays for us, as do saints on earth and perhaps in heaven. Catholic doctrine affirms the intercession of the saints in heaven."

> [The Catholic Council of Trent] affirmed that it is good and useful to invoke the saints and to have recourse to their prayers and help in obtaining God's benefits through Jesus Christ, "who alone is our Savior and Redeemer." But neither Trent nor any other council or pope has imposed upon the individual Catholic the obligation of venerating saints or of invoking them. Vatican II ... described it as "supremely fitting" ... to invoke the saints and have recourse to their prayers.

> Catholics deny that the practice in and of itself is idolatrous or injurious to the honor of Christ the one Mediator, even though the practice must be protected against abuses. The Catholics of this dialogue recognize that abuses have occurred and that the doctrine of the sole mediatorship of Christ provides one critical principle for identifying abuses ... The Lutherans of this dialogue are of the opinion that the practice is not church-dividing provided that the sole mediatorship of Christ is clearly safeguarded.[49]

Indulgences

One of the most challenging elements of Catholic piety for other Christians to understand is the practice of gaining indulgences. In fact, it is not always a clear practice for Catholics themselves, and certainly not central to the devotional life of most, at this time of biblical and liturgical renewal.

However, it remains a component of the Catholic system of penance and reconciliation. In fact, in order to fully understand indulgences it would be necessary to comprehend the history and theology of Catholic penitential discipline, the reconciliation and reintegration of

---

49. H. G. Anderson et al., eds., *The One Mediator*, 56–58.

sinners into the Christian community.[50] At the Reformation, Lutherans[51] and Anglicans reformed, but did not totally reject confession and the penitential practice of the church. All Christian communities have ways of reconciling those who have fallen away from the faith and of providing discipline conducive to growth in Christian discipleship.

Within the Catholic system, the reconciled sinner is obliged to provide restitution to those from whom goods have been stolen if he or she has been a thief. After contrition and reconciliation the sinner is also provided a punishment or a penance to help restore the relationship with God and with the community. These penances do not justify the sinner, who has been reconciled by the grace of Christ. Rather they are part of the sanctification process engendered by union with Christ.

In ancient times, these could be lengthy and public penances for serious failings against God and the community. However, as the church moved further away from the rigors of the persecuted community into a settled and ordinary existence, many of these strict penalties were commuted, or "indulged" by grant of an "indulgence" a devotional practice or prayer to replace long and public penance.[52]

In the Middle Ages, these indulgences, or "pardons" as they were often called in England, became much desired by the pious faithful, as a special blessing. Modern historiography has begun to move beyond the polarizing polemics of the post-Reformation era and to correct the prejudice "that those who acquired and accumulated indulgences in the 250 years or so before England experienced Reformation [are to] be dismissed as gullible dupes because they made indulgences part of their spiritual life and used them as part of their social cement."[53]

---

50. Dallen, *Reconciling Community*. For some of the ecumenical implications and interpretive difficulties, see Osborne, *Reconciliation and Justification*, especially 120ff. Also Marty, "In Defense of Indulgences," 735.

51. See McDonnell, "Luther and Trent on Penance," 26–276. Bagchi, "Luther's *Nintey-five Theses* and the Contemporary Criticism of Indulgences," 331–56.

52. Shaffern, *Penitents' Treasury*. See also Swanson, *Promissory Notes*, "Whatever their centrality to medieval religious practice . . . indulgences were not central to medieval religious doctrine, or among the kinds of activity which would be regularly recorded in the administrative records of the medieval church," 4.

53. Swanson, *Indulgences in Late Medieval England*, x. "Current anxieties, prejudices, and presumptions provide grounds on which to criticize and condemn medieval indulgences, but are not firm foundations for historical assessment. Whatever difficulties indulgences raise when examined from the outside, considered from within the medieval catholic world they make a great deal of sense," 518.

When indulgences emerged in the early Middle Ages, they were under the supervision of local bishops, and papal oversight came into play to regulate abuses, promote the crusades, and coordinate this pious practice. The image of "treasury" was developed to explain how Christ's goodness and that of the members of his Mystical Body were made available. Much of the Reformation polemic, while warranted for specific abuses, was overly generalized, inattentive as it was to the history and the proper understanding, which was not totally lost among the faithful and their pastors.[54]

The original practice of gaining indulgences had nothing to do with the after life or the departed.[55] Likewise, the granting of indulgences for a good work, like giving alms, was also a later development. However, indulgences, when rightly understood, were always seen as a private devotional practice for the already justified and reconciled Christian, and never a means of gaining salvation, always a freely given grace of God in Jesus Christ. This orthodox understanding of the faith did not, however, exclude all abuses, as Chaucer's pardoner, or the preaching of John Tetzel (1465–1519) demonstrate, but central to the practice and its application to the deceased was an exercise of Christian charity and a desire for union with Christ, for one's self or one's loved ones.[56]

The Council of Trent treated indulgences quickly, toward the end of the final session, with little dialogue.[57] It was concerned more with their reform against superstition and their defense against the Reformers, than with providing a positive explication, about which there was no con-

---

54. Swanson, *Indulgences*, 18–19.

55. This application of indulgences to the departed probably started in popular piety before being sanctioned by church leadership. One author suggests it was as late as 1497, on the eve of the Reformation, that papal application of indulgences for the dead was sanctioned, Swanson, *Indulgences*, 21, 519, Shaffern, "The Medieval Theology of Indulgences," 36. Others attribute the first papal application of indulgences to the dead to the Jubilee of 1300, Goff, *Purgatory*, 330. "One glaring exception [to the consensus] stands. Clear disagreements existed in the Latin Christian intellectual tradition over the interpretation of indulgences for the dead. The origins of indulgences for the dead are somewhat mysterious." Shaffern, "Learned Discussions of Indulgences for the Dead in the Middle Ages," 368.

56. Shaffem, 522.

57. December 4, 1563, in Tanner, ed., *Decrees of the Ecumenical Councils*. See Peter, "Communion of Saints in the Final Days of the Council of Trent," in H. G. Anderson et al., eds., *The One Mediator*, 219–33.

sensus in the sixteenth century.[58] It was not until the twentieth century that a more nuanced ecclesial explanation was given, by Pope Paul VI in 1967.[59] Theologians of the stature of Karl Rahner (1904–1984) have given their hand to explicating the devotion for the modern context.[60] The *Catechism of the Catholic Church* gives an accurate, if succinct, statement of the current official teaching on the subject.[61]

However, I think the most helpful official explanation came with the 2000 Jubilee year proclamation, a statement that makes perfectly clear that an indulgence is not to be seen as good works, which somehow merits salvation from God:

> 9. The indulgence discloses the fullness of the Father's mercy, who offers everyone his love, expressed primarily in the forgiveness of sins. Normally, God the Father grants his pardon through the Sacrament of Penance and Reconciliation. Free and conscious surrender to grave sin, in fact, separates the believer from the life of grace with God and therefore excludes the believer from the holiness to which he is called . . . It is precisely through the ministry of the Church that God diffuses his mercy in the world, by means of that precious gift which from very ancient times has been called "indulgence."

> The Sacrament of Penance offers the sinner "a new possibility to convert and to recover the grace of justification" won by the sacrifice of Christ . . . From the first centuries, however, the Church has always been profoundly convinced that pardon, freely granted by God, implies in consequence a real change of life, the gradual elimination of evil within, a renewal in our way of living . . . Reconciliation with God does not mean that there are no enduring consequences of sin from which we must be purified . . . With the indulgence, the repentant sinner receives a remission of the temporal punishment[62] due for the sins already forgiven as regards the fault.

58. Ratzinger, *Eschatology*, 220.

59. *Apostolic Constitution on the Doctrine and Practice of Indulgences*. See Palmer and Tavard, "Indulgences," vol. VII, 436–41.

60. "Remarks on the Theology of Indulgences," *Theological Investigations*, vol. 2. See also Phan, *Eternity in Time*.

61. CCC numbers 1471–78, 1498.

62. "Temporal punishment" often confuses Catholics and their critics, because it is sometimes mistakenly taken in the sense of "time," often time in Purgatory. In fact, "temporal" is meant in contrast to "eternal punishment." That is, this "punishment" is a discipline that increases union with Christ as opposed to hell, which is eternal separa-

10. Because it offends the holiness and justice of God and scorns God's personal friendship with man, sin has a twofold consequence. In the first place, if it is grave, it involves deprivation of communion with God and, in consequence, exclusion from a share in eternal life. To the repentant sinner, however, God in his mercy grants pardon of grave sin and remission of the "eternal punishment" which it would bring.

In the second place, "every sin, even venial, entails an unhealthy attachment to creatures, which must be purified ... This purification frees one from what is called the "temporal punishment" of sin.

Revelation also teaches that the Christian is not alone on the path of conversion. In Christ and through Christ, his life is linked by a mysterious bond to the lives of all other Christians in the supernatural union of the Mystical Body ... His superabundant love saves us all. Yet it is part of the grandeur of Christ's love not to leave us in the condition of passive recipients, but to draw us into his saving work and, in particular, into his Passion.

Everything comes from Christ, but since we belong to him, whatever is ours also becomes his and acquires a healing power. This is what is meant by "the treasures of the Church," which are the good works of the saints. To pray in order to gain the indulgence means to enter into this spiritual communion and therefore to open oneself totally to others. In the spiritual realm, too, no one lives for himself alone ... This is the reality of the communion of saints.

Furthermore, the truth about the communion of saints which unites believers to Christ and to one another, reveals how much each of us can help others—living or dead—to become ever more intimately united with the Father in heaven.[63]

Indeed, this explanation did not satisfy all of critics of this Catholic devotional practice in 2000.[64] However, it did enable representatives of churches, Methodist and Lutheran, who share with the Catholic Church

---

tion from God. The quantitative imagery of the period may be unfortunate, but was probably inevitable given the rise of counting skills and literacy among Christians in the twelth and thirteenth centuries. See Swanson, *Indulgences*, 11, 19; Shaffern, "Medieval Theology," 21–26; Goff, *Purgatory*, 209, 227, 290.

63. 2000 Jubilee Year Proclamation.

64. For example, see Stanley, "Urging Millennial Penitence, Pope Is Offering Indulgences," A1; and response "Indulge Us." 6.

the *Joint Declaration on the Doctrine of Justification*, to recognize that this optional practice of personal piety should not be seen as a church-dividing issue.[65]

Pentecostals with their wide variety of pious practices will have to make their own judgments as to whether such personal devotions can be seen as compatible with the common core of their eschatological faith shared with Catholics. Certainly the enthusiastic thirst for blessings among the pious faithful, without concern for theological reflection or a critical reading of the Bible, is not unknown in Pentecostal piety.

CONCLUSION

We have looked at what the most recent Pentecostal Catholic dialogue has had to say about the last things as part of the Christian experience, and at elements of Christian piety significant in the history of the two traditions. A common systematic approach to Christian eschatology could be given together with elements like those suggested by Peter Phan, In the in-between time, from Christ's ascension to his glorious return, the church is a pilgrim people living in hope, responding to God's gift of self, in the power and under the guidance of the Holy Spirit, so that the kingdom of God may be realized in the world. In other words, eschatology was centered on Christ (Christological), the church (ecclesial), and the cosmos (cosmic). These are the dimensions that must be retrieved in our reconstruction of eschatology."[66] Would it not make sense for Pentecostals and Catholics together to give a common account of the church's thinking about the end time throughout history,[67] to develop a common formulation—as much as possible—of the biblical understanding of eschatology, and to pursue a common witness in society to that future to which we are called, as a pilgrim people, in Christ? Is there not an authentic positive core to both pieties, which continues to need explication for our time? Do we not have a massive educational task to help our people appreciate one another, both in their formal biblical faith and in the most extravagant expressions of their popular piety?

---

65. Root, "Jubilee Indulgence and the *Joint Declaration on the Doctrine of Justification,*" 460–75.

66. Phan, *Responses*, 18.

67. As the dialogue suggests, "Future dialogue should take up this crucial question of how we read history in different ways and explore why we do so." *On Becoming a Christian,* number 280.

As the most recent dialogue affirms: We have discovered that in hearing each other, and in witnessing each other's faith, hope, and love we are drawn more deeply to Christ. We hope through the power of the Spirit that our mutual recognitions will enhance our communion with each other and strengthen our common witness to the world. Each has some experience of what has traditionally been prized by the other. This affords us another way forward in our dialogue, as "spiritual ecumenism" becomes more and more the basis for theological conversations. Most of all spiritual discernment alerts us to the providential possibilities that God offers in his freedom and grace towards us.[68]

Catholics and Pentecostal pieties have been blessed by rich and imaginative approaches to what the Spirit is doing in their history as she leads them as a pilgrim people toward that mysterious horizon, which points to the ultimate unity in Christ to which all are called.[69] The piety of both communities helps them avoid falling into technological determinism or ideological utopianism as they approach history and God's future.[70] For many in society, planning has supplanted providence in approaching time and human development, faith in progress replaced hope in God's future.[71]

While neither community may be disposed to take on the piety of the other, all should feel called to a deeper understanding in Christ and a common hope in the future, which can only be given by the power of the Holy Spirit. "It is precisely the Christian who is able to look on the powers of evil realistically and without fear and stand firm against them because he or she is aware of the greater power of redemption, which is the only thing that can still guarantee hope in the face of the universal need of salvation."[72]

68. *On Becoming a Christian*, numbers 191, 278.

69. The ecumenical encounter itself can be seen as a sign and foretaste of the eschatological calling, as Ratzinger notes, "[T]he dialogue of human beings with each other now becomes a vehicle for the life everlasting, since in the communion of saints it is drawn up into the dialogue of the Trinity itself. This is why the communion of saints is the locus where eternity becomes accessible for us. Eternal life does not isolate a person, but leads him out of isolation into true unity with his brothers and sisters and the whole of God's creation." Ratzinger, *Eschatology*, 159–60.

70. See Ratzinger, *Eschatology*, 210, 273.

71. Ratzinger, *Eschatology*, 209, *Spe Salvi*, numbers 17–22.

72. Kasper, *Faith and the Future*, vii.

The words of Hans Urs von Balthasar (1905–1988) capture nicely what all Christians, Pentecostals and Catholics among them, can share in their eschatological faith, "God is 'the last thing' for the creature. Gained, God is heaven; lost, hell; testing, judgment; purifying, purgatory. God himself is that in which the finite dies and through which it rises again in God and to God. God is such that God turns himself to the world, namely, in his Son Jesus Christ, who is the manifestation of God and therefore also the sum of the 'last things.'"[73] "Catholics and Pentecostals recognize that the thirst for salvation is at the same time a work of the Spirit and a human response."[74]

73. Quoted in Phan, *Responses*, 29.

74. *On Becoming a Christian*, number 190.

12

"Discerning the Times"

The Victorious Eschatology of the Shepherding Movement

DAVID MOORE

LOOKING BACK

In the summer of 1977, over 45,000 charismatic Christians nearly filled Kansas City's Arrowhead Stadium every evening for four successive nights, worshipping God, praying together, and listening to speakers in a show of remarkable ecumenism. The Conference on Charismatic Renewal in the Christian Churches (CCRCC) brought together Roman Catholics, mainline Protestants, independent charismatics, and some classical Pentecostals, all celebrating together the Lordship of Jesus Christ centered in their shared experience of renewal in the Holy Spirit. In daytime meetings, the various denominational expressions of the burgeoning Charismatic Renewal met separately in their own confessional gatherings and in the evening everyone met together at the Stadium.[1] The conference participants were part of a movement, which swept through the historic churches in the 1960s and 1970s, emphasizing "baptism in the Holy Spirit" and a new focus on spiritual gifts, especially speaking

---

1. The conference dates met on July 20–24, 1977 with evening meetings Wednesday through Saturday and denominational gatherings in various venues on Sunday morning to conclude events. Moore, "Kansas City hears 'Jesus is Lord,'" 50–53; Kauffman, "Separate, But United in Spirit," Hawn, "Kansas City: Conference Heard 'Round the World,'" 24.

with tongues. The weeklong conference was the "high water mark" of the charismatic renewal.[2]

In the Friday evening meeting, Bob Mumford, a popular neo-Pentecostal leader, was the plenary speaker. Midway through his message "Helps and Hindrances to Holiness," Mumford paused, "opened his Bible to the book of Revelation and said, 'If you take a sneak look at the back of the book, Jesus Wins!'" Immediately the stadium crowd erupted into spontaneous praise and worship, which lasted for ten minutes. Mumford stood on the platform dumbfounded and simply joined the worshippers until finally resuming his message after the "Holy Spirit breakdown" finally faded away.[3]

Mumford's words that July 1977 night reflected his victorious eschatology, a conviction he shared with his close associates in the Shepherding or Discipleship movement, a movement that threatened the very ecumenical character of the Kansas City conference and the broader charismatic renewal.[4] For nearly two years, controversy had raged over the teachings of the five widely known and traveled authors and Bible teachers: Bob Mumford, Don Basham, Ern Baxter, Derek Prince, and Charles Simpson. Turmoil over their teachings tore at the fabric of the ecumenical idealism, which had been so central to the charismatic renewal for nearly a decade. The controversy, though hardly visible to the CCRCC participants, had forced Kansas City conference organizers to create two separate tracks for independent charismatics, who were

2. The popular origin of the charismatic renewal, or neo-Pentecostalism, as it was also called, is usually associated with Episcopalian priest Dennis Bennett. While pastoring St. Mark's Episcopal parish in Van Nuys, California, a large, affluent congregation, Bennett was filled with the Holy Spirit, speaking with tongues, and after announcing it to his congregation in the spring of 1960, he received national press coverage, which helped popularize renewal in the mainline Protestant Churches. One of the distinctive marks of the Charismatic Renewal was renewal of existing churches. This was particularly the case with the 1967 birth of the Roman Catholic Charismatic Renewal. Unlike early Pentecostals who often left their churches to form new churches or denominations, neo-Pentecostals were encouraged to stay within their churches and to work for renewal. In addition, the movement had a large independent sector of charismatic prayer groups and churches.

3. Blattner, "Living Prophecy," 4–9. See also: Manuel, *Like a Mighty Wind.*

4. For a thorough history and understanding of the movement see Moore, *Shepherding Movement.*

unwilling to meet jointly in the morning and afternoon sessions because of their disagreements over the Shepherding teachings.[5]

The debate centered in the Shepherding movement's emphasis on pastoral care and discipleship. The five leaders of the movement flatly asserted that everyone needed a personal pastor in a relationship of pastoral care, discipleship and teaching. They also advocated the terms "shepherd" for pastors, and "sheep" for the people cared for by the "shepherds." What was especially galling to some leaders was Mumford and the other four insisted that all leaders needed to be "under authority," having their own shepherd/pastor. Many felt the five teachers were trying to get other leaders to submit to their authority and create a new charismatic denomination, a charge the five men doggedly denied. In addition, many charismatic leaders believed the Shepherding movement's teachings on submission and spiritual authority created unhealthy domination by "shepherds" over their "sheep."[6]

By the summer of 1977, a growing movement indeed had formed around the five teachers, largely drawn from younger independent charismatic leaders and participants, a significant number coming from the Jesus People movement, which had blossomed in the late 1960s and early 1970s. These people came into the Shepherding movement in a quest to be pastored and discipled by one of the five men or their designate. This arrangement caused some to believe that the movement had created a kind of pyramid system with the five teachers at the top, a charge also denied by Mumford and the other leaders. What is certain is the Shepherding movement was driven by a renewal ecclesiology, calling for a revitalization of biblical church life and emphasizing the need to restore the New Testament five-fold ministry of apostles, prophets, evangelists, pastors, and teachers.[7] The office they felt most critical for Christian maturity was the office of pastor, an office they believed had been reduced to no more than a kind of chaplaincy role, robbed of any real authority by accommodation to the culture.[8]

---

5. The two nondenominational groups did meet together in one final session where some efforts were made to heal the division. Nothing lasting was accomplished. Moore, *Logos Journal*, 51.

6. Many opposing leaders had their reported stories of spiritual abuse. Some charges seemed to have merit while others were unsubstantiated and sensationalized hearsay.

7. Moore, "Shepherding Movement," 249–70.

8. Prince, "Vision of the Completed Body," transcript, 4.

Perhaps just as important to the movement's five leaders was their call for covenant relationship among believers. In their view, Christians entered into a covenant relationship with God at conversion through faith in Christ. Along with this committed relationship with God, Christians entered into committed relationship with fellow believers as well. The interpersonal relationships needed to be formalized by stated commitments between shepherds and sheep. All this they believed led to a deeper experience of Christian community by confronting the transient nature of typical church relationships, where people regularly moved from prayer group to prayer group or from church to church, treating church commitment as any other consumer choice.

These perspectives emerged out of the committed relationships between the five leaders of the movement. Basham, Mumford, Prince, and Simpson entered into their own covenant relationship in 1970 after witnessing a fellow leader fall into immorality. They felt their mutual commitments to each other would provide needed counsel and account-ability, protecting them from a similar failure their colleague had experienced. Joined in 1974 by Baxter, the five teachers had in their travels recurrently witnessed extreme independence and individualism, which in their view threatened the charismatic renewal's future viability. This committed association of the five independent charismatic teachers fostered new perspectives on the importance of accountability, mutual submission, covenant relationship, and church life that began to shape their individual and collective teaching ministries.

While never intending to start a movement, their teachings made it inevitable. As they taught on submission and authority, personal pastoral care, covenant relationship, and church renewal at various charismatic conferences and events and especially through distribution of audio and video tapes their writings—particularly in *New Wine Magazine*—they tapped into a leadership void among independent charismatics.[9] Before long, as they went about in their ministry travels, people began to submit to their leadership, sometimes bringing entire churches or charismatic prayer groups with them. At first reluctant to start anything that might be perceived as a denomination of sorts, the leaders eventually yielded to the momentum they were experiencing and a church movement was

---

9. *New Wine Magazine* was, along with the *Logos Journal*, the most widely distribut-ed charismatic periodical with a circulation at point of over 100,000. Basham, "Forum: CGM and New Wine," 31.

born in late spring 1974. In the furor over the movement's teachings on submission and authority, few realized the Shepherding movement understood itself through a distinct eschatological restorationism, reflecting the perspectives the five men shared.[10]

THE FIVE TEACHERS

Informing and shaping the development of their collective eschatological perspectives, the varied backgrounds of the Shepherding movement's five principal teachers created a curious mix, creating tensions where there were disagreements among them. None of the five had a common theological pedigree, making their corporate identity all the more unique. They were first drawn together through their mutual involvement with the Holy Spirit Teaching Mission (HSTM) in Ft. Lauderdale, FL, with its charismatic teaching conferences and popular teaching magazine *New Wine*. Mumford and the others always saw their association as more relational than ideological, as is evident in looking at their backgrounds.[11]

Don Basham, a gifted artist and journalist, trained at Phillips University, a Disciples of Christ school, earning both BA and BD degrees. Through the influence of proto-charismatic, Harald Bredeson, Basham experienced Spirit baptism in 1953 and by the 1960s was traveling widely, emphasizing the ministry of deliverance from demonic spirits as well as the need for Spirit baptism.[12] Basham moved to Ft. Lauderdale in 1968. Throughout his involvement in the movement, Basham had the lowest profile of the five leaders and was not a theological innovator. His main ministry thrust drew on his journalistic gifts as an editor and leader of *New Wine Magazine*, the most recognizable media face of the Shepherding movement.

Bob Mumford, who along with Derek Prince, was arguably among the most popular charismatic Bible teachers in the Charismatic Renewal, did his undergraduate ministry training at an Assemblies of God Bible

10. Restorationism, or primitivism, as used in this chapter, refers to the quest to restore the contemporary church to its pristine form as found in the New Testament, particularly Christian experiences described in the book of Acts. I prefer the term restorationism to avoid the reductionistic connotations that may be associated with the term primitivism. See Hughs, *American Quest for the Primitive Church*; idem, *Primitive Church in the Modern World*; Snyder, *Signs of the Spirit*.

11. Mumford and the others would always argue that God brought them together sovereignly. See my account in Moore, *Shepherding Movement*, 28–32.

12. Moore, "Basham, Don Wilson," 367.

college and later completed an MDiv at Episcopal Reformed Seminary in Philadelphia. Between his undergraduate and graduate training Mumford taught for three years at Elim Bible Institute in New York, serving also as Academic Dean. By the late 1960s Mumford was traveling extensively as a charismatic speaker, teaching for a season at Melodyland School of the Bible in Anaheim, CA before moving to Ft. Lauderdale, FL in 1970. Mumford's popularity and prophetic temperament gave him great influence in shaping the Shepherding movement's theology and practice. Although Mumford's early connection with the Assemblies of God oriented him toward a modified dispensationalism, his time teaching at Elim inaugurated a shift toward a restorationistic eschatology. His involvement with the more diverse charismatic renewal along with his seminary training, and more than anything his discovery of the "message of the kingdom" in the early 1960s, caused him to eventually "throw away his prophetic charts" and reject dispensationalism.[13]

Derek Prince, trained in philosophy at Cambridge University, converted to Christianity and was Spirit baptized through the influence of an Assemblies of God church while serving in the British army in 1941. Stationed in Israel in 1944, Prince met his first wife Lydia and developed an interest in the Holy Land that lasted for the rest of his life. After Prince left the British Army he went on to pastor in London, served as missionary in Kenya, and eventually came to the United States where he pastored in Seattle for several years. Prince began his itinerant charismatic ministry in the 1960s, and moved to Ft. Lauderdale in 1968 to enjoy the warm weather and be closer to the HSTM based there. Prince's proper British style coupled with his precise unemotional Bible teaching made him unique among charismatic leaders.[14] Although Prince would later seek to downplay his role in developing the theology for the Shepherding movement, he was instrumental in shaping the early ecclesiology of the movement. His dispensational premillennialism, however, would create significant differences with his fellow leaders, particularly with Baxter.[15]

13. Mumford, *Forty Years in Ministry 1954–1994*; Moore, "Mumford, Bernard C., Jr. ('Bob')," 911.

14. Moore, "Prince, Peter Derek V.," 999.

15. Like many other Pentecostals, Prince uncritically embraced dispensationalism and adjusted it to fit within his Pentecostal beliefs. For a discussion on the relationship of early Pentecostalism to dispensationalism, see Shepherd, "Pentecostals and the Hermeneutics of Dispensationalism," 5–33.

Charles Simpson, who would become the structural ecclesial architect of the Shepherding movement, was the son of a Southern Baptist pastor. Simpson began his own pastoral ministry at the age of twenty when he assumed the pastorate of Bayview Heights Baptist Church in Mobile, AL. While pastoring, he attended William Carey College and after graduating attended New Orleans Baptist Seminary for two years, although he did not graduate. Simpson was Spirit baptized in 1964 and controversy over his experience brought considerable scrutiny from the Southern Baptist Convention as he sought to keep the church in the denomination. From his base as pastor of the Mobile church, Simpson began traveling widely, speaking at various charismatic events. He resigned the Mobile congregation and moved to Ft. Lauderdale in 1971. Until Simpson became a charismatic when he was Spirit baptized in 1964, he was a self-described "pre-trib-pre-mil" fundamentalist preacher, who only saw the church going "down, down, down."[16] In the years after his introduction to the charismatic experience, Simpson would make dramatic adjustments to his eschatological views.[17]

Mumford, Simpson, Basham, and Prince frequently crossed paths and were well acquainted through their travels to Full Gospel Business Men's Fellowship International events and other charismatic speaking conferences. Nothing, however, was more influential to their eventual association than the HSTM in Ft. Lauderdale, FL where the four had become the core teaching team. One of many charismatic centers that emerged in the sixties, the HSTM regularly hosted teaching conferences in Ft. Lauderdale and at various sites around the nation. In 1969, HSTM started publishing *New Wine Magazine* and sought to be a media center for the growing renewal. When the HSTM's primary leader was forced to resign in 1970, the four were thrust into leadership roles for the HSTM and *New Wine Magazine* by default. As they later told it, the crisis at the mission occasioned a peculiar sense that God had sovereignly joined them together and they were to walk together as a ministry team. In 1972, they changed the HSTM's name to Christian Growth Ministries, which continued to publish *New Wine* until the magazine ended publication in 1986.[18]

16. Simpson, "Destiny of the People of God," 26: idem, "Heavenly Perspective," 9.

17. Moore, "Simpson, Charles Vernon," 1070.

18. In 1981, Christian Growth Ministries changed its name to Integrity Communications.

Canadian Ern Baxter was the latecomer to the group. He joined the other four men at the 1974 Shepherds Conference in Montreat, NC. The conference was an ecumenical event sponsored by Roman Catholic and mainline Protestant charismatic leaders along with Basham, Mumford, Prince, and Simpson. The four leaders hosted a private meeting for the men they were now leading and Ern Baxter was invited as an observer. Baxter, deeply impressed by the unity and depth of relationship he saw among the four men and their followers, formally committed himself to the new movement, publically stating that the kind of relational commitment they shared was something he had "been looking for all [his] years of ministry."

Baxter began his ministry as a classical Pentecostal. A great pulpit orator, he pastored Evangelistic Temple, which grew to be one of the largest churches in Vancouver, BC. In the late 1940s, he came under the influence of the Latter Rain and healing movements.[19] In 1949, Baxter accepted the invitation by healing evangelist William Branham to be the campaign manager and Bible teacher for Branham's healing crusades, traveling extensively while still pastoring his church. The demanding schedule eventually forced Baxter to resign both the church and his role with Branham. After various subsequent ministry assignments, Baxter found his place as a popular speaker in the charismatic renewal, preaching worldwide in Pentecostal and charismatic churches and conferences.[20]

Although Baxter did not have any formal theological training, he was an extremely competent self-taught Bible teacher and theologian, drawing on his massive personal theological library. Increasingly over the years, Baxter became strongly Reformed in his doctrinal orientation while still retaining his commitments to a dynamic charismatic orientation. Baxter liked to say he had seen and participated in the entirety of the twentieth-century renewal through his experience with classical Pentecostalism, the Latter Rain movement, the healing movement, and the charismatic renewal. Baxter's eschatology was deeply influenced by

19. See Harrell, *All Things Are Possible*. Harrell's book is dated but still the best work on the healing movements of the late 1940s and 1950s.; Riss, *Latter Rain*; idem, *Survey of 20th Century Revival Movments*. In the years since writing my monograph on the Shepherding movement, I have become convinced that the Latter Rain movement's emphasis on restoration of the five-fold office ministries of Eph 4 significantly influenced both Baxter and Mumford's thinking and consequently the concepts they later developed.

20. Moore, "Baxter, W. J. E. ('Ern')," 367–68.

his readings of postmillennial authors and he came to believe the church replaced Israel in God's plan. This created significant tensions over the years with the stanchly pro-Israel stance of Derek Prince.

ESCHATOLOGICAL RESTORATIONISM

The confluence of the five leaders' backgrounds and personalities, the contextual realities of the early 1970s, and their practical experiences as teachers in the charismatic renewal, all came together to create a distinct movement. The five leaders of the Shepherding movement were especially focused on "discerning the times" in which they were living. Echoing the tendencies of other radical evangelicals, particularly early twentieth-century Pentecostals, the Shepherding movement's leaders saw themselves as an eschatological movement, a movement God was establishing to restore New Testament Christianity.[21] The primary and unique thrust of the Shepherding movement's restoration was ecclesiocentric, with a quest to establish biblical church government, especially pastor/shepherds, which would help prepare a mature and vibrant church as God's eschatological community. From 1974 onward, the Shepherding movement's central purpose was renewal of church structures. In this, they all five agreed. Other issues of eschatology, however, were dynamic and convoluted, reflecting the eschatological variety of the five teachers' theological perspectives and their association resulted in a blend of aspects of differing traditions.

On one eschatological point Mumford and the other leaders were certain: they were living in the last days. But their interpretation of the last days came with a different understanding than early twentieth-century Pentecostals. Whereas early Pentecostals emphasized the immediacy of Christ's Second Coming, the Shepherding movement's leaders emphasized God's preparation of a glorious church shining with increasing brightness "in the midst of a dark and cloudy day."[22] They tended to play down the idea of an immediate parousia. By the late 1970s, the movement went even further with Baxter championing a brand of postmillennialism and Mumford and Simpson not far behind, emphasizing a victorious church. Jesus would come again, they believed, but no one knew when that would be. Mumford called the dispensationalist pretrib-

---

21. Mumford, *Focusing On Present Issues,* 1–24.
22. Mumford, *Shepherd of a Dark and Cloudy Day,* 5 Audiocassettes.

ulation rapture, "escapism" and believed it created a disengaged church that was simply "holding out" until Christ returned.[23] Charles Simpson was troubled by those who seemed "bent on leaving as soon as Jesus will let them, whether the job [here on earth] is done or not."[24] Prince also acknowledged this concern, though not as strongly as the other four.

Although there were pessimistic aspects to their eschatology, as a whole the movement saw the future optimistically with a triumphant church prepared for Christ's return. This outlook was an extension of the eschatological perspectives of many in the charismatic renewal. As the renewal burst forth, the United States was at the height of Cold War tensions and engaged in a war in Vietnam that divided the nation. While many Christians were lamenting the tumultuous decade of the 1960s, which had brought such sweeping societal unrest and claims that God was dead, many charismatics were excited that the Holy Spirit was "loose in the land" and saw a hopeful future despite societal problems. A 1969 editorial in the inaugural issue of *New Wine Magazine* illustrates well the unflinching optimism despite the difficult times.

> Man has amassed such knowledge and achieved such sophistication that outwardly he pretends to ignore spiritual truth and reality. And because of spiritual neglect, the world teeters on the edge of disaster. . . . We have vastly increased the power to bring destruction on ourselves . . . to reduce the earth to smoking cinder. . . . We stand today where the children of Israel stood when the waters of the Red Sea stretched before them, and the horizon behind them was clouded with the dust from the chariots of the armies of Egypt, bent on their destruction. In the eyes of man, there was no way out. And so it is today. But Christians are meant to worship and serve a miracle-working God who rolled back the waters of the Red Sea and let the Israelites race across dry-shod. The Bible clearly promises that signs and wonders are the marks of the Spirit-led life, and God's supernatural gifts the heritage of every Christian. It is this supernatural brand of Christianity which the Lord is restoring in the world today.[25]

---

23. Mumford, "Hit By a Greyhound Bus," 1–4. This article gives unique perspective on the movement's eschatology as he openly challenges "the 'terminal generation' mentality . . . that buries its head in the eschatological sands of Bible prophecy and believes Christians don't really need to concern themselves with the future since the Lord is going to return and set aside the world system in our generation."

24. Simpson, "Destiny of the People of God," 32.

25. "Editorial," *New Wine Magazine*, 2.

With the charismatic movement's continuing growth in the early 1970s, Mumford and the other Shepherding leaders became certain that God was doing something new within the renewal itself. The earlier dimensions of the Spirit's work in the 1960s, they believed, had been about restoring the experience of Spirit baptism and spiritual gifts among mainline Protestants, Roman Catholics, the Jesus People, and others not affiliated with classical Pentecostal denominations. Now God was taking the next step to restore biblical government in order to bring discipline to a movement and correct its tendency toward independence and individualism. In early 1976, Derek Prince defended the emphasis on discipleship and authority by noting the "outstanding characteristic of the world at the close of [the] age would be 'iniquity,' or 'lawlessness.'"[26] He saw their teachings as a clear antidote bringing about character formation and spiritual maturity.[27]

The five leader's experiences on the charismatic teaching circuit had also convinced them that something more was needed. The lack of integrity they observed among some charismatic leaders and teachers was distressing—not the least of which was the moral failure of their close associate, bringing Basham, Mumford, Prince, and Simpson together in their own mutual submission. Mumford and the others were weary of "charismania"—with many charismatics focused on spiritual experiences and the latest "new" teaching, frequently running from meeting to meeting without any real change of behavior. It came to head at a conference where Prince was teaching when two women got into a fight, hitting each other with handbags, over the last available front row seat at the venue.

It was clear something had to change and they needed to foster church life, which facilitated spiritual formation and accountable relationships. Without this, the renewal would only languish in immaturity and emotionalism. In 1975, Ern Baxter asserted that the charismatic movement's "visitation of the Holy Spirit was not just to give us goose bumps and teach us to play tambourines and sing choruses."[28] At the same time Prince, a champion of the charismatic experience, seemed to

26. "Discipleship: Forum in Ft. Lauderdale," *New Wine Magazine,* Insert, 1. The insert was carried jointly by *New Wine's* and *Logos Journal's* March issues.

27. "Discipleship, 1."

28. Baxter, "Thy Kingdom Come," transcript, 15. This message was adapted and published as a book; Baxter, *Thy Kingdom Come.*

agree when he said, "Charisma is secondary; character is primary. This is a total reversal of the present attitude of the majority of charismatics."[29]

Although contemporary societal and religious issues vitally informed their ecclesiological perspectives, to say the driving forces in the Shepherding movement's developing restorationistic eschatology were primarily contextual is insufficient. The more fundamental drive was their sense that God was speaking to the church a "now word" or what Mumford also termed "present truth."[30] This "present truth," to Mumford, was "a portion of biblical truth which the Lord [was] restoring or emphasizing in the life and practice of the Church during a particular period of history."[31] The view that God was giving fresh vision was central to the Shepherding movement's self understanding. Prince understood this vision "to be an ongoing, scriptural revelation of God's purpose for his people at any given time . . . [and] that God always has a word for his people."[32] As a consequence, the leaders passionately pursued ecclesiological renewal, believing that the church had no time for "business as usual."[33]

In 1981, Mumford reflected on the transition he and the movement's leaders had witnessed in the 1960s charismatic renewal as charismatics initially hoped "that God would bring unity to His fragmented Church and restore its New Testament purity by the outpouring of His Spirit and the administration of His gifts."[34] He summarized their reading of the times and God's "present truth" this way:

> By the time the Charismatic Renewal had reached the late 60's, it had, unfortunately, brought with its blessing and deliverance some emphasis and teaching that was not entirely [b]iblical. An unbalanced presentation of the blessing of God and God's love too often developed into Charismatic humanism and "sloppy agape." The liberty of the Spirit often became spiritual anarchy with every man "doing what was right in his own eyes" and saying, "The Lord told me." To bring about balance to the move of the Spirit and keep the Church from missing the mark, the Lord

29. Prince, "Vision of the Completed Body," transcript, 4.

30. Ibid.

31. Mumford, *Focusing On Present Issues*, 2.

32. Prince, "Vision of a Completed Body," transcript, 3.

33. Mumford, "God's Purpose for His People Today," transcript, 3.

34. Mumford, "Change in the Wind," 2.

began in the 1970s to emphasize order, government, leadership, discipleship, and relationships . . .[35]

THE KINGDOM OF GOD

The Shepherding movement's controlling theological matrix was the kingdom of God and the concepts they taught in this regard led the way in shaping their developing ecclesiology. Mumford and the others saw the kingdom of God as the overarching theme of the Bible and the central message of Jesus. In their view, Jesus inaugurated the kingdom or "new age" with his life and ministry, which served as the radical in-breaking of God's dynamic reign. As they saw it, the last days began with the ministry of Jesus. With Christ's resurrection he commissioned his church to establish and represent God's ongoing rule in the last days.[36]

Ern Baxter was the prominent spokesman for the movement's eschatology with periodic articles appearing in *New Wine* featuring the kingdom of God theme. He made his eschatological convictions most clear. "Eschatology is not as some would say, a particular theory concerning the outcome of history; rather, it is the study of every phase of the end of the world as it is revealed in the life of Jesus Christ. It begins with the inauguration of the kingdom of God at Jesus' birth and ends with the consummation of the Kingdom at His Second Coming."[37] Accordingly, the implications for the church during the "last days" were significant.

At the 1975 National Men's Shepherds Conference, in what many said was one of the most memorable messages of the charismatic renewal, Ern Baxter spoke of God's restoration of the church and triumphally proclaimed, "that at the end of this age, [God] is going to manifest his glory in the redeemed community and this outpouring of the Holy Spirit is not only an outpouring of blessing, but an outpouring of authority . . . in the earth that he may, in this hour, bring into existence his kingdom in power in answer to the prayers of multiplied thousands through the centuries who have interceded by saying, 'Thy kingdom come.'"[38] With

---

35. Mumford, "Change in the Wind," 2.

36. For a sampling of the Shepherding movement's theology of the kingdom of God see Baxter, *Thy Kingdom Come*; idem, "King of Glory," 28–32; Mumford, *LifeChangers Newsletter*, November 1975, 1–8; Simpson, *New Way to Live*.

37. Baxter, "Earth is the Lord's," 25.

38. Baxter, "Thy Kingdom Come," transcript, 15.

Reformed influences evident, Baxter called the church to yield to the totality of Christ's lordship as a key to evangelism. He was convinced this was the "ultimate form of evangelism" in the last days.

Baxter's postmillennial leanings were ever so clear in this same message, a conviction he drew from Ps 110. While saying he did not wish to stir "theological debate," he declared that God's reign would be extended through the church to usher in the Second Coming. "But I believe that when he sat down at the right hand of God, the Father meant what he said . . . sit at my right hand until . . . your enemies are made your footstool."[39] This triumph was to be accomplished in space and time. For Baxter, "the redeemed community" would be the vehicle through which Jesus "would establish God's sovereign right to reign in his own redeemed earth."[40] Despite his claim not to provoke controversy, he nevertheless gave a broadside hit to classic dispensationalism. "I don't know of anything that has paralyzed the purposes of God in earth any more than the delayed activity in bringing about his kingdom in a time, space world."[41] Seeking to challenge concepts that had "been distorted for many, many years," Baxter stated, it is not God's purpose "to redeem a bunch of people to sit at a bus stop and wait . . . for a bus to come along and get them out of the mess, but God has redeemed them and claimed them and put himself into them that he may send them back in to clean up the mess and be the salt of the earth and the light of the world and with [the] power of [the] gospel vindicate the death of God's own son . . . Jesus Christ has all power in [the] earth . . . and he is using that power not only individually but he intends to use that power in the redeemed community . . ."[42]

The reign of God would advance through the church "until the entire earth becomes the scene of the government of God, and our often repeated prayer 'Thy kingdom come' has been fully answered."[43] Baxter wrote in 1985, "Jesus' victorious reign means that all authority opposed to Him must be subjugated to Him *before* the end comes" [emphasis mine].[44] It could not have been clearer as Baxter acknowledged he was

39. Ibid., 12.
40. Ibid., 15.
41. Ibid., 12.
42. Ibid., 14.
43. Baxter, "Earth is the Lord's," 28.
44. Ibid., 29.

"declaring that the gospel is destined to be victorious in time, space, and history; and that Jesus Christ will remain in heaven until all things spoken of by the prophets have come to pass. That means the redeemed community is destined in history to become the visible representative of Jesus Christ's authority on earth, and that all nations will one day walk in the light of that authority . . ."[45]

Given this perspective, the movement took seriously the Great Commission's mandate to disciple the nations and again Baxter led the way in articulating their victorious, ecclesiocentric eschatology. "Before history winds down God will have a people who as the ultimate prophetic community will so obey Him and respond to the authority of His Word as to bring the nations into obedience to Jesus Christ."[46] He argued "the time had come" for the church to realize its call was "to be more than a "soul saving force." It was now time for Jesus' church "to be a nation-saving force—a world saving force! We are to become the prophetic community, represents the God of the prophets, declaring and enacting His eternal Word and discipling the nations. The Word of God declares that all nations will come to Him and we are the prophetic instrument to bring this to pass."[47] Christ's lordship was over all of creation and the Shepherding movement openly challenged the secular/sacred dichotomy. The totality of Christ's Lordship meant the church must "speak into areas of economy, education, culture, and politics." Baxter called for the church to "proclaim truth as it relates to every area of life."[48]

With all the strength of Baxter's declarations regarding Christ's ultimate triumph through the church, he was not specific as to just how it would be accomplished, only that it would be accomplished. He readily acknowledged the difficulty in believing in a triumphant, culture-conquering church given the troubled times in the world at the time. "When God says He's going to bring the nations under His government, my first response might be, 'But I don't know how You're going to do it.' Still, he said, 'I don't know how it's going to happen but I believe it.'"[49] It was a matter of faith in God's sure promises.

45. Baxter, "Earth is the Lord's," 30.
46. Baxter, "'Every Knee Shall Bow,'" 19.
47. Baxter, "Perspective for a Decade," 8.
48. Ibid.
49. Baxter, "Every Knee Shall Bow," 22.

Bob Mumford and Charles Simpson never went as far as Baxter in their teachings regarding a victorious church and never explicitly endorsed his more radical postmillennial perspectives. Mumford, early in their association, drew on the picture presented by Isa 60:1–3 and seems to challenge strict postmillennialism. As he saw it in early 1975, "Light is coming to the church, darkness is coming on the world. Now these two things I think are proceeding in some proportionate way, and I think what we can see here does not mean that we believe things are going to get better and better and all of a sudden the Kingdom of God is going to be on the earth. It doesn't mean that. It means that darkness is coming on the people and light is coming on God's people. Now we call that the redeemed community."[50]

Notwithstanding this perspective, Baxter's influence was significant in tilting Mumford and Simpson toward postmillennialism from 1976 to 1984, although there is no evidence they became fully postmillennial and considerable evidence to the contrary.[51] Despite sounding at times postmillennial, Mumford and Simpson were somewhere in between as they wrestled with just what the Bible taught. Some of their postmillennial sounding rhetoric reflected their frustration with the rapture doctrine, which they thought created a surrender of the earth to Satan as Christians passively awaited the immediate return of Christ. To counter this both Mumford and Simpson, in agreement with Baxter, advocated a full cultural engagement for Christians and for the church's victorious prominence at the end of the age, a church that was "doing business" rather than simply waiting for the Second Coming.[52]

This was linked to the movement's strong emphasis on the present dimensions of the kingdom of God as opposed to an emphasis on a final consummation. This orientation was also prominent in the teachings of

50. Baxter and Mumford, transcript of Elder's Meeting, 1.

51. For example, even as late as 1981, Mumford continues to deal with simultaneous presence of both eschatological light and darkness. Bob Mumford, "Change in the Wind," 4. Both Mumford and Simpson, while having great sympathy to the postmillennial position of Baxter, seem to hold back from a full embrace of the implications of postmillennialism. At times they seem closer to an historic premillennial stance. The fact that neither man took a clearly articulated position only reinforced the statements of Baxter as fully representative of the movement. For a helpful survey on premillennialism see Weber, "Dispensational and Historic Premillennialism as Popular Millennialist Movements."

52. Mumford, "Hit By A Greyhound Bus," 2.

Christian reconstructionist, R. J. Rushdoony, who was regularly featured as a contributor to *New Wine Magazine*.[53] Rushdoony's articles called for the cultural application of God's law, with one article expressing an eschatological theme lamenting the lapse of postmillennial "dominion thinking," suggesting there was going to be renewal of a more positive eschatology.[54] In 1979, Bob Mumford distributed Rushdoony's book *God's Plan for Victory* to hundreds of leaders he oversaw.[55] All of this gave the perception that the entire movement was postmillennial.

Derek Prince, with his strong advocacy of Israel and his staunch premillennialism, was the odd man out and he gradually became theologically isolated from the other teachers. Although other factors may have been more significant—like conflict with the other teachers over his 1978 remarriage[56] and growing disagreement with the idea of personal pastoral care—there is little question the movement's lean toward postmillennialism exacerbated his sense of alienation.[57] Prince and Baxter got into heated disputes about the place of Israel in God's redemptive history.[58] Prince consistently maintained a clear, literal distinction hermeneutically between natural Israel and the church.[59] Conversely, Baxter flatly stated he saw no difference "between Jerusalem and Philadelphia" and that salvation for Israel would come through Jews converting to Christ and becoming incorporated into the church. Baxter's position was that "God had formed a new nation out of Jews and Gentiles alike . . . That has become the nation with which God is dealing redemptively and prophetically, and it is into that nation

53. Rushdoony, "Modern Morality," 22–25; idem, "Wise Men Still Adore Him," 10–11; idem, "Prayer," 11–12; idem, "Marching Orders," 18–19.

54. Rushdoony, "Back to the Future," 24–25.

55. Rushdoony, *God Plan for Victory*.

56. Lydia Prince, his first wife, died in 1975.

57. Derek Prince's dispensational premillennialism is expressed clearly in Prince, *Resurrection of the Dead*.

58. Simpson, telephone interview with the author.

59. As with the other four teachers, he made adjustments to his eschatology over time, but never gave up his Zionist premillennial orientations. On a teaching outline Prince distributed in 1984, entitled "Use of 'Israel' and 'Israelite' in the New Testament," Bob Mumford wrote in the margin "Unabashed Scofieldism." In the recent biography on Prince, Stephen Mansfield says that Prince "understood the whole of his life in terms of Israel." Mansfield, *Derek Prince*, 271. Mansfield's book unfortunately and incorrectly downplays Prince's role in the Shepherding movement. See Prince, "Our Debt to Israel," 26–30.

that ethnic Israel, in the hour of her destiny, will come for salvation."[60] Baxter simply had no interest in natural Israel. For Prince, Baxter's perspectives on Israel were unacceptable. In retrospect, Simpson believes the eschatological differences were a major factor in Prince's quiet exit from the Shepherding movement in 1983.[61]

After Prince left the movement the other four leaders sought to hold their association together but by the end of 1986, they decided it was no longer possible to work together. The controversy over their teachings had been costly, and the leaders, especially Mumford and Simpson, were regularly dealing with situations around the nation where pastoral leaders in the movement had either abused their authority or were accused of doing so. In addition, *New Wine Magazine* began experiencing financial difficulties that continued for years. Finally, tensions and disagreements arose in trying to keep these successful and headstrong leaders in close relationship, which simply proved too difficult to manage any longer. They ended publication of *New Wine Magazine* and dissolved their association. For all the optimism of their eschatological hope, their shared vision could not surmount the movement's own external and internal struggles and pressures.

REFLECTIONS

With the aim of this chapter being an exploration of the Shepherding movement's eschatology, a few issues come to the forefront in assessing the movement in hindsight. As noted, the five teachers saw the church as the center of God's activity in the last days and, accordingly, were passionate about ecclesiological restoration. Interestingly, although they were so focused on structural renewal of the church and the importance of restoration of five-fold governmental leadership, they never developed any formal polity to insure the movement's future. With its highly relational and informal organization, the movement fragmented quickly when the five teachers ended their association. There were no structures to provide institutional cohesion.

---

60. Baxter, "Perspective for a Final Decade," 6.

61. Simpson, interview. In a 1983 letter to Charles Simpson in which Prince detailed many of reasons for not continuing his involvement, he made clear his strong commitment to "Israel and the Jewish People." He acknowledged that "it is well known that not all my fellow teachers fully share these convictions of mine, or the sense of urgency they create in me." Prince, "Letter to Charles Simpson, summer 1983," 1–2.

An even greater contributing factor to the movement's breakup was the lack of a movement wide comprehensive creedal statement. Like many Pentecostals, theological imprecision led to an eschatological hodgepodge that was at times confusing. Only Charles Simpson, and his wing of the movement, developed any clear, unifying statement of faith—and only his sector of the movement survived relatively intact after the teachers ended their association in 1986. Their lack of doctrinal unity meant that disparate beliefs and practices contributed to the movement's inability to hold together, as exemplified by Baxter and Prince's eschatological differences and Prince's resulting exit. The leaders thought their covenantal bonds and ecclesiological emphases would be adequate to keep the movement together. The minimization of their differences proved naïve.

After the movement dissolved, the remaining four teachers believed the painful and distressing fragmentation of the movement was evidence supporting their assertions over the years that they were never intending to be a denomination. This may be true but many people who had made significant investment and commitment to the movement's future were disillusioned when it ended. Many had assumed the movement would endure because of its *de facto* institutional character which was visible through its identifiable leadership, a publishing arm, regional and national conferences, and a triumphal vision of its place as an answer to the world's disintegration. It did not endure. Needless to say, the movement's remnant came to assert a more chastened and balanced eschatological vision.[62]

The Shepherding movement illustrates that Pentecostal and charismatic eschatology is far from monolithic. The very diversity feeding the "century of the Holy Spirit" since the early 1900s created a rich variety of theological perspectives. The idea that all Pentecostals are premillennial, dispensational, and focused on the immediacy of Christ's Second Coming certainly did not apply to the Shepherding movement. It was highly restorationistic and eschatologically focused but with a different orientation as already described. Moreover, while most early Pentecostals in North America were deeply motivated toward evangelism given their expectation of Christ's soon return, the Shepherding movement experienced a gradual loss of passion for evangelism in part because of their heavy emphasis on character formation and a delayed return of

62. Simpson, *The Covenant & The Kingdom*, 394–406.

Christ. Their emphasis on a prepared and triumphant church actually turned the movement inward and away from determined evangelism. They recognized this downside and sought to remedy it, but the lack of evangelistic zeal was no less a consequence of their eschatology.[63]

In the final analysis, whatever the Shepherding movement's deficiencies, it should be commended for its willingness to attempt structural church renewal, a renewal that was eschatologically motivated. It was a valiant but ultimately naïve endeavor, but one that serves our day by the challenge it provides. With the cultural accommodation of much of North American Pentecostalism, both the price and byproduct of its successes, there is need for revisiting the call to Spirit-empowered Christianity and church renewal. At a time when the church in the West has become a vender of religious services and goods more than an eschatological, missional community, change is needed.[64] The Shepherding movement was calling for the church in the last days to stand as God's own countercultural, redeemed people, shining with stellar clarity against the darkness of the surrounding environment. May others take up this challenge and lead the church back to more fully engage Jesus' Great Commission, all the while crying, "Come Lord Jesus."

63. A few years after the movement ended Charles Simpson started a magazine entitled *One on One*, which emphasized personal evangelism.

64. I borrow the phrase "vender of religious services and goods" Hunsberger. See Hunsberger and Van Gelder, *Church Between Gospel and Culture*.

13

Prosperity Already and Not Yet

An Eschatological Interpretation of the Health-and-Wealth
Emphasis in the North American Pentecostal-Charismatic
Movement

MICHAEL J. McCLYMOND

INTRODUCTION

ONE OF THE DISTINCTIVE aspects of Pentecostal and charismatic Christianity since the 1970s has been the so-called prosperity message or health-and-wealth gospel. Originating in North America, and more specifically in a heartland region of Oklahoma and Texas—with Tulsa as capital city—this teaching by the 1980s and 1990s had growing influence in Nigeria, Korea, Brazil, Sweden, and other nations. At the same time, the prosperity message has been subjected to incessant criticism among Pentecostal-charismatic believers as well as external critics. Appraisals of the teaching have generally fallen into three categories.

First, there have been biblical-theological analyses, purport to show the deficiencies of prosperity teaching in light of the scriptural instructions regarding God's blessings and the proper use of wealth. Among the works in this category are Charles Farah's *From the Pinnacle of the Temple* (1979), Gordon Fee's *The Disease of the Health and Wealth Gospel* (1979), Dave Hunt and T. A. McMahon's *The Seduction of Christianity*

(1985), and the recent book-length report by the Evangelical Alliance (UK) on *Faith, Health, and Prosperity* (2003).[1]

Second, there are genealogical analyses that explain the intellectual origins of prosperity teachings in unfavorable terms as due to the influence of New Thought or so-called "cultic" influences. Among the works in this second category are D. R. McConnell's *A Different Gospel* (1988) and H. Terris Neumann's 1990 essay in *Pneuma*. The impact of the writings of E. W. Kenyon on Kenneth Hagin, Sr. has been a matter of special interest. Yet two substantial monographs on Kenyon by Dale Simmons and the Norwegian scholar Geir Lie largely rebutted McConnell's claims. By calling into question the appropriateness of labeling Kenyon as a New Thought teacher, they also cast doubt on comparable interpretations of Kenneth Hagin.[2]

A third genre of writing consists in cultural history or cultural analysis. Most of these works do not seek to assess prosperity teaching as true or false, biblical or unbiblical, beneficial or detrimental, but simply as an aspect of the contemporary religious culture in North America and/or other global regions. Among the works in this third category are David Edwin Harrell's study of the post-war Healing Movement, *All Things are Possible* (1975) and his biography *Oral Roberts* (1985), Simon Coleman's monograph on the Word of Life Church in Sweden, *The Globalisation of Charismatic Christianity* (2000), and Ogbu Kalu's *African Pentecostalism* (2008).[3] Under the third heading, one might create a subheading for works of cultural analysis, which display an adversarial stance and dismiss prosperity teaching as a culturally compromised version of North American Christianity, or as an ideological expression of U.S. neocolonialism in the developing nations. Paul Gifford's early book, *The New Crusaders* (1991), and the work that Gifford co-wrote with

---

1. Charles Farah Jr. was among the first major critics of the 1970s movement in print, having published *From the Pinnacle of the Temple*, and "Critical Analysis," 3–21. See also Fee, *Disease of the Health and Wealth Gospel*; Hunt and McMahon, *Seduction of Christianity*; Evangelical Alliance (UK) Commission on Unity and Truth Among Evangelicals, Perriman, *Faith, Health, and Prosperity*.

2. McConnell, *Different Gospel*; Neumann, "Cultic Origins of Word-Faith Theology within the Charismatic Movement;" Simmons, *E. W. Kenyon and the Postbellum Pursuit of Peace, Power, and Plenty*; Lie, *E. W. Kenyon*.

3. Harrell, *All Things are Possible*; idem, *Oral Roberts*; Coleman, *Globalization of Charismatic Christianity*; idem, "Conservative Protestantism and the Word Order," 353–73; Kalu, *African Pentecostalism*.

Steve Brouwer and Susan Rose, *Exporting the American Gospel* (1996), along with a number of essays on prosperity theology in *The Christian Century*, fall into this subheading.[4]

By way of response, there are recent essays tracing the origins of current prosperity teachings in Africa, Asia, and Latin America to indigenous rather than foreign sources. Allan Anderson's essay on David Yonggi Cho underscores the impact of the Japanese occupation and post-war deprivation in Korea in shaping Cho's conviction that "poverty is a curse."[5] David Maxwell argues that Zimbabwean "prosperity teachings," though not unrelated to developments in North America, "have arisen from predominantly southern African sources and are shaped by Zimbabwean concerns."[6] Even Paul Gifford, though not favorably inclined toward African prosperity preachers, has more recently suggested that the emphasis on health and wealth owes as much to indigenous African concerns as to any non-African influences.[7] *Christianity Today* magazine—though generally ambivalent over the American televangelists—featured a 2007 cover story with a moderately favorable attitude toward prosperity teaching in Africa. While North American prosperity teaching might incline toward opulence, the African prosperity message usually had more modest aspirations. Prosperity meant that the person who used to walk might now ride a bicycle.[8]

Before proceeding to any analysis of prosperity teaching, it is important to note at the outset that there is no single set of ideas that can be isolated and identified under this label. Instead there are families or clusters of related doctrines and teachings, including such elements as the principle of receiving according to one's faith, sowing and reaping, the "seed faith" idea, the hundred-fold return, positive confession, the inherent creative capacity of speech, alignment of one's language with God's written Word, praising God for one's blessing before one has received it,

4. See the following works by Gifford, "'Africa Shall Be Saved,'" 63–92; idem, *New Crusaders*; idem, "Prosperity Gospel in Africa," 20–24; and Brouwer, et al., *Exporting the American Gospel*. See also the essay on the Houston-based prosperity preacher, Joel Osteen by Byassee, "Health and Wealth Gospel," 20–23.

5. Anderson, "Contribution of David Yonggi Cho to a Contextual Theology in Korea," 85–105.

6. Maxwell, "'Delivered from the Spirit of Poverty'"? 350–73.

7. See Gifford's essay in Corten and Marshall-Fratani, eds., *Between Babel and Pentecost*.

8. Phiri and Maxwell, "Gospel Riches," 23–29.

the liberating power of worshipping God amid adversity, the mighty and incomparable name of Jesus, the binding of Satan and evil spirits, warfare prayer, the overcoming of generational curses, and the end-times transference of wealth from wicked to righteous persons. What is called prosperity theology in any given place or time is a complex admixture of many elements. Thus any appraisal of prosperity theology is necessarily context-specific. To give one example, George Folarin notes that American prosperity teaching is often rooted in an understanding of the promises of wealth included in God's covenant with Abraham, while in Nigeria the prosperity message starts from the assumption that poverty is an effect of sin.[9] Moreover, the African approach to overcoming poverty often involves deliverance from evil spirits—not usually a part of American prescriptions for breaking out of poverty.

This chapter is part of a larger project on the Latter Rain revival of the 1940s, a number of successor movements, and their impact on the development of global charismatic Christianity during the latter half of the twentieth century. In some respects this chapter falls into the second genre of literature—i.e., genealogical analysis. My general thesis, simply stated, is that prosperity theology needs to be seen against the backdrop of the Latter Rain movement and as one of the currents of charismatic teaching and practice that emanated from that 1940s revival. Also flowing out of the 1940s revival were a stress on the restoration of prophets and apostles in the church, a new call for spiritual and functional unity among Christians, and an optimistic understanding of eschatology and the end-times. Prosperity theology since the 1970s, as I hope to show, was never simply about wealth or even about human wellbeing in a narrower sense. Underlying the teaching on wealth has been *a preoccupation with dominion or God's reign.* The exercise of dominion, according to Latter Rain theology and later prosperity teachers, is mediated by believing individuals and by the church at large. Those who see prosperity teaching simply as an expression of primitive world-magic, or as a

9. Folarin, "Contemporary State of the Prosperity Gospel in Nigeria," 69–95. Regarding the connection of prosperity theology with deliverance ministry, Jacob Olupona writes regarding African Pentecostalism: "There is a general assumption that the world is inhabited by satanic power that causes misfortunes for believers. Evil spirits are viewed as the major cause of life's problems and crises." Olupona, "Survey of West Africa," 15. Social scientist Birgit Meyer offers an analysis of Christian Ghana in which popular stories link together the themes of temptation by money, witchcraft, and family difficulties, in "Delivered from the Powers of Darkness," 236–55.

self-centered quest for materialistic fulfillment, may be missing some of the deeper elements. Notions of prosperity tie into eschatology—more specifically, a realized eschatology according to which God's kingdom achieves its effect in the present time rather than in some futuristic or heavenly consummation.

Paralleling this eschatological thrust is a distinctive interpretation of redemptive history—including Adam's loss of dominion to Satan, Christ's defeat of Satan, and the saints' role in reclaiming the dominion once held by Adam. According to prosperity teachers, the relationship between Christ and the church as Christ's body is so intimate that a believer can affirm in some qualified sense that "I am Christ," or, with fellow believers, that "we are Christ." This theanthropic teaching, or stress on divine-humanity, underlies much of what prosperity teachers affirm, and the teaching derives from the Latter Rain revival and some of its more radical teachings on the "manifest sons of God." Many key tenets of prosperity teaching are hard to grasp unless one takes account of the Latter Rain background.

In the conclusion to the chapter, I will turn to the historiographic implications of this argument. Not only prosperity teaching, but a number of other major developments in charismatic churches since the 1960s—such as prophetic ministry, the apostolic movement, stress on "body life," newer styles of worship, warfare prayer, and an aggressive posture in reclaiming secular culture for Christ—all find their source and taproot in the 1940s, and not, I might add, in the earlier Pentecostal period from 1900 to about 1945. Moreover the non-denominationalism of the Latter Rain laid the foundation for the ecumenism of the Charismatic Renewal during the 1960s and 1970s. Let me turn first to the Latter Rain itself, then offer an analysis of prosperity teaching in light of the Latter Rain, and finally wrap up with some general reflections.

THE LATTER RAIN MOVEMENT

The terms "Latter Rain," or "New Order of the Latter Rain," as generally used, denote a set of teachings and practices, which emerged from a revival beginning in February 1948 at a small Bible college and orphanage in North Battleford, Saskatchewan, Canada. Among the early leaders were George and Ernest Hawtin. Perhaps the most influential book from the first years of the revival was George Warnock's *The Feast of Tabernacles* (1951). The monthly issues of the *Sharon Star* recount the events in North Battleford from December 1948 through 1952, when the local movement had become more diffuse and more subdued. Richard Riss's monograph, *Latter Rain* (1987)—still the major study on the topic—drew on unpublished correspondence to and from the early leaders of the revival and among pastors and denominational leaders in Canada and the USA who responded positively or negatively to the revival.[10] Another important study of the Latter Rain is an unpublished portion of D. William Faupel's 1989 dissertation at the University of Birmingham.[11]

As the Latter Rain movement developed and spread, certain adherents were rumored to have held to a teaching regarding "manifest sons of God" who had advanced spiritually to the degree that their lifespan extended toward immortality. According to this view, freedom from death was not a gift suddenly bestowed on the saints at the return of Christ but rather an outcome of a process of spiritual growth. The "rapture" of the church—if one used that term at all—was not a rescue operation but more of a graduation ceremony. The church would mature to the point where—like Enoch—it was caught up to God without first undergoing death. The Latter Rain thus showed a remarkable degree of eschatological optimism. The end-times were to witness not the great apostasy of the church but rather a great revival—the greatest, in fact, in its entire history. The miracles performed by end-times saints would rival and surpass those of the first-century apostles. For some proponents of the Latter Rain revival, the glorification of the bodies of the saints had already begun. Franklin Hall's book *Atomic Power Through Prayer and Fasting* (1946) laid a foundation for the 1948 revival by encourag-

---

10. Riss, *Latter Rain*. A major collection of unpublished correspondence and other documents related to the Latter Rain are found at the Flower Pentecostal Heritage Center and Assemblies of God Archives, Springfield, Missouri, in the following files: Assemblies of God, Secretariat, "New Order of the Latter Rain." Correspondence from Joseph D. Mattsson-Boze to J. R. Flower, Nov. 2, 1950, re: denominationalism of the Assemblies of God; defense of Winston Nunes; "New Order of the Latter Rain." Correspondence from Winston I. Nunes to Westly R. Steelberg, Oct. 25, 1950, re: the laying on of hands, Nunes's involvement in the Latter Rain movement; "New Order of the Latter Rain." Announcements, advertisements, statements of position. Copies of Richard Riss's personal correspondence, along with other related documents, are found in the Latter Rain Files, American Religions Collections, Special Collections, Library of University of California, Santa Barbara, Santa Barbara, California.

11. Faupel, "Everlasting Gospel." The bulk of Faupel's dissertation appeared in published form under the same title as the dissertation, *Everlasting Gospel*. Yet the published book did not include an extensive section treating the Latter Rain Revival.

ing the faculty and students in North Battleford to engage in extended fasts for days and even weeks at a time. Hall's later work, *The Return of Immortality* (1976), exhibited the most radical aspects of the "manifest sons of God" teaching. Those truly devoted to God, according to Hall, could overcome the aging process, control the physical elements that produce weather, and even escape the law of gravity.[12]

Yet the majority associated with the Latter Rain in Canada or elsewhere never embraced the more outlandish doctrines. Indeed, the root heresy of the Latter Rain in the eyes of the Pentecostal Assemblies of Canada (PAOC) and the Assemblies of God (AG) in the USA was its overt challenge to denominational authority. Latter Rain teachers held that denominationalism was contrary to God's will and that the earlier Pentecostal movement had failed in its God-given mandate to renew the whole of Christendom when it chose to organize itself into denominations. The ecclesiology of the Latter Rain foreshadowed that of the later Charismatic Movement, with its stress on the overcoming of divisions and the complementary of gifts within the church. Another challenge to the authority of the PAOC and the AG lay in the Latter Rain practice of bestowing spiritual gifts upon the faithful through the laying on of hands. The practice presupposed that rank-and-file Pentecostals were as yet spiritually deficient and needed to enhance their spiritual lives through new experiences of spiritual impartation. Because the Latter Rain contested denominational authority and because of the reports on the radical teachings regarding "manifest sons of God," the movement was rapidly marginalized.

The Latter Rain soon dropped off the radar screen and received little attention among Pentecostal and Charismatic leaders or scholars specializing in Pentecostal-Charismatic studies. Among those who carried forward various Latter Rain teachings and emphases were George

---

12. See the following works by Franklin Hall, *Atlantic Ocean Storms Destroying Many Cities*; *Atomic Power with God with Fasting and Prayer*; *Bodyfelt Salvation*; *Formula for Raising the Dead and the Baptism of Fire*; *Our Divine Healing Obligation*; *Return of Immortality*; *Subduing the Earth Controlling the Elements and Ruling the Nations with Jesus Christ*.

and Ernst Hawtin[13] along with George Warnock[14] in Canada from the 1940s through the 1980s, Bill Britton[15] of Springfield, Missouri and John Robert Stevens[16] of southern California during the 1960s and 1970s, Dick Iverson[17] of Portland, Oregon from the 1960s to the 2000s; Reg Layzell[18] of Vancouver from the 1960s to the 1980s, Earl Paulk[19] of Atlanta in the 1980s and 1990s, Rick Joyner[20] of North Carolina from the late 1980s to the present, Paul Cain[21] and Bob Jones of the Kansas City Prophets from the 1980s until the early 2000s, Bill Hamon[22] of Florida from the

---

13. See the following works by. Hawtin, *According to the Purpose; Treasures of Truth*, vol. 15; "Account of the 1948 Latter Rain Outpouring"; *Beholding the More Excellent Glory; Body of Christ, the House Not Made with Hands; Church Government; Creation, Redemption, and the Restitution of All Things*, vol. 28; *Evil Day; Eschatology, the Doctrine of Last Things; Fragments that Remain; From Glory to Glory; Glory, Honor, and Immortality, Eternal Life; Glory Soon to be Revealed; God's Great Family of Sons; Here Is the Mind that Hath Wisdom; Holy Spirit; Learning from Illustrious Men; Mystery Babylon; Mystery of Christ and Our Union with Him; Nine Gifts of the Spirit; Our So Great Salvation; Pearls of Great Price; Portrait of Things to Come; Thy Kingdom Come; Watchman, What of the Night; When Saints Become the Will of God.*

14. Warnock, *Beauty for Ashes, Part I: The Family of God; Beauty for Ashes, Part II; Crowned With Oil; Evening and Morning; Feast of Tabernacles; "Feed My Sheep;" From Tent to Temple; Seven Lamps of Fire.*

15. Britton, *Apprehended of God; Benjamin; Beyond Jordan; Changed By the Son; Cleansing of the Temple; Climb the Highest Hill; Closer Look at the Rapture; Divine Breakthrough into the Unlimited; Double Portion of the Holy Ghost and Power; Eagle Saints Arise! From the Known to the Unknown; God's Sabbath; God's Two Armies; Hebrews; His Unlimited Glory; Jesus: The Pattern Son; Light Out of Shadows; Noah's Ark; Not as a Servant; Oil on the Beard; One New Man; One Shall Be Taken; Only in His Likeness; Peter's Shadow; Points to Consider; Prophet on Wheels* [biography]; *Purple Hearts and Silver Stars; Reach for the Stars; Sectarianism in the "Move of God"*; "Shepherds, Submission, and Trans-local Authority"; *Songs for Eagle Saints.*

16. Stevens, *Baptized in Fire; Elijah and Elisha; Kingdom Fast; Living Prophecies; Living Word on the Coming Glory; Prophecies of December 1968; School of Prophets; Twelve Keys To Heaven's Best.*

17. Iverson, *Journey*; Iverson and Scheidler, *Present Day Truths*; Iverson and Straza, *Restoration: God's Plan.*

18. Layzell, *Pastor's Pen: Unto Perfection.*

19. Paulk, *Held in the Heavens Until; Ultimate Kingdom; Wounded Body of Christ.*

20. Joyner, *Apostolic Ministry; The Call; Epic Battles of the Last Days; Final Quest; The Harvest; Prophetic Ministry; Shadows of Things to Come; Visions of the Harvest.*

21. Cain and Bickle, *Interview With Paul Cain; Prophetic History of Metro Vineyard Fellowship*; Cain and Kendall, *Word and the Spirit.*

22. Hamon, *Day of the Saints; Eternal Church; Prophets and Personal Prophecy; Prophets, Apostles, and the Coming Moves of God; Prophets, Pitfalls and Principles.*

1980s to the present, and Kelley Varner[23] of West Virginia from the 1990s to the present. Taken collectively, these authors published hundreds of books and tracts. The Latter Rain's paper trail, though not well studied, is impressive. Noteworthy is that the Latter Rain exerted its influence in Oklahoma from an early date. One of the most important Latter Rain periodicals, outside of Canada, was the *Latter Rain Messenger*, published in Oklahoma City beginning in 1950. This periodical offered substantive essays and announcements of regional conferences in Oklahoma and Texas—a likely reason for the influence of Latter Rain ideas in this area during the 1960s and 1970s.

Foundational to many aspects of Latter Rain teaching was an optimistic understanding of eschatology. Rejecting the notion that the church would diminish in its sanctity, power, and influence prior to Jesus' return, the newer kingdom theology insisted that God would establish dominion over the world through the church—not in spite of the church and its departure from the faith. Some Latter Rain teachers continued to hold that there would be an "apostasy" from the faith and an "apostate church" in the last days. Yet this was applied only to one group of professing Christians. There was a further teaching regarding a group variously called "overcomers," "eagle saints," the "Bride of Christ" or the "many-membered Man-Child." These elect and elite saints would exhibit exemplary faithfulness to God amid persecution and perform extraordinary miracles that would surpass those of the early church.[24] Jesus was not going to return until this "mature church" was ready to receive him, to exercise joint dominion with Christ over the world.

Another foundational idea for the Latter Rain teaching was a distinctive idea of divine-humanity. Before Christ returned in power and glory on the clouds of heaven, God would first return—in a manner of speaking—*within the saints* through a deeper manifestation of his pres-

23. Varner, *Chosen for Greatness*; *Corporate Anointing*; *Issues of Life*; *Moses, the Master, and the Manchild*; *Prevail*; *Priesthood is Changing*; *Secrets of the Ascended Life*; *Sound the Alarm*; *Time of the Messiah*; *Understanding Types, Shadows, and Name*; *Life and Times of Haggai the Prophet*; *Whose Right It Is*.

24. The theology of the "overcomers" can be traced back to the speculative theology of Charles F. Parham, who insisted that "the people of redemption will walk as Jesus walked" and that this will include "appearing and disappearing at will" and an ability "to traverse the earth at will . . . to carry the Gospel to many tropical and frigid points." Parham, *Voice Crying in the Wilderness*, 74. Yet this view had little influence in the classical Pentecostal movement.

ence and power among them. Various analogies were used to express this teaching, and the images were generally biological in nature, e.g., references to "seed," "planting," "birthing," "generation," and "reproduction." Some teachers went so far as to claim that believers in Christ are "little gods," or that each Christian is in some manner "a Christ." Optimistic eschatology and the "little god" idea went hand in hand. According to Latter Rain teaching, God's ultimate purpose in creation is the exercise of dominion. With the fall of Adam and Eve—God's appointed vice-regents or representatives on earth—God in a certain sense lost dominion over creation and this dominion passed over to Satan. Yet God, it was said, is raising up a people to reclaim dominion over the earth. They are given the capacity, through faith in God's promises, to reverse the curse over creation and to speak words of life and of healing. The word spoken in faith, and in agreement with God's Word, has the power to banish sickness and death and to create life, health, wellness, prosperity, and abundance.

By the late-twentieth century, many who had been directly or indirectly influenced by Latter Rain teaching believed that they had a mandate to reclaim the secular culture for Christ. They engaged in extended periods of prayer and fasting with a view to ending abortion in the USA, overcoming pornography and sexual temptation, uniting the churches, empowering evangelism, manifesting signs and wonders through healing, and redeeming music, art, and film for kingdom purposes. They were no longer premillennialists, like the typical Pentecostal of the 1920s and 1930s. While they believed that Jesus would return again to establish his kingdom, they also believed that the church's faith and faithfulness was the instrument through which Christ was to establish his reign over the earth. Technically, this might be classified as postmillennialism rather than premillennialism. Its aggressive, outward-looking ethos was more reminiscent of American Calvinism than to the sectarianism of first-generation Pentecostals. The optimistic belief in the capacity of Christians to change secular culture seemed a recrudescence of early Puritan or late nineteenth-century optimistic postmillennialism. One observer of Christian Reconstructionists—a non-charismatic movement seeking to reinstitute Old Testament law in modern times—noted that Reconstructionists and charismatics seemed to be drawing closer relationship to one another.[25] Books have analyzed the political influence of

25. See House and Ice, *Dominion Theology?* esp. "Appendix A: Heat and Light: The Charismatic Connection," 367–95.

Religious Right, but little attention has examined the deeper theological and intellectual roots of the charismatic push to cultural dominion.[26]

PROSPERITY TEACHING IN LIGHT OF THE LATTER RAIN

The analysis offered here will center on such prosperity teachers as Kenneth Hagin Sr.[27]—generally regarded as a central figure—along with Kenneth and Gloria Copeland,[28] Charles Capps,[29] and Jerry Savelle.[30] They are often called "Word-Faith" preachers, and the label seems as apt as any of the alternatives. Fred K. C. Price and Norvel Hayes might be seen as minor figures in the Word-Faith school. Somewhat different in tone is Robert Tilton, whose message is closer to the "positive thinking" of Norman Vincent Peale or the "possibility thinking" of Robert Schuller than to the Word-Faith teaching. Joel Osteen, on my view, is better understood alongside of Peale and Schuller rather than Hagin and Copeland. Osteen's positive message includes relatively few references to scripture or to Jesus Christ.[31] Benny Hinn has at times preached something resembling the Word-Faith message, and yet later disavowed it as a "New Age" teaching—though arguably not in a consistent fashion.[32] Oral Roberts might in certain respects be regarded

---

26. Consider the recent book, *Kingdom Coming*. Author Michelle Goldberg, a self-described "secular Jew and ardent urbanite," wrote her book on dominion theology "in part because I was terrified by America's increasing hostility to the cosmopolitan values I cherish," 21. While the work accurately characterizes certain aspects of the current "dominion theology," Goldberg does not appear to understand the theological nuances and diversity of the movement, and the ways in which this leads to differing strategies and responses to secular culture in America. Even more basically, the work fails to recognize that the quest for a "Christian America" is not new and has been an ongoing preoccupation since the early colonial period of the 1600s. See Handy, *Christian America*.

27. Among the many works by Kenneth E. Hagin, Sr. that are relevant to this paper are: *Believer's Authority*; *El Shaddai*; *Exceedingly Growing Faith*; *How to Turn Your Faith Loose*; *I Believe in Visions*; *Midas Touch*; *Ministry of a Prophet*; *Name of Jesus*; *Present-Day Ministry of Jesus Christ*; *Right and Wrong Thinking*; *Seven Steps for Judging Prophecy*; "Trend Toward Faith Movement," 67–70; *Triumphant Church*; *Understanding the Anointing*; "*You Can Have What You Say!*"; *Zoe: The God-Kind of Life*.

28. Copeland, *God's Will is Prosperity*; *Laws of Prosperity*.

29. Capps, *Authority in Three Worlds*; *The Tongue*.

30. Savelle, *Expect the Extraordinary*; *If Satan Can't Steal your Joy*; *Walking in Divine Favor*.

31. See Byassee, "Health and Wealth Gospel," 20–23.

32. Ferraiuolo, "Christian Leaders Admonish Him," 38–39.

as the fountainhead of prosperity teaching, having first popularized the "seed faith" principle as early as the 1950s and thus well before the ministry of Kenneth Hagin became widely influential. Yet Oral Roberts has retained a premillennial eschatology and his message does not show much affinity to Latter Rain teaching and its distinctive eschatological teachings.[33] T. D. Jakes, too, has sometimes been associated with prosperity teaching.[34] Yet Jakes's preaching is less about prosperity and more about personal breakthrough and empowerment amid difficulty. John Avanzini offers a teaching regarding prosperity, but his primary thrust is toward the wealth transfer idea—i.e., that the wealth of the wicked will be given to the righteous during the end-times.[35] Last, but not least, is the case of Pat Robertson, whose broadcasts and books sometimes show affinity with Word-Faith teaching. Robertson's *The Secret Kingdom* (1982), which he co-wrote with Bob Slosser, sets forth a version of dominion theology.[36] Yet the affinities between prosperity theology and Latter Rain teaching are most apparent in the case of the Word-Faith school, to which we now turn.

A striking feature in Word-Faith teaching is the affirmation that human beings are divine, or may become divine. Such statements are startling indeed to the uninitiated reader. Thus Kenneth Hagin writes, "The believer is just as much an incarnation as Jesus was."[37] Kenneth Copeland states, "You don't have a God living in you; you are one!" Frederick K. C. Price comments, "I believe that . . . God made man a god. A god under God." Charles Capps notes that "Jesus said 'ye are gods.' In other words, Adam was god of the earth." Robert Tilton explains, "You are . . . a God kind of creature. Originally you were designed to be as a god in this world . . . Of course, man forfeited his dominion to Satan who became the god of this world."[38] Many further quotations might be sup-

---

33. For Oral Roberts's eschatological views, see his works *Drama of the End-Time*; *God's Timetable for the End of Time*; *Salvation by the Blood*.

34. Lee, "Prosperity Theology," 227–36.

35. Avanzini writes, "A clear prophecy . . . shows that the world will soon witness a day when there will be a dramatic transfer of the world's wealth, literally ripping the wealth from the control of the wicked and placing it in to the hands of informed people everywhere." Avanzini, *Wealth of the World*, 10. Kenneth Hagin in his later works disavowed the wealth transfer idea. Cf. *Midas Touch*, 170–72.

36. Robertson with Slosser, *Secret Kingdom*.

37. Kenneth Hagin, cited in Randles, *Weighed and Found Wanting*, 49.

38. Hunt and McMahon, *Seduction of Christianity*, 84, citing Copeland's message

plied. Suffice it to say that all the major authors in the Word-Faith school regularly make these sorts of statements. But what do they mean?

Morris Cerrullo in a 1991 televised teaching on "Manifested Sons of God," explained the point this way, "God is duplicating Himself in the earth . . . At last, the time has arrived; God is releasing His life through the Body . . . The fullness of the Godhead dwells in me . . . God has planned for me to be Christ's image on earth."[39] The doctrine of divine-humanity thus ties into God's purposes for manifesting himself in the world. God chooses to work through the church as his intermediary and in such an apparent and unmistakable a fashion that the church may be said to become divine. Earl Paulk comments, "The completion of the incarnation of God in the world must be in His church . . . Jesus is the firstfruits, but without the ongoing harvest, the incarnation will never be complete." Elsewhere Paulk affirms, "We are on earth as extensions of God to finish the work He began. We are the essence of God, His ongoing incarnation in the world."[40]

Such affirmations make sense against the backdrop of the Latter Rain teaching of the 1950s and 1960s. George Warnock wrote that "Christ the head . . . is not complete without Christ; the body . . . Christ is the body, the whole body and not just the head."[41] Note the bald assertion by Warnock's assertion that Christ is the body was just a small step away from the converse that the body is Christ. In *Jesus the Pattern Son* (1966), Bill Britton lays down a basic premise of Latter Rain teaching that "the life of Jesus in His humanity here on earth was a divine pattern for the perfect, end time body of Christ." All that Christ achieved in his human nature will eventually be achieved corporately in the church, and most notably through "eagle saints" or "overcomers," specially intended for the fulfillment of God's purposes.[42] A major tendency in the Latter Rain

---

"The Force of Love," Price's personal letter, Aug. 25, 1982, Capps's personal letter, June 4, 1982, and Tilton's *God's Laws of Success*, 170–71. An early twentieth-century Pentecostal leader who anticipated the Latter Rain teachings on divine-humanity was John G. Lake (1870–1935), who wrote, "Man is not a separate creation detached from God, he is a part of God Himself . . . God intends us to be gods." Lindsay, *God-Men, and Other Sermons of John G. Lake*, 20–21.

39. Cerrullo's 1991 program on "Manifested Sons of God," cited in Randles, *Weighed and Found Wanting*, 50.

40. Randles, *Weighed and Found Wanting*, 50.

41. Warnock, cited in Randles, *Weighed and Found Wanting*, 49.

42. Britton writes, "Although there will be unnumbered multitudes of people saved

teaching was to reduce the disparity between Christ and the church. This line of thinking underlies James Robison's words, "God wants us to see Jesus as merely a big brother in a huge family of brothers and sisters. You have the divine nature, the eternal life of God. God reveals that Christ had to be formed, even in Jesus."[43]

Another way that Latter Rain and Word-Faith teaching softened the distinction between Christ and the church was through a kind of charismatic or Spirit Christology. Jesus during his earthly career performed his miracles and lived an obedient life not through reliance on his divine nature but simply through the perfect yielding of his human nature to the direction and empowerment of the Holy Spirit.[44] Latter Rain and Word-Faith teachers have commonly cited Acts 10:38, "How God anointed *Jesus* of *Nazareth* with the Holy *Ghost* and with power: who went about doing good, and healing all that were oppressed of the *devil*; for God was with him." Jesus is the anointed of God *par excellence*. Yet believers individually, and especially corporately, are anointed as well. One might almost speak of the church as messiah or as Christ. In *Understanding the Anointing* (1983), Hagin makes an intriguing statement, "I'm thoroughly convinced—although you can neither prove nor disprove it by the Bible—that we as the Body of Christ *as a whole* have *the same measure* of the Holy Spirit that Jesus did—but we as individual members of the Body of Christ do not. *The greatest anointing of all is the corporate anointing*."[45] On this view, the Spirit of God acted through Jesus during his earthly life and then, on the day of Pentecost, the same fullness of the Spirit was in effect transferred to the church.

Kenneth Hagin, Sr. is not only a characteristic Word-Faith teacher but also one who clearly shows Latter Rain influences. Consider Hagin's early writing, *The Believer's Authority* (1967). He states here that he came

---

by the Grace of God . . . the real purposes of God are tied up in that group of saints who press their way into the mark of the high calling of God . . . They are the 100 fold fruit of the earth, brought forth by the Latter Rain . . . They are the ones who put Satan under their feet and gain back the inheritance lost by Adam." Britton, *Jesus the Pattern Son*, 16.

43. James Robison, cited in Randles, *Weighed and Found Wanting*, 49.

44. Charles Capps explains, "Yes, Jesus was the Son of God; but, first of all, He was a man. He was not operating in His divine power and glory as God when He destroyed the works of the devil. He was drawing from the anointing God had placed upon Him as a man." Capps, *When Jesus Prays Through You*, 53.

45. Hagin, *Understanding the Anointing*, 149.

to a turning point in his understanding of spiritual authority during 1947–1948—the very time, as it happens, that the Latter Rain movement was emerging. Hagin writes, "A few of us have barely gotten to the edge of that authority, but before Jesus comes again, there's going to be a whole company of believers who will rise up with the authority that is theirs. They will know what is theirs, and they will do the work that God intended they should do."[46] Notice the plural language. Though Hagin and other prosperity teachers later framed their message in terms of individual reliance on God in faith, this earlier text spoke of the church—"a whole company of believers"—who would together exercise spiritual authority. This was entirely in line with the Latter Rain idea of the "overcomers."

Later on in *The Believer's Authority* Hagin states, "We are one with Christ. We are Christ. We are seated at the right hand of the Majesty on High. All things have been put under our feet. The trouble with us is that we have preached a 'cross' religion, and we need to preach a 'throne' religion . . . We died all right, but we're raised with Christ. We're seated with Him." "The elevation of Christ's people" means that we are "sharing not only His throne but also His authority."[47] One notices Hagin's completely realized eschatology. The kingdom is already here—already happening—and there is little emphasis on any time of future fulfillment or a need to be patient and to wait. On the contrary, Hagin insists that the church corporately possesses the power to claim its own rightful authority in Jesus' name and thus to enact the kingdom here and now. On the topic of eschatology, "Our trouble is that we relegate everything to the future! Most church people believe that we will exercise our spiritual authority sometime in the Millennium . . . It's now, when there is something that will hurt and destroy, that we have authority." For Hagin, the church can dominate Satan here and now. The church today does not have any less authority than it did right after Jesus died and rose again.[48]

Hagin's version of redemptive history begins with the idea that God gave dominion over the earth to Adam. "In other words, Adam was the god of this world. Adam committed high treason and sold out to Satan, and Satan, though, became the god of this world. Adam didn't have the moral right to commit treason, but he had the legal right to do so. Now

46. Hagin, *Believer's Authority*, Foreword.

47. Ibid., 16–17.

48. Ibid., 20.

Satan has a right to be here and be god of this world until 'Adam's lease' runs out. Satan had the right to rule over us until we became new creatures and got into the Body of Christ ... That's why Satan has no right to rule us or dominate us."[49] Yet the vast majority of believers do not understand that they have authority over Satan. When Hagin wrote *The Believer's Authority,* he seems not to have been primarily concerned with material prosperity. Instead his emphasis is on dominion. As a corollary of dominion, Hagin occasionally speaks of the believer's triumph over unfavorable circumstances such as poverty. He writes: "God's plan for us is that we rule and reign in life as kings: to rule and reign over circumstances, poverty, disease, and everything else that would hinder us ... We reign by Jesus Christ. In the next life? No, in *this* life."[50] So poverty and wealth seem to play a role—though only a subordinate one—in Hagin's teaching during the 1960s.

Both the notion of divine-humanity and the theme of dominion help us to understand the otherwise unusual idea that human beings— like God—can create reality through the words they speak. Often this teaching on the creative power of language or "positive confession" is

49. Hagin, *Believer's Authority,* 19–20. Charles Capps gives an elaborate account of the redemptive plan in history. "God gave Adam a lease on this planet, and He gave mankind dominion over it. But when Adam sinned, he turned the lease over to Satan. Then God had a problem on His hands. What was He going to do? He had given man a lease on the earth, but Adam had broken God's Word and sold out to the devil. The devil became, in essence, 'the god of this world' (2 Cor 4:4). But God had a plan to get His Word back into this earth. He first made a covenant with Adam. Then He made covenants with Noah and with Moses. But the covenant He made with Abraham was the covenant of *all covenants.* It actually meant that Abraham was given access to what God had ... God's plan was to gain back some control in the earth. To do so He had to get His Son born into this earth with a physical flesh, blood, and bone body. Then Jesus would have legal authority here ... When you realize what the first chapter of Genesis says, you will understand why God doesn't come back to earth and destroy the devil and all evil. To do that at the present time, God would have to violate His Word ... He has the ability to destroy the devil and all evil, but if He were to do it now, before the lease expires, He would violate His Word. The true Church, which is the Body of Christ on earth today, has the authority to enforce Satan's defeat until we are raptured. God has done all that *He will do* about it until the lease runs out on this planet. But when that lease expires, Satan will be put in his place." Capps, *When Jesus Prays through You,* 46.

50. Hagin, *Believer's Authority,* 39. Further discussion of the believer's reign over circumstances is found in Hagin, *Zoe,* "Man was never made to be a slave. He was made to reign as a king under God. That kingly being was created in the image and likeness of God. God made man his understudy ... Man lived in the realm of God. Man lived on terms of equality with God," 36.

taken as *ipso facto* evidence for the influence of New Thought on Hagin and other Word-Faith teachers. Yet a different interpretation is possible. If we understand the church as reigning over the world on God's behalf, then it stands to reason that the human word must align with the divine Word. In such a case, the authority, efficacy, and dignity of the human word are wholly dependent on the divine Word. While certain Word-Faith teachers have given the impression that "positive confession" begins with the desires and longings of the individual believer, there is also a strong countervailing emphasis on the need for the human word to fall into agreement with the divine Word. Without a Word from God to "stand on," the human word cannot achieve its effect. Furthermore, there is a remarkable analogy between divine and human words and the respective roles played by faith. Hagin writes: "God is a faith God . . . God created everything except man by speaking it into existence. He's a faith God. Now, God made man a faith man, because man belongs to God's class. A faith man lives in the creative realm of God."[51]

Much more could be included here regarding the links between Latter Rain doctrines and the Word-Faith teachers on God, Christ, humanity, the church's role, and the kingdom's realization in history. Both Latter Rain and Word-Faith teachers exhibit an optimistic eschatology in which the end-times church will visibly and powerfully manifest God's presence on earth, overcoming the forces of sickness, unbelief, discord, and poverty. Prosperity, to be sure, is part of the picture. Yet in the Latter Rain revival of the 1950s and 1960s, and in the earlier phases of Word-Faith teaching from the 1960s to the early 1970s, prosperity was not distinguished or separated from other aspects of God's kingly reign. The all-important principle was divine dominion over the earth, with the church as God's means for achieving this dominion.

CONCLUSIONS

Two schools of thought emerged from the Latter Rain. One of these has stressed ecclesiology, the "mature church" of the end-times, and the special role to be played by a set of super-saints during the last days. One might call this the *corporatist-elitist school*. The current 24/7 prayer movement and International House of Prayer (IHOP) in Kansas City have upheld many aspects of this tradition, including an enthusiastic

---

51. Hagin, *Zoe*, 36.

prediction that select believers will soon effect miraculous works sur-
passing even the accomplishments of the first-century apostles.[52] A
biblical text from the Gospel of John is often cited in this connection:
"Greater works than these shall he do; because I go unto my Father"
(John 14:12, AV). Mike Bickle, founder of IHOP, later admitted that his
ministry was characterized by spiritual elitism during the 1980s and the
early 1990s.[53] A second current of thought has been more individualistic in orientation. It might be called the *individualist-populist school*.
The basic message of the populists was that any believer—by exercising
his or her faith—might affect miracles. Believers who walked in agreement with God and God's Word could banish sickness and release new
wealth into their lives and into the lives of others. Included in this second school were many Word-Faith teachers, such as Kenneth Copeland
and Robert Tilton. While the corporatist-elitist school stuck closer to

52. John Wimber, speaking in Docklands, England, in 1990, made a sweeping declaration concerning the coming movement of the God and the role to be played by the
"Elijahs": "There will be a time where even as in Acts 2, suddenly, as they were gathered,
in the midst of them, the Lord came and with an anointing beyond anything that has
ever been given to man before. Something astounding, so marvelous that God has kept
it as a mystery as it were, behind his back, and He is about to reveal it to the ages.
He is about to reveal it. With the judgment of all mankind will come this incredible
incarnational enduement of God's spirit and we will see the Elijah's [sic] . . . This end
time army will be made of the Elijah's of the Lord God." Randles, *Weighed and Found
Wanting*, 47–48.

53. Mike Bickle in an essay by Lee Grady in *Charisma* (July 1993), "Kansas City
Churches Reconciled," admitted to a number of errors: "We had an elite spirit. That's
become more and more real to me—it's so repulsive." "We promoted mystical experience in a disproportionate way and it was disastrous." "We were careless in the way we
communicated prophetic words. This was hurtful in a lot of cases." "We were wrong in
the way we promoted the city church concept. I still believe in it, but now I believe it's a
unity based on friendship." Compare Bickle's statement with that of Bob Jones—one of
the Kansas City Prophets who had spoken of the extraordinary capacities to be demonstrated by the end-time saints: "From out of the sands of time I have called the best
of every bloodline in the earth, unto this generation . . . Even the bloodline of Paul . . .
of David . . . of Peter, James and John, the best of their seed is unto this generation. They
will even be superior to them in heart, stature and love for me . . . They will move into
things of the supernatural that no one has ever moved in before. Every miracle, sign
and wonder that has ever been in the Bible, they'll move in it consistently. They'll move
in the power that Christ did . . . They themselves will be that generation that's raised up
to put death itself underneath their feet and to glorify Christ in every way . . . So that
glorious church might be revealed in the last days because the Lord Jesus is worthy to
be lifted up by a church that has reached the full maturity of the God man!" Randles,
Weighed and Found Wanting, 77; citing Bickle and Jones, "Visions and Revelations."

the distinctive themes of Latter Rain teaching from the 1950s and 1960s, the individualist-populist school of thought showed marks of affinity to the Latter Rain through its insistence that "I am a 'Christ'" and that the believer's spoken word may be the means whereby God's dominion is reestablished in the earth. Especially in the case of Kenneth Hagin, Sr. one sees how Latter Rain influences were a factor in the emergence of prosperity teaching.

Some larger historiographical lessons may be gleaned from the above argument. It should be clear that the immediate post-World War II period brought a number of novel ideas and practices into North American Pentecostalism. The Latter Rain movement was extraordinarily important for the development of independent charismatic congregations and para-church ministries, and for the emergence of the Charismatic Renewal in the Roman Catholic Church and among mainline Protestants. One might say that it was the 1940s Latter Rain revival that pushed Pentecostals out of a narrow, sectarian stance, which had become dominant in the 1920s and 1930s. American religious historians today acknowledge that early twentieth-century fundamentalism was largely sectarian in orientation. With the mid-1940s, a sea change occurred in the emergence of neo-Evangelicalism, as marked by the founding of the National Association of Evangelicals (1942), the founding of Fuller Theological Seminary (1947), and the sudden appearance of Billy Graham (1949) as a national spokesman for the Neo-Evangelicals. Not so widely recognized is that "Spirit-filled" Christians underwent a comparable transition at roughly the same time as their evangelical counterparts. The Latter Rain and its subgroups exhibited new confidence, desire, and capacity to penetrate the secular culture with Christian influences.

In focusing on the late 1940s as a time of transition and transformation in the Pentecostal movement, this chapter takes issue with the foremost scholar of early Pentecostal theology, Douglas Jacobsen, who has stated: "In a 25-year burst of creative energy at the beginning of the twentieth century, these [Pentecostal] leaders articulated almost all the basic theological ideas that continue to define the Pentecostal message in the United States and around the world."[54] Jacobsen did a brilliant job of expounding Pentecostal thought prior to 1925 and many of the ideas that have continued to be seminal among Pentecostals during the post-World War II era. Yet it does not seem fair or accurate to assert

54. Jacobsen, *Thinking in the Spirit*, x.

that "almost all the basic theological ideas" had fallen into place by the mid-1920s. Perhaps it is time to do away with the "Big Bang" theory of Pentecostal and Charismatic history. Not everything of significance in Pentecostal and Charismatic history may be traced to the Azusa Street Mission. Not everything of significance for the 1940s and 1970s and 1990s had emerged by the 1920s. As an alternative to a "Big Bang," let me suggest that we think in terms of a "string of firecrackers." Toward the beginning of the 1900s, the Azusa Street Revival in Los Angeles was a crucial event and yet it was but one of a number of spiritual percussions—alongside that of Wales in 1904–1905, India in 1905, Korea in 1907–1908, Manchuria in 1908, Chile in 1909, and west African revivals in Liberia, Ivory Coast, and Nigeria from 1914 to 1922. In the North American context, revivals from 1900 to about 1910 laid a foundation for twentieth-century Pentecostalism. Yet the 1940s Latter Rain revival brought many and deep changes within the larger Pentecostal movement, without which the emergence of prosperity teaching during the 1960s and 1970s might not have occurred.

PART FOUR

Contextual Pentecostal Eschatologies

14

The New Jerusalem versus Social Responsibility

The Challenges of Pentecostalism[1] in Guatemala

NESTOR MEDINA

The emphasis on the end of the world has added a sense of urgency to evangelism, which at least partially accounts for the rapid Pentecostal growth in Latin America—particularly when joined to the comfort it gives the poor and downtrodden. But a constant emphasis on the end of the world can also sap the will of believers to work to improve their lot, and it may even provide a sense of vengeance at the injustices of the world.[2]

INTRODUCTION

IT HAS BEEN OVER twenty years since I left Guatemala and came to Canada. Since then the country has changed enormously. The small town feel that it once had has been replaced with an endless string of

---

1. In Guatemala the label "Pentecostal" is a relatively fluid term and often replaced by the label "evangelical," which does not have the political right-wing connotations in North America, particularly the United States. In Guatemala evangelical is a synonym of Protestant, so Pentecostals are conceived as part of the larger group of denominations, which are different from the more "traditional" Protestant communities, e.g., Presbyterians and Anglicans. At the same time, while in Guatemala the labels "Protestant" and "evangelical" are used synonymously, the label "Christian" has been adopted to distinguish Pentecostalism from Catholicism. Catholics are not considered to be Christians by evangelicals. Yet the label "Christian" also allows for Catholic groups, which have embraced the renewal movement.

2. Moreno, "Rapture and Renewal in Latin America," 33.

315

cars, buses, trucks, infrastructure projects, enormous shopping centers and malls, all of which point in the direction of industrialization. The capital city is now a bustling metropolis, overcrowded, highly urbanized, and rife with corruption and crime; it is a good example of the ambiguous impact of complex processes we now call globalization. Few countries have experienced in such a short time the dramatic changes in the social, political, and religious landscape as Guatemala. Today Catholic and "historical Protestant" churches compete with the rapidly expanding and diverse Pentecostal churches: from the small storefronts, to the medium size temples, to the growing number of mega-churches.[3]

In the midst of these diverse changes, the face of Pentecostalism in Guatemala is also changing dramatically. Broadly speaking, Pentecostals can be categorized in four main groups: (1) Churches directly connected to the classical Pentecostal tradition (like the Assemblies of God, Four Square Gospel Church, the Church of God); (2) Churches connected to classical Pentecostalism but divided over a rejection of foreign leadership thus founding their own Pentecostal fellowship (*Iglesia Príncipe de Paz*); (3) the Charismatic Renewal churches (including historical Protestants and Catholics, which have adopted many of the elements of Pentecostalism), (4) and the neo-Pentecostal groups (independent churches that resist denominational affiliation and opt for self-identifying missions such as Elim, Lluvias de Gracia, Maranatha, El Verbo, Fraternidad Cristiana, El Shaddai).[4] Despite the marked differences between these churches, all of them insist in the power and activity

3. Guatemala is unique in terms of the relationship between religion and the indigenous population. "In a country that is one-half Mayan, competition among religious groups for indigenous converts has been fierce. Folk Catholicism, liberation theology, and various Protestant groups compete and sometimes combine with traditional Mayan religions to form a colorful and contentious religious landscape." Steigenga, "Guatemala," in *Religious Freedom and Evangelization in Latin America*, 150–51.

4. Just as there is debate in the way the label evangelical and Protestant are used synonymously, there is also difficulty in the way the various "Pentecostal" groupings are identified by scholars. For other alternative categorization of Pentecostal groups see Steigenga, *Politics of the Spirit*, 7–11; Miller and Yamamori, *Global Pentecostalism*, 25–28. In the context of Guatemala, however, there is very little difference in the people's perception between "historical" Protestants and Pentecostal groups. Members of both traditions identify themselves as Protestants, and outsiders also make no fast distinctions. Distinctions are made more pronounced when talking about the neo-Pentecostals, given that they resist any denominational affiliation. I am using "Pentecostal" and Protestant almost interchangeably, given the historical chronological connection between the two, unless otherwise noted.

of the Holy Spirit, the reality of miracles and healings, and the priesthood of all believers. While most of them are not wholesale dispensationalist, in various ways they do follow some of Cyrus Scofield's premillennial ideas about the eschaton, inaugurated by the Second Coming of Christ, a time of tribulation, and the cataclysmic end of the world.

The development of the eschatological orientation of Pentecostalism in relation to the social-historical-political context of Guatemala is the concern of this paper. On one hand, I focus specifically on the way Pentecostals adopt an otherworldly eschatological orientation, which at times prevents them from participating in the social-political dimension of life in order to bring about change for the larger population, especially the poor. On the other hand, I highlight how Pentecostals, because of their own interests in evangelism and promotion of Pentecostal Christianity, do enter the social-political arena.[5] For this reason, and because of the very nature of their paradoxical (dis)engagement with politics, Pentecostals in Guatemala do not strictly fall under the category of apolitical, despite their adamant insistence of social-political "non-engagement." This, I propose, is the single biggest challenge that Pentecostals in Guatemala (and the rest of the world) face as they confront the reality of countless social problems of national (and global) proportion, while at the same time seek to maintain an otherworldly eschatological orientation.[6] Knowing that Pentecostal growth has reached a plateau in various countries of Latin America (Guatemala, Chile, Venezuela, etc.), how Pentecostalism makes itself relevant to the larger societies of those countries may determine its future.

Often Pentecostalism is conceived as a young movement, a recent arrival to the socio-religious arena. As I will show, in the case of Guatemala one must frame the development of Pentecostalism within

5. Here I agree with Daniel Míguez's assessment that Pentecostals "paradoxically" engage and disengage from political and social participation. See his "Why Are Pentecostals Politically Ambiguous"? 57–74.

6. While I disagree with Pedro Moreno's generalizing characterization of Latin American social problems, I do believe that many of the social ills he lists are endemic to the social fabric of Guatemala. He writes, that although its people are warm and generous, "Latin America is also a continent marked by great social paradoxes. A land of deep religiosity, but little morality (i.e., institutionalized lying and socially accepted adultery); saturated with "macho" types, but not enough responsible men; with a ruling class ethnically "mestiza" (mix of Indian and European), but out of prejudice, considering itself "white"; where the law is seldom openly challenged, but frequently disobeyed and ignored." Moreno, "Rapture and Renewal in Latin America," 31.

the historical arrival of Protestantism over one hundred and twenty years ago.[7] Similarly, one cannot study the "accelerated" growth of Pentecostalism without paying attention to the socio-political changes in the country over the last century, and the rejection of Catholicism by liberal governments. I suggest, the development of Pentecostalism in Guatemala must be understood as part of the internal complex and un-even process of reconfiguration of the population's religious allegiances in connection with, and reaction and response to the shifting histori-cal and socio-political environment of the nation. This is what Edward Cleary labels a "historical-structural approach": the development of the religious changes occurring in Guatemala must be understood as part of the way in which people interact with the changing conditions of their social, political, and economic environment.[8] I divide the develop-ment of Pentecostalism in four phases: The entrance of Protestantism (Pentecostalism), the monopoly of Catholicism, the silent "explosion" of Pentecostalism, and the involvement of Pentecostalism and neo-Pentecostalism in national politics. In what follows, I discuss these four stages connecting the growth of Pentecostalism and its relation to the accompanying eschatological view.

PROTESTANT PENTECOSTALISM IN GUATEMALA

As expected, the history of Christianity in Guatemala corresponds to the arrival of the Spanish conquistadors. The invasion of the "Americas" by the Spanish brought with it many cultural elements to the lands. Along with the *encomiendas*, the decimation of the indigenous population, and the slavery of indigenous and Africans, the Spanish imposed their ver-sions of Catholicism upon the population. Whether because of true con-version or as a way to survive, many sectors of the populations adopted Catholicism as their religious tradition. But the Spanish did not succeed in eradicating the religious traditions, customs, and practices of the in-digenous peoples, and so what emerged was a new mixture of symbols and practices containing indigenous Mayan and European Christian religious elements. What emerged was a new version of Christianity. Protestants were not welcome. Resistance against Protestantism by insti-

---

7. See Stewart-Gambino and Wilson, "Latin American Pentecostals," 228–32.

8. See Cleary, "Evangelicals and Competition in Guatemala," chapter 9.

tutional Catholicism was so much that during the period from 1556 to 1598, twenty-one Protestants were convicted by the Inquisition.[9]

Catholicism continued being the supreme religion of the region, even after the United Provinces of Central America declared independence from Mexico's monarchy in 1823. In 1824 they drafted a constitution declaring that "the religion of the United Provinces is Catholic, Apostolic, and Roman with the exclusion of all others."[10] It was not until the end of the nineteenth century, when Liberals seized power, that the privileges and power of the Catholic Church in Guatemala were considerably curtailed.[11] The provision of the constitution of 1824 making Catholicism the official religion of Guatemala was cancelled, proclaiming freedom of religion the official position of the Guatemalan government.[12] This was soon reversed for a short time during the government of Rafael Carrera Turcios (dictator from 1840s until 1865) who sought to restore the monopoly of the Catholic Church in Guatemala, but fell short of changing the constitution to the original 1824 conditions.

While Mariano Gálvez had allowed Protestants to enter Guatemala, all of them had returned to their countries by the time of Carrera Turcios. It was not until the Liberal government of Justo Rufino Barrios (1873–1885) that Protestantism became part of Guatemala's religious traditions. In 1882 Barrios travelled to New York and requested the Presbyterian World Missions to redirect one of their missionaries (John Clark Hill) to go to Guatemala. Hill experienced great opposition and was soon replaced by Edward M. Haymaker, a Presbyterian who had been deeply influenced by the Social Gospel connecting social concerns to salvation.[13]

Barrios wanted to shape Guatemala according to the "modern" countries of the nineteenth century. Known as the *Reformador* (the

9. Garrard-Burnett, *Living in the New Jerusalem*, 1.

10. Steigenga, "Guatemala," 152.

11. During the administration of Mariano Gálvez (1831–1838) measures were taken to reduce the Catholic religion and restrict the acquisitive power of land holdings by Catholics. He also facilitated the expropriation of the national diocesan treasury for the national treasury, secularized cemeteries, and made civil marriage compulsory. See Garrard-Burnett, *Living in the New Jerusalem*, 3.

12. The anticlericalism against Catholicism at the end of the nineteenth century under Justo Rufino Barrios has been likened to Mexico's own Porfirio Diaz' contempt against the Catholic Church. See Wilson, "Guatemalan Pentecostals," 141.

13. Garrard-Burnett, *Living in the New Jerusalem*, 16.

Reformer), he and the subsequent Liberal presidents adopted social Darwinism as policy for "progress." They believed that the main obstacles preventing Guatemala from being "modernized" were the indigenous peoples with their "backward" traditions and customs, and the Catholic Church.[14]

Social Darwinism had become the theoretical framework of mission theorists. According to Garrard-Burnett, this eventually contributed to the creation of the notion of the USA having a divine "Manifest Destiny" by which Protestant Christianity came to be seen as the means of arresting "the downward trend of degenerate races."[15] With his work in education the Presbyterian Haymaker became instrumental for the Guatemalan government. He believed that Catholicism "had stunted the process of social evolution, engendering a social environment of oppression, drunkenness, and greed."[16] The solution to the "Indian" problem in Guatemala was their *castellanización* (the instruction of Spanish language and culture).

Protestants enjoyed the support of the liberal governments in Guatemala. As Steigenga puts it, the presence of Protestantism was significant for three reasons: 1) it brought foreign cultural influence, which was crucial to change traditional values; 2) it helped the government undermine the influence of the Catholic Church; and 3) through education projects it helped the government gain control of the indigenous communities.[17] For these reasons, this time marks the arrival of Protestantism to Guatemala: The Presbyterian Church (1882), Central American Mission (1888), The Pentecostal Mission (Later called the Nazarenes) (1901), The Society of Friends (1902), The Primitive Methodist Church (1932), Church of God Cleveland (1916), The Assemblies of God (1920s, formalized in 1934). During this time Seventh Day Adventists and Jehovah Witnesses also came to Guatemala (1916 and 1918 respectively).

With their social projects, which included schools, medical clinics, a hospital, literacy programs, publishing houses, and Bible translation,

---

14. Introducing a coffee based national economy caused irreparable harm to indigenous Guatemalans. Perera affirms that "historians now regard Barrios and the rise of the coffee fincas as the second chapter of the conquest and exploitation of Guatemala's indigenous population." Perera, *Unfinished Conquest*, 9.

15. Garrard-Burnett, *Living in the New Jerusalem*, 22.

16. Ibid., 17.

17. Steigenga, "Guatemala," 153.

Protestants became important resources for Guatemala's national leadership in their "civilizing" agenda of the indigenous people.[18] Whatever the interests behind allowing Protestantism to enter, it remains that during this period Protestants and Pentecostals planted the seeds of the later explosion of Protestantism and Pentecostalism in the country. The focus on premillennial eschatology seems to have emerged later on. Although the growth of Pentecostalism was negligible as Protestants and evangelicals made less than one percent of the population of Guatemala, Kenneth Grubb reports that by 1937 the evangelical community numbered 40,657 committed adult members.[19]

THE MONOPOLY OF CATHOLICISM
AND THE THREAT OF COMMUNISM

Despite their membership running into the thousands, Protestantism was largely unnoticeable in Guatemala even after WWII. Protestantism had not yet been seized by the evangelistic spirit that characterizes this second phase. Most missionaries did not have the intention to go outside of their mission. For the most part they tended their own congregations with a largely European constituency.[20]

As foreigners in a hostile environment, Protestants worked among the population despite significant opposition. They established missions in the interior of the country among the indigenous peoples and worked hard at developing local leaders. This was one of the weakest areas of Catholicism as most of their priests were foreign and did not speak the indigenous languages. In order to address the language barrier Protestants invested in language programs in order to translate the Bible in the local languages of the people. This was cemented with the creation of the "Protestant Indian League" (1921).[21]

Manuel Estrada Cabrera (1898–1920) had come to the presidency at the turn of the century. Popular uprisings ensued and forced him to resign. He was replaced by a series of presidents from the Unionist Party,

---

18. Garrard-Burnett, *Living in the New Jerusalem*, 33.

19. Cleary, "Evangelicals and Competition."

20. Ibid.

21. According to Garrard-Burnett, during this time Central American Mission, Presbyterians, and Nazarenes had launched translation projects in Kaqchiquel, the Kanjobal, the Chuj, the Ki'che, the Mam, and the Kec'chi languages. See her Garrard-Burnett, *Living in the New Jerusalem*, 53, 69.

who were greatly influenced by social Darwinism. These presidents viewed the indigenous peoples as "children that could be turned into adults by way of education, nutrition and medicine . . ." They sought the "cultural and even physical absorption of Indians into latino society at large."[22] Not surprisingly, Protestants were thought useful in the *indigenista* project of "civilizing" the indigenous communities and peoples, due to their work in education.

Admittedly, Protestant missionary work had been financially crippled by the lack of funds due to the 1930s North American Depression. But during the administration of Jorge Ubico y Castañeda (1931–1944) the important work that Protestants were doing was brought to a halt.[23] Being confronted with tremendous economic hardships and the rise of Communism Ubico y Castañeda's military administration adopted unpopular policies, which included brutality, torture, and repression of Guatemalans. He used his fight against Communism as an excuse to intervene in the education work of Protestants among the indigenous. He believed that if the latter learned to read they could "fall prey to subversive ideas . . ."[24] His two main concerns were: Communism and gaining control of the Maya to prevent them from rebelling. He later changed his opinion about Protestantism and decided to take advantage of their education work.[25]

Ubico y Castañeda was finally replaced in 1944 by a military junta, and later by the democratic election of Juan José Arévalo Bermejo (1945–1951). He and his successor Juan Jacobo Árbenz Guzmán (1951–1954) represent a serious nationalist attempt at reforming Guatemala. They devised ways to return Guatemala to Guatemalans.[26] Supporting his social reform, he encouraged the creation of labor and right groups, and the creation of a progressive labor code permitting urban workers

---

22. Garrard-Burnett, *Living in the New Jerusalem*, 68.

23. Ubico y Castañeda came to power through a coup that removed the previous government, and with the help of the US government he staged an election where he was the only candidate, thus assuming power as president of Guatemala in 1931.

24. Garrard-Burnett, *Living in the New Jerusalem*, 74.

25. In supporting of the work of Protestants, many Protestants eventually celebrated his administration connecting civil loyalty with Christian behavior. See Garrard-Burnett, *Living in the New Jerusalem*, 77.

26. Arévalo Bermejo created the Guatemalan Institute of Social Security, and he proposed that indigenous languages be treated with unprecedented equality as Spanish.

to form unions, to strike, and to bargain collectively.[27] His "Spiritual Socialism" was welcome by the poor masses, but the changes threatened the oligarchy. This led to an unprecedented number of failed attempts to oust him.

Árbenz Guzmán continued the reform program of his predecessor. He proposed an agrarian reform in order to improve the unequal distribution of land in the country. His plan permitted the government to reclaim uncultivated portions of arable land from large plantations for which owners received market value compensation. While his plan was also resisted by the powerful, the greatest threat to his reform came "from more powerful sources, the United Fruit Company and the United States."[28]

Some Protestants supported Árbenz nationalist reform. The Central American Mission, the Presbyterian Church, and some Protestants with Communist sympathies supported his program, but later were punished with financial shortage by their USA founders. The attack against Árbenz' administration came from the Catholic Church. *Acción Católica*, an organization composed of Maryknoll Fathers and Salesians, which had its roots in Spain and had arrived to Guatemala in 1935, accused him of being a Communist. In 1951 Carlos Castillo Armas had attempted a rebellion against Árbenz Guzmán but failed.[29] This time, in 1954, Castillo Armas led the forces of the "Liberation Army" with the support of the CIA under the code name "Operation Success" and the Catholic Church. The accusations of "Communist influence" were never proven, but the fear of Guatemala turning into a safe haven for Communism was enough for the USA to help oust the democratically elected president.

Once the president of Guatemala, Castillo Armas sought to reward the Catholic Church for their support in removing Árbenz. In 1955 he drafted a new constitution, which formally revoked the limitations on land acquisition. Yet, he fell short of returning the religious monopoly of Guatemala to the Catholic Church. With their new status, and through *Acción Católica*, Catholics made significant inroads in the highlands of Guatemala. The goal was to make orthodox Catholics out of the indigenous peoples. In order to accomplish that, they resorted

27. Garrard-Burnett, *Living in the New Jerusalem*, 81–83.

28. Steigenga, "Guatemala," 155.

29. In the encounter with the presidential forces he was shot and jailed, until he escaped and went into exile to Honduras.

to undermining the structures of authority and community cohesion of the indigenous communities, but not without great opposition from the local communities.[30] The Protestant Church had lost its favored status. Those who bore the brunt were the indigenous people who had converted to Protestantism. Protestants in the highlands began to be persecuted, run out of villages, attacked physically, and some had their churches burned.[31] Garrard-Burnett writes, as the locals began to see the disintegration of their traditions, structures, and *costumbres* (culture and customs), Communism and Protestantism became the easy targets bearing the blame.[32] Despite opposition, Protestantism continued to grow in the highlands of Guatemala.

The drive for nationalism that began with Arévalo Bermejo and Árbenz Guzmán received concrete expression in Protestantism. Some of the explicitly Pentecostal churches divided because some of the leaders wanted a fully Guatemalan church without foreign missionaries.[33] Although Pentecostals had adopted more assertive ways to preach their message early on, the true effects of their preaching would not be felt until the massive evangelistic campaign launched by the Central American Mission in 1962.[34] It is worth mentioning that the Central American Mission was a fundamentalist interdenominational group with doctrine including premillennial Second Coming of Christ and apocalyptic eschatology. While Protestants were growing significantly, by the end of this period Pentecostals still constituted only a small portion.

---

30. Cleary, "Evangelicals and Competition," 4–5.

31. According to Steigenga, persecution against Protestants was more at the popular level, and was more a backlash of the multiple forces that were undermining the indigenous peoples' "traditional patters of authority" and organization like the *cofradías*. They blamed Protestantism for destroying the indigenous social and cultural structures. See his Guatemala, 156

32. Garrard-Burnett, *Living in the New Jerusalem*, 106.

33. In 1954 the Assemblies of God divided and the mission Príncipe de Paz was born. And in 1962 the *Iglesia Primitiva Metodista* underwent division giving birth to the Mission Elim. Both the *Príncipe de Paz* and *Elim* were organized and shared the same doctrinal stance as their mother churches, with the exception that theirs were "fully" Guatemalan missions. In many ways, this contributed greatly to the exponential growth of these missions.

34. This can be seen by Edward Cleary's allusion to the work of Henry and Susanna Strachan who organized massive evangelization campaigns in Latin America and Guatemala as early as 1920s. See his "Evangelicals and Competition," 9.

THE CHANGING TIDES: THE QUIET "EXPLOSION" OF PENTECOSTALISM

Castillo Armas launched a war against Communism and suppressed labor and right groups, which during Arévalo Bermejo enjoyed freedom. He was replaced by Miguel Ydígoras Fuentes (1958–1963). Guatemala was undergoing serious economic hardships and many disapproved of his close connections to the USA supporting the Bay of Pigs invasion of Cuba. Corruption was another element that characterized his government. As a result of his inability to govern, many disenchanted young army officers sought to oust him; without success in 1961 they formed the *Movimiento Revolucionario* (MR–13). This was the first organized insurrection movement in Guatemala. Ydígoras Fuentes retaliated with martial law and national stage of siege but he was soon replaced by another coup, though by then Guatemala had sunk into a civil war.

Julio César Méndez Montenegro was installed as president in 1966, and in his attempt to eradicate the guerrilla groups he created the famous paramilitary organizations *Mano Blanca* and the *Ejército Secreto Anticomunista* (Secret Anticommunist Army). These groups were the forerunners of the "Death Squads," which reigned in Guatemala during the 70s and 80s, and which were responsible for most of the killings that took place during those years.

Given the conditions of social disruption and political instability Protestants began to (de)politicize their message adopting an anti-Communist stance. The war against Communist insurgents centered on the highlands of Guatemala targeting primarily the indigenous population. Wanting to present a façade of neutrality, they adopted an anti-communist stance, partly because of USA right-wing fundamentalist influence, and partly because they did not want to suffer repression from the Guatemalan government. Many Catholics also identified themselves as *evangélicos* to escape torture and death.[35]

At the same time, some Catholic clerics who worked within the indigenous communities began to adopt the progressive vision of Vatican II. They wanted to help indigenous communities to organize themselves. This was perceived by the government as promoting revolution and having Communist connections.[36] This resulted in a systematic persecution

35. Cleary, "Evangelicals and Competition."

36. According to Timothy Steigenga, by the mid-1970s the growth of popular movement: *comité de unidad campesina*, the committee for Justice and Peace, Labor

and repression of Catholics. In turn, this made Protestantism a more viable option.[37] Many people flooded the Pentecostal churches. People's experience of war, military repression, and social instability echoed the biblical message of the tribulation and the end times. Many also converted to Protestantism to resist the suspicion of sympathizing with Communism; it was a matter of survival! Nevertheless, "the evangelicals' message seems to have offered authentic spiritual conciliation to victims of violence, a solace that the Catholic Church was in poor position to offer, given the absence of priests . . . and the repression of Catholics."[38]

At the same time, the Guatemalan governments were under political pressure from right-wing USA governments; needing their financial support, they were invested in eradicating any "Communist" influence. Social instability by way of unemployment, gross inequities in salary distribution, and the increasing impoverishment of the Guatemalan population ran unfettered. These social ills would be magnified by the 1976 earthquake. During the 1960s Pentecostals were growing steadily, but nothing could compare to their "explosion" in the aftermath of the earthquake that left a dead toll of 20,000 and well over a million people homeless.

Because Protestant churches did not have a central organization as Catholics, they were able to respond more effectively in providing relief to the population. Popular local groups and much needed relief aid from foreign missionaries contributed to Protestants playing a prominent role during this national crisis. No doubt many converted to Protestantism as a result of the extraordinary relief work they offered. And many Pentecostals took advantage of offering relief in exchange of people hearing the evangelical message. This has prompted many to conclude that the expansion of Pentecostalism at this time is related to the material needs of people: *lámina por anima* (loosely translated as "rice Christians"). What is most telling is that the speed of growth of

---

groups, and even Ecclesial Base Communities were perceived as serious threat by the Guatemalan military and the oligarchy, and for this reason they were violently repressed. See his Steigenga, "Guatemala," 158.

37. Timothy Evans found that the presence of the ultra conservative group *Acción católica*, and the eruption of Liberation theology in Catholicism forced the population of the highlands to seek alternative modes of religious affiliation given the political environment of repression. See his "Religious Conversion in Quetzaltenango, Guatemala," chapter 5.

38. Garrard-Burnett, *Living in the New Jerusalem*, 131.

Protestant and Pentecostal churches increased even after the foreign financial relief was stopped.[39] People converted to Protestantism and Pentecostalism because it helped them gain control over their own lives. By the end of the 1970s Protestantism had become a national force without foreign involvement; for some it even became a "vehicle of ethnic expression." At this point, I agree with Cleary's assertion that the growth of Pentecostalism must not be explained as something "especially mysterious or miraculously sudden. . . ."[40] Pentecostalism helped people rebuild their lives and make sense of their reality through apocalyptic lenses. The Pentecostal message of the imminent coming of the Lord, war, suffering, and earthquakes as signs of the end times contributed greatly to people flocking to Pentecostal churches. The eschatological message seemed to fit the social and political context. This was a quiet "explosion," as it would not be until the 1980s that Pentecostalism became conspicuously present in Guatemala's religious landscape. Whatever the Pentecostal motivation and methods for providing relief to the victims of the earthquake, in this moment of national crisis they assumed social responsibility for the rest of the Guatemalan population.

TOWARD A PENTECOSTAL CHRISTENDOM?: PENTECOSTALS AND NEO-PENTECOSTALS IN NATIONAL POLITICS

The abuses against and repression of the Guatemalan population continued under the tenure of Fernando Romeo Lucas García (1978–1982). In 1979, under Jimmy Carter, the US military aid to Guatemala was suspended because of the countless violations of human rights by the Guatemalan government. Lucas García was replaced by another military coup led by the retired General Efraín Ríos Montt (1982–1983).

Ríos Montt played a pivotal role at this time in the history of Guatemala for several reasons: 1) under no other government the destruction, repression, and systematic mass killings of the Guatemalan

---

39. Wilson, "Guatemalan Pentecostals," 150. Miller and Yamamori report that of the churches they studied the most "successful" congregations were not dependent on foreign funding nor led by foreign missionaries. The indigenization of the movement has much to do with the speed at which they increase in numbers. See *Global Pentecostalism*, 199.

40. Cleary, "Evangelicals and Competition."

indigenous population was raised to such heights;[41] 2) while during the 1970s two more guerrilla groups were born,[42] it was during his term that the various guerrilla groups joined and formed the Guatemalan Revolutionary Union (URNG),[43] which put tremendous pressure on the military forces; 3) in no other period was the connection between right-wing fundamentalists in the USA and Guatemala's Pentecostalism so obvious. Not only was Ríos Montt supported by the right-wing backed Reagan administration, but even Pat Robertson's *700 Club* celebrated him as the savior of Guatemala;[44] 4) he forced Pentecostalism to come out of the social closet. His charisma and unashamed confidence as a member of the neo-Pentecostal mission *El Verbo* gave confidence to Pentecostals to inhabit the streets of Guatemala with their heads held high. Several Pentecostal missions and churches collaborated in some of his programs to "rebuild" the villages in which the army had scorched and killed the inhabitants;[45] 5) no other Guatemalan president, before or after, has authorized mass killings in the name of God like he did; and 6) more pertinent for this chapter, in his vision of transforming the heart and soul of the population of the country, Ríos Montt made Pentecostalism in Guatemala globally visible. The world came to know that by the 1980s Pentecostal and Protestant churches had multiplied and a reported ten thousand churches and three hundred denominations colored Guatemala's religious landscape.[46] Until then, Guatemala was considered a bastion of Catholicism; Pentecostalism had become a central part of Guatemalan society without many people noticing.

The short presidency of Ríos Montt did not significantly contribute to the growth of Pentecostalism. His use of God language to justify

41. It is reported that in his first three months in government the army killed twenty six thousand indigenous peoples. And by the end of his term, with his approach of "scorching the earth" (the destruction of everything preventing the advance of the army), four hundred villages were destroyed, and more than a half a million indigenous peoples were relocated. See Steigenga, "Guatemala," 159–60.

42. The Guerrilla Army of the Poor (EGP) and the Organization of the People in Arms (ORPA)

43. *Union Revolucionaria Nacional Guatemalteca.*

44. It is reported that only a week after the coup Ríos Montt was featured at the *700 Club* where he was promised a substantial sum of money (which was never received) for the construction of Guatemala. See Garrard-Burnett, *Living in the New Jerusalem,* 140.

45. Garrard-Burnett, *Living in the New Jerusalem,* 149.

46. Ibid., 155.

the destruction of entire villages and killing of thousands of indigenous peoples did not deter its growth either. Virginia Garrard-Burnett argues that surprisingly enough Pentecostalism grew the most in areas where the arm conflict was most severe. For safety reasons, many became Pentecostal whereas Catholics suffered persecution, tortures, and disappearances.[47] Some Pentecostals functioned as informants of the government and helped the army identify those with "Communist" sympathies.[48] They wanted to present the façade of neutrality, and often were coerced into helping the army, so many became informants also as a measure of survival.[49] More, still, found resonance in their beliefs of tribulation, the imminent coming of the Lord, and apocalyptic end times. These factors must be considered for understanding the development and growth of Pentecostalism in Guatemala.[50]

Pentecostals suffered some levels of persecution in the interior of the country after Ríos Montt was deposed by another military junta led by Óscar Humberto Mejía Víctores in 1983. However, Ríos Montt opened the door for Pentecostals and Protestants to envision having their own evangelical national political leader. It was just a question of having the critical mass for electing such a leader. This did not come to fruition until the election of the evangelical José Antonio Serrano Elías in 1991. Although it appears that Serrano Elías was not elected president

47. Garrard-Burnett notes that the repression was not exclusively against Catholics. Forty seven Protestants were also tried under the secret tribunals (*fueros especiales*) that Ríos Montt created, and four of them were executed during John Paul II's visit to Guatemala. See Garrard-Burnett, *Living in the New Jerusalem*, 149.

48. Ríos Montt displaced hundreds of thousands of ethnically diverse indigenous peoples and lumped them together in what he called *communidades de población en Resistencia* (lit. communities for people in resistance). "In the newly established 'strategic hamlets' . . . [the Protestants] became the preferred liaison between the army and the local community, loading civil defense patrols and weeding out guerrilla sympathizers. In turn, army commanders rewarded this cooperation by appointing evangelicals to posts of authority." Steigenga, "Guatemala," 160.

49. David Stoll claims that "evangelical collaboration was less a siding with the military against the guerrillas than an attempt to simply survive the violence and stake out a position of neutrality." Cited in Steigenga, "Guatemala," 160.

50. As Steigenga puts it, while "Protestants had a long history in Guatemala, the pressures of military repression, increasing landlessness, economic hardship, urbanization, and other forms of social dislocation in the countryside dealing with aggressive evangelization strategies and the dangers associated with being a progressive Catholic, all contributed to the rapid growth of Protestantism (especially Pentecostalism) between the 1950s and the 1980s." Steigenga, "Guatemala," 160.

because of his evangelical affiliations, there is no doubt that his presidency was momentous for the Pentecostals, Protestants, and Catholics of Guatemala. Unfortunately, because of his failed self-coup (*autogolpe*), which he orchestrated just as his contemporary Fujimory in Peru did in the same year, 1993, and the charges of corruption for stealing public funds, his "evangelical" government proved to be a disappointment.

Pertinent is the reconfiguration of Protestantism more in the direction of Pentecostalism. The "Pentecostalization" of the "historic" Protestant and Catholic churches was already an issue of the 1960s and 1970s. This was part of the Charismatic Renewal movement, which impacted North America around the same time, but went largely unnoticed. By the 1980s the accelerated growth and popularity of Pentecostalism and Pentecostal-like churches was impossible to avoid or undermine. The shifting political environment from civil war to signing of the peace accord in 1996 was also paralleled by the profound tectonic shifts in the way Pentecostalism would be configured. It is common knowledge that the majority of the people who converted to Pentecostalism in Guatemala came from Catholicism. By the 1970s and 1980s "historic" Protestant churches were also losing members to Pentecostalism through the Charismatic Renewal. The latest trend in Pentecostalism is the accelerated growth of neo-Pentecostal churches at the expense of classical Pentecostals and "historic" Protestants. The fundamental differences of these neo-Pentecostal churches is that they are growing among the upper social classes of Guatemala, and they show the unapologetic tendency toward adopting foreign (primarily USA) cultural elements including the construction of mega-churches and an emphasis on the prosperity gospel (health and wealth). Pentecostalism is no longer the monopoly of the poor classes of Guatemala![51]

MAKING THE CONNECTIONS: CHURCH, SOCIETY, POLITICS, AND ESCHATOLOGY

Although the Ríos Montt regime did not seem to have a significant negative impact on Pentecostalism in Guatemala, and the election of Serrano Elías was not due to evangelical support but to a well-run campaign, there is little doubt the participation of these two men in public politics

---

51. Pentecostals can no longer claim to be winning the poor exclusively. See Walker, "Where Pentecostalism is Mushrooming," 81.

contributed to a change in attitude in the way Pentecostals in Guatemala conceive the relation between the church and society. This shift in attitude is intimately related to and paralleled by a shift in the eschatology of Guatemalan Pentecostalism.

On one hand, the profound impact of Pentecostalism in Guatemalan society can be appreciated in the various movie theatres, which have ceased to function and now are occupied by churches. The public spaces are bombarded by the many vendors who have the radio tuned in to the local Christian station. The numerous television channels with Pentecostal programming and Christian movies, and the singing of choruses of nearby house churches celebrating their worship services are a clear display that Pentecostalism is very much part of the social fabric. On the other hand, the reality of poverty, gang crime, and corruption at every level of government makes one wonder about the effects of Pentecostalism in society. The pervasive presence of Pentecostalism has not greatly improved the general social condition of Guatemalans. Indeed several responses are put forth by Pentecostals and they can be traced as far back to the inception of Protestantism by the end of the nineteenth century.

As I indicated, eschatology played a secondary role for the Protestant missions, which entered Guatemala at the end of the nineteenth and first quarter of the twentieth century. Their focus was on providing important social services to the communities in diverse ways. During this first stage Protestantism and the later Pentecostal missions were largely insular in nature, geared toward fitting in the social and religious landscape of Guatemala. During the second and third stages there is greater opening toward society in the form of evangelization. This was characterized with a message of an apocalyptic future whereby believers will be finally vindicated.[52] With the emphasis on the future coming of Christ, the church adopted an otherworldly attitude by which social and political participation is unnecessary;[53] and focus on social issues

52. This is what Garrard-Burnett points out stating that "without question, the growth in Protestantism had also to do with Protestant's apocalyptic message of salvation, a rendering of truth that emphasized the time of tribulation to presage the Second Coming of Christ, the rapture of the faithful, and the punishment of the wicked." Garrard-Burnett, *Living in the New Jerusalem*, 132.

53. Miller and Yamamori argue that if the church's emphasis is otherworldly its focus will be on those that are part of the community. They have very little engagement with public policy and social welfare except to maintain their right to worship.

and politics can take away from time well-spent in bringing people to Christ.[54] The sole concern of the church was preaching the Pentecostal message. With its concomitant benefits of people's participation in the church structures, the sense of belonging to a specific local community, the replacing of familial and creation of new relationship networks, the domestication of males, and the added bonus of offering an alternative to alcoholism, drug addiction, and gambling, Pentecostals arrived at the conclusion that they were changing society one person at a time. The assumption behind the apprehension for engaging politics was the idea that the more people convert to Pentecostalism the less the government needed to address social issues, or to send letters or organize because government officials will know what to do.[55]

By the time of Ríos Montt, conversion equated with upward mobility and social and community improvement. This was the operating assumption in Ríos Montt's agenda to transform society. He believed that poverty, inequality, and class conflict were rooted in humanity's rottenness.[56] This all came crumbling down as he used his evangelical message to engage in systematic acts of genocide. Unwittingly, he contributed to Pentecostalism's gaining the courage to reclaim a social space and participation in Guatemalan society on its own grounds.

During this fourth stage, things have become far more complicated. Like the first stage the tradition of offering key social services to the communities is maintained with the preservation of medical clinics, creation of evangelical universities, and local soup kitchens for children and drug addicts. Like the second and third stages the focus on evangelization is still a central part of Pentecostal identity and practice, so the adoption of an otherworldly attitude prevails among many churches.

Persecution is seen by these groupings as divinely ordained. See Miller and Yamamori, *Global Pentecostalism*, 54.

54. Manuela Cantón Delgado finds that millenarism is a pervasive element when people testify about their reasons for conversion to Pentecostalism. According to her, testimony reflects the genuine millenarian urgency, which eagerly anticipates the Second Coming of the Savior, foretold in the Bible with deaths, wars, catastrophes, and that in Guatemala is an everyday reality. This is announced with impacting signs (*prepare, Christ is coming!*). As she comments, "this is the option that I find completely appropriate as description that gives sense to the Guatemalan Pentecostal discourse" Cantón Delgado, "Lo Sagrado y lo Político Entre los Pentecostales Guatemaltecos," 9.

55. Míguez, "Why Are Pentecostals Politically Ambiguous?" 68.

56. Garrard-Burnett, *Living in the New Jerusalem*, 148.

In the fourth stage, contradicting aspects are competing. For some, the emphasis on health and wealth promotes an individualistic approach, in line with the consumerist requirements of globalized capitalism, by which abundance is equated as the result of obedience to God, and lack of material means is explained as lack of faith on the part of believers.[57] Poverty is despised, not for being a social ill that needs to be eradicated, but as an indication of not being "right with God."[58] In this way poverty becomes the divine lot of some people until they become faithful to God, or until God ceases to try their faith. Admittedly, economic improvement and upward mobility have been key elements of Protestantism and Pentecostalism.[59] Money previously spent on alcohol and gambling now helps to address overall family needs. This contributes to the believer's and non-believer's perception that economic im-

57. Here the influence of preachers from the USA is deeply felt as television programs by Oral Roberts, Kenneth Hagin, Frederick Price, Creflo Dollar, John Hagee, and the like are ardently listened to by the Guatemalan population. Adopting the biblical language of "sowing and harvesting" (*siembra y cosecha*) and "first fruits" (*primicias*), people are taught to consider themselves chosen to be prosperous, whereby the size and numbers of a church become the indication of success and measure of customer satisfaction. This is the incorporation of the capitalist mindset translated into religious language: the gospel is turned into a commodity, product to be consumed and which gives back significant dividends. Miller and Yamamori observe that for many Prosperity Gospel churches there is no contradiction "between making claims about God's ability to heal people and bless them financially, and setting up health clinics, developing schools, and the like." Miller and Yamamori, *Global Pentecostalism*, 32. But at the same time, they admit that expression of Pentecostalism is rife with the exploitation of poor people who give money with the expectation that they will be blessed a hundredfold. And it also often exploits people who are desperately ill and are willing to grasp after anything that promises relief from suffering. Miller and Yamamori, *Global Pentecostalism*, 175.

58. Sepúlveda, "Pentecostalism and Liberation Theology" 54.

59. In engaging the indigenous groups and cultures of Guatemala, Amy Sherman adopts the Weberian social framing by which there is an intimate connection between economic upward mobility and conversion to Protestantism and Pentecostalism. She tests the theory, which connects conversion to Protestantism with upward mobility. She blames the Mayan population's mixture of ancestral and Catholic religious affiliations for their low levels of economic growth and development. See her *Soul of Development*. According to Steigenga, however, the Pentecostal population does no display higher levels of economic status. "According to the measures of socioeconomic status, Protestants as a group are not significantly more educated (except for the Neo-Pentecostals in Guatemala), do not have better jobs, are not more wealthy than Catholics and the religiously non-affiliated . . . In fact, Pentecostals tend to score slightly lower than other groups on measures of occupational status, level of education, and literacy, a finding that is consistent from previous studies in the region." Steigenga, *Politics of the Spirit*, 40.

provement has taken place as a result of conversion to Pentecostalism.[60] But this individualistic approach leaves unchallenged the structures of capitalism. Pentecostals have been willing to work at "pecking their way up the ladder of the capitalist economic system, even if the overarching effect of that system is to keep large numbers of people in poverty, but what they leave out is 'the biblical emphasis on social justice.'"[61]

Other Pentecostals take a more escapist, apocalyptic attitude, by which society will never improve until the coming of Christ, and until they inherit the New Heaven and the New Earth. This world and life are seen as temporary and inconsequential after conversion. After all, believers have a glorious future determined for them by God; all they have to do is remain faithful until the end. Any significant attempt at changing their reality becomes futile, because that is something only God can do. While for some Pentecostals this eschatological view functions as escapism from reality, numbing the pain and suffering endured because of tragedy, loss of relatives, and sheer poverty, for most believers this is not the promise of a "deferred gratification," but a "time of vindication, justice, empowerment, and reunion for the poor and oppressed, the inheritors of the earth entitled by Jesus Himself on the Sermon on the Mount."[62]

Yet others are waking up to the harsh reality that the ubiquitous message of Pentecostalism has not improved general social conditions.[63] Juan Sepúlveda states, "It is clear that Pentecostal growth has not by itself brought a commensurate and significant diminution in crucial social problems such as poverty, delinquency, alcoholism, drug addiction, child abuse, domestic violence, etc. This evidence forces Pentecostal churches to ask about the meaning of their growth. Is it enough to evangelize and to grow in order to make the gospel a significant factor in society"?[64]

---

60. This helps explain why many consider that there is a connection between a Pentecostal ethic and a Protestant ethic. The Pentecostal ethic produces people who are "honest, disciplined, transparent in their business dealings" viewing their work as a vocation and calling by God. This prevents them from wasting their money, which in turn will have a positive economic effect. Nevertheless, financial gain is an *unintended* consequence of a changed life. See Miller and Yamamori, *Global Pentecostalism*, 165, 169.

61. Miller and Yamamori, *Global Pentecostalism*, 183.

62. Garrard-Burnett, *Living in the New Jerusalem*, 132.

63. Sepúlveda, "Pentecostalism and Liberation Theology," 54.

64. Sepúlveda, "Future Perspectives for Latin American Pentecostalism," 193.

In light of this, many are beginning to see a direct interconnection between social and political engagement and preaching the gospel.[65] This social shift taking place in Guatemala was concretized in 1987 when the document *The Political Task of Evangelicals: Ideas for a New Guatemala* circulated among evangelicals. Anne M. Hallum claims this is an important document because it "calls for believers to become active in social and political work as well as evangelism," and "recognizes government responsibility for social and economic problems in Guatemala and Christian responsibility for being involved at the local and national level effecting change."[66]

This shows that in Guatemala, some Pentecostals are beginning to see the importance of responding to people's material needs, and the need to change structures of poverty as part and parcel of preaching the gospel message. As Lidia Vaccaro de Petrella pointedly observes, "All those who have had a Pentecostal experience cannot remain with their arms folded before those who are thirsty, starving, homeless or unjustly marginalized, as are so many in this century."[67]

These "Progressive Pentecostals," as denominated by Miller and Yamamori, represent a new direction for Pentecostalism. They are beginning to adopt a more integral or holistic approach to ministry whereby evangelism is never divorced from meeting the needs of the whole individual.[68]

This change in the tides of Pentecostal social engagement is also changing the eschatology of the church. Premillennial and apocalyptic eschatology has been the predominant doctrine taught by Pentecostals and Protestants in Guatemala, with the exception of the Presbyterian Church, but some churches are adopting a post-millennial approach, whereby the Second Coming of Christ is viewed as taking place only

---

65. As Cantón Delgado notes, "The explicit negation of a political conscience, the proclaimed distancing from "the affairs of the world," and alienation in the face of the increasing [literally: *sangrantes*] social problems, all of which are characteristics considered inherent to the discourse and practice of Protestantism, have been put into question and need to be reconsidered." Cantón Delgado, "Lo Sagrado y lo Político Entre los Pentecostales Guatemaltecos: Vivencia y Significación," 1.

66. Steigenga, "Guatemala," 164.

67. Vaccaro de Petrella, "Tension Between Evangelism and Social Action in the Pentecostal Movement," 36.

68. Miller and Yamamori, *Global Pentecostalism*, 60.

after the church has built a thousand year kingdom here on earth.[69] In this emerging position, the kingdom of God is not conceived simply as a future reality. Rather, "the faithful Christian seeking to follow the example of Jesus is also obligated to be an agent of love and compassion in the present moment."[70] This shift in eschatology and orientation toward the larger society represents profound theological changes and a redefinition of traditional Pentecostal understandings of the church, society, politics, and God.

This is a crucial stage in the history of Pentecostalism and Protestantism in Guatemala. Studies are beginning to show that the growth of Pentecostalism has slowed down, and that it cannot be considered without paying attention to the high drop-out rate.[71] In the process of maturity of Pentecostalism some second and third generations are also loosing the intensity of their first generations and displaying indifference.[72] Meanwhile some are leaving Pentecostalism altogether and others are going back to Catholicism.[73] Questions remain for why people shift between their religious traditions without tensions, switching of allegiances depending on their needs and interests.[74]

CONCLUSION

As I have shown, the notion that Pentecostals are apolitical needs to be rethought and rearticulated.[75] The context of Guatemala shows, however,

69. Steigenga, "Guatemala," 165. See also Miller and Yamamori, *Global Pentecostalism*, 213.

70. Miller and Yamamori, *Global Pentecostalism*, 213.

71. Cleary, "Shopping Around," 50–53.

72. Stewart-Gambino and Wilson, "Latin American Pentecostals," 228.

73. Cleary, "Evangelicals and Competition."

74. Green, *Fear as a Way of Life*, 160–62. In her work in rural Guatemala, Green found that shifting between religious allegiances was a practice of some indigenous people. As she sees it, the people perceived no contradiction in being members of the evangelical church, while at the same time staying in contact with Mayan healers, and accepting relief from the Catholic Church.

75. I agree that if most Pentecostals view their lives and social networks as "committed to and built around their religious faith rather than other (particularly partisan) commitments," and if their orientation is that "individual faith should be placed in God, not in social or political movements that promise temporal transformation on the basis of man-made [sic] [ideologies], then Pentecostalism is inherently apolitical." Stewart-Gambino and Wilson, "Latin American Pentecostals," 233. However, this would be a mistake in Guatemala because it dismisses the participation of Pentecostals in the political affairs of the country.

that Pentecostals and Protestants have been involved at the forefront of political issues, sometimes even supporting repressive governments. So from this perspective there is no reason to argue that Pentecostals in Guatemala are apolitical. They are neither politically neutral nor absent from the political arena. Pentecostalism in Guatemala is a social, political, and economic force, but it cannot be simplified as the expression of foreign interests. While during its early stages Pentecostalism received financial support and influence from foreign missions and missionaries, today's Pentecostalism is indigenous to Guatemala.[76] As Garrard-Burnett puts it, Christianity in Guatemala has lost its foreign accent.[77]

Guatemala is undergoing a spiritual/religious revival and this is taking place among Catholics as well.[78] Thus, triumphalist notions of an accelerated "explosive" growth must be tempered with the fact that the growth of Pentecostalism is not something recent, but has been taking place over decades before the arrival of Ríos Montt or Mejía Víctores. Yet, they symbolize the emergence of Pentecostalism into the public arena, and both helped stir the large Pentecostal masses in considering the possibilities of having a democratically elected evangelical president. This has contributed to Pentecostals in Guatemala to reject the historically second-class citizenship status they had, and reclaim their right to full participation in Guatemalan society.

But such claims demand that Pentecostals rethink the way they conceive their relation to the larger society. With an emphasis on a futuristic, millenarian, eschatology, and with Christian life defined as exclusively spiritual in nature, some expressions of Pentecostalism retard

76. Because of its unique historical roots, development, and sociopolitical environment within which it has grown and become such a large force, Everett Wilson argues that Pentecostalism in Guatemala cannot be understood as anything other than something very Guatemalan. While there are some missionary connections to the birth of Protestantism in Guatemala, the present expressions of Protestantism and Pentecostalism are truly indigenous movements. See his "Guatemalan Pentecostals." "Wherever it emerges, Pentecostalism tends to indigenize, absorbing the local culture in the way it worships, organizes itself, and relates to the local community." Miller and Yamamori, *Global Pentecostalism*, 211.

77. Virginia Garrard-Burnett, "'God Was Already Here When Columbus Arrived,'" 126.

78. According to Cleary, there is little ground for anticipating the demise of Catholicism. In fact, he demonstrates that a similar impetus and accelerated growth is overtaking the Catholic Church as well. See Cleary, "Evangelicals and Competition."

social transformation.[79] In fact, argues Pedro Moreno, there are reasons to think that some expressions of Pentecostalism hinder their own potential contributions to improve society.[80] "There are many Pentecostal churches that are mired in legalism and prefer to pray for the salvation of the world rather than to transform it through their actions . . . The major challenge for Pentecostals is whether they can move beyond an individualistic model of social service."[81]

On a positive note, some Pentecostals are already confronting social ills head on but they are certainly few by comparison.[82] There is no doubt

79. It cannot be denied that Pentecostalism must overcome some serious criticisms from outside such as its authoritarian organization and the suppression of women. Here I disagree with Miller and Yamamori as they argue that among Pentecostals women sometimes function even as clergy. But this is a way of sugar coating the endemic and systemic placing of women in positions of subordination to men. Also, they insist that even though Pentecostals have hierarchical structures, the notion of the "priesthood of all believers," and the idea that all are equal in the sight of God feeds in the direction of democracy. But again, this is rife with difficulties not only because Pentecostals tend to and have supported conservative, right-wing repressive governments (e.g., Chile and Guatemala), but they do not operate democratically; women are still relegated to subaltern roles. See Miller and Yamamori, *Global Pentecostalism*, 177. Moreover, according to Alan Walker, Pentecostals must begin to address the issues related to extensive membership losses, emotional excesses, the scandals that come to light "as recently won Christians fail to live up to their new profession of faith," the weak intellectual base of the movement's doctrine, the reasons behind disappointment among the youth and second-generation Pentecostals, and, most important, why Pentecostalism shows little sign of social conscience. See his "Where Pentecostalism is Mushrooming," 82.

80. According to Moreno, there are three reasons for which social change is being hindered by Pentecostals: they draw too sharp a line between the secular and the religious, they unnecessarily reject reason for emotion, and they overemphasize theologically the "call to ministry" and the end of the world. See Moreno, "Rapture and Renewal in Latin America," 32–33. Moreover, in the case of some churches, "their focus on the imminent return of Christ typically restricts them from engaging in more programmatic and long-term expressions of Christian social involvement." Miller and Yamamori, *Global Pentecostalism*, 31.

81. Miller and Yamamori, *Global Pentecostalism*, 67.

82. Miller and Yamamori claim that the "projects that engage issues at a systemic level are the leading edge of Progressive Pentecostalism, but is still an emergent movement." Miller and Yamamori, *Global Pentecostalism*, 213. They insist that while many Pentecostals are developing ministries, approaches, and programs that respond to the needs of the people, attempts to eliminate the causes of poverty by changing social policy are relatively rare among Pentecostals. At the same time, they did "encounter a few clergy who are mobilizing their congregation to fight political corruption as well as to confront economic structures that create poverty." Miller and Yamamori, *Global Pentecostalism*, 42.

that their response will contain a revised eschatology in creative ways. The interconnection of social and theologically eschatological issues, I venture to say, will be the challenge of Pentecostalism in the near future. As long as people simply wait for the coming of Christ and spiritualize all social problems seeing them as demonic forces at work in this world there will be no motivation for changing the community surrounding the church.[83] Ways in which Pentecostals will become relevant to the larger society will be reflected in great measure in the changes to their view of the church, society, and eschatology.

83. Miller and Yamamori, *Global Pentecostalism*, 127.

15

"Se fue con el Señor"

The Hispanic Pentecostal Funeral as Anticipatory Celebration

SAMMY ALFARO

INTRODUCTION

SITTING ON A DIRT mound with a cousin at a cemetery in San Luis, Sonora, Mexico over twenty years ago, I pondered seriously for the first time in my life about the meaning of death and its aftermath. As we observed the interment of our uncle's casket, my cousin asked: "What happens when we die?" At age twelve and with no theological language from which to piece together an adequate response, the only words I could conjure came from an often heard popular Pentecostal euphemism for death: "*Se fue con el Señor*"—"he went with the Lord."[1] To this cliché I now turn with a more nuanced reflection, for I believe it is representative of a much deeper eschatological understanding of death, which can be gleaned from the hopeful hymns and faith-filled testimonies that characterize the Hispanic Pentecostal funeral service.

---

1. The title of a 1981 article in *El Evangelio*—the official magazine of La Iglesia de Dios (the Hispanic ministry of the Church of God, Cleveland, TN)—serves to exemplify the use of this common Hispanic Pentecostal euphemism for death as "going to be with the Lord." The article celebrates the life and work of Jesús Fierro de Perez affectionately known as "Mamá Chuy." She was a humble woman of God who pioneered the establishment of the church in Guasave, Sinaloa, as well as missions in the nearby cities, with her love of personal evangelism. Murrieta, "Mamá Chuy se fue con el Señor," 19.

The aim of this chapter is to demonstrate that the Hispanic Pentecostal funeral service functions as an anticipatory celebration of the coming kingdom of God. By reflecting on the implicit eschatological dimensions expressed in the liturgy of the Hispanic Pentecostal funeral one may lay the foundations for an eschatology that is not simply "otherworldly," as has commonly been asserted of Pentecostals.[2] However, before describing the eschatological dimensions of the Hispanic Pentecostal funeral service, this chapter will consider the sources for a Hispanic Pentecostal eschatology. The purpose of this first step is to outline the popular eschatology expounded within the Hispanic Pentecostal community. Premillennial dispensationalism is an alien eschatological framework, which undermines the eschatological hope contained in the community's inherent expressions of faith. Lastly, this chapter will envision how Hispanic Pentecostalism can reinvent its eschatological understanding.

IN SEARCH OF SOURCES FOR A HISPANIC PENTECOSTAL ESCHATOLOGY

The attentive reader might ask: why focus on popular religious practices and not on theological treatises? The short response to this question is Hispanic Pentecostal theology is necessarily an "organic theology" for it is preoccupied with grassroots understandings of the experience of God.[3] It has long been acknowledged the main sources for a Hispanic Pentecostal theology are not academic in nature; but are expressions of their popular spirituality. In order to understand their distinctive theological contributions, as Eldin Villafañe states, "it would be much more fruitful and in a real sense closer to its indigenous nature to look at the *implicit theology* manifested, above all, in the *"culto."*[4] By *"culto,"* Villafañe refers to the Hispanic Pentecostal service in general and specifically to the activities within the service that serve to express the implicit theo-

2. Eldin Villafañe gives a reason for this popular "other-wordly" eschatological perspective. "It appears that the 'vision of the disinherited' (the Hispanic Pentecostals) rejects those persons and institutions, and their informing values, that have rejected them in the dominant culture. Thus, they too often project the fulfillment of their own vision of a renewed "heaven and earth" to the *eschaton*." Villafañe, *Liberating Spirit*, 152–53.

3. I take my cue for describing Hispanic Pentecostal reflection as an "organic theology" from Ada María Isasi-Díaz who approaches her own *Mujerista* theology in similar terms. Ada María Isasi-Díaz, *La Lucha Continues: Mujerista Theology*.

4 Villafañe, *Liberating Spirit*, 123.

logical discourse—for example, sermons, testimonies, songs, and any other activity practiced by the "community of the Spirit" in or outside the church walls.[5] In a similar fashion, Samuel Solclass identifies the *locus theologicus* of Hispanic theology as the worship service.[6] Earlier in the same chapter, Solclass describes what this entails in more depth, "The worship service is the place and the occasion where the sources and the norms that inform our theology come together. It is in the midst of the *culto* that we hear, see, feel, and reflect upon what God has said, is saying, and is calling us to be. Hispanic Pentecostal theology is incomprehensible apart from this experience of Holy Spirit-filled worship and praise."[7] Thus, the Hispanic Pentecostal service functions as the place where beliefs are expressed in organic terms to the community of faith.

Following this line of thought, I believe the grounding for a Hispanic Pentecostal eschatology can be established by examining the expressions of worship and faith during the funeral service. Hymns and testimonies provide a canvas of eschatological visions from which an organic Hispanic Pentecostal eschatology may surface. Yet, should one simply put aside the published eschatological contributions of Hispanic Pentecostals?

Significantly, if one were to focus solely on the published works of Hispanic Pentecostals in order to outline their eschatological worldview, the result would overlook the key elements of the eschatological hope of the community. The main reason for this is that traditionally Pentecostalism in general has worked with an eschatological paradigm, which was adopted from fundamentalist dispensational eschatology.[8] In a sense, this alien eschatological framework piggybacked its way into Pentecostal doctrine via an uncritical adoption of fundamentalist beliefs

---

5. Villafañe, *Liberating Spirit*, 121.

6. Samuel Solclass, "Sources of Hispanic/Latino American Theology," 142. See also Solclass, "Hispanic Pentecostal Worship" 43–56; Maynard, "In the Spirit of Fiesta," 161–86, esp. 173–77.

7. Solclass, "Sources of Hispanic/Latino American Theology," 140.

8. Peter Althouse argues contemporary popular Pentecostal eschatology has uncritically adopted the dispensational framework as a basis for the belief in the pre-millennial return of Jesus Christ. It is an uncritical borrowing because early Pentecostal eschatological imagination is of "a different type of premillennialism known as the latter rain," which "envisioned the end-time period to be a glorious foretaste of the coming King" and not necessarily included a belief in the rapture. Peter Althouse, "'Left Behind'—Fact or Fiction," 188–89.

in the name of orthodoxy. Perhaps there is no greater evidence for this within the Hispanic Pentecostal community than the use of the *Scofield Reference Bible*[9] and the proliferation of prophetic messages and teachings based on its dispensational framework.[10]

For those of us who grew up attending a Hispanic Pentecostal congregation, it is not a novelty to hear detailed explanations derived from Scofield's notes to the biblical text.[11] With the *Scofield Reference Bible* in hand, it was presumed that one could describe the apocalyptic times in which we were living. Ordinary church members with no biblical training became anointed interpreters of the book of Revelation; unlocking its apocalyptic message by putting together the clues and models provided by Scofield's notes. For instance, I have a very vivid memory of helping my mother piece together a chart, which diagramed a dispensational interpretation of the book of Revelation. Although she was a graduate (and later an instructor) of the Bible Institute, she relied on the "expert" notes of her *Scofield Reference Bible*.

Aside from anecdotal accounts, it has been difficult to document the use of Scofield's Bible in popular Hispanic Pentecostal eschatology.

9. Significantly, it was not until 1966 that the *Scofield Reference Bible* was first translated into Spanish. But, it quickly became the study bible of the Americas, for a time being rivaled only by the Spanish translation of the Thompson Chain Reference Bible. Another Bible that has gained popularity among Hispanic Pentecostal circles, primarily because of its focus on prophecy, is Tim Lahaye's *Biblia de Estudio de Profecia*. C. I. Scofield, *Scofield Reference Bible*.

10. Dale Coulter identifies C. I. Scofield as one of the most influential figures behind the quick advance of dispensationalism in the beginning of the twentieth century. In addition, Coulter documents the use of the Scofield Bible to buttress dispensational teachings within Pentecostal circles. What is utterly surprising about the love affair between Pentecostalism and the *Scofield Reference Bible* is that the latter's dispensational teaching openly affirms the cessation of the spiritual gifts denying the modern Pentecostal focus on them. But as French L. Arrington points out Pentecostals "saw the dispensational system as a helpful aid to emphas[ize] the premillenial Second Coming of Christ, the Rapture of the church, the seven years of the great Tribulation, the Millenium, and the cataclysmic Judgment that will mark the end of the present order." Coulter, "Pentecostal Visions of the End," 83, 87; Alexander, "Scofield Reference Bible," 1044; Arrington, "Dispensationalism," 585.

11. As the two major Spanish-speaking Pentecostal denominations (Assemblies of God and Church of God, Cleveland, TN) tend to follow the lead of their Anglo counterparts, it was to be expected that they too adopted the Scofield Reference Bible as their favorite tool for Bible study. See Thomson, *Waiting for the Antichrist*, 48; Prosser, *Dispensational Eschatology and its Influence on American and British Religious Movements*, 253.

At best, one can deduce the tools Bible teachers used to interpret Daniel and Revelation confirm that a dispensational orientation guided by *Scofield Reference Bible* notes was at the core of their eschatological understanding.[12] For example, the Spanish translation of the dispensational charts and diagrams of Alfred Thompson Eade became the key visual aids in prophetic studies and conferences on the book of Revelation.[13] In addition, among the more popular textbooks used at the Bible Institutes for courses on biblical prophecy was Sunshine Ball's commentary on Daniel and Revelation.[14] Admittedly, this book does not make an ex-

12. In his attempt to demonstrate Pentecostals where not originally dispensationalists and that it is problematic for Pentecostals to embrace dispensationalism, Gerald Sheppard makes some comments regarding Hispanic Pentecostalism and its hesitancy to adopt fully the dispensational framework. In order to establish this, Sheppard points to the literal approach to biblical interpretation as expounded in Eric Lund's *Hermeneutics or the Science and Art of Interpreting the Bible.* (A recent edition of the book was published coupled with Alice Luce's *Introducción Bíblica* as E. Lund and A. Luce, *Hermenéutica, Introducción Bíblica*). First published in Spanish in 1934, it quickly became the textbook for teaching hermeneutics among Hispanic Pentecostals. Sheppard notes that "the book totally ignores the dispensational hermeneutical system" and that "no reference is made to the Scofield Bible or standard dispensational materials." However, the problem with this line of reasoning is it assumes that this hermeneutical orientation solely guided the interpretation of the books of Daniel and Revelation. However, it is more likely that various dispensational sources formed the basis for Hispanic Pentecostals interpretation of biblical prophecy, as can be gleaned from an a close analysis of Hispanic Pentecostal understanding of biblical prophecy in comparison to the main tenets of dispensational eschatology. Sheppard, "Pentecostals and the Hermeneutics of Dispensationalism," 16.

13. One must not underestimate the significance of these visual aids, for they served as the blueprints for the charts and diagrams, which were utilized when teaching biblical prophecy. In the decade of the eighties, it was popular to make large "apocalyptic" diagrams using poster board and newspaper/magazine clippings to illustrate the visions and signs of John's Apocalypse, to provide a pictorial layout of the book of Revelation in order to sketch a literal interpretation of the events that would take place in the near future. Eade, *Panorama de la Biblia.* Also by the same author and publisher: vol. 2 "*La Segunda Venida de Cristo*" (The Second Coming of Christ); vol. 4, "*El Libro de Apocalipsis*" (The book of Revelation).

14. Sunshine Ball was the wife of Henry Ball, an Assemblies of God minister whose name is synonymous with ministry among Mexican immigrants living in the US border of Texas. Together, they served as missionaries, helped organize the Latin American District of the Assemblies of God, and founded Editorial Vida (the official publishing house of the Hispanic ministry of the Assemblies of God). Significantly, it was also on account of their efforts that the Latin American Bible Institute was founded in San Antonio, TX. Although published over fifty years ago, now in its tenth edition Sunshine Ball's book on Daniel and Revelation continues to be the textbook in many Bible Institutes today. Ball, *Daniel y el Apocalipsis.*

plicit reference to dispensational works nor the Scofield Bible. However, judging from the line of interpretation it follows, one can surmise that a dispensational framework undergirds its exegesis.[15]

Another way to assess the dispensationalist dependency of Hispanic Pentecostal eschatological writings is by analyzing the interpretative flow found in the official didactic material used for Sunday School lessons. For instance, in 1992, *El Maestro Pentecostés*—the official manual for adult Sunday School teachers of the Iglesia de Dios (Church of God, Cleveland, TN)—contained lessons plans based "on the fundamental doctrines of the Bible."[16] The tenth to the fourteenth lessons in this exposition covered the rapture of the church, the tribunal of Christ, the seven years of tribulation, the millennium, and the final judgment.[17] Throughout the explanations, the hallmarks of dispensational eschatology are expounded in a way that Scofield and his predecessors would

15. One has to clarify first that many books published over twenty years ago (and even some today!) by Hispanic publishing houses do not always contain bibliographic references or citations, which permit the reader to follow the trail of sources used. That is the case on both accounts in Sunshine Ball's *Daniel y el Apocalipsis*. Despite the lack of references, one may still form an educated guess as to the sources behind the interpretation. For example, Ball's commentary on the letters to the churches in Revelation 2–3 follows a very Scofieldian approach by explaining that the seven churches correspond to seven "distinct periods of the church on earth from apostolic times until the rapture" (author's translation). Aside from other passages where one might 'read between the lines' in order to establish her dependency on dispensational works, there is one place where this is more explicitly evident. In her commentary of Daniel's seventy weeks, she describes the epoch of the church as a dispensation of grace. In the end, one has to conclude that although Hispanic Pentecostal exegetes did not adopt the dispensational system as a whole, of the seven dispensations the sixth (grace) and seventh (millennial kingdom) form the basis of their eschatological worldview. Ball, *Daniel y el Apocalipsis*, 66, 47.

16. In the introductory comments for this edition, the editor comments this will be the first time the editorial house will use its own outlines. Calderón, Wilfredo, *El Maestro Pentecostés: manual para maestros de adultos y jóvenes*, 4.

17. Significantly, the Church of God's *Declaration of Faith* does not refer to the seven-year tribulation. Only the last two statements of faith address eschatological themes: the rapture [rapture is vague in connection to source cited: catch away could simply refer to resurrection], the Second Coming and the millennium. "13. [We believe . . .] In the premillennial Second Coming of Jesus. First, to resurrect the righteous dead and to catch away the living saints to Him in the air. Second, to reign on the earth a thousand years. 14. In the bodily resurrection; eternal life for the righteous, and eternal punishment for the wicked." "Declaration of Faith," The Official Website of the Church of God (Cleveland, TN).

be proud.[18] Furthermore, in a companion manual, which was meant to expand on these Sunday School lessons, most of the references cited mention widely known dispensational scholars.[19] It is worth noting that more recent scholarly works within the same denomination attempt to distance themselves from under the umbrella of dispensational eschatology.[20] Such is the case with Hiram Almirudis' exegetical commentary on the Church of God's statement of faith[21] and two commentaries on the books of Daniel and Revelation by Wilfredo Calderón.[22]

18. In fact, explicit references are made to Charles C. Ryrie (Revised Dispensationalist), J. Dwight Pentecost (Progressive Dispensationalist), as well as other notable dispensational scholars. Calderón, *El Maestro Pentecostés*, 98–99.

19. Along with others, the Charles Ryrie's *Study Bible* and J. Dwight Pentecost's *Events to Come* are signaled as useful tools for understanding biblical prophecy. Calderón, *Doctrina Bíblica y Vida Cristiana*, 204, 206.

20. It was refreshing to read in a more recent Sunday School teaching manual a critique of dispensational eschatology. After outlining the dispensational interpretation, which sees the seven churches of Revelation (Rev 2–3) as representing historical stages of the church, Osvaldo Pupillo comments on the modern church in relation to its dispensational counterpart—the church of Laodicea: "some reject this argument in light of the phenomenal growth of the Pentecostal movement and the greatest missionary effort in the history of the kingdom, which would be incompatible with a blind and lukewarm church" (author's translation). Pupillo, "Cristo, el Eterno Señor," in *El Discípulo Bíblico*," 161.

21. As a careful exegete of the biblical text and the Church of God *Declaration of Faith*, Hiram Almirudis does not make explicit mention of the seven-year period called the "Great Tribulation." In fact, in this commentary he provides a clear and concise articulation of the tradition's statement of faith with no apparent dependency on the dispensational eschatological framework. Almirudis, *Comentario Sobre la Declaración de Fe de la Iglesia de Dios*. Hiram Almirudis, "A Commentary on the Church of God Declaration of Faith for Latin American Churches."

22. Notably, Wilfredo Calderón attempts to distance himself from the dispensational school of interpretation by noting that literal futurists need not be dispensationalists, making explicit reference to the *Scofield Reference Bible*. In spite of this, the author still gives a marked preference for the dispensational outlook of the last days leaning heavily on dispensational scholars. In addition, Calderón also substantiates his interpretation of "the child of the woman" (Rev 12:5, 13) as the 144,000 by alluding to the work of Pentecostal dispensationalist exegete Finis Jennings Dake. Calderón goes out of his way to recognize Dake as a great scholar and dedicated biblical exegete of Pentecostal conviction, whose works he consulted while writing these commentaries. (The works here mentioned are *Dake's Annotated Reference Bible* and *Revelation Expanded*). As a side note, one thing that is still troubling about this work is the anti-Catholic rhetoric of the author, particularly in the identification of the Catholic Church as the whore of Babylon in Revelation 17 and the surprising claim that "millions of Jews were massacred in the Holocaust under the Nazi regime of Catholic Germany" (author's translation) Calderón, *Daniel; El Apocalipsis*, 38, 111, 208, 240, 288, 340.

Lastly, if one were to focus solely on popular Pentecostal writings, which pretend to unlock the mysteries contained in biblical prophecy, the eschatology that would surface would employ a strong anti-Catholic and anti-ecumenical rhetoric. For example, books like Yiye Avila's *El Anticristo* are among the most popular interpretations of the end times for Hispanic Pentecostals.[23] In these writings, it is typical to read interpretations that portray the Catholic Church as the Great Whore of Revelation 17 and the Pope as the false prophet, or even the Antichrist. Concerning the ecumenical movement, Avila writes: "the goal of the ecumenical movement is to fuse all of the churches and religions of the world into one universal church."[24]

This wrongheaded fixation of attempting to identify the characters of the book of Revelation with their historical counterparts reveals the dangers of continuing to propagate an eschatological system without critical analysis. Given the apocalyptic fervor of the tradition, it is not surprising that Hispanic Pentecostals devoured one by one all of the books in the *Left Behind* series.[25]

To conclude from all this that Hispanic Pentecostal eschatology is merely otherworldly and pessimistic is to pass partial judgment because it ignores the more popular expressions of its faith. In part, the problem lies in that Hispanic Pentecostalism has defined eschatology in a very limited way. If eschatology only relates to the historical unfolding of God's plan for the end times, then the mission of a teacher of eschatology is to put together the puzzle of biblical prophecy. However, if one understands eschatology as encompassing "what happens when we die" (individual eschatology) as well as the future manifestation of God's reign (general eschatology), then a more holistic eschatological

23. Yiye Avila is a popular Pentecostal evangelist who has preached extensively throughout Latin America for over the past thirty years and whose ministry has a marked eschatological orientation (¡Cristo Viene Pronto!—Jesus is Coming Soon!). Among the prophetic claims that Avila has made popular through his preaching and writing, he affirms that the Antichrist is already alive and waiting to seize power when the opportunity arises, and identifies the Catholic Church as the great whore of Babylon in Revelation 17. Avila, *El Anticristo*, 35.

24. Avila, *El Anticristo*, 56.

25. Peter Althouse's description of the anti-Catholic themes in the *Left Behind* series serves to highlight the similarities: "the Pope is depicted as anti-Christian, influenced by the Antichrist to establish a relativistic world religion that operates from New Babylon. Attempts at ecumenical and interfaith dialogue are portrayed as futile and influenced by, and a deception of, the Antichrist." Althouse, "'Left Behind'—Fact or Fiction," 188.

worldview will develop. In this sense, how we live and die in this life has everything to do with the coming kingdom of God.

THE ESCHATOLOGICAL DIMENSIONS OF THE HISPANIC PENTECOSTAL FUNERAL SERVICE

In order to discover and assess the popular voices of the Pentecostal community, I conducted a brief survey among Hispanic Pentecostal churches. The survey consisted of three main questions:

> 1) In distinction to the funeral service in the Catholic tradition, how would you describe the proceedings of a funeral service in the Hispanic Pentecostal church? What would be considered the typical order of service?
>
> 2) Which hymns do you remember singing in a recent funeral service? What sentiments did those hymns evoke? What do they say about the death of a Christian?
>
> 3) The funeral service reveals how a particular culture or religion confronts death. In general, with what attitude do you believe the Hispanic Pentecostal church confronts death (resignation, celebration, hopelessness, hope, fear, joy, etc.)?

The survey was written in Spanish and handed out to Hispanic Pentecostal students in a theology course (Teología Bíblica y Sistemática III) I taught at the Seminario Hispano de Misionología—a Bible Institute in Phoenix, AZ—in the Fall of 2008. In addition, I contacted local Hispanic pastors of the Church of God (Cleveland, TN), and they agreed to distribute the survey among their congregants. Of the one hundred surveys distributed, forty-two made their way back and form the data pool for this study.[26]

26. This author is aware the data for this survey is limited in many ways because it is not representative of Hispanic Pentecostals as a whole. For example, in this survey, the Assemblies of God is overshadowed in presence by the Church of God (Cleveland, TN), which goes against the reality of denominational percentages; both AG churches and members outnumber those of the COG. Moreover, the unintended exclusion of members from Apostolic congregations (La Iglesia Apostólica de la Fe en Cristo Jesús) also limits the scope of this data. Another admission is that the designation of independent denomination is somewhat misleading. I say this because I was left with some suspicions. For instance, when asked for denominational membership some of the participants filled out "independent" when their congregation is partially affiliated with the Church of God (Cleveland, TN), being that the churches were started as missions though to this day they are functioning as independent church bodies. Given these

The people who responded to this survey can be classified as follows:

- twenty church leaders, nineteen church members, and three pastors
- sixteen Church of God (Cleveland, TN), twenty-four Independent, two Assemblies of God
- nineteen women and twenty-three men

What follows is a descriptive analysis of the responses to the survey. At times, individual responses will be highlighted, but for the most part the observations will be grouped together.

As representative of the Hispanic Pentecostal funeral services, Eliseo López Cortéz provides this description of a Mexican Apostolic funeral service, "When a believing member of the Church dies, a special vigil service is held for the deceased and biblical passages relating to death and the resurrection to eternal life are read. This service is accompanied by funeral hymns. The casket is positioned in front of the altar with the body present in order to hold a vigil, with the lights turned on but without lighting candles or chandeliers. The next day, when the body is taken to the cemetery, the pastor of the church celebrates another special service with a sermon that is allusive to the act."[27] In essence, one can divide the funeral service into three main elements: song, testimony and sermon. It is a time for remembering the deceased for the life he or she lived. Conducive toward this goal, songs that had special significance for the departed are sung in homage. In addition, there is a time for family and other friends of the deceased to take the pulpit in order to express condolences and share anecdotal testimonies remembering the individual in life. Lastly, an evangelistic sermon is preached, specifically addressing those present who are not believers.

Of the hymns mentioned in the surveys, the one that appears almost with complete consensus is *Mas Allá del Sol*[28] (of the forty-two responses

---

limitations, and others that the reader might note, it is more appropriate to consider this reflection as a foretaste but that a more nuanced and complete study should be undertaken.

27. López Cortéz, *Pentecostalismo y Milenarismo*, 72.

28. The scholarly question here would be: who wrote the hymn? I have yet to find a conclusive answer for the composition of *Mas Allá del Sol*. Per an email conversation with Daniel Ramirez, its composition can be narrowed down to two possible origins:

only four did not mention this hymn). This solemn hymn, which is reserved almost exclusively for funeral services, begins by establishing the contrast of this life with the next. Despite the economic hardship one may encounter in this world (*aunque en esta vida*—although in this life), there is a hope of a new life, which will put an end to all suffering. At the present, though, all the believer can do is long for that heavenly place, which will one day be her or his new home. Thus, the chorus brings a joyful declaration of hope:

//Mas allá del sol//	//Farther than the sun//
Yo tengo un hogar,	I have a home,
Hogar bello hogar,	A home beautiful home
Mas allá del sol	Farther than the sun

CLADIC (Concilio Latino Americano de Iglesias Cristianas) or Mexican Adventist. In addition, the extemporaneous nature of Pentecostal worship is difficult to document who composed a particular hymn. For example, there is no hymnal that consists of only songs composed by Hispanic Pentecostals. Moreover, there is the question of how to determine whether a particular source can be considered to be "Pentecostal." The difficulty of this process can be seen when one considers that many hymns (and *coritos*) were adopted either verbatim or at times with an added Pentecostal slant, and that they were not necessarily written by a Pentecostal, but were adopted because they in some way express the Pentecostal experience. In fact, a large percentage of hymns sung in Hispanic Pentecostal churches were translated from their Anglo counterparts or borrowed from Hispanic Apostolic hymnals. It is common in the traditional Hispanic Pentecostal service for a brother or sister to take the pulpit and offer a testimony, which is then followed by a hymn that goes with what was just said. A personal example of this is from a recollection of my parents' testimony (Quirino and Alicia Alfaro). When we were growing up, it was very common for one of the two to go to the pulpit and testify, and then ask the other to join them with a special song for the Lord. Likewise, I came into the possession of Abundio Saldivar's (my father-in-law) rustic hymnbook. As typical of many Pentecostal psalmists who sing to the Lord, he carried that hymnbook with him and wrote down in it the songs he heard that had a special significance and meaning for his experience of walking with the Lord. In his hymnbook I found evidence for the sort of borrowing mentioned above. Some songs are translations of a classic Pentecostal or evangelical hymn. Others are taken from the repertoire of Hispanic composers. Yet, the most dear to his heart—the ones that were sung the most—and the ones which more characteristically evoke some Hispanic Pentecostal sentiment were those, which unbeknownst to my father-in-law, where penned by one of many Mexican Oneness Pentecostals. This suggests that authorship is less significant than content; what is important to the singer is the song's resonance with his or her experience and its ability to transport the singer to a plain where her or his experience is interconnected with the words of the song. For a statistical study of Latino hymnody with a special focus on Pentecostal hymnody see, Ramirez, "Alabaré a mi Señor," 196–218.

Often the person singing at a funeral, along with the congregation, breaks down in tears because of the vivid portrayal of the homecoming of the loved one as expressed in the lyrics. Thus, the hymn has a two-fold function: on the one hand, to contrast the suffering of this world to the joys of the life to come, and on the other hand, to say farewell to the person who went to be with the Lord. Antonia González, an elderly woman now a Christian for twenty-seven years commented: "Well, in my mother's funeral service, nineteen years ago, the pastor gave a short sermon, made an altar call to the people that did not know Christ, and we sang hymns that were already old. And to close, since we are three brothers who are all Christians we sang *Mas Alla del Sol* to say goodbye to her."[29] Worth noting is how this hymn voices a testimony in first-person narrative, as if the person who died is actually present to calm the sorrow of those present by letting them know he or she is at home with the Lord.

Another song that beautifully conjures a heavenly scene in order to bring comfort to those present at a funeral is *Alegrate Alma Triste* (Rejoice Saddened Soul).[30] The words of the first stanza and chorus follow:

Anhelo en las regias mansiones morar	I desire to dwell in the regal mansions
Do reina mi Salvador	Where my Savior reigns
Escucho los ecos de un dulce cantar	I hear the echoes of a sweet song
De triunfo y de gran loor.	Of triumph and of great joy.

Coro:	Chorus:
A mi Supremo Rey, alegre cantaré	To my Supreme King I will sing joyfully
Mis ojos han de ver, la patria celestial	My eyes will one day see, the celestial country
Feliz y libre soy, y caminando voy	I am happy and free, and I walk
Con júbilo a mi eterno hogar.	With jubilee to my eternal home.

29. "Bueno, en el servicio de mi madre, hace 19 años ya que murio, el pastor dio un corto sermón, llamó a la gente que todavia no conocia a Cristo como su Salvador, cantamos cantos ya viejitos y para cerrar somos tres hermanos todos cristianos y le cantamos *Mas Alla del Sol* para despedirla."

30. Though this hymn is likely of Apostolic origin, it is a very popular hymn at funeral services within Hispanic Pentecostal denominations. I have two special recollections regarding this hymn. A friend, Gamaliel Ruiz, sang it at his mother's funeral (who at the time was the *pastora* at the church I attended), and my mother sang it at my grandmother's funeral.

This hymn also presents a living testimony of a person who already has gone to be with the Lord. Listening to the words of this hymn, one can only imagine the deceased on a journey, which crosses the limits of this world and enters into the next. As Guillermina Barajas points out, "we sing hymns that refer to our celestial citizenship." Also in connection to this sentiment, Graciela Salgado recalls the hope expressed in the apostle Paul's words to the Philippians: "for to me, to live is Christ and to die is gain" (1:21). In this light, death is but a journey, for the one who believes in the Lord.

Briefly, other hymns mentioned in the surveys are: *Cruzando el Valle Voy, La Ultima Milla,* and *En Presencia Estar de Cristo.* Each of these in its own way contains the similar theme of dying as a journey into the afterlife. The first renders life as a journey through the valley in which the destination is a mansion of light where the sojourner begins his or her life with the Lord. The second envisions the last stages of life on this earth as being the last mile of the race. The third anticipates the believer's face-to-face encounter at the moment she or he enters into Christ's presence. What all these hymns have in common is an understanding of life as being transitory and death being the final journey into the presence of God.

Focusing on the testimonial aspect of funeral services, the notion of the priesthood of all believers is evident. There is always a time when anyone present can come forward and give a testimony or words of comfort for the bereaving family. Sometimes the person testifying will allude to a dream or vision of the deceased and comment on their celestial abode.[31] Moreover, as so often happens in Hispanic Pentecostal funerals, anecdotes of the last things the person did in his or her life are remembered in order to bring a word of exhortation to those present. I still remember the emotive words spoken by Victor Pagan—at the time, Superintendent of the Southwestern Hispanic territory of the Church of God—at the funeral of Lita Ruiz, the pastor's wife of the church in which I grew up: "She died with her boots on!" This comment was made in reference to the automobile accident in which she died, for at the time she was accompanying the youth group on their way to an evangelistic

---

31. At the funeral service of Adónica Nuñez, a twelve-year old girl who died after a five-year battle with leukemia, Sister Elsa Castellanos narrated a dream in which she saw Adónica in a playful encounter with angels. Afterward, she commented on how this was true to the young girl's playful attitude in life.

crusade in Ciudad Obregon, Sonora, Mexico. Another example of this is the recollection of the last moments of the life of Francisca García Bázaca: "Every year she promised God that she would read the whole Bible. And that day, December 16, 1981, while she waited for a friend of hers who would take her shopping, she fell asleep with her Bible on her chest and with a page in between her right hand fingers. She finished her life like that hanging on to the dream!"[32] Were it not for the burial casket and the flowers present in the church, one could easily mistake the service for an evangelistic crusade.

Often the preaching at a Hispanic Pentecostal funeral service becomes an evangelistic rally, focusing on non-believing family and friends in attendance. For Hispanic Pentecostals, a funeral service is an opportunity to preach the gospel. In fact, this evangelistic impulse is what brings the service to a close. In a sense, the idea of bringing others to salvation makes the funeral service meaningful, for the person's death is made meaningful; it was an opportunity for unbelieving friends and family members to come to saving knowledge of Jesus Christ. Interestingly, one respondent noted that the order of the funeral service (hymns, remembrances, testimonies, prayer of consolation) makes ready the hearts of the listeners for the preaching of the gospel. Thus, in the midst of death Hispanic Pentecostals find comfort in knowing a loved one's funeral became an opportunity to bring someone to salvation.[33]

To summarize, it is significant to trace how the struggles of this life are juxtaposed with the glories of heaven in all of the expressions of faith present in the funeral service. Whereas suffering describes life on earth, the end of suffering is how heaven is pictured. In the words of the very popular and joyous *corito*:

32. Ruiz, "El Drama Humano," 7.

33. It is worth noting that this evangelistic impulse is also present in many of the hymns sung at a funeral. For example, the last stanza of *Mas Allá del Sol* says: "To all the races of the human lineage/ Christ wants to give full salvation." Another hymn that alludes to the fullness of salvation is *Gozándome Yo Voy* (I am going joyfully). This hymn is sung in a joyful tone and envisions death as a joyful walk to the eternal home where Jesus is present. In the hymn, that walk is made even more joyous with the knowledge that sinners are joining one's journey toward the celestial home.

///Alla en el Cielo///	///Up there is heaven///
No habra mas llanto	There will be no more lament
Ni mas tristeza	nor more sorrow
Ni mas dolor	nor more pain
Y cuando estemos los redimidos	And when we the redeemed are
Alla en el cielo	Up there in heaven
Alabaremos al Señor	We will praise the Lord

Faced with a life of constant struggle, hardship and economic issues, the Hispanic Pentecostal community looks to the afterlife as a time when all suffering ceases and only joy will subsist.

Reflecting on the impact of the struggles of life Samuel Soliván comments:

> The socioeconomic reality of the Hispanic community and the location of the Hispanic Pentecostal church also reflect its world-view. Often Hispanic Pentecostals understand themselves to be a bulwark against death and the forces of evil that are overwhelming the world. They are a fortress against the cultural forces that seek to destroy them and their value system—a system that they understand as reflecting the values of the kingdom of God and their Lord Jesus Christ. This countercultural posture is the counterpart of the attitude that the dominant culture has had and continues to have toward them. This worldview plays an important part in the ethos of their worship, which is fueled by an eschatological—at times even apocalyptic—vision of the future.[34]

This is why the funeral service in Hispanic Pentecostal congregations has come to be celebrated in the spirit of *fiesta*.

Perhaps, there is no truer demonstration of *fiesta* in the Hispanic Pentecostal community than the celebration of a funeral service. It is a true *fiesta* because friends who have not seen each other in a long time are reunited as they come to say farewell to a mutual friend. It is a time where food abounds, for eating together brings comfort to the grieving family and friends. It is a time to laugh in remembrance of the funny things the loved one did in life.[35] In many ways, in the Hispanic

---

34. Soliván, *Hispanic Pentecostal Worship*, 47.

35. In the funeral of my great aunt, the family laughed remembering how *la tia Leja* put on the traditional white dress every night before going to bed in the weeks before her death. She did this because she wanted to be ready but she did not wish to be undressed by someone else.

Pentecostal imagination this is what heaven will be like. As the chorus of a hymn puts it:

A los amigos y vecinos veremos allá:	Friends and neighbors we will see there
Oiremos cantos conocidos en el viaje de afán.	We will hear familiar songs in the journey
Alístate a partir gozoso hacia aquel hogar,	Prepare joyfully to depart toward that home
En donde amigos y vecinos veremos allá.	Where friends and neighbors we will see.

Indeed, more than a farewell service, the funeral is seen as an anticipatory celebration that is symbolic of what the new life in heaven will be like.

HISPANIC PENTECOSTAL ESCHATOLOGY: OTHERWORLDLY OR THIS-WORLDLY?

Having presented the popular eschatological understanding of the end as depicted in the writings of Hispanic Pentecostals, on the one hand, and the main contours of the Hispanic Pentecostal funeral service, on the other, it becomes a significant exercise to analyze the continuity and/or discontinuity between the two. What correlation is there in a movement that decisively sees the *Left Behind* series as an excellent interpretation of the book of Revelation and the same tradition's organic eschatology as typified in their celebration of funeral services? The significance of outlining the dispensational eschatological framework in juxtaposition to various manifestations of popular eschatology is that one can contrast the main attitudes each promotes. The first focuses on the cataclysmic destruction of the world in the end times and as such it presents a very pessimistic view of the fulfillment of the book of Revelation. The second contains a more optimist perspective in that death is seen as a transitory journey from this world to the next. However, one might ask: do not both perspectives present different avenues for escapism? Does the intrinsic eschatological vision of Hispanic Pentecostals elicit the same otherworldliness of premillennial dispensationalism?

Peter Althouse's analysis of *Left Behind* eschatology provides a helpful illustration for understanding the difference between the two: "The pre-millenarianism of fundamentalism with its doctrine of a secret Rapture is opposite to the pre-millenarianism of the early church. Early church apocalyptism included eschatological hope that resisted the powers of sin and oppression, but fundamentalist apocalypticism embodies a spiritual escape from this world. Passive withdrawal in the hope of a secret Rapture abdicates our responsibilities to protest against the powers of sin and oppression in all their personal, social and cosmic dimensions."[36] The same distinction could be made between premillennial dispensationalism and organic Hispanic Pentecostal eschatological expressions of faith. Otherworldly eschatology views the present world as heading toward its apocalyptic fate of cataclysmic destruction. There is nothing to be done to rescue it from its intended future; it is only a matter of time before history runs its course. The only response to this eschatological scenario is escapism; to flee the coming destruction. Though this might be the logical conclusion in premillenarian dispensationalism, it is contrary to the expressions of faith contained in the Hispanic Pentecostal funeral service.

Instead, organic Hispanic Pentecostal eschatology contains liberative implications for this present world, in that it focuses on the future-oriented eschatological signs of the kingdom (spiritual redemption, physical healing, and social liberation), but with an eye on the present. As such, it announces the redemptive aspects of the future reign of God, yet it also denounces the sinful and unjust structures, which militate against its present establishment.[37] Central to this claim is an eschatology, which understands the coming kingdom of God as none other than the present and future fulfillment of the reign that Jesus preached and embodied.

As has been noted in the previous section, in the Hispanic Pentecostal funeral service the eschatological hope of the community is at the forefront of this tragic experience. Yet, the hope is not based on the deceased's escape from the coming apocalyptic catastrophes that await this world. Rather, hope is found in the knowledge the deceased,

36. Althouse, "'Left Behind'—Fact or Fiction," 191.

37. Samuel Cruz provides a helpful reminder of the danger of interpreting beliefs and practices without a careful scrutiny of the context and lived faith of the Hispanic Pentecostal community. He states: "Unproductive overgeneralizations seem to be dangerous when endeavoring to understand the foundational premises of Latino(a) Pentecostal rituals/beliefs as they pertain to Pentecostal notions of cultural, social, political and theological realities. As a participant-observer, I encountered unique manifestations of Pentecostal practices, which are often different from what is sometimes verbalized in Pentecostal discourses during worship services and from what religious scholars frequently assert." Cruz contends that the perception of Latina/o Pentecostals being apolitical is due to the misunderstanding of the unconventional ways in which the community asserts its acts of political resistance vis-à-vis that of the Anglo culture. Cruz, "Rereading of Latino(a) Pentecostalism," 202.

who was a fellow sufferer in this world, has gone to be with the Lord. Thus, the deceased becomes a model for the living; he or she embodies the triumph over the trials of this present world. As the hymns express in various ways, the one going to be with the Lord can join Paul in joyful exclamation: "I have fought the good fight, I have finished the race, I have kept the faith. Now there is in store for me a crown of righteousness, which the Lord, the righteous Judge, will award to me on that day—and not only me, but also all who have longed for his appearing" (2 Tim 4:7–8).

The hymns and testimonies of the funeral service present affirmations of this eschatological hope. They are reminders to the community left behind (pun intended) that they must continue to fight the good fight. Daniel Castelo comments on the eschatological dimensions of the Pentecostal practice of sharing testimonies: "Testimonies are indications that believers are in a perpetual state of tarrying before the Lord, because the act of sharing the way God is present among believers inspires a vision of living 'in between the times,' a vision that demonstrates the way God breaks through the experience of the church in an act foreshadowing His soon-coming reign."[38] What better way to bring comfort to a suffering community than to make them focus on the triumph that death presents for the individual who believes in the Lord. The deceased has not entered purgatory or lies awaiting his or her final destination; he or she is present with the Lord in the heavenly mansions!

During the celebration of a funeral, the Hispanic Pentecostal community focuses on the world to come in order to gain strength to continue surviving in this present age. The hope of a heaven where all pain and suffering will end, however, is not a pie waiting in the sky. The longing for an eternal abode reminds the Pentecostal community of the future reward for the present trials and suffering. Pentecostals are fully aware that the forces of this present age, which brought death to the life of a loved one, do not have the final say in the matter. Whether death was the result of an illness or violence, Pentecostals can rejoice in the knowledge that God will triumph over all the forces of sin and evil at the end of the age. However, in this present age, one can have a foretaste of the heavenly pie. The future signs of the establishment of God's eschatological kingdom are manifested partially as God brings healing, salvation and liberation today. Frank Macchia offers a more nuanced definition of Pentecostal

38. Castelo, "Tarrying on the Lord," 53.

eschatology. "Eschatology for Pentecostals is not simply about the end times as the last chapter of a theological system. It is a living hope that affects the entire Christian life. Christ as the coming king integrates and defines Christ's saving work, Spirit baptism and healing. This is the Pentecostal understanding of the Christian Gospel, and it is eschatological through and through."[39] Significantly, Hispanic Pentecostals make use of biblical apocalyptic imagery in order to become empowered to live in this present age.

For example, the hymn *Marcha de Triunfo*[40] (March of Triumph) presents the Christian life as a military battle between the Christian army and the satanic forces. Reading the lyrics of this hymn against the backdrop of the apocalyptic battles in the book of Revelation, one cannot help but notice the similarities. For instance, the hymn alludes to the blood of the martyrs, which inevitably will be shed in the course of the battle (Rev 7:14: 12:11, 17). Moreover, in the spiritual battle of the hymn, as well as in apocalyptic passages, the saints are assisted by an army of heavenly angels. What is significant to note here is how in the Hispanic Pentecostal eschatological imagination one can envisage the struggles of life using apocalyptic imagery.

Another example of this is the hymn *Ya Se Acerca el Tiempo de Prueba* (The Time of Trial is Getting Close). Most interesting about this hymn is how a pretribulationist can sing it and not notice it goes against the grain of premillennial dispensationalism. The first stanza and the chorus of the hymn read:

Ya se acerca el tiempo de prueba	The time of trial is getting close
El Anticristo muy pronto obrará . . .	The Antichrist will soon do his work
Y después de esta vida de prueba	And after this life of trial
Cosas nuevas Jesús me dará.	Jesus will give me new things
Coro:	Chorus:
//Fiel, fiel al Señor yo seré,	//Faithful, faithful to the Lord I will be,
Y la corona de vida tendré//	and I will have the crown of life//

39. Macchia, "Pentecostal and Charismatic Theology," 282.

40. It is worth noting that this hymn became the official anthem among the youth. I still remember how our youth group went to the altar to testify together during the Sunday night service. Obviously, we had other hymns in our repertoire, but this one was by far our favorite, especially because it portrays the youth as a conquering army.

What is puzzling about the use of this hymn is that, though it teaches that the church will go through the tribulation, Hispanic Pentecostals do not seem to have a problem singing it. In a culture that preaches the pre-tribulation rapture of the church, how can we include in our hymnbooks a song that seeks to give the keys for survival during the tribulation? Aside from the obvious answer (i.e., many times people sing without fully understanding what they sing), I believe it pertains to the meaning the hymn provides for everyday living. This song makes little sense if one sees the tribulation in a fundamentalist dispensational sense, as a period of time in the future in which the church is absent. Tribulations are trials that are ongoing. Could it be that inadvertently Hispanic Pentecostals sing this hymn, in contradistinction to their adopted dispensational framework, simply because the lyrics evoke a sense of trial and suffering that is reminiscent of their present life? In many ways, a re-reading of the book of Revelation with an eye on the suffering of the church past and present would provide a much-needed corrective to popular eschatological visions in the Hispanic Pentecostal community. Similarly, the recovery of biblical and non-biblical apocalyptic imagery could serve to frame our own "apocalyptic" understanding of the present world in a way in which the eschatological vision could truly produce hope for the community of faith.

CONCLUSION

For those of us who grew up in a Pentecostal tradition, the thought of an eschatology that moves away from a premillennial dispensationalist framework is difficult to fathom. In part, this is because the eschatological end-times scenario, which posits a literalistic interpretation of the book of Revelation, is almost impossible to shake. Personally, I have often said eschatology was a theological arena I would rather avoid on account of the fact that I find it difficult to read the book of Revelation without ingrained and preconceived interpretations rushing to mind. However, having looked at the eschatological dimensions present in our funeral services, I am hopeful that a truly organic Hispanic Pentecostal eschatology is feasible.

In part, the road toward rethinking our eschatology will require recovery and rediscovery: recovery, because we need to look back at our roots and build from the intrinsic eschatological hope of our community; rediscovery, because the realization that we were working with an alien eschatological framework should lead us to seek new ones. Therefore, to the question whether Pentecostals can be premillenarians without being dispensational, I add, can Pentecostals be non-literalistic in their interpretation of the book of Revelation? As I begin to respond to this question, I am reminded of the wrongheaded effort of attempting to interpret every detail of an impressionist's painting. Instead of finding meaning in all the little details, one needs to step back and take the whole painting in view. As a painting of an impressionist artist, the broad strokes with which John penned his Apocalypse require more understanding of its symbolic meaning and the hope it evoked for its readers. Likewise, our eschatological musings should always be mindful of the hope they provide to the community of faith. Perhaps, what should be at the forefront of the interpretative task is the connection we share with the original readers: an eschatological hope in the midst of suffering.

16

Constructing an African Pentecostal Eschatology

Which Way?

J. Ayodeji Adewuya

INTRODUCTION

ALTHOUGH AN AFRICAN BY coincidence of birth and of Wesleyan-Pentecostal persuasion in faith confession, the task of writing a chapter about African Pentecostal eschatology has been a difficult one. Part of the difficulty lies with the fact that my training is primarily in the discipline of biblical studies and my knowledge of the history and growth of the Pentecostal movement is, to a great extent, limited in scope and restricted to the Nigerian scene and my personal experience in that setting. As such, my approach in this chapter is reflective. However, the greater challenge is how specifically does one define "African Pentecostalism," and, consequently, from such understanding construct an eschatological view, which is not only distinctively Pentecostal but is particularly African. When one talks of Africa, one must keep in mind that it refers to a continent of over fifty countries, each governed on its own, and many people groups (tribes), each with its own traditional beliefs and practices. However, there is a commonness that runs through the continent. The fact that comments are made on the basis of the common aspects does not mean that there are no exceptions. At the same time, comments that focus on any particular people group do not mean that the same belief or practice is not found elsewhere. This chapter draws from common grounds of beliefs and practices. What has just been said is applicable to Pentecostalism as well. Writing of Pentecostalism as a movement, Kalu rightly and succinctly states that "Pentecostalism is a movement of diverse colors."[1] This is particularly true in Africa. Hence, one must not assume that Pentecostalism in Africa is monolithic, since such an assumption is not only flawed but also simplistic.[2] Nevertheless, there are common areas to all Pentecostals, which enable one to speak of a distinct African Pentecostal spirituality that is part of its eschatological worldview.

Both as an African and as one who focuses on the writings and theology of Paul, defining my understanding of the term "eschatology" is important, not as a separate "locus" of theology, which focuses mainly on "the last things" or the "last days in isolation from the past or present. I do understand all of Christian theology to be eschatological in the sense that it is concerned with God's kingdom and the inauguration of the "new earth," which is becoming a reality in the present. Therefore there is an eschatological aspect to every facet of Christian theology. In the context of the present chapter, African Pentecostal eschatology is understood to be, and treated as an integral part of its spirituality, part of which, in turn, is informed by the African-ness of the writer. Methodologically, the chapter is reflective and proceeds by examining the basic African eschatological worldview since one cannot speak of African Pentecostal eschatology without first delineating the basic African eschatological worldview. It then moves on to discuss African Pentecostal spirituality with attention being paid to specific issues that are of particular significance among African Pentecostals.

AN AFRICAN ESCHATOLOGICAL WORLDVIEW

A comprehensive discussion of African eschatological worldview is not possible in this chapter. As such we shall briefly focus on three areas that may serve as window into the African mind in relation to the discussion at hand. These are the issues that relate to death and after life on the one hand and judgment on the other.

---

1. Kalu, *African Pentecostalism*, 4.

2. Gifford, "Complex Provenance of some Elements of African Pentecostal Theology," 62–79.

Death and After-life

Mbiti in his well-known explanation of the African concept of time argues that for Africans the future extends to a period of about six months, perhaps not more than two years at the most.[3] According to him, events outside this range lie beyond what constitutes actual time. He contends that "at most we can say that this short future is only an extension of the present." Africans, according to Mbiti, cannot "conceive the possibility that the end of the world is an ultra-historical myth which cannot be fitted into the immediate conceptualization of individual men and women."[4] He states:

> In traditional African thought, there is no concept of history moving "forward" towards a future climax, or towards an end of the world. Since the future does not exist beyond a few months, the future cannot expect to usher in a golden age, or a radically different state of affairs from what is in the Sasa and the Zamani. The notion of a messianic hope, or a final destruction of the world, has no place in traditional concept of history. African peoples have no "belief in progress," so the idea that the development of human activities and achievements move from a low to a higher degree. The people neither plan for the distant future nor "build castles in the air."[5]

Mbiti is right in that which he affirms and wrong in that which he denies. The theory that Africans are not future-orientated people is, at best, dubious. Although Africans are enthused with the possibility of a good life "below" and their eschatological view is decidedly this-worldly, they, nevertheless, have a hope for the "above" that is the future. It is to be noted that human existence beyond death is shown by different practices among traditional Africans. An example is that of many people groups burying the dead with personal belongings. In addition to the belief in continued existence beyond death, there is, on the part of some people groups, statements concerning the way life is in the hereafter. Some believe in two categories of heaven, namely, "a heaven of fresh breeze" for the good people and a "heaven of broken pots" for the bad ones.[6] This

---

3. Mbiti, *African Religions and Philosophy*, 16–17.

4. Ibid., 235.

5. Ibid., 23.

6. Parrinder, *African Traditional Religion*, 136.

leads to the discussion on the presence or lack of it of the notion of a final judgment among traditional Africans.

Judgment

Mbiti contends that although traditional Africans believe in a life after death for their ancestors, they are not aware of rewards or punishment in the afterlife. Some scholars agree with Mbiti's assertion. This position is well articulated by Steve Biko. He writes:

> We believed—and this was consistent with our views of life—that all people who died had a special place next to God. We felt that a communication with God could only be through these people. We never knew anything about hell—we do not believe that God can create people only to punish them eternally after a short period on earth ... It was the missionaries who confused our people with their religion. They ... preach a theology of the existence of hell, scaring our fathers and mothers with stories about burning in eternal flames and gnashing of teeth and grinding of bone. This cold cruel religion was strange to us but our fore-fathers [sic] were sufficiently scared of the unknown impending anger to believe that it was worth a try. Down went our cultural values![7]

However, I disagree with this view. As a Yoruba, I know that the notion of *Orun Rere* (good heaven) or *Orun Apaadi* (a heaven that is full of potsherds, something that portends burning), akin to what Parrinder argues, is well known. It is believed that good people are destined for the former and the wicked for the latter. Also interesting to note is that the death of old people is celebrated as a "going home," hence the elaborate burial festivities that follow the death of the aged.[8] With respect to final judgment as taught in Christianity, while there is no parallel in African traditional belief, most Africans would not have a problem of associating judgment with God. However, unlike in traditional theology where all judgment is in the future, Africans make room for punishment here and now. As such, ethics and morality are important.

7. Biko, *Biko*, 49.

8. See also Theo Sundermeier, who, despite agreeing with Mbiti's general assertion, allows for exceptions such as the Koko and Basa peoples of Cameroon who hold the belief that wicked and good people are destined for different places, the former for a cold place and the latter for a place full of light. See also Hammond-Tooke, *Roots of Black South Africa*, 149.

The Influence of Evangelical Theology

Asked for the reason why a young man who attended a school operated by missionaries became an ardent communist, he replied saying, "the missionaries taught us how to read but the communists gave us the materials to read." The latter part of the young man's answer highlights the influence and importance of the printed page. This is a point of great importance as one explores and investigates the issue of African Pentecostal eschatology. The early missionaries to Africa were mainly from the evangelical tradition, most of whose eschatological beliefs are based on dispensationalism. Hence, in the African context, the line between evangelical and Pentecostal "eschatologies" are not as clear as they may be in the West because on the whole Pentecostal theology in Africa remains largely oral, despite many scholarly published works on the Pentecostal movement in Africa. However as I personally reflect on the subject it seems to me that Pentecostal theology in Africa is so close to traditional evangelical theology that the former seems to be no more than "evangelical theology ice cream" often with a "baptism with the Spirit" or "speaking in tongues" veneer. In other words, the Eurocentric distinctions between the evangelical and Pentecostal streams of Christianity are basically blurred, now heightened as many non-Pentecostal churches now embrace signs and wonders as necessary for effective gospel proclamation. This is not to demean traditional evangelical theology but to underscore the need to highlight the differences between the two traditions.

AN AFRICAN PENTECOSTAL SPIRITUALITY

Although the Holy Spirit may have been marginalized in western theology,[9] it goes without saying that the presence and activities of the Holy Spirit in and through the community of believers is at the core aspect of African Pentecostal spirituality. In Africa, rediscovery of Spirit came at a point of deep crisis and turmoil in its history. Nigeria is a case in point. Pentecostal spirituality flourished at a time of socio-economic disintegration and political instability in the late 70s and early 80s. It was widely embraced because its spirituality offers the resources for dealing

9. Moltmann, *Spirit of Life*, 83, draws attention to how the Spirit is seen in Protestant theology only as a subjective principle for the appropriation of the salvation won objectively by Jesus on the cross. Pittinger, *Holy Spirit*, 11–12, sees the marginalization of the Spirit dating back to early Christianity

with despair and undertaking the structural adjustment program necessary for the continual search for greater harmony and prosperity for all. From my experience in Nigeria, "born-again" Christians, as members of the Pentecostal groups (and even evangelical fellowships and groups) are often called, are regarded as standing for moral standards higher than those prevalent in the society. Because of the transnational character of the Pentecostal spirituality[10] and the heterogeneity of Africa, questions can be raised about the propriety of speaking about *African* Pentecostal-spirituality. As I said earlier, I do not intend to give the impression that African Pentecostal spiritualities are monolithic. There is however a family resemblance between them. I recognize the transnational character or more accurately, its North American connection. But while this spirituality is seemingly peripheral in the West in general and North American life in particular, it offers the dominant conceptual framework in Africa.

Salvation

In the traditional African worldview, salvation is understood in terms of relief or help in times of trouble. Thus, salvation is expressed in acts such as healing, deliverance from evil spirits, empowerment of the individual self and success in life. As such, the traditional understanding of salvation, which is not only focused but is also primarily preoccupied with the salvation of the soul from hell, remains inadequate to meet the needs of the African world, especially if that salvation does not provide for happiness and prosperity now. Not surprisingly, the so-called "prosperity" or "health and wealth" gospel derided in the West is very much at home with African Pentecostals, for it fills a void as one attempts to develop a coherent Pentecostal eschatology in the African context. I will argue, on the one hand, that although the prosperity message was articulated in America, it intersects with the holistic vision of salvation in the primal religions of Africa. Well-being is conceived of as touching both life here and the hereafter. On the other hand, this prosperity message induces and at the same time reinforces a strand in the primal religious

---

10. See van Dijk, "From Camp to Encompassment," 142. He writes, "Pentecostalism is historically a transnational phenomenon, which in its modern forms is reproduced in its local diversity through a highly accelerated circulation of goods, ideas and people. The new charismatic type of Pentecostalism creates a moral and physical geography whose domain is one of transnational cultural inter-penetration and flow."

tradition of Africa that discounts human agency in the transformation of society. Finally, I argue that the Pentecostal-charismatic spirituality has resources to overcome this one-sidedness.

Death and After-life

Death is very important in the African worldview.[11] Although there is much disagreement among African scholars about the existence of myths about how death could removed or eventually overcome,[12] there is a consensus of opinion that, basically for the African, death is not the end of human existence. For traditional Africans, death is not viewed as mere separation from the living but merely a transition to the realm of the spirit. As such, the departed one is never separated from the family but always is present and treated with great reverence. As Mana observes, to the African death is the initiatory principle of both individual and communal enrichment of life rather than something to be viewed as a catastrophe. Death, he argues, is part of the new creation, something included in the divine plan.[13] This is an echo of Paul's sentiment in 1 Thess 4:16 where Paul describes the dead saints as being asleep. The point of the metaphor is to show the Thessalonians that in the Lord we express the hope for restoration to life of dead believers on the day of the resurrection. In the same manner as a person who is sleeping can be raised, so too the dead, as "sleeping," have the possibility of being re-created and living again. Heaven is not a distant reality that is far removed from historical experience, but the locus of harmony manifested in the experience of freedom.

An important aspect of the final judgment informing Pentecostal eschatology is that of celebration. In the New Testament, the focus of the last days is not as much on the judgment of the last days as it is on the One who is coming to do the judgment. Herein lays the significance of the emphasis of Pentecostals on Christ as the soon coming king. The theology of the Second Coming of Christ is a common denominator of faith for Pentecostals and evangelicals as well as an important as-

11. Healey and Sybertz, *Towards an African Narrative Theology*, 207.

12. See for example, Mbiti, *Introduction to African Religion*, 117, who states that "there are no myths in Africa about how death might one day be overcome or removed from the world." This viewed is untenable in the light of various African myths that point to a Savior-Redeemer figure.

13. Mana, *Christians and Churches of Africa Envisioning the Future*, 59.

pect of the parousia. What has been neglected is its celebratory nature. Growing up among evangelicals and listening to sermons on Christ's Second Coming, the presentation of Jesus as the Judge is without a doubt one-sided. The notion of final judgment is predominantly presented as a dreadful day of fear. Paul's closing words on the parousia in 1 Thess 4:18 are too often sounded as *terrify one another with these words*, rather than *comfort one another with these words*. Paul's language is actually that of a family reunion, an occasion marked by celebration, which in turn ought to elicit eager anticipation.

Spirits

In traditional African belief, spirits are ubiquitous: there is no area of the earth that does not have a spirit of its own or which cannot be inhabited by a spirit.[14] The African universe "is a spiritual universe, one in which supernatural beings play significant roles in the thought and action of the people."[15] Explaining how a traditional African could hold such a view of the universe, Baeta succinctly states, "On a worldview which assumes the effective presence of numberless spirits, and regards all life as one, with no clear distinctions between the material and the non-material, the natural and supernatural, let alone the secular and the religious, or even between man and other created beings, this could hardly be otherwise."[16]

The belief in the existence of other spiritual beings besides God is widespread. The traditional African lives in a world in which things do not happen by chance. Even when the problems are naturally caused, evil spirits are believed to set in quickly and exploit the situation to the disadvantage of the victim. The general belief is that events have causes. Therefore, when Paul speaks about wrestling with "principalities and powers" or having an "agent of Satan" in his body, he speaks in categories and idioms that are at home with African cosmological ideas. Unfortunately, as Ferdinando has rightly noted, the approach of western scholarship to issues related to "spirit beliefs" in Africa is "dominated by anti-supernaturalistic rationalism in which 'spirits have

---

14. Idowu, *African Traditional Religion*, 175.

15. Gyekye, *African Philosophical Thought*, 69.

16. Baeta, "Christianity and Healing," 19.

no place except as constructions of the human mind."[17] Experiences of demon possession are explained away as either psychological or psychiatric conditions, thus seeing them in terms of mental pathology.[18] Without hesitation Asamoa is right in castigating western missionaries for their casual and rather dismissive attitude of the effects of evil spirits among Africans societies. He writes, "It is no exaggeration to say that the church's attitude towards African beliefs has generally been one of negation, a denial of the validity of those beliefs . . . Anybody who knows the African Christian intimately will know that no amount of denial on the part of the church will expel belief in supernatural powers from the minds of the African people."[19]

Nevertheless, the African, has a deeply rooted belief in a mystical power or force in the universe. People use this power in a variety of ways—medical practice, divination, exorcism, predicting where to find lost articles, and foretelling the outcome of an undertaking. With power they employ the practice of magic, sorcery, and witchcraft. Individuals such as diviners, traditional doctors, and witches know better than other people how to employ this power, sometimes in connection with spirits. The positive use of this mystical power is cherished and plays a major role in regulating ethical relations in the community and in supplying answers to questions about the causes of good luck or misfortunes. For fear of witchcraft and formal curses, people may refrain from stealing, speaking rudely, showing disrespect where respect is expected, committing taboos such as incest, or doing harm to people who are considered to be vulnerable—like women, children, the handicapped, and strangers. This is a positive effect of mystical power in society. However, the fear and torment of these powers highlight the need for deliverance by a higher power. Issues relating to overcoming, or defeating evil powers and breaking through debilitating conditions afflicting people, as seen in the gospels and Acts, are very much at home with Pentecostals who basically see themselves as a restorationist movement. One may indeed suggest that a major difference between Pentecostals and other Christian traditions is not simply "speaking in tongues" but also the emphasis placed upon the power of the Holy Spirit in helping people overcome

17. Ferdinando, *Triumph of Christ in African Perspective*, 70.

18. So, Radin, *Primitive Religion*, 131–32, as noted by Ferdinando, *Triumph of Christ*, 71.

19. Asamoa, "Christian Church and African Heritage," 297.

the debilitating influences of evil by means of the spiritual gifts. Thus, through the demonstration of the power of the Holy Spirit, Jesus becomes a living reality, fulfilling the promise in John 14:16. In this regard, Bediako's observation about Christians in general is true of Pentecostals in particular. He writes, "In this setting of ubiquitous and mysterious powers, the Christian who has understood that Jesus Christ is a living reality can be at home, assured in faith that Jesus alone is Lord, Protector, Provider and Enabler. In the struggles of the battles of life, the Christian discovers that Jesus goes ahead, and that . . . he alone is capable of fighting and conquering, leading his people in triumph."[20]

African Pentecostal eschatology with the sense of the assured and imminent return of Christ must not shy away from but instead continue to promote an approach to evangelism that emphasizes the power of the Holy Spirit as a means of reaching out to unbelievers. This approach, on the one hand, takes demon possession seriously, and on the other hand, as we have previously said, coheres with African world-view. It is a worldview that is radically different from the one that has been "handed down" to Africans by the missionaries. The latter is well summed up by Bediako:

> Coinciding as it did with significant advances in scientific discoveries, the Enlightenment acted to direct intellectual attention away from the realm of transcendence to the empirical world that could be seen and felt, away, that is, from the intangible to the tangible. By and large, Christian theology in the West made its peace with the Enlightenment. It responded by drawing a line between the secular world and the sacred sphere, as it were, and so established a frontier between the spiritual world on the one hand, and the material world on the other, creating in effect a dichotomy between them. Many earnest Christians have been attempting by various means since then to bridge the two worlds.[21]

As Bediako further observes, it is here that Africa, and if I may add, African Pentecostalism in particular, has followed a different path culturally and intellectually from the Enlightenment heritage.[22]

---

20. Bediako, *Jesus and the Gospel in Africa*, 9.

21. Bediako, "Worship as Vital Participation," 3.

22. Ibid.

KEY ISSUES IN PENTECOSTAL ESCHATOLOGY

Although I am personally committed to the fivefold gospel paradigm (some would argue fourfold), my intention in this section is primarily to identify and focus on what I consider as key issues in Pentecostal eschatology, which may be helpful as one attempts to define and develop an eschatological framework that is both African and Pentecostal.

The Certainty of the Return of Jesus

The New Testament is very clear about the certainty of Jesus' return. First, Jesus himself unequivocally declares it in the gospels (Mark 13:24, 26; Matt 24:30). While arguments continue about the time of fulfillment, the focus is nonetheless clear: it speaks unambiguously of the Second Coming. In Mark 13:26, the word *opsontai* "will see" is in the future indicative. People shall see the Son of Man (Jesus) coming in glory. The sense of the word is not a "may be" or a "mere wish," or a kind of "pie in the sky," but is an event that will certainly occur. The present participle *erchomenon* "coming" suggests that its fulfillment will be simultaneous with that of the main verb, that is, "shall see or seeing." The certainty of one guarantees the "certainty" of the other. The certainty expressed in this passage forms the basis of its assumption as a fact in other contexts (Matt 25:31; John 14:3). Second, the return of Jesus was part of the *kerygma* of the early church. The coming again of Christ for judgment and the restoration of all things (Acts 3:20–21; 10:42; 17:31; 1 Cor 15:20–28; 1 Thess 1:10) was proclaimed with earnestness.

The Certainty of Resurrection of All (Believers and Non-believers)

Several passages in the New Testament speak about the resurrection of all (believers and unbelievers). In the interest of brevity, our focus shall be limited to two (1 Cor 15:12–19 and Acts 24:15). Paul begins with the question of resurrection in general—some of the Corinthians were saying that there is no resurrection of the dead (v. 12b). But Paul reasons that if there is no resurrection of the dead, then Christ has not been raised; and, if Christ has not been raised, three conclusions of devastating consequence for the Christian life must follow. First, his message or proclamation is in vain, that is, of no power or consequence. Second, it stands to reason that if Christ has not been raised, every preacher, teacher, and missionary in the world is—willfully or ignorantly—perpetrating a hoax, perpetuating an error, and misleading people to trust in a delusion, not simply with respect to the resurrection as a fact of history, but with regard to the gospel that depends on it. Third, without the resurrection of Christ as an historical reality, Paul tells the Corinthians, their faith is futile, and as such, they are still in their sins (v. 17). If Christ has not been raised, then every person who has trusted in Christ for the forgiveness of sins and, on the basis of faith in Christ, has been assured that his or her sins are forgiven, is in fact miserably deluded. Fourth, if there is no resurrection, there is no hope beyond the grave—those also who have fallen asleep in Christ are lost (vv. 18, 19). The rigors, sufferings, self-denials, greatest hopes, and aspirations of this life have been for nothing. What a pitiable state believers are in!

In Acts 24:15, within the context of his self-defense against Jews' accusations before Felix, Paul said: "And I have the same hope in God as these men, that there will be a resurrection of both the righteous and the wicked." Paul is here listing some characteristics of his belief and message on the basis of which he says in 24:16, "So I strive always to keep my conscience clear before God and man." Belief that there will be resurrection of "me" should have effect in my conduct of life. The main point here is that Paul's position on resurrection is very clear. All will be resurrected—each and every person will be raised; each person will have an existence beyond the grave. However, that is not all. The New Testament also teaches that life to come has direct relationship to the life we have now. Thus, Paul says, believers must keep awake and be sober in anticipation of the parousia (1 Thess 5:1–11).

The Defeat of Satan

Although Pentecostals may sometimes be accused of a "triumphalistic attitude," one cannot shy away from the fact that the basis of such attitude is the triumph of Christ on the cross. Pentecostals take the defeat of Satan seriously and are at home with several passages that mention Christ's exaltation over the powers and their subjection. For example 1 Cor 15:24ff clearly presents Christ's reign as something which is well understood as both present and dynamic. Passages such as Col 2:15 and Mark 16:15–18 feature prominently in the proclamation of the gospel and form the bedrock of Pentecostal belief in and practice of healing and deliverance. This is in addition to various texts in the synoptic gospels where Jesus performs miracles of healing and deliverance. Matthew in particular is careful to show that Jesus fulfils Isa 53:5 both in his person and ministry. The existential meaning of the ministry of Christ becomes clearer among African Pentecostals through the ministries of healing and deliverance, aspects of Christian ministry, which are considered crucial for evangelism.

PROBLEMS ON THE AFRICAN CONTINENT

Whenever one listens to the news today, one is tempted to ask the same question as Nathanael, "Can any good thing come out of Nazareth (Africa)? Africa is a continent that is ravaged by internecine wars, and continues to be economically, politically, and sad to say, religiously exploited. It continues to be devastated by famines, natural calamities, and human induced ecological disasters. Its history is that of oppression, aggression, war, revenge, and counter-revenge, homicide, and genocide. Hence the ultimate and elusive longing of Africans is justice. They long for a form of justice where the oppressed do not triumph over the victim. Corruption seems to be not only a fact of life but is accepted as the norm. In many African countries there is much uncertainty as far as a lasting security goes. The rich flee to the West while the poor are left without a choice other than to remain in the uncertain, precarious situation. The overall picture seems to be of hopelessness and helplessness. What is in store for the believer in this situation? Do the poor have any hope? Do eschatological beliefs have bearing on these matters? The question is: "Is there hope in this state of helplessness"? The answer is yes. Does eschatology provide a basis for a smiling face in that situation? Does ultimate justice, however, exist? Yes, it does, but then God shall provide this justice.

AN AFRICAN PENTECOSTAL ESCHATOLOGY: WHICH WAY?

In conclusion, we must return to the question of how to develop an eschatology that is in line with Pentecostal spirituality and draws from African spirituality. An authentic African Pentecostal eschatology must not have to make a choice between evangelical theology and the African eschatological world-view; otherwise it is doomed to failure because such a choice will lead to irrelevance. While evangelical theology is, and retains its foreignness, aspects of a purely African eschatology remain somewhat superfluous. As such the way forward in developing an authentic African Pentecostal eschatology lies in providing a thorough-going critique of both evangelical theology and African eschatological worldviews, providing a healthy balance between the "here" and the "other-worldly" aspects of the Christian life. Formulating African Pente-costal eschatologies demands seeking "a synthesis between Christian reli-gious commitment and cultural continuity."[23] It requires that the African theologian rethink Christianity within the framework of a non-Western culture without betraying or twisting the gospel. In other words we must recover the usable elements in our culture and reject the others.[24]

African Pentecostals must be liberated from the shackles of indi-vidualism that have held evangelicals and North American Pentecostals captive. The focus on personal rebirth, which has often led to the ne-glect of social rebirth, needs to be shifted. This is because it seems to me Pentecostal spirituality resonates with the African contemporary life-world and has resources on which to reflect, become more involved, and directly engage in social transformation. African Pentecostals must take seriously African worldviews of salvation, which are all embracing and not limited to catering just to the spiritual welfare of Africans. Thus, African Pentecostal eschatology must be holistic and must overcome the other-worldliness that has characterized evangelical theology.

African Pentecostal eschatologies must seek to make sense of the sufferings of the people of Africa and shun the triumphalistic attitude of its Western, particularly North American counterpart. It must maintain a healthy balance between the "already" and "not yet." In conclusion, as I said at the beginning of this chapter, I do not presume to offer more than a cursory treatment of the subject. What is offered here is important for its heuristic value rather than its comprehensiveness. It offers an oppor-tunity for further exploration.

23. Bediako, *Jesus and the Gospel*, 67.

24. Cf. Benoit, *L'actualité des Péres de Leglise*, 79 who espoused this idea in his dis-cussion of the relevance of the church Fathers for the church in the twentieth century.

17

Jesus is Victor

The Eschatology of the Blumhardts with Implications for Pentecostal Eschatologies

Frank D. Macchia

Not many in North America know much about the Blumhardts, father (Johann) and son (Christoph), though in European circles it has been widely known for decades that they played a seminal role in the revival of eschatology in modern theology. I plan to highlight my years of research into the eschatology of the Blumhardts in order to expose their important ideas to a wider audience.[1] Their implied struggle under the rubric of the kingdom of God to move from divine healing to social transformation has implications for a Pentecostal eschatology, which is open to the transformative work of the Spirit among a variety of global contexts. We will begin with the spiritual origins of the Blumhardtian message in Southern German Pietism.

THE KINGDOM OF GOD IN EARLY SOUTHERN GERMAN PIETISM

Pietism came into being in the seventeenth century in large part to augment the emphasis on orthodox confession prevalent among the Protestant churches (especially in Germany) with experiential devotion and missionary zeal. Most importantly, an essential component of this pietist revival was a reinvigorated eschatological hope. Philip

1. I discuss this topic in greater fullness in my earlier work, *Spirituality and Social Liberation*.

Jacob Spener (1635–1705), the progenitor of German Pietism, yearned for a "better time" for the church, which was tied to his hope that "the Kingdom of God will break in more and more among us."[2] In fact, there was in existence "an explosion of similar, eschatological, especially chiliastic, thoughts everywhere in early Pietism."[3] In large measure, it was this eschatological fervency that caused the kingdom of God on earth to become one of Protestant theology's major points of emphasis in the twentieth century.

The Blumhardts in the nineteenth century emphasized this fervency more than anyone else in their pietistic background, including Württemberg or the Southern German context where they lived and were active in ministry. I say this with full knowledge of the fact that early Pietism in Württemberg was especially characterized by various more or less separatist cell groups, which promoted a fervent expectation of the soon-coming kingdom of God in the parousia or Second Coming of Christ. Southern German Pietists saw the oppression caused by royal absolutism, political corruption, and moral laxity on all levels of society that characterized seventeenth- and eighteenth-century Germany as a sign that the end was near.[4]

Feeding this fervor were certain theological influences that directed attention to the eschatological framework of biblical history. There was early on, for example, the federal theology of Johann Coccejus (1603–1669), which connected the notion of the kingdom of God with a strongly covenantal theology. Campegius Vitringa (1659–1722) became a student of Coccejus' kingdom theology and insisted that one ground it on biblical exegesis rather than on philosophical speculation concerning the nature of history and its future end. He mediated these thoughts to the famous pietist biblical scholar, Albrecht Bengel (1687–1752).[5] Bengel's greatness was in his ability to synthesize various biblical insights concerning eschatology into a unified emphasis on the coming king-

---

2. Spener, *Pia Desideria*, 76.

3. Greschat, "Die 'Hoffnung besserer Zeiten' für die Kirche," 288.

4. Lehmann, *Pietismus und Weltliche Ordnung in Württemberg*, 31–32.

5. "Bengel is unthinkable without Coccejus," *Gottlob Schrenk, Gottesreich und Bund im älteren Protestantismus vornehmlich bei Johannes Coccejus*, 314, see esp. 305–18. See also, Stoeffler, *German Pietism during the Eighteenth Century*, 97; and Bauch, "Die Lehre vom Wirken des heilgen Geistes im Frühpietismus," 58.

dom, which was to have a significant impact on Württemberg Pietism for generations to come.

Bengel is not known so much for his eschatological writing as for his work on a scientific approach to discovering a reliable New Testament text, an effort that resulted in his magnum opus, the *Gnomon*.[6] This work influenced generations of exegetes and textual critics. Yet his greatest impact on Württemberg Pietism came through his eschatology, which was also the source of controversy. It would not be inaccurate to say that the book of Revelation played the same role for Bengel that Romans played for Luther.[20] Bengel's commentary on the book of Revelation (*Erklaerte Offenbahrung*, 1740) was widely read throughout Württemberg.[7] He claimed that the book of Revelation represented "things that will absolutely come to pass."[8] The most important technique to be used in interpreting this book was "the deciphering of its chronology."[9] In this, "the main points to be regarded are the facts and numbers."[10]

Bengel attempted to portray the heart of the entire Bible as a salvation-history chronology of events that is fixed and may be discovered through biblical exegesis. Through an elaborate, sometimes fantastic, system of calculation, Bengel predicted the coming of Christ for 1836, along with a number of other preceding events.[11] His larger theological vision, however, was not just historical but cosmic, as an "*oeconomia individualis et universae*." The Bible was essentially an "incomparable report on the divine economy" among all creatures and all generations, "from all times, from the beginning to the end of all things."[12] This cosmic dimension had its origin in the universalistic thrust of the kingdom vision of Coccejus and Vitringa.

A more speculative eschatology was channeled into Southern German Pietism of the eighteenth century through Bengel's most influential follower, Friedrich Christoph Oetinger (1702–1782). Oetinger was

---

6. Albrecht Bengel's original work was *Gnomon Novi Testamenti in quo ex natura verborum vi simplicitas, concinnitas, salubritas, sensuum, caelestium indicator.*

7. A remark by Gottfried Mälzer, *Johann Albrecht Bengel, Leben und Werk*, 316.

8. Bengel, *New Testament Word Studies*, 841.

9. Ibid., 832.

10. Ibid.

11. See Sauter, "Die Zahl als Schluessel zur Welt," 1–36.

12. Bengel, "Die zweite Aufgabe der heiligen Schrift," 49; See also Mälzer, *Bengel und Zinzendorf, zur Biographie und Theologie Johann Albrecht Bengels*, 328.

also deeply influenced by the mystical theology and theosophical speculations of Jakob Böhme. Oetinger found Böhme's insights into the divine
presence throughout nature as a great resource in his struggle with what
he perceived as the mechanistic view of nature, rationalism, and determinism implicit in the philosophies Leibniz and Wolff.[13] In Böhme's
writings, Oetinger found a system, which viewed God as active (*actus
purus*) and the innermost nature of God as life.[14] Contrary to materialism (which views nature as self-sufficient) and pantheism (which simply
identifies nature with God), Oetinger took from Böhme a view of God
as intimately involved in nature, moving it towards its final redemption.
Both God and nature move ever closer together as God realizes God's
self more and more through an ever-expanding realm of spiritual cor-
porality, a corporeality toward which nature is also being transformed.[15]
Though less explicitly biblical than Bengel, Oetinger still centered his
teleological vision of universal transformation in Christ, writing, "A new
power and a new movement have been unleashed in the world through
the resurrection of Christ."[16] "Conversion" became the chief term used to
describe the consummation of all things in Christ.[17]

A third figure worth mentioning at the base of the interest in eschatology in Southern German Pietism is Nikolaus Ludwig von Zinzendorf
(1700–1760). Zinzendorf's impact on Württemberg Pietism was channeled largely through the Herrnhuter. The Bruedergemeinde, called
the Herrnhuter in Europe and the Moravians or Unity of the Brethren
in the United States, was rooted in the Jednota Bratrska founded in the
fifteenth century by followers of Jan Hus. Later known as the Unitas
Fratrum, the community settled in Kunwald, east of Prague, to form
a pietistic community in which morals and conduct were emphasized
over doctrine. By 1467, they had formally seceded from Rome, and by
the seventeenth century engulfed more than half of the Protestants
of Bohemia and Moravia. The Thirty Years' War and the defeat of the
Bohemian Protestants at the Battle of White Mountain in 1620 drove
the Unitas Fratrum underground or into exile. The movement was

13. "In the past, God revealed much about His glory to Jakob Böhme," Oetinger,
Heilige Philosophie, 25; See also Oetinger, *Selbstbiographie*, 36–37, 41–44.

14. Oetinger, *Selbstbiographie*, 36–37; see also, Stoeffler, *German Pietism*, 112–13.

15. Oetinger, *Heilige Philosophie*, 27; see also, Stoeffler, *German Pietism*, 112–13.

16. Oetinger, *Heilige Philosophie*, 82.

17. Ibid., 56–58.

kept alive by the efforts of Bishop Comenius (1592–1672). Eventually, some were exiled to Poland, while others went to Germany, where they sought refuge in Saxony on the estate of an Austrian nobleman, Count Nicholaus Ludwig von Zinzendorf, who then offered himself as their mentor and leader.[18]

With a Christocentrism even more radical than that of Bengel and Oetinger, Zinzendorf made the crucified Christ the beginning and the end of his eschatology, "But what an observation this is, that my Creator has laid down his life for me! All your theology, all your theosophy, insight and knowledge will be caught up in this as the central point. . . . Nothing higher, nothing greater can be thought of."[19] The vision of the suffering Savior was central to Zinzendorf's vision of history and the transformation of all things. One is converted by being confronted with this vision of the crucified one and is encouraged to constant repentance and holiness in remembrance.[20] The goal is reconciliation with God the Creator, resulting in a relationship frequently described in familial terms (with God as Father or Husband).[21] But this communion with God the Creator never surpasses our communion with the suffering Savior, since "one knows of no other presence of the Creator than in the beauty of his sufferings."[22] Revival, piety, and mission were his eschatological accents. He thus had little sympathy for eschatological speculation as an end in itself: "It is not enough for us to call him our Creator and Husband? Is it not enough that a soul in the most perplexed and intricate circumstances, most entangled in the snares of Satan, can think in a happy hour, I am, however, created for him; I am a soul, a creature; therefore I belong to the Creator; he is my Husband; Is this not enough? Must we enter into deep mysteries of God and venture to utter mysteries with an unwashed mouth"?[23]

In the nineteenth century, one was faced with Bengel's literal reading of apocalyptic texts, Oetinger's speculative vision of cosmic trans-

---

18. Lindt Gollin, *Moravians in Two Worlds*, 1–5.

19. Zinzendorf, *Nine Public Lectures*, 39; cf. Aalen, "Theologie des Grafen von Zinzendorf," 343.

20. Zinzendorf, *Nine Lectures*, 66–67, 86.

21. Ibid., 77.

22. Ibid., 84–86; Aalen speaks appropriately of a "passion" and "bride" mysticism in Zinzendorf, "Theologie des Grafen von Zinzendorf," 340ff.

23. Zinzendorf, *Nine Lectures*, 5.

formation, and Zinzendorf's rejection of both in favor of the practical effects of eschatological hope in a Christ-centered piety and mission. These key figures naturally overlapped in their concerns but they still had distinctive emphases that influenced Southern German Pietism in different ways. This diverse kingdom of God expectation fed the rise in the nineteenth century of eschatological discussions, revivalism, cell group formation, and missionary activity and provided the spiritual atmosphere necessary for understanding the eschatological message of the Blumhardts. These developments were so intimately interrelated that it would be difficult to discuss one without including the others.

The major centers for the nurturing of these nineteenth-century developments besides the healing home of the Blumhardts at Bad Boll (near Stuttgart) were the separatist pietist village of Korntal, which cultivated an intense expectation of Christ's soon return, Stuttgart, which was a center for revivalism and revival preachers, and (not far from these southern German centers) the Swiss city of Basel, which became the home of the Basel Missionary Society, a leading center for global mission. It is fascinating when reading the works of major Pietists of Württemberg to notice how often these centers are mentioned and how intense the contacts between them were maintained. They were all united by the idea that the kingdom of God was coming to earth at the return of Christ and that the church must be revived and determined more than ever to missionize the globe in preparation for this fulfillment.[24]

The Blumhardts were directly influenced by these centers and the developments surrounding the pietist proclamation of the kingdom of God and more than any other they highlighted this message prior to the turn of the twentieth century. They would end up taking this kingdom message to another level by accenting it as the all pervasive theme of their preaching and theological reflection. They also directed it not only to piety and mission but most prominently to suffering humanity and to signs of healing possible in anticipation of the new creation. As a result, they helped to change the course of modern theology by making eschatology its all pervasive theme, a fascinating story to which we now turn.

---

24. I discuss these developments in my earlier work, *Spirituality and Social Liberation*, 21–44.

THE ESCHATOLOGY OF THE ELDER BLUMHARDT

The elder Blumhardt (Johann) (1805–1880) studied theology at the University of Tübingen, afterwards taking a pastorate at Iptingen, where he experienced poverty first hand, both in his own life and the lives of most of his parishioners. He then moved to Möttlingen as pastor of its Protestant church, a move that would prove historic, for it was there that he encountered a mentally and spiritually disturbed young woman named Gottliben Dittus and would struggle in prayer for her deliverance, a battle that would heighten and shape the eschatological direction of his message. In 1842, her relatives complained of moving objects and noises in Gottlieben's house and she herself sought relief from what she considered to be spiritual torment and anguish. In Blumhardt's words, "a mysterious and dangerous field opened up before me; I could not but commend the matter to the Lord in my solitary prayers."[25] Investigation into Gottlieben's past yielded evidence of abuse by a guardian aunt who exposed the child to occult practices and vowed to dedicate her to Satan. The aunt died before the wish could be fulfilled. Nevertheless, Gottlieben had difficulty throughout her youth with visions, hemorrhaging, and fainting spells.[26]

The further Blumhardt became involved in Gottlieben's case, the more he realized the seriousness of her condition. At one decisive moment in 1842, Gottlieben began convulsing in Blumhardt's presence. At this moment Johann became convinced that something demonic was at play. He jumped up and said forcefully, "we have seen enough of what Satan can do, now we want to see what Jesus can do." He forced her hands together and had her pray after him, "Jesus help me." The symptoms subsided temporarily, but the "battle" (*Kampf*), as it came to be called, was far from over. For more than eighteen months, Blumhardt spent hours day and night praying (and later fasting) for Gottlieben's deliverance. Meanwhile, she went into fits, bled profusely, attempted suicide, reported having visions of spirits, and spoke with numerous voices that claimed to represent departed souls. The final victory came at the close of an all-night prayer vigil in the early morning of December 28, 1843, when a voice roared through Gottlieben's sister Kathrina (who had begun manifesting similar symptoms), "Jesus is Victor" ("Jesus ist Sieger").

25. Blumhardt, *Blumhardt's Battle*, 12, see 12–16.

26. Bovet, "Zur Heilungsgeschichte der Gottlieben Dittus," 1–7; J. C. Blumhardt, *Battle,* 11–12; Zündel, *Johann Christioph Blumhardt*, 101.

Gottlieben's (and Kathrina's) symptoms permanently subsided. She was later able to marry and to become a trusted and respected member of Blumhardt's extended family at the healing center that they established in Bad Boll.[27]

Gottlieben's deliverance ignited a revival in the church, throughout the village and the surrounding areas. At a service soon after the event, Blumhardt spoke on the theme, "the right hand of the Most High can change everything." This service represented the turning point of the revival. People flooded into his church services from surrounding towns. So many people came to his home for confession and absolution that he was busy in the initial days of the revival from 7 a.m. to 11 p.m., without any significant break. Persons from all walks of life waited in his living room for a chance to be prayed for. Some returned several times. Blumhardt wrote of the visits, "they continued all day long without a break, to the point that I could no longer dwell on anything else."[28] He viewed the revival as the extension of the victory of Gottlieben's healing. In the heat of the revival he wrote: "The more battle there is, the more victory we have. Therefore, I am not about to give up. This being the case, victory is assured."[29]

The revival ground to a near halt due in part to criticism from pastors of surrounding towns and subsequent restrictions of Blumhardt's church consistory. Blumhardt became convinced that his work at Möttlingen was over. He began to seek a context for ministry, which would place him out of the public limelight and the watchful eye of church authorities. Negotiations led to the purchasing of Bad Boll near Stuttgart, a former health spa and theater. The extended family of the Blumhardt's (including Gottlieben Dittus) moved to Boll and turned it into a retreat center, where people could come for prayer and guidance for all of their needs. Johann spent a long and fruitful ministry at Boll, making many friends and corresponding with many others in part through his now famous *Blätter aus Bad Boll*.

At Boll, Johann yearned for a widespread revival, which would spread the reign of the kingdom of God throughout the world in preparation for the Christ's coming. This revival would involve an end-time outpouring of the Holy Spirit leading to repentance, healing, and dis-

27. Blumhardt, *Battle*; F. Zündel, *Blumhardt*, 128–32.

28. Blumhardt, "Möttlingen Mitteilungen," 111, 114.

29. In Zündel, *Blumhardt*, 145.

cipleship. His first impulse then was to wed the renewal of Pentecost in the church to the spread of the kingdom of God in the world. He stated, "The Spirit of Pentecost is directed towards the growth and fulfillment of the Kingdom of God." [30] His eschatology was based on this wedding of Pentecost and the kingdom. One may say that for the elder Blumhardt the Spirit was the very substance of God's kingdom and Christ was its King. The experience of Christ as Victor that Gottlieben Dittus realized in her life would become universally available through the outpouring of the Holy Spirit in the world and the coming of Christ.

In his thinking about the breaking in of the kingdom of God, Johann thus gave the theme of deliverance from suffering a centrality and a force unparalleled in his pietistic background. His uncle, G. C. Blumhardt, who was active in the Basel Mission, had written a moving book on the importance of healing among the poor and downtrodden for the experience of the kingdom of God in the world,[31] obviously influenced Johann. Moreover, Blumhardt's background in poverty, his work among the many poor and sick of Iptingen, and the battle for Gottlieben's healing convinced him that the cry "Jesus is Victor" means that the gospel must lead to deliverance from bondage and suffering.[32] For him, the ascension of Christ and the outpouring of the Spirit of Pentecost were for the purpose of helping the suffering of the earth.[33] It also meant that the phrase "thy Kingdom come" consisted of a battle for the kingdom in the world, which has a history and a future fulfillment that is divine in nature (as Karl Barth saw so well in his commentary on Blumhardt's slogan, "Jesus is Victor").[34] The centrality of liberation from suffering for Blumhardt's understanding of the gospel is revealed in the way he interpreted certain concepts drawn from scripture. The outpouring of the Spirit was compared with the Exodus of Israel from bondage.[35] The "blessed" of the Sermon on the Mount should be translated "delivered."[36]

30. Blumhardt, *Ausgewählte Schriften in drei Baende*, 140; see also *Blätter aus Bad Boll*, Gesammelte Werke, Reihe II, Bd. 4 (1876) 335–36.

31. Blumhardt, *Lazarus, Der Kranke, Sterbende, und Auferweckte, Fuer Leidende und Freunde der Leidenden*.

32. Blumhardt, *Ausgewählte Schriften*, Bd. 2, 33.

33. Ibid., Bd. 2, 25.

34. See Barth, *Church Dogmatics* 4/3, 168–71.

35. Blumhardt, *Blätter*, 347.

36. Blumhardt, *Blätter*, Bd. 3 (1876), 9.

The cry "redeem us" can be translated "set us free."[37] His was not a speculative eschatology but a vibrant hope for liberation and new creation, which affected people's lives in the here and now and pervaded every aspect of his message.

This eschatology was rooted in a classic understanding of the atonement as *Christus Victor*.[38] According to Blumhardt, the victory of Christ on the cross was to conquer the full power of darkness, including both sin and sickness.[39] This victory and liberation were also prefigured in Jesus' charismatic ministry before his death. Jesus' miracles of healing arose out of his empathy with the sick and poor. Blumhardt wrote: "We should always contemplate this limitlessly deep empathy of Jesus for the miserable; then in this lay the power and beauty of his miracles."[40] This hope of deliverance was then rooted in Christ's death and resurrection and was made available through the inauguration of the kingdom of God at Pentecost. Blumhardt yearned from this theological context for the final outpouring of the Spirit in the latter days, which would spread the kingdom of God throughout the earth and prepare the world for Christ's coming.

Healing was at the heart of the coming victory. Blumhardt viewed healing as part of an overall revival of spiritual gifts, particularly those of a miraculous nature. The outpouring of the Spirit of Pentecost was inseparably connected with a revival of spiritual gifts.[41] The gifts represent direct help from God as personal.[42] Hence, the absence of the miraculous gifts from the church is a sign of our distance from the Spirit of Pentecost and from the victory of the kingdom of God.[43] The absence of the gifts was caused by disbelief and disobedience in response to God's personal self-disclosure as near to help.[44] Without healing, everything Jesus said would have been a boring sermon.[45] Blumhardt had a long-standing belief that preaching and healing were "one and the same," since both

---

37. Blumhardt, Ausgewählte Schriften, 43.

38. See Aulen, *Christus Victor*.

39. Blumhardt, *Blätter*, Bd. 2 (1874), 251–52.

40. Ibid., Bd. 2 (1874), 218.

41. Blumhardt, *Ausgewählte Schriften*, Bd. 3, 24.

42. Ibid., Bd. 1, 47; Bd. 3, 287, 291.

43. Ibid., Bd. 1, 47; Bd. 3, 48.

44. Ibid., Bd. 1, 10–11; Bd. 3, 193–94.

45. Blumhardt, *Blätter*, Bd. 2 (1875), 18.

proclaim the gospel of the kingdom.[46] The major issue for Blumhardt, however, was not wonderment at miracles but rather the power of God to transform a life through the breaking in of the kingdom of God. A mere wonder at miracles "is not conversion by a long shot. One does not yet feel the nearness of God with this wonderment that flits away quite easily into nothing."[47]

Contrary to what is generally thought of the elder Blumhardt, there are traces here and there in his writings of a connection between deliverance from poverty or social oppression and divine healing. The phrase, "the meek shall inherit the earth," meant for Blumhardt that the lowly, who are given "hardly a space to live" by the powerful, will one day possess their share, once the kingdom of God effects change on the earth. The powerful will be forced to yield their privileged position and humble themselves.[48] He mentioned abused women and children as among the oppressed.[49] Elsewhere he stated that Jesus died so that we could live "without torturing and oppressing one another for the sake of a better living."[50] The request in the Lord's Prayer for those in need, "give us this day our daily bread," should be "give bread to the poor," if one has enough. "Bread" was viewed as the sustenance of life, for "God has a good ear for those who hunger and thirst and are miserable in any way if it relates to aspects of life in the external realm."[51]

The larger context of the Spirit's work in bringing in the kingdom was a vision of vast cosmic change through Christ and the Spirit. The Oetingerian "transformation" and "restoration" of all things became for Blumhardt the "liberation" of all things from suffering. Blumhardt also referred to universal salvation as the "revival" of all people and of the entire creation![52] This connection of salvation with revival converges with other themes, since revival is referred to as a passion for liberation,[53] and as an awareness of the will of God manifested in the breaking in of the

46. Ibid., Bd. 2 (1875), 185.

47. Ibid., Bd. 2 (1875), 11.

48. Ibid., Bd. 1 (1873), 131–32.

49. Ibid., Bd. 1 (1873), 131–41.

50. Ibid., Bd. 4 (1877), 118.

51. Blumhardt, *Ausgewählte Schriften*, Bd. 1, 283–85, 288–89.

52. Ibid., Bd. 3, 214–15, 265.

53. Blumhardt, *Blätter,* Bd. 2, (1874), 256.

kingdom.[54] A dominant description of universal salvation is that of Jesus as Victor over all the forces of darkness and the curse of sin.[55] Once evil is eradicated and conquered, all of creation can be reconciled to God[56] and God will be "all in all."[57]

Blumhardt differed in several important ways from the later fundamentalist eschatological fervor that emerged in early twentieth-century America and shaped the early evangelical ethos.[58] Johann separated himself from the apocalyptic view of history as gradually becoming worse until total destruction occurs at or before the parousia. Against the "downward slope" apocalyptic view of history, Blumhardt preferred hope for a renewal of creation through the work of the Spirit.[59] In a way more analogous to the early Pentecostal latter rain eschatology, Blumhardt placed the latter-day outpouring and renewal of the Spirit at the heart of eschatological fulfillment and harbored a bright hope for the future. The Lord will not destroy the creation but renew it before he returns; otherwise his return will not be the fulfillment of his present work in creation.[60] The Lord is not simply a "destroyer" (*Kaputmacher*) but one who blesses and renews.[61] Since the creation must glorify God, he cannot destroy it without disgracing himself.[62] All of this did not mean for Johann that the Lord's coming would not usher in a genuinely new creation, only that what the parousia brings will in some sense represent the fulfillment of the present renewal of all things. Hence, what God and we do to realize the presence of the kingdom will contribute something to the new creation at the final end.

Blumhardt also disagreed with the apocalyptic view of history as something foreordained and fixed, without room for a responsible,

---

54. Ibid., Bd. 3, (1875), 279.

55. Blumhardt, *Ausgewählte Schriften*, Bd. 1, 300–301; Bd. 2, 103, 316–17; Bd. 3, 297–98; Blumhardt, *Blätter*, Bd. 1 (1873), 78; Bd. 3 (1876), 151; Bd. 4 (1876), 343.

56. Blumhardt, *Blätter*, Bd. 4 (1876), 221.

57. Blumhardt, *Ausgewählte Schriften*, Bd. 1, 267.

58. See Sandeen, *Roots of Fundamentalism*.

59. Blumhardt, *Ausgewählte Schriften* Bd. 2, 236; Blumhardt, *Blätter*, Bd. 4 (1877), 71.

60. Blumhardt, *Ausgewählte Schriften*, Bd. 2, 218–19.

61. Blumhardt, *Blätter*, Bd. 1 (1873), 200.

62. Ibid., Bd. 1 (1873), 84–85.

prophetic shaping of history in dialogue with God.[63] Johann rejected any attempt to calculate the end, since it hindered zeal and work for the coming kingdom of God.[64] He rejected predictions because they are fatalistic, while true prophecy is always conditional to a degree on what we do![65] In answer to the question about the coming "tribulation," he noted that such speculation only removes proper attention from our responsibility for the present moment. He gave the same kind of answer to a question concerning the millennium.[66]

Moreover, he interpreted Matt 24 (a key passage for apocalyptic speculation on end-time events) as referring to the destruction of Jerusalem in 70 CE.[67] Trying to interpret the book of Revelation for signs of the future is fruitless, since the future cannot be known.[68] He even scoffed at the many attempts in the past to match scriptures with coming events. The future end has been fulfilled one hundred times over![69] He rejected a chiliastic interpretation of Rev 20 on the grounds that it is made with dubious, romantic interpretations of various Old Testament prophecies of the coming kingdom on earth and that the outpouring of the Spirit in history *before* the parousia is all that is needed as a preparation for eternity.[70]

Blumhardt's eschatology affected spirituality by promoting both encouragement to work for the dawning of the kingdom and a willingness to wait on God to bring the fulfillment. Blumhardt's eschatology was thus felt in this accent on "hurrying and waiting,"[71] a feature of his eschatology that attracted the early Karl Barth.[72] Basic to this tension is the conviction that salvation is by grace and begins in the divine initiative. The petition of the Lord's Prayer, "yours is the Kingdom," means

---

63. A modern expression of a similar sentiment can be found in Buber's, "Prophecy, Apocalyptic, and Historical Hour," 172–87.

64. Blumhardt, *Ausgewählte Schriften*, Bd. 1, 147ff.

65. Ibid., Bd. 3, 16.

66. Blumhardt, *Blätter*, Bd. 1 (1873), 109–11; Bd. 4 (1877), 80.

67. Ibid., Bd. 1 (1874), 22.

68. Ibid., Bd. 3 (1875), 414; (1876), 94.

69. Ibid., Bd. 4 (1876), 403.

70. Ibid., Bd. 4 (1877), 102.

71. Ibid., Bd. 1, (1874), 140–47.

72. Barth, *Action in Waiting*.

that God must bring the kingdom, or things on earth will never change.[73] Johann stated unequivocally, "salvation is entirely of the Lord."[74] Yet, there are many references in Johann's works to the essential role that we play in being channels of the breaking in of the kingdom before the final outpouring. He wrote that the Lord will give us the kingdom but "we must win it."[75] Every simple cry to Christ which says "come" "sets the wheel in greater motion."[76] The Lord knocks on the door (Rev 3:20) wanting to return. He will only do so if we open the door and welcome him in.[77] Johann shared the assumption common among his contemporaries that the gospel must be preached throughout the world before the end comes.[78] Faith, hope, and self-sacrifice are also important aspects of our part in the breaking in of the kingdom.[79] He wrote, "if all suffered, fought, and believed, must not the Kingdom of God take an entirely new direction?"[80] Though Johann placed weight on the role of demonic forces in binding humanity, he wrote that these forces only bind us to the degree that we allow them to.[81] We play an essential role in the victory of Christ over evil through wrestling and fighting with importunity and impatience.[82] He stated, "We are not God's slaves or puppets," because God lets us "do something with him before he accomplishes it."[83]

One of the most important ways to participate in the breaking in of the kingdom of God for the elder Blumhardt is through "groaning" for universal redemption (Rom 8). This groaning is not a cry of helplessness but a positive yearning for the liberation of all things from suffering and

---

73. Blumhardt, *Ausgewählte Schriften*, Bd. 2, 321.

74. Blumhardt, *Blätter*, Bd. 2, (1874), 373.

75. Blumhardt, *Ausgewählte Schriften*, Bd. 2, 277.

76. Ibid., Bd. 2, 272.

77. Ibid., 309–10; Blumhardt, *Blätter*, Bd. 1 (1874), 28–29.

78. Blumhardt, *Blätter*, Bd. 4 (1876–77), 404, 412, 413.

79. Blumhardt, *Ausgewählte Schriften*, Bd. 3, 195; Blumhardt, *Blätter*, Bd. 1 (1873), 151.

80. Blumhardt, *Ausgewählte Schriften*, Bd. 3, 199–200.

81. Blumhardt, *Blätter*, Bd. 2 (1874), 262.

82. Blumhardt, *Ausgewählte Schriften*, Bd. 3, 80; Blumhardt, *Blätter*, Bd. 1 (1874), 60; Bd. 2 (1874), 415; Bd. 3 (1876), 124; Bd. 4 (1876), 277.

83. Blumhardt, *Blätter*, Bd. 2 (1875), 38.

bondage.[84] The more we groan, the nearer Christ is to help.[85] Without our yearning, "the Kingdom can not proceed toward its goal."[86] It arises out of our sense of the lack of the kingdom in creation.[87] Christ's suffering on the cross was a yearning and groaning for the redemption of the world.[88] We share the heart of Christ when we groan with him for the suffering creation.[89] In this we also share the pain and yearning resident in the very heart of God.[90] Those who groan with the suffering creation from a situation of unavoidable suffering can suffer constructively.[91] Others may selflessly identify with those who suffer and groan in a kind of priestly representation of them and the creation before God.[92] In fact, the heart of all true prayer should consist in some way of this priestly groaning with the whole creation. He stated in this context: "Your prayer should always be an expression of the entire groaning creation, so that you stand as its representative. This is the right way to pray, and in this way you pray as a child of the Kingdom."[93] The younger Blumhardt inherited the restlessness that this yearning for the kingdom inspired.

THE ESCHATOLOGY OF THE YOUNGER BLUMHARDT

Johann's son, Christoph, grew up in the midst of this burning hope for the latter-day outpouring of the Spirit and the coming of Christ that would soon follow. He studied theology at Tübingen as had his father before him. He had difficulty with his studies, however, particularly in combining what was taught to him by his father with what he was learning at the university. He remarked concerning his professors at Tübingen, "If they would but encounter the One about whom they were pontificating, their faces would turn as white as a sheet!" Near the end of his studies,

---

84. Blumhardt, *Ausgewählte Schriften*, Bd. 1, 23–24; Bd. 3, 82–90.

85. Ibid., Bd. 3, 242, 93.

86. Ibid., Bd. 1, 273.

87. Blumhardt, *Blätter*, Bd. 2 (1874), 230–31.

88. Ibid., Bd. 1 (1874), 100.

89. Ibid., Bd. 1 (1873), 200.

90. Blumhardt, *Ausgewählte Schriften*, Bd. 1, 277; Blumhardt, *Blätter*, Bd. 2 (1874), 316–17.

91. Blumhardt, *Blätter*, Bd. 2 (1874), 237–39.

92. Ibid., Bd. 2 (1874), 251, 278; *Ausgewählte Schriften*, Bd. 2, 266.

93. Blumhardt, *Blätter*, Bd. 1 (1876), 52.

he expressed doubts concerning whether the study of theology was right for him.[94]

Despite continuous doubts about his calling to the pastorate, Christoph was ordained in 1866 in Göppingen and was placed shortly afterward in his first Vikariat in Spoeck near Bruchsal. After brief ministries there and a few other locations, Christoph's father requested that he come to Boll to assist in the work there. At first, Christoph had the lowly tasks of giving devotions to the servants and cleaning. More than a year later (at age twenty-seven) Christoph began to assist his father in secretarial work. Soon, however, he became his father's right hand, taking charge of most of the written correspondence and representing him on certain occasions.[95] During this stage of Christoph's ministry (1880) his father gave him the charge of leadership at Bad Boll shortly before his death with the words, "I bless you for victory."[96] From there, Christoph was to begin developing a career and a message, which would shake the pietistic world and further alter the course of modern theology.

Throughout most of the 1880s, Christoph's ministry at Boll was rather uneventful. After 1888, we find him becoming increasingly frustrated with his role as pastor at Boll. He was tired of the people who came to Boll to find a refuge from the world or to seek answers to needs, which Christoph viewed as self-centered.[97] He became weary with the stress and strain of pastoring at Boll[98] and came to the conclusion that "pastoral care is no longer adequate."[99] He did not oppose pastoral work in principle. He could not bear his own work as pastor and the way that the people at Boll were overly dependent on him.[100] He concluded that he could not continue as pastor at Boll. In 1894, he took off his pastoral gown and ceased to identify himself as a pastor.[101]

Throughout this same time period, Christoph became increasingly restless in his anticipation of a new direction, a new revelation that would be as significant for him as the "battle" was for his father. In his

94. Jäckh, *Blumhardt Vater und Sohn und Ihre Botschaft*, 110–18.

95. Ibid.

96. Reden, *Ansprachen, Predigten, Reden, Briefe*, 37.

97. Blumhardt, *Ansprachen*, Vol. 2: 1890–1860, 67.

98. Ibid., 41.

99. Ibid., 97.

100. Ibid., 115.

101. Ibid., 35–37.

anticipation of a new revelation, he began to characterize his father's message as a stage that prepared the way for that which is to come. In this, he had the tendency to simplify somewhat his father's message as overly spiritual and not this-worldly enough. He came to see the "fight" in his father's day as spiritual and hidden, beyond human help.[102] But now it is time to take the fight out into the world. The father's fight was in the invisible realm but is now over: "Today the fight that occurred then is finished. As for us, we are pulled into the world wherein we cry "Jesus is Victor."[103] Christoph clarified by stating, "Today the fight is worldwide. It goes down the streets, everywhere the poor, abused, and miserable are."[104]

His dissatisfaction with the self-centered piety at Boll made him yearn to go out among the strangers "who obey God's will with great desire."[105] His loyalty must be to the kingdom of God and not primarily to Boll or to the churches.[106] If the great outpouring of the Spirit would not be ushered in simply by Bad Boll and other pietistic missions or churches, it would need to be inaugurated with the aid of worldly movements. Christoph was about to take his "turn to the world" in his understanding of the worldwide fulfillment of the kingdom of God. This turn at the beginning of the twentieth century would cause him to become a passionate socialist and even to enter politics for a brief time. The father's yearning for the outpouring of the Spirit in the latter days especially with gifts of healing was transformed so as to include secular movements for global liberation and social renewal.

There were a few theological developments in Christoph's thinking that led up to his "turn" to the world. First, Christoph came to stress the incarnation as the place where the kingdom begins to penetrate the concrete realities of human life. The emphasis of the elder Blumhardt on Pentecost shifted in the younger Blumhardt to an accent on the incarnation of the presence of God through the person of Jesus Christ. He stated: "We still have religion, we still have Christian morals. But that Jesus has come in the flesh, that our God is here, that has often disap-

---

102. Ibid., 35–37.

103. Ibid., 40; see also Vol. 1, 82.

104. Blumhardt, *Ansprachen,* Vol. 2: 1890–1860, 84.

105. Ibid., 38.

106. Ibid., 67.

peared from us."[107] God is everywhere in the universe like a dammed-up stream ready to burst in upon us, even where this is not supernaturally apparent.[108] For the elder Blumhardt, the work of the kingdom was not to begin on a universal scale until the return of the Spirit of Pentecost. The younger Blumhardt, however, was already assured of the presence of God for universal liberation, not just as the presence of Pentecost, but as the outcome of the incarnation.

The incarnation of God in Christ became for Christoph an ongoing reality in history mediated to us through Christ's resurrection. He wrote, "We must feel the incarnation, take on new flesh through his. The love of God penetrates our flesh, removing sin. The resurrection is now; what separates us from God must die."[109] As did his father, Christoph still hoped for the future transformation of all things through the Spirit. But unlike his father, Christoph laid fundamental stress on the incarnation as the inauguration of God's kingdom in the world and as the guarantee that God is present to bring the growth of the kingdom further. For the elder Blumhardt, the Holy Spirit was the *Spirit* of Christ. For the younger Blumhardt, the Spirit was the Spirit of *Christ*.

This emphasis on "Christ" was not so much on his divinity but on his humanity as the recipient in his flesh of the divine presence and the beginning of the in-working of God in all flesh. Christoph wrote early in his pastorate, "We need something in our flesh and blood that means 'God' and is stronger than the world."[110] The in-working of God's presence must be realized in the corporeal realm in order for the identity of Jesus as the point of union between God and creation to be meaningful. This is the background for his statement that the life of God must be represented bodily, "otherwise Jesus is not Jesus."[111] There is an early tendency here for Christoph to interpret salvation as an Oetingerian kind of divinization of creation, implied in the remark, "Two actions must come together if the Kingdom of God is to be with us: something of God must become visible and, as a result, something divine must be formed around this on the earth—this is the Kingdom of God."[112]

107. Blumhardt, *Ansprachen,* Vol. 1, 123.

108. Ibid., 126.

109. Blumhardt, *Ansprachen,* Vol. 2, 101–2.

110. Blumhardt, *Ansprachen,* Vol. 1, 92.

111. Blumhardt, *Ansprachen,* Vol. 2, 53.

112. Blumhardt, *Ansprachen,* Vol. 1, 234.

The accent of Christoph on the incarnation brought with it a seminal stress on "progress," i.e., the progress of the life of God in Jesus Christ throughout history. He wrote bluntly, "the things of God are developing on the earth."[113] He elaborated on this later by writing that the life of Jesus is on earth and is progressing "more and more." To be faithful, Christoph felt that he "must stand at the place from where it proceeds."[114] The challenge is for us "to be people of progress for the Kingdom of God" because "that which is divine progresses."[115] In this way we fulfill our nature as people created by God: "Humankind is made for progress. For God's sake we must change. That which is purely animalistic must leave us. We come from God."[116] With this we find a budding interest in history "from God outward,"[117] as we seek to "grasp the times of Jesus Christ."[118] This emphasis on progress and history is not the Hegelian dialectical development of the divine spirit. This Hegelian vision meant for Christoph that "everything is of God, even if the devil does it."[119] Progress according to Christoph meant that God is present and active to help us in our suffering and distress.[120] If the crisis in-breaking of the kingdom of God through healing was the accent of the elder Blumhardt, the development of the kingdom in the world in secular contexts became the emphasis of his son.

Though Christoph's accent on the progress of the kingdom through the ongoing incarnation process posited an intimate relation between God and creation, Christoph was still careful to maintain something of his father's stress on the freedom of God. Christoph said early in his pastorate, "the mixing of God and world must cease."[121] Even shortly before the time when Christoph would defend a closer relation between the development of the kingdom and social progress, he was able to praise his father for never mixing the human with the divine.[122] This is because the

113. Blumhardt, *Ansprachen,* Vol. 1, 187.

114. Blumhardt, *Ansprachen,* Vol. 2, 90.

115. Ibid., 21.

116. Blumhardt, *Ansprachen,* Vol. 2, 51.

117. Blumhardt, *Ansprachen,* Vol. 1, 103.

118. Blumhardt, *Ansprachen,* Vol. 2, 62.

119. Blumhardt, *Ansprachen,* Vol. 1, 343.

120. Ibid.

121. Ibid., 61.

122. Blumhardt, *Ansprachen,* Vol. 2, 98–99.

kingdom develops not only within but also removed from the world.[123] The life of God is "a life from above not from humanity."[124]

Although Christoph began in the earlier years to accent the progress of the kingdom more than his father did, we find in Christoph's thought a tension similar to that of his father between the present and future realizations of the kingdom. Christoph claimed early on that we will not be blessed until all peoples are blessed. Hence, we are blessed today in hope.[125] The grace of God has not yet arrived as a visible reality on earth.[126] God's dwelling among us is something for which Christoph can say he still hopes.[127] Yet, as we have noted, he placed considerable stress on the presence of God in the ongoing incarnation of Christ in creation and in history. Thus Christoph regarded as "pessimistic" a faith that resists the darkness of the present moment only with hope for a future world. He also regarded such a faith as darkness.[128] In regards to the final resurrection, Christoph said, "whatever is yet future must be present or it is nothing!"[129] He even spoke of the parousia as having in some sense already begun as a reality that can be experienced.[130] I agree with H. Gollwitzer that for Christoph the incarnation is a dynamic force in history, beginning with the historical person of Jesus and culminating in the parousia.[131] For Christoph, the parousia can be experienced through the incarnate presence of God in Christ and the ministry of the Spirit before the end of the age.

Christoph's incarnational emphasis was gradually augmented by an accent on the cross for defining the direction of Christ's incarnate presence. "Die that Jesus might live" became the slogan for this new "spirituality of the cross."[132] With this stress on the cross in Blumhardt's spirituality came a new emphasis on humility and self-resignation: ". . . be poor and miserable, step back, give up your role, and He will

123. Blumhardt, *Ansprachen*, Vol. 1, 63.

124. Blumhardt, *Ansprachen*, Vol. 2, 127.

125. Blumhardt, *Ansprachen*, Vol. 1, 90.

126. Blumhardt, *Ansprachen*, Vol. 2, 56.

127. Ibid., 63.

128. Ibid., 87.

129. Ibid., 90.

130. Ibid., 112; see also 144 and Vol. 2, 47.

131. Gollwitzer, "Christoph Blumhardt neu sichtbar," 259f.

132. Blumhardt, *Ansprachen*, Vol. 1, 181–84.

appear."[133] Included was God's judgment on all of our church forms and piety.[134] This judgment implied in the cross also rested on our religious and cultural identities, on all that separates us as people from each other. Christoph noted that the Pietists were asking when the anti-Christ is coming without knowing that he comes whenever one does not deny the self. The Catholic grinds his teeth because something Catholic must die, and the Protestant grinds his teeth because something Protestant must die. "Something must die from us again and again until the entire person has died in Christ."[135] The "flesh" must die, not that which God has created, but that which we set up from our won identity, which is contrary to the kingdom of God.[136] Christoph referred to his dying process as being "smashed" so that the truth can be manifested through us as it was through Christ. We should ask God to demolish us to preserve the truth: "The truth is greater than I. Jesus went this route. The truth smashed him."[137]

Self-sacrifice leads to service in the image of the cross. Christoph wrote that salvation is not only by Christ's blood but by our blood too. Salvation is "by our blood through Christ's blood," blood being a symbol of self-sacrifice.[138] Mimicking Jesus in "silent self-sacrifice" is better than any miracle.[139] Christoph did not realize that he was involved in a subtle theological shift in focus from Jesus as a dynamic force in history for healing to Jesus as a symbol for our participation in the progress of the kingdom. Christ's redemption is now by "our blood through his."

Though Christoph's social thinking would not play a dominant role in his message until his "turn" to social involvement in 1900, the discussion thus far has shown that the roots of his thinking were with him from the beginning. A few examples of this early shift in the direction of an accent on the social dimension of the kingdom's affect on the world would be helpful. The elder Blumhardt's "groaning" for the suffering creation became for Christoph a groaning for oppressed farmers.[140] The "sin

133. Ibid., 184.

134. Ibid., 105, 112, 186; Vol. 2, 3–4, 6, 106, 126.

135. Blumhardt, *Ansprachen,* Vol. 1, Vol. 2, 30.

136. Ibid., 30–31.

137. Ibid., 5.

138. Ibid., 9–10.

139. Ibid., 105.

140. Ibid., 16.

against the body" was no longer demonic oppression or sickness but the terrible conditions of the factories.[141] The evil manifest in creation was not shown just in its alienation from its Creator but in poisoned and dying trees.[142] The elder Blumhardt's hesitancy to condemn riches (or willingness to accept the attainment of such through divine blessings) was changed in Christoph's condemnation of riches as part of the spirit of Antichrist.[143] In 1904, Christoph wrote there was then no comfort for those suffering under the sins of society. If the serpent's head is really to be crushed, it is in the context of human society.[144] Christoph's social consciousness was budding prior to his political years.

Christoph became intensely interested in political events during the year 1898. This was the year in which the Kaiser gave his "prison speech" in Oeynhausen. The Kaiser declared that every person who hindered the orderly labor of workers or who went on strike would be punished with a prison sentence. A protest rally against this declaration took place in June of 1899. Pastor Blumhardt was there to express his sympathy with the workers. He called the Kaiser's declaration a "travesty of justice." Blumhardt was also present in October of the same year at a meeting of the Marxist Social Democratic Party in Göppingen in which he expressed the same sympathies. The press announced "Pastor Blumhardt's confession of Social Democracy" immediately following this meeting. The Pietist press sharply criticized him.

Yet, the younger Blumhardt stood head and shoulders above his pietist colleagues who largely ignored social issues in their yearning for the kingdom of God as well as his more socially-minded colleagues preoccupied with the German "social question," who had attempted to interpret the kingdom of God either in service to German nationalism or within a dualistic two kingdoms doctrine, which alienated social involvement from the teachings of Jesus.[145] Christoph's kingdom theology may be termed "dialectical" in the sense that the kingdom of God is revealed through the witness of social analogues to the kingdom without

---

141. Ibid., 39.

142. Ibid., 113.

143. Ibid., 61, 124.

144. Blumhardt, *Ansprachen*, Vol. 2, 43.

145. See my *Spirituality and Social Liberation*, 128–33. See also, Meier, *Christoph Blumhardt*, 46–47, 60; Sauter, *Theologie des Reiches Gottes beim älteren und jüngeren Blumhardt*, 136; Bentley, *Between Marx and Christ*.

assuming either equivalence between the two or dualism. This was the aspect of Christoph's kingdom theology that the young Karl Barth as well as the early Paul Tillich found so enlightening.[146]

During Christoph's years of political involvement (1899–1906) he expanded his kingdom vision to include socialists, atheists, as well as Buddhists and Muslims, all who implicitly yearned for the kingdom of God on earth. His eschatology was broad, involving a vision of the work of the kingdom of God that was fundamentally inclusive of the church but also transcending the church, allowing for the implicit gifts of secular movements for justice and mercy to be involved as well. The kingdom was always centered on Christ for Christoph, even if it was the Christ hidden within movements that implicitly bore witness to the justice and mercy of the cross.[147] Not only Karl Barth, Eduard Thurneysen, and Paul Tillich were seminally influenced by this direction of the younger Blumhardt's eschatology, but also and especially Dietrich Bonhoeffer, Harvey Cox, and Jürgen Moltmann.[148] It was not the adequacy of Christ for the kingdom that Christoph questioned but the adequacy of the institutional church.

After the political years, Christoph seemed less optimistic than before that the socialists will usher in a great move of the Spirit, which would be analogous to that for which his father had long hoped, largely because of the infighting that he witnessed within party politics. Christoph did, however, engage in more mature thinking after 1907 about the relation between the development of the kingdom and the flow of history than he had done previously. He described the transcendence of the kingdom and our relation to it in the following picturesque way, "The Kingdom develops from within itself. We walk alongside it and are happy to recognize this great movement of the reign of God, which does not tolerate

146. See, Barth, "Past and Future," 35–45, and Tillich, *History of Christian Thought from Its Judaic and Hellenistic Origins to Existentialism*, 531–33.

147. *Christus in der Welt*, 22. See also Macchia, *Spirituality and Social Liberation*, 122–47, and also my, "Secular and the Religious under the Shadow of the Cross," 59–77.

148. Thurneysen wrote a book on Christoph Blumhardt and introduced the young Barth to his thought. See, Thurneysen, *Christoph Blumhardt*. On Barth's long-term positive and significant but also somewhat ambivalent regard for the Blumhardts see Collins Winn, *'Jesus is Victor.'* See also Harvey Cox's comment that his classic, *Secular City*, was written with Gerhard Sauter's dissertation on the Blumhardts in mind, *Religion in the Secular City*, 22. Moltmann also gives Christoph Blumhardt the same seminal significance to his own eschatology, see Moltmann, *Church in the Power of the Spirit*, 282f.

any party, at least one that believes it alone has the 'right' faith."[149] Yet, the kingdom is not to be wholly separate from the realm of the natural either.[150] In 1910, Christoph wrote to L. Ragaz that "a movement of the Spirit of Christ proceeds through the times," presenting us with a kernel of truth that will push us ahead into that which is new.[151] In another context he wrote that the future breaks into the present at a point of "harmony" of the latter with the former.[152] This implies responsibility on our part to harmonize our efforts with the coming kingdom of God. In this way, the entire "surface development of peoples" gets "pulled up into" the realm of the kingdom, creating new avenues of growth not present before.[153] Such a perspective is not far removed from the *kairos* event depicted in Paul Tillich's classic work, *The Socialist Decision*.[154] The young Barth also caught the dialectical significance of the younger Blumhardt's eschatology and praised the way in which it avoided both dualistic separatism from the world and a simple identification of the kingdom with social movements or ideologies.[155]

CONCLUDING REFLECTION

The Blumhardts played a major role in the rediscovery of eschatology in modern theology. Barth, Tillich, and Bonhoeffer, not to mention Cox and Moltmann, were seminally influenced by the kingdom preaching of the Blumhardts. European Pentecostal groups have also claimed a heritage in the Blumhardts. These are the relevant issues emerging from the eschatology of the Blumhardts, especially for Pentecostalism.

First, the kingdom of God for the Blumhardts was not a *place* that can be occupied. It was the dynamic and liberating reign of God in the world, accomplishing God's redemptive plan. *Eschatological hope was God centered.* There was a Christological focus but also a robust pneumatological substance to their eschatology. The kingdom was revealed in the Christ who took on flesh and identified with the sinner and the

---

149. Blumhardt, *Ansprachen*, Vol. 3, 70.

150. Ibid., 124.

151. Ibid., 61.

152. Ibid., 91.

153. Blumhardt, *Christus in der Welt*, 233.

154. Tillich, *Socialist Decision*.

155. Barth, "Past and Future."

downtrodden all the way to the cross. The kingdom was revealed in the victory of the resurrection and the presence of the Spirit in the world. The kingdom was revealed in Christ's final triumph at his coming, in fact, the triumph of the Triune God. The elder Blumhardt stressed the identification of God's reign with the victory of Christ in the experience of healing, especially as made possible by the work of the Spirit among those who believe. The younger Blumhardt laid greater weight on the incarnation of Christ in the flesh and on the victory of the cross as the place where Christ descended most deeply into the throws of human suffering and is available as hidden within secular movements for liberation. But whether the stress was on the Spirit as the bearer of Christ's victory to those of faith or on Christ as the one who conquers and continues to conquer in the realm of flesh more generally, the Blumhardts made God's liberating work in the world the location in which eschatology was to be discerned.

Second, our previous point means that the Blumhardts envisioned an eschatology that gave God the decisive and even all-encompassing role to play without diminishing human freedom and responsibility. *In other words, hope in the Spirit was empowering.* "Jesus is Victor" was not a banner under which a sleeping church can rest secure but rather a battle cry by which the people of God must yearn and pray, work and fight, for the teleological move of the kingdom of God in the world. Of course, the church must be humble and discerning as well as dialogical, especially with those who suffer the most and have the most at stake in the hope for the liberation that the kingdom of God brings to the world. This humility is part of the church's patience. But the church's humble discernment and dialogue must serve the larger purpose of its struggle for the reign of God in the world. The spirituality implied by the passionate hope for the kingdom of God in the world was one of "hurrying and waiting," or of active waiting and a patient action.

Third, both Blumhardts believed that eschatology was principally about fresh hope for the renewal of life rather than a curiosity about end-time events. *Eschatological hope was sanctifying in the broadest sense of that term, not confined to personal morals but also extending to social justice and even cosmic transformation.* They had little interest in eschatological speculation but a great deal of interest in where to locate the places where hope is needed to overcome despair. Though the younger Blumhardt made this fight more explicitly secular than did the elder

Blumhardt, they both yearned and struggled in their own way in hope for the forces of renewal in the world. Ultimately, there can be no separation between the elder Blumhardt's passion for personal repentance and healing and the younger Blumhardt's struggle for the liberation of oppressed peoples caught in the grip of poverty and despair. The victory of Jesus and the outpouring of the Spirit in the world must relate to both for they are both inseparably connected in life.

Fourth, our previous point means that the Blumhardts exercised a significant role in liberating eschatology from the confines of narrow piety towards a broad vision of the work of the kingdom of God in the world. *Eschatological hope was diverse and global, open to a variety of struggles, heritages, and tongues.* Eschatology was not an escape from the world by an inner circle of the privileged elect but rather an all-pervasive force for renewal in the world. The gospel is all about life and the renewal of creation on a global scale. The elder Blumhardt maintained the indispensable role of the church at the cutting edge of the breaking in of the kingdom of God in the world, though he also recognized that the institutional church had fallen short of its calling. He thus implied a role of those outside of the church who yearned for the healing effects of the kingdom. The younger Blumhardt applied the kingdom of God theology far more critically towards the church and was more unqualified in his acceptance of nonbelievers at the cutting edge of the kingdom of God. But I agree with those who say that Christoph was against the church in order to be for it. In the end, both Blumhardts struggled with a similar kingdom vision. They only differed in the precise role of the church and how confidently to expand the boundaries of the kingdom's victory beyond the church's walls.

Hebrews 11:1 notes that faith has principally to do with hope for things not seen, things that are not yet fully within our grasp. May the Blumhardts encourage us in our struggle by God's grace to know the unknowable, to grasp the ungraspable, or to speak that which is beyond words. Only then can we know the liberation of the kingdom of God on earth in its deepest sense. Only then can we truly say, "Jesus is Victor."

Bibliography

Aalen, Live. "Die Theologie des Grafen von Zinzendorf: Ein Beitrag zur Dogmengeschichte des Protestatismus." In *Zur Neueren Pietismusforschung,* edited by M. Greschat, 319–53. Darmstadt: Wissenschaftliche Buchgesellschaft, 1955.

Achtemeier, Paul J., et al. *Introducing the New Testament: Its Literature and Theology.* Grand Rapids: Eerdmans, 2001.

Alexander, Kimberly E. *Pentecostal Healing: Models in Theology and Practice.* JPTSup 29. Dorset, England: Deo, 2006.

Alexander, Patrick H. "Scofield Reference Bible." In *DPCM,* 771–72.

Alexander, Paul. *Peace to War: Shifting Allegiances in the Assemblies of God.* Telford, PA: Cascadia, 2009.

Almirudis, Hiram. *Comentario Sobre la Declaración de Fe de la Iglesia de Dios.* San Antonio: Hiram Almirudis, 1997.

———. "A Commentary on the Church of God Declaration of Faith for Latin American Churches." D. Min. thesis, San Francisco Presbyterian Theological Seminary, 1981.

Althouse, Peter. "In Appreciation of Jürgen Moltmann: A Discussion of His Transformational Eschatology." *Pneuma* 28.1 (2006) 21–32.

———. "Left Behind—Fact or Fiction: Ecumenical Dilemmas of the Fundamentalist Millenarian Tensions within Pentecostalism." *Journal of Pentecostal Theology* 13 (2005) 187–207.

———. *Spirit of the Last Days: Pentecostal Eschatology in Conversation with Jürgen Moltmann.* JPTSup 25. London: T. & T. Clark, 2003.

———. "Towards a Pentecostal Ecclesiology: Participation in the Missional Life of the Triune God." *JPT* 18 (2009) 230–45.

Altizer, Thomas J. "Modern Thought and Apocalypticism." In *EA* 3:325–59. New York: Continuum, 1998.

Anderson, Allan. "The Contribution of David Yonggi Cho to a Contextual Theology in Korea." *JPT* 12 (2005) 85–105.

Anderson, C. Colt. "A Catholic and Ecumenical Response to the Left Behind Series." *JPT* 13 (2005) 209–30.

Anderson, H. George, J. Francis Stafford, and Joseph Burgess, editors. *The One Mediator, Mary, and the Saints.* Lutherans and Catholics in Dialogue 8. Minneapolis: Augsburg, 1992.

Anderson, Robert Mapes. *Vision of the Disinherited.* Oxford: Oxford University Press, 1979.

Andreas. "Catena." In *Catena in Epistolas Catholicas,* edited by J. A. Cramer. Oxford: Clarendon, 1840.

Anglican Roman Catholic International Commission. "Mary: Grace and Hope in Christ." http://www.prounione.urbe.it/dia-int/arcic/doc/e_arcic_mary.html.

Apostolic Constitution on the Doctrine and Practice of Indulgences http://www.vatican
.va/holy_father/paul_vi/apost_constitutions/documents/hf_p-vi_apc_19670101_
indulgentiarum-doctrina_en.html.

Aquinas, Thomas. *Summa Theologica*. 5 vols. Translated by Fathers of the English
Dominican Province. Allen, TX: Christian Classics, 1948.

Arrington, F. L. "Dispensationalism." In *DPCM*, 247–48.

———. "Dispensationalism." In *NIDPCM*, 584–86.

Asamoa, E. A. "The Christian Church and African Heritage." *IRM* (1955) 292–301.

Aulen, Gustaf. *Christus Victor: An Historical Study of the Three Main Types of the Idea of
Atonement*. 1931. Reprinted, Eugene, OR: Wipf and Stock, 2003.

Aune, D. E., *Revelation 17–22*. WBC 52. Nashville: Nelson, 1998.

Avanzini, John. *The Wealth of the World: The Proven Wealth Transfer System*. Tulsa:
Harrison House, 1989.

Avila, Yiye. *El Anticristo*. Miami: Carisma, 1994.

Barnes, Robin B. "Images of Hope and Despair: Western Apocalypticism: ca 1500–1800."
In *EA* 2:143–84.

Barrett, C. K. *The First Epistle to the Corinthians*. BNTC. Peabody, MA: Hendrickson,
1968.

Baeck, Leo. *The Essence of Judaism*. New York: Schocken, 1961.

Baer, Richard A. "Quaker Silence, Catholic Liturgy, and Pentecostal Glossolalia—Some
Functional Similarities." In *Perspectives on the New Pentecostalism*, edited by Russell
P. Spittler, 150–64. Grand Rapids: Baker, 1976.

Bagchi, David. "Luther's *Nintey-five Theses* and the Contemporary Criticism of Indul-
gences." In *Promissory Notes on the Treasury of Merits: Indulgences in Late Medieval
Europe*, edited by R. N. Swanson, 331–56. Brill's Companions to the Christian
Tradition 5. Leiden: Brill, 2006.

Ball, Sunshine. *Daniel y el Apocalipsis*. Miami: Vida, 2000.

Bamberger, Bernard J. *The Search for Jewish Theology*. New York: Behrman House, 1978.

Barth, Karl. *Action in Waiting*. Rifton, NY: Plough, 1998.

———. *CD* 4/1. Edited and Translated by. T. F. Torrence and G. W. Bromily. Edinburgh:
T. & T. Clark, 1961.

———. *CD* 4/3. Edited and Translated by T. F. Torrence and G. W. Bromily. Edinburgh:
T. & T. Clark, 1961.

———. *The Epistle to the Romans*. 6th ed. Translated by Edwyn C. Hoskyns. London:
Oxford University Press, 1968.

———. "Past and Future: Friedrich Naumann and Christoph Blumhardt." *The Beginnings
of Dialectic Theology*. Vol. 1. Edited by J. A. Robinson and Translated by K. R. Crim.
Richmond: John Knox, 1968.

Bartleman, Frank. *Another Wave Rolls In!* Edited by John G. Myers. Northridge, CA:
Voice, 1970.

Basham, Don. "Forum: CGM and New Wine." *New Wine Magazine* (December 1976)
31.

Bauch, Harmann. "Die Lehre vom Wirken des Heilgen Geistes im Frühpietismus."
Theologische Forschung 55, 1–153. Hamburg: Reich, 1974.

Bauckham, Richard. *The Climax of Prophecy*. Edinburgh: T. & T. Clark, 1993.

———. "Early Jewish Visions of Hell." *JTS* 41 (1990) 354–62.

———. "Jesus and the Wild Animals (Mark 1:13): A Christological Image for an
Ecological Age." In *Jesus of Nazareth: Essays on the Historical Jesus and the New*

Testament Christology, edited by Joel B. Green and Max Turner, 3–21. Grand Rapids: Eerdmans, 1994.

———. *Jude, 2 Peter*. WBC 50. Waco: Word, 1983.

Baxter, Ern. "The Earth is the Lord's." *New Wine Magazine* (January 1985) 24–30.

———. "'Every Knee Shall Bow.'" *New Wine Magazine* (December 1986) 18–22.

———. "King of Glory." *New Wine Magazine* (April 1982) 28–32.

———. "Perspective for a Decade: Discipling the Nations." *New Wine Magazine* (February 1981) 4–8.

———. "Thy Kingdom Come." The National Men's Shepherding Conference (September 1975), Holy Spirit Research Center, Oral Roberts University, transcript, 15.

———. *Thy Kingdom Come*. Ft. Lauderdale: CGM, 1977.

Baxter, Ern, and Bob Mumford. Transcript of Elder's Meeting, 16 November 1975, private holding.

Beasley-Murray, G. R., *Revelation*. NCB. Grand Rapids: Eerdmans, 1981.

Bede. "On 2 Peter." In *Patrologia Latina*. Vol. 90. Edited by J. P. Migne. Paris: Migne, 1857–1886.

Bediako, Kwame. *Jesus and the Gospel in Africa*. Maryknoll, NY: Orbis, 2004.

———. "Worship as Vital Participation: Some Personal Reflections on Ministry in the African Church." *JACT* 8 (December 2005) 3–7.

Bengel, J. A. *New Testament Word Studies*. Vol. 2. Translated by C. T. Lewis and M. R. Vincent. Grand Rapids: Kregel, 1971.

Benoit, André. *L'actualité des Pères de Leglise*. Neuchâtel: Editions Delachaux et Niestlé, 1961.

Bentley, James. *Between Marx and Christ*. New York: Schocken, 1982.

Bergmann, Sigurd. *Creation Set Free: The Spirit as Liberator of Nature*. Sacra Doctrina: Christian Theology for a Postmodern Age, 4. Translated by Douglas Stott. Grand Rapids: Eerdmans, 2005.

Berry, Wendell. *What Are People For?* New York: North Point, 1990.

Berryman, Phillip. *Religion in the Megacity: Catholic and Protestant Portraits from Latin America*. Marynoll, NY: Orbis, 1996.

Bertone, John A. *"The Law of the Spirit": Experience of the Spirit and Displacement of the Law in Romans 8:1–16*. Studies in Biblical Literature 86. New York: Lang, 2005.

———. "The Function of the Spirit in the Dialectic between God's Soteriological Plan Enacted but not yet Culminated: Romans 8.1–27." *JPT* 15 (1999) 75–97.

———. "The Experience of Glossolalia and the Spirit's Empathy: Romans 8:26 Revisted." *Pneuma* 25 (2003) 54–65.

Best, Ernest. *The First and Second Epistles to the Thessalonians*. BNTC. London: Adam and Charles Black, 1977.

Biko, Steve. *Steve Biko: I Write What I Like: A Selection of His Writings*. Edited by A. Stubbs. Johannesburg: Picador Africa, 2004.

Bilateral Working Group of the German National Bishops' Conference and the Church Leadership of the United Evangelical Lutheran Church of Germany. *Communio Sanctorum: The Church as the Communion of Saints*. Collegeville, MN: Liturgical Press, 2004.

Birch, Bruce C. and Larry L. Rasmussen. *Bible and Ethics in the Christian Life*. Revised and Expanded. Minneapolis: Augsburg, 1989.

Black, Edwin. *War against the Weak: Eugenics and America's Campaign to Create a Master Race*. New York: Four Walls Eight Windows, 2003.

Blaising, Craig and D. L. Block. *Progressive Dispensationalism.* Wheaton, IL: Bridge Point, 1993.

Blattner, John. "A Living Prophecy: Report on the Conference." *New Covenant* (October 1977) 4–9.

Blumhardt, Christoph. *Reden, Ansprachen, Predigten, Reden, Briefe: 1865–1917.* Bd. 1–3, hrsg. J. Harder. Neukirchen-Vlyun: Neukirchener, 1978.

———. *Christus in der Welt.* Zurich: Zwingli, 1958.

Blumhardt, Christoph and G. C. Lazarus. *Der Kranke, Sterbende, und Auferweckte, Fuer Leidende und Freunde der Leidenden.* Basel: Schneider, 1827.

Blumhardt, Johann. C. *Ausgewählte Schriften in drei Baende,* Bd. 1–3, edited by B. Otto. Zurich: Goetthelf, 1947–50.

———. *Blätter aus Bad Boll.* Gesammelte Werke, Reihe II. Göttingen: Vandenhoeck & Ruprecht, 1968–1970.

———. *Blumhardt's Battle.* Translated by F. S. Boshold. New York: Lowe, 1970.

———. *Der Kampf in Möttlingen,* hrsg. G. Schaefer. Göttingen: Vandenhoeck & Ruprecht, 1979.

Bobrinskoy, Boris. *The Compassion of the Father.* Translated by Anthony P. Gythiel. Crestwood, NY: Saint Vladamir's Seminary Press, 2003.

Boesak, Allan. "The Eye of the Needle." *IRM* 72 (January 1983) 7–10.

Bolaji Idowu, E. *African Traditional Religion: A Definition.* Maryknoll, NY: Orbis, 1973.

Bornkamm, Gunther. "μυστήριον μυέω." In *TDNT* 4:802–28.

Bouma-Prediger, Steven. *For the Beauty of the Earth: A Christian Vision for Creation Care.* Grand Rapids: Baker Academic, 2001.

———. *The Greening of Theology: The Ecological Models of Rosemary Radford Ruether, Joseph Sittler, and Jürgen Moltmann.* Atlanta: Scholars, 1995.

Bouteneff, Peter, and Dagmar Heller. *Interpreting Together.* Geneva: World Council of Churches, 2001.

Bovet, T. "Zur Heilungsgeschichte der Gottlieben Dittus." In *Der Kampf in Möttlingen,* hrsg. G. Schaefer. Göttingen: Vandenhoeck & Ruprecht 1979.

Bovon, François. *Luke 1: A Commentary on the Gospel of Luke 1:1—9:50.* Translated by Christine M. Thomas. Hermeneia. Minneapolis: Fortress, 2002.

Boyer, Paul. "The Growth of Fundamentalist Apocalyptic in the United States." In *EA* 3:140–78.

Braun, Herbert. *Jesus.* Stuttgart: Kreuz, 1969. English translation: *Jesus of Nazareth: The Man and His Time.* Translated by Everett R. Kalin. Philadelphia: Fortress, 1979.

Britton, Bill. *Apprehended of God.* Springfield, MO: n.p., n.d.

———. *Benjamin.* Springfield, MO: B. Britton, n.d.

———. *Beyond Jordan.* Springfield, MO: B. Britton, n.d.

———. *Changed By the Son.* Springfield, MO: n.p.,n.d.

———. *The Cleansing of the Temple.* Springfield, MO: n.p., n.d.

———. *Climb the Highest Hill.* Springfield, MO: n.p.,n.d.

———. *A Closer Look at the Rapture.* Springfield, MO: The Church Action, n.d.

———. *Divine Breakthrough Into the Unlimited.* Springfield, MO: n.p., n.d.

———. *A Double Portion of the Holy Ghost and Power.* Springfield, MO: n.p., n.d.

———. *Eagle Saints Arise!* Springfield, MO: B. Britton, 1980.

———. *From the Known to the Unknown.* Springfield, MO: n.p., n.d.

———. *God's Sabbath: The Coming Age of Miracles.* Springfield, MO: n.p., n.d.

———. *God's Two Armies.* Springfield, MO: n.p., n.d.

————. *Hebrews: The Book of Better Things.* Springfield, MO: B. Britton, 1977.

————. *His Unlimited Glory.* Springfield, MO: n.p., n.d.

————. *Jesus: The Pattern Son.* Springfield, MO: B. Britton, 1966.

————. *Light Out of Shadows.* Springfield, MO: The Church Action, 1970.

————. *Noah's Ark.* Springfield, MO: B. Britton, n.d.

————. *Not as a Servant.* Springfield, MO: n.p., n.d.

————. *Oil on the Beard.* Springfield, MO: B. Britton, n.d.

————. *One New Man.* Springfield, MO: B. Britton, n.d.

————. *One Shall Be Taken.* Springfield, MO: n.p., n.d.

————. *Only in His Likeness.* Springfield, MO: n.p., n.d.

————. *Peter's Shadow.* Springfield, MO: n.p., n.d.

————. *Points to Consider.* Springfield, MO: B. Britton, n.d.

————. *Prophet on Wheels.* Shippensburg, PA: Destiny Image Publishers, 1987.

————. *Purple Hearts and Silver Stars.* Springfield, MO: n.p., n.d.

————. *Reach for the Stars.* Springfield, MO: B. Britton, 1970.

————. *Sectarianism in the "Move of God."* Springfield, MO: n.p., n.d.

————. "Shepherds, Submission, and Trans-local Authority." Springfield, MO: n.p., n.d.

————. *Songs for Eagle Saints.* Springfield, MO: n.p., n.d.

Brouwer, Steve, Paul Gifford, and Susan D. Rose. "The Prosperity Gospel in Africa: Expecting Miracles." *Christian Century* 10 (July 2007) 20–24.

Brown, Peter. *The Cult of the Saints: Its Rise and Function in Latin Christianity.* Chicago: University of Chicago Press, 1982.

Brown, Raymond, et al. *Mary in the New Testament.* New York: Paulist, 2001.

Bruce, Frederick F. *The Epistle of Paul to the Romans: An Introduction and Commentary.* Grand Rapids: Eerdmans, 1963.

————. *The Epistles to the Colossians, to Philemon, and to the Ephesians.* NICNT. Grand Rapids: Eerdmans, 1984.

Brueggemann, Walter. *The Psalms and the Life of Faith.* Edited by Patrick D. Miller. Minneapolis: Fortress, 1995.

Bruinius, Harry. *Better for All the World: The Secret History of Forced Sterilization and America's Quest for Racial Purity.* New York: Knopf, 2006.

Buber, Martin. "Prophecy, Apocalyptic, and Historical Hour." In *On the Bible, Eighteen Studies,* edited by N. N. Glatzer, 172–87. New York: Schocken, 1982.

Bulgakov, Sergius. *The Bride of the Lamb.* Translated by Boris Jakim. Grand Rapids: Eerdmans, 2002.

————. *The Comforter.* Translated by Boris Jakim. Grand Rapid: Eerdmans, 2004.

Bundy, David. "Visions of Sanctification: Themes of Orthodoxy in the Methodist, Holiness, and Pentecostal Traditions." *WTJ* 39 (2004) 104–36.

Bruns, J. E., "The Contrasted Women of Apoc 12 and 17." *CBQ* 26 (1964) 459–63.

Busch, Eberhard. *The Great Passion: An Introduction to Karl Barth's Theology.* Translated by Geoffrey W. Bromiley. Edited and Annotated by Darrell L. Guder and Judith J Guder. Grand Rapids: Eerdmans, 2004.

Byassee, Jason. "Be Happy: The Health and Wealth Gospel." *Christian Century* 12 (July 2005) 20–23.

Cain, Paul and Mike Bickle. *An Interview with Paul Cain.* VHS Videorecording. Grandview, MO: Grace Ministries, 1990.

————. *The Prophetic History of Metro Vineyard Fellowship: Updated 1991.* 7 Cassette Tapes. Grandview, MO: Metro Vineyard Fellowship, 1990.

Cain, Paul, and R. T. Kendall. *The Word and the Spirit*. Eastbourne, Sussex: Kingsway, 1996.

Caird, G. B., *The Revelation of Saint John*. New York: Harper & Row, 1966.

Calderón, Wilfredo, *Daniel: Un Mensaje Profético*. Miami: Gospel, 2001.

———. *Doctrina Bíblica y Vida Cristiana*. Cleveland: Editorial Evangélica, 1994.

———. *El Apocalipsis: Un Mensaje Escatológico*. Miami: Gospel, 2003.

———, ed. *El Maestro Pentecostés: Manual Para Maestros de Adultos y Jóvenes* 43.10. Cleveland: Editorial Evangélica, 1992.

Canfield, J. M. *The Incredible Scofield and His Book*. Vallecito: Ross House, 1988.

Cantalamessa, Raniero. *Come, Creator Spirit: Meditations on the "Veni Creator."* Translated by Denis and Marlene Barrett. Collegeville, MN: Liturgical, 2003.

Capps, Charles. *Authority in Three Worlds*. Tulsa: Harrison House, 1982

———. *The Tongue: A Creative Force*. Tulsa: Harrison House, 1976.

———. *When Jesus Prays Through You: Release the Infinite Power of Heaven in Your Life*. Tulsa: Harrison House, 1994.

Carson, D. A. *Showing the Spirit: A Theological Exposition of 1 Corinthians 12–14*. Grand Rapids: Baker, 1987.

Carter, Grayson. *Anglican Evangelicals: Protestant Secessions from the Via Media, c. 1800–1850*. Oxford Theological Monographs. Oxford: Oxford University Press, 2001.

Cassidy, Richard J. *Jesus, Politics, and Society: A Study of Luke's Gospel*. Maryknoll: Orbis, 1978.

Castelo, Daniel. *The Apathetic God: Exploring the Contemporary Relevance of Divine Impassibility*. Milton Keynes: Paternoster, 2009.

———. "Tarrying on the Lord: Affections, Virtues, and Theological Ethics in Pentecostal Perspective." *JPT* 13 (2004) 31–56.

Catechism of the Catholic Church http://www.usccb.org/catechism/text/.

Chan, Simon. "The Language Games of Glossolalia, or Making Sense of the 'Initial Evidence.'" In *Pentecostalism in Context: Essays in Honor of William W. Menzies*. JPTsup 11, edited by Wonsuk Ma and Robert P. Menzies. Sheffield: Sheffield Academic, 1997.

———. *Pentecostal Theology and the Christian Spiritual Tradition*. JPTSup 21. Sheffield: Sheffield Academic, 2000.

———. "Evidential Glossolalia and the Doctrine of Subsequence." *AJPS* 2 (1999) 195–211.

Chappell, Paul G. "The Divine Healing Movement in America." PhD diss., Drew University, 1983.

Charlesworth, James H., editor. *The Messiah—Developments in Earliest Judaism and Chris-tianity*. Minneapolis: Fortress, 1987–1992.

Chafer, Lewis Sperry. *Major Bible Themes*. Revised by John F. Walvoord. Grand Rapids: Zondervan, 1974.

Charette, Blaine. "'Tongues as of Fire': Judgment as a Function of Glossolalia in Luke's Thought." *JPT* 13 (2005) 173–86.

Cheung, P. W. "The Mystery of Revelation 17:5 & 7: A Typological Entrance." *Jian Dao* 18 (2003) 1–19.

Chilton, Bruce. "Resurrection of the Body in Early Judaism and Early Christianity: Doctrine, Community, and Self-Definition." *CBQ* 68 (Jan 2006) 157–60.

Cho, Youngmo. *Spirit and Kingdom in the Writings of Luke and Paul*. Milton Keynes: Paternoster, 2005.

Cleary, Edward L. "Evangelicals and Competition in Guatemala." In *Conflict and Competition: The Latin American Church in a Changing Environment,* edited by Edward L. Cleary and Hannah Stewart-Gambino, 167–95. Boulder, Colorado: Lynne Rienner, 1992. Online: http://www.domcentral.org/library/cleary_books/conflict/conflict09.htm (Accessed November 24, 2008).

———. "Shopping Around: Questions About Latin American Conversions." *IBMR* 28 (April 2004) 50–53.

Cohn, Norman. *The Pursuit of the Millennium: Revolutionary Millenarians and Mystical Anarchists of the Middle Ages.* New York: Oxford University Press, 1970.

Coleman, Simon. *The Globalization of Charismatic Christianity: Spreading the Gospel of Prosperity.* Cambridge: Cambridge University Press, 2000.

———. "Conservative Protestantism and the Word Order: The Faith Movement in the United States and Sweden." *Sociology of Religion* 54 (1993) 353–73.

Collins, John J. *The Apocalyptic Imagination.* New York: Crossroad, 1984.

Collins, John J., Bernard McGinn, and Stephen J. Stein. General Introduction. *EA* 3: ix–xiii.

Collins Winn, Christian T. *"Jesus is Victor": The Significance of the Blumhardts for the Theology of Karl Barth.* Princeton Theological Monograph Series 93. Eugene, OR: Pickwick, 2009.

Conzelmann, Hans. *1 Corinthians.* Translated by James W. Leitch. Hermeneia. Philadelphia: Fortress, 1975.

Copeland, Gloria. *God's Will is Prosperity.* Tulsa: Harrison House, 1978.

Copeland, Kenneth. *The Laws of Prosperity.* Ft. Worth: Kenneth Copeland, 1974.

Cortéz, Eliseo López. *Pentecostalismo y Milenarismo: La Iglesia Apostólica de la Fe en Cristo Jesús.* Iztapalapa: Universidad Autónoma Metropolitana, 1990.

Costas, Orlando E. *The Integrity of Mission: The Inner Life and Outreach of the Church.* San Francisco: Harper & Row, 1979.

Coulter, Dale M. "Pentecostal Visions of the End: Eschatology, Ecclesiology, and the Fascination of the *Left Behind* Series." *JPT* 14 (2005) 81–98.

Crutchfield, L. V. *The Origins of Dispensationalism: The Darby Factor.* New York: University Press of America, 1992.

Cruz, Samuel. "A Rereading of Latino(a) Pentecostalism." In *New Horizons in Hispanic/Latino(a) Theology,* edited by Benjamín Valentín, 201–16. Cleveland: Pilgrim, 2003.

Cullman, Oscar. *Christ and Time: The Primitive Christian Conception of Time and History.* Translated by Floyd V. Filson. Philadelphia: Westminster, 1962.

———. "The Son of Man in First-Century Judaism." *NTS* 38 (1992) 446–52.

Dake's Annotated Reference Bible. Lawrenceville: Dake, 1963.

Dallen, James. *The Reconciling Community: The Rite of Penance.* Collegeville: Liturgical, 1992.

Daniels, David D. "'Gotta Moan Sometime': A Sonic Exploration of Earwitnesses to Early Pentecostal Sound in North America." *Pneuma* 30 (2008) 5–32.

Danker, Frederick W., ed. *A Greek-English Lexicon of the New Testament and Other Early Christian Literature.* 3rd edition based on the 6th rev. ed. of Walter Bauer's *Griechisch-deutsches Worterbuch zu den Schriften des Neuen Testaments und der übrigen urchristlichen Literatur.* Chicago: University of Chicago Press, 2000.

Darby, J. N. *The Collected Writings of J. N. Darby.* 34 vols. Edited by William Kelly. Sunbury, PA: Believers Bookshelf, 1971.

Darwin, Charles. *The Origin of the Species with Introductions and Notes.* The Harvard Classics, 11. Edited by Charles W. Eliot. New York: Collier, 1909.

Davies, W. D. *Paul and Rabbinic Judaism—Some Rabbinic Elements in Pauline Theology.* London: SPCK, 1955

Dayton, Donald W. *Theological Roots of Pentecostalism.* Peabody, MA: Hendrickson, 1987.

"Declaration of Faith." The Official Website of the Church of God (Cleveland, TN), Online: http://churchofgod.org/index.php?page=declaration-of faith&phpMyAd min=EyPnWE74if52AvqTJ13%2COH6xVv1 (accessed February 12, 2009).

De Jonge, Marinus. *Jewish Eschatology, Early Christian Christology and the Testaments of the Twelve Patriarch.* New York: Brill, 1991.

———. "The Use of the Word 'Anointed' in the Time of Jesus." *Novum Testamentum* 8 (1966) 132–48.

———. "The Role of Intermediaries in God's Final Intervention in the Future According to the Qumran Scrolls." In *Studies on the Jewish Background of the New Testament,* edited by O. Mitchel, et al., 44–63. Assen: Van Gorcum, 1969.

Deissmann, Adolf. *Light from the Ancient East: The New Testament Illustrated by Recently Discovered Texts of the Graeco-Roman World.* 1927. Reprinted, Peabody, MA: Hendrickson, 1996.

De Jonge, Marinus, and Van Der Woude. "11Q Melchizedek and the New Testament." *NTS* 12 (1965-1966) 301–26.

De Petrella, Lidia Susana Vaccaro. "The Tension Between Evangelism and Social Action in the Pentecostal Movement." *IRM* 75 (1986) 36–38.

Delgado, Manuela Cantón. "Lo Sagrado y lo Político Entre los Pentecostales Guatemaltecos: Vivencia y Significación." *Gazeta de Antropología* 9 (1992). Online: http://www.ugr.es/~pwlac/G09_14Manuela_Canton_Delgado.html (Accessed December 12, 2008).

Dempster, Murray W. "Christian Social Concern in Pentecostal Perspective: Reformulating Pentecostal Eschatology." *JPT* 2 (1993) 51–64.

———. "The Church's Moral Witness: A Study of Glossolalia in Luke's Theology of Acts." *Paraclete* 23 (Winter 1989) 1–7.

———. "Evangelism, Social Concern and the Kingdom of God." In *Called and Empowered: Global Mission in Pentecostal Perspective,* edited by Murray W. Dempster, et al., 22–43. Peabody, MA: Hendrickson, 1991.

———. "Pentecostal Social Concern and the Biblical Mandate of Social Justice." *Pneuma* 9 (Fall 1987) 129–53.

———. "Presidential Address: Christian Social Concern in Pentecostal Perspective." Presented at the Twenty First Annual Meeting of the Society for Pentecostal Studies, Southeastern College, Lakeland, FL, November 1991.

———. "Soundings in the Moral Implications of Glossolalia." Presented at the Thirteenth Annual Meeting of the Society for Pentecostal Studies, Cleveland, TN, 1983.

———. "The Structure of a Christian Ethic Informed by Pentecostal Experience: Soundings in the Moral Significance of Glossolalia." In *The Spirit and Spirituality: Essays in Honour of Russell P. Spittler.* JPTsup 24, edited by Wonsuk Ma and Robert P. Menzies, 108–40. London: T. & T. Clark, 2004.

———. "A Theology of the Kingdom: A Pentecostal Contribution." In *Mission as Transformation: A Theology of the Whole Gospel,* edited by Vinay Samuel and Chris Sugden, 45–75. Oxford: Regnum, 1999.

Dempster, Murray W., ed. "Church Mission and Social Concern: The Changing Global Face of Classical Pentecostalism." *Transformation* 11 (January/March 1994) 1–33.

Descartes, René. *Discourse on Method.* Translated by Donald A. Cress, 1637. Indianapolis, IN: Hackett, 1998.

Devlin, Christopher, ed. *The Sermons and Devotional Writings of Gerard Manley Hopkins.* Oxford: Oxford University Press, 1959.

"Discipleship: Forum in Ft Lauderdale," *New Wine Magazine* (March 1976) Insert.

Dolan, Jay. *The American Catholic Experience.* New York: Doubleday, 1985.

Duffield, Guy P., et al. *Foundations of Pentecostal Theology.* Los Angeles: L.I.F.E. Bible College, 1983.

Duffy, Eamon. *The Stripping of the Altars: Traditional Religion in England, 1400–1580.* New Haven: Yale University Press, 1999.

Dunn, James D. G. *The Theology of Paul the Apostle.* Grand Rapids: Eerdmans, 1998.

———. *Beginning from Jerusalem.* Christianity in the Making. Vol. 2. Grand Rapids: Eerdmans, 2009.

———. *Romans.* WBC. 38a–38b. Dallas: Word, 1988.

Eade, Alfred Thompson. *Panorama de la Biblia: Curso de* Estudios. Vol. 1. *"El plan de los Siglos."* El Paso: Casa Bautista de Publicaciones, 1975.

———. *"La Segunda Venida de Cristo"* (The Second Coming of Christ) vol. 4, *"El Libro de Apocalipsis"* (The Book of Revelation). El Paso: Casa Bautista de Publicaciones 1976.

Ehlert, Arnold D. *A Bibliographic History of Dispensationalism.* Grand Rapids: Baker, 1965.

Eire, Carlos M. N., *From Madrid to Purgatory: The Art and Craft of Dying in Sixteenth-Century Spain.* Cambridge: Cambridge University Press, 2002.

Eliade, Mircea, and Joseph Mitsuo Kitagawa, editors. *The History of Religions: Essays in Methodology.* Chicago: University of Chicago Press, 1959.

Ellington, Scott A. *Risking Truth: Reshaping the World through Prayers of Lament.* Princeton Theological Monography Series 98. Eugene, OR: Pickwick, 2008.

Ervin, Howard M. *Healing: Sign of the Kingdom.* Peabody, MA: Hendrickson, 2002.

Eusebius of Emesa. "Catena." In *Catena in Epistolas Catholicas,* edited by J. A. Cramer. Oxford: Clarendon, 1840.

Evans, Timothy. "Religious Conversion in Quetzaltenango, Guatemala." PhD diss., University of Pittsburgh, 1990.

Faith and Order Commission, *A Treasure in Earthen Vessels: An Instrument for an Ecumenical Reflection on Hermeneutics.* Paper No. 182. Geneva: World Council of Churches, 1998. Online: http://wcc-coe.org/wcc/what/faith/nature1.html.

Farah, Jr., Charles. *From the Pinnacle of the Temple.* Plainfield, NJ: Logos International, 1979.

———. "A Critical Analysis: The 'Roots and Fruits' of Faith Formula Theology." *Pneuma* 3 (1981) 3–21.

Farmer, Ron. "The Kingdom of God in the Gospel of Matthew." In *The Kingdom of God in 20th-Century Interpretation,* edited by Wendell Willis, 119–30. Peabody, MA: Hendrickson, 1987.

Faupel, D. William. *The Everlasting Gospel: The Significance of Eschatology in the Development of Pentecostal Thought.* Sheffield: Sheffield Academic, 1996.

———. "The Everlasting Gospel: The Significance of Eschatology in the Development of Pentecostal Thought." PhD diss., University of Birmingham, 1989.

———. "The Function of 'Models' in the Interpretation of Pentecostal Thought." *Pneuma* 2 (1980) 51–71.

———. "Whither Pentecostalism?" *Pneuma* 15 (Spring 1993) 9–27.

Fee, Gordon D. *The Disease of the Health and Wealth Gospel*. Costa Mesa, CA: Word for Today, 1979.

———. *The First Epistle to the Corinthians*. NICNT. Grand Rapids: Eerdmans, 1987.

———. "Hermeneutics and Historical Precedent—A Major Problem in Pentecostal Hermeneutics." In *Perspectives in the New Pentecostalism*, edited by Russell P. Spittler, 118–32. Grand Rapids: Baker, 1976.

———. "The Kingdom of God and the Church's Global Mission." In *Called and Empowered: Global Mission in Pentecostal Perspective*, edited by Murray W. Dempster, et al., 7–21. Peabody, MA: Hendrickson, 1991.

Ferdinando, Keith. *The Triumph of Christ in African Perspective: A Study of Demonology and Redemption in the African Context*. Carlisle, UK: Paternoster, 1999.

Ferraiuolo, Perruci. "Christian Leaders Admonish Him: Televangelist Calls Word-of-Faith 'New Age.'" *Christianity Today* 16 (August 1993) 38–39.

Feuerbach, Ludwig. *The Essence of Christianity*. Translated by George Eliot, 1845. Reprint: New York: Harper and Row, 1957.

Fiddes, Paul. *The Promised End: Eschatology in Theology and Literature*. Oxford: Blackwell, 2000.

Fitzmyer, Joseph A. *The Acts of the Apostles*. Anchor Bible 31. New York: Doubleday, 1998.

———. *Paul and His Theology: A Brief Sketch*. Englewood Cliffs: Prentice Hall, 1989.

Folarin, George O. "Contemporary State of the Prosperity Gospel in Nigeria." *Asia Journal of Theology* 21 (2007) 69-95.

Fowler, Robert Booth. *The Greening of Protestant Thought*. Chapel Hill: University of North Carolina Press, 1995.

Fraikin, Daniel. "'Charismes et Ministères' à la Lumière de 1 Cor 12–14." *EgT* 9 (October 1978) 455–63.

Friedlander, Michael. *The Jewish Religion*. London: Shapiro Valentine & Co, 1937.

Gaffin, Richard B. *Perspectives on Pentecost*. Phillipsburg: Presbyterian and Reformed, 1979.

Garrard-Burnett, Virginia. "'God Was Already Here When Columbus Arrived': Inculturation Theology and the Mayan Movement in Guatemala." In *Resurgent Voices in Latin America: Indigenous Peoples, Political Mobilization, and Religious Change*, edited by Edward L. Cleary and Timothy J. Steigenga, 125–53. Brunswick, NJ: Rutgers University Press, 2004.

———. *Living in the New Jerusalem: Protestantism in Guatemala*. Austin: University of Texas Press, 1998.

Gause, R. H., *Revelation: The Stamp of God's Sovereignty on History*. Cleveland: Pathway, 1983.

Gee, Donald. *Concerning Spiritual Gifts*. Springfield, IL: Gospel, 1980.

Gifford, Paul. "'Africa Shall Be Saved': An Appraisal of Reinhard Bonnke's Pan-African Crusade." *JRA* 17 (1987) 63–92.

———. *The New Crusaders: Christianity and the New Right in Southern Africa*. London: Pluto, 1991.

———. *Exporting the American Gospel: Global Christian Fundamentalism*. New York: Routledge, 1996.

————. "The Complex Provenance of Some Elements of African Pentecostal Theology." In *Between Babel and Pentecost; Transnational Pentecostalism in Africa and Latin America*, edited by Paul Gifford, André Corten, and Ruth Marshall-Fratani, 62–79. Bloomington: Indiana University Press, 2001.

Gifford, Paul, André Corten and Ruth Marshall-Fratani, eds. *Between Babel and Pentecost: Transnational Pentecostalism in Africa and Latin America*. Bloomington: Indiana University Press, 2001.

Gill, Anthony. *Rendering unto Caesar: The Catholic Church and the State in Latin America*. Chicago: University of Chicago Press, 1989.

Goff, James. *The Birth of Purgatory*. Chicago: University of Chicago Press, 1984.

Goldberg, Michelle. *Kingdom Coming: The Rise of Christian Nationalism*. New York: Norton, 2006.

Gollin, Gillian Lindt. *Moravians in Two Worlds*. New York: Columbia University Press 1967.

Gollwitzer, Helmut. "Christoph Blumhardt Neu Sichtbar." *Evangelische Theologie* (1981) 259–75.

González, Justo L. *The Story of Christianity*. Vol. 2, *The Reformation to the Present Day*. San Francisco: Harper & Row, 1984.

Gray, Sherman W. *The Least of My Brothers Matthew 25:31–46: A History of Interpretation* SBL Dissertation Series 114. Atlanta: Scholars, 1989.

Greathouse, William M. "John Wesley's View of the Last Things." In *The Second Coming: A Wesleyan Approach to the Doctrine of Last Things*, edited by H. Ray Dunning 139–60. Kansas City: Beacon Hill, 1995.

Green, Joel B. *The Gospel of Luke*. NICNT. Grand Rapids: Eerdmans, 1997.

Green, Linda. *Fear as a Way of Life: Mayan Widows in Rural Guatemala*. New York: Columbia University Press, 1999.

Green, William Scott. "Messiah in Judaism: Rethinking the Question." In *Judaisms and Their Messiahs at the Turn of the Christian Era*, edited by Jacob Neusner, et al., 1–13. New York: Cambridge University Press, 1987.

Gregory of Nazianzus. *On God and Christ: The Five Theological Orations and Two Letters to Cledonius*. Popular Patristics. Translated by Frederick Williams and Lionel Wickham. Crestwood, NY: St. Vladimir's Seminary Press, 2002.

————. *The Life of Moses*. The Classics of Western Spirituality. Translated by Everett Ferguson and Abraham J. Malherbe. New York: Paulist, 1978.

Greschat, Martin. "Die 'Hoffnung Besserer Zeiten' für die Kirche." In *Zur Neueren Pietismus Forschung*, edited by M. Greschat, 224–39. Darmstadt: Wissenschaftliche Buchgesellschaft, 1977.

Gribben, Crawford. *Writing the Rapture: Prophecy Fiction in Evangelical America*. Oxford: Oxford University Press, 2009.

Gros, Jeffrey. "Towards a Hermeneutics of Piety for the Ecumenical Movement." *Ecumenical Trends* 22 (January 1993) 1–12.

Grudem, Wayne. *The Gift of Prophecy in 1 Corinthians*. Washington, DC: University Press of America, 1982.

Gyekye, Kwame. *African Philosophical Thought: The Akan Conceptual Scheme*. Philadelphia: Temple University Press, 1995.

Haarbeck, H. "Word, Tongue, Utterance." In *NIDNTT*, 1078–146.

Haenchen, Ernst. *The Acts of the Apostles: A Commentary*. Translated by Bernard Noble et al. Philadelphia: Westminster, 1971.

Hagin, Kenneth E., Sr. *The Believer's Authority.* Tulsa: Faith Library, 1984.

———. *El Shaddai: The God Who Is More Than Enough, the God Who Satisfies Us with Long Life.* Tulsa: Faith Library, 1980.

———. *Exceedingly Growing Faith.* Tulsa: Faith Library, 1983.

———. *How to Turn Your Faith Loose.* Tulsa: Faith Library, 1979.

———. *I Believe in Visions.* 2nd ed. Tulsa: Rhema Bible Church, 1989.

———. *The Midas Touch: A Balanced Approach to Biblical Prosperity.* Tulsa: Kenneth Hagin Ministries, 2000.

———. *The Ministry of a Prophet.* Tulsa: Faith Library, 1979.

———. *The Name of Jesus.* Tulsa: Kenneth Hagin Ministries, 1986.

———. *The Present-Day Ministry of Jesus Christ.* Tulsa: Kenneth Hagin Ministries, 1983.

———. *Right and Wrong Thinking.* Tulsa: Faith Library, 1966.

———. *Seven Steps for Judging Prophecy.* Tulsa: Faith Library, 1986.

———. "Trend Toward Faith Movement." *Charisma* (August 1985) 67-70.

———. *The Triumphant Church.* Tulsa: Rhema, 1993.

———. *Understanding the Anointing.* Tulsa: Faith Library, 1983.

———. *"You Can Have What You Say!"* Tulsa: Faith Library, 1979.

———. *Zoe: The God-Kind of Life.* Tulsa: Hagin Ministries, 1981.

Hall, Franklin. *Atlantic Ocean Storms Destroying Many Cities: New Continents Coming Forth.* Phoenix: n.p., 1973.

———. *Atomic Power With God with Fasting and Prayer.* Phoenix: n.p. 1973 [1946].

———. *Bodyfelt Salvation: The Eradication of the Adamic Sickness.* Phoenix: Hall Deliverance Foundation, 1983 [1968].

———. *Formula for Raising the Dead and the Baptism of Fire.* San Diego, CA: n.p., 1960.

———. *Our Divine Healing Obligation.* n.p., n.d.

———. *The Return of Immortality.* Phoenix: Hall Deliverance Foundation, 1976.

———. *Subduing the Earth Controlling the Elements and Ruling the Nations with Jesus Christ.* Phoenix: n.p., 1966.

Handy, Robert T. *A Christian America: Protestant Hopes and Historical Realities.* New York: Oxford University Press, 1984.

Hammond-Tooke, D. *The Roots of Black South Africa.* Johannesburg: Jonathan Ball, 1993.

Hamon, Bill. *The Day of the Saints.* Shippensburg, PA: Destiny Image, 2005.

———. *The Eternal Church.* Santa Rosa Beach: Christian International, 1981.

———. *Prophets and Personal Prophecy.* Shippensburg: Destiny Image, 1987.

———. *Prophets, Apostles, and the Coming Moves of God.* Santa Rosa Beach: Christian International, 1997.

———. *Prophets, Pitfalls and Principles.* Shippensburg, PA: Destiny Image, 1991.

Harink, Douglas. *Paul among the Postliberals: Pauline Theology beyond Christendom and Modernity.* Grand Rapids: Brazos, 2003.

Harper, Michael. *Walk in the Spirit.* Plainfield, NJ: Logos International, 1968.

Harrell, David Edwin. *All Things Are Possible,* Bloomington: Indiana University Press, 1975.

———. *Oral Roberts: An American Life.* Bloomington: Indiana University Press, 1985.

Harshbarger, Luther H., and John A. Mourant. *Judaism and Christianity—Perspectives and Traditions.* Boston: Allyn & Bacon, 1968.

Hawn, Robert. "Kansas City: Conference Heard 'Round the World.'" *Charisma* (September/ October 1977) 10–11.

Hawtin, George R. *According to the Purpose*, n.d.

———. *The Treasures of Truth*. Vol.15. Battlefield, SK: G. R. Hawtin, n.d..

———. "Account of the 1948 Latter Rain Outpouring" [Flower Center].

———. *Beholding the More Excellent Glory*. Battlefield, SK: G. R. Hawtin, 1980.

———. *The Body of Christ, the House Not Made With Hands*. Battlefield, SK: G. R. Hawtin, 1980.

———. *Church Government*. Battlefield, SK: G. R. Hawtin, 1949.

———. *Creation, Redemption, and the Restitution of All Things: The Treasures of Truth*. Vol. 28. Saskatoon, Saskatchewan: Modern, 1980.

———. *The Evil Day*. Battlefield, SK: G. R. Hawtin, 1980.

———. *Eschatology, the Doctrine of Last Things*. Battlefield, SK: G. R. Hawtin, 1980.

———. *Fragments that Remain*. Battlefield, SK: G. R. Hawtin, 1980.

———. *From Glory to Glory*. Battlefield, SK: G. R. Hawtin, 1980.

———. *Glory, Honor, and Immortality, Eternal Life*. Battlefield, SK: G. R. Hawtin, 1980.

———. *The Glory Soon to Be Revealed*. Battlefield, SK: G. R. Hawtin, 1980.

———. *God's Great Family of Sons*. Battlefield, SK: G. R. Hawtin, 1980.

———. *Here Is the Mind That Hath Wisdom*. Battlefield, SK: G. R. Hawtin, 1980.

———. *The Holy Spirit*. Battlefield, SK: G. R. Hawtin, 1980.

———. *Learning from Illustrious Men*. Battlefield, SK: G. R. Hawtin, n.d.

———. *Mystery Babylon*. Battlefield, SK: G. R. Hawtin, 1980.

———. *The Mystery of Christ and Our Union with Him*. Battlefield, SK: G. R. Hawtin, 1980.

———. *The Nine Gifts of the Spirit*. n.d.: n.p.

———. *Our So Great Salvation*. Battlefield, SK: G. R. Hawtin, n.d.

———. *Pearls of Great Price*. Battlefield, SK: G. R. Hawtin, n.d.

———. *Portrait of Things to Come*. Battlefield, SK: G. R. Hawtin, 1980.

———. *Thy Kingdom Come*. Battlefield, SK: G. R. Hawtin, 1980.

———. *Watchman, What of the Night*. Battlefield, SK: G. R. Hawtin, 1980.

———. *When Saints Become the Will of God*. Battlefield, SK: G. R. Hawtin, 1980.

Healey, Joseph, and Donald Sybertz. *Towards an African Narrative Theology*. Maryknoll, NY: Orbis, 1996.

Hegel, G. W. F. *Phenomenology of Spirit*. Translated by A. V. Miller. Analysis by J. N. Findlay. Oxford: Oxford University Press, 1977.

Hill, C. *In God's Time: The Bible and the Future*. Grand Rapids: Eerdmans, 2002.

Hocken, Peter. "Charismatic Movement." In *NIDPCM*, 477–519.

Hogan, J. Philip. "Because Jesus Did." *Mountain Movers* 31 (June 1989) 10–11.

Holdcroft, L. Thomas. *The Holy Spirit: A Pentecostal Interpretation*. Springfield, IL: Gospel, 1979.

Hollenweger, Walter J. *Pentecostalism: Origins and Developments Worldwide*. Peabody, MA: Hendrickson, 1997.

Horton, Harold. *The Gifts of the Spirit*. London: Assemblies of God Publishing House, 1962. Reprint Springfield, IL: Gospel, 1975.

Horton, Stanley M. *What the Bible Says about the Holy Spirit*. Springfield, IL: Gospel, 1976.

House, H. Wayne, and Thomas Ice. *Dominion Theology: Blessing or Curse?* Portland, OR: Multnomah, 1988.

Howard, T. "The Literary Unity of 1 Thessalonians 4:13—5:11." *GTJ* 9 (1988) 163–90.

Hughes, Richard T. editor. *The American Quest for the Primitive Church.* Urbana: University of Illinois Press, 1988.

———. *The Primitive Church in the Modern World.* Urbana: University of Illinois Press, 1995.

Hunsberger, George, and Craig von Gelder, eds. *The Church Between Gospel and Culture.* Grand Rapids: Eerdmans, 1996.

Hunt, Dave, and T. A. McMahon. *The Seduction of Christianity: Spiritual Discernment in the Last Days.* Eugene, OR: Harvest House, 1985.

"Indulge Us." *Commonweal.* 125 (18 December 1998) 6.

Isaac, Ephraim. "1 (Ethiopic Apocalypse of) Enoch." In *The Old Testament Pseudepigrapha,* edited by James H. Charlesworth, 1:5–89. New York: Doubleday, 1983.

Isasi-Díaz, Ada María. *La Lucha Continues: Mujerista Theology.* Maryknoll, NY: Orbis, 2004.

Israel, Richard D. "Joel 2:28–32 (3:1–5 MT): Prism for Pentecost." In *Charismatic Experiences in History,* edited by Cecil M. Robeck, Jr., 1–14. Peabody, MA: Hendrickson, 1985.

Iverson, Dick. *The Journey: A Lifetime of Prophetic Moments.* Portland: Bible Temple, 1995.

Iverson, Dick, and Bill Scheidler. *Present Day Truths.* Portland: Bible Press, 1975.

Iverson, Dick, and Daniel Straza. *Restoration, God's Plan.* Regina, Canada: Maranatha Christian Centre, 1984.

Jäckh, Werner. *Blumhardt Vater und Sohn und Ihre Botschaft.* Stuttgart: Steinkopf, 1925.

"Jacobo Árbenz Guzmán." Online: http://en.wikipedia.org/wiki/Jacobo_Arbenz_Guzm %C3%A1n (Accessed December 18, 2008).

Jacobsen, Douglas. *Thinking in the Spirit: Theologies of the Early Pentecostal Movement.* Bloomington: Indiana University Press, 2003.

Jeremias, Joachim. *Rediscovering the Parables.* Translated by S. H. Hooke and Frank Clarke. New York: Scribner, 1966.

———. *The Sermon on the Mount.* Facet Books Biblical Series. Philadelphia: Fortress, 1963.

"Joaquinismos, Utopías, Milenarismos y Mesianismos en la América Colonial." In *Teología En America Latína (1493–1715).* Vol. I, edited by Josep Saranyana Closa, 613–88. Madrid: Iberoamericana, 1999.

Johnson, Aaron P. "Resurrection of the Body in Early Judaism and Early Christianity." *JECS* 14 (Summer 2006) 235–36.

Johnson, Luke T. *The Acts of the Apostles.* Sacra Pagina 5. Collegeville: Liturgical, 1992.

Joyner, Rick. *The Apostolic Ministry.* Wilkesboro, NC: MorningStar, 2004.

———. *The Call.* Charlotte: MorningStar, 1999.

———. *Epic Battles of the Last Days.* Charlotte: MorningStar, 1997.

———. *The Final Quest.* Kensington, PA: Whitaker House, 1996.

———. *The Harvest.* Pineville, NC: MorningStar, 1989.

———. *The Prophetic Ministry.* Charlotte: MorningStar, 2006.

———. *Shadows of Things to Come: A Prophetic Look at God's Unfolding Plan.* Nashville: Nelson, 2001.

———. *Visions of the Harvest.* Charlotte: MorningStar, 1994.

Kaiser, Walter C. *Toward Old Testament Ethics.* Grand Rapids: Zondervan, 1983.

Kalu, Ogbu. *African Pentecostalism: An Introduction.* Oxford: Oxford University Press, 2008.

Kasper, Walter. *Faith and the Future.* New York: Crossroads, 1982.

Kauffman, Rick. "Separate, But United in Spirit." *National Courier* (August 19, 1977) 1.

Kelly, Anthony. *Eschatology and Hope.* Theology in Global Perspective Series. Maryknoll, NY: Orbis, 2006.

Kiddle, M., *Revelation.* MNTC. London: Hodder and Stoughton, 1947.

Klausner, Joseph. *The Messianic Idea in Israel: From Its Beginning to the Completion of the Mishnah.* Translated by W. F. Stinespring. New York: MacMillan, 1955.

Knight III, Henry H. *The Presence of God in the Christian Life: John Wesley and the Means of Grace.* Metuchen, NJ: Scarecrow, 1992.

———. "God's Faithfulness and God's Freedom: A Comparison of Contemporary Theologies of Healing." *JPT* 2 (1993) 65–89.

———. "From Aldersgate to Azusa: Wesley and the Renewal of Pentecostal Spirituality." *JPT* 8 (April 1996) 82–98.

Kuzmič, Peter. "History and Eschatology: Evangelical Views." In *Word and Deed: Evangelism and Social Responsibility,* edited by Bruce J. Nichols, 135–64. Grand Rapids: Eerdmans, 1985.

———. "Kingdom of God." In *DPCM,* 521–26.

Kydd, Ronald A. N. *Healing through the Centuries: Models for Understanding.* Peabody, MA: Hendrickson, 1998.

Ladd, George E. *The Gospel of the Kingdom: Popular Expositions on the Kingdom of God.* Grand Rapids: Eerdmans, 1959.

———. *Jesus and the Kingdom: The Eschatology of Biblical Realism.* Waco, TX: Word, 1964.

———. *Revelation.* Grand Rapids: Eerdmans, 1972.

———. *The Presence of the Future.* Grand Rapids: Eerdmans, 1974.

Lahaye, Tim. *Biblia de Estudio de Profecia.* Nashville: Broadman & Holman, 2002.

Land, Steven J. *Pentecostal Spirituality: A Passion for the Kingdom.* JPTSup 1. Sheffield: Sheffield Academic, 1993.

Lawrence, B. F. *The Apostolic Faith Restored.* St. Louis, MO: Gospel Publishing House, 1916.

Layzell, Reginald. *The Pastor's Pen: Early Revival Writings of Pastor Reg. Layzell.* Vancouver: Glad Tidings Temple, 1965.

———. *Unto Perfection: A Sequel to "The Pastor's Pen."* Yuba City, CA: Glad Tidings Missionary Church, 1981.

Lee, Shayne. "Prosperity Theology: T. D. Jakes and the Gospel of the Almighty Dollar." *Cross Currents* (Summer 2007) 227–36.

Lehmann, H. *Pietismus und Weltliche Ordnung in Württemberg.* Stuttgart: Kohlhammer, 1969.

Lenhard, H. "Ein Beitrag zur Übersetzung von II Ptr 3.10d." *Zeitschrift für die neutestamentliche Wissenschaft* 52 (1962) 128–29.

Lie, Geir. *E. W. Kenyon: Cult Founder or Evangelical Minister?* Oslo: Refleks, 2003.

Lightfoot, J. B. *The Apostolic Fathers.* Part 1. Vol. 2. London: Macmillan, 1890.

Lindars, Barnabas. *New Testament Apologetics: The Doctrinal Significance of the Old Testament Quotations.* Philadelphia: Westminster, 1961.

Lindsay, Gordon, editor. "Spiritual Hunger." In *The God-Men, and Other Sermons of John G. Lake.* Dallas: Christ for the Nations, 1978.

Luce, Alice. *Introducción Bíblica* In *Hermenéutica, Introducción Bíblica*, edited by Eric Lund, et al. Miami: Vida, 1964.

Macchia, Frank D. *Baptized in the Spirit: A Global Pentecostal Theology*. Grand Rapids: Zondervan, 2006.

———. "Discerning the Truth of Tongues Speech: A Response to Amos Yong." *JPT* 1 (1998) 67–71.

———. "Pentecostal and Charismatic Theology." In *The Oxford Handbook of Eschatology*, ed. Jerry L. Walls, 280–94. Oxford: Oxford University Press, 2008.

———. *Spirituality and Social Liberation: The Message of the Blumhardts in the Light of Württemberg Pietism*. Metuchen, NJ: Scarecrow, 1993.

———. "Tongues as a Sign: Towards a Sacramental Understanding of Pentecostal Experience." *Pneuma* 15 (1993) 61–76.

———. "Sighs Too Deep for Words: Toward a Theology of Glossolalia." *JPT* (1992) 47–73.

———. "The Tongues of Pentecost: A Pentecostal Perspective on the Promise and Challenge of Pentecostal/ Roman Catholic Dialogue." *JES* 35 (Winter 1998) 1–18.

———. "The Question of Tongues as Initial Evidence: A Review of *Initial Evidence*, edited by Gary B. McGee." *JPT* 2 (1993) 117–27.

———. "The Secular and the Religious under the Shadow of the Cross: Implications in Christoph Blumhardt's Kingdom Spirituality for a Christian Response to World Religions." In *Religion in a Secular City: Essays in Honor of Harvey Cox*, edited by Arvind Sharma. 59–77. Philadelphia: Trinity, 2001.

———. "The Time is Near! Or, Is It? Dare We Abandon Our Eschatological Expectation?" *Pneuma* 25 (2003) 161–63.

Maddox, Randy L. *Responsible Grace: John Wesley's Practical Theology*. Nashville: Kingswood, 1994.

Mälzer, Gottfried. *Bengel und Zinzendorf, zur Biographie und Theologie Johann Albrecht Bengels*. Witten: Luther, 1968.

———. *Johann Albrecht Bengel, Leben und Werk*. Stuttgart: Calwer Verlag, 1970.

Mana, K. *Christians and Churches of Africa Envisioning the Future*. Glasgow: Regnum, 2002.

Mansfield, Stephen. *Derek Prince: A Biography*, Lake Mary, FL: Charisma House, 2005.

Manuel, David. *Like a Mighty River*. Orleans, MA, Rock Harbor, 1977.

Marshall, I. Howard. *The Gospel of Luke: A Commentary on the Greek Text*. NIGTC. Exeter, UK: Paternoster, 1978.

Marty, Martin E. "In Defense of Indulgences." *Christian Century* 111 (1994) 735.

Maxwell, David. "'Delivered from the Spirit of Poverty?': Pentecostalism, Prosperity and Modernity in Zimbabwe," *JRA* 28 (1998) 350–73.

Maynard-Reid, Pedrito U., editor. "In the Spirit of Fiesta." In *Diverse Worship: African-American, Caribbean & Hispanic Perspectives*, 161–86. Downers Grove: IVP, 2000.

Mbiti, John. *Introduction to African Religion*. Nairobi: East African Educational Publishers Limited, 1992.

———. *African Religions and Philosophy*. London: Heinemann, 1969.

McClung, L. Grant, Jr. "Missiology." In *DPCM*, 606–9.

McConnell, D. R. *A Different Gospel*. Peabody, MA: Hendrickson, 1988.

McDonnell, Kilian. "Luther and Trent on Penance." *Lutheran Quarterly* 7 (1993) 261–76.

McDowell, D. H. "The Purpose of the Coming of the Lord." *Pentecostal Evangel* (May 2, 1925) 2.

McGinn, Bernard. *Apocalyptic Spirituality.* New York: Paulist, 1979.

———. "Apocalypticism and Church Reform: 1100–1500." In *EA* 2:74–109.

———. *Visions of the End.* New York: Columbia University Press, 1979.

———. *AntiChrist: Two Thousand Years of the Human Fascination with Evil.* San Francisco: HarperSanFrancisco, 1994.

———. *The Calabrian Abbott: Joachim of Fiore in the History of Western Thought.* New York: Macmillan, 1985.

McGinn, Bernard, and Jeffrey Burton Russell. "The Last Judgment in Christian Tradition." In *EA* 2:361–401.

Meier, K. J. *Christoph Blumhardt: Christ, Sozialist, Theologe.* Bern: Lang, 1979.

Menzies, William W. *Anointed to Serve: The Story of the Assemblies of God.* Springfield, MO: Gospel, 1971.

———. "Synoptic Theology: An Essay on Pentecostal Hermeneutics." *Paraclete* 13 (Winter 1979) 14–21.

Metzger, Bruce M. *A Textual Commentary on the Greek New Testament.* New York: United Bible Societies, 1971.

Meyer, Brigit. "Delivered from the Powers of Darkness: Confessions of Satanic Riches in Christian Ghana." *Africa* 65 (1995) 236–55.

Míguez, Daniel. "Why Are Pentecostals Politically Ambiguous? Pentecostalism and Politics in Argentina, 1983–1995." *European Review of Latin American and Caribbean Studies* 67 (1999) 57–74.

Miller, Donald E., and Tetsunao Yamamori. *Global Pentecostalism: The New Face of Christian Social Engagement.* Los Angeles: University of California Press, 2007.

Millgram, Abraham Ezra, editor. *Great Jewish Ideas.* Washington, DC: B'nai B'rith Dept. of Adult Jewish Education, 1964.

"Minutes of the General Council of the Assemblies of God in the United States, Canada and Foreign Lands, 1916." Flower Pentecostal Heritage Center. Online: http://ifphc .org/DigitalPublications/USA/Assemblies%20of%20God%20USA/Minutes%20 General%20Council/Unregistered/1916/FPHC/1916.pdf [accessed November, 2009].

Moltmann, Jürgen. *The Church in the Power of the Spirit.* Translated by Margaret Kohl. New York: Harper & Row, 1977.

———. *The Coming of God: Christian Eschatology.* Translated by Margaret Kohl. Minneapolis: Fortress, 1996.

———. *God in Creation: An Ecological Doctrine of Creation.* Translated by Margaret Kohl. London: SCM, 1985.

———. *In the End—The Beginning: The Life of Hope.* Translated by Margaret Kohl. Minneapolis: Fortress, 2004.

———. *Science and Wisdom.* Minneapolis: Fortress, 2003.

———. *Theology of Hope: On the Ground and the Implications of a Christian Eschatology.* Translated by James W. Leitch. London: SCM, 1967.

———. *The Spirit of Life: A Universal Affirmation* trans. Margaret Kohl. Minneapolis: Fortress, 1992.

———. *The Way of Jesus Christ: Christology in Messianic Dimensions.* Translated by Margaret Kohl. London: SCM, 1990.

Montefiore, C. G. *Rabbinic Literature and Gospel Teachings.* New York: Ktav, 1970.

Moo, D. *The Epistle to the Romans*. NICNT. Grand Rapids: Eerdmans, 1996.

Moore, Carey. "Kansas City Hears 'Jesus is Lord.'" *Logos Journal* (September/October 1977) 50–53.

Moore, David. "Basham, Don Wilson." In *NIDPCM*, 367.

———. "Baxter, W. J. E. ("Ern")." In *NIDPCM*, 367–68.

———. "Mumford, Bernard C., Jr. ("Bob")." In *NIDPCM*, 911.

———. "Prince, Peter Derek V." In *NIDPCM*, 999.

———. "Simpson, Charles Vernon." In *NIDPCM*, 1070.

———. "The Shepherding Movement: A Case Study in Charismatic Ecclesiology." *Pneuma* 22 (Fall 2000) 249–70.

———. *The Shepherding Movement: Controversy and Charismatic Controversy*. London: T. & T. Clark, 2003.

Moorhead, James H. "Apocalypticism in Mainstream Protestantism, 1800 to the Present." In *EA* 3:72–107.

Moreno, Pedro C. "Rapture and Renewal in Latin America." *First Things* 74 (Jan-July 1997) 33.

Moss, Vernon. "I Corinthians xiii.13." *ExpTim* 73 (1962) 93.

Mott, Stephen Charles. *Biblical Ethics and Social Change*. New York: Oxford University Press, 1982.

Mounce, R. H. *The Book of Revelation*. Grand Rapids: Eerdmans, 1977.

Mowinckel, Sigmund. *He That Cometh: The Messiah Concept in the Old Testament and Later Judaism*. Translated by G. W. Anderson. Nashville: Abingdon, 1956.

Mumford, Bob. "Change in the Wind." *LifeChangers* (January/February 1981) 1–4.

———. "Focusing On Present Issues." *LifeChangers* (1979).

———. *Forty Years in Ministry 1954–1994*. Raleigh, NC: LifeChangers, 1994.

———. "God's Purpose for His People Today." The National Men's Shepherding Conference, September 1975. Holy Spirit Research Center, Oral Roberts University, transcript.

———. "Hit by a Greyhound Bus." *Lifechangers* (August 1979) 1–4.

———. *LifeChangers Newsletter*. November 1975, 1-8. Holy Spirit Research Center, Oral Roberts University, Tulsa.

———. *Shepherd of a Dark and Cloudy Day*. Audiocassettes; Ft. Lauderdale: LifeChangers, n.d.

Murray, Paul D., editor. *Receptive Ecumenism and the Call to Catholic Learning Exploring a Way for Contemporary Ecumenism*. Oxford: Oxford University Press, 2008.

Murrieta, Leopoldo. "Mamá Chuy se fue con el Señor." *El Evangelio* 36 (October 1981) 19.

Murphy, F. J., *Fallen Is Babylon*. Harrisburg, PA: Trinity, 1998.

Myland, D. Wesley. "Latter Day Lectures." *The Latter Rain Evangel* 1 (May-October 1909), n.p.

———. *The Latter Rain Covenant and Pentecostal Power*. Chicago: The Evangel Publishing House, 1910.

Niebuhr, H. Richard. *The Responsible Self*. New York: Harper & Row, 1963.

Neumann, H. Terris. "The Cultic Origins of Word-Faith Theology within the Charismatic Movement." *Pneuma* 12 (1990) 32–55.

Neusner, Jacob. *Handbook of Rabbinic Theology—Language, System, Structure*. Leiden: Brill, 2002.

———. *Theological Dictionary of Rabbinic Judaism.* Parts 1–3. Lanham, MD: University Press of America, 2004.

———. *Theology of Normative Judaism.* Boulder: University Press of America, 2005.

Neusner, Jacob, and Bruce Chilton. *Jewish and Christian Doctrines—The Classics Compared.* London: Routledge, 2000.

———. *Jewish-Christian Debates.* Minneapolis: Fortress, 1998.

Noth, Martin. *The Old Testament World.* Translated by Victor I. Gruhn. Philadelphia: Fortress, 1966.

Oberman, Heiko Augustinus. *Luther: Man between God and the Devil.* New Haven: Yale University Press, 1990.

Oecumenius. "Commentary on 2 Peter." In *Patrologia Graeca.* Vol. 119, edited by J. P. Migne. Paris: Migne, 1857–1886.

Oetinger, Friedrich Christoph. *Heilige Philosophie.* Württemberg: Metzinger, n.d.

———. *Selbstbiographie.* Württemberg: Metsinger, 1961.

Olupona, J. K. "Survey of West Africa." In *NIDPCM*, 13–21.

On Becoming a Christian. http://www.prounione.urbe.it/dia-int/pe-rc/e_pe-rc-info.html.

Osborne, Kenan. *Reconciliation and Justification.* New York: Paulist, 1990.

Palmer, Parker. *The Courage to Teach: Exploring the Inner Landscape of a Teacher's Life.* San Francisco: Jossey-Bass, 2007.

Palmer, P. F., and G. A. Tavard. "Indulgences." *The New Catholic Encyclopedia.* Vol. VII. 2nd ed. Washington, DC: Catholic University Press, 2002.

Pannenberg, Wolfhart. *Anthropology in Theological Perspective.* Translated by Matthew J. O'Connell. Philadelphia: Westminster, 1975.

Parham, Charles F. *A Voice Crying in the Wilderness.* 4th ed. Joplin, MO: Joplin Printing, 1944.

Parrinder, G. *African Traditional Religion.* London: Hutchinson's, 1961.

Patai, Raphael. *The Messiah Texts.* Detroit: Wayne State University Press, 1979.

Paulk, Earl. *Held in the Heavens Until.* Atlanta: K-Dimension, 1985.

———. *Ultimate Kingdom.* Atlanta: K-Dimension, 1986.

———. *The Wounded Body of Christ.* Atlanta: K-Dimension, 1983.

Pearlman, Myer. *Knowing the Doctrines of the Bible.* Springfield, IL: Gospel, 1981.

Pentecost, J. Dwight. *Things to Come: A Study in Biblical Eschatology.* Grand Rapids: Zondervan, 1958.

Perera, Victor. *Unfinished Conquest: The Guatemalan Tragedy.* Los Angeles: University of California Press, 1993.

Perriman, Andrew, editor. *Faith, Health, and Prosperity: A Report on "Word of Faith" and "Positive Confession" Theologies.* Carlisle: Paternoster, 2003.

Pervo, Richard I. *Acts: A Commentary.* Hermeneia. Minneapolis: Fortress, 2009.

Peter, Carl J. "The Communion of Saints in the Final Days of the Council of Trent." In *One Mediator, the Saints, and Mary,* edited by George H. Anderson, et al., 219–33. Minneapolis: Augsburg, 1992.

Petersen D. L., and G. W. Nickelsburg. "Eschatology." In *ABD* Vol.2. New York: Doubleday, 1992.

Petersen, Douglas. *Not By Might Nor Power: A Pentecostal Theology of Social Concern in Latin America.* Oxford: Regnum, 1996.

Phan, Peter. *Eternity in Time: A Study of Karl Rahner's Eschatology.* Sesinsgrove, PA: Susque-hanna University Press, 1988.

———. *Responses to 101 Questions on Death and Eternal Life.* New York: Paulist, 1997.

Phiri, Isaac and Joe Maxwell. "Gospel Riches: Africa's Rapid Embrace of Prosperity Pentecostalism Provokes Concern and Hope." *Christianity Today* (July 2007) 23-29.

Pittinger, Norman. *The Holy Spirit.* Philadelphia: Pilgrim, 1974.

Plevnik, Joseph. *Paul and the Parousia: An Exegetical and Theological Investigation.* Peabody, MA: Hendrickson, 1997.

Poloma, Margaret. *The Charismatic Movement: Is There a New Pentecost?* Boston: Twayne, 1982.

————. "The Future of American Pentecostal Identity: The Assemblies of God at a Crossroad." In *The Work of the Spirit: Pneumatology and Pentecostalism,* edited by Michael Welker, 147-65. Grand Rapids: Eerdmans, 2006.

Pomerville, Paul. *The Third Force in Missions.* Peabody, MA: Hendrickson, 1985.

Pupillo, Osvaldo. "Cristo, el Eterno Señor." In *El Discípulo Bíblico: manual para maestro de adultos.* 4.1. Cleveland: Editorial Evangélica, 2006.

Prigent, P. *L'Apocalypse de Saint Jean.* Geneva: Labor et Fides, 2000.

Prince, Derek. "Letter to Charles Simpson." (Summer 1983), private holding 1-2.

————. "Our Debt to Israel." *New Wine Magazine* (June 1978) 26-30.

————. *Resurrection of the Dead.* Ft Lauderdale, FL: Derek Prince Publications, n.d.

————. "The Vision of the Completed Body." The National Men's Shepherds Conference, September 1975. Holy Spirit Research Center, Oral Roberts University, transcript.

Prosser, Peter E. *Dispensational Eschatology and its Influence on American and British Religious Movements.* TSR 82. Queenston, NY: Mellen, 1999.

Radin, P. *Primitive Religion.* New York: Dover, 1957.

Rahner, Karl. "Remarks on the Theology of Indulgences." *Theological Investigations.* Vol. 2. Baltimore: Helicon, 1955.

Ramirez, Daniel. "Alabaré a mi Señor: Hymnody as Ideology in Latino Protestantism." In *Singing the Lord's Song in a Strange Land: Hymnody in the History of North American Protestantism,* eds. Edith L. Blumhofer and Mark A. Noll, 196-218. Tuscaloosa: University of Alabama Press, 2004.

Randles, Bill. *Weighed and Found Wanting: Putting the Toronto Blessing in Context.* Marion, IA: Believers in Grace Fellowship, 1995.

Rasmussen, Larry L. "Creation, Church, and Christian Responsibility." In *Tending the Garden: Essays in the Gospel and the Earth,* edited by Wesley Granberg-Michaelson, 114-31. Grand Rapids: Eerdmans, 1987.

Ratzinger, Joseph. *Eschatology: Death and Eternal Life.* Washington, DC: Catholic University of America Press, 1988.

————. *Theology of History in St. Bonaventure.* Chicago: Franciscan Herald, 1971.

Reymond, Robert L. *What about Continuing Revelations and Miracles in the Presbyterian Church Today?* Phillipsburg: Presbyterian and Reformed, 1977.

Riss, Richard. *Latter Rain: The Latter Rain Movement of 1948 and the Mid-Twentieth Century Evangelical Awakening.* Mississauga, ON: Honeycomb Visual Productions, 1987.

————. *A Survey of 20th Century Revival Movements.* Peabody, MA: Hendrickson, 1988.

Robeck, Cecil M. *The Azusa Street Mission and Revival.* Nashville: Nelson, 2006.

————. *Witness to Pentecost: The Life of Frank Bartleman.* In HCL 5.

Roberts, J. W. "A Note on the Meaning of II Peter 3.10d." *Restoration Quarterly* 6 (1962) 32-33

Roberts, Oral. *The Drama of the End-Time*. Franklin Springs, GA: Publishing House of the Pentecostal Holiness Church, 1941.

———. *God's Timetable for the End of Time*. Tulsa: Heliotrope, 1969.

———. *Salvation by the Blood*. Franklin Springs, GA: Pentecostal Holiness Publishing House, 1938.

Robertson, Pat with Bob Slosser. *The Secret Kingdom*. Nashville: Nelson, 1982.

Robins, R. G. *A. J. Tomlinson: Plainfolk Modernist*. Oxford: Oxford University Press, 2004.

Root, Michael. "The Jubilee Indulgence and the *Joint Declaration on the Doctrine of Justification*." *Pro Ecclesia* 9 (Fall 2000) 460–75.

Rossing, B. *The Rapture Exposed: The Message of Hope in the Book of Revelation*. Boulder: Westview, 2004.

Ruiz, Mario. "El Drama Humano." *El Evangelio* (May 1982) 6–7.

Rusconi, Roberto. "Antichrist and Antichrists." In *EA*, 2:287–325.

Rushdoony, Rousas John. "Marching Orders." *New Wine Magazine* (September 1986) 18–19.

———. "Modern Morality: Tampering with God's Law." *New Wine Magazine* (October 1981) 22–25.

———. "Prayer: Talking with Someone You Love." *New Wine Magazine* (May 1984) 11–12.

———. *God Plan for Victory: The Meaning of Postmillennialism*. Fairfax, VA: Thaburn, 1977.

———. "Back to the Future: A Historical Look At Eschatology." *New Wine Magazine* (November 1986) 24–25.

Rybarczyk, Edmund J. *Beyond Salvation: Eastern Orthodoxy and Classical Pentecostalism on Becoming Like Christ*. Milton Keynes, UK: Paternoster, 2004.

———. "Spiritualities Old and New: Similarities between Eastern Orthodoxy and Classical Pentecostalism." *Pneuma* 24 (2002) 7–25.

Ryrie, Charles C. *Dispensationalism Today*. Chicago: Moody, 1965.

———. *The Basis of the Premillennial Faith*. Neptune, NJ: Loizeaux Brothers, 1953.

Sasse, H. "αἰων αἰώνιος." In *TDNT* 1:197–209.

Sauter, Gerhard. *Die Theologie des Reiches Gottes beim älteren und jüngeren Blumhardt*. Zürich: Zwingli, 1962.

———. "Die Zahl als Schluessel zur Welt." *Evangelische Theologie*, Heft 1, Bd. 26 (1966) 1–36.

Savelle, Jerry. *Expect the Extraordinary: Thinking in the Image of Christ*. Tulsa: Harrison House, 2000.

———. *If Satan Can't Steal Your Joy . . .* Tulsa: Harrison House, 1982.

———. *Walking in Divine Favor*. Crowley, TX: Jerry Savelle Publications, 1997.

Schechter, Solomon. *Aspects of Rabbinic Theology*. New York: Schocken, 1972.

Schmid, L. "κέλευσμα." In *TDNT* 3:656–59.

Schneider, G. "δείκνυμι δεικνύω." In *EDNT* 1:280–81.

———. "πάρειμι." In *EDNT* 3:36.

Scholem, Gershom. *The Messianic Idea in Judaism*. New York: Schocken, 1971.

Schonborn, Christoph. *From Death to Life: The Christian Journey*. San Francisco: Ignatius, 1988.

Schrage, Wolfgang. *The Ethics of the New Testament*. Translated by David E. Green. Philadelphia: Fortress, 1988.

Schrenk, Gottlob. *Gottesreich und Bund im älteren Protestantismus vornehmlich bei Johannes Coccejus, zugleich ein Beitrag zur Geschichte des Pietismus und der heilsgeschichtlichen Theologie.* Gütersloh: Bartelsmann, 1923.

Schüssler Fiorenza, Elizabeth. *The Book of Revelation: Justice and Judgment.* Philadelphia: For-tress, 1985.

Schwarz, Hans. *Eschatology.* Grand Rapids: Eerdmans, 2000.

Scofield, C. I. *Rightly Dividing the Word of Truth.* Fincastle, VA: Scripture Truth Book Co., n.d.

———. *Scofield StudyLeaflets.* Philadelphia: Philadelphia School of the Bible, 1935.

———, editor. *Oxford NIV Scofield Study Bible.* New York: Oxford University Press, 1984.

Sepúlveda, Juan. "Future Perspectives for Latin American Pentecostalism." *IRM* 87 (2006) 189–95.

———. "Reflections on the Pentecostal Contribution to the Mission of the Church in Latin America." *JPT* 1 (1992) 93–108.

———. "Pentecostalism and Liberation Theology: Two Manifestations of the Work of the Holy Spirit for the Renewal of the Church." Translated by J. M. Beaty. In *All Together in One Place: Theological Papers from the Brighton Conference on World Evangelization,* edited by Harold D. Hunter and Peter D. Hocken, 51–64. Sheffield: Sheffield Academic, 1993.

Senior, Donald, and Carrol Stuhlmueller. *The Biblical Foundations for Mission.* Maryknoll, NY: Orbis, 1983.

Selter, F., and C. Brown, "Other." In *NIDNTT,* 739–42.

Shaffern, Robert. "Learned Discussions of Indulgences for the Dead in the Middle Ages." *Church History* 61 (December 1992) 367–81.

———. "Reflections on the Pentecostal Contribution to the Mission of the Church in Latin America." *JPT* 1 (1992) 93–108.

The Penitents' Treasury: Indulgences in Latin Christendom, 117–1375. Scranton: University of Scranton Press, 2007.

Sheppard, Gerald T. "Pentecostals and the Hermeneutics of Dispensationalism: The Anatomy of an Uneasy Relationship." *Pneuma* 6 (1984) 5–33.

Sherman, Amy. *The Soul of Development: Biblical Christianity and Economic Trans-formation in Guatemala.* New York: Oxford University Press, 1997.

Sider, Ronald H. *Rich Christians in an Age of Hunger.* Downers Grove, IL: IVP, 1984.

"Sidetracked!" *Mountain Movers* 31 (March 1989) 3.

Simmons, Dale. *E. W. Kenyon and the Postbellum Pursuit of Peace, Power, and Plenty.* Metuchen, NJ: Scarecrow, 1996.

Simpson, Charles. "A Heavenly Perspective: Proclaiming a Victorious Church." *New Wine Magazine* (November 1986) 8–10.

———. *A New Way to Live.* Greensburg, PA: Manna Christian Outreach, 1975.

———, editor. *The Covenant & The Kingdom.* Kent: Sovereign World, 1995.

———. "The Destiny of the People of God." *New Wine Magazine* (December 1979) 26–33.

Skaggs, Rebecca. *1 Peter, 2 Peter, Jude.* The Pentecostal Commentary. Cleveland: Pilgrim, 2004.

Skeat, W. W. *An Etymological Dictionary of the English Language.* Oxford: Clarendon, 1946.

Smalley, Stephen S. "Spirit, Kingdom and Prayer in Luke-Acts." *Novum Testamentum* 15 (1973) 59-71.

———. *The Revelation to John.* Downers Grove, IL: IVP, 2005.

Smith, Brian. *Religious Politics in Latin America: Pentecostal vs Catholic.* Notre Dame: University of Notre Dame Press, 1998.

Smith, A. Christopher. "The Eschatological Drive of God's Mission." *Review & Expositor* 82 (Spring 1985) 209-16.

Smith, Morton. "What is Implied by the Variety of Messianic Figures"? *JBL* 78 (1959) 66-72.

Snyder, Howard A. *Signs of the Spirit.* Grand Rapids: Zondervan, 1989.

Soliván, Samuel. "Sources of Hispanic/Latino American Theology: A Pentecostal Perspective." In *Hispanic/Latino Theology: Challenge and Promise,* edited by Ada María Isasi-Díaz and Fernando F. Segovia, 134-18. Minneapolis: Fortress, 1996.

———. "Hispanic Pentecostal Worship." In *¡Alabadle!: Hispanic Christian Worship,* edited by Justo L. González, 43-56. Nashville: Abingdon, 1996.

SpeSalvi. http://www.vatican.va/holy_father/benedict_xvi/encyclicals/documents/hf_ben-xvi_enc_20071130_spe-salvi_en.html # 15.

Spener, Jacob. *Pia Desideria.* Translated by T. G. Tappert. Philadelphia: Fortress, 1964.

Stackhouse, Reginald. *The End of the World?: A New Look at an Old Belief.* New York: Paulist, 1997.

Stagg, Frank. "Glossolalia in the New Testament." In *Glossolalia: Tongue Speaking in Biblical, Historical, and Psychological Perspectives,* edited by Frank Stagg, et al., 20-44. Nashville: Abingdon, 1967.

Stanley, Alessandra Stanley. "Urging Millennial Penitence, Pope Is Offering Indulgences." *New York Times* 148 (28 November, 1998) 1.

Stauffer, Ethelbert. *Christ and the Caesars.* London: SCM, 1955.

Steigenga, Timothy J. "Guatemala." In *Religious Freedom and Evangelization in Latin America: The Challenges of Religious Pluralism,* edited by Paul E. Sigmund, 150-74. Maryknoll, NY: Orbis, 1999.

———. *The Politics of the Spirit: The Political Implications of Pentecostalized Religión in Costa Rica and Guatemala.* New York: Lexington, 2001.

Stevens, John Robert. *Baptized in Fire.* North Hollywood: Living Word, 1977.

———. *Elijah and Elisha.* North Hollywood: Living Word, 1975.

———. *The Kingdom Fast.* North Hollywood: Living Word, 1975.

———. *Living Prophecies.* North Hollywood: Living Word, 1974.

———. *The Living Word on the Coming Glory.* North Hollywood: Living Word, 1976.

———. *Prophecies of December 1968.* Sepulveda, CA: Living Word, 1969.

———. *The School of Prophets.* North Hollywood: Living Word, 1976.

———. *Twelve Keys To Heaven's Best.* North Hollywood: Living Word, 1959.

Stewart, Roy A. *Rabbinic Theology.* Edinburgh: Oliver & Boyd, 1961.

Stewart-Gambino, Hannah W., and Everett Wilson. "Latin American Pentecostals: Old Stereotypes and New Challenges." In *Power, Politics, and Pentecostals in Latin America,* edited by Edward L. Cleary and Hannah W. Stewart-Gambino, 228-32. Boulder, CO: Westview, 1997.

Stoeffler, F. Ernest. *German Pietism during the Eighteenth Century.* Studies in the History of Religions 24. Leiden: Brill, 1973.

Streiff, Patrick. *Reluctant Saint? A Theological Biography of Fletcher of Madeley.* Translated by G. W. S. Knowles. Peterborough, UK: Epworth, 2001.

Stronstad, Roger. *The Charismatic Theology of St. Luke.* Peabody, MA: Hendrickson, 1984.

Sutcliffe, Edmund F. *The Old Testament and the Future Life.* London: Burns, Oates and Washbourne, 1947.

Swanson, R. N. *Indulgences in Late Medieval England.* Cambridge: Cambridge University Press, 2007.

———. *Promissory Notes on the Treasury of Merits: Indulgences in Late Medieval Europe.* Leiden: Brill, 2006.

Swinton, John. *Raging with Compassion.* Grand Rapids: Eerdmans, 2007.

Tannehill, Robert C. "What Kind of King? What Kind of Kingdom? A Study of Luke." *Word & World* 12 (1992) 17–22.

Tanner, N. P., editor. *Decrees of the Ecumenical Councils.* Vol. 2. Washington: Georgetown University Press, 1990.

Tavard, George H. *The Contemplative Church: Joachim and His Adversaries.* Milwaukee: Marquette University Press, 2005.

Telushkin, Joseph. *Jewish Literacy.* New York: Morrow, 1991.

Tertullian. *Of Patience.* Whitefish, MO: Kessinger, 2004.

"The Object of the Baptism in the Holy Spirit." *The Latter Rain Evangel* 3 (May 1911) 8–9.

Thomas, John Christopher. "The Kingdom of God in the Gospel According to Matthew." *NTS* 39 (1993) 136–46.

———. *Spirit of the New Testament.* Blandford Forum, UK: Deo, 2005.

Thomas, R. L. "Tongues . . . Will Cease." *JETS* (1974) 81–89.

———. "Contemporary Issues in the Doctrine of the Holy Spirit: IV, Spiritual Gifts Today." *BSac* 130 (October 1973) 315–28.

Thompson, Damian. *Waiting for the Antichrist: Charisma and Apocalypse in a Pentecostal Church.* Oxford: Oxford University Press, 2006.

Thompson, Matthew K. *Kingdom Come: Revisioning Pentecostal Eschatology.* JPTSup. Blandford Forum, UK: Deo, 2010.

Thurneysen, Eduard. *Christoph Blumhardt.* Münich: Kaiser, 1926.

Tillich, Paul. *A History of Christian Thought from Its Judaic and Hellenistic Origins to Existentialism.* Edited by C. E. Braaten. New York: Harper & Row, 1967.

———. *The Socialist Decision.* Translated by F. Sherman. New York: Harper & Row, 1977.

Trocmé, André. *Jesus and the Nonviolent Revolution.* Translated by Michael H. Shank and Marlin E. Miller. Scottsdale, PA: Herald, 1973.

Turner, Max. "The 'Spirit of Prophecy' as the Power of Israel's Restoration and Witness." In *Witness to the Gospel: The Theology of Acts,* edited by I. Howard Marshall and David Peterson, 327–48. Grand Rapids: Eerdmans, 1998.

Tutu, Desmond. "Forward." In *The Earth Story in the New Testament,* edited by Norman C. Habel and Vicky Balabanski. London: Sheffield Academic, 2001.

Truesdale, Al. "Last Things First: The Impact of Eschatology on Ecology." *Perspectives on Science and Christian Faith* 46 (June 1994) 116–22.

Van de Walle, Bernie A. *The Heart of the Gospel: A. B. Simpson, the Fourfold Gospel, and the Late Nineteenth-Century Evangelical Theology.* Princeton Theological Monograph Series 106. Eugene, OR: Pickwick, 2009.

Van Dijk, Rijk A. "From Camp to Encompassment: Discourses of Transsubjectivity in the Ghanaian Pentecostal Disapora." *JRA* 27 (1997) 135–59.

Varner, Kelly H. *Chosen for Greatness: Discover Your Personal Destiny.* Shippensburg, PA: Destiny Image, 2003.

———. *Corporate Anointing: Christ Manifest in the Fullness of His Body.* Shippensburg, PA: Destiny Image, 1998.

———. *The Issues of Life.* Shippensburg, PA: Destiny Image, 1992.

———. *Moses, the Master, and the Manchild: Every 2000 Years God Has a Son.* Shippensburg, PA: Destiny Image, 2001.

———. *Prevail: A Handbook for the Overcomer.* Little Rock, AR: Revival Press, 1982.

———. *The Priesthood is Changing.* Shippensburg, PA: Destiny Image, 1991.

———. *Secrets of the Ascended Life.* Shippensburg, PA: Destiny Image, 2006.

———. *Sound the Alarm: The Apocalyptic Message from the Book of Joel.* Shippensburg, PA: Destiny Image, 2005.

———. *The Time of the Messiah: A Prophetic Picture of the End-Time Church.* Shippensburg, PA: Destiny Image, 1996.

———. *Understanding Types, Shadows, and Names: A Biblical Guide.* Shippensburg, PA: Destiny Image, 1996.

———. *Unshakeable Kingdom: The Life and Times of Haggai the Prophet.* Shippensburg, PA: Destiny Image, 1994.

———. *Whose Right It Is? A Handbook of Covenantal Theology.* Shippensburg, PA: Destiny Image, 1995.

Verhey, Allen. *The Great Reversal: Ethics and the New Testament.* Grand Rapids: Eerdmans, 1984.

Villafañe, Eldin. *The Liberating Spirit: Towards an Hispanic American Pentecostal Social Ethic.* New York: University Press of America, 1992.

Volf, Miroslav. "Materiality of Salvation: An Investigation in the Soteriologies of Liberation and Pentecostal Theologies." *JES* 26 (1989) 447–67.

———. "On Loving with Hope: Eschatology and Social Responsibility." *Transformation* 7 (July-September 1990) 28–31.

———. *Work in the Spirit: Toward a Theology of Work.* 1991. Reprint, Eugene, OR: Wipf and Stock, 2001.

Wacker, Grant. "A Profile of American Pentecostalism." In *Pastoral Problems in Pentecostal-Charismatic Movement,* edited by Harold D. Hunter, 1–47. Cleveland: Society for Pentecostal Studies, 1983.

———. "Are the Golden Oldies Still Worth Playing? Reflections on History Writing among Early Pentecostals." *Pneuma* 8 (Fall 1986) 81–100.

———. *Heaven Below: Early Pentecostals and American Culture.* Cambridge, MA: Harvard University Press, 2001.

Waddell, Robby. "Revelation and the (New) Creation: A Prolegomenon on the Apocalypse, Science, and Creation." In *The Spirit Renews the Face of the Earth: Pentecostal Forays in Science and Theology of Creation,* edited by Amos Yong, 30–50. Eugene, OR: Pickwick, 2009.

Walker, Alan. "Where Pentecostalism is Mushrooming." *Christian Century* 85 (17 January 1968) 81–82.

Wall, R. W. *Revelation.* NIBC 18. Peabody, MA: Hendrickson, 1991.

Walvoord, John F. "Dispensational Premillennialism." *Christianity Today* 15 (September 1958) 11–13.

Warnock, George H. *Beauty for Ashes, Part I: The Family of God.* Cranbrook, BC: n.p., 1985.

———. *Beauty for Ashes, Part II.* Cranbrook, BC: n.p., 1986.

———. *Crowned With Oil.* Cranbrook, BC: n.p., 1987.

———. *Evening and Morning.* Cranbrook, BC: n.p., 1979.

———. *The Feast of Tabernacles.* Springfield, MO: n.p., 1951.

———. "*Feed My Sheep.*" Cranbrook, BC: n.p., 1980.

———. *From Tent to Temple.* Cranbrook, BC: n.p., 1984.

———. *Seven Lamps of Fire.* Cranbrook, BC: n.p., 2001.

Warrington, Keith. *Pentecostal Theology.* New York: T. & T. Clark, 2008.

Weber, Timothy. "Dispensational and Historic Premillennialism as Popular Millennialist Movements." In *Historic Premillennialism: An Alternative to "Left Behind" Eschatology,* edited by Craig L. Bloomberg, et al., 1–22. Grand Rapids: Baker Academic, 2009.

———. *Living in the Shadow of the Second Coming: American Premillinialism.* Chicago: University of Chicago Press, 1987.

———. *On the Road to Armageddon: How Evangelicals Became Israel's Best Friend.* Grand Rapids: Baker Academic, 2005.

Wesley, John. *The Works of John Wesley: Sermons.* 4 Vols. Edited by Albert C. Outler. Nashville: Abingdon, 1984–1987.

White, Lynn. "The Historical Roots of Our Ecological Crisis." *Science* 155 (1967) 1203–7.

Williams, Stephen N. "The Partition of Love and Hope: Eschatology and Social Responsibility." *Transformation* 7 (1990) 24–27.

Wilson, Dwight J. "Eschatology, Pentecostal Perspectives on." In *DPCM,* 264–68.

Wilson, Everett. "Guatemalan Pentecostals: Something of Their Own." In *Power, Politics, and Pentecostals in Latin America,* edited by Edward L. Cleary and Hannah W. Stewart-Gambino, 139–62. Colorado: Westview, 1997.

Wilson, W. E. "Εὑρεθησεται in 2 Peter iii.10." *Expository Times* 32 (1920–21) 44–45.

Witherington, Ben, III. *Revelation.* New Cambridge Bible Commentary. Cambridge: Cambridge University Press, 2003.

———. *Jesus, Paul, and the End of the World: A Comparative Study in New Testament Eschatology.* Downers Grove, IL: IVP, 1992.

———. *Jesus the Seer: The Progress of Prophecy.* Peabody, MA: Hendrickson, 2000.

Wolf, Ron. "God, James Watt, and the Public Lands." *Audubon* 83 (May 1981) 58–65.

Wood, A. S. "Ephesians." In *The Expositor's Bible Commentary.* Vol. 11. Grand Rapids: Zondervan, 1982.

Wood, Laurence W. *The Meaning of Pentecost in Early Methodism: Rediscovering John Fletcher as John Wesley's Vindicator and Designated Successor.* Pietist and Wesleyan Studies 15. Lanham, MD: Scarecrow, 2002.

Wright, N. T. *The Climax of the Covenant: Christ and the Law in Paul.* Minneapolis: Fortress, 1992.

———. *Justification: God's Plan and Paul's Vision.* Downers Grove, IL: IVP, 2009.

———. *The New Testament and the People of God.* Minneapolis: Fortress, 1992.

———. *Paul: In Fresh Perspective.* Minneapolis: Fortress, 2005.

———. *Surprised by Hope: Rethinking Heaven, the Resurrection, and the Mission of the Church.* New York: HarperOne, 2008.

Yong, Amos. *The Spirit Poured Out on All Flesh: Pentecostalism and the Possibility of Global Theology.* Grand Rapids: Baker Academic, 2005.

———. "'Tongues of Fire' in the Pentecostal Imagination: The Truth of Glossolalia in Light of R. C. Neville's Theory of Religious Symbolism." *JPT* 6 (1998) 39–65.

Zinzendorf, L. *Nine Public Lectures on Important Subjects in Religion.* Translated by G. W. Forell. Iowa City: University of Iowa Press, 1973.

Zmijewski, J. "Βδέλυγμα." In *EDNT* 1:209–10.

Zündel, Friedrich. *Johann Christioph Blumhardt.* 19th ed. Basel: Brunnen, 1979.

Made in United States
Orlando, FL
13 January 2025

57289842R00245